LIVING WITH THE ARMY II

The Results of Remote Sensing and Fieldwalking Surveys in Novae (Lower Moesia)

by Agnieszka Tomas

with contributions by

M. Jaworski, P. Jaworski, M. Pisz, P. Wroniecki,
P. Dyczek, E. Gencheva, P. Janik, B. Kontny, M. Kot, W. Małkowski, K. Misiewicz,
Sz. Modzelewski, M. Moskal-del Hoyo, T. Sarnowski (†), R. Stachowicz-Rybka, H. Winter

BREPOLS

Brepols Publishing 2022

Warsaw Studies in Archaeology
Volume 4

Coordinating editor: **Dorota Dzierzbicka**

Translation and English proofreading by **Miłosława Stępień** and **Ian Marshall**

Drawing of the figures and plates: **Emil Jęczmienowski**, **Agnieszka Tomas**, **Aleksandra Kalinowska**

Typesetting and layout by **Piotr Lewandowski**

The book is based on the results of the project entitled Research on the settlement structures near the Roman legionary fortress at Novae (Lower Moesia) using non-destructive prospection methods (No. UMO-2011/01/D/HS3/02187), financed by the Polish National Science Centre and realised in 2012–14.

Financial support for the publication of this book was provided by the Centre for Research on Ancient Civilizations (University of Warsaw)

Printed in the EU on acid-free paper.

ISBN 978-2-503-60399-5
e-ISBN 978-2-503-60401-5
D/2022/0095/345
DOI: 10.1484/M.WSA-EB.5.132109

List of Contents

Introduction and acknowledgments

The ruins of Novae were for the first time described by the Italian scholar, emissary and soldier, Luigi Ferdinando Marsigli, who saw the remains of walls visible on the southern bank of the Danube. In his book *Danubius Pannonico-Mysicus* first published in 1726, and later published in French as *Description du Danube*, he described the ruins, which he named as Merlan, probably mistakenly, as the village Marlean was on the Romanian side of the Danube.[1] Novae with its monuments was later described by other travellers and scholars, among others by the Romanian general and antiquarian Nicolas Mavros, who transported epigraphic monuments from Novae to Bucharest,[2] Friedrich Kanitz, an Austrian traveller who visited Svishtov, Novae, and other nearby sites,[3] or a Czech scholar Karel Škorpil who prepared a sketch presenting a plan of the site and marking the ruins outside the fortress.[4] These included a building to the west of the West Gate (the remains of an early Christian basilica), a water conduit running to the west of the fortress and a cemetery on the Bobata Hills to the east of Novae, on the right bank of the Dermen dere river.[5] The same basilica was described in the list of old churches prepared by Violeta Ivanova in the 1920s.[6] Erich Polaschek published a quite precise description of the publications and finds from Novae, along with some brief historical information about Novae in the Pauly-Wissowa Realäncyklopedie.[7] Before and after the WWII, the site was investigated by Stefan Stefanov, who was a teacher of history and the head of the Historical Museum in Svishtov for more than 20 years. Stefanov prepared a plan of the site showing the course of three aqueducts, and published a series of communications on stray finds made on the site and in the area.[8] In 1958 Stefanov published some observations about the neighbouring site in the place Ostrite Mogili.[9] Based on the topography of numerous analogous sites along the Roman frontiers, Bulgarian historian Boris Gerov suggested that there may have been a second settlement (*vicus*).[10]

Novae has been excavated by the Polish (now three teams) and Bulgarian archaeologists since 1960. The results of investigations have been published in regular reports and many different articles.[11] Up to the 80s of the 20th century, the location and the legal status of civilian settlements near Novae was the subject of mainly theoretical considerations.[12] Several buildings in the extramural area have been explored, however, with some of them, much the same as the cemeteries, only having been investigated during rescue excavations. Apart from the regular excavations of the extramural residence (the so-called *villa extra muros*) explored since 1978, these buildings include among others the mithraeum excavated in 1984–85, the shrine of Dionysus and a few burials excavated in 1960 or a part of the *vicus* at Ostrite Mogili and the farm near Vardim.[13] The aqueducts were surveyed by S. Stefanov (before 1930) and M. Biernacka-Lubańska (in the 1960s). The field surveys in the vicinity of Novae were carried out by a Polish team in 2000.[14] The broad area around Novae was also surveyed by the German-Bulgarian team in the springs of 1999 and 2000.[15]

As a result of the many years of observations of the terrain surrounding the camp, which in recent years has begun to rapidly change from being a rural area into a suburban one, we have arrived at the conclusion that any archaeological activities undertaken in the nearest vicinity of the camp will be very significant as these will document remains that are disappearing before our very eyes. The formation of large amounts of recreational plots in the area has led to the development of local infrastructure such as asphalt roads, pylons and fencing, and – during the next stage – littered and modified the landscape. These difficult conditions have been made all the worse by illegal looting. In 2008, Novae was added to the list of 100 most threatened sites in the world according to the international organisation World Monuments Fund. Taking this into account, we came to the decision to document the remains of the settlement located next to the camp and the sites around Novae as quickly as possible as this may be the final opportunities for such activities. Three two-week seasons had been planned within the framework of our project, and it was during this short time that we took on the daunting task, fully aware that we would be seeing

1. Marsigli 1726, vol. II; 1744, vol. II, 36 and Tab. 16, Fig. XLI and cf. Škorpil 1905, 456, fn. 2; Kolendo 2008a, 5; Lemke 2015, 178–79
2. Kolendo 1968.
3. Kanitz 1879, 193–96.
4. Škorpil 1905, 456; Majewski 1962, 76
5. Škorpil 1905, 456–57, Tab. XCIXe and Tab. CII, 1 and the list of stamped clay pipes (CIL III 756–760, 785).
6. Ivanova 1926, 463.
7. Polaschek 1936, col. 1125–29.
8. Stefanov 1930-31; 1958, 345 and communications published in Izvestiya na Arheologicheskiya Institut (Sofia).
9. Stefanov 1958, 351.
10. Gerov 1964, 128–33; 1977, 300, fn. 4.
11. Kolendo 2008a.
12. Sarnowski 1976, 61–62; Gerov 1977; Parnicki-Pudełko 1981; Mrozewicz 1981b; 1982, 61; Mrozewicz 1984, 296; Sarnowski 1976, 61-62; Tomas 2012, 120; Tomas 2017: 159–61.
13. See Tomas 2017: 41–92.
14. Tomas 2012.
15. Conrad, Stančev 2002.

some of the features for the last time moments before they were destroyed.

Reconstructing the exact layout of the *canabae* is practically impossible in the light of this situation. Gathering as much archaeological information as possible in such a short time required a well thought-through research plan. We decided to use a few research methods jointly to enable at least a partial reconstruction of the settlement's character. Following in the footsteps of the researchers conducting non-invasive studies in the areas in the vicinity of the Roman legionary camps, e.g. in Viminacium, Caerleon, Carnuntum, and Troesmis,[16] we decided to do a geophysical prospection, knowing full well that Novae was not one of those sites that would provide unequivocal results. On the other hand, we were aware that any positive results in the case of Novae would be extremely significant. Simultaneously with the geophysical prospection, surface prospecting and the mapping of metal finds were also done in an attempt to achieve as complete a picture of the individual sections of the settlement near the camp and of the nearby sites as possible. We tried to record both the finds coming from earlier epochs and those from later ones. In order to provide a more complete reconstruction of the settlement landscape, a series of analyses were also conducted, including the testing of plant pollen and macroremains, aiming to provide as complete a reconstruction of the past environment in this area as possible. As a result, we were able to gather an incredibly rich set of information, which – even though it does not all in total come from the Novae settlement complex – reflects its complexity and multiphase character.

The following book presents the results of the project realised in 2012–14,[17] but it contains also the materials from Ostrite Mogili collected in 1979 and in 2000. The description of the finds is given after the original documentation and may vary in details. The samples for palynological analyses were collected in 2009 from the layers in the deep trench near the northern defensive wall,[18] and the macrobothanic remains were collected from the trench in the retentura in summer 2014.[19]

A long-term collaboration between Polish and Bulgarian archaeologists made it possible to carry out these surveys. I would like to thank to Lyudmil Vagalinski for the possibility of field works in spring 2012–14 in the area outside the Archaeological Park and his kind support in the following years. I owe my special gratitude to Evgenia Gencheva who was always supportive and helpful to our team, gave advice and valuable observations about recent discoveries. We could also visit the local Museum in Svishtov and document the finds stored there thanks to the kindness of Marin Marinov, curator of the archaeological department. We received a strong support from Tadeusz Sarnowski who visited Novae during our investigations and provided his valuable remarks. The content of the present volume is enriched thanks to the kindness of Tadeusz Sarnowski and Piotr Dyczek who allowed publication of the results of their field surveys carried out in 1979 and 2000. I also would like to thank Pavlina Vladkova-Baicheva who allowed us to carry out the geophysical surveys in her sector (extramural residence).

My special personal thanks go to the team who were involved in the project, particularly to Piotr Wroniecki who was responsible for the managing and elaboration of the non-invasive investigations. All members of the fieldwork were devoted to the ideas of the project and made great efforts to do the best they could: Piotr Jaworski, Marcin Jaworski and Michał Pisz who were working on the site each spring, and also those who participated once, but were similarly engaged in the investigations: Karolina Juszczyk, Krzysztof Misiewicz, Wiesław Więckowski, Stanisław Rzeźnik and Katarzyna Dejtrowska. It would be also unfair not to mention students of the University of Warsaw who were working very hard despite the intensive research programme and challenges made by spring weather conditions.

This book presents the results of six weeks of fieldwork. One can say that it is a very short period of time to collect all necessary data, and probably one would be right. On the other hand, we felt that such an opportunity may be the last chance to document the remains which may disappear due to the intensive human activities, including illegal looting, and urbanization of the area where Novae is placed. The vicinity of the site turned out to be difficult to investigate with non-invasive methods, but we did not feel discouraged by these special and difficult conditions, but on the contrary, felt challenged and mobilized to solve endless obstacles which gave us a lesson in archaeological life.

Agnieszka Tomas, Warsaw 14.10.2021

16. Mikić, Stojanović, and Mrdić 2006; Guest et al. 2012; Doneus, Gugl, and Doneus 2013; Alexandrescu, Gugl, and Keinrath 2016.

17. The project entitled "Badania struktur osadniczych przy rzymskim obozie legionowym w Novae (Mezja Dolna) przy użyciu niedestrukcyjnych metod prospekcji terenowej" / "Research on settlement structures near the Roman legionary fortress at Novae (Lower Moesia) using non-destructive prospection methods" received financial support from the Polish National Science Centre (dec. No. 2011/01/D/HS3/02187).

18. Sarnowski, Kovalevskaja, and Tomas 2010, 163–169.

19. Sarnowski et al. 2016, 188–89.

I

The site and its surroundings

Agnieszka Tomas

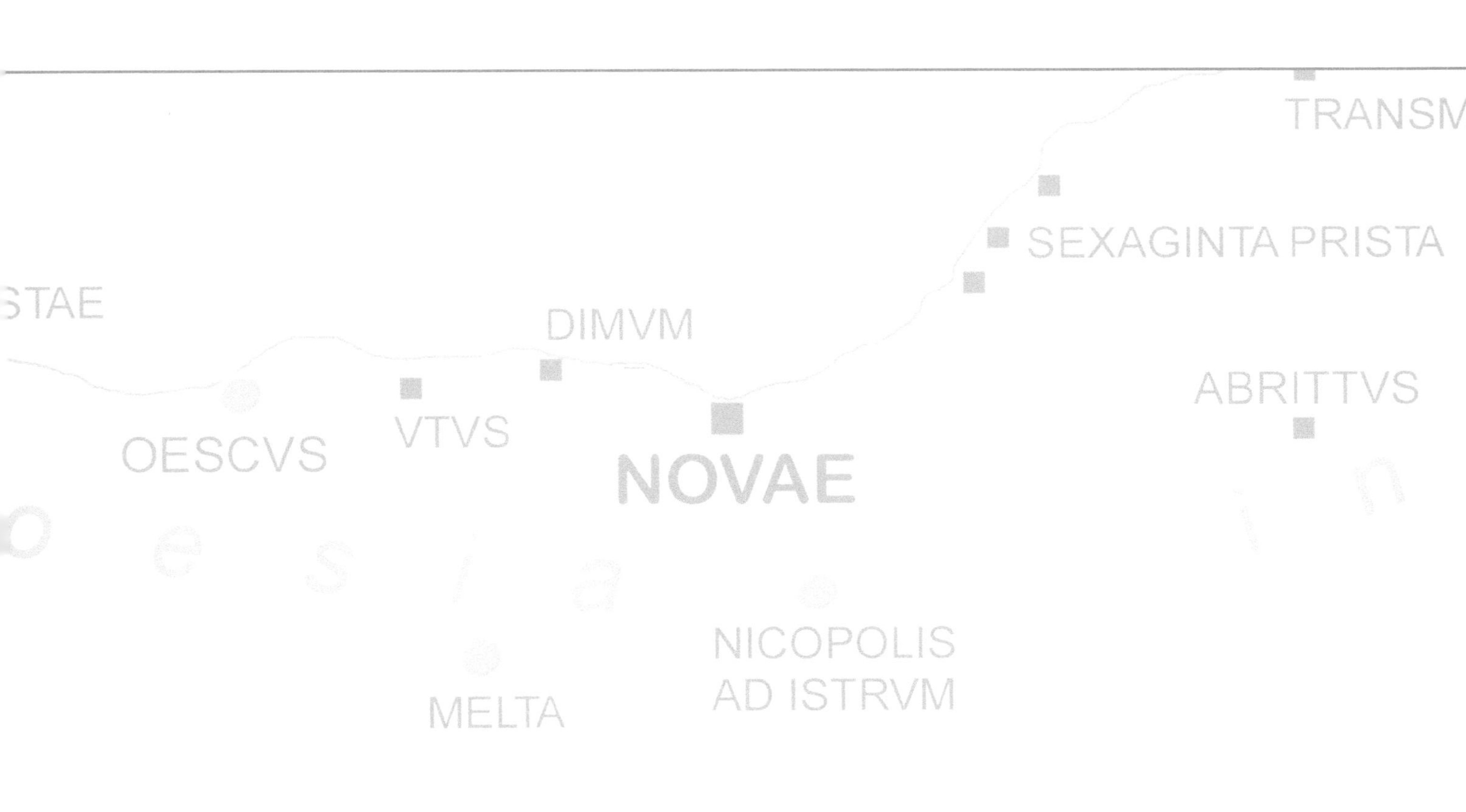

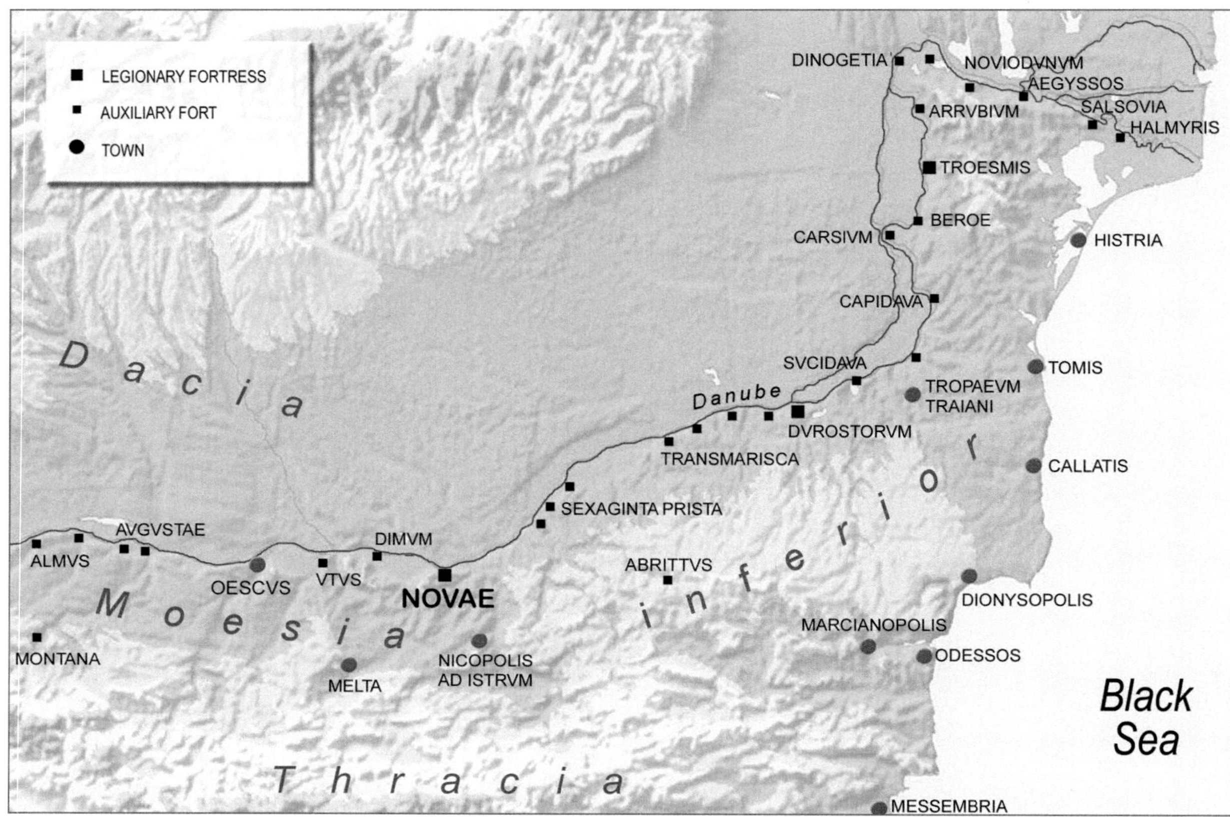

Fig. 1. The location of Novae in Lower Moesia (by A. Tomas).

Novae, a Lower Moesian Roman legionary fortress and late Roman town, is located in northern Bulgaria, on the southern bank of the Danube, at the point where the river has its southernmost bend (**Fig. 1**). The coordinates of the site are from N 43°37'04" E 25°22'20" to N 43°36'57" E 25°24'20" in the North, and N 43°36'22" E 25°22'15" to N 43°36'11" E 25°24'15' in the south.

The Danube at Novae is about 2.1 km wide with waters at about 20–25 m a. s. l. (**Fig. 2**). The southern bank of the Danube near Novae is 20 m high and densely covered with bushes and trees, while the northern is swampy, with elevated areas lying at a distance of about 3–3.5 km from the river. The right tributaries of the Danube flowing from the south to the north intersect the high riverbank in the form of deep valleys and gullies.

The deep valley carved out by the small river Dermen dere (formerly called Tekir dere) surrounds Novae from the east and south-east, with its waters flowing into the Danube via a broad outlet providing access to the river. The *castra* were located at a spot where the riverbank is quite wide, with hills rising up beyond the camp's southern defensive walls. Additionally, for the support of monumental architecture this terrain was adapted by cutting out flat terraces (**Fig. 3**). The northern part of the site lies at 40–46 m a. s. l., while the southern one lies at 70 m a. s. l. The area to the west of the *castra* is flat with only one hill at a distance of 300 m south-west of the West Gate. The south-eastern and southern sides of the camp are surrounded by hills and elevated areas.

The mouths of the Dermen dere provide convenient access to the high riverbank, and this feature was used during the Turkish-Russian war, when the imperial troops landed on 27th June 1877 (**Fig. 4**). This historical event was commemorated by a park and several monuments named Pametnitsite, one of which is very large in size, placed to the east of Novae in the naturally low grounds of Dermen dere's left bank. The archaeological park and historical monuments form one complex, currently popular with tourists.[1] A museum pavilion and small private lots are located on the western side of the fortress. Larger lots also extend to the south and east of Novae.

Historical outline

Novae lies halfway between the two right tributaries of the Danube – the Osum and the Yantra, flowing almost parallel to each other. This part of the Danube Plain was a borderland between tribes influenced by the La Tène culture and northern Thracians. The possible

1. Sarnowski et al. 2012.

Fig. 2. Danube near Novae (photo by M. Pisz).

different status of the Moesian and Thracian tribes is expressed well by a series of boundary stones set up in AD 136 under Hadrian, who ordered the division of the *Moesi* and *Thraces* tribal territories probably along the lower course of the Yantra and its left tributary – Eliya.[2] According to our present state of knowledge, local settlement in the 1st century BC was rather scarce, and during the Roman conquest the Novae area was not densely settled.[3] Moesia was organized as a province by Tiberius, probably in AD 15, although the process started toward the end of Augustus' reign.[4] The attested legates of Moesia acted in AD 6 and 10/11 repelling Dacians attacks,[5] and the Mysians were obliged to pay tribute to Rome starting from Tiberius' reign, which would mean that Moesia and Treballia came under Roman control in this period, but as a *praefectura civitatium*.[6] Even before Rhoimetalces' death in AD 12, the Romans controlled Laevus Pontus, as the epigraphic evidence indicates.[7] This might have been conducted by sending the prefects to the western Pontic Greek colonies (*praefecti orae maritimae* or rather *praefecti civitatium*),

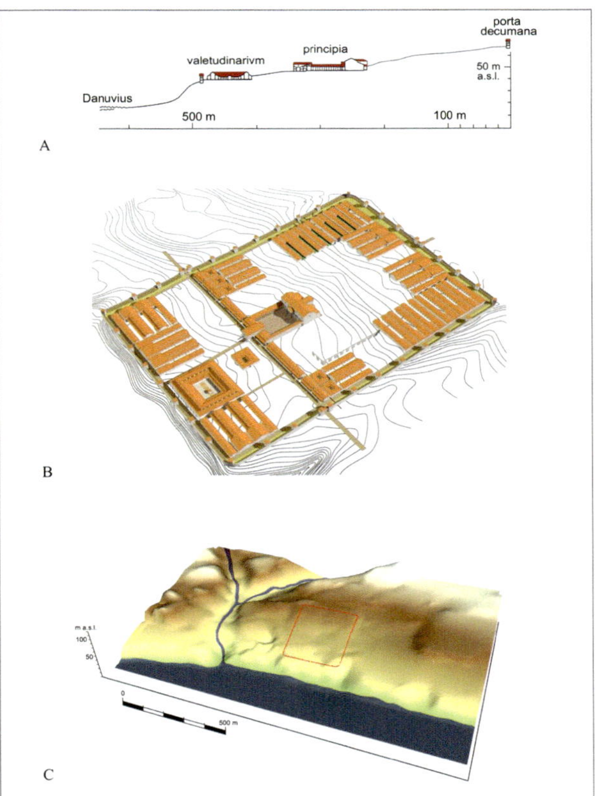

Fig. 3. Novae. The shape of the terrain and the location of the fortress. A – cross section along the N–S axis; B – visualization of the legionary fortress' buildings; C – the shape of the terrain compared to the size of the camp (by J. Kaniszewski, P. Zakrzewski).

2. Tomas 2009, 31.
3. Tomas 2018.
4. Syme 1999; Matei-Popescu 2014.
5. Cass. Dio LV 29.3; Strabo VII 3.10.
6. CIL V 1838 and 1839 (*praefectus civitatium Moesiae et Treballiae*).
7. Avram and Ionescu 2013; Matei-Popescu 2014, 460; Bărbulescu and Buzoianu 2014.

Fig. 4. Crossing of the Russian army over the Danube at Zimnicea/Svishtov June 15, 1877. A painting by N. Orenburgsky, 1883, Artillery Museum, Petersburg (Wikimedia Commons).

but also to areas along the Danube (*praefecti Danuvii*).[8] It was Gaius Poppaeus Sabinus who was the first governor of a province in AD 14/15.[9] Since Thracian rule over northern Thrace was still in place after this date, Poppaeus' *provinciae* must have encompassed Macedonia, Moesia and Treballia, the Danubian riverbank, and the Laevus Pontus.[10] It was only around the mid-1st century after the Thracian uprising had been quelled and the Thracian Kingdom incorporated into the Empire in AD 44 that north-eastern Thrace came under Roman military control.

The 1st century AD on the Lower Danube is characterised by large resettlement actions which changed Moesia's ethnic composition. Scholars continue to debate the number of peoples moved by the Romans and the areas where they were located.[11] The earliest Roman military presence in Novae is attested by layers dated by T. Sarnowski to the Claudian-Neronian period and linked to the Eighth Augustan Legion dispatched to Thrace during the Thracian uprising.[12] However, a permanent and long-term garrison was established after AD 69, by the *legio I Italica*.[13] During Domitian's rule, Moesia saw the destructive attacks of the Dacians, ending in long military campaigns (84–89).[14] In AD 86 the province was divided into two parts, and Novae became one of two legionary bases in Lower Moesia.[15]

The earliest epigraphic evidence of the *ripa Thraciae* customs district, which included stations from Novae to the mouths of the Danube is dated to AD 100.[16] Trajan's Dacian campaigns (101–102 and 105–106) resulted in rapid changes and the growth of the province continued by Hadrian.[17] The Fifth Macedonian Legion from Oescus was moved downriver to Troesmis, and the Eleventh Claudian Legion was dispatched to Durostorum. The legionary fortress in Novae was rearranged and rebuilt in stone and the former legionary camp at Oescus was granted a colony status.[18] The newly founded town of Nicopolis in northern Thrace[19] largely covered

8. Sarnowski 2006b, 90–91; Ruscu 2014, 164; Tomas 2017, 100. On the idea of *praefecti civitatium* presented by A. von Domaszewski and the later discussion, see Matei-Popescu 2014, 463.

9. Tac. *Ann.* VI 39; Cass. Dio LVIII 25; Matei-Popescu 2014; Tomas 2016, 20.

10. The *horothesia* of Dionysopolis dated to AD 15 mentions the presence of publicani; see Slavova 1998. According to F. Matei-Popescu, Moesia as governed by Poppaeus was divided into two separate areas: Moesia and Treballia, and Laevus Pontus as a second district (see Matei-Popescu 2014, 458). In my opinion, lack of control over the Danube including its riverbanks would be illogical from the strategic point of view, hence it must have been under the control of a *praefectus classis*; see Sarnowski 2006b, 90–91.

11. Mrozewicz 2013; Tomas 2018.

12. Mrozewicz 1981c, 106; Sarnowski 1988, 26; Sarnowski 1991, 348.

13. Sarnowski et al. 2014, 82.

14. On the problem of the critical assessment of literary sources and rich literature regarding the Dacian campaigns, see Wheeler 2010; Wheeler 2010; 2011.

15. Tomas 2016, 29.

16. Tomas 2016, 100 with further literature.

17. Tomas 2016, 21, 25, 66.

18. CIL III 753; Ivanov, R. 1993, 27; Tomas 2016, 58.

19. A. Poulter, In *Nicopolis I*, 10; Tomas 2016, 11 and fn. 95.

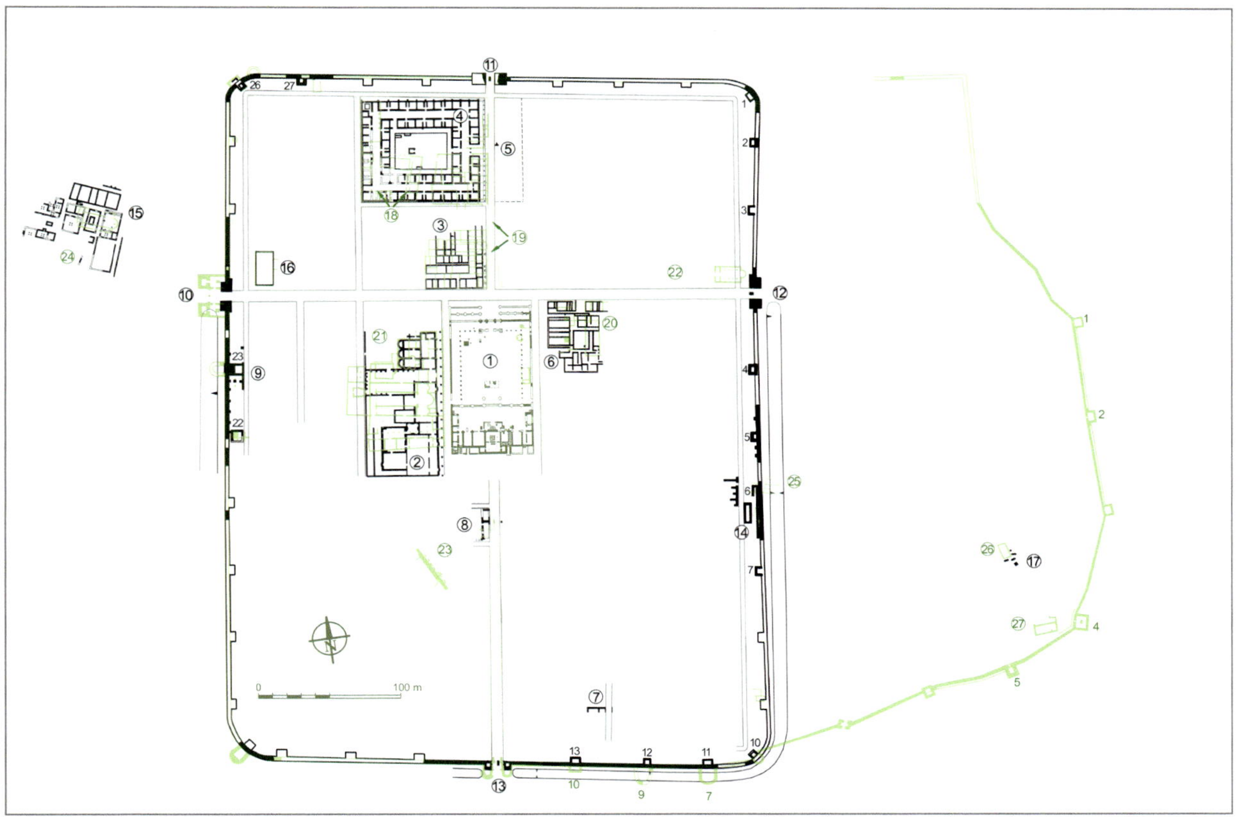

Fig. 5. Novae 2019. The legionary fortress and the late Roman town. 1 – the headquarters building (principia); 2 – the legionary baths (thermae); 3 – the officer's house; 4 – the military hospital (valetudinarium); 5 – granary (horreum) (?); 6 – residence in the latera praetorii; 7 – cavalry barrack; 8 – building in the retentura (praetorium) (?); 9 – workshop (fabrica) (?); 10 – West Gate (porta principalis sinistra); 11 – North Gate (porta praetoria); 12 – East Gate (porta principalis dextra); 13 – South Gate (porta decumana); 14 – water cistern; 15 – extramural residence; 16 – schola (?); 17 – the graves excavated in 2016–19; 18–20 residential quarters; 21 – Episcopal complex with cathedral; 22, 24 – churches; 23 – massive wall; 25–27 utility buidlings. Figures along the curtain wall refer to the numbers of towers (drawing by E. Jęczmienowski, after the partial drawings published by the expeditions: Faculty of Archaeology, University of Warsaw, National Archaeological Institute with Museum, BAN Sofia, Antiquity of Southeastern Europe Research Centre, University of Warsaw; International Interdisciplinary Archeological Expedition University of A. Mickiewicz in Poznań).

local demand for craft products, selling its goods, among others, to Novae.

The reign of Hadrian and Antoninus Pius was a time of consolidation and development, not only in the towns but also in the rural areas.[20] Shifting the provincial border southwards by the end of the 2nd century made economic contacts easier and stimulated the development of both urban centres and their rural hinterlands, as well as resulting in new roads and provincial infrastructure being constructed. The second half of the 2nd and the beginning of the 3rd centuries were a time of great prosperity for the region until the disastrous Costobocs' invasion in AD 170/171, which caused great damage to the rural areas.[21]

The commanders of the First Italic Legion were loyal to Septimius Severus during the civil war in 192/193.[22] Imperial favour and gratitude, combined with economic development and prosperity, are observable in the archaeological evidence. A sudden collapse occurred in AD 238 and 250/251, when the Barbarian raids did great damage to the suburban areas and rural territories. As stated by various ancient authors, Novae was besieged by the Goths of Cniva in AD 250/251, and although the Germanic chieftain did not succeed in conquering the fortress, it is very probable that his warriors plundered the vicinity of Novae.[23] The permanent threat resulted in the withdrawal of Roman troops and administration from Dacia during Aurelian's rule (270–275). These dramatic events caused a significant change in the layout of Novae. The extramural area along the eastern side of the camp was surrounded by a new line of defensive walls, which enlarged the fortress area almost by 50%. According to T. Sarnowski this could have happened around 300 AD.[24] The layer under one of the towers

20. Tomas 2016, 66–67; 129.

21. Tomas 2016, 22 and 27.

22. Tomas 2015b, 83–84.

23. Kolendo 2008b, 118.

24. Sarnowski, Kovalevskaja, and Tomas 2010, 170.

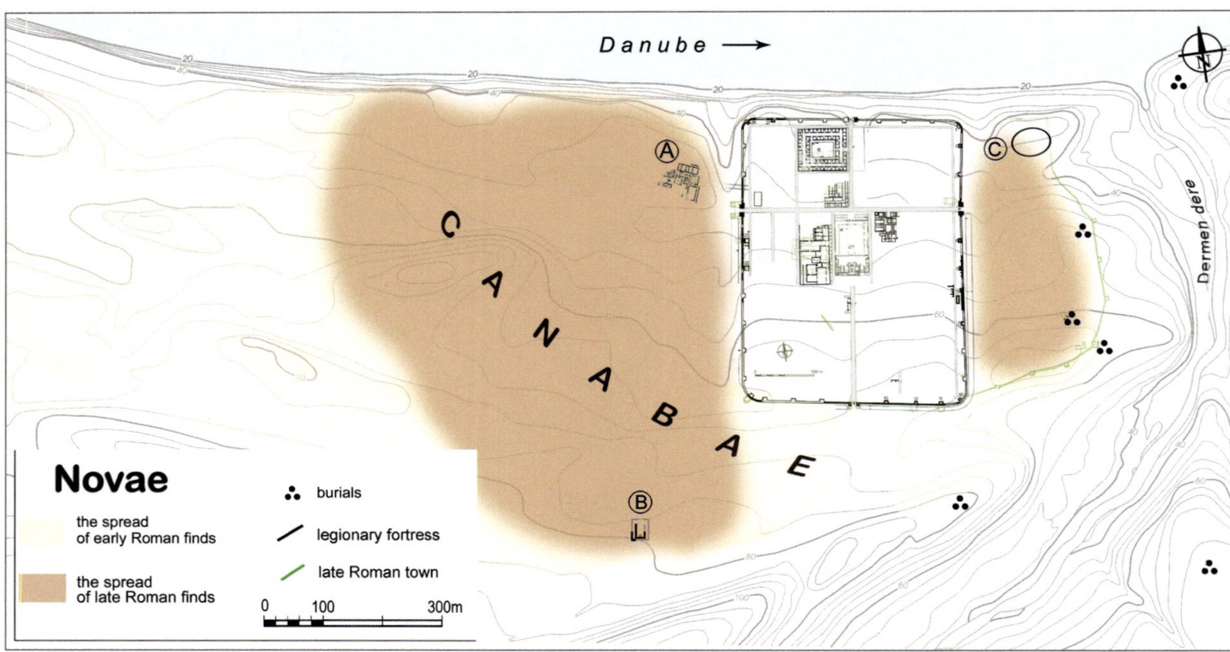

Fig. 6. Novae. The legionary fortress and the *canabae legionis (*by A. Tomas).

of these defences' southern gate contained a coin issued in the second half of the 3rd century.[25] However, the fortifications may have been built later, and certainly underwent at least one reconstruction and the addition of some towers. Radical changes in provincial administration were introduced by Diocletian and continued by his successors.

The north-eastern part of Lower Moesia formed the new province of Scythia Minor manned by two legions, *II Herculia* and *I Iovia*, while the western borders of the province neighboured the newly created Dacia ripensis. Lower Moesia was soon renamed Moesia II. At that point, the military units were dispatched to numerous forts, and the Lower Moesian legionary prefects (*praefecti ripae*) were stationed in Novae, Transmarisca, Sexaginta Prista and Durostorum. The new military commanders (*duces*) of the riparian part of Moesia had the frontier troops (*limitanei*) and the reconditioned fleet under their command. Novae was transformed into a fortress inhabited by soldiers and civilians, now a fortified town with a military garrison, which became part of the Moesia II province. Building activities during the House of Constantines' period, and later during the reign of Valentinian and Valens, strengthened the defensive attributes of many military bases. Nevertheless, the Gothic *foederati* settled by the later Emperor in the Balkans rebelled and defeated the Roman army at Adrianople, prowling the province long after the battle.

The long-term destructive ravage of the rural hinterland resulted in the collapse of local crafts and trade[26]. In the 430s, Novae and Oescus were supplied by the Mediterranean provinces according to the *pastus militum* system, which is well attested by a series of inscriptions.[27] The invasions of the Huns from the 420s up to the mid-5th century had a great impact on local settlement. Although it is not clear whether Attila's demands concerning the subjugation of lands to the west of Novae were actually executed, the destruction and abandonment of rural territories and many towns is well attested. The Lower Danubian towns, including Novae, were revitalised by Theodoric the Great's Goths between 478 and 488. Although in the 6th century the town witnessed a final period of development and revival, a large mass of Slavs and Avars approaching the Balkans pressed the scarce Roman population into finally migrating, and at the beginning of the 7th century they ultimately left their homeland.

Topography of the site

The main part of the site is formed by the legionary fortress (*castra*) which has quite regular shape of a playing card (**Fig. 5**). The inner surface of the camp measures 17.99 ha with some irregularities in the line of the eastern and southern defensive wall.[28] The NS axis of the *castra* is shifted by 8° to the East from the geographical North. The whole site has deep, complex stratigraphy. Among the main buildings inside the fortress which were unearthed by archaeologists is the headquarters building

25. Dimitrov et al. 1970, 60–63.

26. Poulter 2008, 82.

27. Sarnowski 2013; Łajtar 2013, and see Summary and conclusions in this volume.

28. Sarnowski, Kovalevskaja, and Kaniszewski 2005, 141.

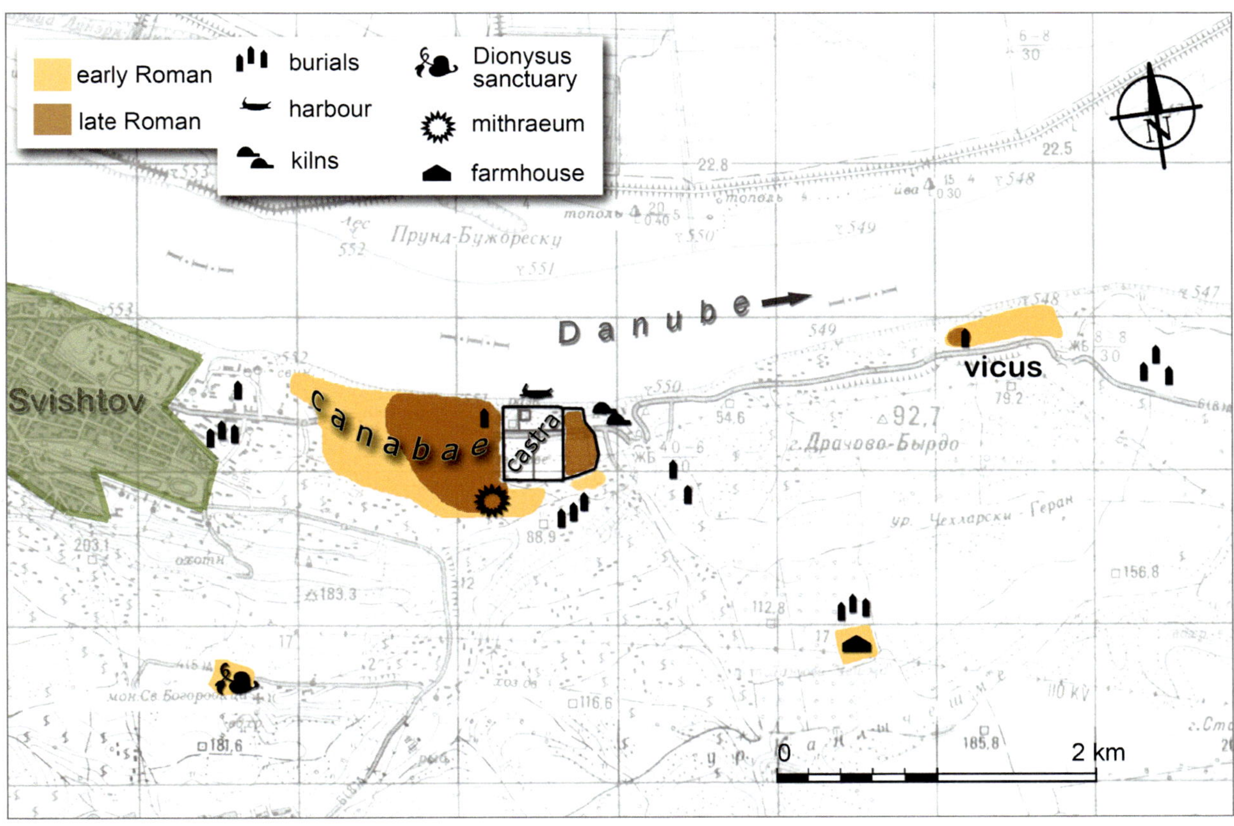

Fig. 7. Novae and its surroundings in Antiquity (by A. Tomas).

(*principia*), the officer's house in the *scamna tribunorum*, the early legionary baths (*thermae legionis*) which existed in the Flavian period, which were superposed by the Trajanic military hospital (*valetudinarium*), and the late Roman residential quarter. The 2nd-century legionary baths unearthed to the west of the headquarters building were replaced by the Episcopal complex.

Recent excavations unveiled architectural remains to the east and to the west of *principia*, as well as rear rooms in the headquarters building unknown so far and large 1st-century pits[29]. Rescue excavations in the *principia* produced a series of inscriptions.[30]

The line of the eastern legionary fortifications is marked by the remains of towers, ghost walls, and ditches, as this side of the former legionary fortress wall was dismantled when the fortress was enlarged by the area to the east of the camp forming the so-called annexe. The late Roman town of Novae received a new layout with this new extension covering ca. 8.85 ha. It was possible to establish the surface of the annexe in 2013-2016 when the measurements with the use of GPS RTK were made along the eastern fortifications.[31]

Traces of human activity including cemeteries and places of manufacture during the early Roman period stretch over the area of 80 ha around the camp (**Fig. 6**). Few buildings outside the fortress have been excavated so far at Novae. The only long-term excavations are being conducted outside the West Gate, where two residential buildings have been unearthed. The buildings outside the West Gate of the fortress were identified as the extramural residence, which was built up by a new large building, and finally overbuilt by a church with a cemetery.[32] Rescue excavations revealed a mithreum and a Liber Pater shrine, some burials, and the remains of water supply facilities.[33] Common dwellings dated to the period when the *canabae* existed have not been excavated by archaeologists.

A possible *vicus* is situated 2.5 km to the east of the fortress' East Gate, in the place called Ostrite Mogili (**Fig. 7**), but traces of the Roman presence were recorded in many places around Novae.[34] In the late Roman period the extramural area was partly abandoned, and unequivocal traces of human presence appear in the annexe.

29. Sarnowski et al. 2014; Sarnowski et al. 2016.
30. Sarnowski et al. 2016.
31. The surface was measured within the fortifications, without a deep gully to the east of the *praetentura dextra*. Including the gully adds another 0.15 ha.

32. Chichikova 1992, 240; Vladkova 2003, 226–27; Tomas 2017, 53–57.
33. Tomas 2017, 50–73.
34. Tomas 2017, 41–92.

II

Introductory remarks on civil settlement near Roman legionary bases and the case of Novae

Agnieszka Tomas

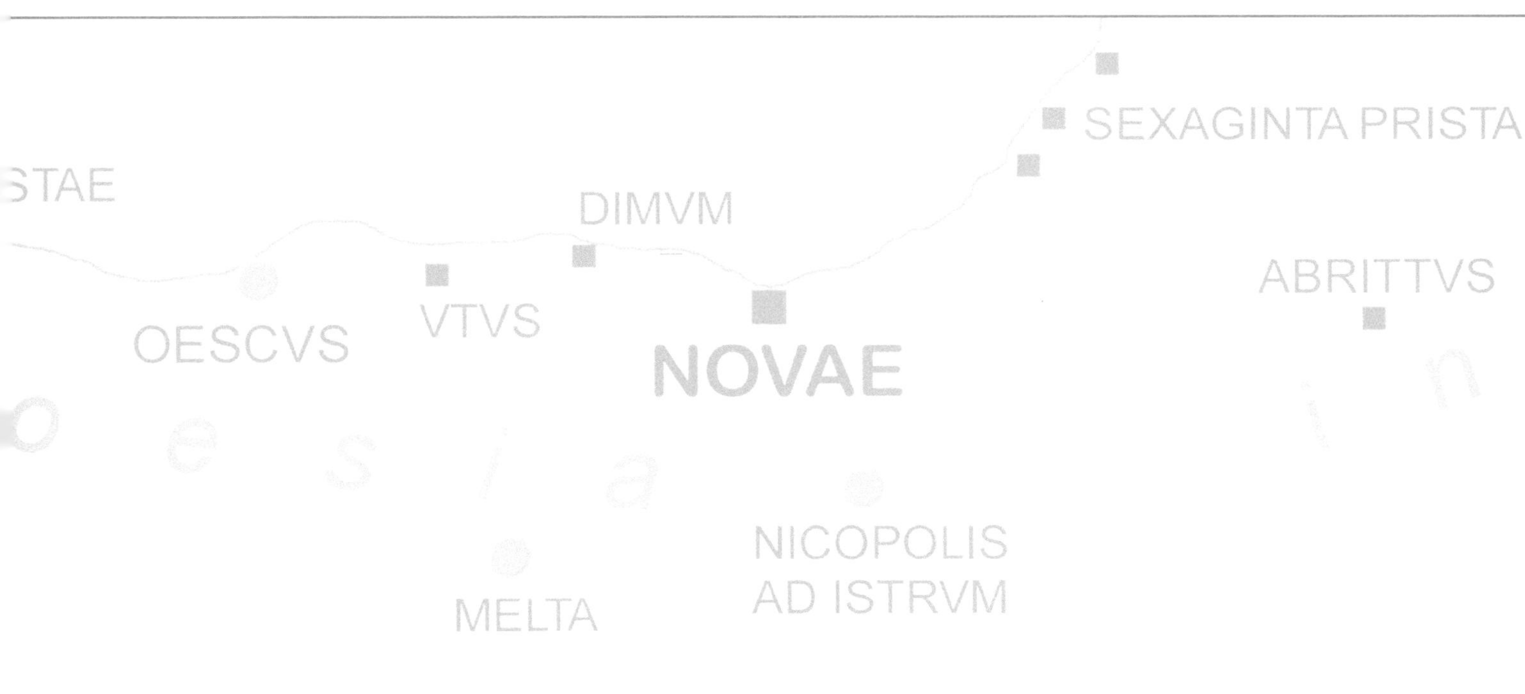

Civilians who followed the army during military campaigns created temporary settlements where they lived in tents and huts. Many of them served food and beverages or provided various services. Such temporary food huts, booths, stalls or tents, particularly with wine,[1] were called *canabae*, as the plural form of the word *canaba*.[2] The unofficial character of such settlements is well illustrated by the fact that the term *canabae* does not appear with reference to military bases in the literary sources from the Principate period. It was first attested in a series of inscriptions dated to AD 100, which refer to the *canabae Dimensis* – civil settlement near Dimum.[3] But more numerous epigraphic pieces of evidence come from Hadrian's times.[4] *Canabae* developed outside camp fortifications, while another associated settlement (*vicus*) was located at a certain distance from the military base, usually about 2–3 km. Such a phenomenon, attested for many European sites, is described in modern literature as settlement duality, but it was mainly true in the case of military bases founded before the end of the 2nd century.[5] The same phenomenon has been observed at Novae, where a second settlement was identified 2.7 km to the east of the camp, at the Ostrite Mogili site.[6]

The majority of the inhabitants consisted of tradesmen, merchants, artisans, and people providing services and entertainment. Apart from Roman veterans and Roman citizens attached to the *canabae*, one could encounter *peregrini* living in the fortress surroundings, and people of low social status, among them musicians, dancers, and gladiators. A substantial number of *canaba* residents were members of soldier and veteran families. The social strata observed at Novae fit this model very well. The inscriptions dated to the first three centuries name 22 veterans, 25 members of military families and 79 civilian inhabitants, among them a significant group of freedmen and people of servile origin.[7]

The *canabae* usually streched out around the camp, reaching as far as the ditches surrounding the fortress. At Chester / Deva, apart from the defensive ditch and patrol track (*berma*), there was a *ca*. 150-m-wide zone which seems to have remained empty.[8] The size of the average legionary fortress (18–25 ha) is not proportional to the surface of its *canabae*. The layout and positioning of the extramural settlement depended also on the local terrain, access to water, and other factors. It usually extended along the streets, starting from the gates. Contrary to some written sources, the extramural settlements were very rarely positioned along the *porta decumana*.[9] The street network could be quite regular, with minor streets crossing at a right angle, or had more developed layouts.[10] Although aqueduct sections have been discovered in many *canabae* settlements, it is not clear whether the same pipelines were feeding the camp and the civil settlement.[11] Drainage and sanitation facilities were of great importance, and such drains are known from Deva and other sites.[12] In some cases, the settlement was encircled by ditches, palisade or masonry walls.[13] Burial grounds were located at a certain distance from the settlement, along the roads. Preliminary findings made during the field surveys by Bulgarian, Polish and German archaeologists at Novae indicated that the archaeological material found around the legionary camp covered an area of 80 ha, including the cemeteries along the main roads.[14]

We can encounter various public and private buildings within the area of the *canabae*. Military amphitheatres, both earth-and-timber and stone constructions, very often occupying an area of about 3 ha, were located not far from legionary and auxiliary bases.[15] Open areas outside the camp are considered to have possibly been parade or training grounds for the infantry and cavalry,[16] but sometimes open spaces within the *canabae* could have been market-places. The location of the amphitheatre at Novae is presumptive and requires further investigation, but it is very possible that it was placed on the north-east

1. TLL, vol. III.1, p. 222–223 (*tabernacula, vicus stativis vicinus, cella vinaria, penaria*); Ernout-Meillet, 91 (tente, barraques, cabarets); DAGR, p. 867; Walde-Hofmann, p. 150 ("Krämerbude beim Heer, Lagerdorf; Vorratskammer für Wein, Schuppen als Warenniederlage, Schutzhütte u. dgl."), DE II, p. 59ff. ("una baracca, un edificio che facilmente si può togliere"). Etymological analysis in Mommsen 1873, 303–305, esp. fn. 5. Ernout-Meillet (see. p. 91 and cf. p. 94) indicated possible connections with the word capanna, which means the hut of someone employed in the wine cellars.
2. Mommsen 1873, 303, fn. 4; DAGR, p. 867 with literature concerning late Roman sources. According to some scholars, this Latin term originates from the Greek word κάν(ν)αβος, denoting a wooden frame or scaffolding; see Liddell and Scott, p. 874; Ernout-Meillet, p. 91.
3. ISM I, 67, 68.
4. Mommsen 1873, 303, fn. 4; Bohn 1926, 29–30; Vittinghoff 1971, 299; DAGR, p. 867 with literature concerning late Roman sources.
5. Mócsy 1954, 183; Mrozewicz 1984; Mason 1988, 178.
6. For an analysis of the topography near Lower Moesian legionary fortresses, see Tomas 2017, esp. for Novae, see 41–79.
7. Tomas 2015a (military families); Tomas 2017, 127–29 and Tab. 8 (all inhabitants).
8. Carrington et al. (eds) 2012, 308.
9. Sommer 1984, 42–44.
10. Evans 2000, Fig. 125.
11. Tomas 2011.
12. Tomas 2013, 145–50; Carrington et al. (eds) 2012, 307.
13. von Petrikovits 1981, 172–73.
14. Tomas 2017, 41–44.
15. von Petrikovits 1979, 229; Hanel 2007, 412.
16. von Petrikovits 1979, 229; 1981, 169; Davis 1968; Sommer 1997, 50–52.

side of the fortress.[17] Other open areas are difficult to trace due to the modern land use around the site.

It has been noted that the location of baths was one of the most significant factors in the development of civil settlements near military bases.[18] They were frequently situated just outside the military base, near the gates, with good access to efficient water sources. We can find spectacular residences in the *canabae*, considered to have been the legate's quarters or the temporary residences of high officials and guesthouses for people travelling on official trips.[19] Common mansions were very often provided with bathhouses and stables and offered a comfortable place to stay. Workshops producing pottery, building materials, terracotta lamps, metal products, as well as granaries and storehouses were always present in the extramural areas.[20] *Tabernae*, i.e., small shops frequently offering food and beverages,[21] were buildings which must have been located outside fortress walls. Some sanctuaries, like Mithraea and Dolichena, were always located outside the fortress, but the official Roman deities were worshipped both inside and outside the military gates. Temples dedicated to Neptune, Diana, Jupiter, Hercules, and others are known from various *canabae*.[22] H. von Petrikovits lists *aediculae* among the *canaba* buildings.[23] Dwellings and residential houses in the western part of the Empire had the form of striphouses along the street. Houses with timber framing (Fachwerk) were often built alongside stone houses. In the former case, the roofs were not covered with tiles.[24] Some private buildings had the form of residences. It is quite striking that not one known extramural settlement had a town centre with a *curia*, *basilica* and main temple, such as are normally found in civilian towns.[25] Inscriptions also do not give any hints as to this issue. While the legionary legate could act as a judge in the *basilica principiorum*, the quasi-municipal and later municipal authorities in the *canabae* would not have their seat.[26]

Military bases were built on public land,[27] and hence their provisioning needs required some space and the surroundings of a camp must have occupied a certain territory.[28] The legion must have had access to resources situated sometimes in distant places; thus, the surface of such military territories could have varied, e.g., depending on the availability of resources or density of the local settlement and its urbanization. The recreation of the territories controlled by a certain legion, based on stamps on building materials and other epigraphic evidence,[29] may be misleading, since the soldiers exercising non-military tasks, including building activities, had multiple opportunities to leave traces.[30] Even if we agree that vast territories were controlled by the legions, such areas must have shrunk with time, as the process of urbanization transformed provincial lands into territories divided among towns, *civitates*, and military bases.[31] The former military territories thus had numerous exterritorial areas with necessary resources,[32] including quarries, meadows or mines. Basic needs, apart from outside supply systems, must have been met by provisions based in the surroundings. Apart from their use as meadows for breeding and husbandry,[33] stone, wood and clay were certainly acquired from legionary territories. The emergence of civil settlement providing basic supplies and residences for military families, particularly in non-urbanized provinces, was an obvious process.

The nearest camp surroundings understood as legionary territory in epigraphic sources are described as *territorium legionis*,[34] *prata legionis / cohortis* or simply *territorium*.[35] The new reading of two inscriptions discovered in the sanctuary of Jupiter on Pfaffenberg Hill near Carnuntum has provoked some discussion concerning the size and limits of the territory around Roman legionary camps. The inscriptions mention a space *intra leugam primam*, i.e., within the first *leuga*, a Gallic measure corresponding to 1.5 Roman mile and 2.222 km.[36] Ioan Piso, who presented this new reading, suggested that the *canabae* with their own self-government were located within the limits of the *leuga*, while another civil settlement, usually just outside its border, was to be found beyond the lands under military

17. Tomas 2017, 76–77.
18. Sommer 1984, 46.
19. von Petrikovits 1979, 235.
20. von Petrikovits 1981, 170–71.
21. Fagan 2002, 32–33 and fn. 51.
22. von Petrikovits 1981, 172–73.
23. von Petrikovits 1979, 235.
24. von Petrikovits 1981, 166.
25. von Petrikovits 1981, 171.
26. In Argentorate the legate of the Eighth Augustan Legion ruled in a controversial inheritance case in AD 186, but it is not clear whether the case was ruled in the camp or in the municipium Arae Flaviae (Rottweil); AE 1956, 90, Wilmanns 1981.
27. ISM V 135, AD 163 (Troesmis); AE 1987, 783 (see Mehl 1986).
28. In the literature, such territory is described as 'military territory', 'Militärland', 'territoire militaire / legionnaire', 'zone d'action', 'zone de surveillée' or 'militärisches Nutzland'; Sarnowski 1988, 71–72; Bérard 1992, 75.
29. E.g. von Gonzenbach 1963; LeRoux 1982, 109–14 (Hispania); Wilkes 1969 (Dalmatia); Baatz 1989, 170–72 (Germania inferior).
30. Rüger 1968, 56–60; Sarnowski 1988, 87; Hanel 2013, 81–82. In the Severan period, the soldiers of the legio I Italica were sent to help in building the fortifications of Salona in Dalmatia; see Wilkes 1969, 119.
31. Such an idea was presented for the first time in 1894 by Adolf Schulten (1894, 483); cf. doubts were presented by Fr. Bérard (1992, 76).
32. Vittinghoff 1974, 113; also Bérard 1992, 86.
33. von Petrikovits 1979, 231–32.
34. CIL III 10489; Mócsy 1974, 347 (Aquincum).
35. Hanel 2013; Kovács 2013.
36. Piso 1991; idem, 2003, 12 and Nos. 6–11, 19.

control.[37] He pointed out, however, that in some cases, this model seemed to not have been implemented; thus, the theory raises some doubts. The Gallic measure used in Carnuntum, as well as in *Galliae* and *Germaniae*, is not surprising, but it was not so commonly used outside these territories.[38] The application of both measures is also possible, since 1 *leuga* corresponds more or less to 1.5 Roman miles. In the case of a dispute, Roman measures would be treated as more reliable.[39] But the crucial argument against this theory is that the topography of Carnuntum itself does not fit this model, and neither do those of other sites, such as Apulum, Durostorum, and Lambaesis.[40] Further doubts arise if we consider the implementation of a land measure in the form of a circle, which is rather impossible and absurd in land surveying.[41] Another question can be raised concerning the point from which a *leuga* would be delimited – *locus gromae*, the fortification line or both points in various places.[42] Perhaps the term *leuga* should be understood as a metonymy of an area,[43] among other words meaning *territorium*.[44] Warwick Rodwell has shown that the major towns in Britain were surrounded by considerable territories, not necessarily symmetrical, which could span a river or be defined by artificial boundaries.[45] The emergence of no-man's-land zones (*agri vacuos*) on the barbarian side of the river during the Roman conquest[46] created favourable conditions for their use by the army. Boundary markers of the *prata legionis primae Minerviae* and stamped building materials were discovered on the other side of the Rhein.[47] On the other hand, the army (or rather a unit) could have leased private land for public (military) use.[48]

The *canabae* and *vicus* each had their own independent administrations. A number of epigraphic finds mention members of the magistratus in the context of civil settlements near military bases. We do not know whether the *canaba* could have its own *territorium*,[49] although the *vicus* certainly could. If we agree that the *canabae* developed on legionary territory, i.e., most likely on *ager publicus*, public land owned by the emperor (*solum Caesaris*), it would have been impossible. Nonetheless, the questions concerning which of these two settlements and when was granted municipal rights remain open in the case of the majority of legionary bases. Regrettably, epigraphic evidence mentioning the status of extramural settlements at Novae is very scarce, with one inscription discovered so far. It consists of only one letter 'M', which has been interpreted as an abbreviation of 'municipium', and it remains a matter of debate which settlement was granted this privilege.[50] The size and quality of the remains, as well as the low amount of epigraphic evidence, seem to indicate that it was the *canabae* which was granted this status, and the fact that it happened relatively late may explain why there were so few inscriptions.[51]

For many years the civil settlements accompanying the camp at Novae have been the subject of mainly theoretical considerations regarding their location and the possible receipt of municipal rights. Settlement duality, the location of the municipium and the moment when Novae was granted municipal rights were also analysed by L. Mrozewicz and other authors.[52] The site of Ostrite Mogili first attracted the attention of Stefan Stefanov, and later Boris Gerov, who identified the *vicus* as an element of settlement duality, known from analogous Roman legionary bases. The state of research known at the moment when we started the project was presented in 2017.[53]

One of the main goals of the non-destructive investigations conducted outside the legionary camp at Novae was to establish whether the idea of an applied settlement pattern could be traced archaeologically and what kind of pattern was adopted at that site. The short six-week period of investigations was not fully sufficient, but some important observations and measurements were made and the results of this research are presented in the following chapters.

37. Piso 1991.
38. Kovàcs 2000, 40; Gugl 2012, 414. Its use in one town in Colonia Canopitana in Africa (AÉ 1979, 658) is an exception, possibly due to the fact that the municipal aristocracy originated from Gaul; Beschaouch 1979, esp. 404–405.
39. Hyg. 91.36–39 "[…] we must watch out (for the practices of) different regions in case we seem to be doing something unusual. For our profession will retain its integrity if we also conduct our investigations principally according to the practice of the region"; transl. by Campbell 2000, 95 and see the note about the author on p. XXXV.
40. Sommer 2004, 313; Gugl 2012, 414.
41. Piso 2003, 12; Sommer 2004, 315.
42. Sommer 2004, 312; Kovàcs 2000, 43–44.
43. Beschaouch 1979, 403–07, Abb. 5; Kovács 2000, 40–42 and 48–50; Gugl 2012, 414, 417; Doneus, Gugl, and Doneus 2013, 175–86, esp. 182.
44. A list of terms referring to *territorium* was collected by Leveau 1993, 463–466.
45. Rodwell 1975, 90.
46. Tac. *Ann.* XIII 54.1: eoque Frisii iuventutem saltibus aut paludibus, imbellem aetatem per lacus admovere ripae agrosque vacuos et militum usui sepositos insedere; Cass. Dio LXXII 3.2; 15; 16.1. Dio suggested that it was a five-to-ten-mile (10–20 km) wide zone; see Potter 1997; Austin and Rankov 1995, 180.
47. von Petrikovits 1979, 239–40.
48. CIL III 14356.3a = AE 1900, 156, Carnuntum: *C(aius) Iul(ius) Catul/linus mil(es) / leg(ionis) XIIII G(eminae) M(artiae) V(ictricis) / cond(uctor) prat(i) / Fur(iani)*, and see Harmatta 1974, 83; Tibiletti 1974, 100.

49. Bérard 1992, 88ff.
50. AÉ 1964, 224 = ILBulg 282 = IGLNov 39; Tomas 2017, 160 and Fig. 60.
51. Tomas 2017, 159–62.
52. Gerov 1977; Parnicki-Pudełko 1981; Mrozewicz 1981b; 1981c; 1982, 61; 1984, 296; 2008; Tomas 2017, 159–64.
53. Tomas 2017.

III

The present and the past environment

Magdalena Moskal-del Hoyo, Renata Stachowicz--Rybka, Agnieszka Tomas, and Hanna Winter

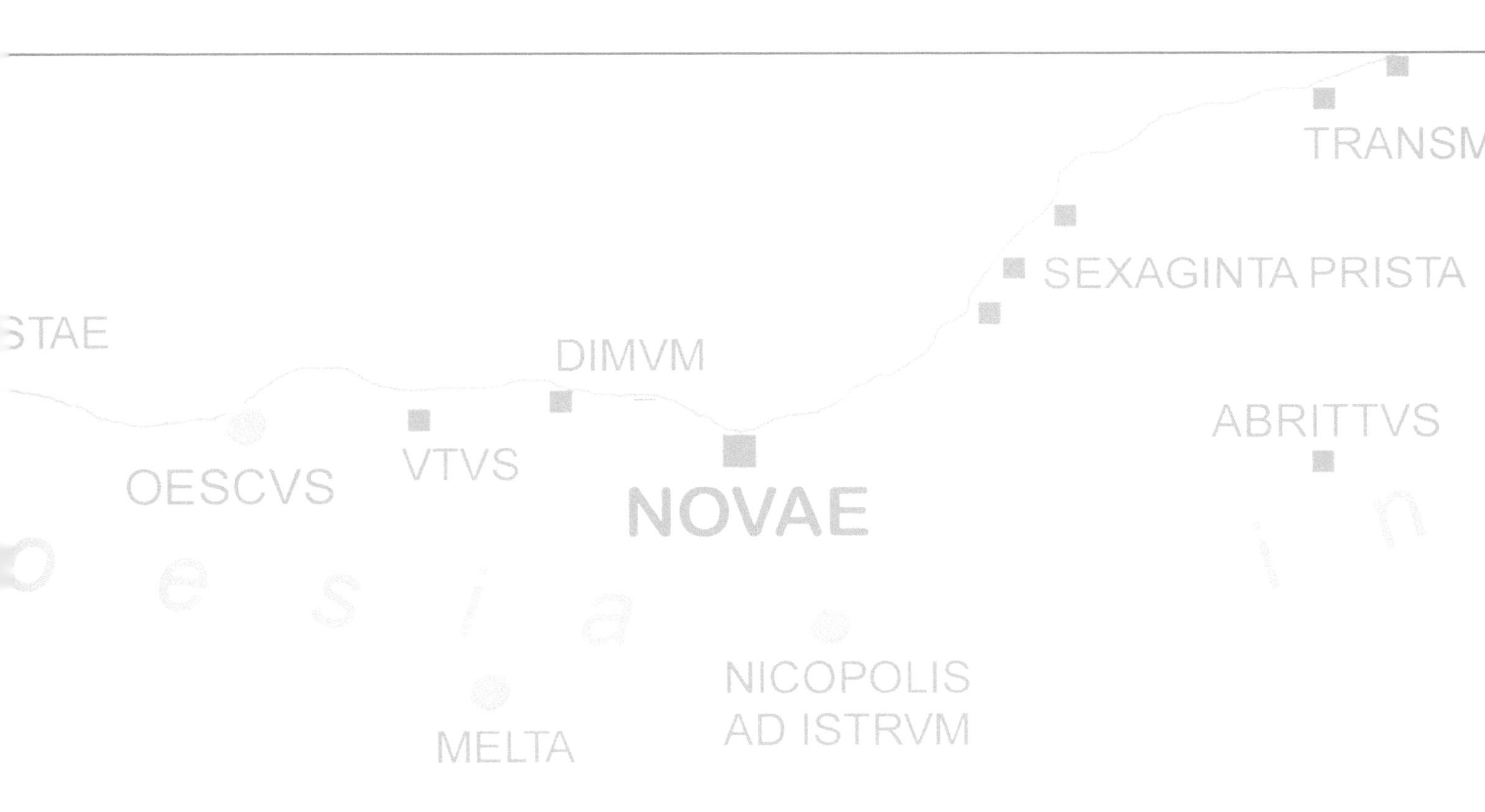

1. The environment at present

Agnieszka Tomas

The climate closely resembles a continental one with a dry and very warm summer and cold winter.[1] The highest temperatures reach +43°C, and the lowest temperatures in January may drop to –34.5°C and are the lowest in the whole Lower Danubian area. Despite the river being quite wide in this section, the waters of the Danube can sometimes freeze and become unnavigable, even overnight.[2] The average winter temperatures amount to slightly less than 0°C and in the summer ca. +23°C, with August being the warmest month (+24°C). The temperatures remain relatively high until late autumn, but the early autumn frosts, which are harmful to crops, may come as early as at the end of August. The largest rainfall occurs in the early summer and in winter,[3] while droughts occur in the early spring (February–March) and late summer (August–September). Strong gales may appear in winter and the snow cover remains for *ca.* 50 days. The strip of land stretching along the Danube has rather harsh climate conditions as compared to the area surrounding Nicopolis ad Istrum.[4]

The entire area is rich in springs with wells and public water intakes (Bulg. *cheshmi*). A large, 1.5-km wide and 3-km long underground water reservoir yielding 3500 litres per second is located to the west of Svishtov. The area of the modern-day town and its surroundings has resources of artesian thermo-mineral waters with a temperature between 44–47°C and water flow of 50–80 litres per second.[5]

The surroundings of Novae are covered with alluvial-riparian and riparian-silty soils with 20-m thick loess layers.[6] Chernozem and brown earths can be found farther to the south.[7] The thick loess layers, well visible in the high bank of the Danube, contain siltstone and calcareous or quartz sandstone blocks, with thick outcrops near the village of Oresh, around 18 km west of Novae. Layers of soft and hard limestone are present in the whole area.[8] The nearest lime quarries are located within a 5-km radius, near the villages of Tsarevets, Oresh, and Vardim, while the larger ones are situated near the outlets of the Yantra and Osum rivers.[9] Better-quality metamorphosed limestone

1. Gylybov et al. 1960, 8, 128.
2. Tomas 2016, 9.
3. Gylybov et al. 1960, 129.
4. Tomas 2016, Tab. II.
5. Vasilev et al. 1974, 7.
6. Gylybov et al. 1960, 84; Smalley et al. 2009, 8.
7. Vasilev et al. 1974, 10; Tomas 2016, 6.
8. Skoczylas 1995, 98.
9. Tomas 2016, 37–38.

Fig. 8. Novae 2012. The aerial view of the south-eastern part of the site and the valley of the Dermen dere river (photo by M. Pisz).

used at Novae in monumental architecture and public monuments was quarried near Hotnitsa, in the rural territory of Nicopolis.[10] Novae is located in a seismically active region. Although earthquakes are not frequent now, it is very possible that were in Antiquity, especially between the 3rd and 4th centuries AD.[11]

At present, the entire area is covered with forest steppe with wood enclaves (**Fig. 8**), mainly pine and mixed woods, including such trees as elm, hornbeam, poplar, linden, ash, walnut, mulberry, yew, birch, chestnut, sycamore and hazel, as well as oak in the Oresh area.[12] The northern part of Novae is forested, but this was not the case in the mid-20th century. The trees were planted during the creation of the park at the beginning of the 1960s. The hills to the south of Novae are favourable for cultivating vine and large, opened fields are used for growing cereals, sunflowers and corn.

The recreation of the past environment was a very important element of the project, as settlement patterns are influenced not only by human activities, but also by the flora and fauna and the past landscape. The issue of the changes in the local landscape which occurred after the Roman conquest constitute a most intriguing question, requiring long-term palaeoenvironmental analyses.

10. Škorpil 1905, 476–77; Skoczylas 1999; Tomas 2016, 37.
11. Sarnowski, Kovalevskaja, and Tomas 2010, 169 and fn. 66.
12. Gylybov et al. 1960, 89; Vasilev et al. 1974, 11.

2. Palynological study of the samples from the archaeological site at Novae

Hanna Winter

The samples and the method

Using the pollen analysis method, twelve samples were tested, all of which had been taken in 2009 from archaeological layers dated to the period between the 1st century and the beginning of the 7th century, while – for comparison – one sample was collected from the layer superposing the virgin soil (12/09) and one from the humus (6/09) (**Tab. I** and **II**). Samples collected during excavations in the northern defensive walls and the *intervallum*[13] originated from (1/09) the early street (*via sagularis*), (10/09) a ramp (*ascensus*),

13. For a discussion of the excavation results in this section, see Sarnowski, Kovalevskaja, and Tomas 2010, 163–69. The analysis was conducted within the framework of the project financed by the Polish National Science Centre 2011/01/D/HS3/02187. Prepared by Dr Hanna Winter, Polish Geological Institute – National Research Institute.

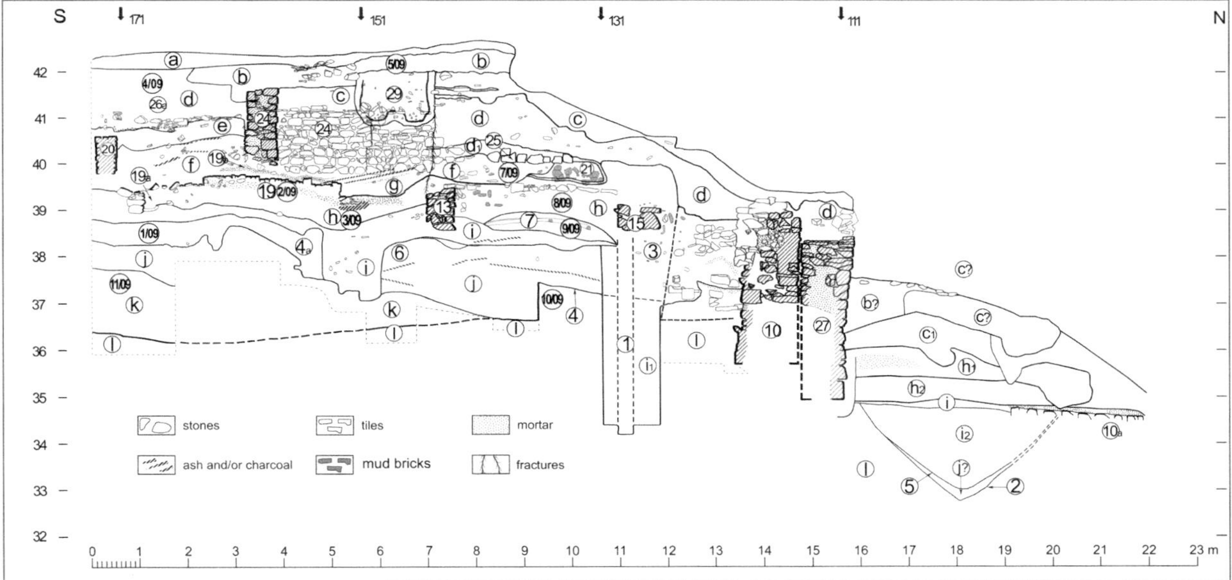

Fig. 9. Novae 2009. Northern defences. Section P1 (by A. Tomas, P. Zakrzewski with minor corrections by A. Tomas). 1: Post hole, 2: 1st-century ditch, 3: Rampart, 4: Ramp (*ascensus*), 4a: 1st-century street (*via sagularis*), 5: late 1st-century ditch, 6: Ghost wall(?), 7: Smashed oven, 10: Trajanic curtain wall, 10a: Soil reinforcing stones, 15: Northern wall of rectangular structure, 19: 2nd–3rd-century street (*via sagularis*), 19a: Street sewer, 19b: late 3rd-century street, 20: Northern wall of a centurial barrack; 21: Oven, 24: Southern wall of a late-3rd century building, 26a: 4th-century street, 27: Late retaining wall, 29: 6th-century pottery kiln; a: Top soil with the 6th-century finds, b: Layer with the 5th-century finds, b(?) – possibly 5th-century layer; c, d, d1: Layers with the late 4th-century finds, c? – possibly the late 4th-century layer, d, d1: Layers with early 4th-century finds, e: Layer with early 4th century finds, e? – possibly early 4th-century layer, f – Layer with the 3rd-century finds, g – Layer with the 2nd century finds, h – Layer with the early 2nd-century finds, i – Layer with the late 1st-century finds; j, k: Layers with the 1st-century finds (Flavian?), l: virgin soil. Numbers 1/09 – 10/09 refer to the numbers of the samples (sample no. 11/09 was extracted from the place not illustrated here).

(11/09) a layer under the stone foundation of the Flavian barracks, (2/09) a late Flavian *via sagularis*, (3/09) a Trajanic levelling layer under the *via sagularis,* (9/09) an oven in the *intervallum*, (8/09) a building layer dated to Trajan's reign, (7/09) a layer outside the oven, (4/09) a thick levelling(?) layer outside a late Roman building, (5/09) a layer above a 6th-century pottery kiln (**Fig. 9**).

The various pollen specimens were in different states of preservation. They were often torn with blurred reliefs and corroded, while Cerealia grains were frequently very strongly crumbled and eroded. The bad state of preservation and the crumbling of the specimens made it impossible for the cereal pollens' genus to be established. Especially tricolpate and tricolporate grains have undergone extensive damage, making it impossible to identify them. Pollen destruction is characteristic for settlements that were subjected to the influence of air, located above water level. The pollen frequency was variable, from very low to very high. The presence of pollen clusters and anther fragments were especially prominent. Charcoal and fragments of charred tissue, fungus spores and other non-pollen fossils, including phytoliths were also encountered within the specimens.

The laboratory analysis of the samples involved the removal of calcium carbonate using 10% of HCl, after which the samples were boiled in a 7% KOH solution. The separation of mineral fractions from the organic ones occurred through the use of heavy liquids (an aqueous solution of cadmium and potassium iodide) of a density of 2,1g/cm^3 The appropriate maceration was conducted by using a modified version of E. Erdtmann's acetolysis method. The analysis was done using a Carl Zeiss Axioskop microscope. The entire microscopic section covering a surface of 22×22mm was counted. Atlases were used in the process of marking the pollen and spores.[14]

The results of the analyses have been presented in the form of a table containing the absolute and percentage values. In the case of percentage calculations, the sum of the tree and shrub pollen (AP – arboreal pollen) and land herbaceous plant pollen (NAP – non-arboreal pollen) come to a base sum total of 100%. The percentage of aquatic plants, spores, damaged or unmarked pollen was calculated in relation to the base sum total (**Tab. I**).

The results

The samples for pollen analysis were taken from various spots at the site attributed to different periods. The permanent or periodical drying up of the sediment resulted in the selective destruction of pollen and high Cichorioideae and Chenopodiaceae values, but also in the low percentage of other taxa. The possibility of spectrum disruptions as a result of the digging of stone foundations might have occurred in the case of sample 11/09. It is assumed that pollen penetration did not take place through vertical transport. The very low frequency resulted from the selective destruction of the pollen grains in samples 7 and 8/09.

The spectra of the pollen from the archaeological sites reflect the local vegetation. This is attested by the domination of herbaceous plant pollen (NAP) in relation to tree and shrub pollen (AP) in all the spectra. In some samples, Cichoriodeae, Chenopodiaceae and Poaceae achieve very high values, while it was simultaneously easy to identify damaged specimens and the occurrence of pollen clusters, as indicated by their overrepresentation.

Taking into account the presumed deposition time, the results of the analysis have been divided into groups consisting of samples similar in age.

1st – 2nd centuries

The frequency of the pollen in sample 1/09 was very low, of which the majority was that of Cichorioideae (82.5%). There were also quite numerous taxon pollen belonging to the *Tragopogon pratensis* family (4.8%), the *Crepis* type (6.3%) and *Lactuca sativa* (1.6%). Aside from the dominant Cichorioideae pollen, the only other pollen present was that of Poaceae (1.6%) and Chenopodiaceae (1.6%) pollen.

Plants representing the Cichorioideae subfamily are cosmopolitan and can be encountered throughout the world, but they are the most diverse in the Mediterranean climate and in the cold climate in the northern hemisphere. Even though such a high share of such plant pollen may be linked to the presence of human beings,[15] they could also occur in various open habitats. In the Mediterranean region, they have been noted in large numbers in settlements from the previous glaciations and from the Holocene.[16]

Within the spectrum of sample 2/09, NAP pollen with a prevalence of Poaceae (42.6%) are predominant, along with a high share of Chenopodiaceae, Cichorioideae, *Cerealia* and Brassicaceae, *Anthemis* t., *Tragopogon pratensis* t., *Taraxacum officinale* t., *Aster* t., *Cirsium* t., Chenopodiaceae and *Plantago*

14. Punt et al. 1976–2009; Moore et al., 1991; Reille 1992–98; Beug 2004.

15. Behre 1981.

16. Combourieu et al. 2009.

lanceolata. Tree pollen are more abundant, especially *Pinus sylvestris* t. and *Carpinus.*

The diversity of the herbaceous plant pollen indicates the occurrence of different plant communities. Cereal (*Cerealia*) pollen attests to the fact that such plants were cultivated. Crops were the source of Cichorioideae, Poaceae, Brassicaceae, Chenopodiaceae and Asteroideae pollen, including *Anthemis* t., *Aster* t. and *Cirsium* t. Wet meadows and pastures were covered with ribwort plantain (*Plantago lanceolata*), hoary plantain (*Plantago media*), *Rumex acetosa* t., Poaceae and Asteraceae. At dry natural sites, Poaceae, Brassicaceae, Apiaceae and various complexes (Asteraceae: Asteroideae and Cichorioideae) were encountered.

Within the spectrum of sample 9/09, NAP were represented mainly by Cichorioideae (37.1%), Poaceae (5.4%), *Cirsium* t. (4.7%), *Anthemis* t. (4.0%), *Artemisia* (4.3%), Asteroideae (3.3%), *Aster* t. (3.3%), Chenopodiaceae (2.3%), Cerealia (1.7%), Brassicaceae (1.7%), *Centaurea jacea* t. (1.7%), *Centaurea scabiosa* t. (1%), and others.

The presence of *Cerealia* pollen attests to the cultivation of cereals. Cichorioideae, *Artemisia, Centaurea jacea* t., *Cirsium* t. pollen came from these plant communities and from ruderal communities. *Centaurea* and *Cirsium* pollen can also probably be linked to pastures. The strong influence of steppe vegetation can be indicated by the presence of Asterioideae, *Aster* t., *Anthemis* t., Cichorioideae, *Cirsium* t., Chenopodiaceae and Apiaceae, as well as psammophyte and halophyte taxa: *Artemisia,* Brassicaceae and Chenopodiaceae.[17] Tree pollen is represented by *Pinus sylvestris* t., *Quercus* and *Tilia.* There were probably clusters of trees consisting of pine, oak, linden, and perhaps also hornbeam.

The spectrum from sample 11/09 is characterised by a prevalence of Chenopodiaceae pollen (64.1%), which is linked to the presence of anther fragments. The presence of anther in the settlement might be attested by the presence of the same type of pollen grains both scattered within the settlement and present in concentrations. Nonetheless, pollen of another type was also present; thus, it should be assumed that such a high frequency was not linked to the described phenomenon, but testifies to the abundant occurrence of Chenopodiaceae in the plant communities. There were also Poaceae and Cichorioideae pollen clusters, but their share was much lower, i.e. 9.7% and 4.4% respectively. The listed pollen came from very different habitats – fields, meadows and pastures, but also from natural communities.

It is worth noting the high share of pollen from plants of the goosefoot family (Chenopodiaceae), which are more abundantly present in places that are dry and salinated, associated with dry steppes, frequently in desert regions. Some of the pollen might also have been connected to ruderal and trampled habitats. Such pollen as *Centaurea jacea* t., Brassicaceae, Poaceae, *Centaurea scabiosa, Geranium* might have come from wet meadow communities. Wet communities may be linked to such pollen as *Polygonum persicaria* t., *Polygonum bistorta* t., Apiaceae, while dry habitats can be associated with *Knautia* and Asteroideae pollen.

A high share of Cichorioideae pollen (43.1%), as well as a substantial percentage of *Artemisia* (13.7%), Chenopodiaceae (8.8%) and Cerealia (5.9%) are characteristic for the spectrum of sample 12/09. Among the NAP, Cyperaceae (4.9%), Asteroideae (3.9%), Brassicaceae (2.0%), Apiaceae, *Centaurea nigra* t., *Valeriana officinalis* t. and others are more numerous. Tree pollen is represented primarily by *Pinus sylvestris* type, *Quercus* and *Carpinus.*

4th – 6th/7th centuries

Sample 4/09 shows a high share of Cichorioideae (48.6%) and a lower one of Poaceae (14%), Chenopodiaceae (9.3%), *Artemisia* (3.7%), Asteroideae (3.7%), *Cirsium* t. (3.7%), Apiaceae (2.7%). The spectrum represents various local communities of Cichoriodeae, Poaceae, Chenopodiaceae and *Artemisia.* Nitrophyte communities can also be linked to the pollen of Cichorioideae, *Artemisia,* Chenopodiaceae and Apiaceae.

Within the spectrum of sample 5/09, high values are characteristic for the pollen of herbaceous plants, such as Cichorioideae (37.3%), Chenopodiaceae (22.7%), Poaceae (11.8%), *Artemisia* (5.5%) and *Cirsium* t. (4.3%). As in the case of the previous sample, the presence of Chenopodiaceae, Cichorioideae, *Artemisia* might indicate a nitrophyte environment. The presence of cereals (*Cerealia*) attests to the existence of farmland, from which such pollen as Cichorioideae, Poaceae and *Cirsium* t. might originate. Ruderal and trampled communities might be the source of *Artemisia*, Chenopodiaceae, Poaceae and Cichorioideae pollen.

Pollen samples from the humus

The pollen spectrum from sample 6/09 predominantly consists of Brassicaceae (39.4%), Cichorioideae (28.2%) and Chenopodiaceae (22.2%) pollen. There

17. Marinova and Atanassova 2006.

is a small share of *Artemisia* (1.8%) and *Cirsium* t. (1.6%).

In the case of the Brassicaceae and Chenopodiaceae pollen, marking their genus is impossible. It should be assumed that Cichorioideae are encountered in open ecologically-diverse habitats. The presence of *Artemisia* and *Centaurea jacea* t. pollen, as well as that of Chenopodiaceae can be linked to open communities, and rather dry ones. The pollen of Brassicaceae, Cichorioideae, *Cirsium* t., Cyperaceae, *Anthemis* t. and *Polygonum aviculare* t. came from fresh and wet habitats.

Plants belonging to the Brassicaceae family are cosmopolitan in character; however, in Europe they preferably grow in Mediterranean areas. Many of these plants can be used by humans, but the lack of any indication of human activities may confirm that they were present in natural local plant communities.

Conclusions

As already mentioned, the prevalence of NAP over AP is characteristic for archaeological sites and attests to the distortion of the regional vegetation, or perhaps even microregional, due to the overrepresentation of herbaceous plant pollen. The taxonomic composition of the tree pollen, aside from sample 6/09 that comes from the contemporary humus, includes the pollen of deciduous trees, such as *Quercus*, *Carpinus*, *Tilia* and *Ulmus*. The remaining *Alnus*, *Fagus* and *Betula* taxa are only encountered sporadically. The pollen of conifers, *Pinus sylvestris* t., *Picea* and *Abies*, are much more abundant. Such a taxonomic composition might indicate the presence of forest communities with oak (*Quercus*), spruce (*Picea*), hornbeam (*Carpinus*) and linden (*Tilia*) at fresh sites, with elm and alder in wet places. A similar pollen image is noted in the diagram from the Durankulak-2 drilling,[18] but Marinova suggests that the conifer (*Pinus*), spruce (*Picea*) and fir tree (*Abies*) came from distant transports.[19]

The role of pine trees remains uncertain as they might have constituted part of the communities, but such pollen may have actually originated only from distant transports.[20] Oak, hornbeam and linden are also anemophilous trees, heavily pollinating, and their source might have been distant transport. Spruce and elm pollen, i.e. trees with lower pollen productivity, as well as the pollen of spruce, consisting of heavy seeds not easily transported over large distances, should be considered to have occurred *in situ*, but transports to the discussed area are not excluded. Similarly, the presence of fir-tree pollen (*Abies*), a weak pollen producer characterized by short-distance transport, is indicated by the occurrence of individual specimens of this tree in forest communities.[21] It is also obvious that beech (*Fagus*) pollen taxon is linked to mountain sites. It is considered that the pollen of this tree is subrepresented in spectra,[22] and thus individual seeds might indicate the presence of this tree. In this context, the individual occurrence of this tree pollen in sample 6/09, in the modern-day sample, might signify very heavy deforestation or selective pollen destruction.

In the pollen spectra from the studied samples, the following pollen is present at very high values: Cichorioideae, Chenopodiaceae, Asteroideae, Poaceae and Brassicaceae. Both in present times and in the past, the presence of Brassicaceae, Chenopodiaceae, Cichorioideae and Asteroideae is characteristic for the Mediterranean region.[23] The occurrence of Chenopodiaceae and *Artemisia* is linked to steppe communities, but in the spectra from Novae there is no *Ephedra* pollen, which has been noted at other sites in Bulgaria.[24] In all probability, the spectra reflect the occurrence of natural local steppe-like communities and xerothermic herbaceous flora. The ecological requirements of the plants belonging to Cichorioideae, Asterioideae, Brassicaceae, Poaceae, Cyperaceae but also to Chenopodiaceae are undetermined and they can be present in very diverse habitats – from wet to dry ones, as well as those that are nitrophytic. This attests to the occurrence of diverse local habitats, with the vegetation occurring in mosaics, i.e. in small patches.

The following pollen, i.e. *Aster* t., *Saussurea* t., *Centaurea scabiosa* t. and *C. jacea* t., *Scabiosa, Ambrosia, Bupleurum* and *Viccia*, originated in dry habitats. Cyperaceae, Apiaceae, various species of *Cirsium, Knautia, Geranium, Valeriana, Polygonum persicaria* t., *P. bistorta, Campanula, Dipsacus* and *Convolvulus* grew at fresh and wet sites. *Malva neglecta* was present in dry sandy soil.

A variable share of cereal pollen (*Cerealia*) was encountered in the pollen spectra from the studied samples as an indicator of human activities. The percentage of the remaining indicators of the first

18. Bozilova and Tonkov 1998.
19. Marinova 2003.
20. Latałowa et al. 2004.
21. Obidowicz et al. 2004; Suszka 1983.
22. Sugita et al. 1999.
23. Bozilova and Tonkov 1998; Marinova 2003; Marinova and Atanassova 2006; Noti et al. 2009; Combourieu-Nebout et al. 2009.
24. Marinova 2003.

order[25] is very low and represented by the pollen of ribwort plantain (*Plantago lanceolata*), common sorrel (*Rumex acetosa* t.) and common knotgrass (*Polygonum aviculare* t.). As weeds, Cichorioideae, Asteroideae, Brassicaceae, Poaceae, Cheonopodiaceae, *Artemisia*, Apiaceae, Caryophyllaceae, *Plantago lanceolata* occupied various synanthropic communities: farmland, meadows, dry swards and pastures, as well as ruderal and trampled habitats.[26]

The low percentage of indicating taxon pollen may attest to low anthropogenic activity, while the presence of cereals and synanthropic plants might largely be linked to airborne pollen blown in from some distance, of even up to 1 km away, to a deforested area. The pollen spectra probably primarily reflect local natural flora.

3. Plant macro-remains from Novae

Renata Stachowicz-Rybka,
Magdalena Moskal-del Hoyo

The six samples containing plant macro-remains analysed and presented in this paper were taken from a trench in the rear part (retentura) of the legionary fortress at Novae (**Fig. 10**).[27] Sample 1 (primarily interpreted as virgin soil) was taken from a layer which was first described as virgin soil, Samples 2 (Neronian(?)–Flavian) and 3 (Flavian) originate from a 1st-century layer – including the content of a vessel found in this layer (**Fig. 11**), Sample 4 is dated to the early 2nd century, Sample 5 is dated to the 2nd–3rd centuries, while Sample 6 is dated to the 4th century (**Tab. III**).

Material and research methods (Tab. III)

After the sediment samples were measured, they were water-sieved using a sieve with a mesh diameter of Ø = 0.18 mm. The material obtained after drying was sorted under a stereoscopic microscope, in order to select seeds, fruits, and vegetative plant fragments suitable for taxonomic identification. The sediment volume and lithological characteristics of each sample are provided in Table III. The presence of seeds, fruits and charcoal fragments was recorded in all the analysed samples.

Plant macro-remains, such as fruits and seeds, were determined on the basis of morphological features visible with a binocular magnifier at 10x and 16x magnifications. Various fruits and seeds were identified using keys, atlases, and other publications, as well as a comparative collection of modern diaspores and fossil flora from the National Biodiversity Collection of Recent and Fossil Organisms at W. Szafer Institute of Botany, Polish Academy of Sciences (herbarium KRAM) in Kraków.

The charcoals were identified with a metallographic microscope using magnifications of 100–500x and compared with anatomical atlases and specimens from the reference collection housed in the Department of Palaeobotany at the W. Szafer Institute of Botany, Polish Academy of Sciences. The identification of individual fragments of the charcoals is based on the observation of fresh fractures in three anatomical sections: a transverse section, a longitudinal radial section and a longitudinal tangential section. In order to observe all the anatomical details characteristic of the respective species, it is recommended to examine fragments larger than 4 mm3; however, smaller specimens are usually also identifiable.[28] From the Novae site, only pieces of burnt wood larger than 1 mm in transverse-section were analysed. Micrographs were taken in the Laboratory of Scanning Electron Microscopy and Microanalysis at the Institute of Geological Sciences, Jagiellonian University (HITACHI S-4700).

Analysis of the seeds and fruits (Tab. IV)

The state of the plant remains from the site in Novae was diverse and depended mainly on how they had been preserved. In four samples, various seeds and fruits occurred mainly as mineralized specimens: Sample 1, 2, 3, and 4. In two samples, Samples 5 and 6, they occurred only in the form of charred specimens. As a rule, the mineralized specimens were well or very well preserved, while the charred specimens and some of the mineralized ones were not suitable for identification to the species level. A total of 15 taxa of varying levels were identified in the samples analysed: 9 identified to species level, 1 probably to species, 1 to genus, 1 to phylum, and 2 to family. Most of the grains were generally classified as Cerealia indet cereals. Detailed results of the identifications are presented in Tables IV and V.

The remains of cultivated plants were preserved. They occurred in the form of mineralized kernels, grains and seeds, as well as in the form of burnt

25. Behre 1990.
26. Behre 1981.
27. Sarnowski et al. 2016, 188–189 and Figs. 13–14. Figure 14 published in the excavation report from 2017 contains an erroneous description of the layers. This publication presents the corrected version of the drawing and a new interpretation of the layer described in 2017 as virgin soil.
28. Chabal et al. 1999.

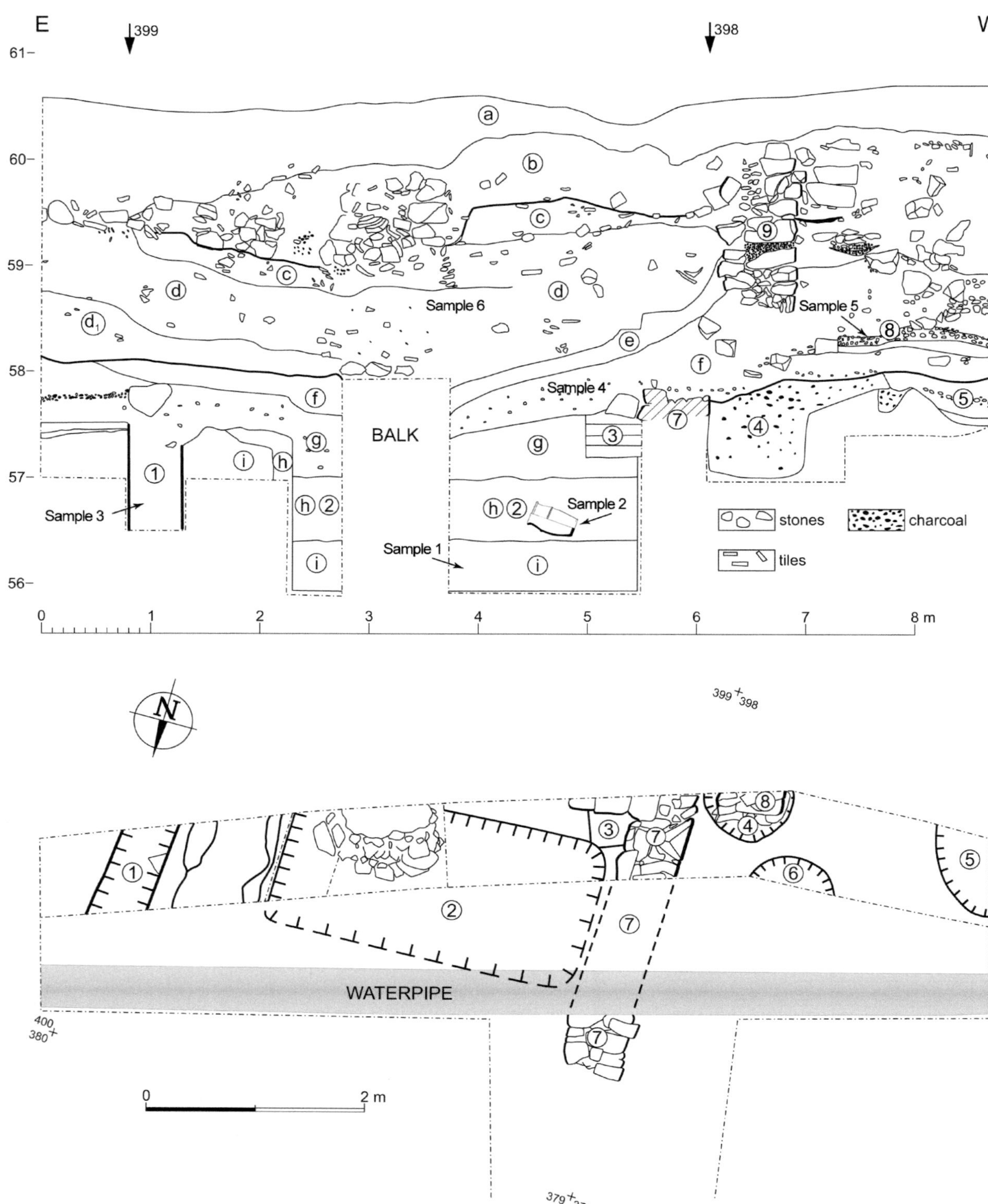

Fig. 10. Novae 2014. Water pipeline trench in the left *retentura* (by A. Tomas, P. Zakrzewski). Plan and section – 1: Foundation trench, 2: Cellar, 3: Mud-bricks, 4: Storage(?) pit (yellow-brownish loess with large amounts of charcoal), 5–6: Early pits, 7: Early wall (stones in yellow loess bonding), 8: 2nd – mid-3rd-century street, 9: Late wall (stones in grey earth bonding), a: Humus, b: Light grey earth with stones, broken tiles and large lumps of yellow mortar, c: Light orange earth with large amounts of broken tiles, charcoal and lumps of white mortar, d: Grey and dark grey (d1) earth with charcoal and small fragments of broken tiles, e: Light yellow loess with white mortar and charcoal, f: Grey-yellow earth with charcoal, broken tiles, white mortar and stones, g-i: Earthen filling of the cellar (g: dirty grey-yellow loess, h: Grey loose loess with large amounts of animal bones), i: Light yellow loess (virgin soil?).

diaspores. On this basis, several cereals were distinguished, such as common barley *Hordeum vulgare* L., (**Fig. 12:6a–c**) proso millet *Panicum miliaceum* L. (**Fig. 12:7**), probably buckwheat *Fagopyrum* cf. *esculentum* Moench (**Fig. 12:5**), and various undetermined – due to their poor state of preservation – *Cerealia* indet cereals (**Fig. 12:8a, b; 9**). Various useful plants were also identified, such as the European olive *Olea europaea* L. (**Fig. 12:15,16**), the common grapevine *Vitis vinifera* L. (**Fig. 12:1**), the common fig *Ficus carica* L. (**Fig. 12:2, 3**), edible lentil *Lens culinaris* Medik. (**Fig. 12:14**), peas *Pisum* sp. (**Fig. 12:13**) and the Fabaceae legume. Weeds include white quinoa *Chenopodium* t. *album* L. (**Fig. 12:10**), false cleavers *Galium spurium* L., sticky cleavers *G. aparine* L. (**Fig. 12:12**) and hawkweed oxtongue *Picris hieracidoides* L. (**Fig. 12:11**).

Most of the listed taxa are not very numerous, as a rule represented by individual specimens in the samples. The abundant amounts of common grapevine pips *Vitis vinifera* L. are an exception, found mainly in Sample 2, and those of the common fig *Ficus carica* L., most numerous in Sample 3. Ergot is also abundant (**Fig. 12:4**), especially in Sample 1. The remains of various cereals, such as common barley *Hordeum vulgare* L., millet *Panicum miliaceum* L., buckwheat *Fagopyrum* cf. *esculentum* Moench, were discovered mainly in Samples 1, 2 and 3.

Comparing the taxonomic composition, one can note the similarity between the four samples: Samples 1, 2, 3, and to some extent sample 5. These four samples mainly contained very numerous grapevine pips *Vitis vinifera* L., single grains of unspecified cereals, and relatively numerous ergots. The samples also contained the common fig *Ficus carica* L. and the European olive *Olea europaea* L. The ratio of useful plants to weeds in these samples indicates a definite predominance of the former. Adding Sample 5, containing only two grains of *Cerealia*, to this group may be debatable; however, they are charred, which somehow places them closer to the second group, in which charred finds are more frequent.

The situation is quite different for the group of remaining samples: 4 and 6. They contain less fruits and seeds; however, charred specimens are more frequent and primarily the occurrence of weeds increases as compared to that of the remains of cultivated plants.

Anthracological analysis (Tab. V)

The size of the charcoal fragments, their state of preservation, and their anatomical characteristics affect the analysis results, and a given fragment may be

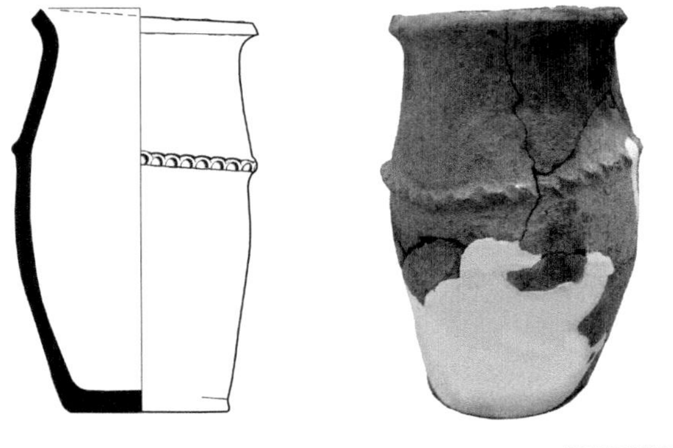

Fig. 11. Reconstructed Thracian vessels found in the oldest cultural layers at Novae (by A. Tomas).

designated to the level of species, genus, family, or may generally be included into the group of deciduous or coniferous trees and shrubs.[29] Due to the lack of clear diagnostic features, the charred wood of trees and shrubs occurring in Europe is most often categorized to the genus level, and species names are usually given if there is one species representing the genus in the local flora (e.g., *Cotinus coggygria*).[30] In the material from the Novae site, in the case of the *Carpinus* genus, one species was marked, i.e., *Carpinus orientalis*, which differs from *Carpinus betulus* due to the presence of scalariform perforation plates in the vessels (**Fig. 13:1b**), next to the dominant simple perforations.[31] The taxa marked as cf. *Quercus* sp. indicates the absence of wide multiseriate rays, which is a feature that may indicate the presence of *Castanea sativa*. Less well-preserved fragments were classified to deciduous trees, while specimens lacking distinctive anatomical elements were included into the group of indeterminate fragments.

For the anthracological material from Novae, the basis for any compilation is counting the charcoal fragments in the sample. Typically, every charcoal fragment found in a sample, regardless of size, is determined. The charcoals found in Sample 2 were thus identified, while a different method was used for the charcoals found in the other samples, mainly due to secondary fragmentation and the large abundance of remains. The essence of this method is to count a certain equal number of fragments in relation to fragments of a certain limit value. These values are known after initial charcoal identification, which involves indicating the relationship between the number of taxa and the number of determined charcoal fragments. An indication of the relationship between the number of taxa and the number

29. Schweingruber 1990a; Chabal et al. 1999; Asouti and Austin 2005; Lityńska-Zając and Wasylikowa 2005.

30. Lityńska-Zając and Wasylikowa 2005.

31. Schweingruber 1990b.

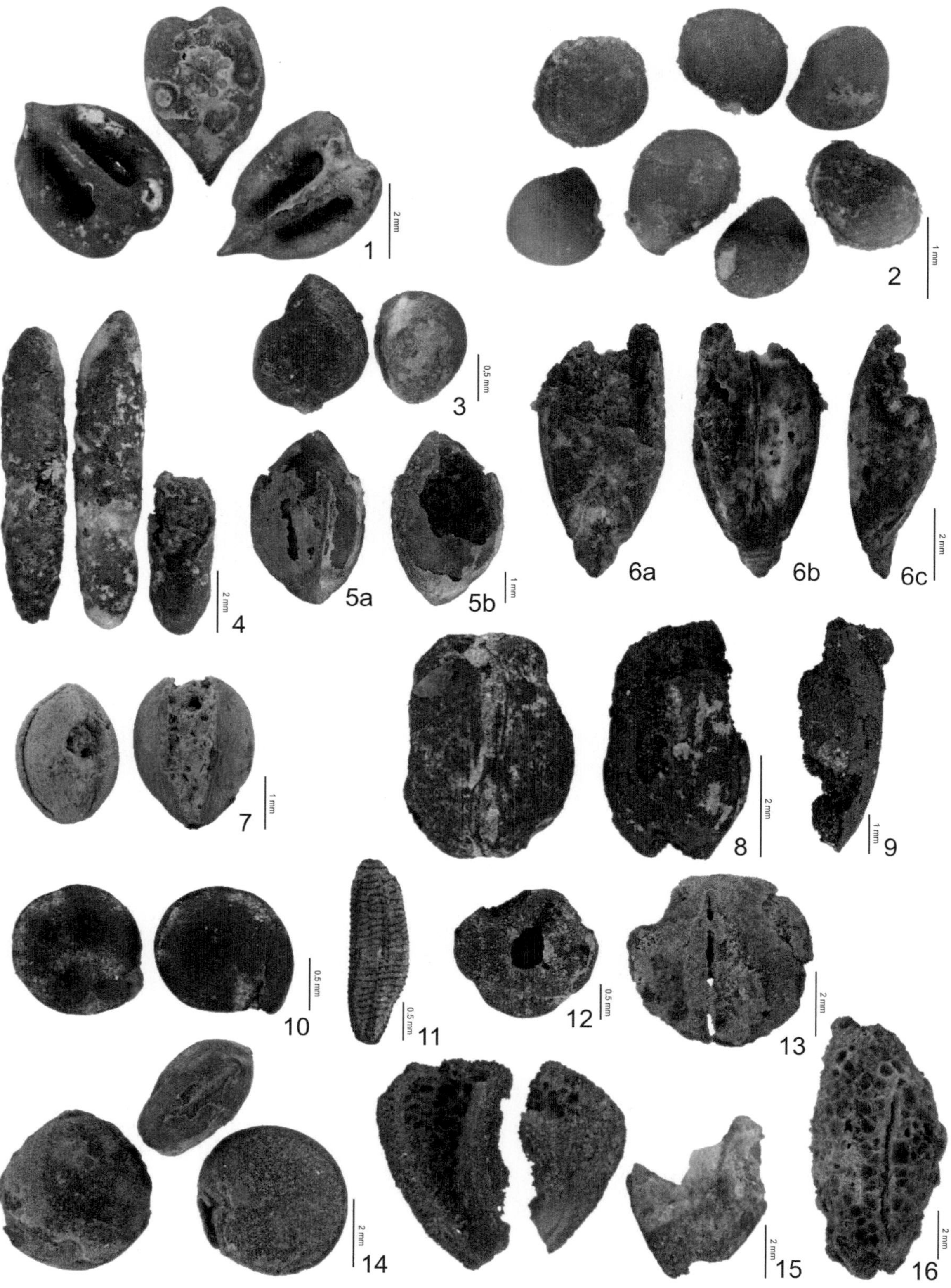

Fig. 12. Novae. Examples of mineralized and charred remains of cultivated and wild plants. 1. *Vitis vinifera* L. – Thracian vessel, 2, 3. *Ficus carica* L. – Thracian vessel, 4. Ergot – Thracian vessel, 5. *Fagopyrum* cf. *esculentum* Moench – virgin soil (canal B), 6a, b, c. *Hordeum vulgare* L., grain on three sides – virgin soil (Layer i), 7. *Panicum miliaceum* L. – Thracian vessel, 8a, b. Cerealia, grain on both sides – street level in layer (f), 9. Cerealia – foundation trench, 10. *Chenopodium* typ. *album* L. – Layer (f), 11. *Picris hieracioides* L. – Layer (f), 12. *Galium aparine* L. – Layer (f), 13. *Pisum* sp. – Thracian vessel, 14. *Lens culinaris* Medik. – virgin soil (Layer (i), 15. *Olea europaea* L. – virgin soil (Layer i), 16. *Olea europaea* L. – foundation trench (photos by K. Stachowicz).

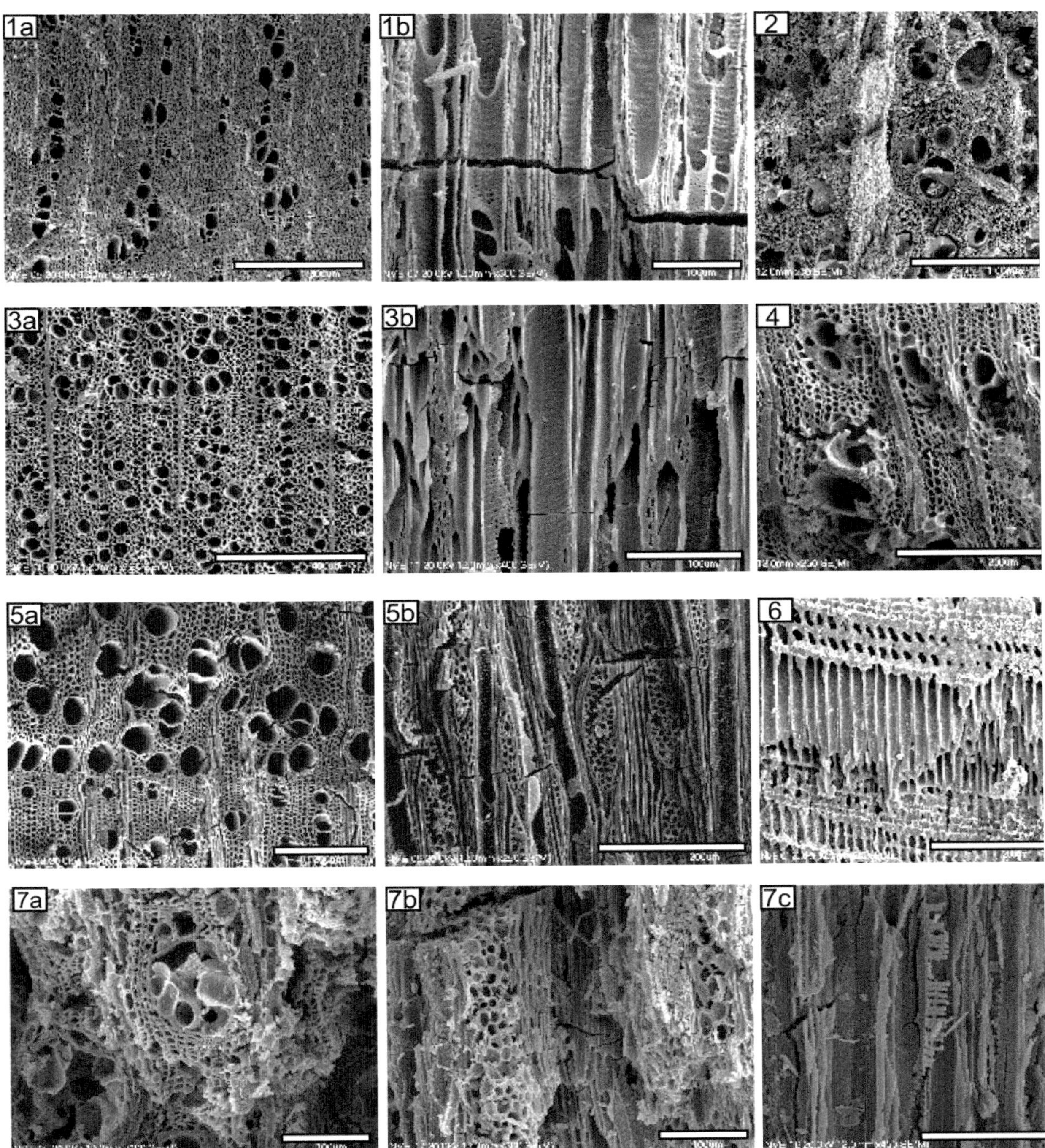

Fig. 13. Novae. Selected charcoal fragments.1. *Carpinus orientalis*: a. transverse section, b. longitudinal radial section – Thracian pot; 2. *Quercus* sp.: transverse section – Layer (f); 3. *Tilia* sp.: a. transverse section, b. longitudinal tangential section – Layer (f); 4. *Fraxinus* sp.: transverse section – Layer (f); 5. *Acer* sp.: a. transverse section, b. longitudinal tangential section – Thracian vessel; 6. *Pinus* sp. type *sylvestris-nigra*: transverse section – Layer (f); 7. *Vitis vinifera*: a. transverse section, b. longitudinal tangential section, c. longitudinal radial section – Layer F. Scale bar: 300 μm (1a), 100 μm (1b, 3b, 7a, 7b, 7c), 1.00 mm (2), 400 μm (3a), 200 μm (4, 5a, 5b, 6). Sample 1: 1 and 5; Sample 3: 2 and 3; Sample 5: 4, 6 and 7 (by M. Moskal-del Hoyo).

of identified charcoal fragments can be obtained by using taxonomic curves.[32] Such a curve is a graphic representation of the course of the analysis marking the appearance of individual taxa (Y axis) along with the number of analysed charcoal fragments (X axis). The most abundant taxa are usually found first, while the rarest may appear at the beginning of the analysis, or – as is most common – after a larger number of fragments have been marked. Figure 14 presents this dependency, as the most frequently encountered charcoal fragments, in this case those

32. Chabal 1988; 1997; Badal Garcia 1992; Ntinou 2002; Carrión Marco 2005.

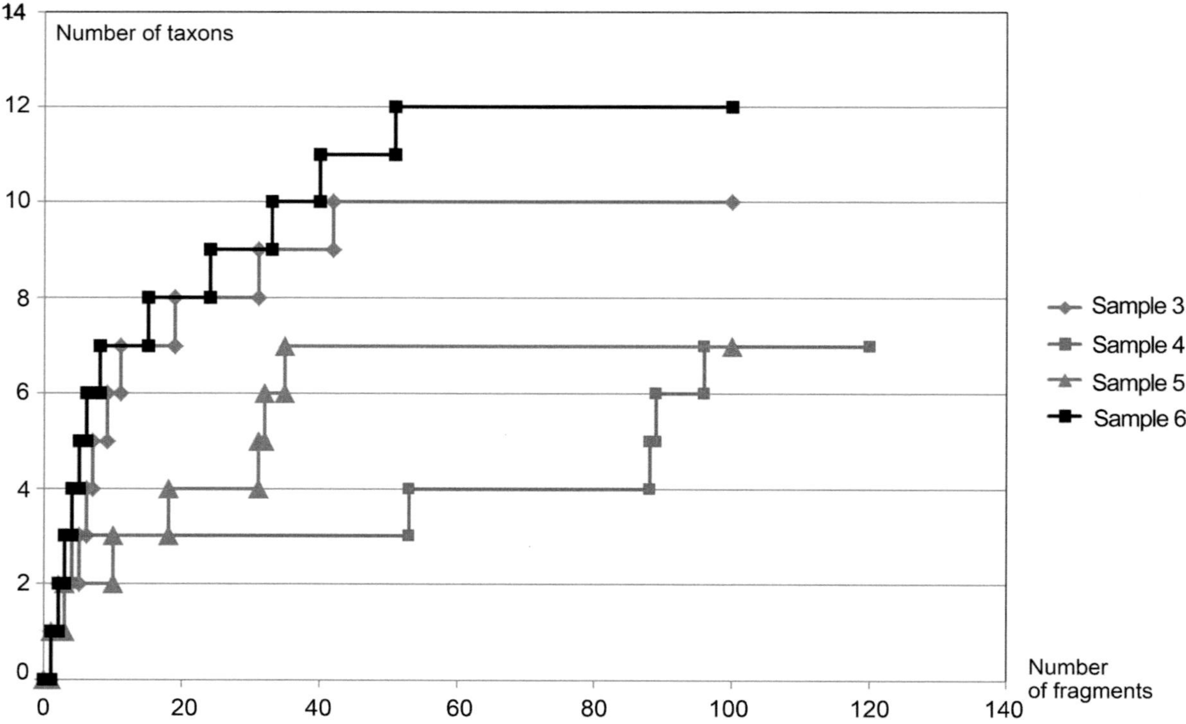

Fig. 14. Taxonomic curve presenting the dependency in three samples between the amounts of taxa determined and the number of analysed charcoal fragments (by M. Moskal-del Hoyo).

of the oak *Quercus* sp. and hornbeam *Carpinus* sp., occurred in the group formed by the first five fragments. The next appeared in the first 10–20 fragments analysed, while the last and rarest occurred after analysing a much larger number of specimens ranging between 30 and 50 (**Fig. 14**). Only in Sample 4 were new taxa found between 85 and 96 analysed fractions. The graph presented here takes into account four exemplary samples in which the last taxon appeared after 35 and 42 analysed fractions (Samples 3 and 5) or after 51 (Sample 6). Thus, it could be assumed that the minimum number of fragments analysed to obtain taxonomic diversity should be 100. In Sample 4, due to finding new taxa at the end of the analysis of the first 100 charcoal fragments, the decision was made to extend the analysis to 120 fragments. On the other hand, if mainly one taxon was found in the sample in the first 50 fragments (Sample 1), then the analysis ceased, as it was apparent the sample contained one larger piece of burnt wood that had undergone secondary fragmentation.

Among the charcoals found at the archaeological site in Novae 16 taxa were discovered (defined as a minimum number of taxa, with no broader categories such as deciduous), including 3 identified to the species level (oriental hornbeam *Carpinus orientalis* (**Fig. 13:1**), grape vine *Vitis vinifera* (**Fig. 13:7**), the European smoketree *Cotinus coggygria*), 1 determined as a pine of the Scots common pine variety or the black pine *Pinus sp.* type *sylvestris/ nigra* – Fig. 13:6, distinguished based on the presence of large fenestriform pits in the cross-fields, 10 marked to the genus level (maple *Acer* – **Fig. 4:5**, hornbeam *Carpinus*, dogwoods *Cornus*, ash *Fraxinus* – **Fig. 13:4**, plum *Prunus*, oak *Quercus* – **Fig. 13:2**, elm *Ulmus*, willow *Salix* and lime *Tilia* – **Fig. 13:3**), 1 taxon was identified as poplar or willow (*Populus* vel *Salix*), and 1 to the subfamily level (the Maloideae apple subfamily).

The remains of oak *Quercus* sp. and hornbeam *Carpinus* sp. stand out in terms of the frequency of taxa in the samples, as they were found in all layers. Considering this feature, the remains of maple *Acer* sp. and ash *Fraxinus* sp. also appeared in 4 samples. The charcoal remains of the oriental hornbeam *Carpinus orientalis* and poplar *Populus* sp. or willow *Salix* sp., lime *Tilia* sp. and Maloideae were relatively frequent, i.e., in 3 samples. The remnants of pine *Pinus sylvestris*/*Pinus nigra*, dogwoods *Cornus* sp., *Prunus* sp., elm *Ulmus* sp. were less common (2 samples), while occasionally charcoal fragments of other taxa were found.

Discussion of the fruits and seeds analysis results

The low number of samples and of the plant remains preserved in them do not allow for reliable reconstructions of the diet of the camp inhabitants; however, they indicate the use of particular plants during the different settlement phases of the site.

In the backfill of a Thracian vessel (Sample 2), as well as in the sediment of a foundation trench (Sample 3), primarily the remains of grape pips (*Vitis vinifera*), unspecified remains of cereals (Cerealia), single grains of millet, buckwheat and peas were found among the cultivated plants. Common millet *Panicum miliaceum* L. is a light- and heat-loving cereal that is also drought-resistant. In terms of soil, it is not too demanding and succeeds even in poor soils. Millet cultivation has been recorded since the Neolithic period in central Asia, Iran, Iraq, Armenia and Georgia,[33] while in Europe an increase in millet production has been confirmed as having occurred since the second half of the 2nd millennium BC.[34] The presence of buckwheat *Fagopyrum* cf. *esculentum* Moench, found in the form of a single and not very well-preserved specimen, is also significant. Its origin is disputable and it is assumed that it may come from Manchuria, Siberia, China or India. In Europe, as a cultivated plant, it has been encountered since the Middle Ages.[35] The cultivation of buckwheat in Europe is associated with the Tartar invasions in the 13th century. However, at archaeological sites in southern Ukraine in the Azov Sea region and on the steppes north of the Black Sea, it appeared much earlier, around the 7th century BC.[36] Peas *Pisum sativum* L., similarly as lentils *Lens culinaris* Medik., are some of the longest cultivated legumes in Bulgaria, as they have been present since the early Neolithic.[36] The samples from Novae provide rather few remains of cultivated plants, though it can be assumed that the spectrum of such plants was much richer, as evidenced by archaeobotanical material from other Roman-period archaeological sites from northern Bulgaria, such as Abritus (originally a legion military camp), the Roman town Nicopolis ad Istrum and the Dichin hillfort.[37] The main cereal grains include naked wheat identified as *Triticum compactum* Host, *T. aestivum* L. or *T. aestivo/compactum* when it was not possible to distinguish the two species. Rye *Secale cereale* L. was also recorded, as was common rye *Avena sativa* L. and glumed wheats, such as einkorn *T. monococcum* L. and emmer *T. diccoccum* Schrank. *Sorghum bicolor* (L.) Moench was also encountered. Of the legumes, lentils and peas were the most frequent, while broad bean *Vicia faba* L. and bitter vetch *V. ervilia* L. (Willd.) were also in use.

In the material from the 1st century AD, sclerotia of ergot appeared, i.e., proliferated grain or grass seed, the ascospore of a parasitic fungus stimulated to growth by *Claviceps purpurea* (Fr.) Tul. of the tubercle family *Hypocreaceae*, which attacks cereal grains, e.g., rye, barley, wheat and rice. When ripe, it falls to the ground and, after the winter, around the time of the flowering of the cereals and grasses, it develops into red sclerotia. Ergot contains various toxic substances and causes an illness known as ergotism, which affects the nervous system and may result in death. Ergot follows the cereal harvest and invariably gets mixed with cereals during threshing. It can only be removed from the harvest by picking it by hand.[38] Currently, ergot is almost non-existent in crops thanks to various crop protection products.

Fruit pips were also identified in the samples from Novae, such as grapevine *Vitis vinifera* L. and the common fig *Ficus carica* L., in material dated to the 1st century AD. Grapevines have often been found at Neolithic sites in southern Europe (Greece, Italy, Spain, France), but it is difficult to determine when they became a cultivated species. On the basis of the archaeobotanical material compiled to date, it is assumed that fairly certain evidence of vine cultivation dates from the 6th millennium BP.[39] Seeds and fruit fragments have been found from this period at archaeological sites in the Middle East. In ancient Rome, viticulture was a very important branch of the economy and it was widespread in the countries of central Europe within and beyond the borders of the Empire, although viticulture in Gaul and among the Celtic tribes had already been known earlier.[40] In turn, the common fig tree has been cultivated since the Bronze Age. The first documented cultivation was recorded in Sumer, later in Egypt, where the fig was one of the most important crops in the 9th century BC. In Greece, fig cultivation began on the Aegean islands and later spread throughout the Mediterranean. Both species were also found at sites in northern Bulgaria, at Abritus and Nicopolis ad Istrum from the Roman period.[41]

Fragments of poorly preserved, mineralized seeds of the European olive *Olea europaea* L. were also found in two samples from the 1st century AD (Samples 2 and 3) and in Sample 1. The beginning of olive cultivation has been located in the Near East.[42] From there, their cultivation spread to spread to Central and Western Mediterranean region during second millennium BC.[43] The olive has not

33. Lityńska-Zając and Wasylikowa 2005.
34. Filipović et al. 2020.
35. Körber-Grohne 1988; Lityńska-Zając and Wasylikowa 2005.
36. Marinova 2007; Marinova and Krauß 2014.
37. Popova 1999; Popova and Marinova 2000.
38. Vanhanen S., 2012.
39. Zohary and Hopf, 2000.
40. Lityńska-Zając 2005 with cited literature.
41. Popova 1999; Popova and Marinova 2000.
42. Zohary and Spiegel-Roy 1975; Liphschitz et al. 1991.
43. Langgut et al. 2019.

been identified at nearby sites from this same period in Abritus, Nicopolis ad Istrum and Dichin;[44] however, a few seeds of *Olea europaea* L. have been recorded at Kapitan Andreevo from the Iron Ages in southern Bulgaria.[45]

The edible lentil *Lens culinaris* Medik was present in material dating to the 4th century AD (Sample 6). Beginning around 7000 BP, lentils were found at many archaeological sites in the Near East in association with crops. In Europe, domesticated lentils appeared together with cereals around 6000 BP and spread all over Europe, as evidenced by numerous finds of lentils associated with different cultures in the area from France to Ukraine and Georgia, including Bulgaria. During the Roman period, lentils became very common, as evidenced by the appearance of lentils at numerous sites in the Roman Empire and at its borders.[46]

It is possible that leguminous crops included a seed described as the legume Fabaceae indet. (Sample 4), especially since a pea seed *Pisum* sp. was also found in the same sample. The specimens were deposited in material dating to the early 2nd century AD.

Herbaceous plants, which had in the past spontaneously developed in the vicinity of the studied site at Novae, were represented by the goosefoot *Chenopodium* t. *album* L., false cleavers *Galium spurium* L., sticky cleavers *G. aparine* L., and hawkweed oxtongue *Picris hieracidoides* L. Most were found in the sample dated to the beginning of the 2nd century AD, whereas single goosefoot seeds occurred in the samples from the 1st century AD and the 4th century AD (Fig. 12:10). *Chenopodium* t. *album* remains are among the most frequently occurring in archaeological material. This species is found today primarily in ruderal habitats, although it also appears in cultivated fields. It may have been collected and used for consumption. Both diaspores and young shoots were suitable for such applications.[47] Typical field weeds[48] include false cleavers *Galium spurium* L. (one berry in a sample from the 4th century AD) and sticky cleavers *G. aparine* L. (**Fig. 12:12**) (three berries deposited in a sample from the beginning of the 2nd century AD). The hawkweed oxtongue *Picris hieracidoides* L., identified in materials from the early 2nd century AD, may also have occurred in the surrounding meadows, in dry places, but also in segetal habitats (**Fig. 12:19**). All these species probably occurred in the past as weeds in the vicinity of the site. Their presence may indirectly indicate local cereal cultivation. Numerous remains of herbaceous wild plants corresponding to 31 taxa were found at Abritus, most of which represented weeds.[49]

Discussion of anthracological analysis results

The charcoals found at Novae are relatively well preserved, with the exception of a sample taken from Sample 1, in which strongly vitrified charcoal fragments were found. It is not clear what caused this type of vitrification. Presumably, it is the result of high temperatures or the burning of moist wood.[50] The few fragments found in Samples 2, 4, and 5 showed the presence or traces of microorganisms and wood-boring insects.

Typically, charcoals preserved at archaeological sites are a source of valuable ethnographic information because they indicate a variety of uses of wood. When found in the form of charred objects or the remains of wood used for construction purposes, they are most often characterized by low taxonomic diversity resulting from the selection (human choice) of particular species (referred to as "concentrated charcoal", "charcoal concentrations" or short-lived deposits).[51] It is worth noting that charcoals, if the appropriate research method is applied, can also serve as material for environmental reconstruction. In this case, they should be the result of the use of firewood, the remains of which are numerous and come from the long-term deposition of such remains (referred to as "dispersed charcoal", "charcoal scatters" or long-term deposits).[52] Charcoals that are the residue of wood collected for firewood have been shown to represent a specific sample of local forest vegetation, as for this purpose wood was chosen that was available, easy to collect, and could be quickly transported to the settlement or encampment site. Therefore, the list of taxa obtained from the analyses of the charcoals deposited in archaeological layers or waste sites tends to be distinguished by the relatively high species richness and randomness of assemblages the taxonomic set. Nevertheless, in order for charcoal assemblages to be used to reconstruct ancient

44. Popova 1999; Popova and Marinova 2000.
45. Hrisrova, Atanassova, and Marinova 2017
46. Körber-Grohne 1988; Marinova 2007; Marinova and Krauß 2014.
47. Łuczaj 2004; Mueller-Bieniek et al. 2019.
48. Lityńska-Zając 2005 with cited literature.
49. Popova and Marinova 2000.
50. Théry-Parisot 2001; Lityńska-Zając and Wasylikowa 2005.
51. E.g. Badal Garcia 1992; Chabal 1988, 1997; Ntinou 2002; Asouti and Austin 2005; Carrión Marco 2005; Moskal-del Hoyo 2013; Kabukcu 2018; Kabukcu and Chabal 2021.
52. Badal Garcia 1992; Chabal 1988, 1997; Ntinou 2002; Asouti and Austin 2005; Carrión Marco 2005; Moskal-del Hoyo 2013; Kabukcu 2018; Kabukcu and Chabal 2021.

forests, representative samples should be obtained from which at least 250–400 charcoal fragments per cultural level can be determined.[53] Therefore, the materials from Novae are not representative samples as they only come from individual samples representing different periods.

The results of the quantitative analysis based on fragment counts are very consistent with the results obtained by calculating the frequency of taxa occurrence in the samples, suggesting that mainly oak, hornbeam, maple and ash wood were used by the population, most likely as fuel, judging by the high taxonomic diversity of the samples. Moreover, a high similarity can be observed between the results of the qualitative analysis of the sample obtained from the backfill of the Thracian vessel (Sample 2) and the results obtained from the other samples, as the vessel contained the remains of 6 taxa, of which oak and hornbeam were the most numerous. On this basis, it can be assumed that charcoal remains should not be related to the original contents of the vessel and may have entered it with the soil filling the layers.

Taking into account the taxonomic composition of the anthracological samples, their local origin can be assumed. The analysed materials are definitely dominated by oak and hornbeam. Numerous anthracological analyses have shown that most often the wood residues of species and genera most abundant in the samples reflect the trees and shrubs quantitatively dominant in the surrounding forest stands.[54]

The high proportion of oak and hornbeam, especially in the same samples, may indicate the presence of deciduous forest. Maples, limes and trees of the Maloideae subfamily may also be a component of this type of forests. On the other hand, the presence of ash, elm, alongside the willow may suggest wood extraction also from habitats where riparian forests could have developed. Moreover, trees or shrubs from the Maloideae subfamily are heliophilous and may indicate the occurrence of more open forests, fringe edge communities or even partially deforested areas.[55]

Taking into account the potential natural vegetation,[56] in particular, mixed oak forests, mixed oak-hornbeam forests and thermophilous mixed deciduous broadleaf forests should have developed near the archaeological site, while along the Danube – sub-meridional hardwood alluvial forests with oak, elm and ash and willow-poplar alluvial forests. In the mixed oak forest, the dominant oak species include *Quercus pedunculiflora*, *Q. cerris*, *Q. pubescens* and *Q. frainetto*. In the layer of trees, the following are encountered: *Acer tataricum*, *Fraxinus ornus*, *Ulmus minor*, *Carpinus orientalis*, *Pyrus pyraster*, *Sorbus domestica*, while in the understory layer, we mainly encounter *Crataegus monogyna*, *Cornus mas*, *Prunus spinosa*, *Ligustrum vulgare*, *Cotinus coggygria* and *Euonymus europaea*. In turn, in the oak-hornbeam forests, the *Q. petraea* is predominant among the oaks, while other important components of such forests include *Carpinus betulus*, *Q. robur* and *Tilia cordata*. Sporadically, *Tilia tomentosa*, *Carpinus orientalis* and *Fagus sylvatica* subsp. *orientalis* are encountered.

The results of the anthracological analysis are in line with the general characteristics of the forests that may have developed in the vicinity of the archaeological site, which are mainly mixed oak-hornbeam forests, predominantly with various oak species and with frequent occurrences of both hornbeam species. Wood was also sourced from local floodplain forests in the vicinity of the Danube. The occurrence of thermophilous forests, possibly related to oak woods, is indicated by the appearance of xerophilous, warm-loving and heliophilous species, such as the European smoketree. The taxonomic composition of the archaeobotanical samples mostly confirms the local character of the harvested wood. At the sites at Nicopolis ad Istrum, Dichin and Abritus, mainly the remains of *Quercus*, *Ulmus*, *Fraxinus*, *Acer*, *Corylus*, *Carpinus*, *Cornus*, *Prunus* and Pomoideae (Maloideae) were found among the charcoals.[57] At Nicopolis ad Istrum, *Vitis vinifera* charcoals were also encountered along with grape pips.[58] At Novae, burnt *Vitis vinifera* wood was encountered in Sample 6 from the 4th century AD, while mineralized *V. vinifera* pips occurred in Sample 1, and in Samples 2, and 3 from the 1st century AD. Based on the anatomical structure, it is impossible to determine whether the wood corresponds to a wild or cultivated grape variety. The presence of *V. vinifera* in present-day Bulgaria was confirmed as early as during the Neolithic period, including sites from the Lower Danube, where it is associated with riverine vegetation.[59]

53. E.g. Chabal 11997; Kabukcu and Chabal 2021.

54. Badal Garcia; 1992; Chabal 1997; Ntinou 2002; Carrión Marco 2005; Lityńska-Zając and Wasylikowa 2005.

55. Medwecka-Kornaś 1972; Matuszkiewicz J.M. 2005.

56. Doniţă et al. 2004.

57. Popova 1999; Popova and Marinova 2000.

58. Popova 1999.

59. Marinova and Krauß 2014; Marinova et al. 2012/2013.

Table I. Novae 2013. Retentura sinistra. Palynological samples and the basis for their dating. Quantitative values (by H. Winter).

DATING	Pre-Flavian or early Flavian	Pre-Flavian or early Flavian	Pre-Flavian or early Flavian	Pre-Flavian or early Flavian	Late Flavian	late Flavian / Trajanic	early 2nd c.	Trajanic	late 2nd – first half of 3rd c.	4th c.	late 6th – early 7th c.	Humus
Sample No.	12/09	1/09	10/09	11/09	2/09	9/09	3/09	8/09	7/09	4/09	5/09	6/09
Context / Taxon	**l** - layer directly on the virgin soil near Tower no. 27	**4a** - via sagularis?	**4** - ramp (ascensus)	**k** - under the foundations of the military barracks	**19** - via sagularis	**7** - smashed oven	**h** - layer under the via sagularis	**h** - building layer of almost clean loess	**f** - layer with charcoal near the oven	**d** - thick layer outside the building	**b** - layer over a pottery kiln	top soil
AP												
Abies			7	9	1	1					1	
Alnus			1	1	7	1						
Betula										2	1	
Carpinus	2		1	1	11	2	1				1	
Corylus				1	1							
Cupressaceae						1						
Fagus					2			1				
Picea				7	2	2	6			2		
Pinus sylvestris type	7	1	12	7	15	40	7			3		10
Quercus	2		78	2		26	3	1	1	1		1
Tilia	1		3		3	3	4	1			1	1
Ulmus			2		2			2		1		
cf *Vitis*						1						
Sum												
NAP												
Ambrosia							1		1			
Androsaceae												1
Anthemis type			6		16	12	5	1				3
Apiaceae	1		2	11	7	2	1			3	3	
Armeria type B				5						1		
Artemisia	14		45	3	8	13	5		1	4	6	9
Aster type			9	1	11	10		2	1			
Asteraceae	4		3	4	6	10				4		3
Brassicaceae	2		1	2	20	5	1					193
Bupleurum falcatum type				1								
Caryophyllaceae			1	1	1	2						
Centaurea scabiosa				1		3	1					
Centaurea nigra	1			1								
Cerastium type				1			2					
Cerealia	6			25	89	5	4				2	
Chenopodiaceae	9	1	1	588	10	7	1		1	10	25	109
Cichorioideae	44	52	408	36	77	111	160	21		52	41	138
Cirsium type	1		5	19	12	14	1	2	4	4	14	8
Convolvulus				1								
Crepis type		4										
Cyperaceae	5				4	1	1					1
Dipsacaceae							1					
Dipsacus fulonum type			4								1	
Fabaceae	1				2							
Geranium				1						1		1
Knautia				1			1					
Lactuca sativa type		1					11					
Malva neglecta											1	
Plantago			2									1
Plantago lanceolata					6				1			

DATING	Pre-Flavian or early Flavian	Pre-Flavian or early Flavian	Pre-Flavian or early Flavian	Pre-Flavian or early Flavian	Late Flavian	late Flavian / Trajanic	early 2nd c.	Trajanic	late 2nd – first half of 3rd c.	4th c.	late 6th – early 7th c.	Humus
Sample No.	12/09	1/09	10/09	11/09	2/09	9/09	3/09	8/09	7/09	4/09	5/09	6/09
Context / Taxon	**l** – layer directly on the virgin soil near Tower no. 27	**4a** – via sagularis?	**4** – ramp (ascensus)	**k** – under the foundations of the military barracks	**19** – via sagularis	**7** – smashed oven	**h** – layer under the via sagularis	**h** – building layer of almost clean loess	**f** – layer with charcoal near the oven	**d** – thick layer outside the building	**b** – layer over a pottery kiln	top soil
Plantago media					1							
Poaceae		1	39	89	265	16	28	5	1	15	13	4
Polygonum				1	1							2
Polygonum aviculare type								1				2
Polygonum bistorta type				1								
Polygonum persicaria type												
Pycnocomon				1			1					
Ranunculaceae												
Rumex acetosa type					1							
Secale					2							
Silene type					2							
Sonchus arvensis					6		1					
Taraxacum officinale type					14							
Tragopogon pratensis type		3		1	15	5	1			3		
Valeriana			1									
Valeriana officinalis type	1											
Sum	102	63	633	917	622	299	249	37	11	107	110	490
Spores												
Anthoceros	1						3			1		
Bryales		12										
Lycopodium annotinum						1						
Polypodiaceae	2	1	13	3	2	7	4		1	2		5
Pteridium aquilinum			1				1					
Aquatic plants												
Potamogeton							1					
Damaged	5	11	27	14	63	51	14	13	4	10	15	10

Table II. Novae 2013. Retentura sinistra. Palynological samples and the basis for their dating. Percentage values (by H. Winter).

DATING	Pre-Flavian	Pre-Flavian	Pre-Flavian	Pre-Flavian or early Flavian	Late Flavian	late Flavian / early Trajanic	early 2nd c.	Trajanic	late 2nd – first half of 3rd c.	4th c.	late 6th –early 7th c.	HUMUS
Sample No.	12/09	1/09	10/09	11/09	2/09	9/09	3/09	8/09	7/09	4/09	5/09	6/09
Context / Taxon	**l** – layer directly on the virgin soil near Tower no. 27	**k** – via sagularis?	**4** – ramp (ascensus)	**k** – under the foundations of the military barracks	**j** – via sagularis	**7** – smashed oven	**h** – layer under the via sagularis	**h** – building layer of almost clean loess	**f** – layer with charcoal near the oven	**d** – thick layer outside the building	**b** – layer over pottery kiln	top soil
AP												
Abies			1.1	1.0	0.2	0.3					0.9	
Alnus			0.2	0.1	1.1	0.3						
Betula										1.9	0.9	
Carpinus	2.0		0.2	0.1	1.8	0.7	0.4				0.9	

DATING	Pre-Flavian	Pre-Flavian	Pre-Flavian	Pre-Flavian or early Flavian	Late Flavian	late Flavian / early Trajanic	early 2nd c.	Trajanic	late 2nd - first half of 3rd c.	4th c.	late 6th -early 7th c.	HUMUS
Sample No.	12/09	1/09	10/09	11/09	2/09	9/09	3/09	8/09	7/09	4/09	5/09	6/09
Context / Taxon	**l** - layer directly on the virgin soil near Tower no. 27	**k** - via sagularis?	**4** - ramp (ascensus)	**k** - under the foundations of the military barracks	**j** - via sagularis	**7** - smashed oven	**h** - layer under the via sagularis	**h** - building layer of almost clean loess	**f** - layer with charcoal near the oven	**d** - thick layer outside the building	**b** - layer over a pottery kiln	top soil
Corylus				0.1	0.2							
Cupressaceae						0.3						
Fagus					0.3			2.7				
Picea				0.8	0.3	0.7	2.4			1.9		
Pinus sylvestris type	6.9	1.6	1.9	0.8	2.4	13.4	2.8			2.8		2.0
Quercus	2.0		12.3	0.2		8.7	1.2	2.7	9.1	0.9		0.2
Tilia	1.0		0.5		0.5	1.0	1.6	2.7			0.9	0.2
Ulmus			0.3		0.3			5.4		0.9		
cf Vitis						0.3						
Ambrosia							0.4		9.1			
Androsaceae												0.2
Anthemis type			0.9		2.6	4.0	2.0	2.7				0.6
Apiaceae	1.0		0.3	1.2	1.1	0.7	0.4			2.8	2.7	
Armeria type B				0.5						0.9		
Artemisia	13.7		7.1	0.3	1.3	4.3	2.0		9.1	3.7	5.5	1.8
Aster type			1.4	0.1	1.8	3.3		5.4	9.1			
Asteraceae	3.9		0.5	0.4	1.0	3.3				3.7		0.6
Brassicaceae	2.0		0.2	0.2	3.2	1.7	0.4					39.4
Bupleurum falcatum type				0.1								
Caryophyllaceae				0.1	0.2	0.7	0.2					
Centaurea nigra	1.0			0.1								
Centaurea scabiosa				0.1		1.0	0.4					
Cerastium type				0.1			0.8					
Cerealia	5.9			2.7	14.3	1.7	1.6				1.8	
Chenopodiaceae	8.8	1.6	0.2	64.1	1.6	2.3	0.4		9.1	9.3	22.7	22.2
Cichorioideae	43.1	82.5	64.5	3.9	12.4	37.1	64.3	56.8		48.6	37.3	28.2
Cirsium type	1.0		0.8	2.1	1.9	4.7	0.4	5.4	36.4	3.7	12.7	1.6
Convolvulus				0.1								
Crepis type		6.3										
Cyperaceae	4.9				0.6	0.3	0.4					0.2
Dipsacaceae							0.4					
Dipsacus fulonum type			0.6								0.9	
Fabaceae	1.0				0.3							
Geranium				0.1						0.9		0.2
Knautia				0.1			0.4					
Lactuca sativa type		1.6					4.4					
Malva neglecta											0.9	
Plantago			0.3									0.2
Plantago lanceolata					1.0				9.1			

DATING	Pre-Flavian	Pre-Flavian	Pre-Flavian	Pre-Flavian or early Flavian	Late Flavian	late Flavian / early Trajanic	early 2nd c.	Trajanic	late 2nd – first half of 3rd c.	4th c.	late 6th –early 7th c.	HUMUS
Sample No.	12/09	1/09	10/09	11/09	2/09	9/09	3/09	8/09	7/09	4/09	5/09	6/09
Context / Taxon	**l** - layer directly on the virgin soil near Tower no. 27	**k** - via sagularis?	**4** - ramp (ascensus)	**k** - under the foundations of the military barracks	**j** - via sagularis	**7** - smashed oven	**h** - layer under the via sagularis	**h** - building layer of almost clean loess	**f** - layer with charcoal near the oven	**d** - thick layer outside the building	**b** - layer over a pottery kiln	top soil
Plantago media					0.2							
Poaceae		1.6	6.2	9.7	42.6	5.4	11.2	13.5	9.1	14.0	11.8	0.8
Polygonum				0.1	0.2							0.4
Polygonum aviculare type								2.7				0.4
Polygonum bistorta type				0.1								
Polygonum persicaria type												
Pycnocomon				0.1			0.4					
Ranunculaceae												
Rumex acetosa type					0.2							
Secale					0.3							
Silene type					0.3							
Sonchus arvensis					1.0		0.4					
Taraxacum officinale type					2.3							
Tragopogon pratensis type		4.8		0.1	2.4	1.7	0.4			2.8		
Valeriana			0.2									
Valeriana officinalis type	1.0											
Sum	100.0	100.0	100.0	100.0	100.0	100.0	100.0	100.0	100.0	100.0	100.0	100.0
Spores												
Anthoceros	1						3			1		
Bryales		12										
Lycopodium annotinum						1						
Polypodiaceae	2	1	13	3	2	7	4		1	2		5
Pteridium aquilinum			1				1					
Aquatic plants												
Potamogeton							1					
Damaged	5	11	27	14	63	51	14	13	4	10	15	10

Table III. Novae 2013. Retentura sinistra. The archaeobotanical samples and the basis for their dating (by R. Stachowicz-Rybka).

	Sample 1	Sample 2	Sample 3	Sample 4	Sample 5	Sample 6
	Layer (i)	Thracian vessel	Foundation trench (1)	Layer (f)	street level in layer (f)	Layer (d)
Dating	pre-Roman or early Roman	Neronian(?)–Flavian	Flavian	early 2nd century AD	early 2nd–3rd centuries AD	4th century AD
Capacity [ml]	2000	650	1700	2400	1700	1600

Description of the sample	Light beige-yellowish loess with sparse fragments of mineralized wood fragments, bone fragments, and pieces of carbonate rocks	Light beige loess with sparse charcoal pieces, mineralized wood fragments, burned clay lumps, bone fragments, and pieces of carbonate rocks	Light beige loess with sparse charcoal pieces, mineralized wood fragments, bone fragments, and pieces of carbonate rocks	Grey yellow loess with charcoal fragments, burned clay lumps, and pieces of carbonate rocks	Light beige loess with fragments of pottery and pieces of carbonate rocks	Light beige loess with big fragments of pottery and tiles, bone fragments, pieces of carbonate rocks and plant roots

Table IV. Novae 2013. Retentura sinistra. List of identified seeds and fruits and the basis for their dating (min. – mineralised; charr. – charred). Quantitative values (by R. Stachowicz-Rybka).

Sample No.	Sample 1	Sample 2	Sample 3	Sample 4	Sample 5	Sample 6
Context	Layer (i)	Thracian vessel	Foundation trench (1)	Layer (f)	street level in layer (f)	Layer (d)
Dating / Taxon	Pre-Roman or early Roman	Neronian (?) –Flavian	Flavian	early 2nd century	2nd – early 3rd	4th century
	Number/State of preservation	Number/State of preservation	Number/State of preservation	Number/State of preservation	Number/State of preservation	Number/State ofpreservation
Chenopodium t. *album* L.	2/ min.	1/min.		5/charr.		1/charr.
Ficus carica L.	3/min.	2/min.	58/min. 1/charr.			1/min.
Fagopyrum cf. *esculentum* Moench			2/min.			
Galium aparine L.				3/min.		
Galium spurium L.						1/charr.
Hordeum vulgare L.	1/min.					
Lens culinaris Medik.	27/min.					6/charr.
Olea europaea L.	3/min.	1/min.	2/min.			
Panicum miliaceum L.		2/min.				
Picris hieracioides L.				1/min.		
Vitis vinifera L.	207/min.	125/min.	63/min.			
Pisum sp.		5/min.		1/charr.		
Fabaceae				1/charr.		
Cerealia	1/charr.	1/min.	1/charr.		2/charr.	
Undetermined chaff		1/min.				
Ergot	27/min.	4/min.				
Sum of diasporas	**271**	**142**	**127**	**11**	**2**	**9**
Undetermined	1					3

Table V. Novae 2013. Retentura sinistra. List of taxa identified in anthracological assemblages. Number of charcoal fragments and their percentage value (by M. Moskal-del Hoyo).

Sample No.	Sample 1		Sample 2		Sample 3		Sample 3		Sample 4		Sample 5	
Context	Layer (i)		Thracian vessel		Foundation trench (1)		Layer (f)		Street level in layer (f)		Layer (d)	
Context	Layer (i)		Thracian vessel		Foundation trench (1)		Layer (f)		Street level in layer (f)		Layer (d)	
Dating / Taxon	Pre-Roman or early Roman		Neronian (?)–Flavian		Flavian		early 2nd century		2nd – early 3rd		4th century	
	Number	%	Number	%	Number	%	Number	%	Number	%	Number	%
Carpinus orientalis			3	8.6	7	7					1	1
Cotinus coggygria					1	1						
Acer sp.			1	2.9	7	7			24	24	3	3
Carpinus sp.	46	92	7	20.0	13	13	68	56.7	17	17	7	7
Cornus sp.			9	25.7					1	1		
Fraxinus sp.			2	5.7			2	1.7	1	1	3	3
Pinus type *P. sylvestris/P. nigra*					3	3					1	1
Populus sp.					1	1	1	0.8			10	10
Populus sp. *vel Salix* sp.							1	0.8			1	1
Quercus sp.	1	2	10	28.6	56	56	32	26.7	49	49	50	50

Sample No.	Sample 1		Sample 2		Sample 3		Sample 3		Sample 4		Sample 5	
Context	Layer (i)		Thracian vessel		Foundation trench (1)		Layer (f)		Street level in layer (f)		Layer (d)	
Context	Layer (i)		Thracian vessel		Foundation trench (1)		Layer (f)		Street lev-el in layer (f)		Layer (d)	
Dating / Taxon	Pre-Roman or early Roman		Neronian (?)–Flavian		Flavian		early 2nd century		2nd – early 3rd		4th century	
	Number	%	Number	%	Number	%	Number	%	Number	%	Number	%
cf. *Quercus* sp.							1	0.8	1	1		
Salix sp.											1	1
Tilia sp.					1	1	7	5.8	1	1		
Ulmus sp.					1	1					5	5
Vitis sp.											4	4
Maloideae					1	1	2	1.7			7	7
Broad-leaved	3	6	3	8.6	8	8	6	5	6	6	7	7
Needle-leaved					1	1						
Monocotyledons											1	1
Sum of charcoal fragments	**50**	**100**	**35**	**100**	**100**	**100**	**120**	**100**	**100**	**100**	**100**	**100**
Undetermined	2				1		1				4	

IV

Research programme

Marcin Jaworski, Piotr Jaworski, Wiesław Małkowski, Krzysztof Misiewicz, Michał Pisz, Agnieszka Tomas, and Piotr Wroniecki

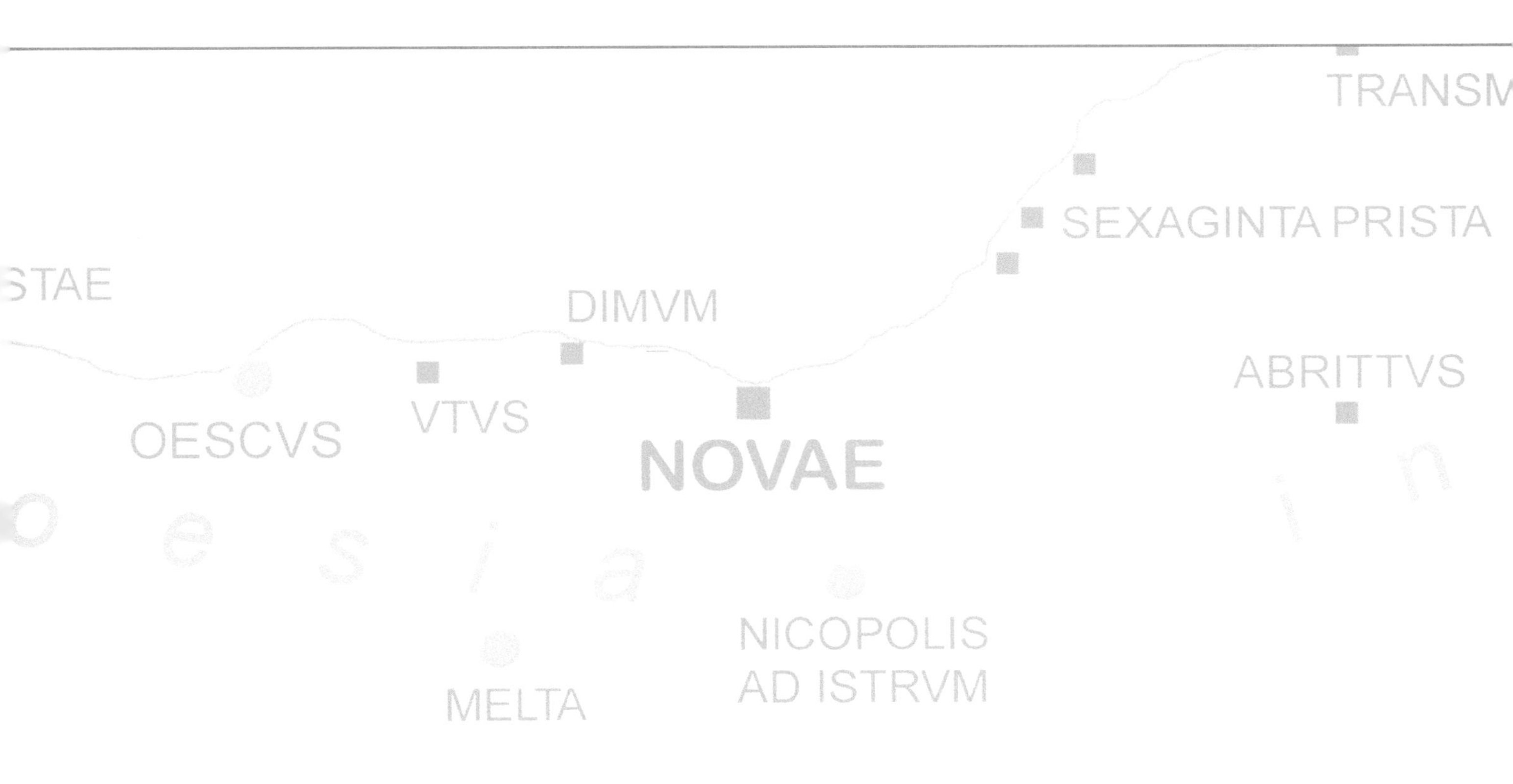

The idea behind non-invasive prospection in Novae was to investigate select components of the archaeological landscape by introducing a multi-method, large-scale approach. This involved the application of geophysical methods supplemented by remote sensing techniques. The outcome of the procedures was aimed at producing a complementary and integrated data resource as a basis for further analysis, leading to the identification of unknown archaeological resources and future fieldwork planning. In many aspects, the present research programme can be considered to be pioneering work in terms of the studies conducted at Novae; hence, expected and unexpected obstacles may be encountered and we aim to prepare the grounds for further investigations into the landscape around the site.

1. The landscape and research limitations

Agnieszka Tomas, Piotr Wroniecki, Marcin Jaworski

Novae and its surroundings are not easy terrain for geophysical prospection. The site is located on the outskirts of Svishtov and the immediate surroundings of Novae are occupied by residential plots and small, intensively cultivated fields. Moreover, the main part of the *canabae* is located in an area of contemporary plot parceling and crops. A similar situation occurs at the site of Ostrite Mogili – although residential buildings are not as numerous as in the area of the *canabae*, it is partly covered by small parcels, where vegetables and vines are cultivated. The best conditions for geophysical prospection are offered by the wide, arable fields further to the east and south of the fortress. These open areas are covered by the monoculture cultivation of cereals.

The area under investigation is located on the high Danubian embankment, which is subject to river water erosion resulting in landslides. The area adjacent to the riverbed of the Danube is located on loess, sand, and gravel covering the bedrock, while fertile plains covered with chernozem stretch further to the south. This is reflected in the results of the geophysical surveys, especially with the use of a magnetometer, due to the magnetic properties of local stones, mainly sandstone, limestone, and basalt.

Despite these unfavorable conditions, integrated non-invasive methods make it possible to detect some traces of human activity. Various artifacts, mainly pottery sherds and fragments of building materials, are visible on the ground. The analysis of the topography and satellite imagery provides indications of traits related to transformation and land use in the past, as well as allowing a selection of areas potentially attractive for settlement and cultivation to be made.

Fig. 15. Google Earth satellite image with the georeferenced layout of Novae. The areas chosen for the prospection are marked with the letters. A – *retentura* and the southern annexe; B – Ostrite Mogili; C1 – extramural residence quarter; C2 – *canabae*; D – field to the south-west of the fortress; E – fields to the south of Ostrite Mogili; F – presumed villa at Kanlu cheshme (by A. Tomas).

2. Organization of work and general settings

Agnieszka Tomas

The project of non-intrusive investigations was preceded by a query and museum studies in the National Museum in Sofia and the Museum in Svishtov conducted by Agnieszka Tomas, who had the opportunity to study the old museum inventories. In 2011 and 2014, a series of photographs were taken in the Museum in Svishtov with the help and kindness of the curator Marin Marinov. The query was focused on finds documented before the start of the excavations, which might have originated from the extramural areas.

Based on the field observations and satellite imagery, several areas were chosen for ground prospection and marked with the letters A–F (**Fig. 15**). Area A1 is located in the central and south part of the annexe and Area A2 is located in the *retentura dextra* and across the eastern fortifications of the legionary fortress. The fields inside the fortress, where we expected to detect the remains of military barracks, were included in the prospection area for the purpose of comparison and verification of images created as a result of geomagnetic measurements. Area B covers the eastern part of the Ostrite Mogili site, a possible *vicus* near Novae.[1] Area C1 is a small lot near an extramural residence, while C2 is a small field surrounded by private summer houses. Area D is a field on a terrace to the south-east of the fortress. Areas E and F are situated on open fields to the south and south-west of Ostrite Mogili. Large fields located more than 1 km to the south-east of the South Gate were also investigated but with negative results, i.e. with no traces of Roman presence found. They were marked as N1 and N2.

The procedure of prospection started with a visit to the fields, including interviews with local people if possible. The owners of the private properties were informed about the nature of the non-intrusive investigations and the legal regulations and permits required for our investigations. The chosen area was measured with a total station and the grids were set out on the field. Extensive field walkings were implemented as the first method, and – depending on the density of the finds – intensive field walkings (mapping finds) with the use of metal detectors were carried out on a chosen set of grids. After field walkings, geomagnetic measurements were taken, and the results were elaborated every day after work. Depending on the results, some grids were chosen for electrical resistivity survey.

Complementary to the work on the ground, aerial photographs were taken with the use of a helium balloon and drones. One series of photographs was taken in autumn 2011 and three series in the springs of 2013–14.

Some data used for the purpose of recreating the ancient landscape were obtained during summer excavations. Samples for palynological and anthracological analyses were taken from high trench profiles in the *retentura* of the legionary camp and in the area of the northern defensive walls. The results of these analyses are presented in Chapter III.

3. Previous non-intrusive investigations at Novae

Agnieszka Tomas, Michał Pisz

Apart from the historical records on Novae and the pioneer work conducted there,[2] more detailed prospection of the site and its surroundings was carried out in 1960 before the start of the Bulgarian-Polish excavations headed by Kazimierz Majewski and Dimitr Dimitrov. The archaeologists observed that the main part of the extramural settlement was on the western side of the fortress, and other observations concerning traces of human activity were made during the prospection carried out simultaneously with the excavations.[3] They also observed remains in the vicinity of Novae, including the site of Ostrite Mogili.[4] A catalogue of finds discovered before the start of the excavations was prepared by Maria Nowicka.[5]

Field walking surveys

In 1961, Polish archaeologists headed by Witold Hensel carried out a series of field walking surveys, among others, near Novae. They localised three sites in the vicinity of Ostrite Mogili, within the supposed Roman *vicus*, with archaeological material dated from the Neolithic (Boian culture) up to the Medieval period.[6] The publication presented drawings of pottery and other finds, but without a plan.

The site was subject to intensive field walking and mapping finds in 1977 carried out by Tadeusz Sarnowski.[7] The surveying archaeologists used squared

1. Tomas 2017, 77–79.

2. Especially those done by Stefan Stefanov, the long-time director of the Museum in Svishtov; see Stefanov 1930-31; Stefanov 1958. For the history of research prior to the start of the excavations, see Kolendo 2008a.

3. Majewski 1962, 75–92 and see above, Introduction.

4. Majewski 1962, 92.

5. Catalogued by M. Nowicka in Majewski 1962, 151–56.

6. Hensel et al. 1965, 235–87, esp. 281–84. The archaeologists identified fragments of pottery which they attributed to the Neolithic Boian culture, as well as Thracian, Roman and Slavic artefact sherds from the First Bulgarian Empire (681–1018).

7. T. Sarnowski 1979, 210, Fig. 77.

paper notebooks with a scale, where they marked each type of material with a different symbol and a number referring to the quantity of finds. The results of these investigations are included in this volume as Area B.

Sarnowski applied this method in a place named Kanlu cheshme (in his publications referred to as Kulna cheshma), after the discovery of two funerary monuments.[8] The finds were registered along 6-m wide ploughed field strips, crossed by 1-m wide bounds of fruit trees. The prospection covered an area of 3 ha, but fragments of building materials and pottery were found only on the surface covering 140×150 m. This led T. Sarnowski to the conclusion that it might have been a farmhouse. In this volume, the site was named Area F.

Between 1997 and 2003, large-scale extensive field walking surveys in the area between Novae and the late Roman fort of Iatrus were conducted by German and Bulgarian archaeologists, who carried out excavations at the latter site.[9] The researchers estimated the surface of the extramural settlement at Novae as amounting to 70–80 ha in the early Roman period, and presented two general plans in chronological division – of the early and late Roman periods.[10] The surveyors visited the site of Ostrite Mogili (here named Area E), the supposed farmhouse at Kanlu cheshme mentioned above (Area F), and another small settlement to the south of Ostrite Mogili, in the place known as Chehlarski geran, here referred to as Area E.

In spring 2000, field walkings around Novae were carried out by Piotr Dyczek.[11] The surveys were done in several places, including the area to the east of the fortress, on the fields to the north of the Nursing Home where the researchers thought they would find a hippodrome, but the field walkings and trenches there did not provide any substantial evidence.[12] Some concave terrain to the south-west of this place was identified by P. Dyczek as possibly the spot mentioned in a 19th-century Bulgarian text, which refers to the ruins of a theatre.[13] However, the trenches made there excluded such an identification.[14] Surveys were also carried out on the western edge of the modern village of Vardim, where late Roman finds were recorded,[15] and to the south of the fortress. Traces of a supposed road to the south of Novae, 5 km from the village of Bulgarsko Slivovo, were never confirmed, although some pottery sherds were found there.[16]

Intensive field walkings were also conducted again at the Ostrite Mogili site, which provided several detailed maps of finds.[17] The method applied then was similar to the method used by T. Sarnowski, but the distances were measured with an odometer. Ten surveyors walked in transects at a distance of 5 m from one another. Each person had a squared paper notebook, where each type of material was marked with a different symbol.

Extensive field walking surveys in an area to the south and to the east of Novae were done by Bulgarian archaeologists in 2017. Within the framework of the "Archaeological Map

8. T. Sarnowski 1979.

9. Vagalinski et al. 2001a; Vagalinski et al. 2001b; Stanchev 2002; Conrad and Stančev 2002; Conrad 2006.

10. Conrad and Stančev 2002, 674 and Fig. 5; Conrad 2006a, 319–21, Figs. 8, 10, 11.

11. Gencheva 2001, 75–76; Tomas 2006, 115.

12. Gencheva 2001, 75.

13. Tomas 2017, 76–77 and App. 1 on p. 170; cf. Gencheva 2001, 75.

14. Dyczek 2003.

15. Gencheva 2001, 76.

16. Gencheva 2001, 76. The places where the researchers had expected to find the remains of the road leading to the south were subjected to trenching in 2009, but the results were once again negative; see Gencheva and Reclav 2010.

17. Gencheva 2001, 75; Tomas 2006, 115–28, Figs. 2, 6, 8 and 9.

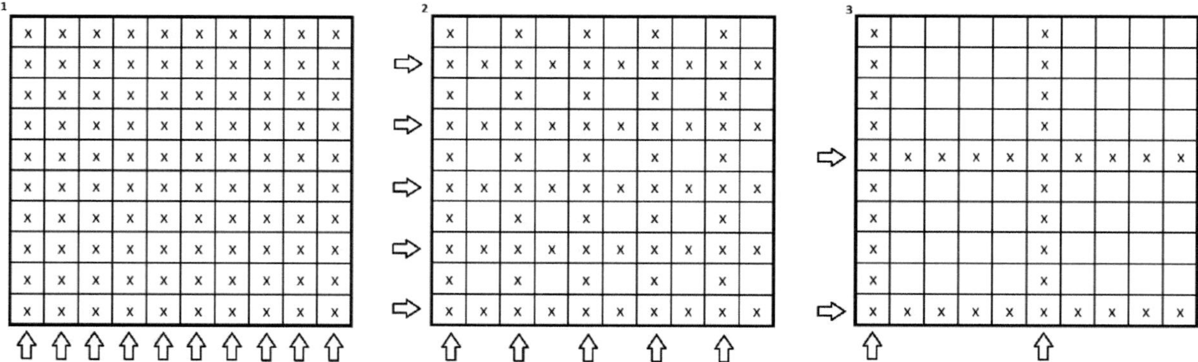

Fig. 16a – Sampling pattern presented on exemplary 10×10 m grid. Left: 1. Widely used today 1×1 m sampling resolution, profiles along one axis; 2. Sampling pattern applied in the principia area – 1×2 m, 2 m intervals between profiles measured along two axes; 3. Sampling pattern applied in the extra mural area – 1×5 m, 5 m intervals between profiles measured along two axes (by M. Pisz).

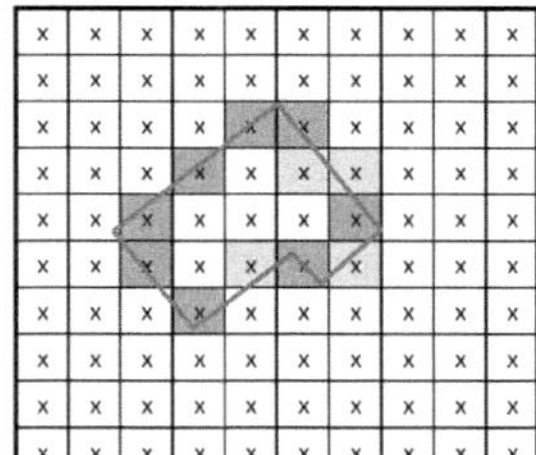
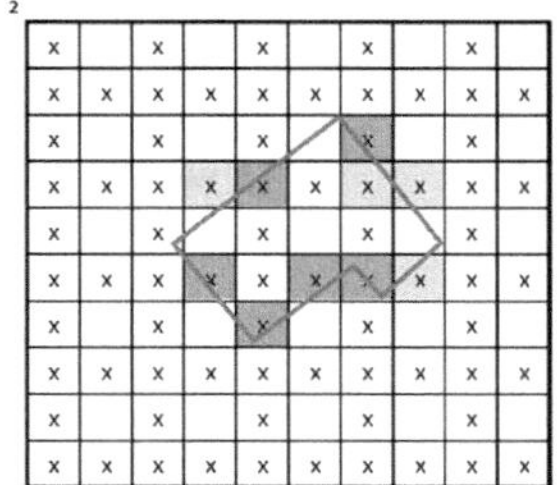
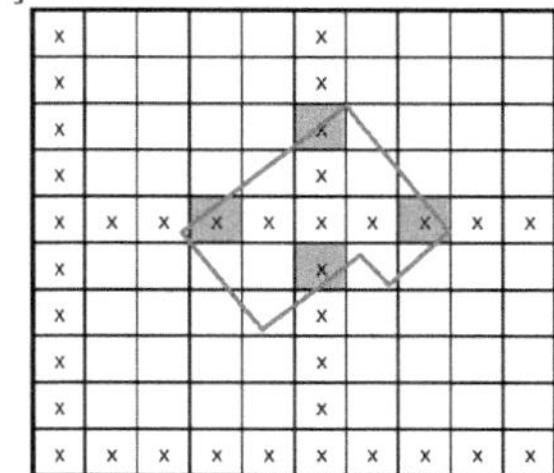
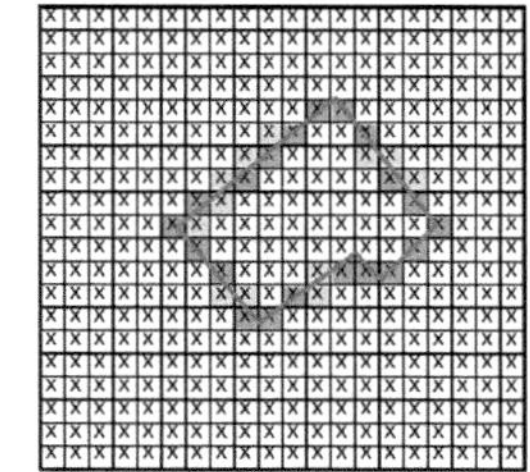

Fig. 16b – Electrical resistivity survey sampling pattern over hypothetical high-contrasting architectural remains. With (1×1 m) samples marked. Grey-coloured grids represent theoretical highly resistive response measured by the instrument. 1 – 1×1 m sampling; 2 –1×2 m sampling; 3 –1×5 m sampling; 4 –0.5×0.5 m sampling (M. Pisz).

of Bulgaria" programme, the team surveyed areas near the villages of Tsarevets and Vardim and managed to register 19 sites, including 13 burial mounds, three cemeteries, two settlements, and one *villa rustica*.[18]

Aerial photography

A series of aerial photographs were taken in the 1970s, when the images were used to construct a 1:5000 topographical map of Bulgaria.[19] The first analysis of the aerial and satellite imagery of the area where Novae is located was made towards the end of the 1990s, and one of them was published by Szymon Lipa.[20] The author used two series of panchromatic vertical aerial photographs from 1957 and 1982 and one monochromatic oblique photograph made in the summer of 1979.[21] Based on the analysis of the river's cut-off and oxbows visible on the satellite imagery, Lipa presented a possible reconstruction of the Danubian riverbed in ancient times.[22] Such an interpretation obviously contained a flaw, caused by the fact that the comparative material was very poor, which the author himself admitted. Apart from the changes of the Danubian riverbed, the author tried to identify the archaeological features unearthed during excavations, and thereafter, tried to determine other traces of ancient human activity using vegetation and soil marks. Lipa identified a number of line marks, which he tried to compare to the main roads of the fortress.[23] Aerial photographs were also published by S. Conrad.[24]

18. Andreeva et al. 2018a; 2018b. The second series of field walkings were done along the planned gas pipeline, but they included sites further to the south, with the nearest one located in the vicinity of the present-day village of Kozlovets, about 10 km to the south of Novae.
19. E. Gencheva (2001) mentions the photographs on p. 75.
20. Lipa 2000.
21. Lipa 2000, 133.
22. Lipa 2000, 136–38.
23. Lipa 2000, 143–46.
24. Conrad 2006a, Fig. 7.

Geophysical and geological surveys

The first electrical resistivity survey was carried out in Novae in July 1965 in the area of the West Gate and the west defensive wall.[25] Some of the results were confirmed by later excavations.[26] In 1977, two specialists from the AGH University of Science and Technology in Cracow conducted an electrical resistivity survey in the area of the headquarters building (*principia*) and outside the fortress, at a distance of 90 to 160 m from the western defensive wall.[27] Back then, an electrical profiling method was implemented. Measurements were taken using a PKE-7 resistivity meter, with a 400V battery supply. Geophysicists applied a pole-dipole electrode array, with a 1 m electrode spacing. In the area of the partly excavated headquarters building, the interval between traverses was 2 m and the profiles intersected. Sampling along the profiles was done every 1 m (**Fig. 16a/2**). Such a sampling pattern resulted in the uneven covering of the surveyed area in terms of the conducted measurements. 25 out of 100 measurement points were doubled. Another area, located outside the camp walls, was considered as a preliminary research spot, and hence the interval between the profiles was increased to 5m (**Fig. 16a/3**). It is noteworthy that state of the art for archaeological prospection with the electrical resistivity profiling method advises not to decrease the sampling resolution to below 1×1 m.[28] The graphic comparison of the sampling resolution effectiveness in prospecting on hypothetical architectural remains is illustrated in **Fig. 16b**. Considering the times and the technological capabilities, the results and interpretation of the geophysical research conducted in 1977 in the headquarters area were very good.

25. Stopiński 1968. The surveys were done by Wojciech Stopiński from the Polish Academy of Sciences, who worked on the medieval site in Sturmen on the Yantra River.
26. Stopiński 1968, 206–07.
27. Matuszyk, Szybiński, and Sarnowski 1979.
28. Schmidt et at. 2015, 10–13.

The results in the extramural area were interpreted as the remains of architecture, and were followed by the start of excavations in this sector.[29]

Over the years, various geological and petrographic investigations were carried out by J. Skoczylas, Z. Walkiewicz and N. Cholakov.[30]

4. Field walking surveys and documentation of structural remains

Agnieszka Tomas

Field walking is usually carried out in early spring or autumn, when the arable fields have been ploughed and vegetation has not appeared yet. In Bulgaria, this period lasts only two weeks in early spring, i.e., the second part of March. In autumn, many fields and meadows are still densely covered with vegetation. Even on arable fields, the remains of cultivated crops, like the green parts of sunflowers or corn, are very often left on the field until spring. In such cases, the field chosen for archaeological surveying must be cleared prior to the field walking, as well as prior to the geophysical prospection.

29. Matuszyk, Szybiński, and Sarnowski 1979, 216.

30. E.g., Skoczylas and Tcholakov, and Walkiewicz 1979; Skoczylas 1995.

Our objective was to verify the sites recorded in the past and to discover new ones situated within a radius of 3–4 km around the legionary camp. Theoretically, this area is large, but in fact the grounds available for surveying are located only to the south, south-east and east, in the form of limited arable fields.

For the purpose of detecting new sites or searching for the edges of a site, we implemented extensive field walking (the transect method). A chosen area was divided into a series of parallel transects, of which each was 10 m wide (**Fig. 17**). One person acting as a guide had a notepad to make a sketch of the site, to write remarks concerning the visibility, surveying limitations, etc., but he or she also monitored the walking tempo and the intervals between the walkers. To cover as much of the area as possible, the surveyors walked in a zig-zag. In order to maintain the azimuth and even intervals, at least two people were provided with hand-held GPS devices. They also marked the edges of the surveyed site. Each person carried a bag with a label containing the name of the place, its position, surveying date, and the person's name (**Fig. 18**). The entire area was scanned for artefacts, i.e., pottery and glass shards, fragments of building material, metal waste, bone remains, etc. The finds were classified

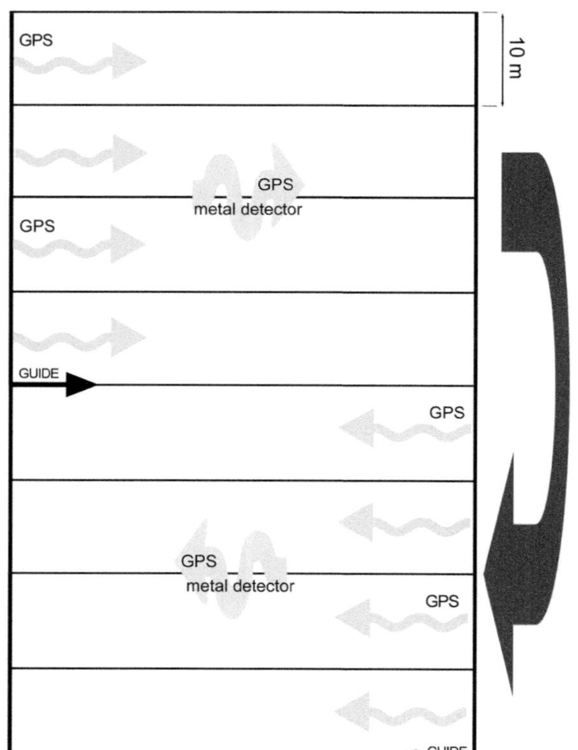

Fig. 17. Scheme of the extensive field walking (transect) method implemented in 2012–14 (by A. Tomas).

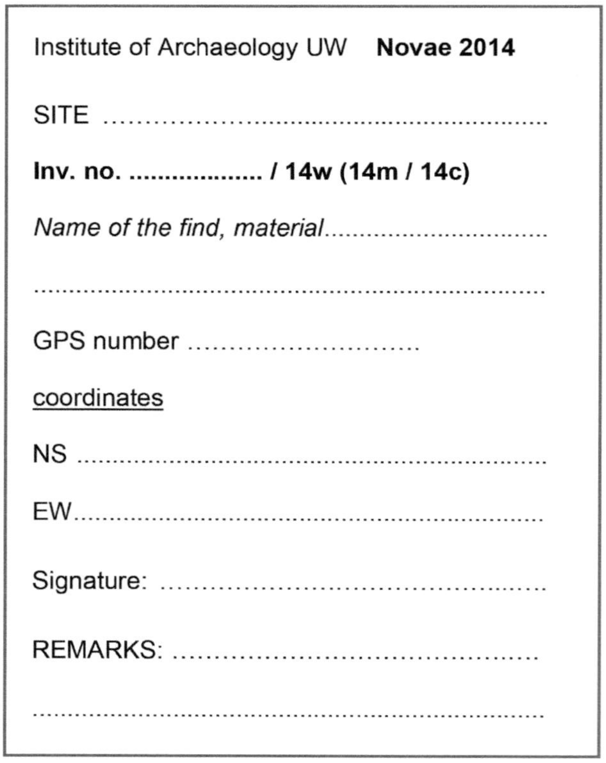

Institute of Archaeology UW **Novae 2014**

SITE ....

Inv. no. .... / 14w (14m / 14c)

Name of the find, material...............................

....

GPS number ....

coordinates

NS ....

EW...

Signature: ....

REMARKS: ....

....

Fig. 18. Novae 2012–14. Label used during field walkings in 2012–14 (by A. Tomas).

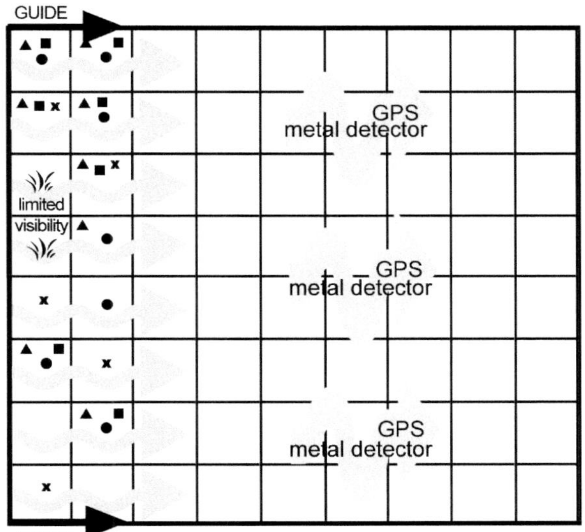

Fig. 19. Scheme of intensive field walkings (grid) method implemented in 2012–14 (by A. Tomas).

as 'selected' and 'mass'. Each of the selected finds (Polish: *wydzielone*) was documented separately and marked with the letter 'w' (e.g., 17/12w; 18/12w, etc.). The spatial location of the selected finds was marked with a hand-held GPS. Mass finds (Polish: *masowe*) were documented in groups with the letter 'm', and each find received its own number within its group (e.g., 3/12m/1; 3/12m/2, etc.). They were collected within the investigated areas (transects) and put into a bag provided with a label. The finds of stamped building materials were marked as 'bricks' (Polish: *cegły*) with the letter 'c' (e.g., 12/13c). A person with a metal detector walked in front of the two–three lines, and marked metal finds with a GPS device, filling in a label for selected finds. After each transect, the bag was closed.

Intensive field walkings (grid method) were applied on the sites selected after carrying out extensive field walkings. The grid method makes it possible to create maps of different categories of finds (building materials, pottery, glass, etc.), along with their density in certain places. The general rules of the method follow the transect method, but the collection of finds is more accurate and done within 5×5 m squares (grids). During the field walking, each person marked the number and class of the finds in every grid (**Fig. 19**). Two guiding persons walked on both sides of a line of walkers to maintain the tempo and azimuth. Limitations of visibility, e.g., grass or field paths, were also marked within every grid in order to compare the maps of finds with the visibility during field walking and the features of the terrain, such as valleys, hills, etc. The finds were labelled the same as in the extensive method. This method was used twice at the Ostrite Mogili site (in 1979, 2000) and at area F – Kanlu cheshme (in 1979). In 1979, the grids were marked with the number of steps taken, in 2000 with an odometer, and in 2012–14 by GPS devices.

The field walkings within the project presented in this volume were carried out in the springs of 2012, 2013 and 2014, and combined both intensive and extensive methods. They covered all the areas where magnetic prospection was applied, as well as the large fields to the south of Novae, a broad area to the east of Ostrite Mogili, and the fields to the south of this site, which were excluded from the geophysical prospection, after the negative results of the field walkings.

The remains of architecture visible in Area C1 and in the illegal trenches within the annexe were photographed and registered with hand-held GPS devices. Apart from standard photography, photogrammetric orthophotoplans were created for the architectural remains.

The accuracy of the precise location of the annexe's eastern fortifications had to be verified for the purpose of future investigations and the creation of a correct plan of the entire site. Preliminary prospection made along the eastern fortifications with the hand-held GPS showed that topographical surveying with modern geodesy instruments (GPS RTK) should be done to establish the accurate position of the towers and the outline of the defensive wall. In 2012 this task, however, was left to be done in the nearest future, since the fortifications were covered with vegetation, trees and rubbish. The measurements were made from 2014 to 2018.[31]

5. Geophysical prospection methods

Piotr Wroniecki, Marcin Jaworski, Michał Pisz, Krzysztof Misiewicz, Wiesław Małkowski

Research carried out in the three seasons of 2012–14 was preceded by small-scale tests of magnetic and electrical resistivity methods in 2011, which helped to evaluate the applied methodology as suitable, despite hindrances, such as urban sprawl and agriculture. The most accessible areas for geophysical measurements were chosen, i.e., a non-wooded area located at the rear of the headquarters, a small plot within the headquarters, and a small field west of the camp. The tests produced positive results for the further implementation of the methods.

31. The present publication presents plans based on the measurements made in 2018. For the results see Chapter V.

Magnetic prospection with a Bartington Grad601-2 gradiometer

Piotr Wroniecki, Marcin Jaworski

Magnetic gradiometry offers the fastest area coverage of all available methods. This type of prospection may register architectural relicts lying underground, but also traces of other human activity. Thermoremanent magnetization was also applied, which is created through submitting ferric oxides to high temperatures and characterises such archaeological features as hearths, kilns, brick structures, structures with clay mortars or burned daub. Various archaeological features (pits, ditches) generate magnetic anomalies described in nanotesla units (nT). Magnetic anomalies identified as typical cut and fill features generate point anomalies, locally increasing the vertical component of the magnetic field, whereas architectural relics and in general remains of buildings erected with the use of thermally processed materials generate variously shaped dipolar anomalies.

The disadvantage of this method is its vulnerability to additionally registering the magnetic fields of ferromagnetic objects, such as steel or iron structures and parts of modern infrastructure. Such elements with their own strong magnetic field tend to cover anomalies with less distinct magnetic features, like the ones that originate in places containing archaeological deposits. As a result, the possibilities of archaeological prospection using magnetic surveys are limited in urban environments or places heavily transformed by modern human activity that has led to the introduction of strongly magnetic ferrous objects into the landscape.

During subsequent campaigns between 2012–14, magnetic prospection was the main geophysical method applied in the survey of the *canabae* and other sites in the vicinity of the legionary fortress. The measurements were conducted in parallel profiles within a network of square grids (usually 30×30m or 40×40m) set up individually for each site through the prior application of a GPS STK Azus Star with a DF5232 antenna (2013–14), a GPS RTK Trimble 5800 (2014), and a Total Station Leica TS02 7" (2012–14) in the field.

Electrical resistivity prospection

Michał Pisz

Electrical resistivity surveys complement magnetic measurement data with information on the approximate depth of the deposition of anomalous subsoil structures and potential archaeological features and provide information on their electrical properties. Its application enhances the overview of buried architectural remains and can provide data on the underlying stratigraphy of studied areas. One of the advantages of this method is the possibility of applying various electrode configurations, which make it possible to control the maximum depth of electric current penetration. The major disadvantage is the influence of natural conditions beyond the surveyors' control, such as soil humidity and hence electrical conductivity / resistivity.

Electrical resistivity method allows to capture high and low resistivity anomalies, that might be interpreted as archaeological features. In general, low resistivity areas may be usually identified as filled pits, ditches and other filled-in anthropogenic interferences in the natural stratigraphy. On the contrary, high resistivity areas can be identified as an indicator of the presence of compact structures (such as, e.g., rows of bricks, stones or rubble) or hollows. Surveys in Novae were conducted with an ADA-5 instrument in dipole-dipole (2 m) or twin-probe (0.5 m) configurations in polygons overlying areas of special interest located within larger polygons researched previously through magnetic measurements.

In the study of the surroundings of Novae, electrical resistivity was chosen as a complementary geophysical method to magnetic prospection. It was carried out in the annexe and to the west of Novae at Areas A1, C1 and C2 (**Fig. 15**). Grids within Area A1 were measured for the purpose of verifying the results obtained from the magnetic measurements. Areas C1 and C2 are small fields close to the extramural residence, located on parcels among the private summer houses to the west of the fortress.

Magnetic prospection with a caesium Geometrics G858 Magmapper

Krzysztof Misiewicz, Wiesław Małkowski

Geophysical measurements were executed using a caesium magnetometer, which functioned with the probes in a horizontal alignment (horizontal gradient), simultaneously registering the intensity level values of the magnetic field's complete vector. The applied horizontal measuring system enables the calculation of the values of the horizontal gradient – the difference in the values of the magnetic field, measured at the same time by probes in a metric gauge. The measurement cycle was set to every 0.1 second. Simultaneously with the magnetic prospection, height measurements were conducted using the GPS RTK system. Merging the GPS function and the magnetometer into one device enables a precise determination of the location of the changes in the values of the magnetic field to be determined, while simultaneously registering the height of the surveyed terrain. The RTK work mode allows for a very precise establishment of the position, both vertically and horizontally, which – in connection with the visualisation of the motion path – allows fieldwork to be conducted without using other systems supporting the locating process, e.g., it is possible to forego staking orthogonal nets in the field and extending tape measures.

The measuring set consists of three elements: two GPS receivers (the base receiver and the mobile receiver) and a caesium magnetometer. The GPS receivers communicate with each other through radio modems. The mobile GPS receiver, which is connected to the magnetometer, receives reference corrections from the base receiver via radio on the radio frequency UHF 410-470 MHz at (0.5W–1.0W). This enables working in open territory with a radius significantly exceeding 1km. During the measurements, the CMR (Compact Measurement Record) correction format is transmitted. Within the frame of this data stream, package information is sent about the GPS satellite L1, L2 signals, GLONASS, as well as the location (coordinates) and parameters of the base receiver's antenna. The mobile receiver, working in the RTK mode, is connected via an RS-232 serial port with a G-858 caesium magnetometer. The mutual configuration of the connections (the speed of sending and synchronising data bits) makes it possible to send data about the geographical coordinates and the heights from the GPS receiver and receive it on the magnetometer's datalogger, while maintaining equipment precision/errors (GPS measurements have a horizontal precision of H: ±10 mm + 1 ppm and a vertical one of V: ± 15 mm + 1 ppm). The transmission of the data from the GPS in NMEA (National Marine Electronics Association) format contains GGA (Global Positioning System Fixed Data), providing information about the geographical longitude and latitude, as well as the altitude with a measurement precision of 1mm. The data from the GPS is sent at a time interval of one second, and then interpolated to the magnetometer measurement depending on the settings – in the case of the described site, every 0.1 second. The position data are archived in the memory of the magnetometer according to the time column next to the synchronized magnetic field data/records. The registered data collected after taking the measurements are transmitted using the MagMap2000 programme, in which the geographical coordinate values in degrees (BLH Breite Länge Höhe) are converted to the metric system (UTM – Universal Transverse Mercator), according to the parameters adopted for the site (offsets on the N-S and E-W axes, establishing the central meridian, the grossing-up factor). Eventually, it should be possible to perform the conversion from the global coordinate system to the local system adopted for the archaeological work conducted at a particular site. To this purpose, a minimum of three points of contact (common points) can be used for both systems. The initial coordinate system is then the UTM metric system (with a defined central meridian), while the target coordinate system is the local one. In the case of Novae, the horizontal position was determined based on cylindrical angle-preserving UTM as zone 35, central meridian 27, while the heights were measured in the GPS system using the satellite system. As a result of this solution, it was later possible to find the position of the research results, e.g., magnetic anomalies using one-frequency GPS receivers set in the metric measurement mode of the appropriate zone in the UTM mapping system.

6. Satellite imagery and aerial photography

Michał Pisz

High-resolution (0.41 m per pixel) orthorectified satellite imagery from the WorldView-2 satellite encompassing the entire area of the fortress and its surroundings was used as a supplementary tool to aerial photography. A substantial part of Novae is covered with high trees limiting the visibility of the ground. The trees and two power lines crossing the site on the east-west axis were obstacles for the use of a balloon or drones.

The satellite imagery has served not only as a base map for the GIS database, but also as a tool for planning the fieldwork, spatial analyses, a reference point for observations of the changing landscape, and a way

Fig. 20. Novae 2013. Hexacopter DJI S800 equipped with a Canon 5D MkII camera with a 14–70 mm lens (photo by J. Pisz).

Fig. 21. Novae 2014. Parallel transects used for mapping finds with the use of metal detectors (photo by P. Jaworski).

of documenting the state of preservation of the site. The images helped to analyze the relations between the site's layout and the landscape, the environment and human activities. The satellite images were also very helpful in planning and interpreting the results of our surveys.

A series of low-altitude aerial photographs were performed using a remote-controlled camera platform attached to various unmanned aerial vehicles (UAV). Back in the beginning of the 2010s, multirotor aircrafts were not yet very developed. During the first research seasons (2011–12), we used a helium balloon, to which a remote-controlled AeroSurveyor1 platform was attached. A spherical balloon made from latex could contain up to 5m^3 of helium, as a result of which it was able to lift a photographic platform (2 kg load) to a height of ca. 230 m (the height was limited by steering cords). The platform AeroSurveyor1 consisting of an aluminium frame attached to the balloon by a Picavet suspension,[32] was fitted with servos allowing for the rotation of the camera in relation to the two axes (pan-tilt). The platform had a signal transmitter (on the 2.4 GHz frequency) and the image transmitter from the video feed (on the 5.8 GHz frequency). A Canon 550d DSLR camera equipped with a 14–70 mm lens was mounted onto the platform. The platform was also fitted onto a photographic kite of the flowform type; however, this type of aircraft did not work in Novae due to the topographical obstacles (trees, electric wires etc.).

In 2013, aerial prospection was conducted using two types of aircraft. The first of these was the AeroSurveyor2 drone – a self-propelled, radio-controlled plane Delta Wing-type drone, equipped with a stabilizing system, autopilot and an MFT Olympus E-PL3 camera with 17 mm lens. The camera was directed perpendicularly downwards, without the possibility of it being regulated, as a result of which it was possible to only take perpendicular or slightly diagonal photographs. The second device was a hexacopter DJI S800 equipped with a Canon 5D MkII camera with a 14–70 mm lens (**Fig. 20**). Its biggest asset was the possibility of maintaining full control of the platform and the camera settings; however, there are certain features which should be seen as its main flaws: its susceptibility to wind effects, short flight time and unreliability, due to the large amount of unshielded electronic elements affected by the field conditions.

Since 2013 we have experienced a technological revolution in the matter of Unmanned Aerial Vehicles.[33] Currently, multirotor platforms have become widely available, and they are superior to all the platforms used during the research in 2013–14 done at Novae in terms of their technological advancement.

Regarding the processing of collected aerial images, some were processed in order to compose high-resolution orthophotomaps. Just like in the case of UAVs, a rapid development has taken place in the area of 3D photogrammetry. Nowadays, there are a number of programmes which allow for the production of orthophotomaps and 3D surface models out of a set of pictures almost automatically. In the first half

32. Picavet 1912

33. Campana 2017.

of the 2010s, the workflow of processing the pictures was manual and this method was used in Novae. During the first stage, the pictures were devoid of distortion and calibrated with ground control points (GCP), measured with geodesy instruments. For this purpose, we used the Autodesk Raster Design and applied the polynomial algorithm method of calibration. Calibrated pictures were manually merged into an orthophotomap using graphic software.

The orthophotomaps generated based on aerial photographs taken using UAV at a low altitude are characterized by a much higher resolution than the aerial and satellite images. In turn, their main flaw is their limited territorial range. In the case of Novae, some areas were inaccessible for photographs taken at a low altitude. In particular, this applied to terrains covered by trees, private property whose owners had not given permission for the platform to fly over, and other areas through which energy lines run. It was assumed that while preparing images from the air, any spots at which high-resolution photographs could not be taken would be filled in using satellite imagery.

It should be emphasized that the work done within the framework of the discussed project was of a pioneering nature, while the use of modern aerial photography techniques with the application of UAV took place there even before the development of broadly available multirotor platforms. The most important part, however, is that we were able to document a rapidly changing landscape near Novae.

7. Mapping of metal finds

Piotr Jaworski

A metal detector is a standard tool for searching for metal artefacts both during excavations and during surveys. However, it should be remembered that artefacts deposited on the surface or in the humus in most cases lack an archaeological context due to a variety of factors and the fact that they had been separated from their original place of deposition in various periods. Even though in most cases retrieving metal artefacts from hummus layers using a metal detector provides material that had already earlier lost its archaeological context, this type of activity, conducted in accordance with a strictly followed procedure, may provide important information in the light of this dilemma, which – on the one hand – is linked to the problems resulting from leaving such artefacts in layers significantly accelerating their corrosion and destruction and the possibility of them being taken by the wrong people, and – on the other hand – to ensuring that all the metal artefacts are collected in a methodical manner so that they can be studied and published, an archaeologist should undertake the immediate and proper acquisition of such material. At sites where the history of archaeological research is old, and Novae is undoubtedly one such place, the finds collected on the surface and in the hummus layers with metal detectors generally do not change the chronology of the individual find categories. A good example of this are monetary finds, of which a few thousand were acquired at this site and which have been the subject of many studies. Such individual finds of unique or rare artefacts, even though they have their own – sometimes very high – relevance, do not nonetheless change the overall analysis of the situation.

During methodically conducted prospection, metal artefacts are acquired through intensive searches conducted on smaller areas (mapping finds). In the case of the mapping of finds conducted in Novae, it was decided to gather all the metals on the previously delineated area, which enables a precise estimation of the proportions between artefacts and modern metallic debris, as well as the statistics of the finds themselves within their category or type of metal. The prospections were conducted at designated research polygons, while every find was recorded separately. This method allows for the near-complete coverage of the investigated area at high-resolution.[34]

Preparing the area was preceded by a meticulous selection of the research area and measuring the research polygons in the form of parallel transects (**Fig. 21**). All the areas subjected to searches of metal objects were located within a grid used in geophysical studies. In the terrain, they were designated using bench marks which already had their coordinates, and tape measures. The strips were 2.5 m wide, while their lengths were dependent on the accessibility of the terrain. Attempts were made to avoid areas directly adjacent to modern roads and the fences of private properties to avoid retrieving excessive amounts of contemporary scrap.

Three metal detectors were used for the research: two models of the Garrett Ace 150 type and one MineLab x-Terra 705. Two people worked on each of the strips. One – operating the metal detector and the other – preparing the field documentation. Each of the couples would begin at opposite ends of the studied areas so as to not disrupt the work of the remaining detectors. In the course

34. Connor and Scott 1998, 81–82.

of the surveys, the devices worked in the "all metal" mode, as a result of which artefacts made of non-ferrous metals as well as ferrous and leaden ones were collected. The locations of all the finds were registered with handheld GPS devices. The surveyors classified each find as a selected or mass find. Each selected find received its own label. Mass finds from each strip were collected into one bag with one label.

The selected finds were identified, described, drawn and photographed. Data recorded by the handheld GPS devices were exported as .shp files to the GIS environment, where they received additional attributes, such as identification, a description of the material, and dating. This made it possible to produce a series of maps with the distribution of finds in chronological divisions.

8. GIS database and spatial analyses

Piotr Wroniecki

The final goal of the prospection was to integrate all the acquired data into one consolidated geospatial environment. The GIS database makes it possible to collect, analyze and present different kinds of data, including the results of present investigations, but also other sources, such as cartographic and topographic material, mapping, etc. The previous excavation results in the form of plans of the unearthed buildings and fortifications were integrated with the imagery obtained during the recent investigations. The analyses allowed detection inaccuracies or false interpretations made in the past, when archaeologists did not have such convenient, modern tools of spatial measurement, to be identified. Another aspect of the GIS database was the possibility of conducting advanced spatial analyses, such as the Voronoi diagrams/Thiessen polygons or visibility analysis for any areas within the studied region. For the latter, additional software was applied in the form of the open-source Saga GIS and Digital Elevation Model, obtained from the NASA operated Aster satellite.

The satellite image produced by the WorldView-2 satellite sensor purchased for the purpose of the project covered the area of the fortress and its surroundings, ca. 3.2 km to the West and ca. 1 km to the East; hence, without the Ostrite Mogili site, which is not as densely covered with vegetation as the area of the fortress and – therefore – is a more convenient site for aerial photogrammetry. In 2012, a spatial database was created using the Quantum GIS programme and integrated with the georeferenced satellite image and plans of the architectural remains discovered so far. The plans were corrected and georeferenced with data obtained from GPS measurements using static (GPS Azus Star) and Real Time Kinematic (Trimble 5800) systems, total station theodolite, and hand-held GPS devices. Further added data included the known structures unearthed or visible in the extramural area, and the various spots marked with hand-held GPS devices, e.g., the limits of the sites defined by the archaeological material visible on the surface, the results of the previous field walking surveys, topographical maps, etc. The satellite imagery was enhanced by adding the rectified orthophotomaps taken in 2012–14. The results of the non-invasive investigations and other data acquired during the project were added to this basic spatial model in the form of separate raster and vector layers.

V

The results of the prospection

Marcin Jaworski, Wiesław Małkowski, Krzysztof Misiewicz, Michał Pisz, Agnieszka Tomas, and Piotr Wroniecki

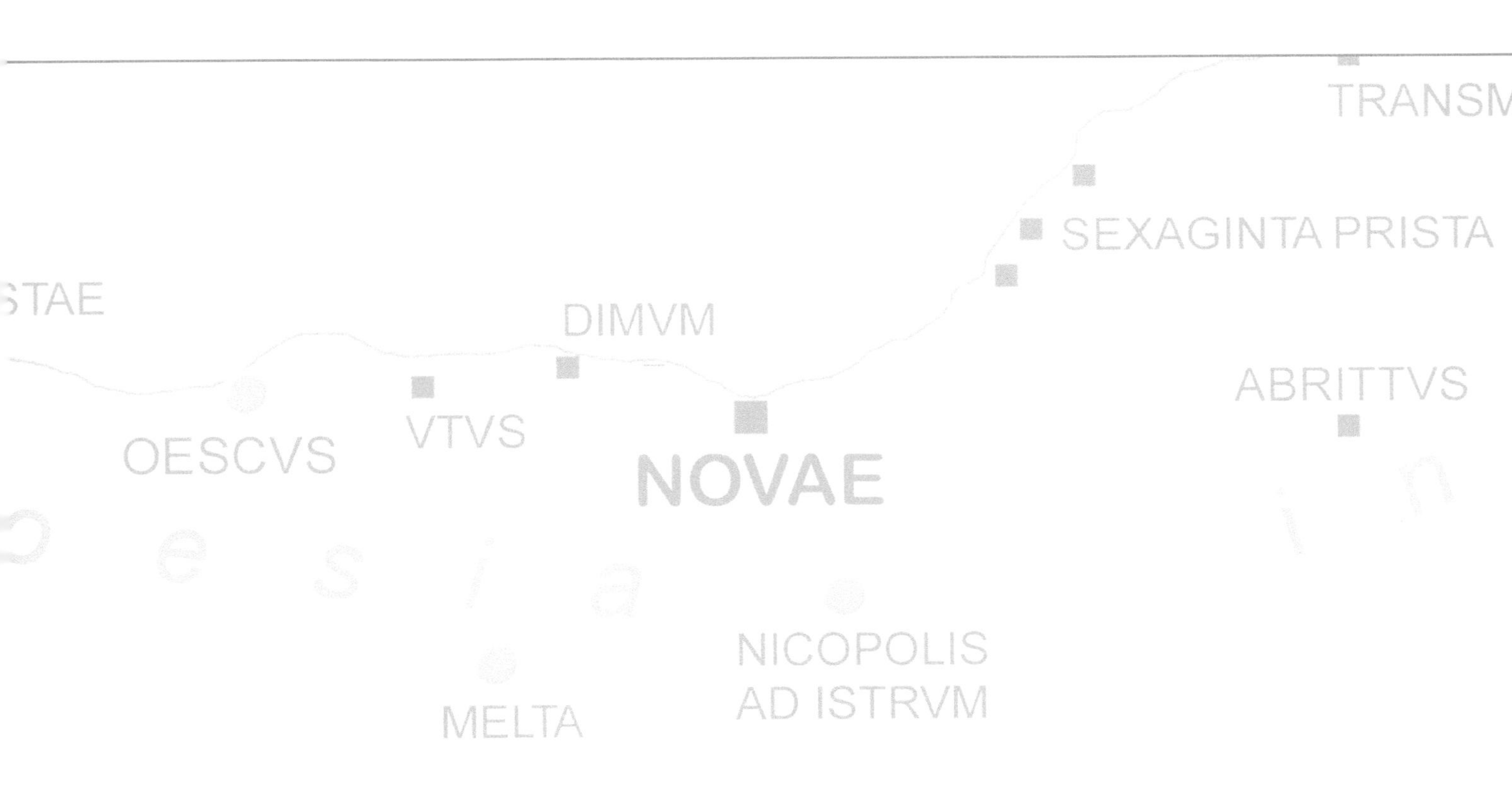

1. Satellite imagery and aerial photography 2011–14

Michał Pisz

The topographic conditions in Novae, vegetation at the site and dense private lots, make archaeological feature detection based on remote sensing data hardly possible. However, in the case of Novae, aerial photography provides some additional data for other spheres of the conducted archaeological activities. The images from the air allow us to observe and document its state of preservation or any hazards related to human activities and nature, but – above all – to create a GIS database using the georeferenced remains of walls, geodesy reference points and the newly acquired data. This was no easy task if we take into account the fact that the position of the features unearthed in past years was not established with such precision as can be done now with state of the art measuring instruments. Some features which look meaningless from the ground show clearly from the air.

The first step to creating the orthophotomap of Novae was the purchase of a satellite image, which was a useful tool for planning the flights and estimation of the efforts required to cover a maximum area of the site. However, in 2021, when this publication is being published, satellite imagery of much better quality is widely available, so the results will be presented on the new Google Earth images, but taken in a year of prospection – 2013.

High-altitude oblique photographs were taken over the entire area of Novae and to the south of it (**Fig. 22**). Low-altitude photographs were taken over the southern part of the annexe, the southern part of the legionary fortress (*retentura*), over the headquarters building (*principia*), the cathedral and Episcopal residence, the military hospital with superimposed remains of a Late Roman urban villa, as well as an extramural residence and the late Roman basilica beyond the western walls of the fortress. Outside Novae, low-altitude photographs were taken over the site of Ostrite Mogili.

The first flights were conducted in September 2011. A series of photographs were taken from a helium balloon. This first session made it possible to create the orthophotomap of the fortress' centre with the headquarters building (**Fig. 23**). A number of oblique photographs over the broad area around the site provided images useful for remote sensing prospection. Flights over Novae were continued in 2012 and 2013, but the balloon was replaced by drones. The aerial vehicles made it possible to take photographs in places where the use of balloons would be inconvenient.

In 2012 and 2013 high-resolution vertical photographs were taken both over the intra- and extramural area. The accurately defined position of the camp's fortifications and the architectural remains were useful reference points for further measurements in the extramural area. The fortifications of the annexe and the southern part of the annexe

Fig. 22. Novae 2012. The southern part of the annexe and the view on the Dermen dere Valley (photo by M. Pisz).

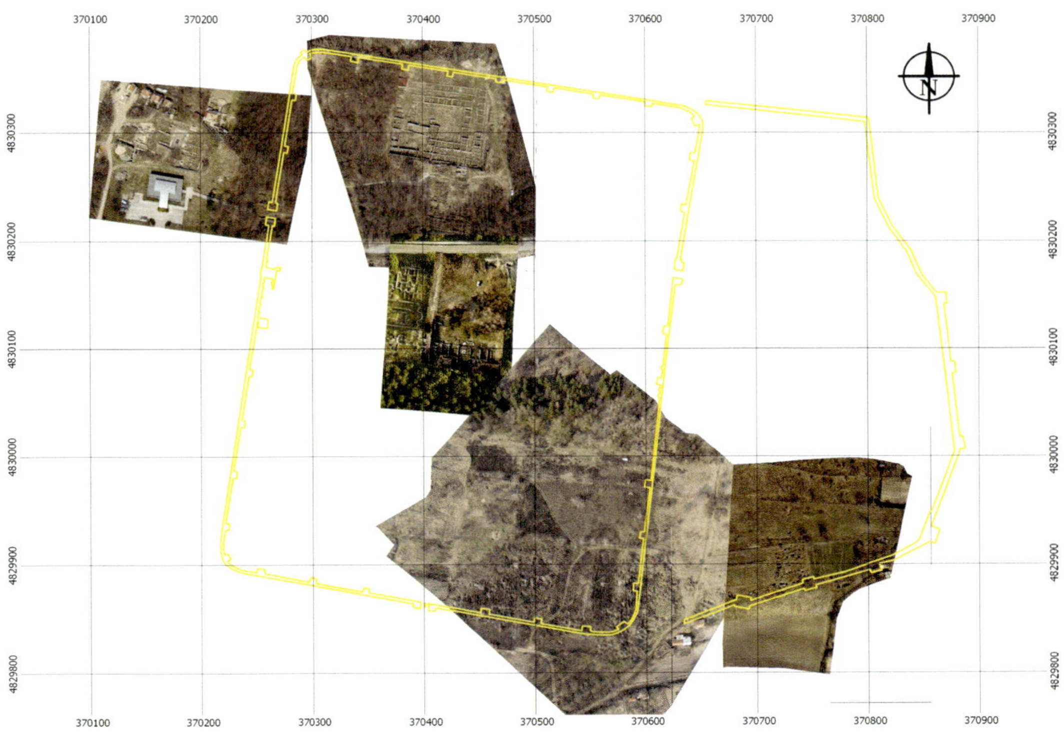

Fig. 23. Novae 2011–12. The orthophotomap presenting the site with the fortress' schematic layout marked in yellow (by M. Pisz).

were areas where we especially focused our interest. In some places, crucial points, such as the south-eastern corner of the fortress, where the former legionary fortifications join the annex's curtain, were clearly visible. In 2013, we documented the unearthed *forum militare,* and the newly discovered buildings to the east of the *principia* were included into the orthophotomap of Novae.

In 2013 and 2014, flights were conducted over Ostrite Mogili. It was the first time that the site was documented from the air. The northern and eastern parts of Ostrite Mogili are open fields, but there are

Fig. 24. Novae 2013. The orthophotomap of the site superimposed over satellite imagery (by M. Pisz).

Fig. 25. Ostrite Mogili 2014. The orthophotomap of the site (by M. Pisz).

some private buildings in the western part. The entire site is divided into small lots and fields which make the visibility very limited. All these inconveniences and the character of the cultivation hindered observation of soil marks, despite the fact that some fields were recently ploughed. In some places, high grass and bushes were left dry over the winter and covered the surface, which was completely indistinct from the ground. The image from the air showed a number of illegal trenches, some of them buried. This information turned out to be very important for the interpretation of the geophysical research.

Over the course of four seasons, several thousand oblique and vertical photographs in JPEG and RAW formats were taken. Based on the vertical images, three georeferenced orthophotomaps of Novae were prepared. The first one covered almost the entire area of the legionary fortress (**Fig. 24**); the second one – the Ostrite Mogili site (**Fig. 25**), while the third one – the southern part of the annexe (**Fig. 26**). The places where high trees and power lines made it difficult to fly with drones were supplemented with satellite imagery.

The moment when the photographs were taken turned out to be very significant for the modern history of the site. In 2011, Novae was still an archaeological site with unearthed remains of architectural structures visible in some places as ruins. In 2013, the local authorities started an EU-funded project aimed at creating an archaeological park with superstructures built on top of the ancient buildings. Aerial photographs of the site

Fig. 26. Novae 2013. The orthophotomap of the southern part of the annexe (by M. Pisz).

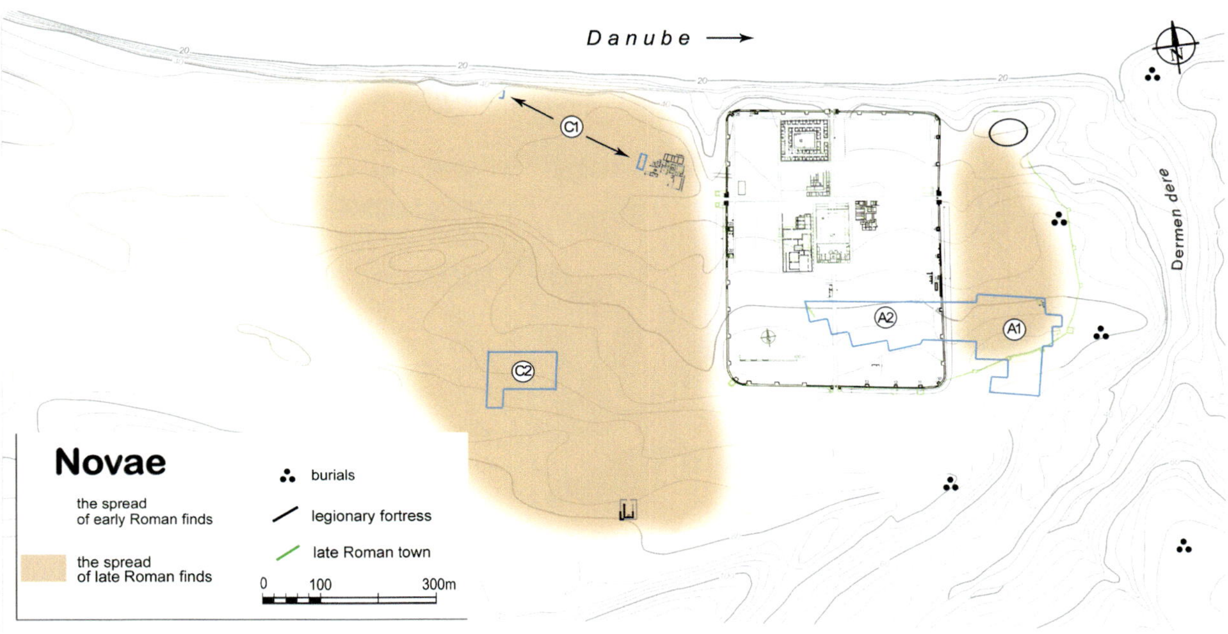

Fig. 27. Novae. The surveyed areas in the close vicinity of the fortress (by A. Tomas).

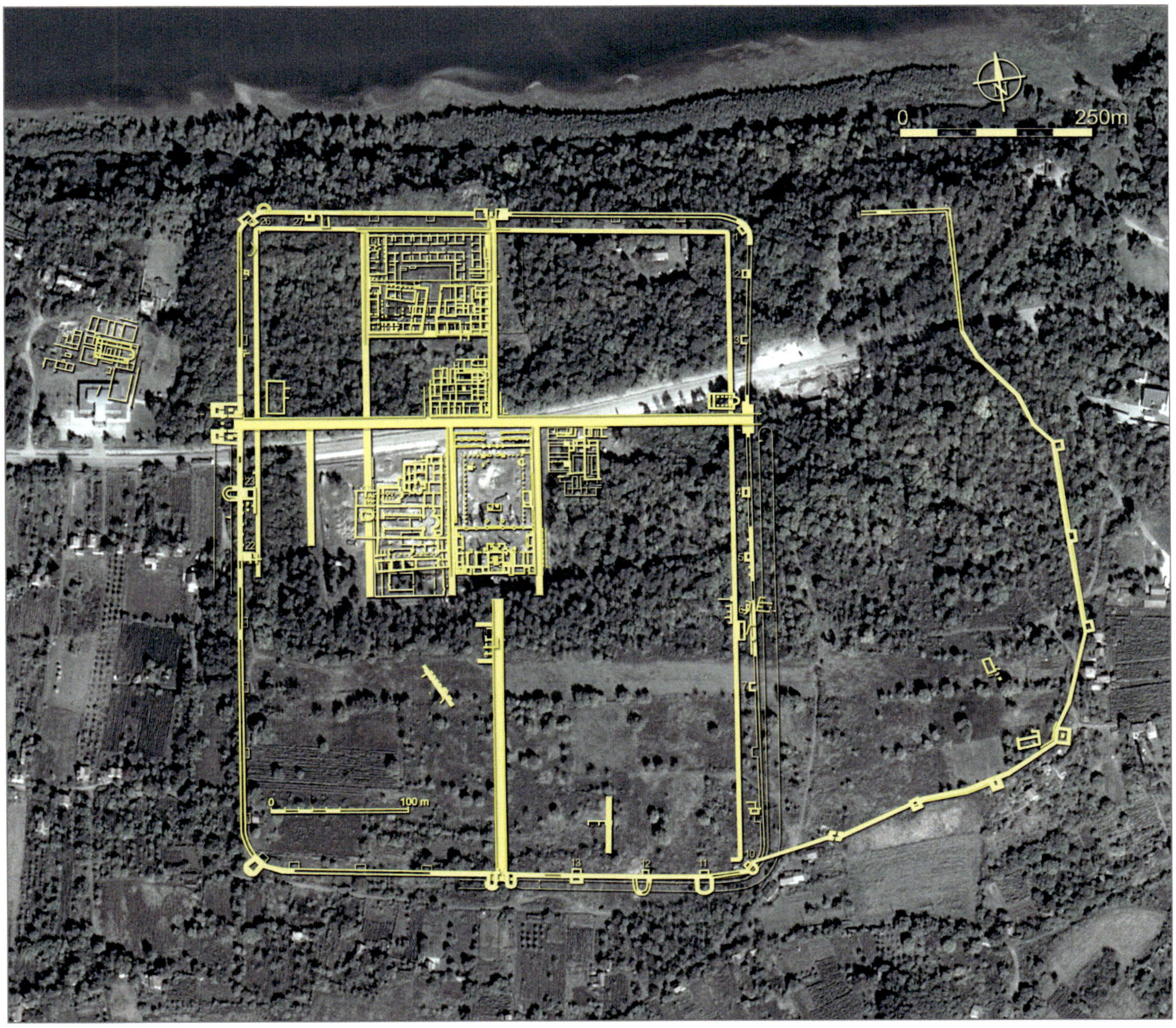

Fig. 28. Novae 2014. Plan of the *castra* and the outline of the annex's eastern defensive walls (by A. Tomas, E. Jęczmienowski).

taken before, during and after its transformation are now priceless documents. Apart from the archaeological remains and the heritage protection activities, we documented over 200 illegal trenches, the majority of them located in the southern part of the fortress, which was documented more accurately due to the prospects of further investigations.

2. Fortification measurements, field walking, mapping finds and documentation of structural remains

Agnieszka Tomas

Field walking prospections were carried out over the course of three seasons (2012–14), although some observations and measurements with the use of hand-held GPS devices were made in earlier years preceding the start of the project. One of the objectives of the reconnaissance was to estimate the extent of the sites, to establish their exact location, and to document the datable finds collected from the surface.

The reconnaissance around the fortress made it possible to estimate the total size of the area where archaeological material is visible on the surface as measuring 70–80 ha, including the area within the annexe (**Fig. 27**). After completing the project, it was possible to create a detailed plan of Novae with the accurate course of the eastern defensive walls of the annexe (**Fig. 28**).

Thanks to the measurements taken along the late Roman fortifications it was possible to establish that the annexe surrounded 9 ha, including a deep gully on its northern edge whose surface covers 0.15 ha, therefore, the new area which could have been used for habitation was 8.85 ha. Together with the surface of the former *castra* (17.99 ha)

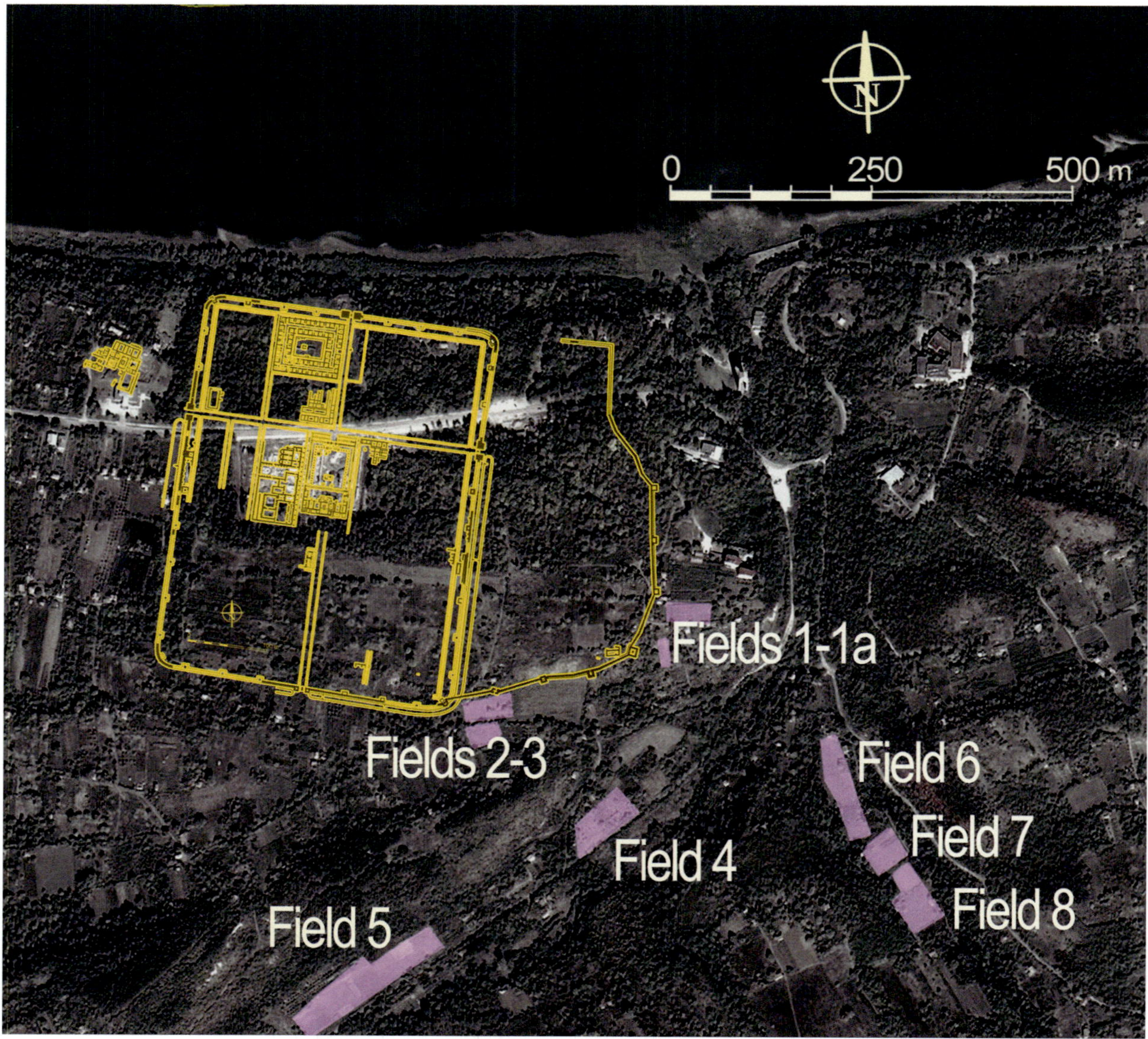

Fig. 29. Novae 2012–14. Fields surveyed in Area D (by A. Tomas).

the late Roman Novae covered an area of about 26.84 ha.

The areas available for more intensive field walking surveys and geophysical measurements outside the fortifications were limited to small arable plots located mainly to the east of the camp. In our documentation, they were marked as Area D (**Figs. 15** and **29**).

In 2012, we conducted intensive mapping of the finds in the south-eastern part of the fortress extension and on the available fields to the west of the camp. In 2013 and 2014, field walkings were done within a radius of 3–4 km around the fortress. The major part of the *canabae* is located to the west of the fortress, but densely built-up private summer houses make archaeological surveys very difficult. In contrast, large open arable fields situated further to the south and east of the fortress were available, but there were few finds. Such vast areas with no traces of past human activity lie 1.6 km to the south-east of the *groma* and to the south-west of Ostrite Mogili. Although the investigated fields were ploughed and the field walkings were made during very good visibility conditions, we did not find any archaeological materials.

The western side of the fortress (Area C2)

The prospection on the western side of the fortress is extremely limited by the existence of small and densely located private parcels. However, every

Fig. 30. Novae 2013. Area C2 (photo by A. Tomas).

year ploughing or digging reveals new finds there. Pottery sherds, worked stones or pieces of marble are visible all over the area.

Due to the character of modern habitation and changes in the landscape, the collection of archaeological finds was random and made within irregular spatial units. The pottery and glass were collected in two fields chosen for geophysical measurements (**Fig. 30**). Despite intensive modern agricultural activities, pottery and glass fragments are quite numerous there. We also found a marble piece bearing the fragmentarily preserved letter of an inscription (see Chapter VI.11, **Fig. 94**). Detailed mapping of metal finds was not carried out in Area C2 due to high modern metal pollution, but one fragment of a bronze strigil was found during prospection (see Chapter VI.6).

Fig. 31. Novae 2013. Area C1. The arrows mark the remains of walls,a possible line of the western aqueduct of Novae (by A. Tomas, photo by M. Pisz).

Fig. 32. Novae 2013. Area C1. The remains of a wall (photo by S. Rzeźnik).

Fig. 33. Novae 2012. Northern part of the annexe. Thick arrows mark towers 1 and 2 and thin arrows mark the line of the annex's defensive walls (by A. Tomas, photo by M. Pisz).

Fig. 34. Novae 2012. Southern part of the annexe. The view from the west (photo by M. Pisz).

The remains of the western aqueduct

The remains of walls and constructions are visible in three places on the Danubian escarpment to the west of the fortress. These remains were documented and published by P. Vladkova in 2015.[1] Three separate structures were found at a distance of ca. 40, 80, and 250 m respectively from the western wall of the fortress (**Fig. 31**). The remains located 40 m to the west from the north-western corner of the camp belong to a rectangular structure 4×3.5 m made of stones mixed with mortar and the inner surface covered with a 0.20 m layer of rubble. The second place was reported by a private property owner in 2006. It is situated 38 m to the west of the first structure. The original size of the preserved walls was 4.70×3.14 m, and its width was 0.60–0.88 m. The height was preserved up to 1.14 m and the upper part of the wall was built from bricks. Primarily, the floor was covered with clay suspensura floor with LEG I ITAL stamps (0.405×0.41×0.07 m), and the entire inner wall surface was covered with hydraulic mortar.

1. Vladkova 2015 (named Towers No. 1, 2 and 3).

In 2012, we visited the third structure, which was documented by Pavlina Vladkova in 2008. The two perpendicular walls of a solid south-eastern corner of deeply dug foundations were preserved to a height of 1.50 m and a width of 0.90 m, but the remains of the parallel E–W and N–S walls presented in Vladkova's publication were not preserved anymore (**Fig. 32**).

The first two afore-mentioned structures belong to the western aqueduct of Novae described by K. Škorpil and S. Stefanov and documented by M. Biernacka-Lubańska in the early 1960s.[2]

Areas A1 and D: The annexe and to the east of the annexe

The terrain on the eastern side of the fortress is more varied. Almost directly outside the *praetentura dextra*, there is a deep gully, 35 m wide and 45 long, covering an area of *ca*. 0.15 ha. A section of the northern curtain wall of the extension is traceable in front of a monument dedicated to Russian soldiers along the East–West axis, but it ends *ca*. 20

2. Škorpil 1905, 457; Stefanov 1930-31, 266; Majewski 1963, 99–104, esp. Fig. 84; Majewski 1964, 183–86 (Trench C); cf. Vladkova 2015, 189, Fig. 3. For discussion, see also Tomas 2017, 54.

m before the ridge of the gully (cf. **Figs. 5** and **33**). We attempted to find a place where the north-eastern camp's curtain wall and the extension's fortifications merged, similar as in the south-eastern corner of the fortress, but the verification was negative. The surface of the area to the south of the northern curtain wall is irregular, forming a shape reminiscent of a *cavea* (**Fig. 33**), but it is densely forested with high trees which made it impossible to measure the accurate position of the round convex shape. This place may well have been an amphitheatre.[3] Further to the east, at the mouth of the Dermen dere, pottery kilns were documented in the past.[4]

The central and southern part of the annexe is elevated terrain more conveniently accessible for surveyors, but partly forested. The southern edge of the extension rises gently reaching one of the highest points in the area at its south-eastern corner (**Fig. 34**). This part of the site is covered with illegal trenches, and in three of them we documented the remains of walls and architectural elements (**Fig. 35**).

Small pottery fragments were collected in two open fields situated directly to the south and south-east

3. Tomas 2017, 76–77.

4. Tomas 2015c.

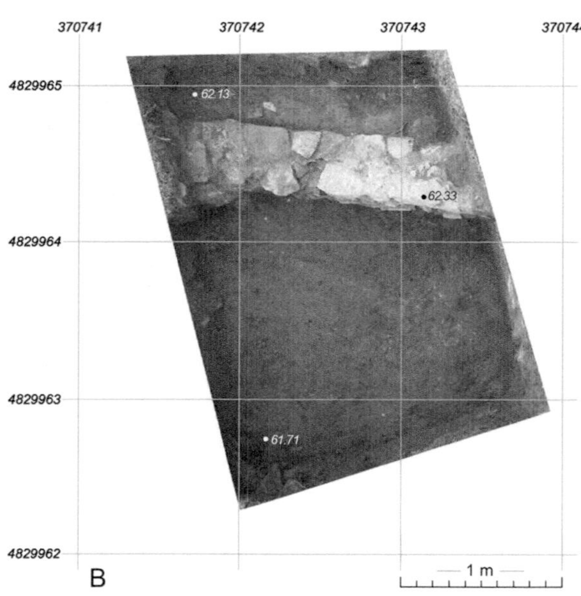

C

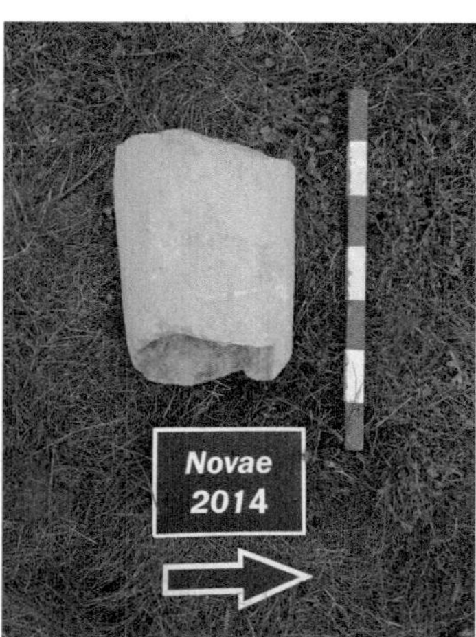

D

Fig. 35. Novae 2012. Illegal trenches in the annexe (photo by S. Rzeźnik).

Fig. 36. Novae 2013. The location of a stone structure and the remains visible in the high scarp of the Dermen dere Valley (by A. Tomas).

Fig. 37. Novae 2013. The view on the southern part of the *canabae* (photo by M. Pisz).

Fig. 38. Novae 2011. Illegal excavations in the southern *canabae* (photo by A. Tomas).

Fig. 39. Novae 2014. The remains of the mithreum. The view from the east (photo by M. Lemke).

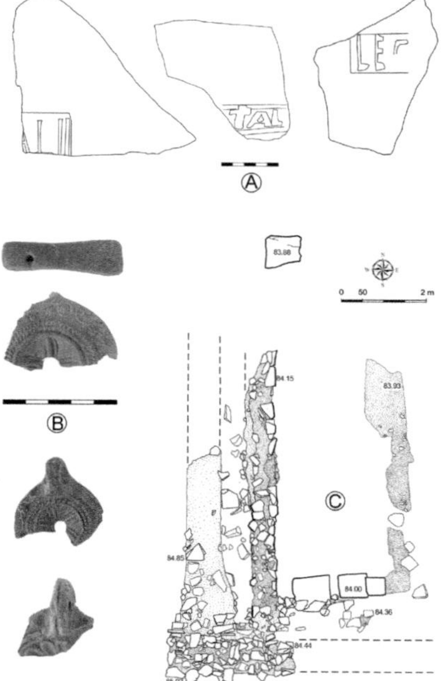

Fig. 40. Novae 2014. The finds from the mithraeum and plan of the building. A – stamped bricks; B – fragments of clay lamps; C – plan of the mithraeum (photo by A. Tomas, drawing by E. Jęczmienowski, A. Tomas).

of the annexe, in Area D – Fields 1, 1a and 2 (**Fig. 29**), but most of them were very fragmented due to the agricultural activities performed on the fields. Further to the south, we surveyed six open arable fields on both sides of the river valley. A few pottery fragments, mostly from the 2nd–3rd centuries, were collected from four of them, and they were also very fragmented.

The main purpose of field walkings carried out along the Dermen dere River was to find possible crossings through the valley. On the left bank of the Dermen dere, about 550 m to the south of the legionary camp, we found the remains of an old structure made of stone, bricks, and pottery fragments. Remains of a stone structure, 3 m wide and ca. 0.50 m thick, were visible in a steep slope adjacent to the river. The structure is located 550 m to the south of the South Gate, almost at the N–S axis (**Fig. 36**).

The terrain to the south of the fortress gently rises up to the line of an elongated forested hill, oriented E–W (**Fig. 37**). The southern necropolis was identified on the eastern slope of this hill in the early 1960s.[5] Buildings of the *canabae* existed in the area between the fortress and the hill. Illegal trenches were visible in some of the parcels and in one of them we found the remains of a building with a well (**Fig. 38**).

Some 100 m from this place, the ruins of the mithraeum are visible in a small forested parcel (**Fig. 39**). In the summer of 2014, we visited the site for the first time,[6] and in spring 2015, we conducted the first reconnaissance. Fragments of pottery, oil lamps, glass vessels and stamped building material were collected and documented there (**Fig. 40A-B**). The said sanctuary is located at the southernmost edge of the main part of the *canabae*, at a distance of ca. 300 m from the fortress, i.e., 240 m to the south and 150 m to the west of its south-western corner, on the gentle slope of a terrace at a height of 80 m a.s.l. Its remains were still visible, with the south-western corner and western bench preserved to a height of ca. 60 cm. In August 2015, the place was revisited with the purpose of preparing a detailed plan (**Fig. 40C**). The results of our survey and the analysis of the former archaeological excavations conducted there have been summarized in a separate publication.[7]

The central part of the annexe within Area A1 were chosen for the mapping of metal finds. An area covering 0.5 ha in total was selected for detailed prospection. The surveys provided 58 small metal finds which were identified as ancient and selected for

5. S. Kołkówna in Majewski 1962, 123–28.

6. I owe this information to Mr Peti Donevski who guided me to the spot and informed me about some important details concerning the discovery.

7. Tomas and Lemke 2015, and also Tomas 2017, 57–60.

detailed documentation, among them 22 finds related to armour and military equipment (Chapter VI.5), 11 pieces of jewelry and cosmetic items (Chapter VI.6), and 25 other metal finds (Chapter VI.7). Another 367 metal mass finds (including ancient and modern) were only counted and photographed for statistical analyses (see Chapter VI.7, **Fig. 76**). Among them, nails and items possibly used as construction elements were prevalent (213 pieces). The number of unspecified copper alloy fragments is significantly low (12) due to looters' activities. The amounts of lead fragments and waste (21) are higher, but it is possible that some such finds were also looted.

Fig. 41. Ostrite Mogili 2000. The view from the west (photo by A. Tomas).

Area B: Ostrite Mogili

Ostrite Mogili is a very well-known site, with the remains stretching across an area of more than 10 ha (**Figs. 26** and **41**). Its size and location indicate that this could have been a civilian *vicus* or even a *vicus* which was granted municipal rights, as some scholars believe.[8] The place is now occupied by private parcels, arable fields and vineyards along the modern Svishtov – Vardim asphalt road.

The site of Ostrite Mogili was subject to field surveys in 1948, and subsequently in 1961,[9] 1977,[10] 1999 and 2000,[11] with test excavations carried out there in 1990.[12] About 500 m to the east of the small gully in the eastern part of the site, there is a cemetery excavated in 1961–62.[13] The finds collected in the course of the 1977 field surveys headed by T. Sarnowski, the 2000 surveys headed by P. Dyczek and during the excavations carried out by P. Donevski are presented in this volume.[14] All these investigations have provided archaeological material dated from the Stone Age up to the Medieval Period.

Field walkings and mapping finds in 1977

In the summer of 1977, T. Sarnowski and a group of young researchers and students conducted the first regular investigations at the site. The mapping of the finds was done with the use of the grid method. Each of the surveyors had a notebook with a grid in scale and a legend where each type of material was marked with a different symbol. The quantity of the finds was marked with a symbol and a number written next to it. The results are presented on a plan showing the density and spread of the finds (**Fig. 42A**).[15]

During the surveys, a number of pottery sherds was mapped, but only a few dozen were chosen for detailed documentation. Among them, pottery, sherds and a fragment of a marble relief depicting the leg of a rider, most probably that of the Thracian Horseman (Chapter VI.14, **Pl. XLV.3**).

Field walkings and mapping finds in 2000

The field walkings carried out in 2000 at Ostrite Mogili were conducted by a group of students under the supervision of P. Dyczek.[16] The applied methods were comparable to those used in 1977. A series of plans were produced, each one showing the density of various types of finds – building materials (**Fig. 42A**), pottery (**Fig. 43A**), and other finds (**Fig. 43B**). At the site where excavations were conducted in 1990, within the deep and wide trenches, we found square bricks from a heating system and large worked stones (**Fig. 42B**). Based on these maps and findings, one plan of the site was created (**Fig. 44**). In the western part of the site, we found some pieces of glass slag and numerous window glass fragments. At least one illegally robbed and damaged grave was found at the site, not far from the present Svishtov-Vardim road. The grave goods, which included pottery and a brick with a LEG I ITAL stamp (Chapter VI.2, **Pl. XVII**) had been scattered around and were mixed with human bones.

Field walkings and mapping metal finds in 2014

In 2013, the biggest obstacles for intensive prospection and geophysical measurements were the new

8. Tomas 2017, 77–81.
9. Hensel et al. 1965, 47–84.
10. Sarnowski 1979.
11. Gencheva 2001, 75–76; Tomas 2006.
12. Donevski 1991.
13. Vulov 1965, 31–34.
14. The materials were kindly shared with us by the listed researchers.
15. The documentation was kindly made available to us by the late Prof. Tadeusz Sarnowski.
16. Tomas 2006.

vineyards in the south-eastern part of the site, small bushes, and deep robbery trenches in the western part of the site. Before beginning our activities, we had to clear 2 hectares of the field to prepare it for geophysical investigations. One essential issue involved the identification of the eastern and southern extents of the Roman site. To this purpose, a field survey was carried out in the area to the east of a gully in the eastern part of the site and to the south of the asphalt road. The prospection was carried out in conditions of very good visibility, on a recently ploughed field.

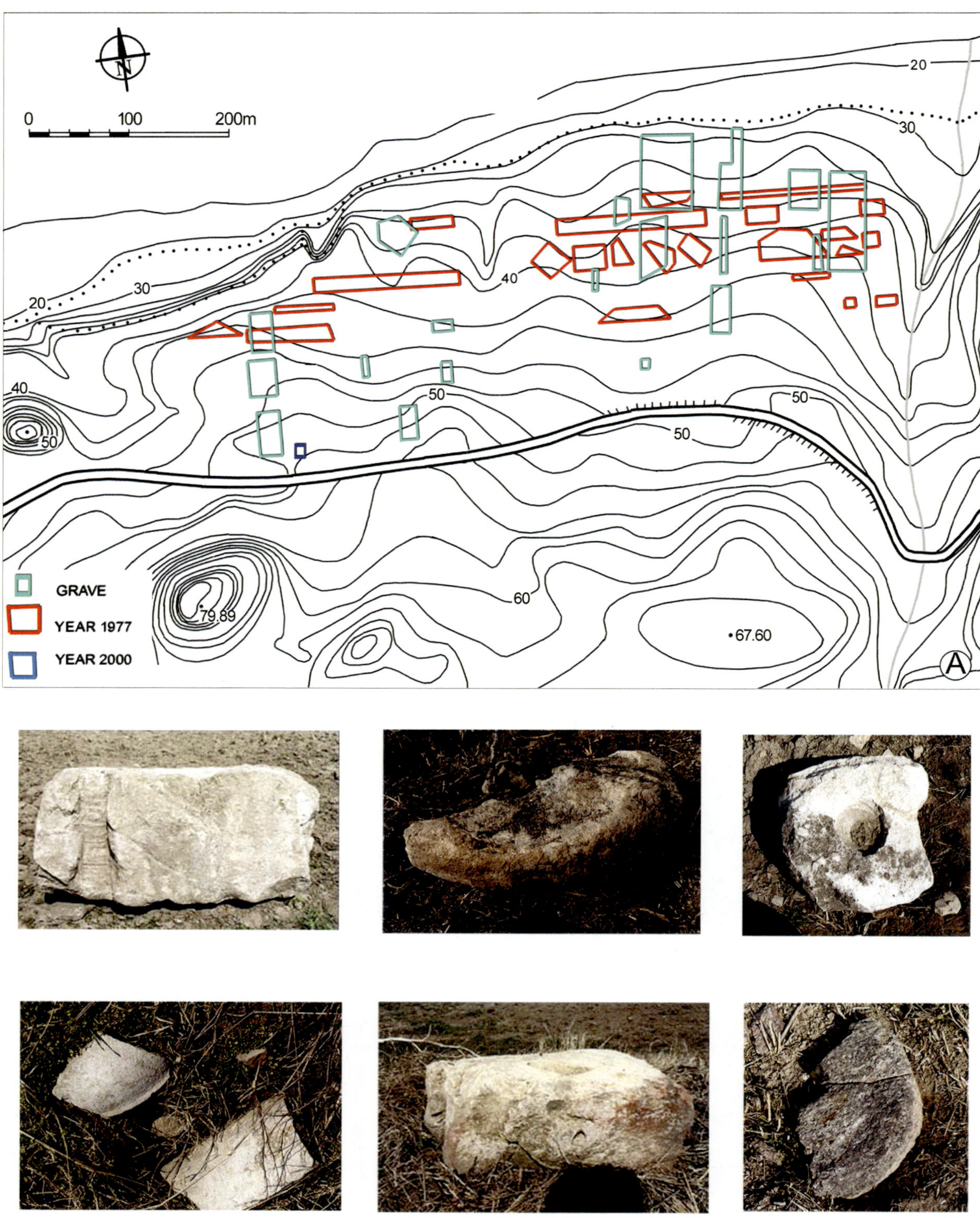

Fig. 42. Ostrite Mogili 1977 and 2000. A – the spread of debris; B – stone finds (drawing and photo by A. Tomas).

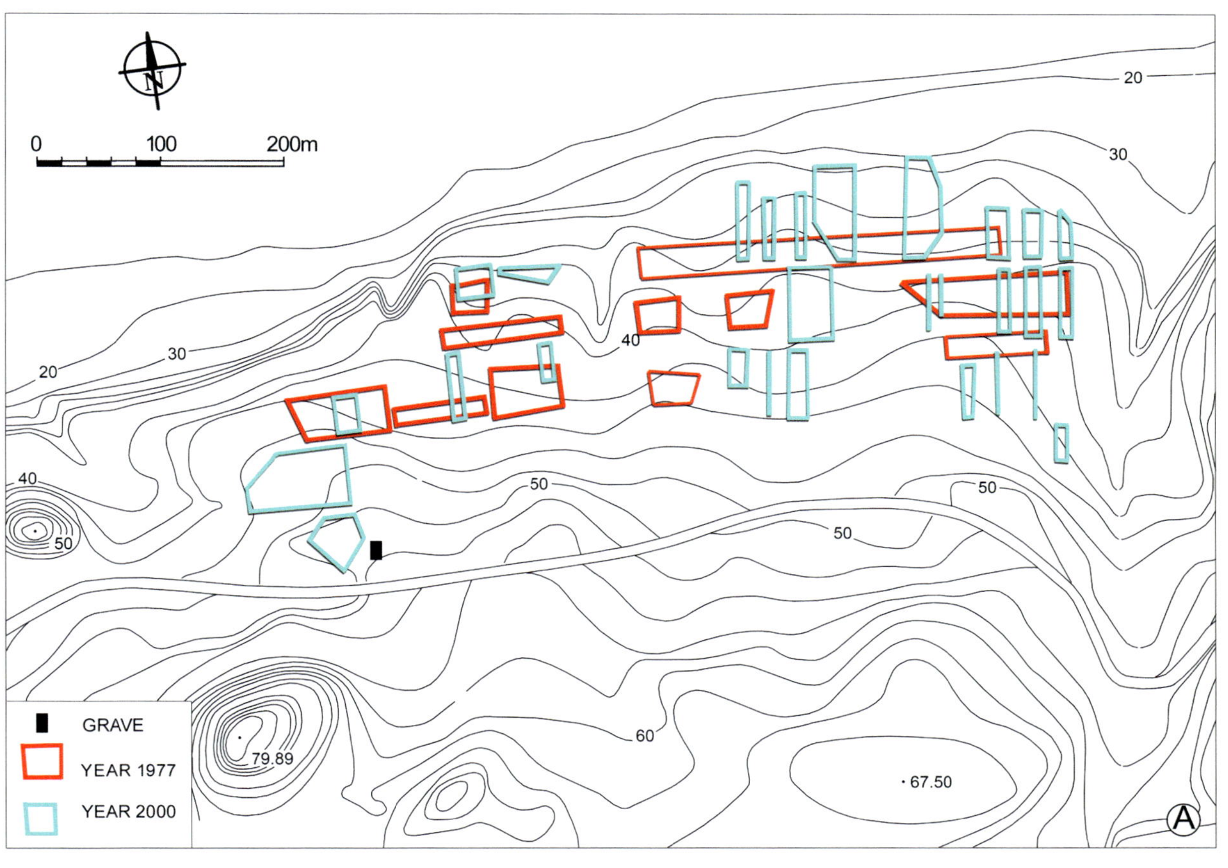

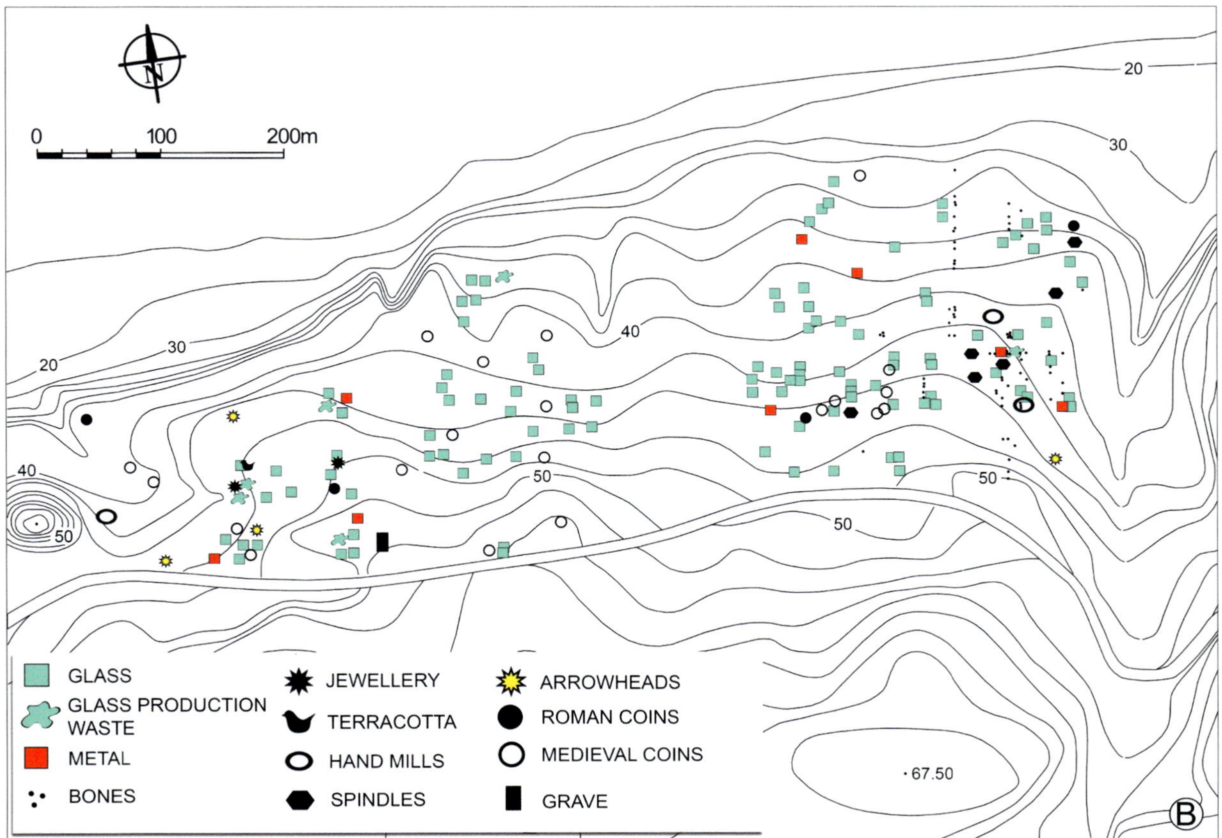

Fig. 43. Ostrite Mogili 1977 and 2000. A – the spread of pottery; B – the spread of other finds (drawing and photo by A. Tomas).

The western part of the site has been intensively robbed and damaged. Deep, densely dug trenches cover a substantial part of the area. A number of large robbery trenches were also identified in the eastern part of the site in the forest. In one of these, we documented a stout and partially dismantled masonry wall made from sandstone and crushed limestone (**Fig. 45**). The wall oriented N–S was quite solid and bound with mortar. It contained two fragments of an inscription dated to AD 196 and a fragment of a cornice (Chapter VI.11, **Pl. XLII**), published in a separate paper in 2014.[17]

The area where the archaeological material is visible on the ground, including medieval-period items, lies between a single hill in the west and vast arable fields beyond a small gully in the east. It was established that to the east of the mentioned gully there were almost exclusively fragments of Slavic pots and Stone Age tools. Further to the east, a few fragments of amphorae and bricks dated to the Roman period were found, and they were collected in the vicinity of the cemetery discovered in the 1960s. To the south of the asphalt road, where the terrain is slightly elevated above the roadway, we found no pottery, although such finds were noticed by German and Bulgarian colleagues in 2000.[18] However, in 2015, the surface covered by Roman finds could be assessed as at maximum 15 ha. It is noteworthy that the grave (or graves) documented in 2000 was found within the area of the site, so the settlement may have been even smaller.

Two areas, covering 0.5 ha in total, were chosen for the detailed mapping of metal finds. Both these areas provided 575 metal finds, including 46 items selected for detailed documentation. The majority of the finds are related to agriculture and manufacturing (35), while 11 finds were linked to military activities, and 1 to hygienic activities. Interestingly, the military-related finds are all arrowheads, which may be evidence of fighting or some attacks. The lack of other military equipment is quite surprising, as the proximity of the legionary fortress should have had some influence on these statistics. Nevertheless, the civilian character of the site is mirrored by their hypothetically low quantity. The remaining 543 mass finds were divided into two groups: modern waste (210) and unspecified, possibly ancient items (333). The metal items were mostly made of iron (Chapter VI.7, **Fig. 77**), while copper alloy and lead finds were much less frequent.

17. Tomas 2014.

18. Conrad and Stančev 2002; Conrad 2006a, Fig. 12.

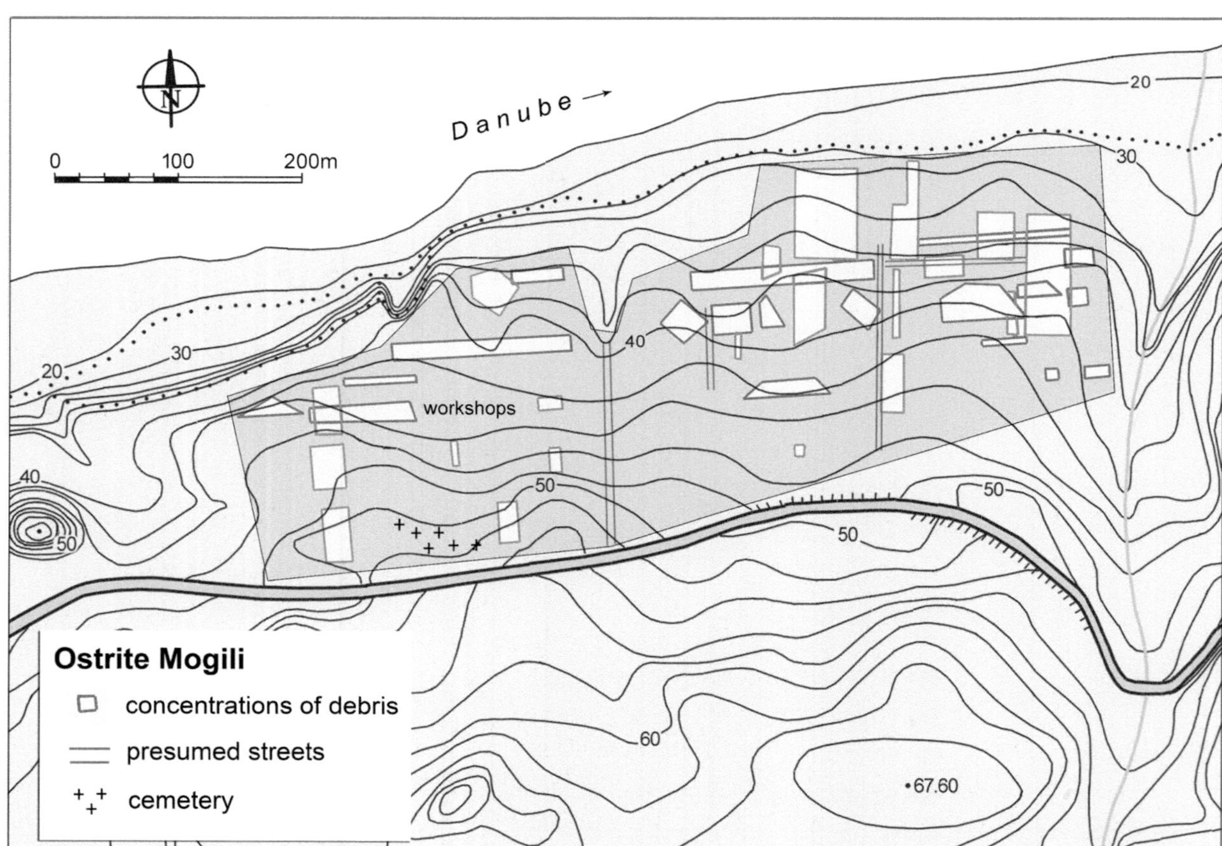

Fig. 44. Ostrite Mogili. Hypothetical reconstruction of the site (by A. Tomas).

Area E

During the reconnaissance conducted within a broader area around Ostrite Mogili, we found several concentrations of pottery and debris visible on the surface of the fields to the south of the *vicus*. Intensive field walkings done by four people walking in transects at a distance of 5 m from one another were made within the entire area, and – as a result – we located three big concentrations of archaeological material.

Two concentrations were identified 500 and 700 m to the south-west of Area B, and named Area E (**Fig. 15**). The largest concentration was found in an area covering 0.3 ha in the western part of the arable fields. The building materials and pottery sherds found there were very damaged by intensive ploughing, some of them crushed into pieces, and only a few finds were collected for drawing (Chapter VI.2. **Pl. XXI**). This place was chosen for the detailed geophysical measurements described in Chapter IV.3.

Two separate strips, covering 0.5 ha in total, were selected for detailed prospection within Area E. Among the selected finds, there were 3 arrowheads, 2 iron knives, 1 copper alloy bracelet, and 1 unspecified copper alloy item. The mass finds (Chapter VI.7, **Fig. 78**) consisted mainly of very corroded iron items (240), including modern waste (164).

Area F: Kanlu cheshme

The site of Kanlu cheshme is located 2 km from the fortress' *groma* (**Fig. 15**), on the right side of the Dermen dere, on open arable fields. The site was surveyed in 1979 by T. Sarnowski, who prepared a density map of the fields.[19] During an unsystematic reconnaissance done at the site, we saw a few fragments of bricks and vessels, and no traces of worked stone. In 2014, we found this location (**Fig. 46**) and decided to check the site by applying geophysical prospection.

Area F was very polluted with modern waste (35 items). Twelve iron items were identified as possibly Roman or medieval, among them 5 were nails (Chapter VI.7, **Fig. 78**). Only one knife was selected for detailed documentation. No finds related to the military activities were found there.

The Sanctuary of Liber Pater

Field walkings in the surroundings of Novae encompassed an area situated to the south of the fortress and

19. T. Sarnowski 1979.

Fig. 45. Ostrite Mogili 2014. Stone wall in the western part of the site (photo by S. Rzeźnik).

along the road leading to the site where in the past a shrine of Dionysus / Liber Pater had been discovered.[20] The archaeological material was very scarce there, but some pottery sherds were collected along the modern beaten path.

It was not possible to establish the exact location of the sanctuary remains, i.a., as a result of the vague description in the publication and due to the fact that its location and plan have never been published. Nevertheless, we identified the place described by the discoverer. We found pottery fragments and building materials in several robbery trenches dug around this place.

Burial in the principia

The construction works in the Archaeological Park of Novae carried out in the spring of 2013 included the restoration of the headquarters building and the earth works in the courtyard. A single grave was found in the south-western part of the courtyard (**Fig. 47**). The exact position of the grave was measured with a total station and compared

20. Dzhonova 1961, 21–24; Tomas 2015d.

Fig. 46. Kanlu cheshme. The oblique view on the site and the 1977 results (elaborated by M. Pisz based on a drawing by T. Sarnowski. Google Earth satellite image).

with the layout of the headquarters building. The burial was made very close to the line of pillars and the stylobate of the *basilica principiorum*. The pillars and the stylobate were not preserved there, although a large stone slab was found not far away (**Fig. 48A**).

The 1.6×0.45 m grave pit was covered with large half-round roof tiles (*tegulae*), arranged in the form of "roofing", i.e., what is referred to as "alla cappuccina" or "tile graves". The covering was very damaged at the moment of its discovery (**Fig. 48B**). The tiles were broken – or rather crushed – and the central part of the grave was robbed probably in Antiquity, as the tiles in the centre must have been broken a long time ago. The grave pit was oriented East-West with the deceased's head directed towards the West.[21] It is possible that originally the grave pit was surrounded by small stones. Some were preserved at the foot and in certain places around the pit. No grave goods were found. The burial contained a skeleton of a 1.4-m-tall individual, lying in a supine position. The bones were in a very poor state of preservation (**Fig. 48C**).

Graves with analogous "roof-like" coverings were widespread across the Empire.[22] Tile graves were discovered in the eastern necropolis of Novae[23] and in the surroundings – ca. 4 km east of the fortress, at the necropolis of the *vicus* at Ostrite Mogili.[24] They contained both skeletal and cremation burials. However, the discussed grave seems to be of a later date.

The deceased person could have been buried at the time when the headquarters building had changed its primary function of being an exclusively military and administrative centre, and become a late Roman provisioning coordination spot. If this is true, this place could have been chosen due to its closeness to the Cathedral.

Christian burials dated to the second half of the 5th century discovered near the extramural basilica at Novae were also oriented to the West, but only five or six out of 111 graves were covered with tiles, and one out of these five or six contained a coin of Nero.[25]

The lack of grave goods in the burial found in the principia makes dating impossible. On

21. Cf. Sarnowski et al. 2012, 198 (who mistakenly gives an eastward orientation).

22. Toynbee 1996, 102.

23. Tomas et al. 2020.

24. Vulov 1965, 32–34, Fig. 13.

25. Vladkova 2006.

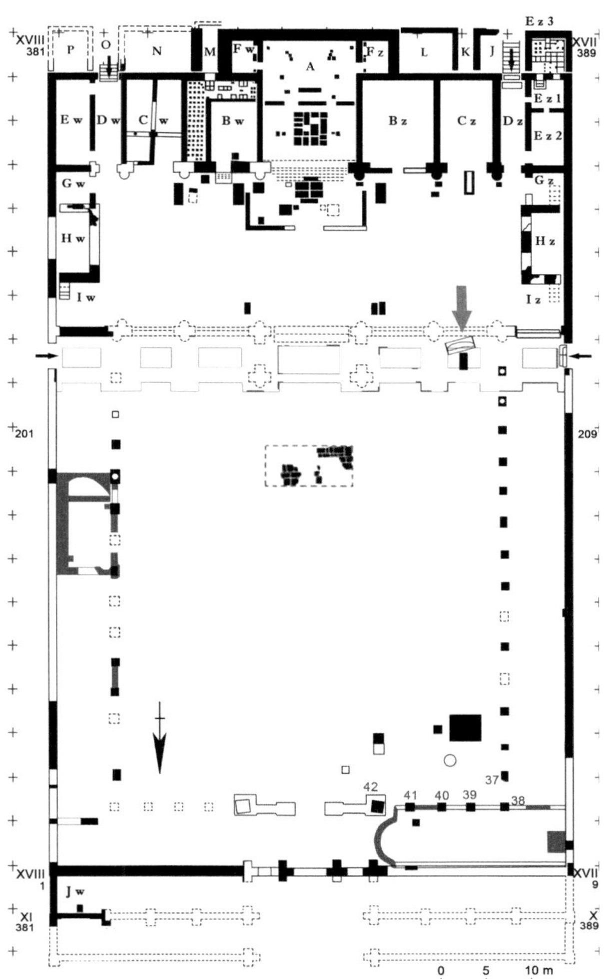

Fig. 47. Novae 2013. The headquarters' building and the location of the grave. The rooms added in the 3rd century and later are marked in grey. The grey arrow indicates the place where the grave was found (drawing by E. Jęczmienowski, A. Tomas, based on the plan by T. Sarnowski).

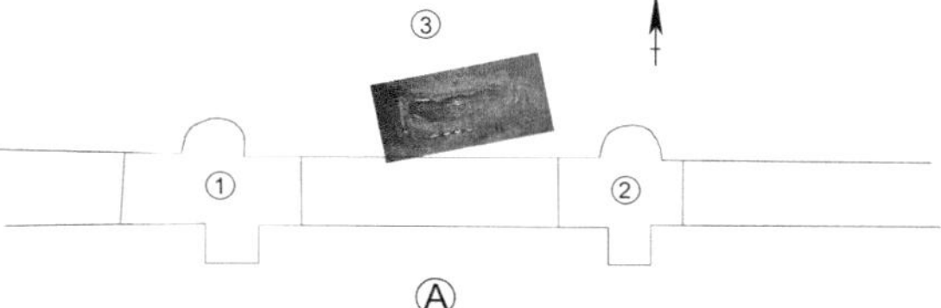

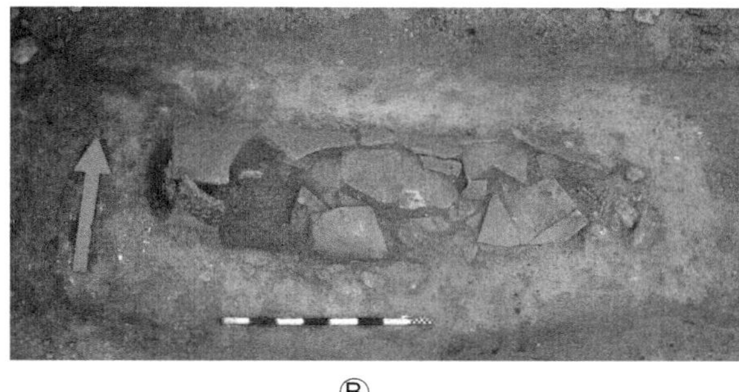

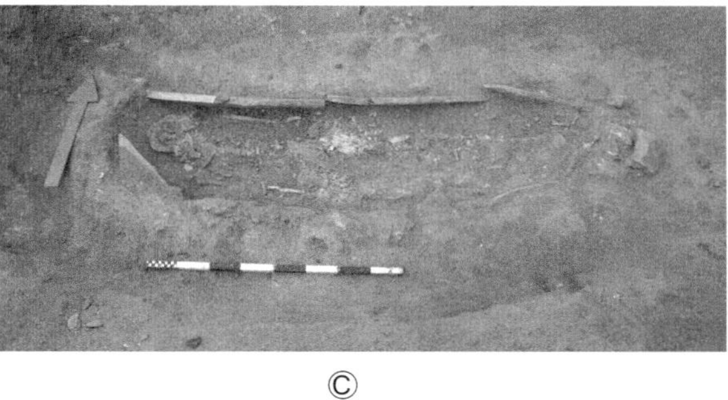

Fig. 48. Novae 2013. The headquarters' building. A – the location of the grave near the stylobate: 1, 2 – the hypothetical layout of the stylobate pillars; 3 – the location of a large stone slab north of the stylobate; B – the grave after discovery; C – the grave after removing the tile covering (drawings by A. Tomas, photo by S. Rzeźnik).

one hand, covering with roof tiles seems to be a non-Christian custom at Novae, on the other – a grave in such a place would indicate the second half of the 5th or 6th centuries.

3. Geophysical measurements

Piotr Wroniecki, Marcin Jaworski, Michał Pisz, Krzysztof Misiewicz, Wiesław Małkowski

The areas chosen for geophysical measurements are situated in the south-eastern part of the site (Areas A1 and A2), in two available lots west of the fortress (Areas C_1 and C_2), and at the Ostrite Mogili site (Area B), as well as in two places to the east of Novae (Areas E and F) chosen after fieldwalking surveys (**Fig. 15**).

Terrain conditions within the annexe (Area A1) are not very favourable. The entire area is divided by sloping terraces and two power lines on its western and northern ends. The highest terrace has largely been destroyed by densely packed illegal trenches. The south-eastern corner of the annexe was excavated in the 1960s, and in 2012–14 this place was inaccessible due to dense vegetation and rubbish. The area to the south of the annexe, along its southern edge, was relatively flat and accessible. The only obstacle was a power line running along its eastern edge (**Fig. 26**).

In order to compare the results in the intramural and extramural areas, prospection was also done in the camp, in the area of the *retentura dextra*, referred to as Area A2. Ghost walls and the remains of the eastern camp's fortifications, as well as the possible existence of barracks in the *retentura dextra* could potentially be helpful in verifying the results obtained in the annexe and other places outside the fortress. In 2012, various methods were applied in order to compare

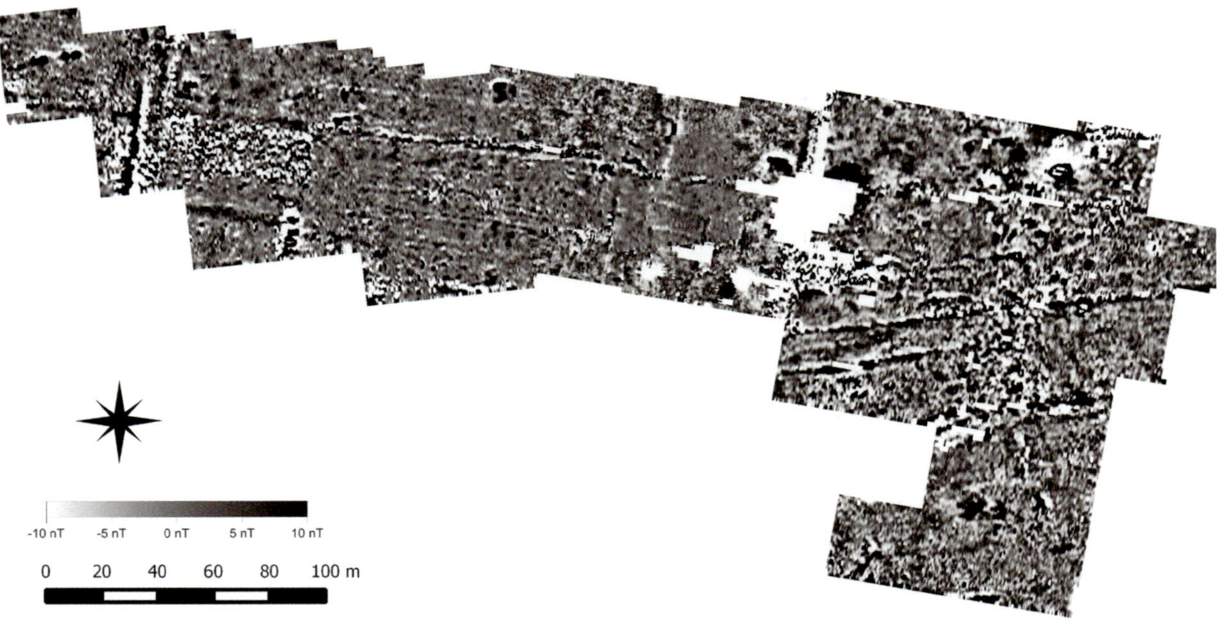

Fig. 49. Novae 2012. Combined results of the geophysical survey in Area A1 – the annexe and Area A2 – the *retentura* (greyscale, -10/10nT) (by P. Wroniecki).

the results. The southern part of the annexe (Area A1) was measured with a gradiometer and a caesium magnetometer.[26]

Prospection at Ostrite Mogili (Area B) was possible only in the eastern part of the site. In 2014, when the surveys were conducted, the eastern part was covered with deep illegal trenches, while the central part was occupied by a house with vineyards. Magnetic prospection was conducted there on an area covering 4.5 ha.

Geophysical prospection on the western side of the fortress was done on two opened fields among the private parcels – one situated ca. 100 m to the west of West Gate, north of the extramural residence (Area C1), and another, situated ca. 280 m to the south-west of the fortress (Area C2). The total surveyed area in the *canabae* covered ca. 0.7 ha, which is not much when compared to the estimated

26. Resistivity spacing in both measuring tools was set at 0.5 m. The results were presented in the same colour conventions. Differences between images can result from the varied depth penetration and the various height of the probes above the surface.

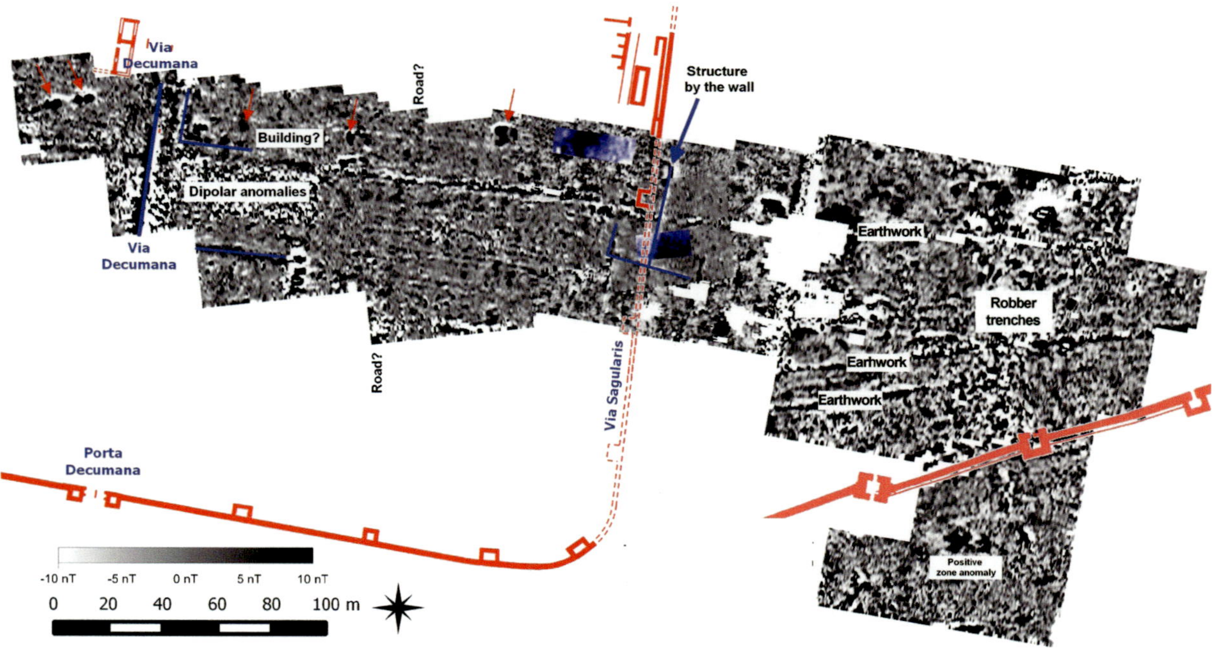

Fig. 50. Novae 2012. Interpretation of the anomalies detected in Areas A1 – the annexe and Area A2 – the *retentura* (magnetic: greyscale, -10/10nT; electrical resistivity: Highpoints2, 50–125 Ω·m, 37–147 Ω·m) (by P. Wroniecki).

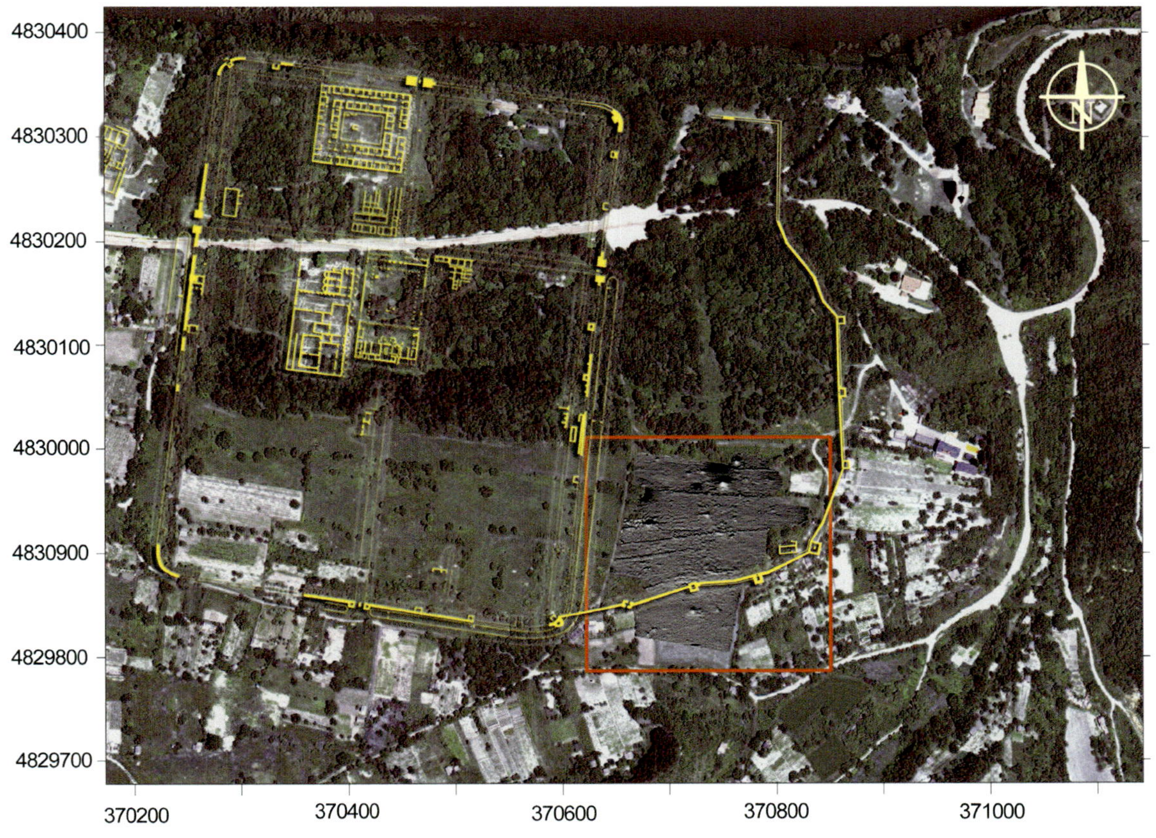

Fig. 51. Novae 2012. The location of the caesium magnetometer measurements in Area A1 and the image showing the results (by W. Małkowski).

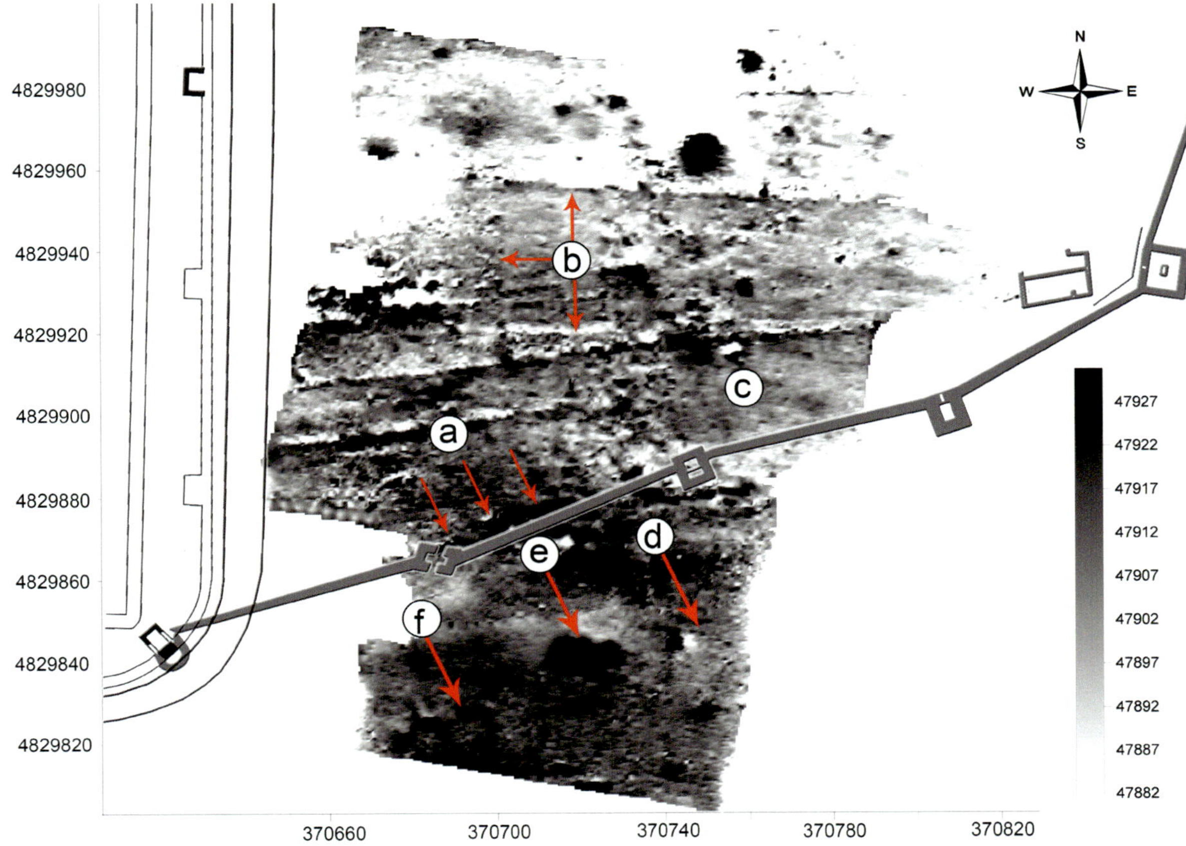

Fig. 52. Novae 2012. The results of caesium magnetometer measurements in Area A1 a, c – traces of overfiring of the objects; b, d-f – linear anomalies (by W. Małkowski).

surface of the whole site marked by the archaeological finds visible on the ground (80 ha). The western side of the fortress is now within privately owned parcels containing buildings, fences, and power lines. Only a few places – arable fields – are accessible for geophysical measurements, yet these remain limited due to metal fences and buildings. In order to reduce the potential for errors and unclear results, the two lots were investigated with magnetic and resistivity survey simultaneously.

Electrical resistivity surveys were conducted in Areas C1 and C2, but also in one place within Area A2, to enhance the results obtained through magnetic measurements. Additionally, a GPS RTK was used to create a Digital Terrain Model (DTM) of the southern part of the annexe with high accuracy.

Area A1: The annexe. Gradiometer measurements

(Piotr Wroniecki, Marcin Jaworski)

The surveyed area is limited to the north by trees and thick vegetation and to the south by a steep slope and modern buildings which continue on the eastern side. The south and central part of the annexe consists of three levels of terraces descending to the north. The terraces are divided by linear earthworks composed of stone rubble and earthenware sherds. In the south part, the measurements were continued on the slope and in the available area at its foot, which lies outside the annex's defensive wall.

The edges of the terraces are formed by stones and fragments of Roman bricks and tiles. The total area surveyed there covered 2.4 ha, divided into 30×30 m grids. Resistivity spacing was set at 0.5 m with readings taken every 0.25 m (0.5×0.25 m probing).

A group of linear anomalies were detected there, some of which run along the East – West axis (**Figs. 49 and 50**). Both groups of anomalies are created by earthworks more or less prominent in the terrain. The origin of these rows of banks seems to be connected with the previous agricultural transformation of the area, but some of the linear anomalies, registered within the boundaries of the annexe, might suggest the presence of architectural remains. An archaeological study aimed at identifying the origins of these anomalies and their correlation with either modern transformations or ancient settlement would be beneficial.

Numerous dipolar anomalies were registered in the central part of the annexe and their density increases in the area adjacent to the edge of the slope. Their location is connected with the presence of numerous robbery trenches that formed during the systematic plundering of the site. This process led to the repositioning of the soil with magnetic material on top of the ground, clearly visible in geophysical maps.

Another zone of dipolar anomalies is located by the western edge of the surveyed area. It is connected with the presence of a large quantity of brick rubble and roof tile sherds. These remains suggest the presence of a building here that may have been connected with the agricultural use of the area.

At the bottom of the southern slope, within a small field covered with magnetic measurements, a positive zone anomaly was registered. This type of response may suggest that this area has been subjected to anthropogenic transformation and may contain archaeological deposits.

Within the same area at the bottom of the slope, as in the centre of the annexe, numerous point positive anomalies have been registered. This type of response is typical for sunken archaeological features, such as pits. Their presence indicates that there might be archaeological sources located in the subsoil that should become the subject of excavations, especially since the area is consistently robbed by treasure hunters.

Area A1: The annexe. Caesium magnetometer measurements

(Krzysztof Misiewicz, Wiesław Małkowski)

Caesium magnetometer measurements were taken in Area A1 (**Fig. 51**). Both on the greyscale maps and the coloured ones, significant differences are observable in the values of the magnetic field intensity. They are caused by the unevenness of the terrain in the surveyed area, the presence of modern metal objects in the subsurface layers, the remains of past excavations, interferences in places with modern installations (water supply systems), electric traction lines with metal abutments, and finally – the aspect of most interest to us – the remains of archaeological objects.

The registered anomalies can be divided into three groups: dipolar anomalies with increases and decreases in values in regions with the presence of objects causing changes, linear anomalies (some can also be of a dipolar character), and – finally – localized rising and falling in the registered values of the magnetic field intensity.

Along the annex's fortifications at the edge of the scarp (y=4829880), a linear anomaly is observable, which in places assumes a dipolar character attesting to the overfiring of the objects (**Fig. 52**, loc. **a**). The existence of this clear anomaly in a place where fortification remains were assumed provides basis for the supposition

Fig. 53. Ostrite Mogili 2014. The results of geophysical prospection (greyscale, -5/5nT) shown on the orthophotomap of the site (by M. Wroniecki, M. Pisz).

that the material used in the foundation construction might provide enough of a contrast in relation to the surroundings. However, it should be taken into account that the other remains of buildings might have a less contrasting image, due, for example, to the less sound technique used to make them or the use of breakstone or brick sherds for their construction. Thus, aspects that were more significant for the conducted analysis and interpretation included the shape, scope and location of the anomalies in relation to each other rather than the value of the magnetic field intensity.

Clear parallel linear dipolar anomalies are visible along the East – West axis within the entire area where measurements were taken (y=4829890–940). The dipolar character of these anomalies results primarily from the fact that stones and fragments of ancient ceramic building material were collected from the fields and put in lines, as when they were scattered across these places it was more difficult to conduct agrotechnical activities.

At metres x= 370700–750; y=4829910–950, a group of linear anomalies can be observed (**Fig. 52** loc. **b**) that might be caused by the remains of roads on the East – West axis, but also running at a slight angle to the road along a North – South line. Fragments of buildings visible in the form of anomalies may have been preserved here along the roads. Among these, we can distinguish a group of anomalies that might have been caused by the remains of two parallel structures 12×20 metres in dimension, located along the North-South axis, linked at a height of ca. 1/3 to the wall running from the east to the west. The wall, probably the northern border of the complex's eastern wing, has been better preserved, causing a strong dipolar anomaly with a lowering of the magnetic field value from the north and an increase from the south. Due to the anomaly diversification in this spot (linear anomalies, strong dipolar anomalies, numerous clusters of small anomalies), it is difficult to determine the depth of the remains deposited here with any precision. At least some of the remains discovered during prospection may be located in layers lying at a depth of more than 1 m beneath the modern ground surface. Linear anomalies are also observable at metres x=4829890–4829920; y=370750–370790 (**Fig. 52c**), but they may be the remains of poorly preserved or low-quality walls.

In the southern, lowermost part of the studied terrain, three regular linear anomalies are visible (**Fig. 52** loc. **d–f**), caused by the remains of the foundations of former buildings, located at quite a shallow depth (up to 1 m). The best visible object is a regular rectangular structure located at metres x=370705–723; y=4829840–848, approximately 8×16 m in dimension. To its east, there is a second similar anomaly,

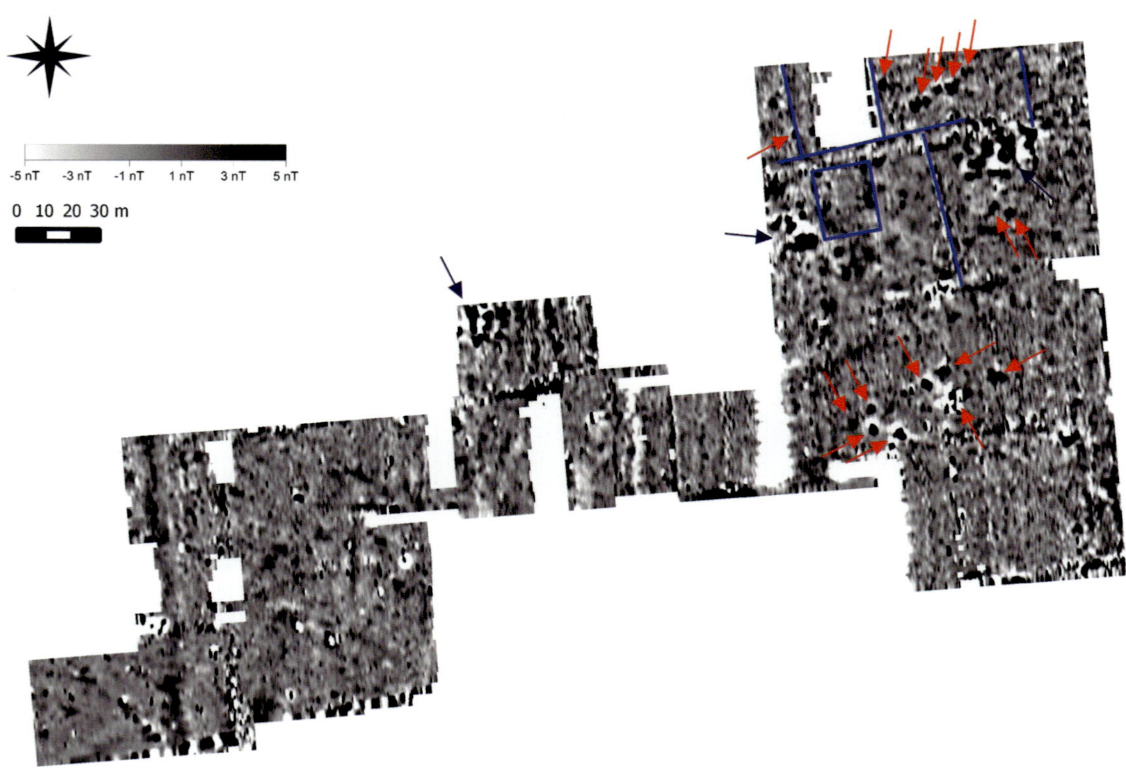

Fig. 54. Ostrite Mogili 2014. The interpretation of anomalies detected at the site during the geophysical prospection (greyscale, -5/5nT) (by M. Wroniecki).

Fig. 55. Novae 2014. Area C1. The results of electrical resistivity survey, dipole-dipole, d=1 m, D=6m shown on the orthophotomap of the site (by M. Pisz).

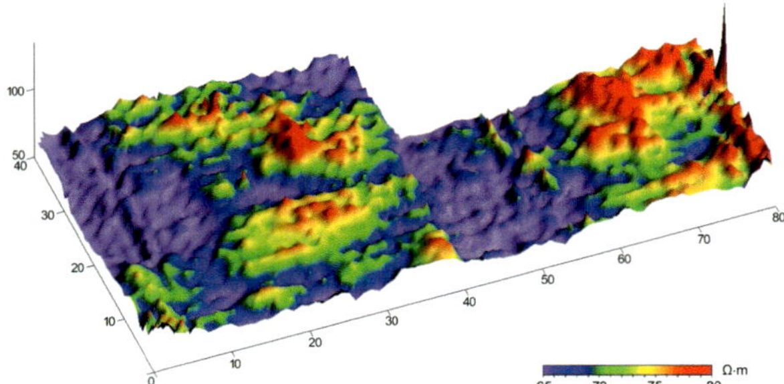

Fig. 56. Novae 2013. Area C2. Results of geophysical prospection: electrical resistivity: Rainbow2, 65-80 Ω·m (by M. Pisz).

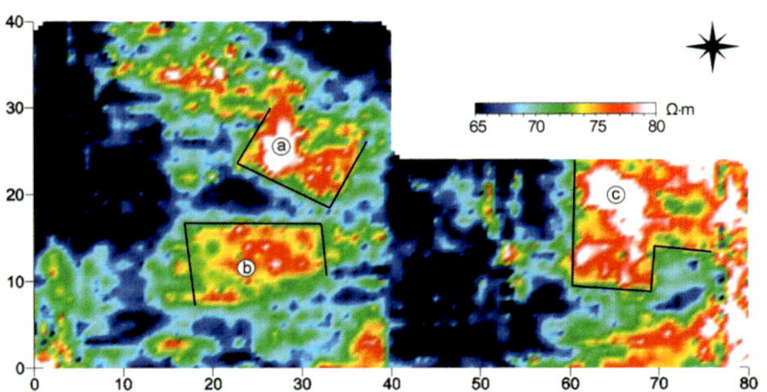

Fig. 57. Novae 2013. Area C2. Interpretation of anomalies detected at the site: electrical resistivity (Rainbow2, 65-80 Ω·m) (by M. Pisz).

observable as a rectangle ca. 11×17 m in dimension, with clear borders on each side, and one can also see a strong dipolar anomaly in the north-western corner of this zone (x=370738–745; y=4829812–818). The last zone of anomalies was located at metres x= 370670–700; y=4829818–830, where two regular rectangular structures can be distinguished. A few elongated dipolar anomalies with blurred borders might have been caused by remains located at a depth of more than 1 m or ones that are not very thick.

Area A2: *Retentura dextra*

(Piotr Wroniecki, Marcin Jaworski)

The grids were laid out on an area relatively clear of obstacles, located in the south-eastern part of the legionary fortress (**Fig. 49**). Magnetic prospection covered 1.5 ha, divided into 30×30 m grids, with sensor horizontal spacing at 0.5 m and readings taken every 0.25 m (0.5×0.25 m probing). The electrical resistivity covered an area of approximately 490 m^2, with 10×30m and 10×20 m grids, in a 1×1m dipole-dipole (2 m) configuration.

The magnetic prospection revealed numerous linear anomalies that run along two distinct axes – North – South and East – West (**Fig. 50**). The first group may be connected with the layout of the communication tracts within the fort walls. This is suggested by the fact that the anomalies run parallel to the west and east walls. The most distinct is the anomaly in the western part, which is located on the axis leading from the *porta decumana* to the *principia*. It may therefore be possible that the magnetic response is generated by structures related to one of the main roads leading through the Roman fortress, the *via decumana*. On its eastern side, other linear anomalies were detected, which may be interpreted as the remains of architectural structures. Another very clear linear anomaly is located 80 m further to the east of the above, and may be connected with the remains of another road or tract.

Other linear anomalies were recorded at the place along which the eastern wall runs, and parallel to it on the inner and outer side of the fortress. This might suggest that the area was transformed by the presence of communication tracts running

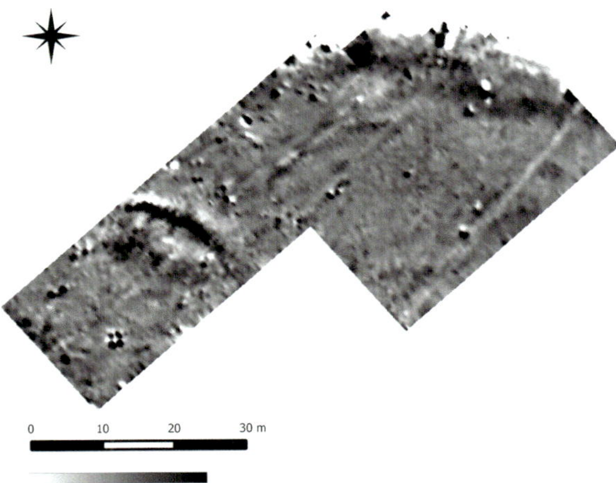

Fig. 58. Novae 2014. Area D. Results of geophysical prospection at the site (greyscale, -10/10nT) (by P. Wroniecki).

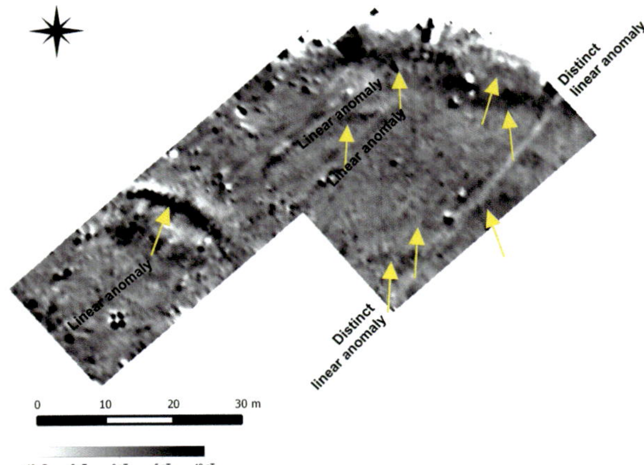

Fig. 59. Novae 2014. Area D. Interpretation of anomalies detected at the site (greyscale, -10/10nT) (by P. Wroniecki).

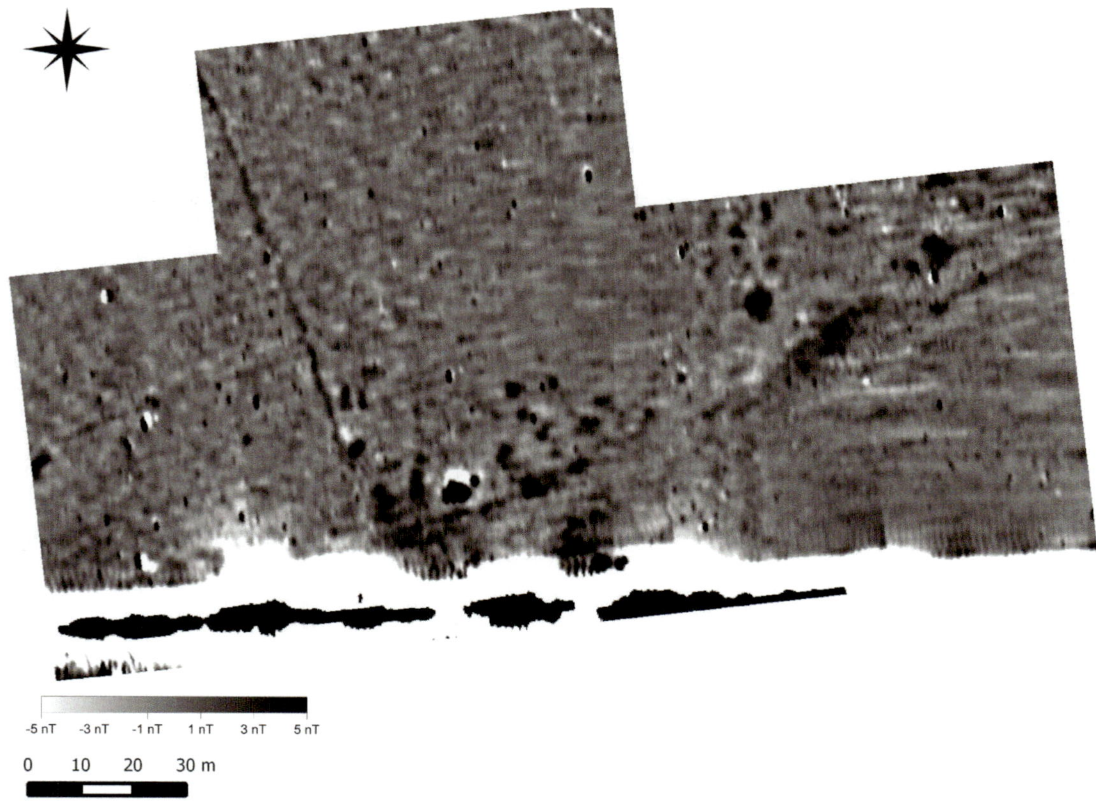

Fig. 60. Novae 2014. Area E. Results of geophysical prospection at the site (greyscale, -5/5nT) (by P. Wroniecki).

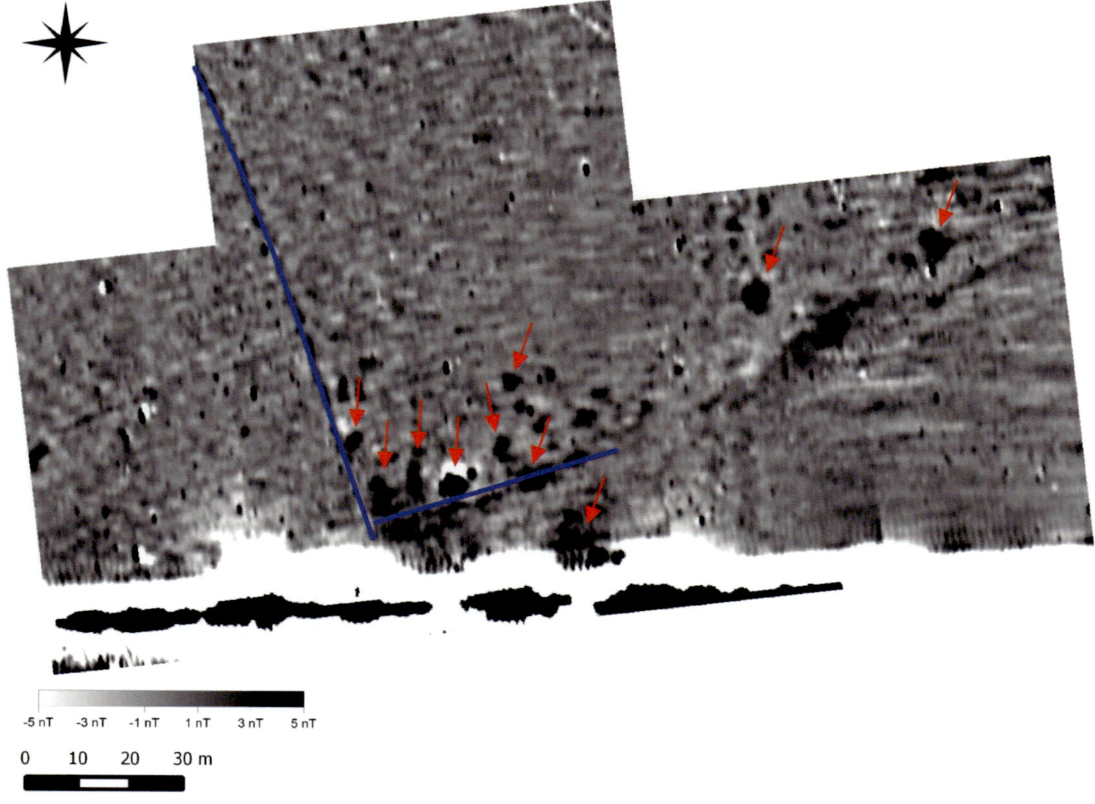

Fig. 61. Novae 2014. Area E. Interpretation of anomalies detected at the site (greyscale, -5/5nT) (by P. Wroniecki).

along the walls, including the *via sagularis*, which ran circumferentially along the wall on its inner side. Electrical resistivity measurements were conducted over the area where the wall was supposed to run and confirmed its presence. These results allowed the anomalies detected here to be placed, whether located in the vicinity of the fortification wall or connected with its presence. This is especially important in the case of the enclosed magnetic anomaly located north of the area surveyed by electrical resistivity. This rectangular anomaly may suggest the presence of a building adjoining the wall or which is a part of the fortifications on their outer side.

Another group of linear anomalies is located at the eastern end of the surveyed area. They run along the hypothetical outline of the fort's defensive wall on its outer side. In the southern end, the anomalies run perpendicularly to the wall, crossing it to the inner space of the fort and shifting direction by 90 degrees to the north. This might indicate the presence of architectural remains connected with buildings in the direct vicinity of the fortifications.

On the other hand, the anomalies oriented on the East – West axis may be generated by modern or post-medieval transformations of the area, including earthworks composed of magnetic material – stone rubble and clay shards. Their origin may be connected with modern agricultural use of the area and a process aimed at flattening and clearing it of stones and rubble. Less distinct linear anomalies at this stage of field evaluation may correspond to relics of tobacco farming dating to the Ottoman times. Yet the outline of these anomalies tends to correspond with the general layout of the fort; therefore, their origins and precise dating should become the subject of future investigations.

In the central area of the surveyed part of the *retentura dextra*, a rectangular zone of dipolar anomalies can be distinguished. Such anomalies occur when there are numerous small magnetic objects present in the topsoil. This might suggest that relics of architectural structures may be present there. Other dipolar anomalies detected at the site are located along the northern boundary of the surveyed space. They have the form of high amplitude point anomalies and are present as separate features with the exception of the two westernmost ones, which seem to indicate a linear pattern. Further investigation of these features is necessary as they might potentially indicate the location of archaeological structures, such as hearths or burnt structures.

The biggest factor hampering a wider multi-method survey in this part of the Novae complex is terrain inaccessibility. Modern infrastructure (roads, field boundaries), sloping terrain and heavy thorny vegetation allow only for select parts of the *retentura dextra* to be studied. Indeed, if these factors can be overcome, a follow-up geophysical investigation would be essential.

Area B: Ostrite Mogili

(Piotr Wroniecki, Marcin Jaworski)

The site is stretching over numerous small fields, of which many are abandoned and others used for grapevine cultivation. In some places, numerous metal fences and agricultural installations composed of steel wires that aid in vine cultivation are visible on the ground. Magnetic prospection was conducted on the best available and "clean" area covering 4.5 ha (**Fig. 53**). The tests were made in grids of 40×40 m, and 0.5×0.25 m probing.

Most of the registered magnetic features consist of high amplitude point positive and point dipolar anomalies. Both groups are present in the entire surveyed area. Point positive anomalies can be connected with the presence of pits and dipolar anomalies with ferrous or thermoremanent features. Most distinct groups of both types are present in the eastern part, where they form more or less compact clusters. The origins of both groups in this vast site need to be investigated, yet at this point it can be suggested that they correspond with traces of past human activities here.

There are at least three areas where dipolar zones can be observed. They consist of dense clusters of numerous dipolar anomalies and cover a limited area. Their presence might be connected with industrial activities or places where architectural remains form piles of magnetic rubble. In an area so strongly transformed by modern agriculture, special care must be taken during the future evaluation and identification of the sources of these anomalies.

Linear anomalies were registered throughout all of the surveyed area (**Fig. 54**). The most complex cluster of positive and negative linear anomalies is present in the north-east corner. These anomalies are concentrated at the northern edge of the surveyed space, forming enclosures with the mentioned zones of dipolar anomalies adjoining them. These linear anomalies might indicate the presence of archaeological structures and settlement boundaries.

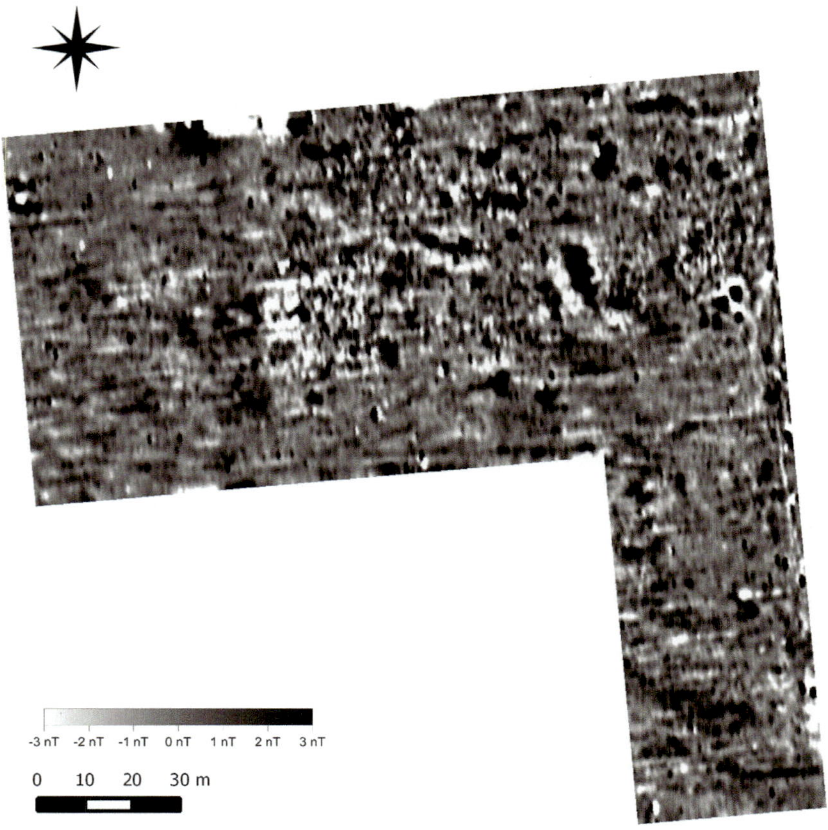

Fig. 62. Novae 2014. Area F. Results of geophysical prospection (greyscale -3/3nT) (by P. Wroniecki).

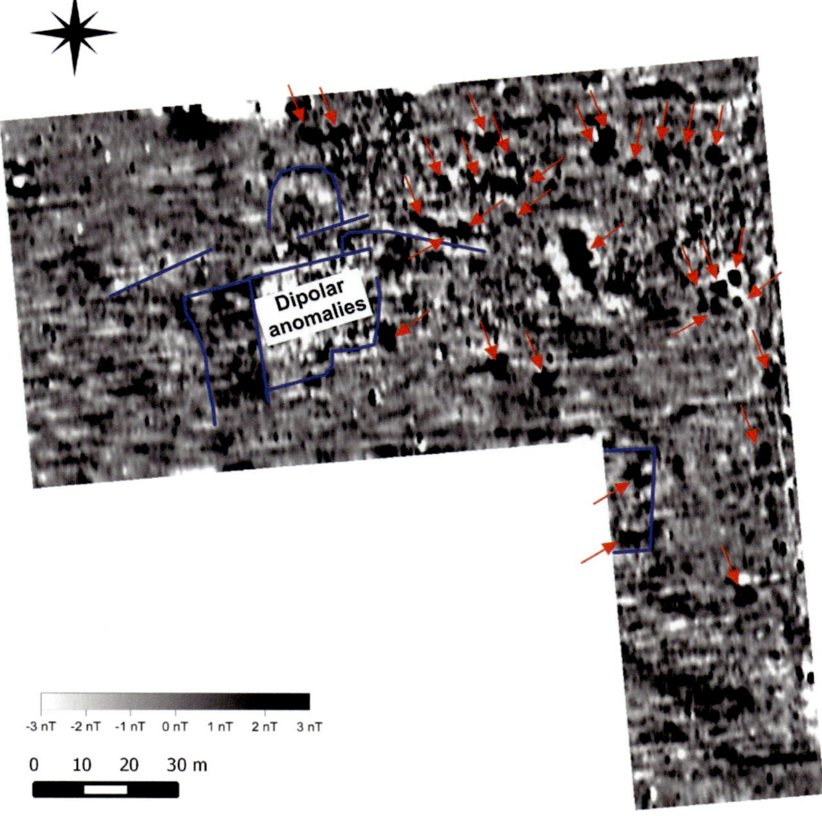

Fig. 63. Novae 2014. Area F. Interpretation of anomalies detected at the site (greyscale -3/3nT) (by P. Wroniecki).

In the western part, linear anomalies form a less complex pattern. A distinct anomaly to the far west on the North – South axis might be generated by the remains of a presumed communication tract which is parallel to a modern dirt road (manifested by a line of numerous dipolar anomalies to the east of it). The many linear anomalies detected in this part of the site need to be carefully studied and their origins investigated through other methods of prospection.

Area C1: Canabae – residential quarter
(Michał Pisz)

The area outside the West Gate, to the south of the extramural residence, was chosen for sample testing.[27] The results showed that the electrical resistivity method applied in the quarter occupied by solid buildings may provide promising results. The anomalies detected in 2013 were verified later by excavations confirming the non-intrusive results. In two places, the remains of walls on the East – West axis were found (**Fig. 55**). A strong linear anomaly running along the North – South axis may either belong to an aqueduct or a modern pipeline and a modern road to the north of it.

Area C2: Canabae
(Michał Pisz)

The lot chosen for the geophysical prospection is located ca. 300 m to the west of the legionary fortress. The area available for the survey was very limited, due to the presence of modern buildings and fences. It consisted of a cultivated field adjacent in the north to a dirt road and to metal fences at its other sides. The presence of such infrastructure had a negative influence on the results of the survey. The magnetic prospection covered an area of 0.4 ha (**Fig. 56**), with probe horizontal spacing of 0.5 m and readings taken every 0.25 m (0.5×0.25 m probing). The electrical resistivity survey prospection covered 0.26 ha, surveyed with a gradiometer, in 1×1 m twin probe (0.5 m) configuration. Both prospections were made in 40×40 m grids.

The surveyed area contained numerous point dipolar and positive anomalies. They are probably generated by smaller magnetic objects, possibly fragmented stone material or pieces of ferrous objects, among which potential archaeological sources might be present.

The electrical resistivity survey conducted on most of the area resulted in the detection of three zones of higher resistivity than the surroundings (**Fig. 57** loc. **a-c**). The three zones are characterised by a rough rectangular shape in each case, measuring somewhat close to 10×10 m. Judging from the properties of these anomalies, the presence of collapsed architectural structures can be suggested. They might consist of either stone or dirt that does not produce magnetic contrasts, since there were none detected. These high resistivity features may therefore be the relics of structures or other forms of the anthropogenic transformation of the area.

Area D: To the east of the annexe
(Piotr Wroniecki, Marcin Jaworski)

Area D is a small arable field located ca. 120 m to the south-east of the annex's south-eastern corner (**Fig. 15**). It was chosen for geophysical prospection during fieldwalking surveys due to the amount of pottery sherds visible on the surface. It is enclosed by a metal fence and descends towards the west. At its northern corner, it is adjacent to an ascending slope with a dirt road running along its top. Magnetic prospection was conducted on an area of 0.25 ha, which was divided into 40×40 m grids, with 1×0.25 m probing.

This limited area contains very distinct magnetic anomalies (**Fig. 58**). There are two types of linear anomalies present here – linear and curvilinear. The first group is oriented parallel and runs in three rows. This type of anomaly may be connected with modern transformations and the agricultural use of this area.

The second group consists of curved linear anomalies, protruding to the north and northeast. The arrows on (**Fig. 59**) indicate the direction in which each anomaly protrudes. These anomalies correspond with the topography of the site and the shape of its northern boundary. Their origins might therefore be connected with geological, agricultural or other modern processes, and transformations connected with contemporary anthropogenic activities.

Area E
(Piotr Wroniecki, Marcin Jaworski)

Area E is located, on an arable, intensively cultivated field to the south-west of Ostrite Mogili (**Fig. 15**). This site was selected based on earlier fieldwalking surveys that suggested the existence of the potential remains of Roman structures in the topsoil. The site was limited to the north by thick vegetation. To the south, it was adjacent to a system of water pipes located throughout the farmland. Magnetic prospection covered an area of 2 ha (**Fig. 60**), divided into 40×40 m grids, which were measured in 1×0.25 m probing.

27. The authors would like to thank to Dr Pavlina Vladkova-Baicheva, who kindly allowed us to conduct the surveys in the sector of her excavations.

The strong linear anomalies detected at this site might be connected with the agricultural use of the land and repeated ploughing (**Fig. 61**). However, it is also possible to distinguish linear positive anomalies that might be connected with the potential existence of archaeological features. Such anomalies form a single line oriented along a North–South axis, perpendicular to the plough lines, and also parallel linear anomalies on a very similar axis as the ploughing. It could also be possible that these anomalies are connected with the water pipe system running to the south of the site, and the area of anomalies caused by lesser water installations, such as drains.

Point positive and dipolar anomalies were also registered in the central and eastern part of the surveyed area. The central zone consists of both types of anomalies, while outside this area only three other distinct positive anomalies are present – two to the east and one to the south. It is also interesting to note that the central zone is located in the area where two linear anomalies cross. This might indicate a pattern that suggests the presence of structures or traces of activity in the topsoil, which might include archaeological features.

Area F: Kanlu cheshme

(Piotr Wroniecki, Marcin Jaworski)

Area F is an open arable field located on a vast agriculturally used plain, *ca.* 1.7 km to the south-east of the fortress. The selection of this site was based on the discovery of two inscriptions and the fieldwalking surveys done in 1977 that suggested the existence of a potential Roman settlement there.[28] Magnetic prospection covered an area of 1.6 ha, divided into 40×40 m grids, and with 1×0×25 m probing. The grids were set on a very deeply ploughed field, limited to the north and east by thick vegetation. Deep ploughing has had a visibly negative effect on the acquired results (**Fig. 62**).

The site contains numerous point dipolar anomalies in the central area. It is clearly distinguishable that there are two types of anomalies – smaller ones and ones covering larger areas. It can be presumed that there might be relics of architecture in advanced stages of destruction present in the topsoil. This is indicated by the detection of numerous smaller point dipolar anomalies, which suggest fragmented magnetic material. On the other hand, the larger anomalies indicate the presence of places and structures that might be connected with high temperatures, such as kilns or hearths. Based on these results, it is possible to pinpoint places of future archaeological evaluations and the type of expected archaeological features, as well as narrowing the area where architectural remains may be located, such as a rectangular-shaped zone of compact dipolar anomalies slightly to the west of the central area (**Fig. 63**).

A different group of anomalies registered at this site consists of linear anomalies spread throughout the central and western part of the surveyed area. These anomalies form enclosures and run in both parallel and perpendicular patterns, which might further indicate the presence of architectural remains. Moreover, a larger group of linear anomalies to the north encompasses a zone of dipolar anomalies and a zone of higher magnetic values. Such a pattern suggests that the remains of a building and zones of past human activities may still be present at the site and the linear anomalies form an enclosure around them. A smaller group of linear anomalies to the south encompasses point dipolar anomalies and might be connected with architectural remains.

Conclusions

All of the surveyed areas are characterized by highly fragmented magnetic material, which strongly impedes the reading of the prospection results. This is especially visible in the analysed area encompassing the *canabae* (Areas C1, C2), the annexe (Area A1) and the Ostrite Mogili site (Area B). Therefore, the interpretation of the results has been limited to finding anomalies with characteristic features and shapes that can be linked to underground archaeological structures. In connection with agricultural usage, the surveyed terrain continues to undergo numerous transformations, while the magnetic material is subjected to growing fragmentation, as a result of which the anthropogenic remains may become increasingly more indistinct.

It should also be emphasized that all the surveyed areas show a high density of small dipolar anomalies, which can be identified as small magnetic items, e.g., small fragments of ferrous objects. The numerous anomalies might be caused both by modern items linked to the usage of these lands by farmers or by shallowly deposited archaeological artifacts made from iron.

The non-invasive analysis of the area of the *canabae* (Areas C1, C2) has brought to light a series of anomalies that can at this initial phase be linked to archaeological structures. The correlation of the magnetic

28. T. Sarnowski 1979

anomalies with the electrical resistivity images is especially interesting, as they partially overlap at the edges of the zones of higher apparent ground resistivity. The characteristically rectangular anomalies at the edges of the zone are separated from each other by spaces with lowered apparent ground resistivity. At this initial stage of interpretation, they can be identified as subsurface archaeological structures.

The non-invasive survey of the annexe over the course of the three-year-long prospection brought results collected during different seasons and in varied environmental conditions. As a result, it was possible to capture linear anomalies arranged into elongated shapes, which could initially be interpreted as subsurface architectural structures. Unfortunately, the anomaly with a rounded outline registered through magnetic prospection has not been confirmed through electrical resistivity prospection, which can be explained by the unfavourable environmental conditions, i.e., the high amount of soil moisture. The prospection confirmed the course of the eastern camp wall, as well as of a structure adjacent to it.

The prospection at the Ostrite Mogili site is also impeded. The extensive land parcelling and accompanying numerous infrastructural elements disrupt the magnetic measurements, masking weaker anomalies of probable archaeological origins. Interesting structures were observed in the eastern part, where land parcelling is not so extensive. These especially include some linear structures with a concentric layout and strong dipolar anomalies and smaller linear ones in their presumed interior. At the current state of knowledge, the existence of architectural structures with zones of human activity can be assumed, as can the presence of clusters of places with the prevalence of high temperatures. Spots with the highest possible archaeological potential can be indicated in this part of the site, with future archaeological investigations probably based on the interpretation of this area, surveyed non-invasively, by searching for analogies. These include clusters with strong dipolar anomalies (probably places of thermal processing), as well as point and linear anomalies with elevated magnetic susceptibility (stratigraphic breaches and architectural structures).

The above interpretation of the geophysical results should be approached with caution due to the lack of possibility of verifying the registered anomalies through excavations and the impossibility of creating an archaeological prospection key. The difficult terrain with numerous limitations in accessibility due to modern infrastructure impact the possibility of conducting an open and extensive investigation of the surveyed sites. The strong magnetic field dynamics caused by modern infrastructure makes it impossible to detect objects of an assumed archaeological nature due to the weaker field being masked by newer elements. This signifies that a one hundred percent certain interpretation of the anomaly is not possible. At the current state of knowledge, based on the results of the non-invasive prospection, the only aspect that can be indicated is the probable location of anomalies caused by the existence of archaeological structures. It should be remembered that these anomalies might also be caused by modern or contemporary structures. This situation can only be resolved by further repeated non-invasive verification in different environmental conditions, as well as conducting either excavations or surveying probes.

VI

The finds

Piotr Dyczek, Evgenia Gencheva, Paweł Janik, Piotr Jaworski, Bartosz Kontny, Małgorzata Kot, Szymon Modzelewski, Magdalena Moskal-del Hoyo, Tadeusz Sarnowski (†), Renata Stachowicz-Rybka, Agnieszka Tomas, and Hanna Winter

1. Stone Age artefacts
Małgorzata Kot

Stone tools were discovered in Novae and to the east of Ostrite Mogili near the small gully of Kouru dere (**Fig. 64**).[1] They were discovered in a southern Danube terrace,[2] which recently has taken the form of a wide spur surrounded from the north and the east by the Danube (**Fig. 65**). The artefacts were found on the eastern slopes of the small gully of Kouru dere cutting the terrace and leading north into the Danube.

Stone artefacts had already been known from the Ostrite Mogili site.[3] Kowal and Kozłowski have recently published an Epigravettian backed point found during the surveying conducted in 2000. The artifacts found in 2000 were collected on the western side of the Kouru dere (**Fig. 64**).

The surveying conducted in 2013 brought eight more stone artefacts from the same location. All the artefacts are described based on their photographs and drawings; therefore, providing their detailed technological description and chronological/cultural attributions was not possible.

Catalogue

Inventory No. 8/13m/OM. Pl. I.1.

Description: a small distal part of a partly cortical flake.

Raw material: the artefact is made of yellowish-bronze, slightly translucent flint with irregular whitish dots – probably "Balkan flint."[4] The beige cortex is 1mm thick.

Inventory No. 2a/13m/OM. Pl. I.2.

Description: a big flat oval flake with different states of preservation of the dorsal and ventral faces. The butt and near-the-bulb part have not been preserved. There is an irregular scar pattern on the dorsal face; moreover, the artefact's size and shape may suggest that the flake comes from the core preparation stage.

Raw material: the artefact is made of yellowish-bronze, slightly translucent flint with irregular whitish dots – probably "Balkan flint". The artefact is heavily patinated, achieving a whitish-blue colour.

Inventory No. 2b/13m/OM. Pl. I.3.

Description: a partly cortical chunk with several semi-steep, far-reaching removals forming a kind of convex working edge.

Raw material: grey, badly silified flint or chert[5] of a heterogeneous structure, with beige discolourations. The beige-white cortex is 1mm thick.

Inventory No. 3/13m/OM. Pl. I.4.

Description: an endscraper with a regular convex front prepared with the use of a single step retouch. Both sides of the endscraper were shaped and blunted with

1. Majewski et al. 1961, 86 and cat. No. 21 on p. 152 (=Dobruski 1900, 130); Kowal and Kozłowski 2011, 7–13.
2. Enciu, Balteanu and Dumitrica 2015, 58–69.
3. Kowal and Kozłowski 2011, 7–13.
4. Gurova et al. 2016, 422–441; Bonsall et al. 2010, 9–18.
5. Andreeva, Stefanova, and Gurova 2014, 25–45.

Fig. 64. Ostrite Mogili 2013–14. The location of the Stone Age site (by A. Tomas based on Google Earth image).

Fig. 65. Ostrite Mogili 2013. View of the Stone Age site from the south-west (photo by A. Tomas).

the use of double step, abrupt, marginal removals. The tool was additionally thinned on both the dorsal and ventral faces in its proximal part, probably in order to prepare it for hafting. The artefact was made on a thick, slightly bent oval flake with a regular parallel scar pattern on the dorsal face.

Raw material: the artefact is heavily patinated into a blueish-white colour, which renders a detailed description of the flint raw material impossible.

Inventory No. 9a/13m/OM. Pl. I.5.

Description: the medial part of a small cortical flake or an irregular blade. The regular parallel scar pattern and triangular cross section indicate that the artefact comes from the blank production or rejuvenation phase of blade core exploitation.

Raw material: the artefact is made of dark grey, almost black, opaque flint with irregular dots. The 2mm-thick cortex is beige. It is slightly patinated into a whitish hue.

Inventory No. 9b/13m/OM. Pl. I.6.

Description: a big oval flake with a bipolar scar pattern on the dorsal face. The artefact is a core tablet and comes from a blade core of a substantial size.

Raw material: the artefact is made of yellowish-bronze, slightly translucent flint with irregular whitish dots – probably "Balkan flint."[6]

Inventory No. 18/13m/OM. Pl. I.7.

Description: a short endscraper made on the distal part of a thick, broken, partly cortical flake. The convex front was prepared with an abrupt double step retouch. The right edge of the endscraper was additionally shaped with the use of a semi-abrupt removal. The butt and the near-the-bulb parts have not been preserved. The tool was made on a big, thick flake with an irregular scar pattern, which suggests that the flake comes from the early stages of core preparation.

Raw material: the artefact is made of slightly translucent flint of indeterminable colour and structure due to its heavily patinated state of preservation. The artefact is heavily patinated into a blueish-white colour. The cortex is greyish-beige hue.

Inventory No. 45/13w/OM. Not illustrated.

Description: a distal part of a wide blade or flake.

Raw material: the artefact is made of yellowish-grey, slightly translucent flint with irregular whitish dots – probably "Balkan flint."[7] It is patchily patinated into a blueish-white colour.

Summary

The chronological and cultural attribution of the above-mentioned artefacts is very problematic. The Ostrite Mogili site is mostly known for its Mediaeval and Roman age findings, although a single Gravettian or Epigravettian backed point has been published lately by Kozłowski and Kowal.[8]

The regular endscraper inv. No. 3/13m/OM (Pl. I.4) fits into the Epigravettian horizon,[9] as long as one takes into consideration its regular shape and ventral thinning. The rest of the described artefacts do not provide grounds for any further chronological and cultural interpretations apart from the suggestion that their Epigravettian attribution cannot be excluded.

6. Gurova et al. 2016, 422–41.

7. Gurova et al. 2016, 422–41.

8. Kowal and Kozłowski 2011, 7–13.

9. Tsonev 1997; Kozłowski and Kaczanowska 2004, 5–18.

Pl. I. Stone Age artefacts from Area B

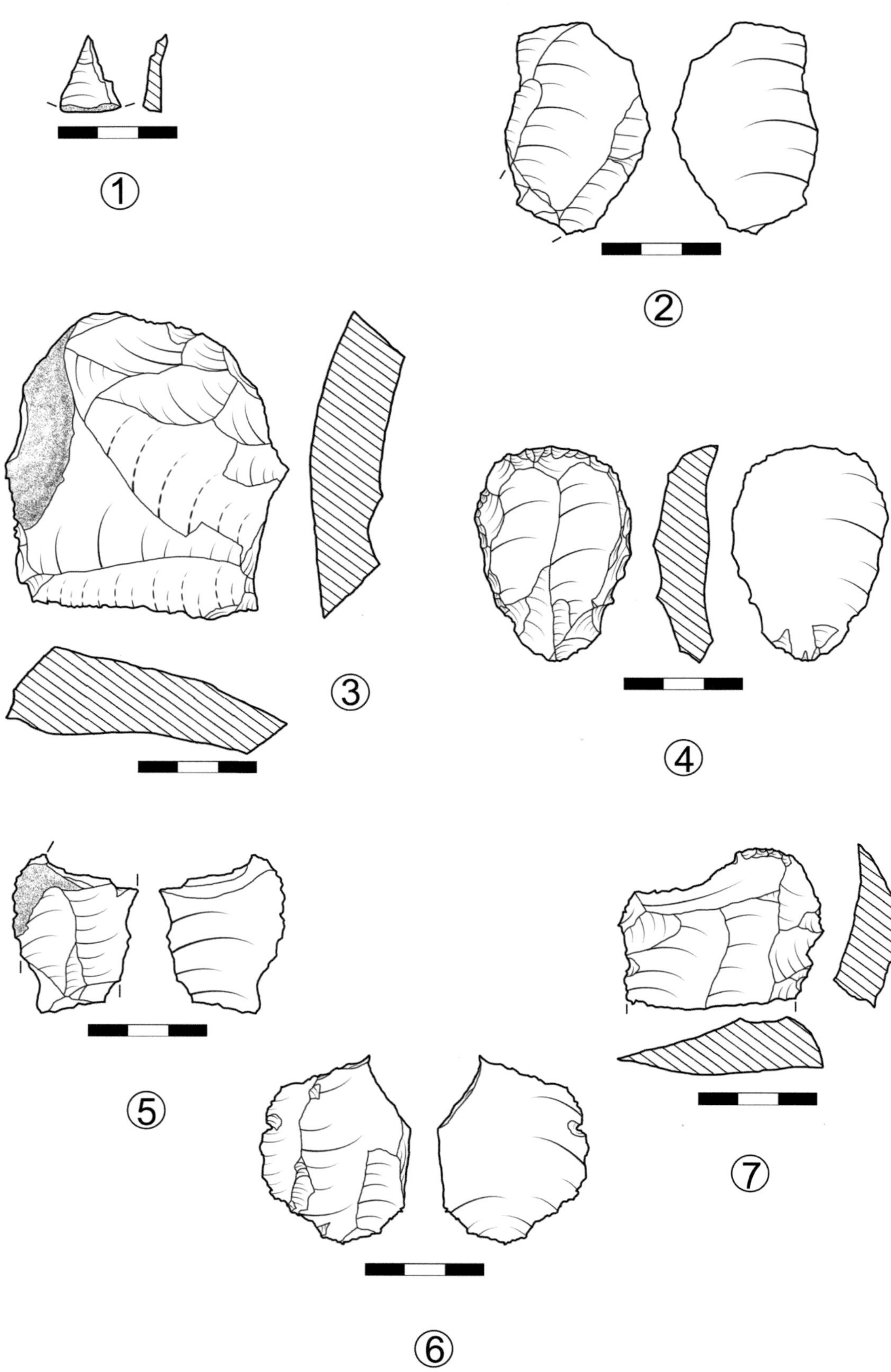

2. Pottery

Agnieszka Tomas

The pottery finds presented here were collected during field surveys carried out in 1979, 2000 and 2012–14. Each fragment received its own catalogue number indicating the inventory number and the year when it was found (e.g., 1/79m, 1/00m or 1/13m). The sherds were collected in seven areas, which in 2012 were named Areas A (*retentura*), A1 and D (east of the camp), B (Ostrite Mogili), C2 (west of the camp), E and F (south of Ostrite Mogili). The finds from Area B come from the surveys in 1979, 2000, and 2014. The finds from Area E were collected during the surveys in 1979 and in 2014.

During our surveys in 2012, the visibility in Area A1 was very limited by dense and high grass. Only 13 diagnostic pottery fragments were collected from illegal robbery trenches. The largest group of finds was collected in Area B during field walkings in 2000 and 2013. Pottery fragments collected in Areas C2 and F were very often small and non-diagnostic. Area E produced the smallest quantity of pottery sherds.

The large amounts of vessel fragments collected during excavations enabled the definition of nineteen basic types of wares numbered I–XIX (Table I). Of course, this classification was based on naked-eye observations made in the field, and only some of these groups can be connected with the samples analysed in the laboratories. The main goal of the present classification was to determine the basic groups of wares. One has to keep in mind that only laboratory analyses may define the proper chemical composition and more sophisticated differences within each fabric type.

During the prospections done in 2000 and 2012–14, sherds of several types of wares listed in Table I were absent. Wares numbered IV (orange tableware known from the early Flavian contexts), VII (kitchenware imported from Phocaea in the early Flavian period) and IX (yellowish tableware) are known from the fortress' 1st-century contexts (see Table I). They were found in the early layers and the above-mentioned pits. Yellowish-pinkish imported vessels defined as ware X are known from the 2nd– and early 3rd-century layers unearthed in the fortress. These classes of wares have not been discussed below.

Medieval finds, including sherds, were also collected from the surroundings of Novae. The settlement pattern and the nature of the finds differ so much from the Roman period that we have decided to discuss this period in a separate text. The pottery finds dated to the early Medieval and post-Medieval period, defined as two groups of wares (wares XVIII and XIX), are discussed in Chapter VI.15.

The classification of wares was prepared according to the fabric type, form, and finishing, following a standard as advised in pottery textbook recommendations.[1] A set of distinct ware samples was collected during the excavations in 2007–09, which produced finds from layers dated to between the Neronian or early Flavian period and the late 6th century, and during the excavations of the well-dated pits discovered in the headquarters building.[2] This set of wares was compared to pottery fragments collected during the field walking surveys in 2000 and 2012–14. In the case of finds documented in 1979, we had to rely only on the descriptions and drawings from the archives.

During fieldwalkings in 2000 and 2012–14, diagnostic pottery fragments were collected and compared to ware samples. The sherds which could be ascribed to the defined ware class were marked with a proper symbol (e.g., ware XIII). Fragments which did not fit any of the defined wares were described in detail. The colours of all sherds were described according to the Munsell Soil Color Charts numbering system. The description of the finds documented in 1979 follows the original documentation, since the Munsell standard was not applied before 2000. It is also worthwhile to keep in mind that the colour of sherds which lay on the surface for a long time may have faded or even changed significantly.

The fabric descriptions took into account the temper density (singular particles, small, middle, large; the evaluation by mutual comparison of particular fabrics), size (coarse-, middle- and fine-grained), the kind (e.g., mica, lime), the grain shape (particles, chips, flakes), the porosity (porous, slightly porous, rather dense, dense), and the surface texture (powdery, smooth, coarse). Coarse-grained temper is temper with grain sized double the average as determined by Shepard (0.25–0.5 mm). Fabric (firing) hardness was evaluated on the ten-point Mohs scale recommended by Orton, where pottery hardness falls in the 2–6.5 range. Mohs' hardness can be measured by scratching the surface with substitutes of minerals: a fingernail (soft clay; below 2.5 on the Mohs scale), a copper coin (moderately soft, below 3), a piece of plastic (moderately hard, 3–4.5),[3] a window glass (hard, below 4.5), and a steel blade (very hard, 6).[4] The term "slip" used in the descriptions of vessel surface

1. Shepard 1976; Orton, Tyers, and Vince 1993.
2. Sarnowski, Kovalevskaja, and Tomas 2010; Sarnowski et al. 2014, 77–83. There are plans to publish the finds from these excavations in a separate publication.
3. Plastic was not listed by Orton, but included by the author of the present paper into the measuring procedure adapted for the pottery from Novae.
4. Orton, Tyers, and Vince 1993, 69 and 138.

coats refers to a coat of diluted clay, which is matt or semi-glossy after firing, but not vitrified. The tactile and visual sensations regarding the surface were also described, as the texture and general appearance of these surfaces is a factor of different elements that cannot be strictly defined.[5] A surface is "smooth" when it resembles a piece of wood, "coarse"– when it is like fine sandpaper, while "powdery"– when it is most like an object dipped in talcum powder.

Imported tableware

At Novae, imported tableware[6] is more frequently found during excavations than during field walkings. Our surveys produced only small amounts of sherds which could be identified as tableware imports. Only one fragment of a bowl was found in Area D (**Pl. II/1**), but in the open field to the west of the camp (Area C2), where the visibility during prospection was better, we collected five fragments of imported vessels, including a Drag. 37 bowl (**Pl. XVIII, 1–6**). The sherds belonged mainly to red slip ware imported from Rheinzabern, most probably in the late 1st and in the 2nd century. A variety of imported vessel types, including *terra nigra*, red slip ware, Pannonian thin-walled vessels, have been found in Area B – the *vicus* at Ostrite Mogili (**Pl. III, 1–15**). It is very probable that the green-glazed pottery which was classified as ware XVI could also be imported vessels (**Pl. XV, 285–288**), but forms which were found during prospection cannot be defined as early Roman tableware.

Ware I: Hand-formed pottery

Vessels defined as this ware include pots, small jars, and one handle cup (*cupa Dacica*), made from poorly sorted fabric with an uneven surface and hand-made fingertip-incised decorations. The pots and jars are usually ovoid, with thick walls. The bottoms frequently have thicker walls at the periphery and thinner ones at the centre. Some are hand-formed and wheel-thrown, rarely wheel-turned. Hand-formed vessels have traces of soot and fire on the outer surface, indicating primitive burning-on-the-stove technology. Some jars could also have been used for direct-heat cooking over fire.

The hand-formed vessels defined as ware I follow Iron-Age forms known from the Middle and Lower Danubian lands – from Pannonia, through Upper and Lower Moesia and south Dacia (Oltenia).[7] In the 1st-century contexts at Novae, this type of pottery is abundant. Fragments of this type were discovered in the layers dated to the last quarter of the 1st century AD, as well as in the pits dated to the early Flavian period discovered in different parts of the site.[8] The issue of who manufactured them and where has been a matter of some debate. Some scholars have interpreted them as vessels of local origin, manufactured in Novae by an indigenous population who was still living there after the arrival of the Romans.[9] However, despite theoretical postulates, archaeological remains indicating local settlement have not yet been discovered, and perhaps mass finds of hand-formed pottery in the layers dated only to the Flavian period have some other explanation. It is possible that they were made by members of the population resettled after the Roman conquest – in the late Neronian or early Flavian period – from more distant areas, perhaps from the northern side of the Danube. Such an interpretation would fit the mass displacements supervised by Ti. Plautius Silvanus in AD 60–67.[10]

Interestingly, at Novae such vessels are not present later than during the last quarter of the 1st century AD, while in Nicopolis ad Istrum they were found in layers dated to the early 2nd century.[11] Their mass production was continued in pottery manufacturing centres at Boutovo and Pavlikeni in the 2nd and early 3rd centuries.[12] The laboratory analysis conducted on one sample from Novae has shown that the clay had "regional" rather than "local" features; thus, at least some of the vessels may have been manufactured outside of Novae,[13] and this conclusion would fit the later production at Boutovo. The appearance of characteristic hand-formed pottery in Novae and in Nicopolis and nearby production centres can be indeed interpreted as the presence of non-local population resettled from the transdanubian areas, and this phenomenon seems to be marked by the Dacian-sounding names among the inhabitants of the rural areas of Nicopolis.[14] On the northern

5. Shepard 1976, 120–21.
6. Imported tableware sherds were identified and dated by Krzysztof Domżalski, whom I would like to thank.
7. Soultov 1984, 186; 1985, 87–88; Tab. XLV; Karasiewicz-Szczypiorski 1998, 194, No. 7; Bichir 1984, 30–33, Pl. X–XII; Grünewald 1979, 51–53, Taf. 38.7–40.4; Rusu-Bolindeţ 2007, 102–13, Tab. XIV–XX; Popilian 1976, 285, Figs. 2, 1–4; Popilian 1997, 15, Pl. XXXVI; Cvjetičanin 2005, Fig. 4.
8. E.g. Karasiewicz-Szczypiorski 1998; Domżalski 1998; Gencheva 2002, esp. 41; Chichikova 2013, 227–46.
9. Sarnowski 2009, 19; Chichikova 2013, 242.
10. Tomas 2018, esp. 15.
11. Falkner 1999, 65 (Wares 25 and 30/31); Tomas 2015c.
12. Soultov 1984; 1985, 87–88.
13. Daszkiewicz, Bobryk, and Schneider 2006.
14. Matei-Popescu 2017.

side of the Danube, this pottery was also manufactured as late as in the 2nd and 3rd centuries.[15]

In the close extramural area, fragments of ware I vessels were found outside the southern part of the annexe (Area D, **Pl. II, 6–7**). Many of them were shredded and non-diagnostic. Farther outside the fortress, such pottery sherds were found in the *vicus* (Area B, **Pl. III, 16–27**), and in the presumed farmhouse to the south of the *vicus* (Area E, **Pl. XXI, 1–2**). Interestingly, almost all of the fragments found outside the fortress were hand-formed and wheel-thrown. This can be regarded as evidence of the manufacturers' skill development.

Wares II and III: Early tableware and kitchenware

Wares II (tableware and vessels of everyday use) and III (kitchenware) are two groups of vessels made from the same high-quality fabric, containing abundant silver mica. Their forms and finishings are modest and simple. The vessels are not coated with a slip, and narrow horizontal grooves left by small sparse sand crumbs during the wheel-turning process can be observed on the surface. Ware II are jugs with a spherical body and bowls, and these are the most common forms among those collected during prospection, but other forms, such as censers, inkwells or *unguentaria*, are known from the excavations.[16] Kitchenware defined as ware III was made from the same fabric, but tempered with crushed sherd. Pots and large bowls are predominant forms.

The most numerous early kitchenware sherds were collected in the *canabae* (Area C2, **Pl. XIX, 33–48**). In other prospected areas, wares II and III were infrequent finds. The early tableware was not identified in the annexe and only one fragment of early kitchenware was found there (Area A1, **Pl. II, 5**). In the *vicus*, only one fragment of early tableware and two fragments of early kitchenware were found (Area B, **Pl. XII, 218–220**). One well-preserved fragment of early tableware was identified in the presumed farmhouse (Area E, **Pl. XXI, 3**).

In the camp, these two groups of vessels appear in contexts dated to the third quarter of the 1st-early 2nd century AD. Ware II fragments were found in pits dated to the early Flavian period.[17] Early layers in the test trench across the northern fortifications of the camp also provided some sherds identified as wares II and III. The latest fragments were discovered together with ESB form 60, which is dated to between the end of the 1st and the early 2nd century AD.[18]

The modest quality of these vessels may indicate that they could have been produced in local workshops, most probably in the *canabae* outside the West Gate. Local pottery production dated to such an early period has not been confirmed yet, but kilns for firing lamps, building materials and vessels dated to later periods have been discovered.[19]

Ware V: Orange burnished tableware

Only one fragment identified as ware V was found during field walks outside the camp, belonging belonged to a large amphora-like jug found in the *vicus* (Area B, **Pl. XVI, 328**).

This type of vessel was defined during excavations in the fortress as a group of very distinctive, although infrequent vessels. Cups, beakers, jugs, bowls, and particularly flat-based amphora-like jugs are the most common forms. Thanks to their characteristic light orange colour and burnished surface, they are very easy to identify. Analogous vessels, referred to as *orange und glatt Keramik*, have been found in Carnuntum in the layers dated to the Flavian and Trajanic periods.[20] The sherds found at Novae during excavations of the Flavian pits located in the centre of the camp and in the trench near the northern defensive walls can be dated to the same period. The provenance of ware V is not known, although the Eastern influence suggested by Mathilde Grünewald cannot be excluded.

Ware VI: Early burnished pottery

Pottery described in the relevant literature as burnished pottery (*geglättete Keramik*, *izlăskana keramika*) occurs throughout Antiquity. Nevertheless, there are strong arguments for dividing this type of pottery into two separate groups: early Roman burnished pottery (ware VI) and late Roman burnished pottery (ware XV). According to Lyudmil Vagalinski, early dated vessels have thick slip which flakes easily, and the burnished bands are mostly straight, not with a wavy or zigzag pattern as the sherds dated to the late Roman period.[21] However, thick-walled vessels decorated with wavy burnished lines were discovered in the early contexts

15. Popilian 1976.
16. Domżalski 1998, 149–50, nos. 22, 24, 28–31, Tab. III–IV.
17. Domżalski 1998, 148–53, nos. 22–54, Tab. III–VI.
18. The fragments of terra sigillata vessels were identified by Krzysztof Domżalski, whom I would like to thank.
19. Klenina 2006, 25–28 and Tab. 1; Tomas, 2015.
20. Grünewald 1983, 22, Taf. 20.8–14.
21. Vagalinski 2007, 53.

in Novae.[22] In fact, sometimes it is difficult to state whether a fragment of a vessel with a burnished decoration collected during field walkings is early or late Roman. This is particularly difficult in the case of fragmented vessels or non-distinctive fragments. Some sherds with a burnished surface collected during prospection were very damaged and not always easy to identify, so it is possible that some fragments classified as ware XV should actually be ascribed to ware VI.

Ware VI vessels are usually thick-walled and thickly slipped, with a burnished and glossy surface which very often flakes. A distinctive feature of their fabric is abundant small silver mica and small lime particles. They are usually greyish or greyish-brown in colour. Three fragments identified as ware VI were found in Area B, i.e., in the *vicus* (**Pl. XVI, 320–322**).

Despite vessels of this type being relatively frequent in the middle and Lower Danubian provinces, their origin has not been specified. They are found at sites associated with La Tène, Germanic and Sarmatian traditions,[23] and occur in the so-called classic phase of the Geto-Dacian culture.[24] Parallel forms were discovered in Muntenia, which was inhabited by the tribes defined as the Chilia-Militari culture.[25] Small round fragments of *dolia* were found in the pits discovered at Novae[26] and in the 1st-century layers near the northern defensive wall. Such vessels were also identified in Nicopolis in the contexts dated to the 2nd century AD.[27]

Ware VIII: Norico-Pannonian coarse ware

Ovoid hand-formed pots with a thickened triangular rim and a characteristic shiny and "pimply" surface often appear in the camp, in contexts dated to the early Flavian period.[28] This pottery was most probably not manufactured locally, as it has very close analogies in the Norico-Pannonian tradition. In Noricum, Pannonia and north Italy these vessels are known as pottery with a so-called *Kammstrich* decoration. During the prospection outside the fortress, only one fragment was collected, i.e., the rim of a pot found in the *canabae* (Area C2, **Pl. XIX, 32**).

Wares XI and XII: Boutovo/Pavlikeni tableware

The production of the Moesian sigillata is relatively well-recognized thanks to the discovery of manufacturing centres in Boutovo, Pavlikeni and Hotnitsa in the *chora* of Nicopolis. The earliest production most probably started at Pavlikeni in the early Flavian period, and in Boutovo in the early 2nd century.[29] The finds of vessel fragments are widespread in the region. In Nicopolis, they were referred as to ware 8.[30] They are represented by a wide variety of forms, such as dishes, plates, bowls, jugs, beakers and cups, among which there are high-quality thin-walled table vessels.[31]

The fabric of these two wares compared with the naked eye is very similar, and an archaeologist in the field can only rely on differences in form, quality and finishing. The vessels collected during prospection were generally described as wares XI/XII to mark that they were produced in more than one production centre, but it was not possible to determine the origin of each sherd. Laboratory tests have showed that the fabric of the vessels produced in Pavlikeni and Boutovo may vary slightly in chemical composition, especially the content of silicium (Si), aluminium (Al), and magnesium (Mg), but the difference is detectable only by chemical analysis.[32]

Vessels produced in Boutovo and Pavlikeni are mass finds in Novae, and during prospection they were found in all the investigated places. In Area B, wares XI/XII were very frequent with bowls and dishes which form the biggest group of tableware (**Pl. VI–XI**). Other frequently found forms include medium-sized vessels, such as beakers, and closed forms, such as jugs (**Pl. IV, V**). Some of the collected fragments could be identified as types known from manufacturing centres, e.g. jugs (**Pl. IV, 29–30**), dishes (**Pl. IX, 180–189**), bowls (**Pl. VIII, 137–141**) or one- and two-handled cups (**Pl. V, 56–62**),[33] forms similar to those published by Soultov (e.g. **Pl. X 193–194**),[34] and forms which seem to be so far unknown (**Pl. IV, 31–40**). They are also present at other nearby sites, including Area F (**Pl. XXII, 1, 2**). There are also some interesting forms which

22. Personal experience.

23. Vagalinski 2007, esp. 23–25.

24. Crişan 1969, 143.

25. Bichir 1984, Pl. XIII, 6; XIV, 1,3,7; XX, 6; XXIV, 1–3; XXVII, 4, 13; XXVIII, 8; Teodor 2015.

26. Vagalinski 2007, 102–03, КУ130; 125, Г254; 136, Д313.

27. Falkner 1999, 85 (ware 78).

28. Sarnowski 1983b, 159, Tab. I, 7; Karasiewicz-Szczypiorski 1998, 192, group IIE, Tab. I, 15; III, 43–46.

29. Soultov 1983, 119–20; 1985, 33–60; Vladkova 2011, 45 (the earliest building phase of the villa at Pavlikeni is dated to the early Flavian period, but the pottery kilns are not dated so precisely).

30. Falkner 1999, 74–84 (ware 8).

31. Soultov 1985, Tab. XXVII–XXXVIII.

32. Daszkiewicz, Naumann, Schneider, and Baranowski 2013, 170. For the technological remarks, see Nacheva 1981.

33. Soultov 1985, Tab. XXXIV, 2 (jug); XXXVII, 6; XXVI, 13 (dishes); XXX, 2 and 6 (bowls); XXXII, 4, 8, 9 (one-handled cups); XXXVII–XXXVIII (two-handled cups).

34. Cf. Soultov 1985, Tab. XXVII, 1, 2, 4.

are rather rare, e.g., a rim with a handle, probably of a *patera* or a skillet (**Pl. V, 92**), and a fragment of an inkwell found in the presumed villa at Kanlu cheshme (Area E, **Pl. XXI**, 7).

Ware XIII: Boutovo/Pavlikeni kitchenware

The same production centres provided Novae with kitchenware. This pottery was made from fabric which is the same as that of wares XI and XII, but it contains coarser tempers, such as coarse sand with small white stones. The execution and quality of the pots are good. All the forms, mainly pots with lids, are wheel-turned, sometimes ribbed, but never decorated.[35]

Ware XIII vessels were found in the vicinity of the camp (Area D, **Pl. II, 16–17**; C2, **Pl. XX, 49–53**) and at the *vicus* (Area B, **Pl. XII-XIV**). Surprisingly, they were not found in the farther surroundings (in Area E and F), where fragments of ware XIV kitchenware were discovered.

Ware XIV: Lower Danube Kaolin ware

Ware XIV is very characteristic and easy to recognize, due to the fabric and finishing of the vessels. Kitchenware of a yellowish colour is predominant, although beakers are also very frequent. The surface of the vessels is usually ribbed on the belly, while the handles are flat, very often decorated with two shallow grooves. The rims are concave in section.

These characteristic vessels were referred to as Lower Danube Kaolin ware by Piotr Dyczek, who suggested their provenance from Dobrudja and indicated Axiopolis as their production centre.[36] According to Elena Klenina, the pottery was manufactured in Singidunum.[37] Laboratory analyses could not exclude or support either supposition, since the authors did not have any comparable raw clay samples.[38] In fact, the fabric of ware XIV may be confused with ware X, mainly large *oinochoai* made from coarse fabric, which is similar at first glance, but their surfaces have pinkish discolorations. This pottery could have been manufactured somewhere in the Danubian delta region.[39]

The finds of ware XIV are quite common in Novae, unlike to ware X. Ware XIV sherds were found outside the annexe (Area D, **Pl. II, 18**; Area C2, **Pl. XX, 54–57**), and in the surroundings of Novae (Area B, **Pl. XVI, 303–319**; Area E, **Pl. XXI, 9–10**; Area F, **Pl. XXII, 3**).

At Novae, the earliest dated sherds were recorded during the excavations in the fortress near the northern defensive walls, in layers dated to the beginning of the 2nd century AD, while in the military hospital they were found in a context dated to the mid-2nd century, and the latest dated sherds were found in layers dated as late as the 6th century AD.[40]

They were classified as ware 24 in Nicopolis.[41] Their mass appearance may indicate some non-distant manufacturing centre,[42] which flourished in the 2nd and 3rd centuries AD. It is worth noting that quite similar forms but made from different fabric were found in the Boutovo, Hotnitsa and Pavlikeni production centres.[43]

Ware XV: Late Roman burnished pottery

Ware XV are vessels made from fine-grained, very micaceous, medium soft and porous fabric, which is greyish-brown in colour. Closed forms decorated with burnished lines, waves and zigzags, but also with a grooved decoration are the most common. In contrast to the early Roman burnished pottery defined here as ware VI, the late Roman vessels are very often thin-walled, with a wide rim and flat bottom. Some features, such as a collar on the neck, flat handles, burnished surface and colour, seem to imitate metal vessels.

This type of micaceous burnished pottery is very often associated with the barbarians, especially with the Goths and Sântana de Mureș / Chernyahov culture; therefore, it is often called "Foederati ware".[44] Laboratory analyses seem to indicate that some of these vessels were manufactured locally,[45] and the same conclusions can be drawn based on some forms and the naked-eye observations of the fabric.[46] Although the association with the barbarians is an appealing theory, one cannot exclude that at least some of the vessels were produced in local workshops, and their forms and finishing followed the fashion and the expectations of the purchasers.[47]

35. Soultov 1985, XLII–XLIII.
36. Klenina 2006, 109–19; Dyczek 2009, 168.
37. Klenina 2006, 114–15, 164, 178.
38. Daszkiewicz et al. 2010, esp. 37.
39. Radulescu 1975, 341–43, no. 10 and Pl. VIII; Tomas 2003, 123, ware E.
40. Dyczek 2009, 156–157.
41. Falkner 1999, 72–73 (ware 24).
42. Local production was also suggested based on the results of laboratory analyses; see Daszkiewicz et al. 2010, 38.
43. Soultov 1985, 86, tab. XLIII, 2, 4, 5.
44. Poulter 1999, 44; Falkner 1999, 111–12; Vagalinski 2007, esp. 9-17, 27.
45. Baranowski and Daszkiewicz 2009, 147 (N2).
46. Falkner 1999, 112.
47. The same conclusion was reached by M. Grünewald (1980, 29–30).

In the extramural area of Novae, ware XV is not as frequent as in the fortress. During our surveys, several sherds were found in the *vicus* (Area B, **Pl. XVI, 323–327**). Burnished vessels are also known from Iatrus[48] and Nicopolis.[49]

Ware XVI: Late Roman glazed pottery

Glazed pottery does not appear in the early contexts in Novae, although such technology was well-known for the Romans, who followed the Hellenistic tradition, and whose manufacturing centres in Asia Minor had been active since the mid-1st century BC. Glazed vessels were produced in north Italy since the Augustan era, and in the following two centuries this technology was applied also in the Gaulish and middle Danubian provinces.[50] Contrary to the early Roman Late glazed pottery, which was luxurious and rare tableware, late Roman glazed pottery was mass produced. In Moesia it is well-known from the second half of the 3rd century until the mid-5th century.[51]

For the purpose of the present classification, late Roman glazed pottery was described as ware XVI. This ware appeared to be infrequent in the extramural area. Only three fragments were collected in the *vicus*, belonging to a bowl, two *mortaria* and a jug (Area B, **Pl. XV, 285–288**). Two *mortaria* seem to resemble the vessels imported from north Italy or produced in Moesia I, but none of these vessels can be treated as close analogies.[52]

This type of pottery seems to be rare in Nicopolis,[53] but more frequent in the 4th- and 5th-century layers in Novae[54] and in Iatrus.[55] Moesian production centres have been suggested by Tatjana Cvjetičanin, who indicated 5th-century production in Marcianopolis.[56]

Ware XVII: Late Roman pottery

The vessels classified as ware XVII are actually a broad group of kitchenware and tableware, which should be divided into several groups. However, ware XVII is rare in the surroundings of Novae; thus, for the purpose of this publication, two sub-groups were defined: subgroup A – vessels carefully made from good quality but sandy fabric, with 5-cm-thick walls and a well-finished surface; subgroup B – vessels with usually 0.2–0.4-cm-thick walls and an uneven surface, made from fabric containing abundant lime particles. Among the forms known from the excavations in Novae there are characteristically bulbous pots with lids, jars with wide, grooved necks and usually everted rims, but also jugs with trefoil rims, and bowls.[57] Two pottery kilns have been discovered in Novae so far.[58] They were found in occupation layers dated to the second half of the 5th century – late 6th century AD.[59]

Only one example of subgroup A was found during prospection and it belonged to a flask (Area B, **Pl. XV, 289**). The fabric and form resemble a set of flasks discovered in *principia* Room Bz, but it certainly was not one of this set, since the said form is slightly bigger and broader in section. The set from the *principia* was dated to the early 4th century and it is considered to be a provision distributing vessel for the army.[60]

Vessels of subgroup B are quite common in the fortress, but rare in the surroundings. Two rims were found in the *vicus* (Area B, **Pl. XV, 290–291**).

Vessels of similar forms to those from Novae are known from Iatrus and Nicopolis ad Istrum. In Iatrus, they were defined as Töpfe VII, dated to period D.[61] In Nicopolis, where the fabric was defined as ware 1 (grey coarse ware), they are dated to AD 450–600.[62] The forms of the pots should be regarded as common in the 6th century,[63] and their low quality indicates local production in each town.[64]

48. Böttger 1967; 1982, 123–24, Töpfe V, Taf. 47, 494–99.
49. Falkner 1999, 73–74 (Ware 14).
50. Cvjetičanin 2006, 18.
51. Cvjetičanin 2006, 193.
52. Cvjetičanin 2006, 30, LRG 11 and 12b.
53. Falkner 1999, 87.
54. E.g., Majewski et al. 1961, 147, Tab. X, 18–20; 1962, 112, Tab. VI.
55. Böttger 1982, 33ff.
56. Cvjetičanin 2006, 180, 193.
57. Klenina 1999, esp. Fig. 4, 5 and 7; Klenina 2006, 79–88, Tab. 41–46, esp. types 21, 22; Tomas 2015c.
58. Kotecki 1978.
59. Klenina 2006, 117, type 5; Tomas 2015c.
60. Sarnowski, Kovalevskaja, and Tomas 2000.
61. Böttger 1982, 141–42, Töpfe VII, period "D".
62. Falkner 1999, 66–72 (ware 1).
63. Kouzmanov 1985, 47–54 and Tab. 28–32.
64. Klenina 1999, 93; Klenina 2006, 172; Poulter 1999, 46; Böttger 1982, 84; cf. the results of laboratory analyses by Daszkiewicz, Bobryk, and Schneider 2006, 194–95.

Catalogue of pottery

A detailed description of the defined wares is included in Table I. The sherd fabric classified to ware types were not described in detail, unless they showed some features different than those described in Table I. The colours of each specimen were described according to the Munsell Color Charts. Descriptions of pottery from surveys carried out in 1979 are given in the original version copied from the old archives. Medieval finds classified as wares XVIII and XIX were not included in the present catalogue, but elaborated in a separate text by Paweł Janik in Chapter VI.15.

Pl. II. Pottery finds from Areas A1 and D

Area A1. Various wares.

1. Rim of a terra sigillata bowl. 4/11/14m/can. Medium-hard, fine-grained fabric without visible inclusions, compact; thick, shiny slip. Imported tableware. Break 10 R 6/6, slip 10 R 4/8.
2. Rim of a bowl with an incised decoration. Discovered in a robbery trench. 42/12/13m/can. Sparse small-sized lime inclusions. Rather soft, slightly porous fabric, an abraded surface. Ware XI? Break 5 YR 5/4, surface 7.5 YR 5/4.
3. Bottom of an opened vessel. 30/1/13m/can. Found in the humus during the mapping of metals. Ware XI/XII. Break 7.5 YR 6/4, slip 10 R 6/6.
4. Upper part of a vessel (without bottom). 4/5/14m/can. Ware XI/XII. Break and surface 5 YR 6/6.
5. Rim and bottom of a pot. 4/9-10/14m. Ware III. Break and surface 10 YR 5/1–5/2.

Area D (outside the annexe). Ware I (hand-formed pottery).

6. Rim of a jar. 4/7/12m/can. Hand-made and wheel-thrown. Hard, fine-grained compact fabric, tempered with crushed sherd. Powdery surface. Decorated with grooves made before firing. Break and surface 7.5 YR 7/4.
7. Rim of a pot. 4/6/12m/can. Hand-made and wheel-thrown. Medium-hard fabric with moderate lime inclusions, tempered with large amount of sand; porous. Surface uneven, rough. Traces of fire around the rim. Break two-coloured—outer 10 YR 7/1, inner 2.5 YR 6/6, surface 7.5 YR 6/4.

Area D. Wares XI/XII (local tableware).

8. Rim of a censer rim with a decoration in the form of a wavy edge. 3/2/12m/can. Hard fabric tempered with coarse sand with sparse grains of stones (up to 2 mm), and abundant small-sized lime inclusions; rather porous. Surface rough and powdery, without slip. Traces of fire inside. Break and surface 7.5 YR 7/4.
9. Rim of a censer with an incised decoration made before firing. 1/1/12m/can. Break and surface 7.5 YR 7/3.
10. Rim of a bowl. 1/15/12m/can. Break 5 YR 6/3, slip 5 YR 4/3.
11. Rim of a bowl decorated with the *en barbotine* technique. 4/11/12m/can. Break 5 YR 6/6, slip 5 YR 4/4.
12. Rim of a bowl. 3/12/12m/can. Fabric without visible inclusions. Break and surface 2.5 YR 6/6.
13. Upper part of a pot. 4/8/12m/can. Powdery surface, worn slip. Break and slip 10 YR 8/4.
14. Rim with an incised decoration. 4/5/12m/can. Break 5 YR 7/6, surface 10 YR 5/6.
15. Rim. 3/1/12m. Break 2.5 YR 6/4, slip 2.5 YR 4/8.

Area D. Ware XIII (Boutovo/Pavlikeni kitchenware).

16. Rim of a kitchen pot. 5/4/12m/can. Fabric tempered with sherds, porous. Surface rough and powdery, with traces of wheel-turning. Break and surface 7.5 YR 7/4.
17. Rim of a kitchen bowl. 5/3/12m/can. Fabric tempered with large amount of coarse sand with small stones, porous (with single large pore spaces); surface rough and powdery. Break and outer side surface GLEY 1 4/N, inner side surface 2.5 Y 6/1.

Area D. Ware XIV (Lower Danube Kaolin Ware).

18. Three fragments of a pot. 4/9/12m-5/10/12m-2/1/12m. Traces of fire on the outer surface, burned bottom. Break 2.5 Y 5/1–10YR 4/4, surface 10YR 4/4 to 10 YR 8/2.

Pl. III. Pottery finds from Area B – Ostrite Mogili

Imported tableware

1. Fragment of a bowl (*terra nigra*). Fine-grained fabric with a moderate quantity of small-sized silver mica flakes, rather dense. 37/4/00/OM. Break 10 YR 5/1, glossy slip 2.5 YR 5/1.
2. Rim (*terra nigra*). 141/2/00/OM. Medium-hard fabric with sparse, small-sized lime particles and silver mica flakes, slightly porous; worn slip. Break 2.5 Y 5/2, slip 2 FG 2.5 / 5 PB.
3. Rim of a bowl. 154/1/00/OM. Hard fine-grained fabric with a moderate quantity of medium-sized sand, slightly porous; worn slip. Break 5 YR 6/6, slip 2.5 YR 5/8.
4. Rim. 145/4/00/OM. Fine-grained fabric with no visible inclusions, dense; worn slip. Break 5 YR 6/6, inner slip 2.5 YR 5/8, outer slip 2.5 YR 5/8 – 6/8.
5. Upper part. 1/7/00/OM. Medium-hard fabric with sparse, small-sized lime particles, rather dense. Break 2.5 YR 6/6, slip 2.5 YR 6/8.
6. Rim. 5/3/14m/OM. Fine-grained, hard, compact. Break 5 YR 6/6, thick glossy slip 5 YR 5/8.
7. Fragment of an everted rim with decoration. 33/79/OM. Fine-grained fabric. Slip dark reddish.

Pl. II. Pottery fragments from Areas A1 and D

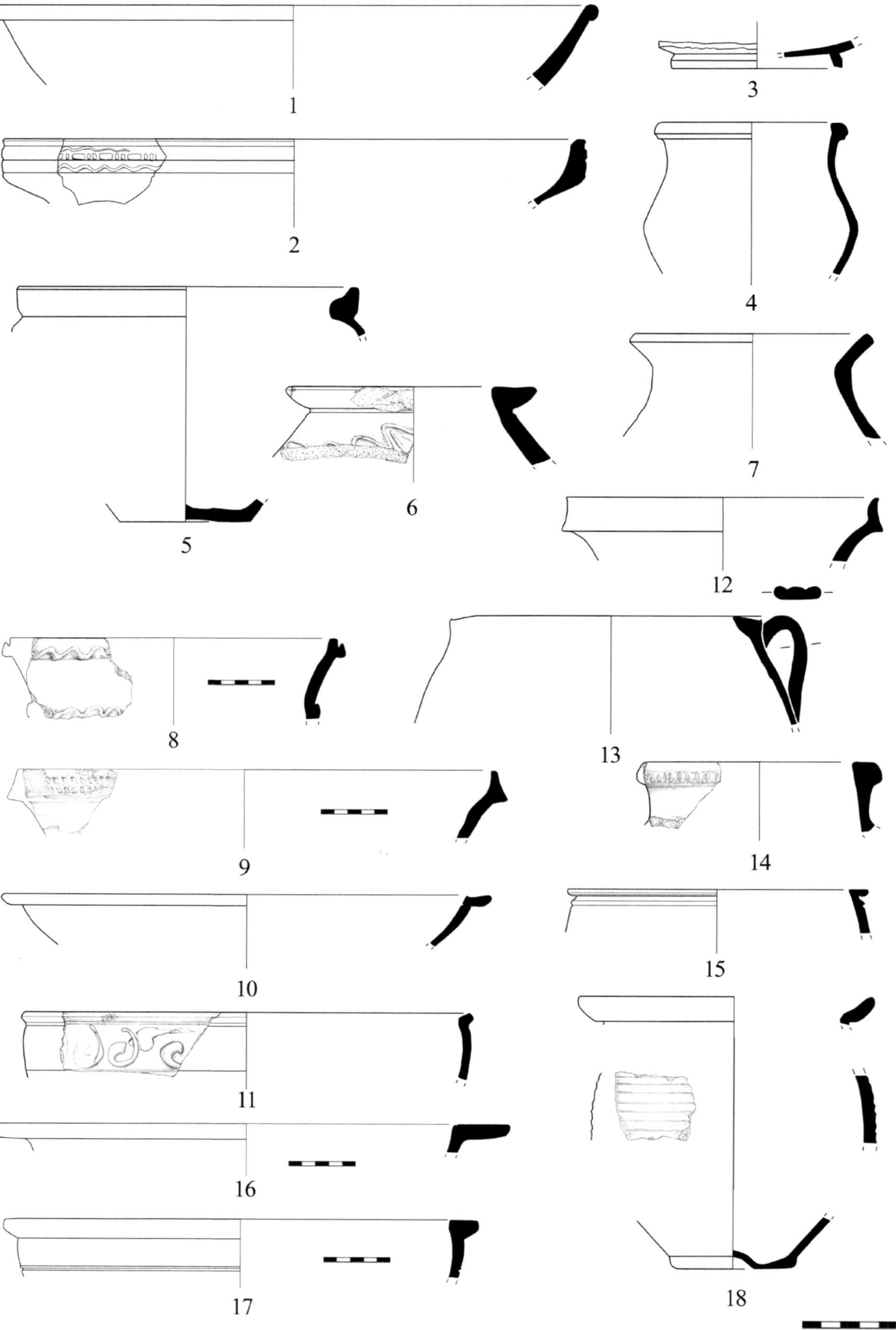

Pl. III. Pottery finds from Area B

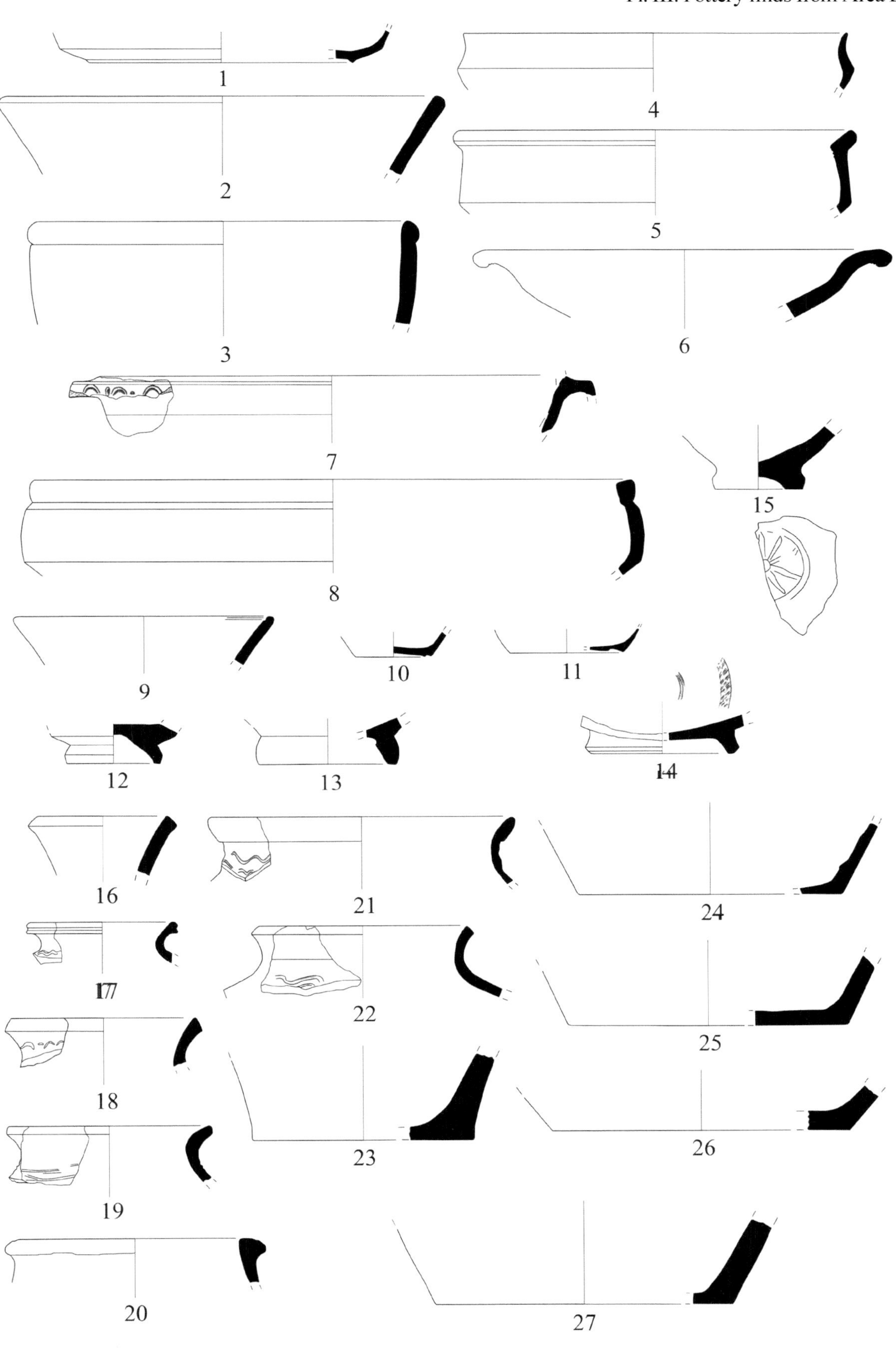

8. Rim. 50/2/00/OM. Hard, fine-grained fabric with abundant, small-sized silver mica flakes and small-sized lime particles, rather dense. Break 7.5 YR 6/6, slip 10 R 5/6.
9. Rim of a *terra sigillata* vessel. 8/2/00/OM. Medium-hard, fine-grained fabric without visible inclusions, compact; glossy slip. Break 7.5 YR 7/4, slip 5 YR 4/2. Consp. Form 8. *Published:* Tomas 2006, cat. no. 5, fig. 13.5.
10. Bottom of a cup. 21/3/00/OM. Fabric with sparse, small-sized lime particles, rather dense, opalescent slip. Break and slip 7.5 YR 5/3 – 5/4. Pannonian thin-walled tableware.
11. Bottom of a cup. 24/4/00/OM. Hard fine-grained, fabric with no visible inclusions, compact. Break 7.5 YR 7/4, slip 5YR 6/2. Pannonian thin-walled tableware.
12. Bottom. 104/4/00/OM. Fine-grained fabric with sparse small-sized lime particles, compact. Break 2.5 YR 6/6, slip 2.5 YR 4/8.
13. Bottom. 148/8/00/OM. Fine-grained fabric with sparse, small-sized lime particles, dense. Break 7.5 YR 7/3, slip 10 YR 7/3.
14. Bottom with a grooved decoration. 5/10/14m/OM. Hard, fine-grained fabric without visible inclusions, compact. Break 5 R 5/6, slip 5 R 5/8.
15. Bottom of a closed form with a potter's stamp on the outer side. 145/1/00/OM. Fabric with sparse lime inclusions and silver mica flakes, tempered with fine-grained sand, slightly porous. Break 5 Y 5/1, thick matt coating 10 YR 5/1 – 4/1. *Published:* Tomas 2006, cat. no. 9, fig. 13.9.

Ware I (hand-formed pottery)

16. Rim. 8/1/00/OM. Fine-grained soft fabric with sparse, small-sized silver mica flakes; hand-made and wheel-turned, surface covered with poor-quality slip, slightly porous. Break 2.5 Y 6/2, slip 2.5 Y 6/3 – 6/4.
17. Rim with an incised waved decoration. 3/2/00/OM. Medium-hard, coarse fabric with abundant, small-sized silver mica flakes, tempered with sand with small stones, rather dense; hand-made and wheel-turned; rough surface. Break 1 for GLEY 3/N, surface 10 YR 6/2.
18. Rim with an incised decoration made with nails. 9/79/OM. Fine-grained and well-sorted fabric. Break and surface reddish.
19. Rim with an irregular grooved decoration. 30/6/00/OM. Medium-hard fabric with sparse, small-sized lime particles, slightly porous. Break 1 FG 4/N, surface 7.5 YR 6/4.
20. Rim. 150/2/00/OM. Medium-hard fabric tempered with large amounts of coarse sand; rough surface, slightly porous. Break and surface 5 YR 6/8.
21. Rim with an incised wavy decoration. 22/d1/00/OM. Hard fabric with abundant small-sized lime particles and silver mica flakes, tempered with coarse sand; slightly rough surface. Break 5 YR 6/2, surface 2.5 Y 3/1.
22. Rim with a grooved decoration. 7/3/14m/OM. Hand-made and wheel-turned. Medium-hard fabric tempered with coarse sand. Smoothened surface. Break 2.5 Y 6/2, slip 2.5 Y 6/3.
23. Bottom. 8/4/00/OM. Medium-hard fabric with sparse, small-sized silver mica flakes and abundant small-sized lime particles, tempered with coarse sand, porous; uneven surface. Break 2.5 Y 6/2, surface 10 YR 6/3.
24. Bottom. 25/1/00/OM. Medium-hard fabric with abundant small-sized silver mica flakes, lime particles and broken shells, slightly porous. Break 5 YR 5/1, surface 5 YR 7/6.
25. Bottom 15/1/00/OM. Soft fabric with abundant small-sized silver mica flakes, medium-sized lime particles, tempered with coarse sand with small stones, porous. Break and surface 7.5 YR 7/4 – 6/6.
26. Bottom. 30/7/00/OM. Medium-hard fabric with abundant medium-sized silver mica flakes, coarse lime particles, tempered with coarse sand, porous. Break 5 YR 6/8, surface 5 YR 6/4.
27. Bottom. 42/1/OM. Medium-hard fabric with moderate quantity of small-sized silver mica flakes and lime particles, porous. Break 1 FG 4/N, surface 5 YR 6/3.

Pl. IV. Pottery finds from Area B – Ostrite Mogili

Wares XI/XII (local tableware). Jugs and other closed forms

28. Rim of a jug. 132/79/OM. Fabric tempered with medium-sized sand. Break and surface brownish.
29. Rim. 117/1/00/OM. Worn slip. Break 10 YR 7/4, slip 10 YR 5/2.
30. Rim. 21/9/00/OM. Worn slip. Break 7.5 YR 8/4, slip 2.5 YR 6/6.
31. Rim decorated with outer horizontal grooves. 23/6/00/OM. Smooth surface. Break 5 YR 6/8, slip 2.5 YR 5/8.
32. Rim. 2/d1/00/OM. Fabric tempered with large amounts of fine-grained sand, porous; smooth surface, without slip. Break 5 YR 6/1, surface 5 YR 6/2.
33. Rim. 71/1A/00/OM. Break 7.5 YR 7/4, slip 5 YR 5/6.
34. Rim. 70/10/00/OM. Break and slip 7.5 YR 7/4.
35. Rim with horizontal grooves. 60/79/OM. Slightly shiny slip. Break pinkish, slip red-brownish.
36. Rim with horizontal grooves. 63/79/OM. Slightly shiny slip. Break pinkish, slip red-brownish.
37. Rim. 2/k1/00/OM. Hard, fine-grained fabric without visible inclusions, compact; worn slip. Break 5 YR 5/5, slip 2.5 YR 4/6. *Published:* Tomas 2006, cat. no. 19, fig. 14.7.
38. Rim with a fragment of a handle. 164/8/00/OM. Break 5 YR 6/6, slip 2.5 YR 5/8.
39. Rim. 45/8A/00/OM. Smooth surface. Break and surface 10 YR 7/4.
40. Rim. 67/7/00/OM. Break and slip 2.5 YR 6/8.
41. Bottom with a foot and a body. 8/d1/00/OM. Smooth surface without slip. Break 2.5 YR 6/8, slip 2.5 YR 6/8.

Pl. IV. Pottery finds from Area B

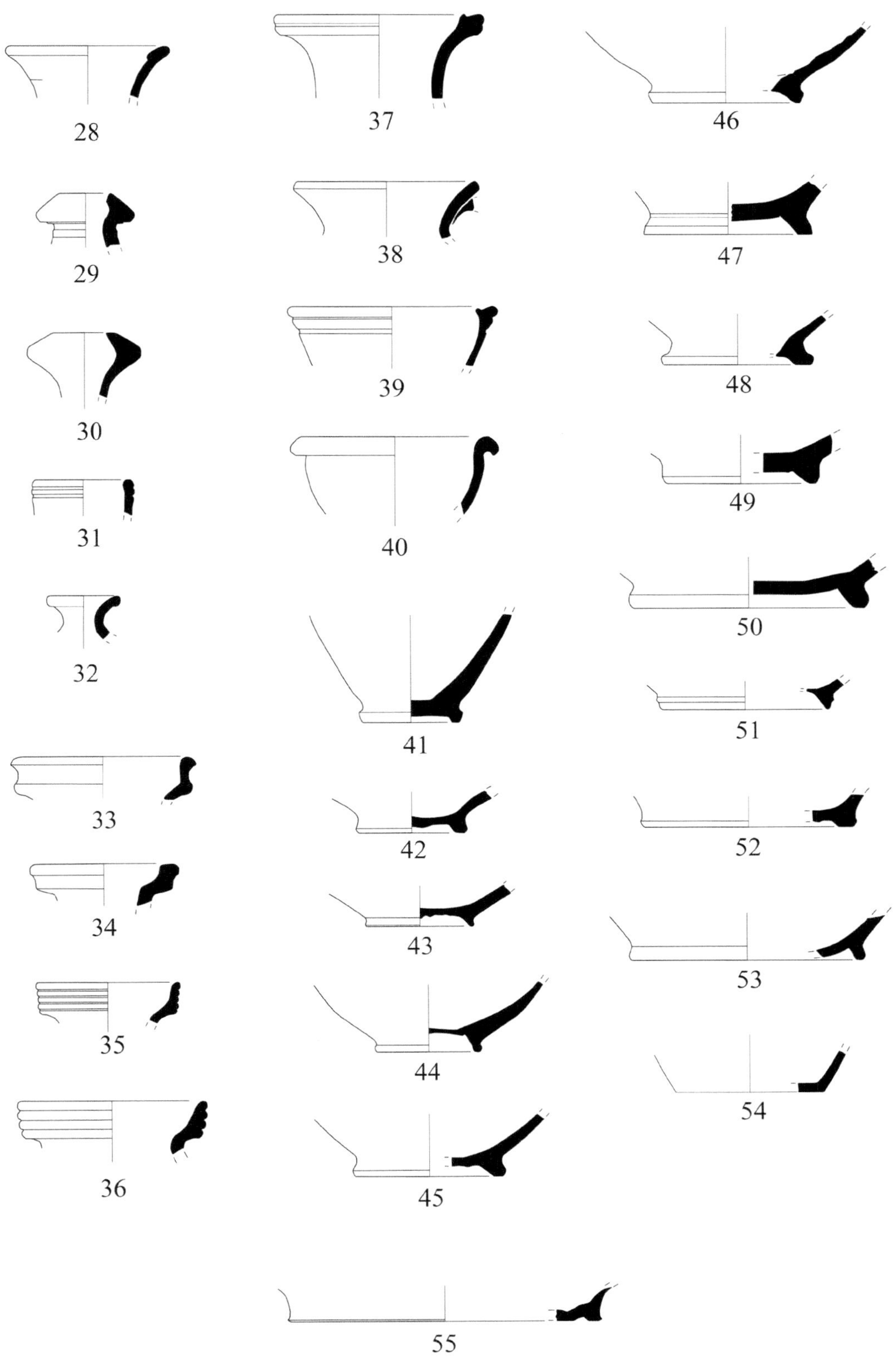

42. Bottom with a foot. 31/1A/00/OM. Break and surface 2.5 YR 6/6.
43. Bottom with a foot. 32/1/00/OM. Fabric tempered with fine-grained sand. Break 7.5 YR 7/4, surface 7.5 YR5/6.
44. Bottom with a foot and a body. 42/3/00/OM. Very smooth surface. Break 10 R 6/6, surface 2.5 YR 6/8.
45. Bottom. 71/5A/00. Break and surface 5 YR 6/6.
46. Bottom with a foot and a body. 13/4/00/OM. Break 10 R6/6, slip 10 R 5/2.
47. Bottom with a foot. 131/10/00/OM. Break and surface 2.5 Y 7/3.
48. Bottom. 13/5/00/OM. Break and surface 2.5 YR 7/4 – 6/6.
49. Bottom with a foot. 73/5/00/OM. Rather porous; slightly rough surface. Break and surface 10 YR 7/4.
50. Bottom with a foot and a body. 67/1/00/OM. Rather porous. Break 7.5 YR 6/4, surface 2.5 YR 7/3.
51. Bottom. 45/3A/00/OM. Break 5 YR 6/6, slip 2.5 YR 5/8.
52. Bottom with a foot and a body. 71/7A/00/OM. Break 7.5 YR 7/4, surface 7.5 YR 6/6.
53. Bottom with a foot (production waste?). 40/10/00/OM. Rough surface. Break 2 YR 6/8, surface 5 YR 6/6.
54. Bottom. 144/1/00/OM. Smooth surface. Break 2.5 YR 5/6, slip 7.5 YR 6/4.
55. Bottom (production waste?). 168/4/00/OM. Fabric tempered with medium amounts of sand; slightly rough surface. Break 10 YR 7/4.

Pl. V. Pottery finds from Area B – Ostrite Mogili

Wares XI/XII (local tableware). Cups and beakers.

56. Rim. 106/1/00/OM. Rather porous. Break 7.5 YR 6/6, slip on inner surface 2.5 YR 5/8, slip on outer surface 2.5 YR 8/2.
57. Rim. 7/9/14m/OM. Slightly worn slip. Break 5 YR 6/6, slip 5 YR 5/8.
58. Fragment of a vessel with an everted rim. 35/2/00/OM. Slightly porous. Break 2.5 Y 6/4, slip 5 YR 6/3.
59. Fragment of a vessel with an everted rim. 101/8/00/OM. Slightly porous. Break 5 YR 6/6, slip 2.5 YR 5/6.
60. Rim with a body fragment. Rim decorated with horizontal grooves and a body decorated in the *en barbotine* technique. 120/1/00/OM. Break 2.5 YR 6/8, slip 2.5 YR 5/8 – 6/8.
61. Fragment of a vessel with applique decoration of 'fish scales' made with finger-tips. 71/3A/00/OM. Break 5 YR 6/4, slip 2.5 YR 4/6. *Published:* Tomas 2006, cat. no. 13, fig. 14.1.
62. Fragment of a vessel with applique decoration made with finger-tips. 171/1/00/OM. Worn slip. Break 2.5 Y 7/2, slip 5 YR 6/8.
63. Rim with a fragment of a handle. 136/2/00/OM. Break 7.5 YR 7/6, slip 7.5 YR 6/6.
64. Bottom. 62/1/00/OM. Break 5 YR 5/4, inner slip 7.5 YR 5/3, outer slip 7.5 YR 6/6.
65. Bottom with a foot. 101/5/00/OM. Break 2.5 YR 6/8, slip 2.5 YR 6/6.
66. Bottom. 78/9/00/OM. Break 2.5 YR 5/6, outer slip 2.5 YR 5/8.
67. Bottom. 112/3/00/OM. Worn slip. Break 2.5 YR 6/8, outer slip 2.5 YR 5/8.
68. Bottom with a foot. 45/2A/00/OM. Break 5 YR 7/4, slip 2.5 YR 5/8.
69. Bottom with a foot. 8/5/00/OM. Break 2.5 YR 6/8, surface 5 YR 6/8.
70. Upper part decorated with the *en barbotine* technique. 109/2/00/OM. Break 10 YR 6/3, slip 5 YR 5/4.
71. Upper part with applique decoration. 59/4/00/OM. Porous. Break and slip XI/XII, 2.5 YR 6/8.
72. Rim. 92/1/00/OM. Rather porous. Break 5 YR 7/6, slip 2.5 YR 6/8.
73. Upper part. 5/17/14m/OM. Break 5 YR 6/4, slip 2.5 YR 4/4.
74. Rim with horizontal grooves. 8/7/00/OM. Soft but compact fine-grained fabric. Break 5 YR 6/4, slip 2.5 YR 4/4.
75. Rim. 127/2/00/OM. Break 5 YR 6/4, slip 2.5 YR 4/4.
76. Rim with horizontal grooves. 11/79/OM. Smooth surface. Break light brownish, inner slip dark brownish, outer slip light brownish.
77. Rim with horizontal grooves. 7/8/14m/OM. Break 5 YR 6/4, slip 2.5 YR 4/4.
78. Rim decorated with horizontal grooves. 88/8/00/OM. Break and slip 5 YR 6/6.
79. Rim decorated with horizontal grooves. 19/2/00/OM. Fabric without visible inclusions, slightly porous. Break 5 YR 7/6, slip 5 YR 4/4.
80. Rim. 59/6/00/OM. Break 1 FG 4/N, slip 10 YR 6/4.
81. Rim. 41/79/OM. Fine-grained fabric. Break red, slip dark red.
82. Rim. 65/79/OM. Fine-grained fabric. Break pinkish, slip red.
83. Rim. 40/9/00/OM. Slightly worn slip. Break 7 YR 6/6, slip 7 YR 7/6.
84. Rim. 134/5/00/OM. Break 5 YR 6/6, slip 2.5 R 6/8.
85. Rim with horizontal grooves. 148/2/00/OM. Soft, fine-grained fabric, compact; opalescent inner surface. Break 5 YR 7/6, slip 5 YR 6/6.
86. Rim. 24/1/00/OM. Break 7.5 YR 8/4, slip 5 YR 6/4.
87. Rim with traces of two handles. 4/6/00/OM. Rather porous. Break 7.5 YR 8/4, slip 5 YR 6/6.
88. Rim with horizontal grooves. 134/2/00/OM. Fabric tempered with sherd. Break 5 YR 7/6, slip 10 R 5/6.
89. Upper part. 37/1/00/OM. Slightly porous. Break 2.5 YR 6/6, slip 10 R 6/8.
90. Rim. 150/1/00/OM. Very worn slip. Break 5 YR 6/6, slip 5 YR 7/4.
91. Rim. 7/2/14m/OM. Break and surface 10 R 5/3
92. Rim with a handle. 37/8/00/OM. Slightly porous. Break 2.5 YR 5/8, slip 2.5 YR 5/6.

Pl. V. Pottery finds from Area B

Pl. VI. Pottery finds from Area B

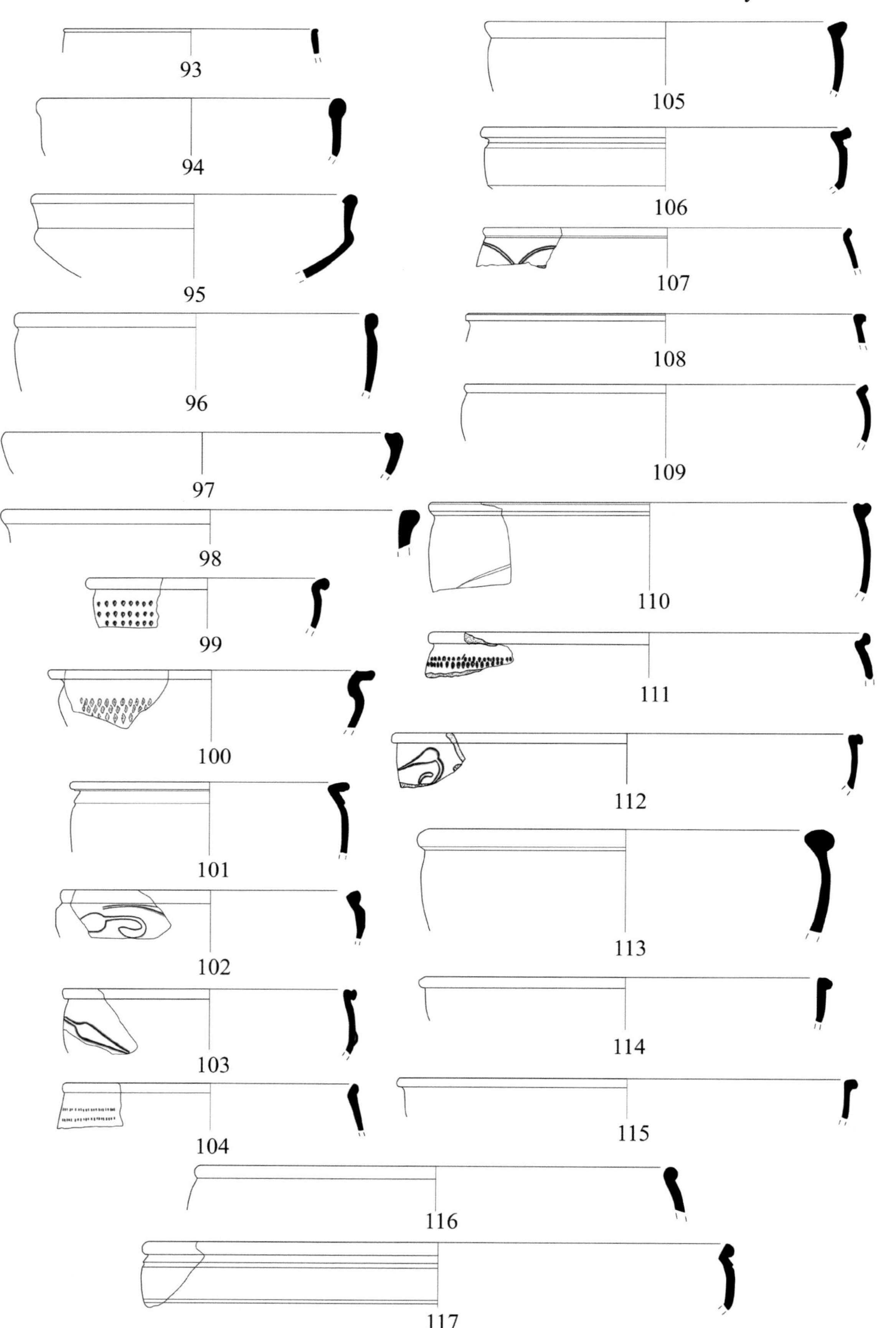

Pl. VI. Pottery finds from Area B – Ostrite Mogili

Wares XI/XII (local tableware). Bowls

93. Rim. 31/9/00/OM. Slightly porous. Break 5 YR 6/4, slip 2.5 YR 4/8.
94. Rim. 146/3/00/OM. Slightly porous. Break 2.5 YR 6/8, slip 2.5 YR 4/8.
95. Rim. 168/1/00/OM. Break 5 YR 6/4, slip 2.5 YR 4/8.
96. Rim. 59/2/00/OM. Fabric without visible inclusions, slightly porous. Break 5 YR 4/6, slip 5 YR 5/6.
97. Rim. 146/2/00/OM. Break 2.5 YR, slip 7.5 YR 7/3.
98. Rim. 88/6/00/OM. Break 10 YR 7/4, slip 2.5 YR 5/8.
99. Rim with incised decoration in the form of singular ovals. 21/2/00/OM. Abundant small-sized silver mica flakes. Break 5 YR 6/8, slip 5 YR 5/8.
100. Rim decorated with three rows of incised ovals. 167/1/00/OM. Break 7.5 YR 6/6, slip 7.5 YR 6/8.
101. Rim with a body. 104/1/00/OM. Break 5 YR 6/6, slip 2.5 YR 4/8.
102. Rim. 9/11/14m/OM. Break 7.5 YR 6/6, slip 7.5 YR 6/8.
103. Rim with a body decorated in the *en barbotine* technique. 13/7/00/OM. Break 5 YR 6/6, 2.5 YR 5/8. *Published:* Tomas 2006, cat. no. 15, fig. 14.3.
104. Rim with incised decoration in the form of two rows of short vertical lines. 111/1/00/OM. Break 5 YR 5/6, slip 2.5 YR 5/8.
105. Rim. 147/2/00/OM. Break 5 YR 6/8, slip 5 YR 5/8.
106. Rim. 21/1/13m/00/OM. Break 7.5 YR 6/6, slip 7.5 YR 6/8.
107. Rim decorated in the *en barbotine* technique. 43/79/OM. Break and slip light red.
108. Rim. 55/79/OM. Fine-grained fabric. Break pinkish, inner slip orange-red, outer slip red-brownish.
109. Rim. 9/12/14m/OM. Break 7.5 YR 6/6, slip 7.5 YR 6/8.
110. Rim decorated in the *en barbotine* technique. 47/79/OM. Fine-grained fabric. Break pinkish, inner slip red, outer slip dark reddish.
111. Rim with incised decoration in form of two rows of ovals. 40/79/OM. Fine-grained fabric, opalescent slip. Break red, slip dark red.
112. Rim decorated in the *en barbotine* technique. 49/79/OM. Fine-grained fabric. Break pinkish, inner slip dark orange, outer slip dark brownish.
113. Rim. Break 7.5 YR 6/6, slip 7.5 YR 6/8.
114. Rim. 70/8/00/OM. Break 5 YR 7/4, slip 2.5 YR 5/8.
115. Rim. 12/4/00/OM. Break 5 YR 6/6, slip 5 YR 5/8.
116. Rim. 145/2/00/OM. Break 5 YR 5/4, outer slip 7.5 YR 4/4 – 5/4, inner slip 5 YR 4/6.
117. Rim decorated in the *en barbotine* technique. 45/79/OM. Opalescent slip. Break and slip orange-reddish.

Pl. VII. Area B - Ostrite Mogili

Wares XI/XII (local tableware). Bowls

118. Rim. 56/79/OM. Fine-grained fabric, shiny slip. Break light brownish, slip brownish.
119. Rim. 59/79/OM. Fine-grained fabric, opalescent slip. Break orange-reddish, slip dark brownish.
120. Rim decorated with the *en barbotine* technique. 4/7/00/OM. Break 7.5 R 6/4, slip 10 R 5/8. *Published:* Tomas 2006, cat. no. 16, fig. 14.4.
121. Rim. 34/79/OM. Fine-grained fabric, opalescent slip. Break light orange-reddish, slip red.
122. Rim. 40/6/00/OM. Slightly worn slip. Break 5 YR 6/6, slip 2.5 YR 4/6.
123. Rim. 70/9/00/OM. Break 2.5 YR 6/4, slip 2.5 YR 5/6.
124. Rim. 37/79/OM. Fine-grained fabric, inner slip opalescent. Break pinkish, inner slip red, outer slip dark red.
125. Rim. 61/79/OM. Fine-grained fabric. Break pinkish, slip orange-reddish.
126. Rim. 96/1/00/OM. Break 5 YR 6/6, slip 2.5 YR 6/8.
127. Rim. 160/2/00/OM. Slightly porous. Break 7.5 YR 7/6, slip 2.5 YR 6/8.
128. Rim. 38/79/OM. Fine-grained fabric. Break light-brownish, slip dark brown.
129. Rim. 58/79/OM. Fine-grained fabric, shiny slip. Break and slip orange-red.
130. Rim. 136/4/00/OM. Slightly porous; smooth surface, slightly worn slip. Break 7.5 R 7/4, slip 5 YR 5/4.
131. Rim. 3/6/00/OM. Slightly worn slip. Break 5 YR 6/6, slip 10 R 5/6.
132. Rim. 1/1/00/OM. Slightly worn fabric. Break 5 YR 6/6, slip 5 YR 5/6 – 3/4.
133. Rim. 45/3/00/OM. Porous, without slip. Break and surface 2.5 Y 8/3.
134. Rim. 70/1/00/OM. Break 10 YR 7/4, slip 5 YR 5/8.
135. Rim. 70/6/00/OM. Slightly porous. Break 7.5 YR 6/4, slip 2.5 YR 6/8.
136. Rim. 133/79/OM. Fine-grained fabric. Break pinkish, slip reddish.

Pl. VIII. Pottery finds from Area B – Ostrite Mogili

Wares XI/XII (local tableware). Bowls

137. Rim. 137/3/00/OM. Fabric tempered with small-sized crushed sherds. Break 5 YR 5/3, slip 5 YR 5/2.
138. Rim. 123/1/00/OM. Fabric without visible inclusions; surface smooth and shiny. Break 2.5 YR 7/4, slip 2.5 YR 5/8.
139. Rim. 18/5/00/OM. Fabric without visible inclusions. Break 10 YR 5/3, slip 5 YR 5/3.
140. Rim decorated with horizontal grooves. 101/7/00/OM. Slightly porous. Break and slip 7.5 YR 8/4.
141. Rim. 57/2/00/OM. Fabric without visible inclusions. Break 2.5 YR 6/8, slip 2.5 YR 5/8.
142. Rim. 73/3/00/OM. Compact. Break 7.5 YR 7/4, slip 2.5 YR 6/8.
143. Rim. 57/1/00/OM. Fabric without visible inclusions. Break 2.5 YR 6/4, slip 5 YR 4/4 – 2.5 YR 5/8.
144. Rim. 5/8/14m/OM. Fabric soft, slightly porous; powdery surface. Break 5 YR 7/1, surface 5 YR 6/6.

Pl. VII. Pottery finds from Area B

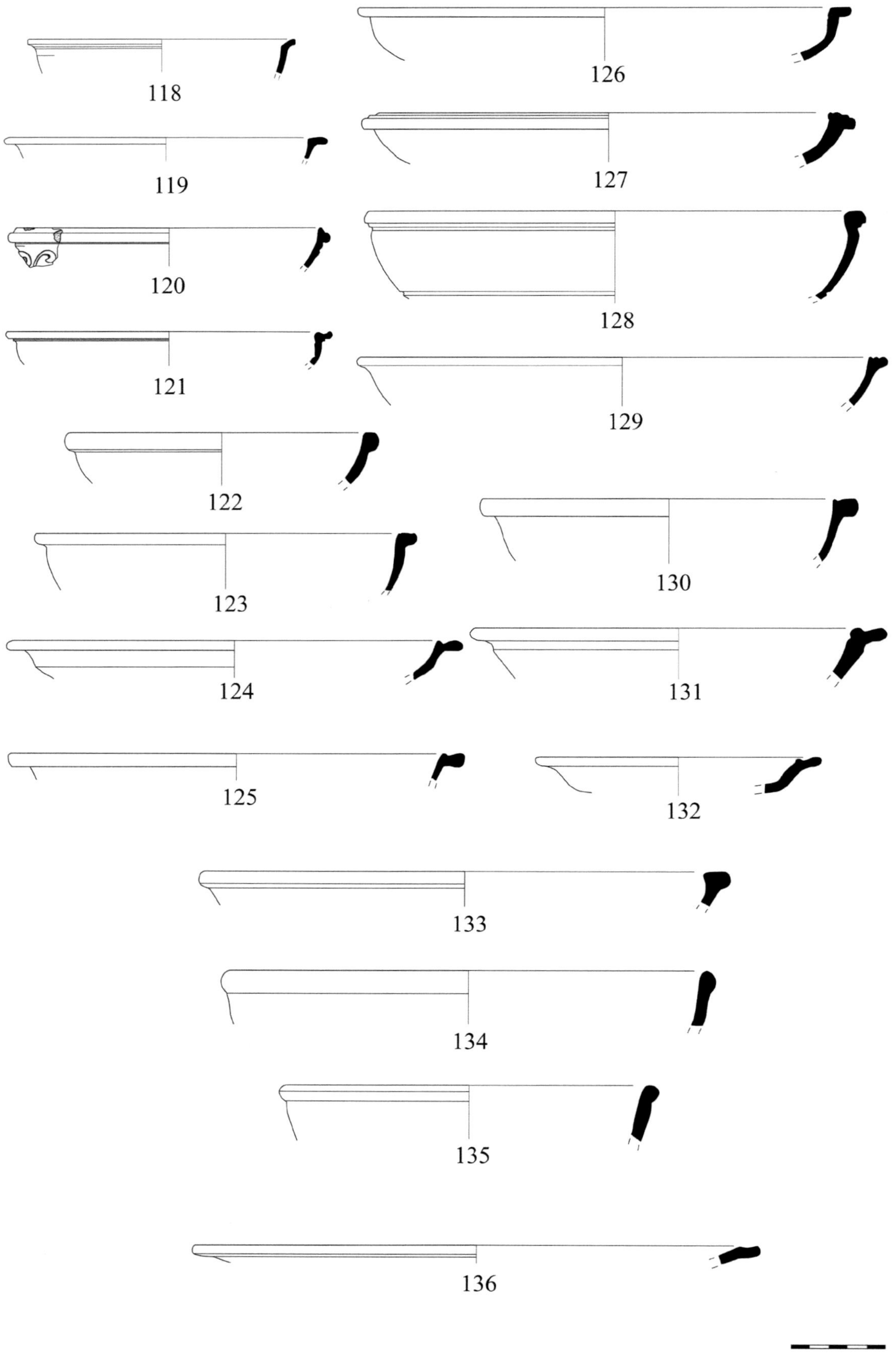

118

126

119

127

120

128

121

129

122

130

123

104

124

131

125

132

133

134

135

136

Pl. VIII. Pottery finds from Area B

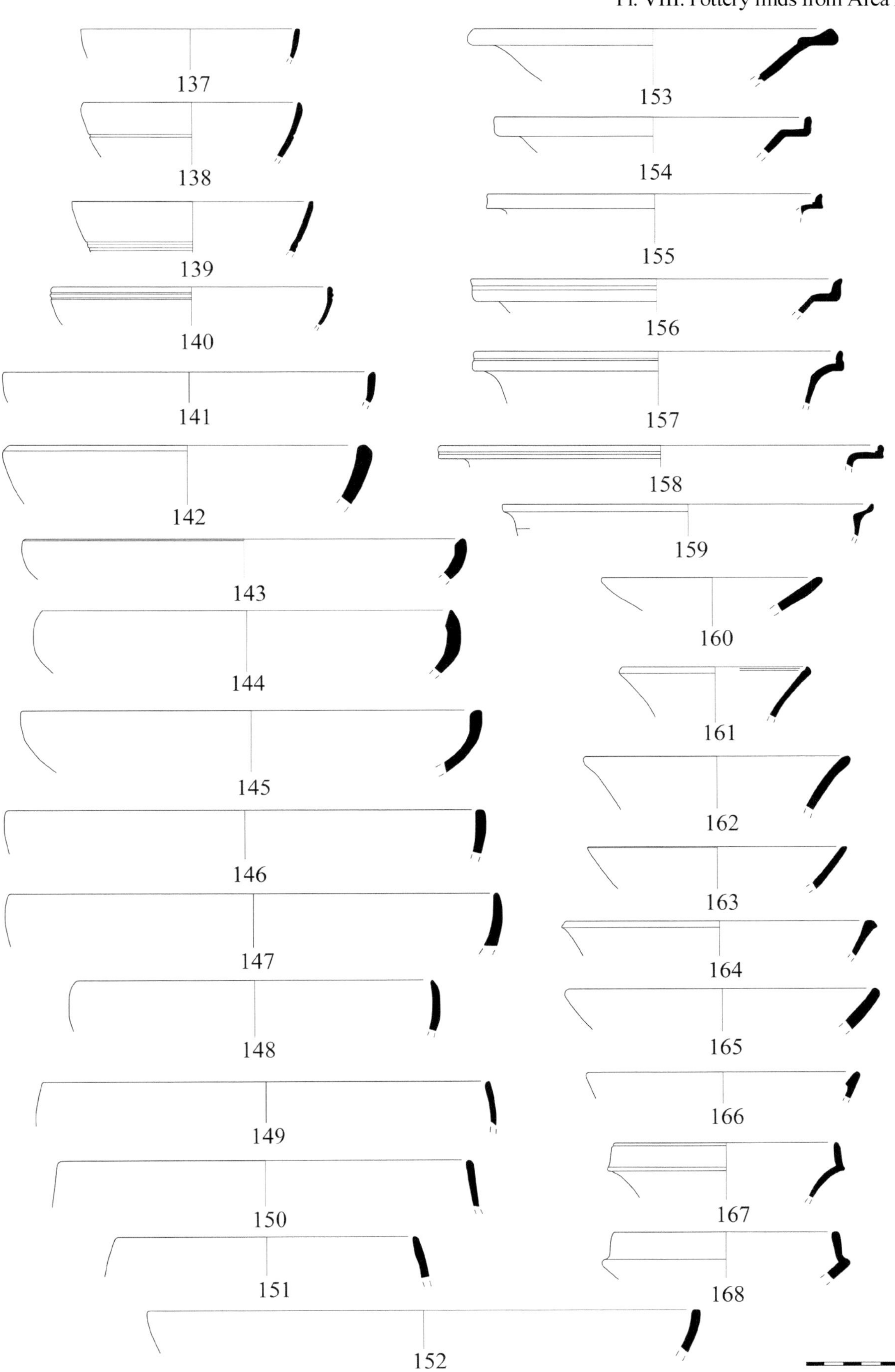

Pl. IX. Pottery finds from Area B

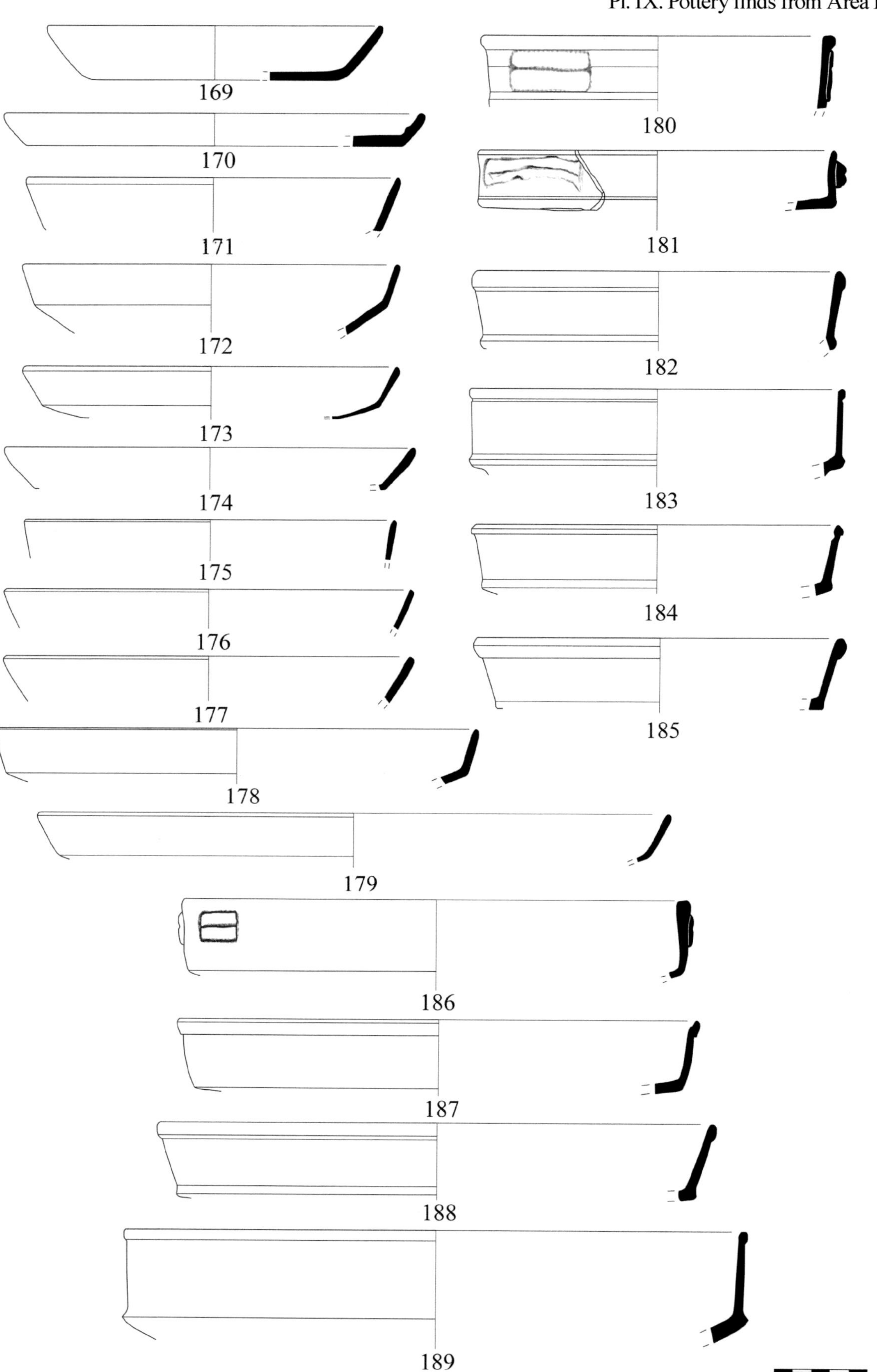

145. Rim. 101/4/00/OM. Fabric slightly porous. Break 5 YR 6/6, slip 2.5 YR 6/8.
146. Rim. 96/2/00/OM. Fabric slightly porous. Break 5 YR 6/8, slip 2.5 YR 5/8.
147. Rim. 93/2/00/OM. Break 5 YR 5/6, slip 2.5 YR 4/8.
148. Rim. 5/11/14m/OM. Break 2.5 YR 5/8 – 6/8, slip 2.5 YR 4/8.
149. Rim. 141/6/00/OM. Break 2.5 YR 5/8, slip 2.5 YR 5/6.
150. Rim. 32/8/00/OM. Break 2.5 YR 5/8, slip 5 YR 5/8.
151. Rim. 58/3/00/OM. Break 5 YR 5/3, slip 2.5 YR 5/8.
152. Rim. 145/3/00/OM. Break 2.5 YR 5/8 – 6/8, inner slip 2.5 YR 5/8, outer slip 2.5 YR 5/8 – 3/6.
153. Rim. 151/5/00/OM. Slightly porous. Break 2.5 YR 5/6, slip 2.5 YR 5/8.
154. Rim. 1/3/00/OM. Slightly worn slip. Break 5 YR 6/4, slip 5 YR 7/8.
155. Rim. 21/4/13m/OM. Break 7.5 YR 6/8, slip 5 YR 7/8.
156. Rim 18/4/00/OM. Break 2.5 YR 6/6, slip 2.5 YR 4/8.
157. Rim. 96/3/00/OM. Break 5 YR 6/6, slip 2.5 YR 4/4.
158. Rim. 57/79/OM. Fine-grained fabric, slightly shiny slip. Break red, slip orange-reddish.
159. Rim. 53/79/OM. Fine-grained fabric. Break pinkish, slip orange-reddish.
160. Rim. 49/1/00/OM. Slightly porous. Break 7.5 YR 6/4, slip 10 YR 7/3.
161. Rim. 11/1/13m/OM. Break 7.5 YR 6/8, slip 5 YR 7/8.
162. Rim. 104/5/00/OM. Opalescent slip. Break 7.5 YR 7/4, slip 7.5 YR 5/4.
163. Rim. 67/2/00/OM. Break and slip 7.5 YR 5/4.
164. Rim. 68/4A/00/OM. Smooth surface. Break 5 YR 6/8, slip 2.5 YR 5/8.
165. Rim. 44/9/00/OM. Break and slip 10 R 5/6.
166. Rim. 39/3/00/OM. Smooth surface without slip. Break and surface 5 YR 6/6.
167. Rim. 5/7/14m/OM. Break 10 YR 5/3, slip 5 YR 5/3.
168. Rim. 160/6/00/OM. Fabric without visible inclusions. Break and slip 2.5 YR 4/8.

Pl. IX. Pottery finds from Area B – Ostrite Mogili

Wares XI/XII (local tableware). Plates and dishes

169. Fragment of a vessel. 21/7/00/OM. Shiny slip with discolorations. Break 7.5 YR 6/3, slip 2.5 YR 5/6 – 6/6.
170. Fragment of a vessel. 12/7/00/OM. Uneven inner surface. Break 7.5 YR 6/6, slip 2.5 YR 6/8.
171. Rim. 10/d1/00/OM. Opalescent surface. Break 10 YR 6/3, slip 2.5 YR 6/8.
172. Rim. 73/4/00/OM. Break 7.5 YR 6/3, slip 2.5 YR 5/6.
173. Rim. 5/d1/00/OM. Smooth and opalescent surface. Break 7.5 YR 6/3, slip 2.5 YR 4/6.
174. Rim. 75/79/OM. Fine-grained fabric. Break pinkish, slip red-brownish.
175. Rim. 134/6/00/OM. Break 2.5 YR 6/6, slip 2.5 YR 4/8.
176. Rim. 101/6/00/OM. Break 2.5 YR 6/6, slip 2.5 YR 4/8.
177. Rim. 67/3/00/OM. Break 10 R 5/8, slip 10 R 6/8.
178. Rim. 134/8/00/OM. Shiny slip. Break 2.5 YR 7/6, slip 2.5 YR 5/8.
179. Rim. 39/79/OM. Fine-grained fabric. Break pinkish, slip reddish.
180. Rim decorated with a horizontal applique. 152/2A/00/OM. Fabric with no visible inclusions. Break 5 YR 6/4, slip 2.5 YR 5/8.
181. Rim decorated with a horizontal applique. 2/2/13m/OM. Break and slip 2.5 YR 6/8.
182. Rim. 70/7/00/OM. Break 2.5 YR 6/6, slip 2.5 YR 5/8.
183. Rim. 21/3/13m. Break 2.5 YR 6/6, slip 2.5 YR 5/8.
184. Rim. 50/79/OM. Fine-grained fabric, slightly opalescent slip. Break and slip red.
185. Rim. 148/6/00/OM. Break 5 YR 7/4, slip 5 YR 5/3.
186. Rim decorated with a horizontal applique. 18/6/00/OM. Worn slip. Break 2.5 YR 6/6, slip 5 YR 6/8.
187. Rim. 69/79/OM. Fine-grained fabric. Break pinkish, inner slip orange-reddish, outer slip dark orange-reddish.
188. Rim. 24/2/00/OM. Shiny slip. Break 2.5 YR 6/6, slip 2.5 YR 5/8.
189. Rim. 5/1/14m/OM. Break 2.5 YR 6/8.

Pl. X. Pottery finds from Area B – Ostrite Mogili

Wares XI/XII (local tableware). Plates, dishes and other vessels

190. Rim. 101/3/00/OM. Break 2.5 YR 5/8, slip 2.5 YR 5/6.
191. Rim. 10/7/00/OM. Break 2.5 YR 6/6, slip 2.5 YR 5/8.
192. Everted rim decorated with two rows of incised semi-ovals. 48/79/OM. Fine-grained fabric. Break orange, slip orange-reddish.
193. Fragment of a vessel with an everted rim, decorated with a row of incised vertical lines. 101/9/00/OM. Matt surface. Break 5 YR 6/6, slip 2.5 YR 6/6.
194. Rim. 1/2/00/OM. Slightly porous; worn slip. Break 5 YR 6/6, slip 5 YR 5/8.
195. Rim. 12/6/00/OM. Break 5 YR 6/4, slip 5 YR 5/3 – 6/8.
196. Rim. 31/6/00/OM. Break and slip 2.5 YR 5/8.
197. Rim. 5/2/14m/OM. Break 7.5 YR 6/6, slip 7.5 YR 6/8.
198. Everted rim decorated with a row of incised ovals and round appliqués. 127/5/00/OM. Matt surface. Break 7.5 YR 6/4, slip 7.5 YR 7/4.
199. Rim with a relief decoration. 104/2/00/OM. Break 5 YR 7/8, slip 2.5 YR 6/8.
200. Rim with a relief decoration. 157/1/00/OM. Break 5 YR 7/4, worn slip 5 YR 6/8.
201. Bottom with a foot. 73/6/00/OM. Break 5 YR 6/4, slip 2.5 YR 5/8.
202. Bottom with a foot. 125/2/00/OM. Smooth surface. Break 2.5 YR 4/8, slip 2.5 YR 7/6.
203. Bottom with a foot. 71/8A/00/OM. Break 5 YR 6/6, slip 2.5 YR 5/8.
204. Bottom with a foot. 134/1/00/OM. Break two-coloured, core 2 FG 5/10G, inner and outer sides 2.5 YR 4/3, surface 5 YR 6/4.

Pl. X. Pottery finds from Area B

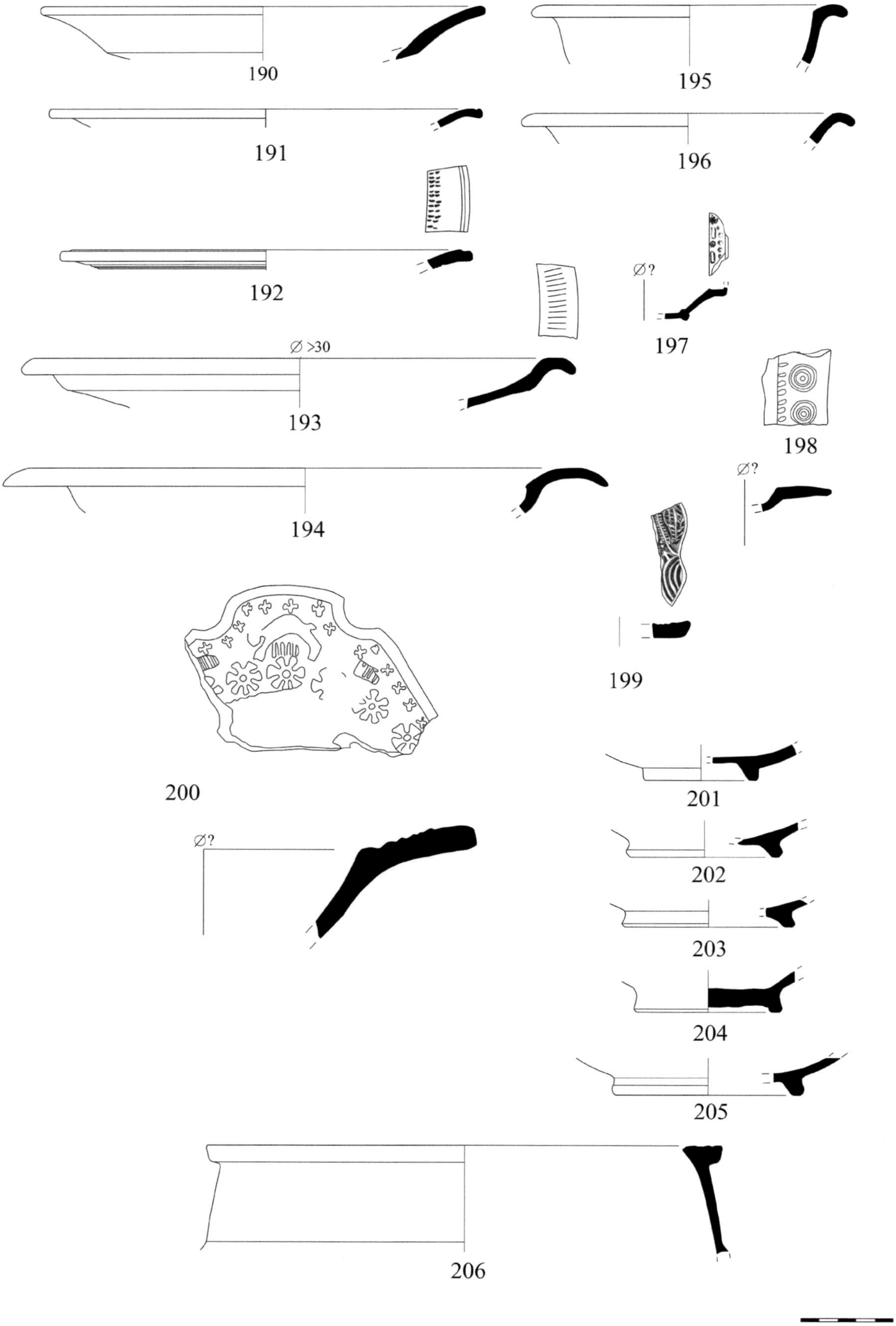

190

195

191

196

192

Ø?

197

Ø >30

193

198

194

Ø?

199

200

Ø?

201

202

203

204

205

206

205. Bottom with a foot. 71/6A/00/OM. Break and slip 5 YR 6/4.
206. Rim. 18/3/00/OM. Slightly porous; worn slip. Break 5 YR 6/6, slip 5 YR 5/8.

Pl. XI. Pottery finds from Area B – Ostrite Mogili

Wares XI/XII (local tableware). Decorated flatware

207. Bottom decorated with two rows of incised lines. 67/8/00/OM. Break 2.5 YR 6/6, slip 5 YR 5/8.
208. Bottom decorated with one row of incised lines. 24/5/00/OM. Break 2.5 YR 6/6, slip 2.5 YR 6/8.
209. Bottom decorated with three rows of incised lines. 47/4/00/OM. Break 2.5 YR 6/4, slip 2.5 YR 5/6.
210. Bottom decorated with two rows of incised lines. 160/7/00/OM. Break 7.5 YR 6/4, slip 2.5 YR 4/3.
211. Bottom decorated with three rows of incised semi-ovals. 92/2/00/OM. Break 5 YR 6/6, slip 5 YR 5/6.
212. Bottom decorated with three rows of incised lines. 37/7/00/OM. Break 7.5 YR 7/4, slip 2.5 YR 5/4.
213. Bottom decorated with one row of incised irregular lines. 153/1/00/OM. Break 5 YR 6/4, slip 5 YR 6/8.
214. Bottom decorated with one row of incised vertical lines. 136/3/00/OM. Break 10 YR 7/2, slip 2.5 YR 4/6.
215. Bottom decorated with two rows of short incised vertical lines. 104/3/00/OM. Break 10 YR 6/1, slip 10 YR 4/2.
216. Bottom decorated with one row of incised semi-ovals. 12/d1/00/OM. Break 5 YR 6/6, slip 5 YR 5/8.
217. Bottom with a foot decorated with one row of incised irregular lines. 59/5/00/OM. Slightly porous; shiny slip on inner surface. Break 2.5 YR 6/3, slip 10 R 6/4.

Pl. XII. Pottery finds from Area B – Ostrite Mogili

Ware II (legionary tableware)

218. Bottom. 45/1/13m/OM. Slightly porous. Break 2.5 YR 6/8, surface 5 YR 6/8.

Ware III (legionary kitchenware)

219. Rim. 9/1/13m/OM. Break and surface 5 YR 5/1.
220. Rim. 5/18/14m/OM, Break and surface 10 YR 5/1.

Ware XIII (local kitchenware)

221. Rim. 159/2/00/OM. Fabric with abundant fine-grained sand. Break and surface GLEY 10 YR 4/1.
222. Rim. 64/79/OM. Fine-grained fabric. Break pinkish, slip red-brownish.
223. Rim. 30/3/00/OM. Break 7.5 YR 2.5/1, surface 2.5 Y 4/2. *Published:* Tomas 2006, cat. no. 21, fig. 14.9.
224. Rim. 30/10/00/OM. Rough surface. Break 2.5 YR 6/6, surface 2.5 YR 6/8.
225. Rim. 23/3/00/OM. Very porous. Break 2.5 Y 5/1.
226. Rim. 4/1/00/OM. Rough surface. Break 2.5 YR 5/6, surface 10 R 5/8.
227. Rim. 42/1/00/OM. Slightly porous. Break 10 YR 5/2, surface 5 YR 5/3.
228. Rim. 37/2/00/OM. Slightly porous. Break 1 FG 3/N.
229. Rim. 164/4/00/OM. Slightly porous. Break GLEY 10 YR 3/1, surface GLEY 1 2.5/N.
230. Rim with an incised decoration. 18/9/00/OM. Slightly porous. Break 5 YR 4/1, surface 7.5 YR 6/4.
231. Rim. 111/2/00/OM. Sparse, medium-sized lime particles, slightly porous. Break 7.5 YR 5/4, surface 1 FG 6/N.
232. Rim. 41/1/00/OM. Fabric tempered with coarse sand, slightly porous. Break 5 YR 7/3, surface 7.5 YR 7/4.
233. Rim. 127/4/00/OM. Sparse lime particles; porous. Break and surface 2.5 YR 6/6.
234. Rim. 1/9/13m/OM. Slightly porous. Break 7.5 YR 3/1 – 5 YR 6/4.
235. Rim. 18/10/00/OM. Slightly porous. Break 5 YR 4/1, surface 7.5 YR 6/4.
236. Rim. 141/5/00/OM. Slightly porous. Break 10 YR 6/2, surface 7.5 YR 7/6.
237. Rim. 21/4/00/OM. Fabric tempered with coarse sand, porous. Break and surface 7.5 YR 8/4.
238. Rim. 9/8/00/OM. Abundant small-sized silver mica flakes and sparse lime particles; slightly porous. Break 1 for GLEY 5/1, surface 5 YR 5/4.
239. Rim. 18/8/00/OM. Slightly porous. Break 7.5 YR 3/1 – 5 YR 6/6.

Pl. XIII. Pottery finds from Area B – Ostrite Mogili

Ware XIII (local kitchenware)

240. Rim. 40/7/00/OM. Break 10 YR 6/4, surface 10 YR 7/4.
241. Rim. 27/8/00/OM. Smooth surface. Break and surface 10 YR 5/1 – 5 YR 6/4.
242. Rim. 76/2/00/OM. Break and surface 10 YR 6/3 – 7/3.
243. Rim. 73/1/00/OM. Break 7.5 YR 8/3, surface 1 FG 4/N.
244. Rim. 2/79/OM. Fabric tempered with small amounts of medium-sized sand. Break and surface gray.
245. Rim. 31/3/00/OM. Fabric tempered with coarse sand. Break 10 YR 8/1, surface 10 YR 6/4.
246. Rim. 151/1/00/OM. Break 1 FG 6/10 Y, surface 5 YR 2.5/1.
247. Rim. 40/2/00/OM. Break 5 YR 6/8, surface 5 YR 6/6.
248. Rim. 22/2/00/OM. Porous. Break and surface 10 YR 6/4 – 3/1.
249. Rim. 168/3/00/OM. Break and surface 5 YR 6/6.
250. Rim. 27/4/00/OM. Break 5 YR 6/6, surface 5 YR 6/2.
251. Rim. 27/3/00/OM. Break 10 YR 8/4, surface 7.5 YR 7/8.
252. Rim. 7/7/14m/OM. Break and surface 5 YR 5/1.
253. Rim. 165/1/00/OM. Break and surface 7.5 YR 6/2.

Pl. XI. Pottery finds from Area B

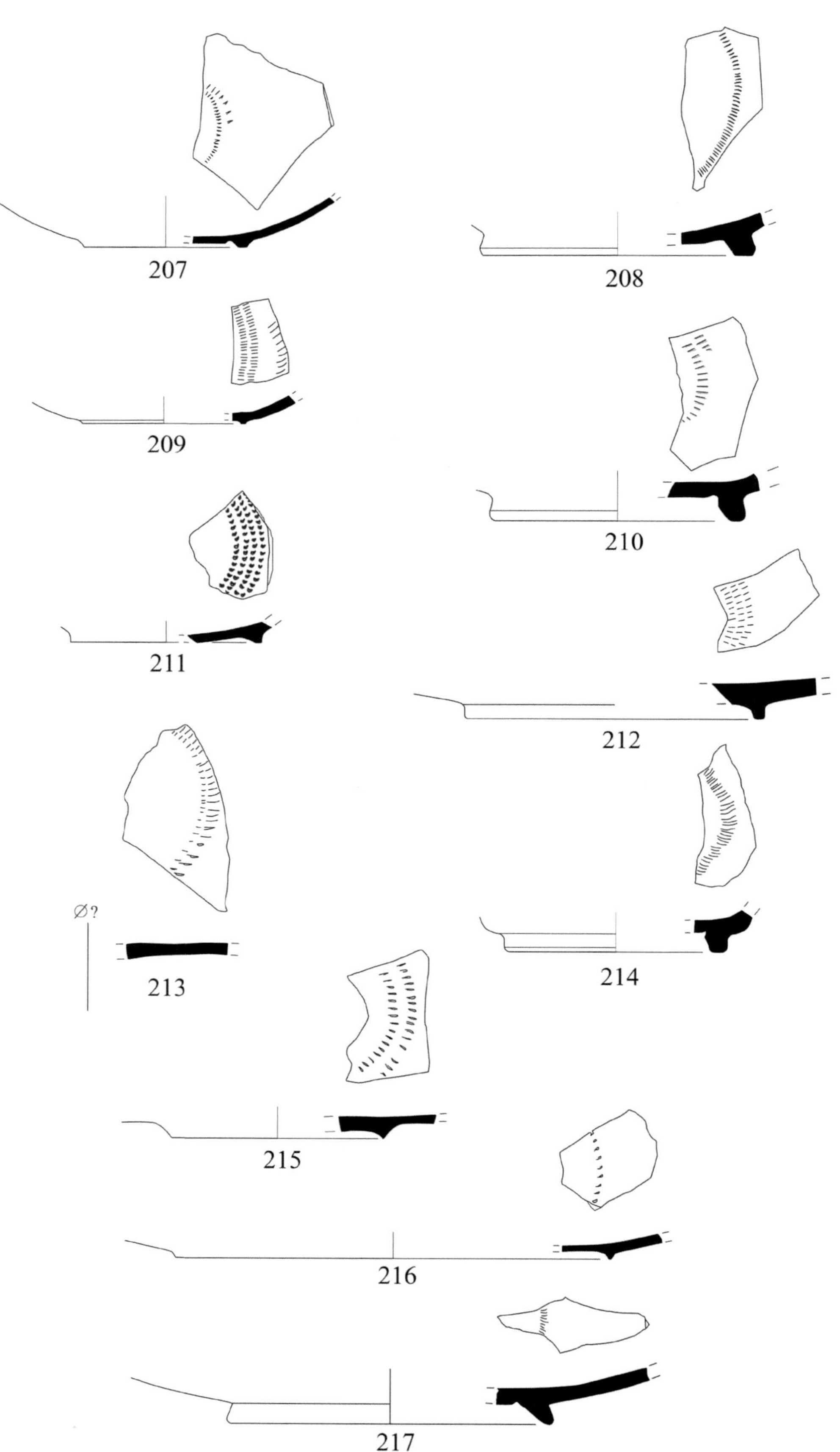

Pl. XII. Pottery finds from Area B

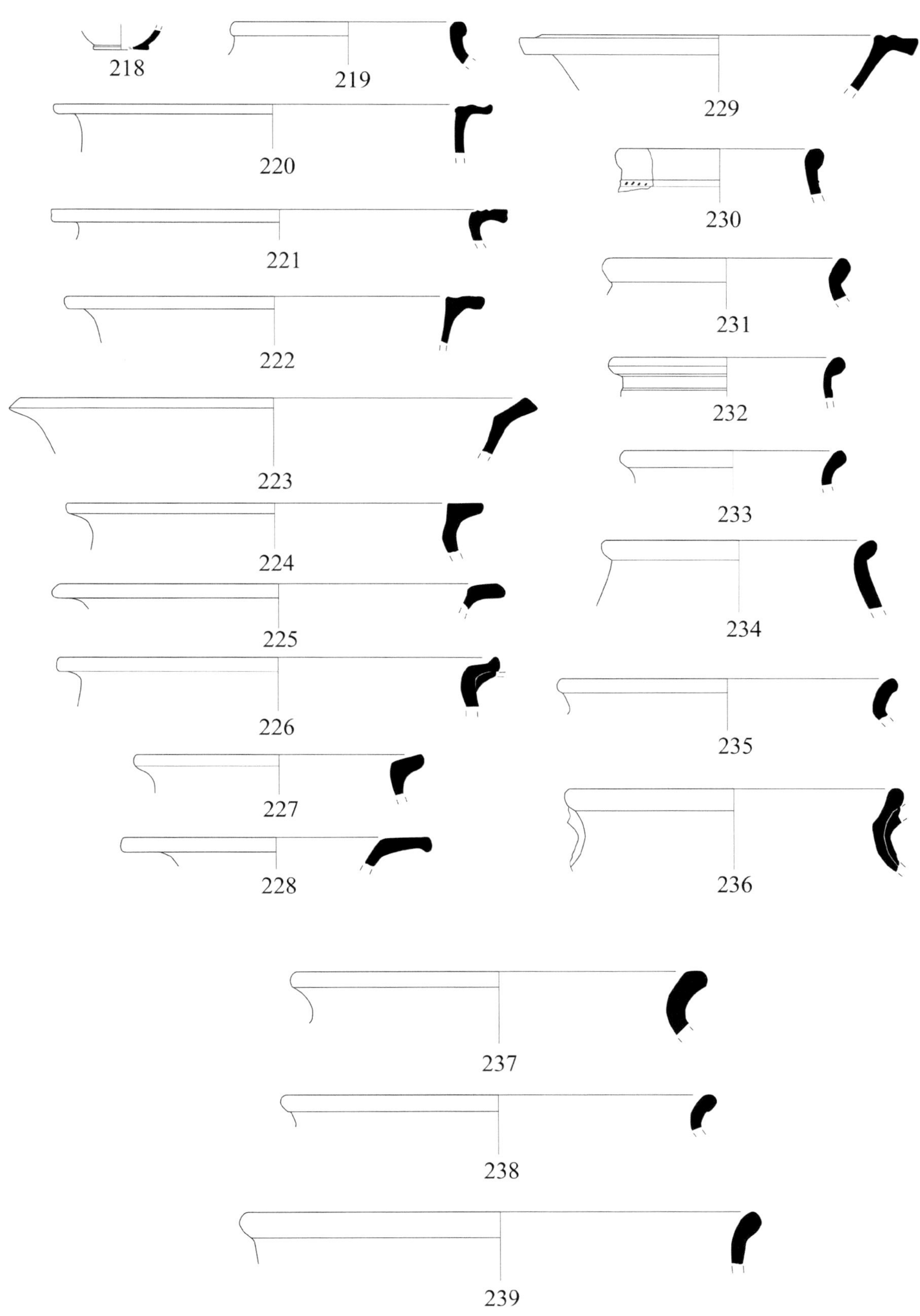

Pl. XIII. Pottery finds from Area B

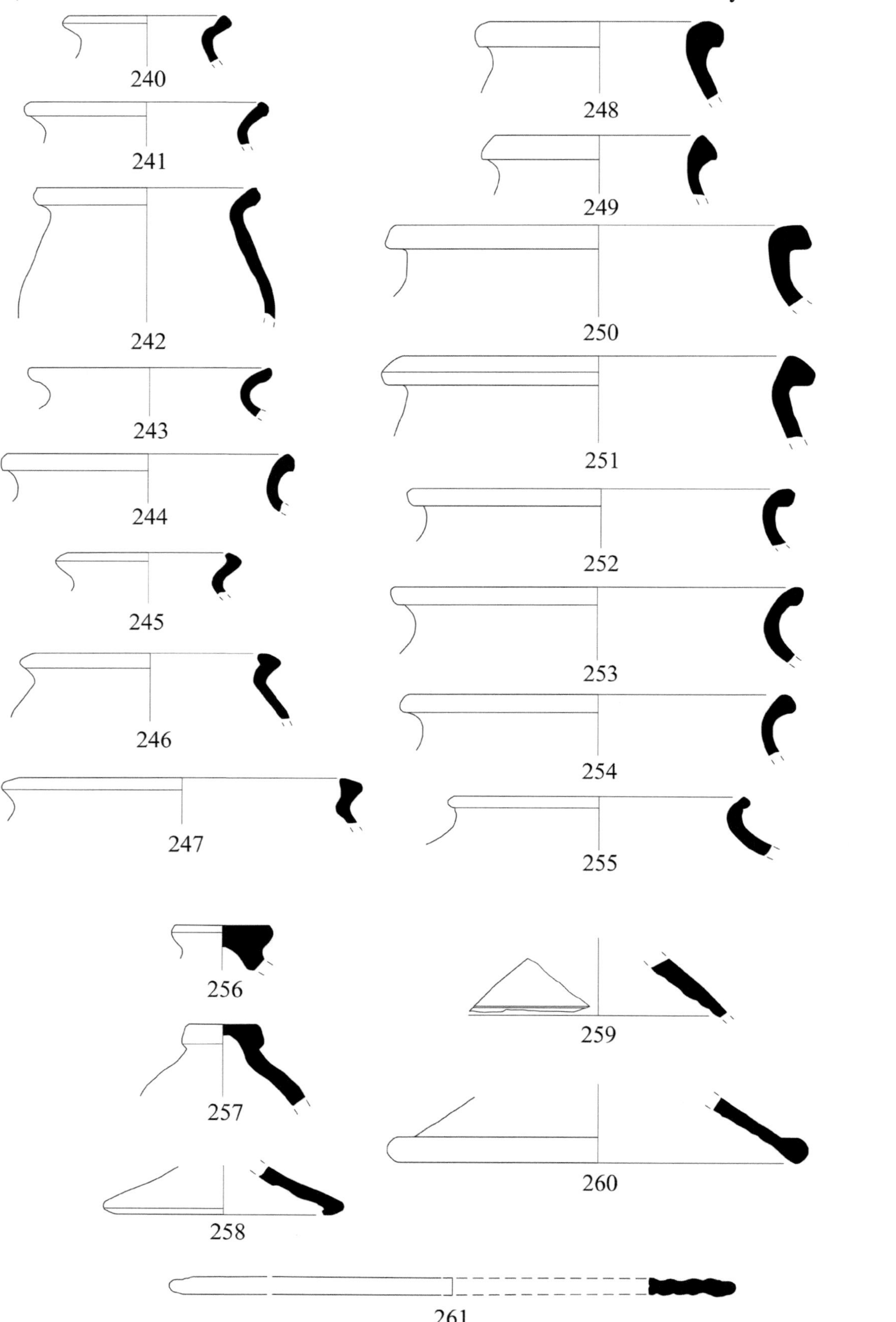

254. Rim. 5/12/14m/OM. Fabric tempered with coarse sand. Break 2.5 Y 2.5/1, surface 5 Y 6/3.
255. Rim. 68/3A/00/OM. Hand-made and wheel-turned. Fabric tempered with coarse sand with abundant lime particles and silver mica flakes. Break 2. Y 2.5/1, surface 5 Y 6/2.
256. Lid handle. 156/1/00/OM. Break and surface 10 YR 7/2.
257. Lid handle. 42/5/00/OM. Break and surface 5 YR 6/6.
258. Lid. 6/8/00/OM. Porous. Break and surface 10 YR 3/3.
259. Lid. 23/1/13m/OM. Powdery surface; traces of fire on the inner side. Break and surface 7.5 YR 5/1.
260. Lid. 6/1/14m/OM. Porous; rough surface with traces of repeated heating. Break and surface 5 YR 6/8.
261. Fragment of a cooking pot-pad. 60/3/00/OM. Fabric tempered with large amounts of fine-grained sand, porous; secondarily burned with fire. Break two-coloured 10 YR 8/9 and 10 YR 6/1.

Pl. XIV. Pottery finds from Area B – Ostrite Mogili

Ware XIII (local kitchenware. Bottoms)

262. Bottom. 71/4A/00/OM. Porous. Break 2.5 Y 5/2, surface 5 YR 6/6.
263. Bottom. 88/3/00/OM. Compact. Break and surface 10 YR 6/3.
264. Bottom. 131/9/00/OM. Fabric XIII with crushed sherds, porous. Break 5 Y 6/1, surface 7.5 YR 5/4.
265. Bottom. 6/9/00/OM. Sparse large lime particles, tempered with coarse sand with small stones, porous. Break 5 Y 6/2, surface 10 YR 5/2.
266. Bottom. 132/1/00/OM. Porous. Break 1 FG 5/N, surface 10 YR 5/3.
267. Bottom. 78/5/00/OM. Break 1 FG 5/5 GY, surface 7.5 YR 6/4.
268. Bottom. 130/2/00/OM. Porous. Break 2 FG 4/5B, surface 5 YR 6/6.
269. Bottom. 166/1/00/OM. Porous. Break 2 FG 3/5 PB, surface 2.5 Y 6/2.
270. Bottom. 15/9/00/OM. Break and surface 10 YR 6/1.
271. Bottom. 88/1/00/OM. Porous. Break 1 FG 5/N, surface 7.5 YR 6/4.
272. Bottom. 127/6/00/OM. Break 1 FG 6/10Y, surface 5 YR 6/6.
273. Bottom. 88/4/00/OM. Break 1 FG 7/10 Y, surface 5 YR 6/6.
274. Bottom. 88/2/00/OM. Porous. Break 1 FG 6/10 Y, surface 7.5 YR 6/3.
275. Bottom. 88/5/00/OM. Porous; Break 2 FG 6/10 B, surface 2.5 YR 5/6.
276. Bottom. 15/4/00/OM. Break 10YR 6/1, surface 5 YR 7/6.
277. Bottom. 127/8/00/OM. Break 1 FG 6/10 Y, surface 7.5 YR 5/4.
278. Fragment of a bowl. 140/3/00/ Break 10 R 5/6, surface 5 YR 6/6.

Wares XI/XII/XIII (Boutovo/Pavlikeni utility vessels)

279. Fragment of a mortarium. 138/4/00/OM. Hard fabric with a medium percentage of fine-grained sand, lime, slightly porous; rough surface. Break 2.5 Y 6/2.
280. Rim of a censer. 134/79/OM. Fabric tempered with small amounts of medium-sized sand, porous. Break light pinkish.
281. Rim of a mortarium. 154/1/00/OM. Hard fabric tempered with small amounts of fine-grained sand, slightly porous, smooth surface. Break 7.5 YR 6/3, surface 10 YR 6/6.
282. Bottom of a mortarium. 6/7/00/OM. Medium-hard fabric containing sparse small-sized lime particles and small-sized silver mica flakes, slightly porous. Break 5 YR 6/1 – 7/4.
283. Bottom of a mortarium. 13/1/00/OM. Medium-hard fabric containing sparse small-sized lime particles and small-sized silver mica flakes, slightly porous. Ware XI. Break 7.5 YR 4/1 – 7/4, slip 2.5 YR 5/4.
284. Rim of a mortarium with a spout. 118/1/00/OM. Medium-hard fabric containing medium-sized lime particles and small amounts of small-sized silver mica flakes, tempered with coarse sand with small stones, porous; rough surface. Break 2.5 Y 7/2 – 6/2, outer slip 5 YR 6/6, inner slip 7.5 YR 7/4.

Pl. XV. Pottery finds from Area B – Ostrite Mogili

Ware XVI (glazed pottery)

285. Rim. 125/4/00/OM. Well-sorted fabric with sparse silver mica flakes, compact. Break 1 FG 6/10 Y, glaze 10 YR 3/2.
286. Rim. 168/5/00/OM. Break 2.5 Y 7/1, glaze 2.5 Y 8/2.
287. Rim. 162/3/00/OM. Hard fabric without visible inclusions, rather dense; glazed surface. Break 5 R 4/2, glaze 2.5 YR 5/8.
288. Rim of a mortarium. 95/79/OM. Fabric tempered with coarse sand. Fabric light brownish, slip brownish-green.

Ware XVII (late Roman pottery)

289. Neck of a flask. 3/k1/00/OM. Abundant, small silver mica flakes; slightly rough surface. Break 5 Y 4/2, surface 5 Y 5/2.
290. Rim. 155/1/00/OM. Break 5 Y 6/1, surface 10 YR 6/4.
291. Rim. 1/5/00/OM. Hard fabric with a moderate quantity of small-sized silver mica flakes, tempered with large amounts of medium-sized sand containing black round particles (pyroxene?). Rather dense; rough surface. Break and surface 7.5 YR 6/1.

Unclassified kitchenware

292. Rim. 9/13/14m/OM. Break and surface 5 YR 6/1.
293. Rim. 47/3/00/OM. Compact. Break and surface 2.5 YR 6/6.
294. Rim. 42/2/00/OM. Break and surface 5 YR 6/6.

Pl. XIV. Pottery finds from Area B

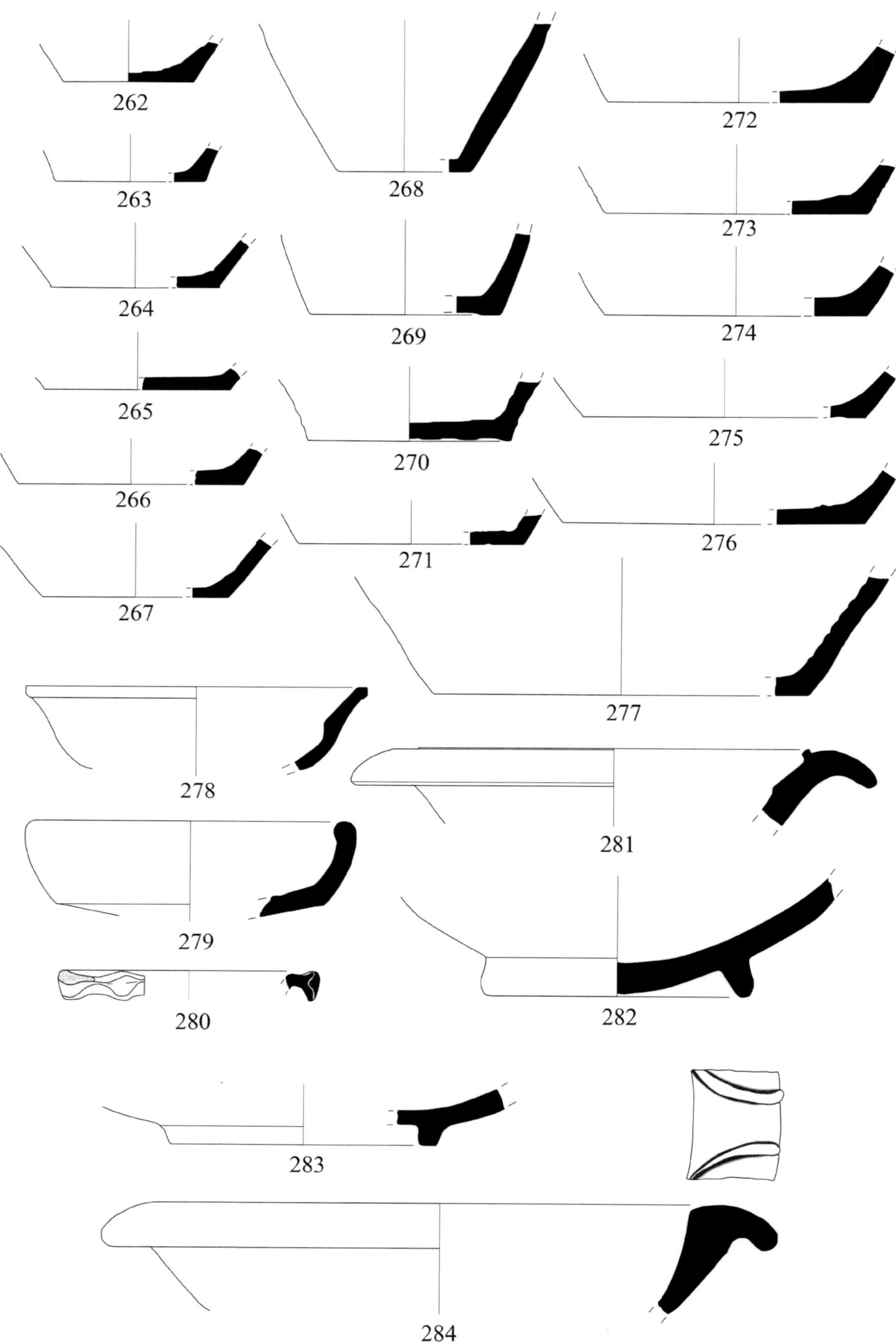

Pl. XV. Pottery finds from Area B

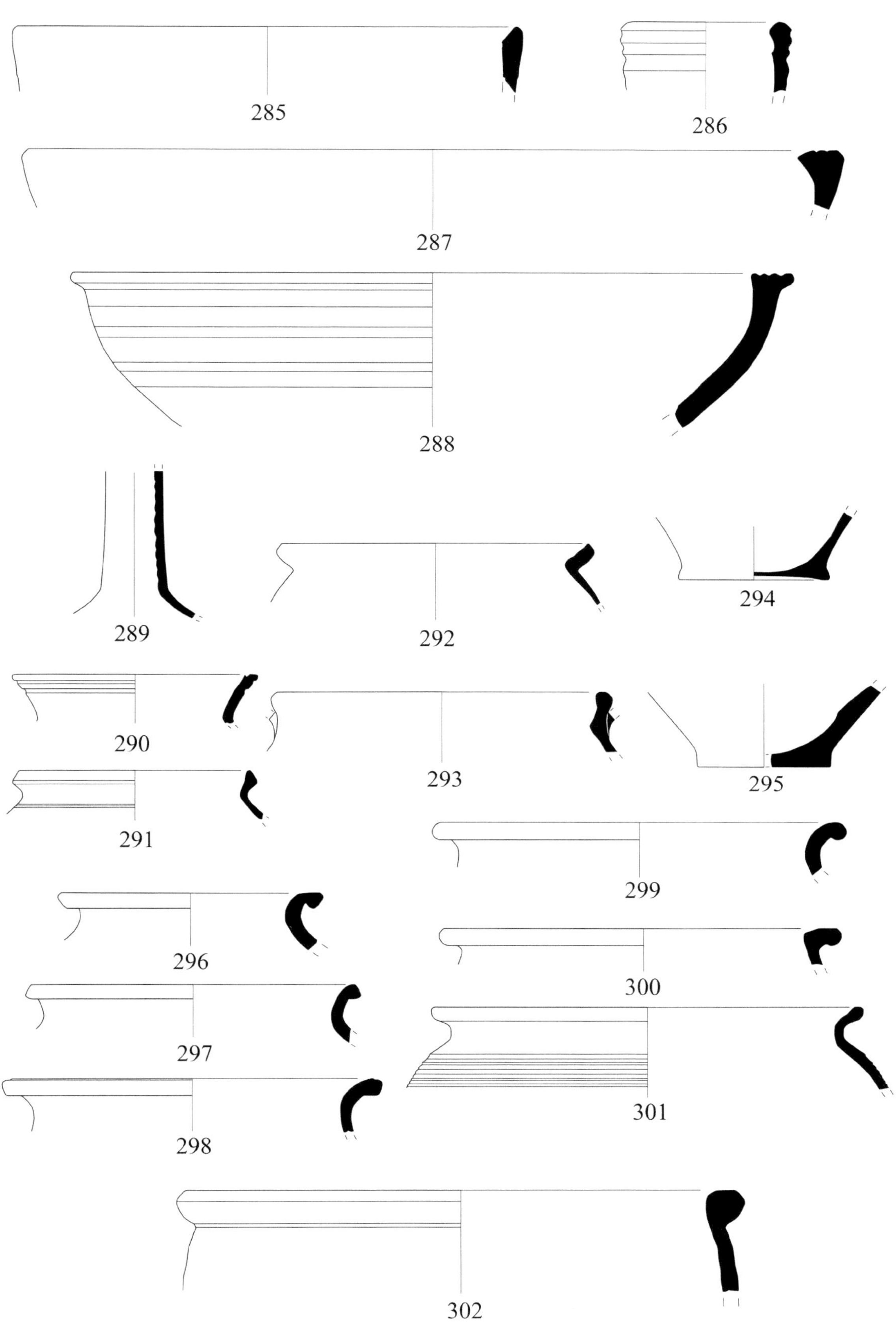

Pl. XVI. Pottery finds from Area B

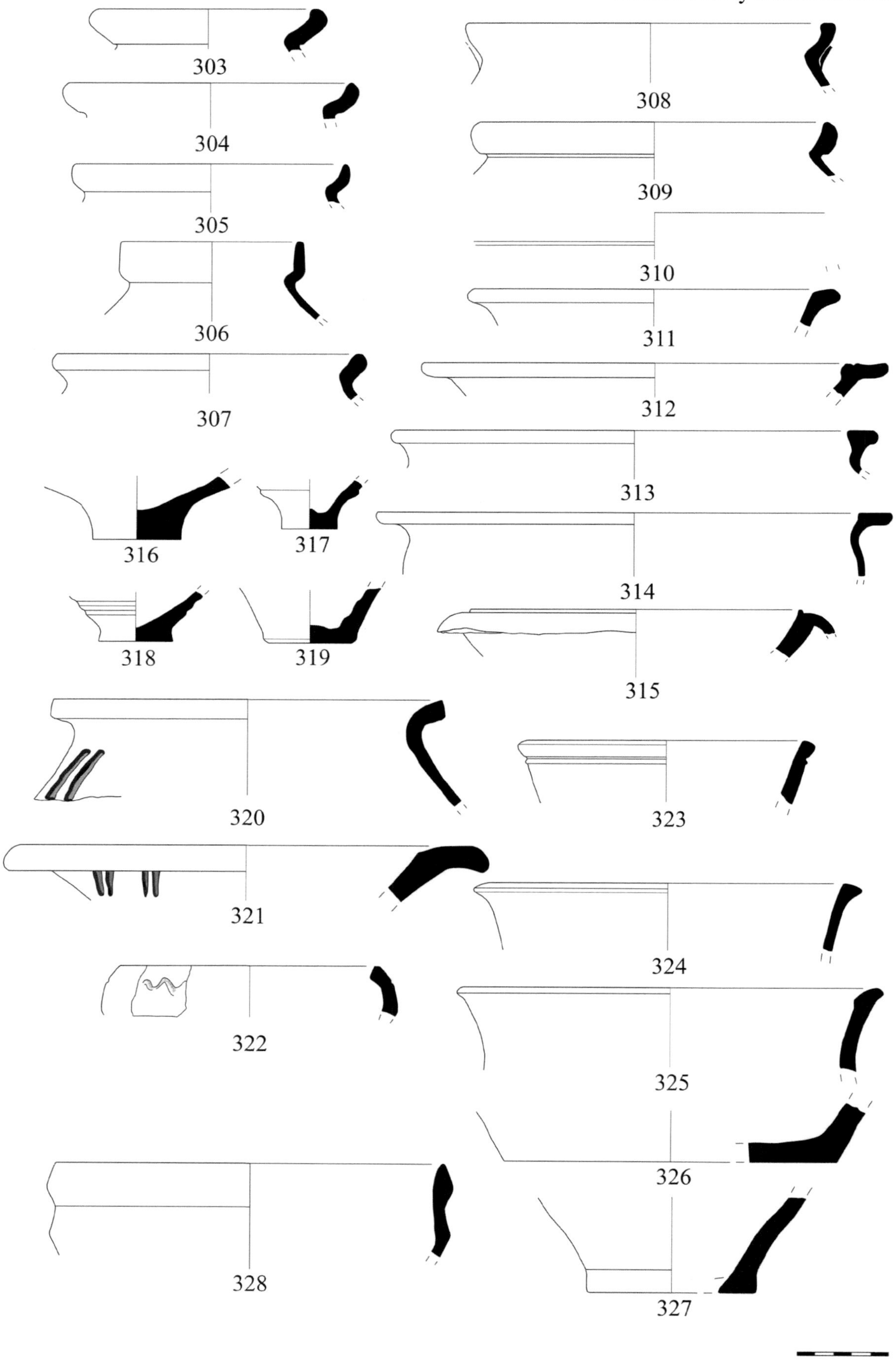

303
304
305
306
307
308
309
310
311
312
313
314
315
316
317
318
319
320
321
322
323
324
325
326
327
328

295. Bottom of a closed vessel. 18/7/00/OM. Break and surface 10 YR 7/4 – 2.5 YR 6/6Rim. 1/6/00/OM. Hard fabric with a moderate quantity of small-sized silver mica flakes, tempered with medium-sized sand containing black round particles (pyroxene?). Slightly porous; rough surface. Break and surface 5 YR 4/1 – 7/3.
296. Rim. 127/1/00/OM. Hard fabric with a moderate quantity of small-sized silver mica flakes, tempered with medium-sized sand containing black round particles (pyroxene?) and crushed sherds; slightly porous; rough surface. Break and surface 2 FG 3/10B – 7.5 YR 5/2.
297. Rim. 12/9/00/OM. Hard fabric with a moderate quantity of small-sized silver mica flakes, tempered with medium-sized sand containing black round particles (pyroxene?) and crushed sherds; slightly porous; rough surface. Break and surface 5 YR 4/1 – 7/3.
298. Rim. 6/1/00/OM. Hard fabric with a moderate quantity of small-sized silver mica flakes, tempered with medium-sized sand containing black round particles (pyroxene?) and sparse crushed sherds; slightly porous; rough surface. Break and surface 1 for GLEY 4/N.
299. Rim. 40/5/00/OM. Fabric with sparse medium-sized lime inclusions, tempered with medium-sized sand containing black round particles (pyroxene?), slightly porous; rough surface. Break 5 YR 5/8, surface 5 YR 6/6.
300. Rim 9/7/00/OM. Hard fabric with abundant small-sized silver mica flakes and lime particles, tempered with medium-sized sand with black round particles (pyroxene?); rather dense. Break 7.5 YR 5/1, surface 7.5 YR 6/4.
301. Rim of a storage vessel. 68/2A/00/OM. Hand-made and wheel-turned. Fabric with abundant small-sized silver mica flakes and medium-sized lime particles, tempered with large amounts of coarse sand; porous. Break 2.5 Y 2.5/1, surface 7.5 YR 6/4.
302. Rim of a storage vessel. 60/2A/00/OM. Wheel-turned. Fabric with small-sized silver mica flakes and medium-sized lime particles, tempered with small amounts of medium-sized sand; porous. Break 2.5 YR 2.5/1, surface 5 YR 6/6.

Pl. XVI. Pottery finds from Area B – Ostrite Mogili

Ware XIV (Lower Danube Kaolin Ware)

303. Rim. 27/6/00/OM. Break and surface 2.5 Y 8/2.
304. Rim. 10/1/14m/OM. Break and surface 2.5 Y 8/4.
305. Rim. 5/3/00/OM. Break and surface 2.5 Y 8/4.
306. Rim. 8/10/00/OM. Break and surface 2.5 Y 8/4.
307. Rim. 10/3/00/OM. Break and surface 10 YR 7/4 – 2.5 Y 7/1.
308. Rim. 13/3/00/OM. Break and surface 2.5 Y 7/3.
309. Rim. 5/5/14m/OM. Break and surface 2.5 Y 8/4.
310. Rim. 64/1/00/OM. Break and surface 10 YR 8/3.
311. Rim. 8/3/00/OM. Break and surface 10 YR 8/3 – 8/4.
312. Rim. 6/6/00/OM. Break 2.5 Y 3/1, surface 2.5 Y 7/2
313. Rim 1/4/00/OM. Break and surface 10 YR 8/4 – 10 YR 7/6.
314. Rim. 12/1/00/OM. Break and surface 2.5 Y 8/3.
315. Rim of a mortarium. 5/4/14m/OM. Break and surface 2.5 Y 8/4.
316. Bottom. 18/d1/00/OM. Break and surface 10 YR 8/3.
317. Bottom. 32/3/00/OM. Break and surface 10 YR 8/2.
318. Bottom. 50/6/00/OM. Break and surface 7.5 YR 8/4.
319. Bottom. 147/3/00/OM. Break and surface 10 YR 7/2 – 7/3.

Ware VI (ER burnished pottery)

320. Rim and upper part decorated with double vertical grooves. 109/1/00/OM. Break 5 YR 5/8, surface 5 YR 4/2.
321. Rim of a bowl with a burnished decoration. 112/4/00/OM. Break 1 FG 3/N, surface 5 YR 5/4.
322. Rim decorated with a grooved wave. 4/2/13m/OM. Break 1 FG 6/10Y, slip 10 Y 6/1.

Ware XV (LR burnished pottery)

323. Rim. 23/2/00/OM. Break and surface 2.5 Y 4/1.
324. Rim. 20/79/OM. Fabric tempered with small amounts of medium-sized sand. Break and surface gray.
325. Rim. 112/2/00/OM. Break 1 FG 6/10Y, surface 7.5 YR 5/2.
326. Bottom of an opened vessel. 9/1/00/OM. Outer surface coarse, inner surface smooth, burnished. Break and surface 2.5 Y 8/2.
327. Bottom of a closed vessel. 15/2/00/OM. Ware VI or XV. Break and surface 7.5 YR 7/6 – 10 YR 6/3.

Ware V (Orange burnished pottery)

328. Rim. 158/1/00/OM. Hard, fine-grained fabric without visible inclusions, compact, burnished surface. Fabric 10 YR 6/2, surface 2.5 YR 5/6.

Pl. XVII. Pottery finds from Area B – Ostrite Mogili

The grave goods

1. Lid or an amphora stopper. GR/7/00/OM. Hard, fine-grained fabric with sparse small-sized lime particles; hand-made; smooth, powdery surface. Ware XI. Break 5 YR 6/2, surface 7.5 YR 7/1. *Not published.*
2. Bottom of a closed vessel. GR/8/00/OM. Very hard fabric with sparse small-sized lime particles; porous; rough surface. Ware XIII? Break and surface 5 Y 7/1. *Not published.*
3. Bottom of a closed vessel. GR/4/00/OM. Hard, sandy fabric with abundant tiny lime; porous; rough surface. Ware XIII? Break and surface 2.5 YR 7/1. *Published:* Tomas 2006, cat. no. 32, fig. 16.6.
4. Bottom of an opened vessel. GR/5/00/OM. Hard, well-sorted fabric without visible inclusions; rather

Pl. XVII. Grave goods from the grave in Area B

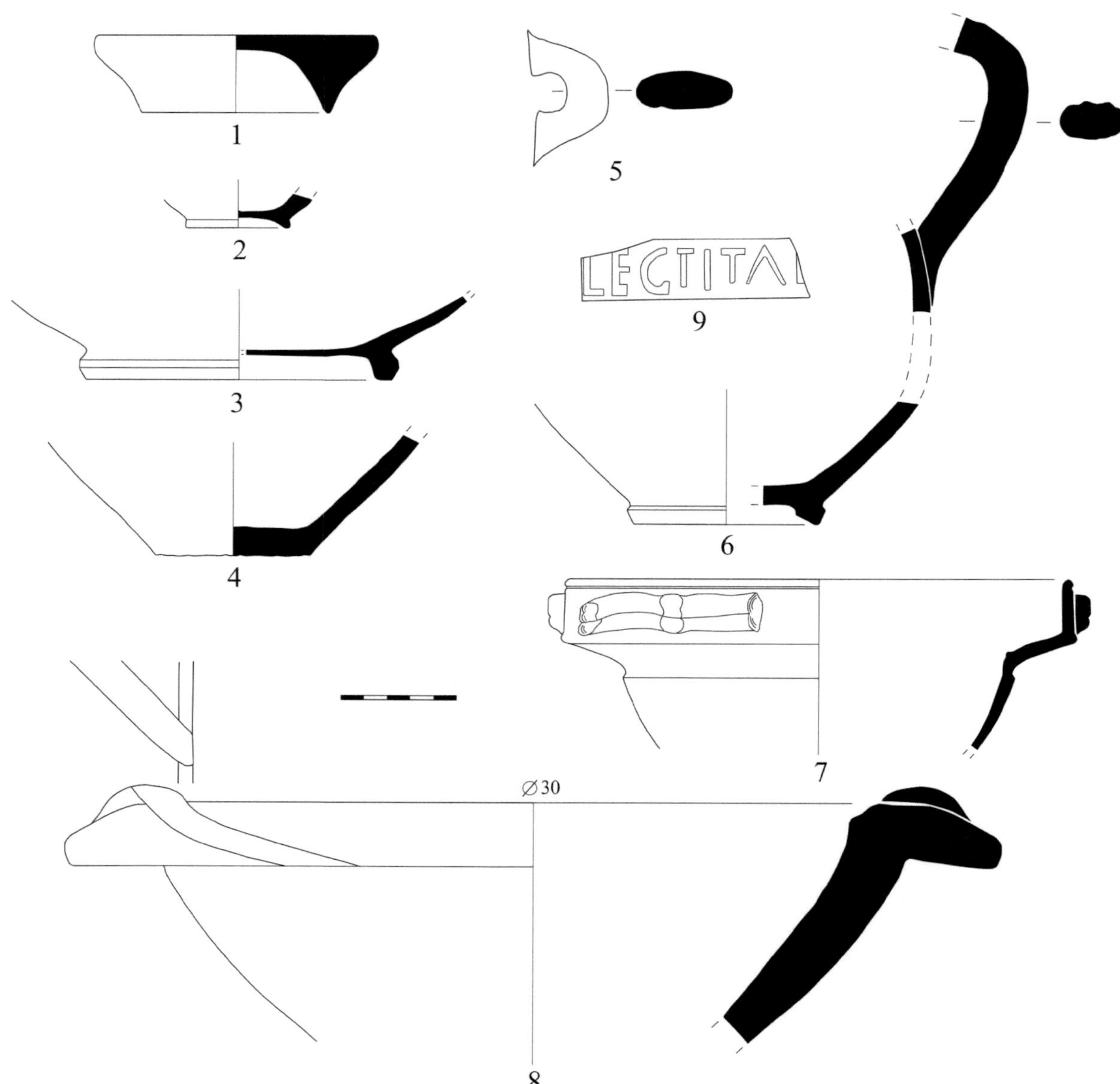

dense; matt coating inside. Ware XI/XII. Break and surface 7.5 YR 6/2. *Published:* Tomas 2006, cat. no. 33, fig. 16.5.

5. Fragment of a handle. GR/6/00/OM. Hard fabric with a moderate quantity of silver mica flakes and black round particles (pyroxene?), tempered with fine-grained sand and large amounts of crushed sherds; slightly porous; rough, but powdery surface. Break and surface 10 YR 6/4. *Not published.*
6. Two fragments of a jug. GR/3/00/OM. Worn slip. Ware XI/XII. Break 7.5 YR 7/3, slip 7.5 YR 6/4. *Published:* Tomas 2006, cat. no. 31, fig. 16.2.
7. Rim of a bowl with an applique decoration. GR/2/00/OM. Worn slip. Ware XI/XII. Break 7.5 YR 6/4, slip 7.5 YR 6/8. *Published:* Tomas 2006, cat. no. 30, Fig. 16.1.
8. Fragment of a mortarium. GR/1/00/OM. Hard fabric with an abundant quantity of mica flakes and sparse lime particles, tempered with coarse sand; porous; rough surface. Ware XIII. Fabric Break 7.5 YR 7/3. *Published:* Tomas 2006, cat. no. 29, Fig. 16.4.
9. Fragment of a brick with a stamp LEG I ITAL. GR/6/00c/OM. *Published:* Tomas 2006, cat. no. 34, fig. 16.3.

Pl. XVIII. Pottery finds from Area C2

Imported tableware

1. Rim of a *terra sigillata* bowl with a grooved ornament. 4/1/13m/can. Break and slip 2.5 YR 5/4. Rheinzabern, the end of the 2nd century.

Pl. XVIII. Pottery finds from Area C2

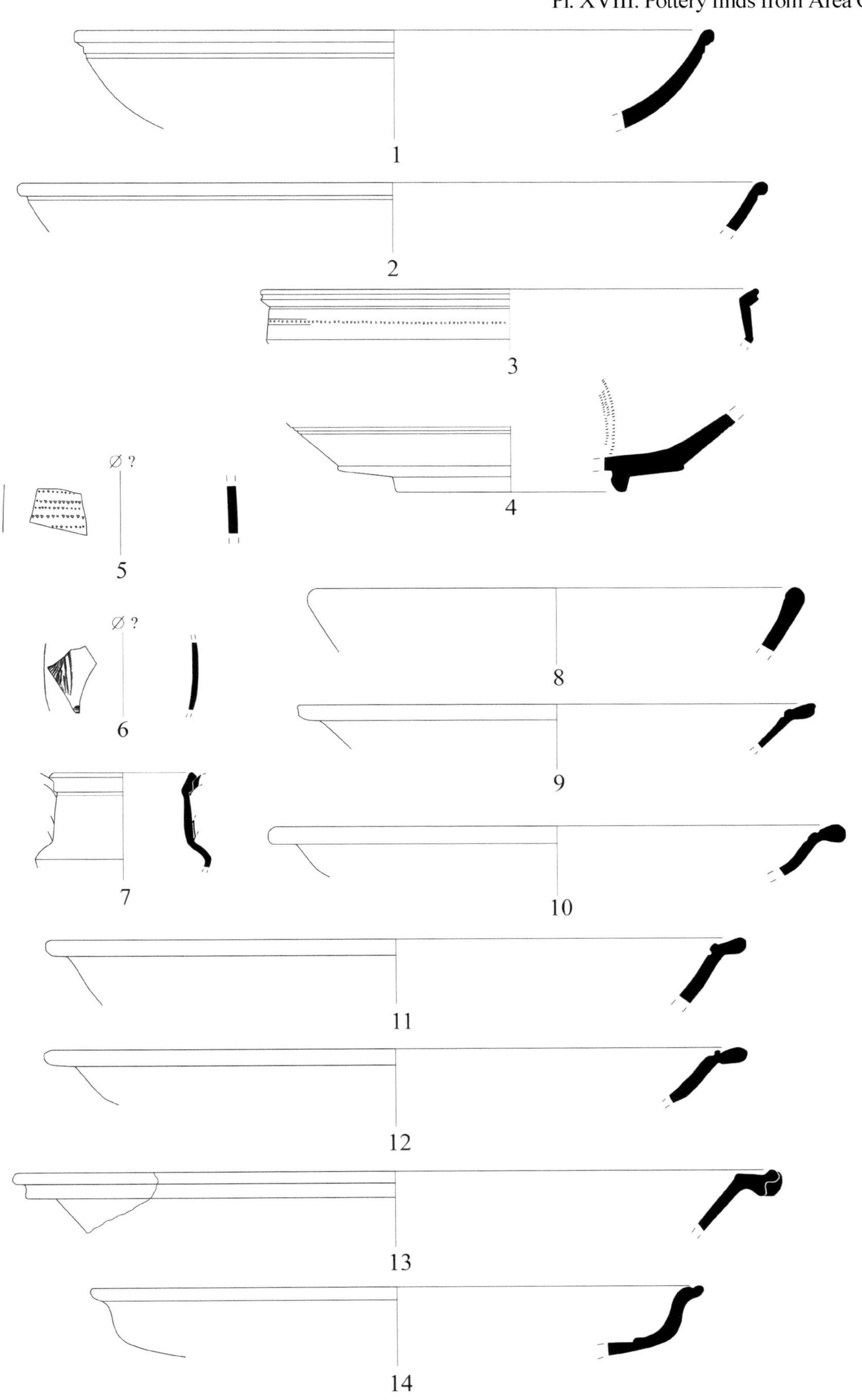

Pl. XIX. Pottery finds from Area C2

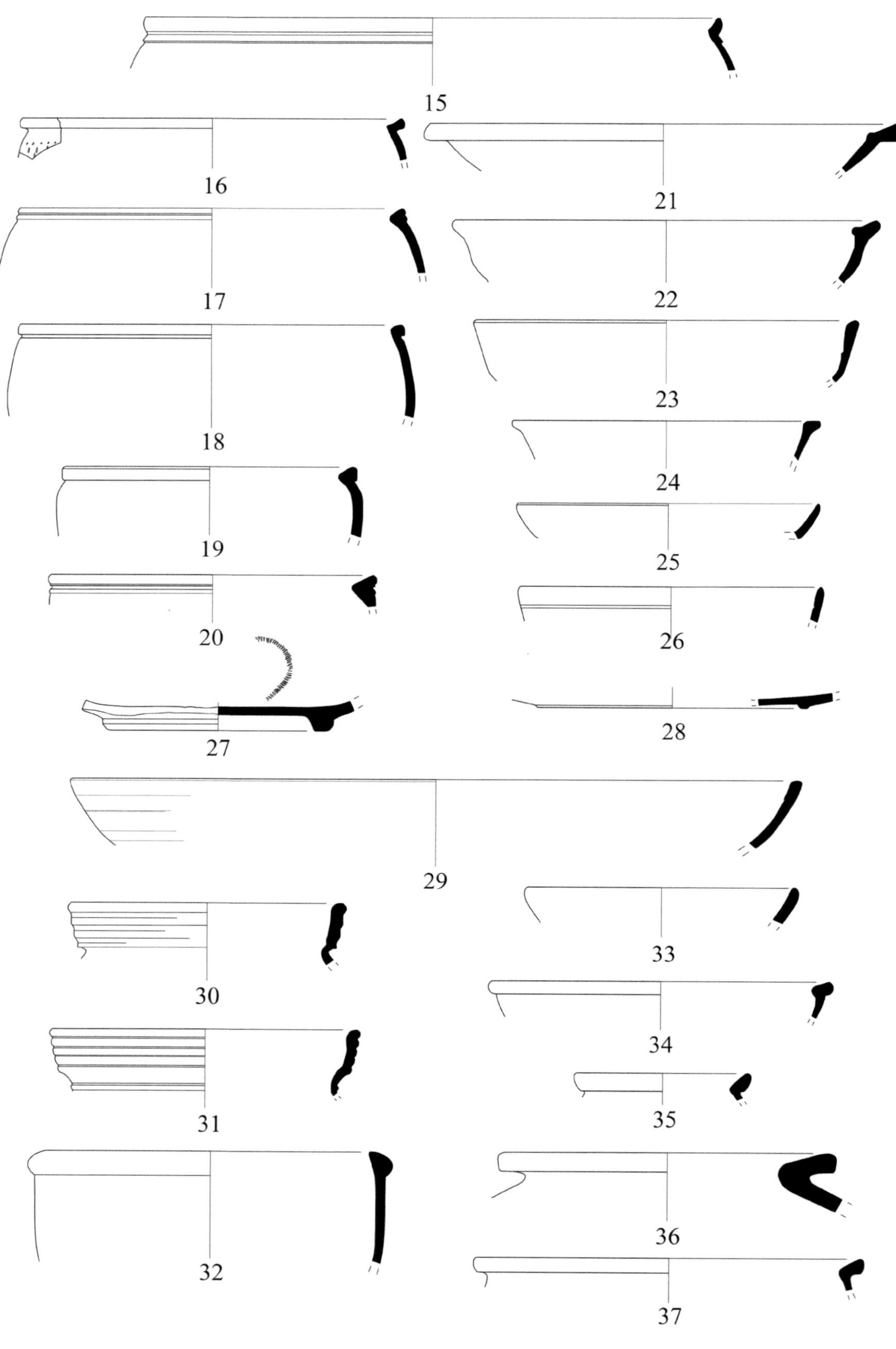

2. Rim of a bowl. 4/3/12m/can. Break and slip 2.5 YR 6/6. Rheinzabern.
3. Rim of a bowl. 4/7/13m/can. Break 10 YR 4/1, slip 4/2. Thin-walled. Pannonian?
4. Bottom of a *terra sigillata* vessel with an incised decoration. 4/31/13m/can. Break 7.5 YR 7/4, slip 5 YR 6/8.
5. Fragment of a body with an incised decoration. 4/8/13m/can. Break 7.5 YR 5/1, slip 7.5 YR 5/3. Thin-walled. Pannonian?
6. Fragment of a body with an incised decoration. 4/2/13m/can. Break and slip 2.5 YR 5/8. Gaulish or Rheinzabern.

Wares XI/XII (local tableware)

7. Upper part of a two-handled vessel. 4/18/13m/can. Break 2.5 YR 6/6, slip 2.5 YR 6/8.
8. Rim decorated with an inner groove. 4/11/13m/can. Break and slip 5 YR 6/8.
9. Rim decorated with an inner groove. 4/10/13m/can. Break 10 YR 6/6, slip 5 YR 6/6.
10. Rim decorated with an inner groove. 4/16/13m/can. Break 10 YR 7/3, slip 10 YR 6/4.
11. Rim decorated with an inner groove. 4/9/13m/can. Break 10 YR 7/2, slip 10 R 5/6.
12. Rim. 4/10/13m/can. Break 10 YR 7/2, slip 10 R 5/6.
13. Rim with an applique decoration. 4/33/13m/can. Break 10 YR 7/2, slip 10 YR 6/6.
14. Rim. 4/14/13m/can. Break 5 YR 7/4, slip 5 YR 5/6.

Pl. XIX. Pottery finds from Area C2

Wares XI/XII (local tableware)

15. Rim. 4/12/13m/can. Break 5 YR 6/6, slip 5 YR 6/8.
16. Rim with an incised decoration. 4/22/13m/can. Break 5 YR 6/6, slip 5 YR 6/8.
17. Rim.4/23/13m/can. Break 5 YR 6/6, slip 5 YR 6/8.
18. Rim. 4/17/13m/can. Break 5 YR 6/6, slip 5 YR 6/8.
19. Rim. 4/27/13m/can. Break 7.5 R 4/6, slip 5 R 6/6.
20. Rim. 4/30/13m/can. Break and slip 5 YR 6/6.
21. Rim. 4/21/13m/can. Break 7.5 R 6/6, slip 5 YR 6/8.
22. Rim. 4/24/13m/can. Break 7.5 YR 6/4, slip 7.5 YR 5/6.
23. Rim. 4/26/13m/can. Break 7.5 6/4, slip 5 YR 6/6.
24. Rim. 4/25/13m/can. Break and slip 7.5 YR 6/6.
25. Rim. 4/29/13m/can. Break 5 YR 5/6, slip 5 YR 6/6.
26. Rim. 4/34/13m/can. Break 5 YR 5/6, slip 5 YR 6/6.
27. Bottom with an incised decoration. 4/32/13m/can. Break 7.5 YR 7/6, slip 7.5 R 6/8.
28. Bottom with an incised decoration. 4/39/13m/can. Break 5 YR 6/4, slip 5 YR 6/6.
29. Rim. 4/15/13m/can. Break 7.5 YR 7/4, slip 5 YR 5/6.
30. Rim with a grooved decoration. 4/19/13m/can. Break and slip 5 YR 6/8.
31. Rim with a grooved decoration. 4/20/13m/can. Break and slip 7.5 YR 6/8.

Ware VIII (Norico-Pannonian)

32. Rim of a pot. 4/49/13m/can. Break 5 YR 5/2, coating 5 YR 2/2.

Ware III

33. Rim. 4/65/13m/can. Break and surface 10 R 5/1.
34. Rim. 4/52/13m/can. Break and surface 2.5 YR 5/2.
35. Rim. 4/54/13m/can. Break 2.5 YR 5/1, surface 10 YR 4/1.
36. Rim of a pot. 4/66/13m/can. Break 10 YR 5/2, surface 10 YR 3/2.
37. Rim of a pot. 4/55/13m/can. Break and surface 7.5 YR 6/1.

Pl. XX. Pottery finds from Area C2

38. Rim of a bowl. 4/61/13m/can. Break and surface 5 YR 5/1.
39. Rim of a pot. 4/44/13m/can. Break and surface 5 YR 7/1.
40. Rim of a pot. 4/71/13m/can. Break 10 YR 4/4, surface 10 YR 3/1.
41. Rim of a pot. 4/57/13m/can. Break and surface 5 YR 6/2.
42. Rim of a pot. 4/45/13m/can. Break and surface 10 YR 6/1.
43. Rim of a pot. 4/69/13m/can. Break 10 YR 7/1, surface 10 YR 5/1.
44. Lid. 4/47/13m/can. Break and surface 5 YR 6/2.
45. Lid. 4/43/13m/can. Break and surface 2.5 YR 5/1.
46. Lid. 4/42/13m/can. Break and surface 10 YR 5/1.
47. Lid. 4/41/13m/can. Break and surface 5 YR 6/2.
48. Lid. 4/62/13m/can. Break and surface 2.5 YR 5/1.

Ware XIII (local kitchenware)

49. Rim. 4/51/13m/can. Break 1 FG 5/N, surface 10 YR 5/3.
50. Lid. 4/58/13m/can. Break 7.5 YR 4/1, surface 7.5 YR 3/1.
51. Bottom. 4/59/13m/can. Break 1 FG 6/10Y, surface 5 YR 6/6.
52. Fragment of a lid. 4/35/13m/can. Break and surface 7.5 YR 6/8.
53. Rim of a mortarium. 4/40/13m/can. Break and surface 10 YR 7/4.

Ware XIV (Lower Danube Kaolin Ware)

54. Rim of a pot. 4/50/13m/can. Break and surface 10 YR 8/3.
55. Rim of a pot. 4/56/13m/can. Break and surface 2.5 Y 8/4.
56. Rim of a pot. 4/53/13m/can. Break 2.5 Y 8/4, surface with discolorations 10YR 4/4 to 10 YR 8/2.
57. Rim of a pot. 4/67/13m/can. Break and surface 2.5 Y 7/3.

Pl. XX. Pottery finds from Area C2

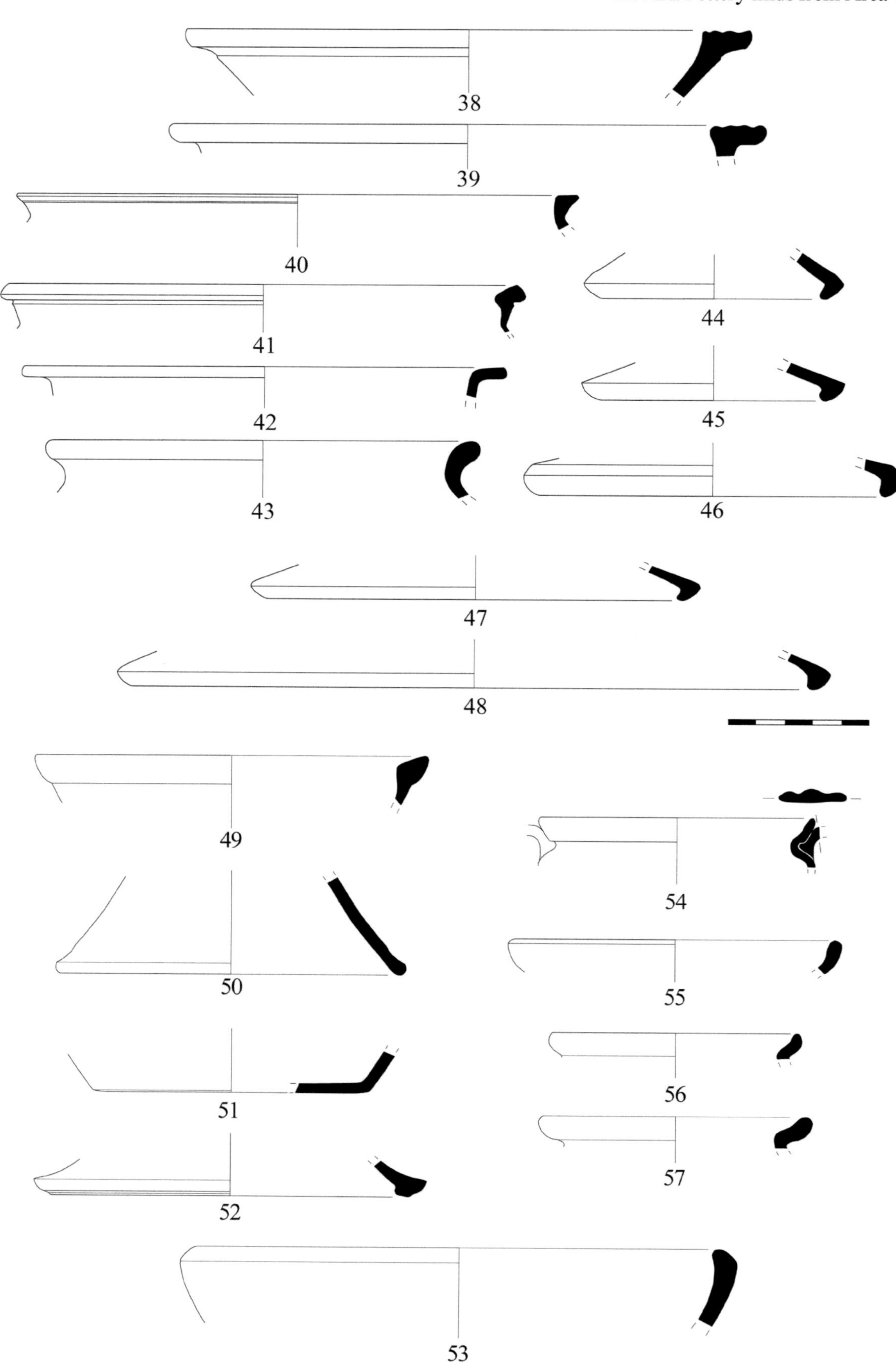

Pl. XXI. Pottery finds from Area E

Ware I (hand-formed)

1. Rim with two handles. 3/8/14m/OMS. Hand-made and wheel-turned. Break and surface 7.5 YR 7/4 – 6/6.
2. Rim. 3/1/14m/OMS. Hand-formed and wheel-turned. Break 5 YR 6/2, surface 2.5 Y 3/1.

Ware II (legionary tableware)

3. Bottom of a jug. 1/6/14m/OMS. Break and surface 2.5 YR 7/2.

Wares XI/XII (local tableware)

4. Rim of a bowl. 3/3/14m/OMS. Break 5 YR 6/3, slip 5 YR 6/4.
5. Rim of a bowl. 1/7/14m/OMS. Break 5 YR 6/3, slip 5 YR 6/6.
6. Rim. 3/4/14m/OMS. Worn slip. Break 5 YR 6/4, slip 5 YR 6/6.
7. Rim and bottom of an inkwell. 3/6-7/14m/OMS. Break 10 R 6/3, slip 10 R 5/6.
8. Bottom of a plate with an incised decoration. 1/8/14m/OMS. Break 2.5 YR 6/4, slip 2.5 YR 5/8.

Ware XIV (Lower Danube Kaolin Ware)

9. Cap of a lid. 1/5/14m/OMS. Break and surface 2.5 Y 7/3.
10. Rim. 1/4/14m/OMS. Break and surface 2.5 Y 8/4.

Pl. XXII. Pottery finds from Area F - Kanlu cheshme)

Ware XI/XII

1. Rim of a bowl. 2/6/14m/Kč. Worn slip. Break 10 R 6/3, slip 10 R 5/6.
2. Bottom 2/5/14m/Kč. Break and surface 5 YR 6/4.

Ware XIV

3. Rim of a vessel. 2/4/14m/Kč. Break and surface 2.5 Y 8/4.

Pl. XXI. Pottery finds from Area E

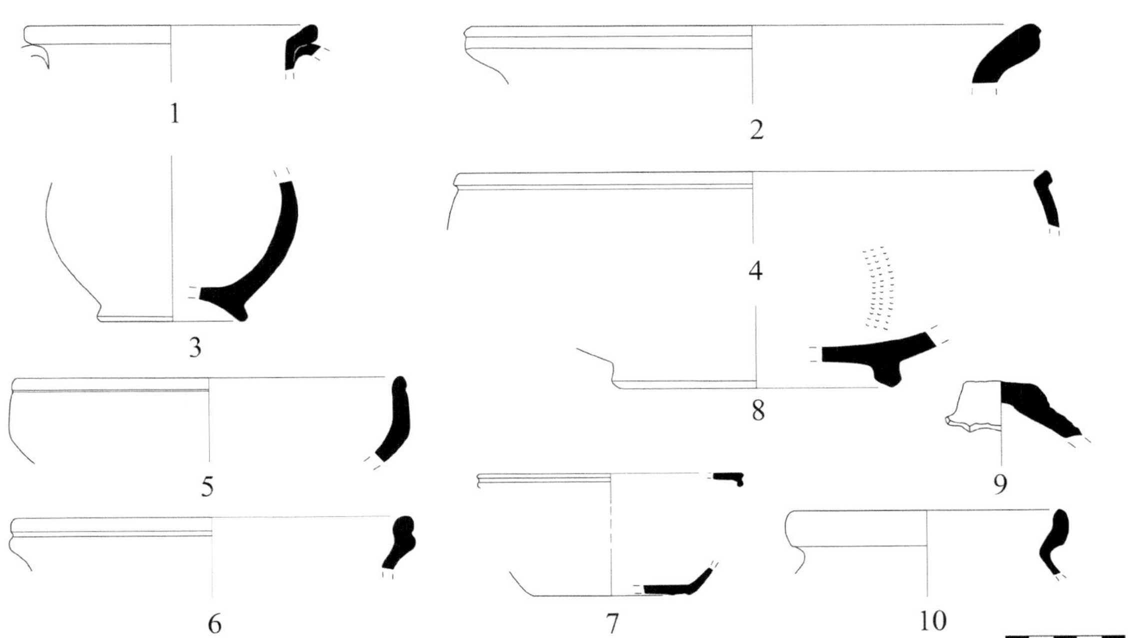

Pl. XXII. Pottery finds from Area F

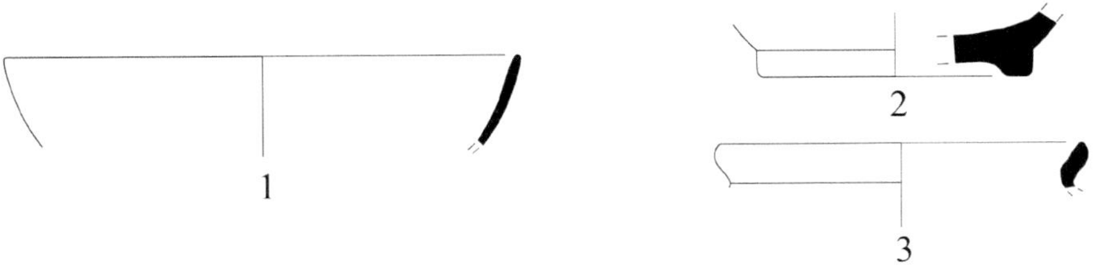

Table I. Classification of wares (by A. Tomas).

Fabric descriptions from surveys carried out in 2000 and 2012-14 were based on sherd samples collected during excavations and field walkings. The sherds were classified after mutual comparison of fabrics, forms, and finishing. For the convenience of the research process, each of the wares were also given specific names (e.g., Norico-Pannonian, Early Roman burnished pottery etc.). The description includes the temper density (sparse, moderate, abundant), the inclusions or temper size (small-sized or fine-grained, medium, coarse), the grain shape (particles, chips, flakes), the porosity (porous, slightly porous, rather dense, dense, compact), the surface texture (powdery, smooth, coarse). Coarse-grained temper is such with grain sized double the average determined by Shepard (0.25-0.5 mm). Fabric (firing) hardness is evaluated on the ten-point Mohs scale recommended by Orton, where pottery hardness falls in the 2-6.5 range, scratched successively with a nail (soft clay; 2-2.5 on the Mohs scale), piece of plastic (medium hard), glass shard (hard), piece of steel (very hard). Colours described according to the Munsell Color Charts are included in the catalogue in Chapter V.1.

Classification	Fabric, technology, and forms	Examples in the present publication	Reference to the laboratory analyses, published excavated examples and analogies
Ware I (Hand-formed)	Fabric very often with small to medium-sized lime inclusions, and small-sized silver mica flakes, tempered with coarse sand containing small quartz stones or crushed sherds or organic temper, recognizable as empty holes in the break. The fracture in section can be porous (with medium to large pore spaces) or quite dense, soft to medium hard. The surface is uneven, but not rough. The colour varies from pale brown, greyish to black. The most common decoration is an applique fillet with impressed finger-tipping, punching or incising with finger-nails around the body or rim. Some specimens are smeared with white clay. Hand-formed (variant A), hand-formed and wheel-finished (variant B). Variant B vessels are made from well-sorted fabric, rather dense, and their shapes are more sophisticated.	Pl. II, 6–7; III, 16–27; XXI, 1–2	Daszkiewicz, Bobryk, and Schneider 2006; Gencheva 2002, esp. 41; Chichikova 2013, 227–246
Ware II (Early tableware)	Well-sorted fabric with medium-sized lime inclusions, frequent to very frequent fine silver mica flakes, tempered with sand containing small quartz stones. The fracture is very often porous (with frequent small pore spaces), hard to very hard. The walls are usually 0.4-1 cm thick. The surface is usually burnished but slightly rough to the touch, with horizontal scratches made by small stones during the wheel-turning process. The surface is not slipped. The colour is usually pinkish, reddish to very pale brown. Similar to Ware III, but of better quality (better-sorted and finished).	Pl. XII, 218; XXI, 3	Domżalski 1998
Ware III (Early kitchenware)	Fabric very similar to Ware II, but very often containing sherd temper. The fracture is porous (with frequent small pore spaces), hard. The surface is rough. The colour can be reddish (variant A), greyish to very pale brown (variant B). The rims are usually everted, while the bottoms flat. Kitchenware.	Pl. XII, 219–220	Domżalski 1998
Ware IV (Early local tableware?)	Fabric with moderate to frequent fine silver mica, sparse small lime inclusions, tempered with fine sand and / or sherd. The fracture in section is lightly porous, medium hard to hard. The surface–slightly rough but powdery, even, covered with very worn slip. Finishing of medium quality. The colour is light orange. Tableware.	Not found during prospection	Not published
Ware V (Orange burnished pottery)	Very fine silty fabric, with moderate quantity of small-sized lime inclusions and silver mica flakes, sparse small, round black and red particles. The fracture is compact. The surface is carefully finished, burnished and smooth, although without slip. A characteristic light orange colour. Thin-walled (up to 0.5 cm). Tableware (cups, mugs) and big jars.	Pl. XVI, 328	Not published; cf. Grünewald 1983, 22, Taf. 20, 8–14
Ware VI (ER burnished pottery)	Medium hard to hard, well-sorted fabric with abundant small-sized silver mica flakes and lime inclusions. The fracture is porous. The surface is covered with thick burnished slip, sometimes flaking (grey pottery) or non-slipped (reddish dolia). The surface is smooth. Colour–greyish brown or pale reddish. Heavy pots, with thick solid walls. Burnished or incised ornaments of wavy lines.	Pl. XVI, 320–322	Vagalinski 2007, 102–103, КУ130; 125, Г254; 136, Д313
Ware VII (Phocaea kitchenware and tableware)	Fabric with abundant small-sized silver mica flakes and sparse golden mica flakes, visible on the surface. Lime and sparse pyroxene inclusions are also visible in the break. Fine temper containing sandstones and sherds. The fracture is slightly porous, very hard. The surface is rough or slightly rough, sometimes with lime sediments, uneven. The colour is red to brown in section, with grey surface. Kitchenware in three variants: variant A–thin-walled kitchenware (0.2-0.4 cm) with a richly profiled rim concave in section; variant B–massive pots with a slightly rough surface; variant C–thick- or thin-walled tableware, with a slightly rough surface, sometimes ornamented.	Not found during prospection	Not published (cf. kitchenware published by Heath, S., and B. Tekkök (eds.), 2012)
Ware VIII (Norico-Pannonian)	Fabric with abundant medium-sized sand temper containing sparse black crushed particles (sherd?) and white, crushed feldspar. Hand-formed and wheel-finished. The surface is finished with a dark greyish-brown to black shiny coating, which is uneven and "pimply", but smooth to the touch. The section is very often brownish. The vessels are often ornamented with semi-circular, parallel lines made with a comb (Kammstrich) or a brush (Besenstrich). Ovoid pots and beakers.	Pl. XIX, 32	Karasiewicz-Szczypiorski 1998, 192, group IIE, Tab. I, 15; III, 43–46
Ware IX (Yellowish pottery)	Very well-sorted fabric with sparse fine sherd temper and small-sized lime inclusions, black, round particles (pyroxene?) and silver mica flakes. Fracture–medium-hard, rather compact. Surface–smooth, slightly powdery, with yellowish slip. Break–yellowish. Fabric–yellow reddish with discolorations. Mainly bowls.	Not found during prospection	Not published

Classification	Fabric, technology, and forms	Examples in the present publication	Reference to the laboratory analyses, published excavated examples and analogies
Ware X (Yellow-pinkish tableware)	Fabric containing small amounts of small-sized silver mica flakes, tempered with large amounts of coarse sand with hard round reddish particles (hematite?), and tempered with medium-sized sherds. The break is yellowish to pinkish, the surface–yellowish to light brownish. Wheel-turned vessels, very often with a flat uneven bottom and slippery surface. Large jugs (oinochoai), cups and bowls.	Not found during prospection	Not published
Wares XI/XII (Boutovo/Pavlikeni) w	Usually dense or compact, hard or medium-hard fabric with lime inclusions and small-sized silver mica flakes. The fabric is well-sorted and tempered with fine-grained sand or (rarely) with crushed sherds. The surface is finished with a thick layer of good-quality slip, which is smooth. Table vessels can have walls 0.2-0.3-cm thick, but most of the specimens have walls about 0.4–0.6 cm. The break is usually pinkish or orange in colour, the slip–orange to reddish and brownish, sometimes opalescent. Jugs or bowls can have an uneven coating with streaks at the bottom. Some vessels are decorated with various techniques. Beakers and bowls are forms decorated with the en barbotine, incised, roulette or applique techniques. Opened vessels are often decorated with grooves forming parallel lines. Wheel-turned tableware: bowls, jugs, cups, beakers, plates and platters, and mortaria are the most common. Ware XII fabric, forms and finishing are very similar to Ware XI, but some vessels of Ware XII can be made of poorly-sorted fabric with large lime particles and can have a more porous fracture than Ware XI. However, in many cases, it is not possible to classify the sherd to Ware XI or Ware XII.	Pl. II, 3–4; IV–XI; XVII, 4, 6–7; XVIII, 7–14; XIX, 19–31; XXI, 4–8; XXII, 1, 2	Nacheva 1981; Daszkiewicz et al. 2013; many examples published in the excavation reports in Archeologia (Warszawa); cf. Soultov 1985 tab. XXVII – XXXVIII; Falkner 1999, 74 (Ware 8)
Ware XIII (Boutovo/Pavlikeni kitchenware)	Medium-hard or hard fabric with inclusions of small-sized silver mica flakes and lime particles (similar to Wares XI/XII), often tempered with sand, sometimes coarse, containing small-sized white stones. Usually slightly porous, but sometimes compact fracture; the surface is rough but carefully finished. The break is usually brownish, surface dark brownish to black, rarely light brownish or reddish. Undecorated, wheel-turned kitchen pots, lids, bowls, jars, and mortaria.	Pl. II, 16–17; XII, 221–239; XIII, 240–261; XIV, 262–278; XX, 49–53	Many examples published in the excavation reports in Archeologia (Warszawa); cf. Sultov 1985, tab. XLII–XLIII.
Ware XIV (Lower Danubian Kaolin Ware)	Very hard to hard fabric with small-sized silver mica flakes, sparse golden mica flakes, and small brown particles (hematite?), tempered with fine-grained sand. The fracture is usually porous (numerous small pores), very rough, the surface is "pimply", with visible particles of sand, but well-finished and rather even. The break is often light brownish, surface yellowish, light brownish to yellowish-grey, without coating. The vessels are quite well-finished. The forms have flat bottoms, characteristic short, flat handles, decorated with wide grooves and a rim concave in section. Wheel-turned kitchen pots and beakers.	Pl. II, 18; XVI, 303–319; XX, 54–57; XXI, 9–10; XXII, 3	Daszkiewicz, Bobryk, and Radan 2010, esp. 37; Klenina 2006, 109–119; Dyczek 2009
Ware XV (LR burnished pottery)	Medium-hard to hard fabric with abundant small-sized silver mica flakes and small-sized lime particles. Fracture–porous. The surface is burnished, often decorated with broad and shallow lines made with a bone or a wooden tool. The break and surface are very often greyish to greyish brown. Very carefully finished. Wheel-turned, rarely hand-formed and wheel-finished tableware, but also jars or mortaria.	Pl. XV, 323–327	Vagalinski 2007, 53, К16, К38, К113–114, Ч241, Г257, Г305–306, Ф350–353, 356–359; cf. Böttger 1967; Falkner 1999, 73 (Ware 14)
Ware XVI (LR glazed pottery)	Medium-hard to hard fabric, usually with abundant, small-sized silver mica flakes and small-sized lime particles, and rather porous fracture, but some sherds are made from well-sorted fabric, which is dense and contains less inclusions. The surface is finished with a glaze yellowish, greenish or brownish in colour, very often rugged and uneven. The break is usually dark brownish. Wheel-turned tableware, very often jugs, cups and bowls.	Pl. XV, 285–288	cf. Falkner 1999, 87.
Ware XVII (LR pottery)	Divided into two sub-groups: A–medium-hard, porous, well-sorted micaceous fabric, with a large quantity of small-sized lime particles, tempered with large amounts of fine sand. The walls are usually 0.5 cm thick. Wheel-turned pottery. B–rather hard, porous, sandy fabric, with small-sized silver mica flakes and lime inclusions, tempered with medium-grained sand containing quartz and small, white stones. Breaks are sometimes visible near lime intrusions. Some sherds have white eruptions on the surface. The walls are often crusty and relatively thin in proportion to the size and capacity of the vessels. The break and surface are usually greyish to reddish grey or brownish grey. Wheel-turned pottery. Jars, pots and jugs with a wide and short neck decorated with horizontal grooves.	Pl. XV, 289–291	Klenina 2006; cf. Böttger 1982, 141–142, Töpfe VII; Falkner 1999, 66–67 (Ware 1)
Ware XVIII (Early Medieval Slavic)	Poorly-sorted, medium-porous and medium-hard fabric with abundant small-sized silver mica flakes and lime particles, which can be sometimes large, tempered with coarse or fine-grained sand containing abundant small white stones. The surface is soft but uneven, very often decorated with a deeply grooved comb decoration in the form of horizontal lines or perpendicular waves or incised with finger-nails, cords, and wooden or bone tools all over the body. Usually hand-formed or hand-formed and wheel-finished ovoid vessels.	Pl. XLVI (decorations); XLVII; XLVIII, 31–36; LI, 58–59	Hensel et al. 1965
Ware XIX (Mediaeval/post-Mediaeval glazed)	Hard fabric with abundant silver mica flakes and small-sized to medium-sized lime particles and black grits. The break is greyish and grey-yellowish, but red-brownish is also possible, the surface is always covered with thick green or green-and-white glaze. Plates, jugs, bowls.	Pl. XLVIII, 37–39; L	Hensel et al. 1965, esp. Fig. 24.

3. Amphorae

Agnieszka Tomas, Piotr Dyczek

Amphora and pitcher sherds are very numerous finds in the extramural area; however, they are usually preserved in the form of body fragments, frequently difficult to identify. The present publication is a selection of the most characteristic and interesting finds, chosen from a number of collected amphora fragments.

Seven fragments of amphorae presented here come from the nearest neighbourhood of the fortress, three of them from the southern part of the annexe and its vicinity (Area A1, **Pl. XXIII, 2, 6, 7**), and five from the *canabae* (Area C2, **XXVI, 1–5**). The finds from the nearest vicinity of the fortress, especially on its western side, are badly preserved and shredded due to modern land use. The low number of finds from the annexe results from the vegetation limiting visibility during the prospection.

The majority of finds from Area A1 come from the period after the 3rd century AD. Probably the earliest find is a piece of a Kapitän II amphora (**Pl. XXIII, 2**), a container known in several variants, quite common along the Danube.[1] Such amphorae were probably used as containers for wine, produced in the Aegean area and in Asia Minor from the late 2nd century to the 4th century, when they were very common.[2] Analogous forms are known from Nicopolis, but their find context is broadly dated from AD 250 to 600.[3] A fragment found in Area A1 belonged to an interesting variant, perhaps an early form produced from the late 2nd to the 3rd century.[4]

The second fragment is the rim (**Pl. XXIII, 6**) of a pan-Roman amphora type imitating Koan containers, once defined as a pseudo-Koan or Zeest 77 type, and now attributed to Heracleia and Sinope.[5] Such amphorae were broadly distributed along the Lower Danube.[6] Fabric of the presented piece fits the Sinopean variant Sin III, dated to between the mid-1st century BC and the third quarter of the 1st century AD;[7] therefore, the sherd from Novae would be from the latest period of their production. The Sinopean amphorae manufactured during the Roman period can only be broadly dated to between the late 1st and the early 3rd century, when their form changed dramatically.[8] The third fragment collected there is the rim of a table amphora, perhaps Soultov 1 (**Pl. XXIII, 7**), produced in the Boutovo/Pavlikeni workshops in the 2nd–3rd centuries.[9]

Area D to the south of the annexe provided four finds. Two or three fragments of LR 1 amphorae (**Pl. XXIII, 1, 3** and possibly **4**) are dated to the 4th–6th centuries.[10] Such amphorae could have been used as containers for wine or olive oil.[11] In the extramural area, amphorae Zeest 90 = Dressel 24 *similis*, common from the 1st to the 3rd centuries at military sites along the Danube,[12] have been found in high numbers of body fragments and handles. These containers, produced in the central Aegean area and used for the transport of olive oil, became predominant at Lower Danubian military sites.[13] Fragments of LR 2 amphorae are also frequent finds in Novae and other Lower Danubian sites, and therefore, are considered to serve as containers for the *annona*.[14] Unfortunately, we did not collect any diagnostic fragments in the prospected areas. The fragment of a small, wheel-turned stopper (**Pl. XXIII, 5**) resembles stoppers known from northern Dalmatia and regio Venetia. Analogous stoppers have been found in the Flavian pits at Novae.

Five fragments of amphorae found in the *canabae* to the west of the camp (Area C2) are dated significantly earlier than those from the annexe. The rim of a Zeest 64 = Shelov C IV amphora (**Pl. XXVI, 4**), found also in Nicopolis,[15] was produced probably on the south-eastern Black Sea coast, and was widespread from Italy to the far East and Barbaricum in the second quarter of the 2nd century.[16] The rim of a Soultov 1 table amphora (**Pl. XXVI, 5**) is another example of a common type of local container from the 2nd–3rd centuries AD. The rim of a Kapitän II amphora (**Pl. XXVI, 2**) is a relatively early example, dated to the beginning of the 3rd century AD.[17] The second fragment (**Pl. XXVI, 3**) belongs to the same type, but made from different fabric with a creamy-buff slip.[18]

The highest number of amphora sherds were collected in the *vicus* (Area B, **Pl. XXIV and XXV**). The earliest specimens are dated to the Flavian period, and they belonged to a Dressel 6A amphora (**Pl. XXIV, 6**), which

1. Dyczek 2001, 144; Dyczek 2010; Biernacki and Klenina 2015, 103; Opaiţ and Ionescu 2016, 62.
2. Riley 1979; Keay 1984, 137; Auriemma and Quiri 2004, 53; Carandini and Panella 1981; Empereur and Picon 1989, 233.
3. Falkner 1999, Fig. 9.54 nos. 1093–95.
4. Cf. Negru, Bădescu and Avram 2003, 209 and Fig. 1.1, 2; Opaiţ 2022.
5. Zeest 1960, 113, Tab. XXXII, 77e; Vnukov 2004, 409–11 and Fig. 2.
6. Opaiţ 2013, 38–45, Figs. 5–6.
7. Vnukov 2004, 410; 2011, 364.
8. Vnukov 2011, 362.
9. Soultov 1985, 74, Tab. XXXIV, 3.
10. Empereur and Picon 1989, 236.
11. Piéri 2005.
12. Dyczek 2001, 174, type 25; Opaiţ and Tsaravopoulos 2011, 317–18.
13. Opaiţ and Tsaravopoulos 2011, 318.
14. Biernacki and Klenina 2015, 105. Karagiorgou 2001.
15. Falkner 1999, Fig. 9.52, no. 1065.
16. Vnukov 2016, 36, 42, 4.1–10.
17. Dyczek 2001, 144; 2010, 994.
18. Bezeczky 2005.

served as a container for fish sauce and wine produced on the Adriatic coast of Italy.[19]

The fragment of a small, wheel-turned stopper (**Pl. XXIV, 10**) resembles stoppers known from northern Dalmatia and regio Venetia, the same as the stopper found in Area D discussed above.[20] Analogous stoppers have been found in the Flavian pits at Novae, as well.

A Dressel 2 wine amphora (**Pl. XXIV, 7**) is of a similarly early date, produced in Hispania Tarraconensis.[21] The rim of a Pascual 1=Peacock/Williams 6 amphora (**Pl. XXIV, 2**), which served as a container for Spanish wine, is dated no earlier than to the Flavian or even Trajanic period.[22] The rim (**Pl. XXIV, 3**), perhaps of a Dressel 12 = Beltran 3 amphora, which was a container for fish-based products imported from Spain from the mid-1st to the late 2nd century.[23]

A Rhodian-type amphora (**Pl. XXIV, 9**) originating from the Aegean region and Asia Minor served for transporting sweet wine up to the early 2nd century AD.[24] Rhodian amphorae, together with Dressel 6A and Dressel 2–4, were predominant types along the Danubian border from the Flavian to the Hadrianic period.[25] A small toe (**Pl. XXIV, 8**) probably belonged to an imitation of a Rhodian-type amphora or a smaller vessel related to amphorae, like an *amphoriskos* or *unguentarium*.[26]

A Beltrán 2A amphorae (**Pl. XXIV, 1**) produced from AD 10–15 to the mid-2nd century served for storing Spanish fish products.[27] A massive wide rim (**Pl. XXIV, 5**) belonged to a variant of a Zeest 75 amphora, a container for fish products from the north Black Sea coast.[28] In Nicopolis, the same type was found in a context dated to AD 175–250.[29] A Dressel 24 amphora has been identified in one fragment (**Pl. XXIV, 13**). Such containers were present in the Balkans, Danube region and the Black Sea from the 1st to the 3rd centuries.[30] The most frequent are fragments of the Zeest 90 type, as well as their later variant, LR2 amphora (**Pl. XXIV, 14–17**).[31] The bottom was found of a Dressel 23 amphora (**Pl. XXIV, 18**), which served as a container for olives, olive oil and olive-based products imported from Spain, and it is dated to between the 3rd and the 6th century.[32]

An Agora M273 amphora is represented by a rim (**Pl. XXIV, 20**). Such amphorae, which probably served as wine containers produced in the East, are dated to the 4th and the 5th centuries AD and were also found in Scythia and north of the Danube.[33] Three fragments, a rim with handles, a handle and a base (**Pl. XXIV, 22–24**), belonged to the Heracleian / Sinopean amphorae mentioned above. It is difficult to identify the subtype of handle no. 22, but the rim and the base (nos. 23 and 24) probably belonged to the late Heracleian subtype S IVb, dated to between the second half of the 2nd and the first quarter of the 4th century AD.[34]

A number of sherds found in Novae belong to table amphorae and / or pitchers (**Pl. XXIV, 25–26; XXV, 27–39**). Their rims may differ, but a common characteristic is fine fabric and reddish or brownish slip, similar to that of local tableware. A quite common type of a table amphora in Novae is what is referred to as Dinogetia table amphora. These vessels were made from well-sorted fabric and covered with reddish coating. The rim is everted, triangular in section, with a characteristic internal bevel (**Pl. XXV, 27–29**), and the handles are oval in section or twisted.[35] Such vessels are present at other sites on the Lower Danube and their fabric may vary, so various manufacturing places are possible.[36] Table amphorae with handles oval in section like the item found in Ostrite Mogili were identified in Troesmis and defined as Type 2, while those with twisted handles and the characteristic rim described above are known from Dinogetia.[37] Both these types appear at these sites in 2nd-century contexts. Very similar table amphorae with twisted handles are known from Sagalassos (Type 4P100), where they are dated to no earlier than the second half of the 4th up to the 7th century.[38] It is noteworthy that the upper part resembles Galoise 6 type, but contrary to the Gaulish original, which was made from well-sorted fabric orange in section and beige on the surface, its fabric is coarser, rather porous, and red.

Table amphorae were also produced in the Boutovo/Pavlikeni workshops in the 2nd and 3rd centuries AD. They were defined by the discoverer, Bogdan Soultov, as Type 1.[39] These vessels were made from

19. Piccottini 1997; Bezeczky 1998.
20. Lipovac Vrkljan, Konestra, and Ožanić Roguljić 2013, 129–35 (pottery workshop of Sex. Metilius Maximus); Cipriano, Mazzocchin 2013, 94, type 3, Fig. 3.3 and Fig. 4.2.
21. Millet 2015, 194, Fig. 3 (type 2).
22. Tschernia 1986; Ciotola et al., 1989.
23. Beltrán 1970, type 3.
24. Peacock 1977, 266–70; Egri 2007, 47–48.
25. Egri 2007, 48.
26. Cf. forms of the examples from Chios workshop: Opaiţ and Tsaravopoulos 2011, 294, Fig. 20.
27. Beltrán 1970; Peacock 1984.
28. Opaiţ 2007, 109–12; Opaiţ and Ionescu 2016, 69.
29. Falkner 1999, Fig. 9.54, no. 1106.
30. Auriemma and Quiri 2004; Bezeczky 2004.
31. Dyczek 2001, 174, type 25.
32. Becker, Constantin, and Vielledieu 1989, 657–58.
33. Bonifay and Piéri 1995, 114; Opaiţ 1996, 211.
34. Vnukov 2004, 412, Figs. 7.5, 6; Vnukov 2011, 364 and Fig. 1.5 and cf. an earlier variant in: Vnukov 2003, 117–28, esp. Fig. 47 (S IV, variant S p IB)
35. Opaiţ 2003, 216, Fig. 6.
36. Opaiţ et al. 2020, 160, Fig. 2.1
37. Opaiţ 2003, 216.
38. Degeest 2000, 160–62, 379–81, Figs. 186–93; Corremans et al., 2010, 289.
39. Soultov 1985, 74, Pl. XXXIV, 3.

fine fabric, the same as fabric used for the production of tableware (see Chapter VI.2, Tab I, Ware XI/XII; cf. **Pl. XXV, 38**). The break is usually light reddish, pinkish or light brownish with reddish or brownish shiny slip. The rims are thickened, everted, usually triangular or round in section, the handles are flattened, and the bottom is flat. Their mass production started in the second half of the 2nd century in Boutovo, Pavlikeni and Hotnitsa; thus, the shape of the rims may vary. It is also possible that some of these rims belonged to pitchers – relatively large vessels, with a capacity smaller than that of amphorae, well-known from the Danubian delta.[40]

During our research, such vessels were found in the *vicus* (Area B, **Pl. XXV, 30–38**) and near the camp (Area A1, **Pl. XXIII,** 7 and C2, **Pl. XXVI, 5**). This group of vessels is still not well-recognized. Two fully preserved table amphorae, with different rims were found in Novae in a pit dated to the 3rd–4th centuries.[41] Analogous vessels but with handles round in section were found in Troesmis in a context dated to the first half of the 2nd century, and are similar to Galoise 5 amphorae.[42]

Only one fragment of a container was found in Area F (**Pl. XXVI, 6**). The atypical, foreign fabric indicates an imported vessel, but no analogies have been identified.

40. Opaiţ 2003; Opaiţ and Ionescu 2016, 65–66.

41. For two finds from Novae, see Majewski et al. 1965, 222, Figs. 9 and 10, 247–48, Figs. 75 and 76.

42. Opaiţ 2003, 216, Type 2, Fig. 5.

Prospection in Area E did not provide any fragments of amphorae or containers, but their absence may result from the bad preservation of the site.

Catalogue of amphorae

Pl. XXIII. Area A1 and D

1. Amphora (upper part). 4/10/14m/can. Clay containing small-sized lime. Medium-hard fabric containing medium amount of coarse sand with stones. Surface smooth. Fabric and surface 10 YR 7/6. Area D.
2. Amphora (upper part). 6/4/12m/can. Clay containing medium-sized lime. Hard fabric containing medium amount of coarse sand with stones and brownish inclusions, porous (with medium pore spaces). Surface uneven and rough. Fabric and surface 10 YR 5/6. Area A1.
3. Amphora (rim and neck). 4/6/14m/can. Fabric the same as No. 4. Area D.
4. Amphora (rim and neck). 4/3/14m/can. Hard fabric containing medium amount of medium- and large-sized lime particles, small amount of small silver mica flakes and medium-sized pyroxene particles, tempered with sand with small and medium-sized stones and brown inclusions, porous; uneven surface. Fabric and surface 10 YR 5/6. Area D.
5. Lid or amphora stopper. 4/8/14m/can. Clay containing small-sized lime. Medium-hard fabric containing medium amount of coarse sand with stones. Surface slightly rough. Fabric and surface 6/5. Area D.
6. Rim with a neck. 3/14/12m. Hard fabric containing large quantity of lime and black round particles, tempered with medium-sized sand and sherds, compact. Fabric and surface 5 YR 6/6. Area A1.

Pl. XXIII. Amphorae from Areas A1 and D

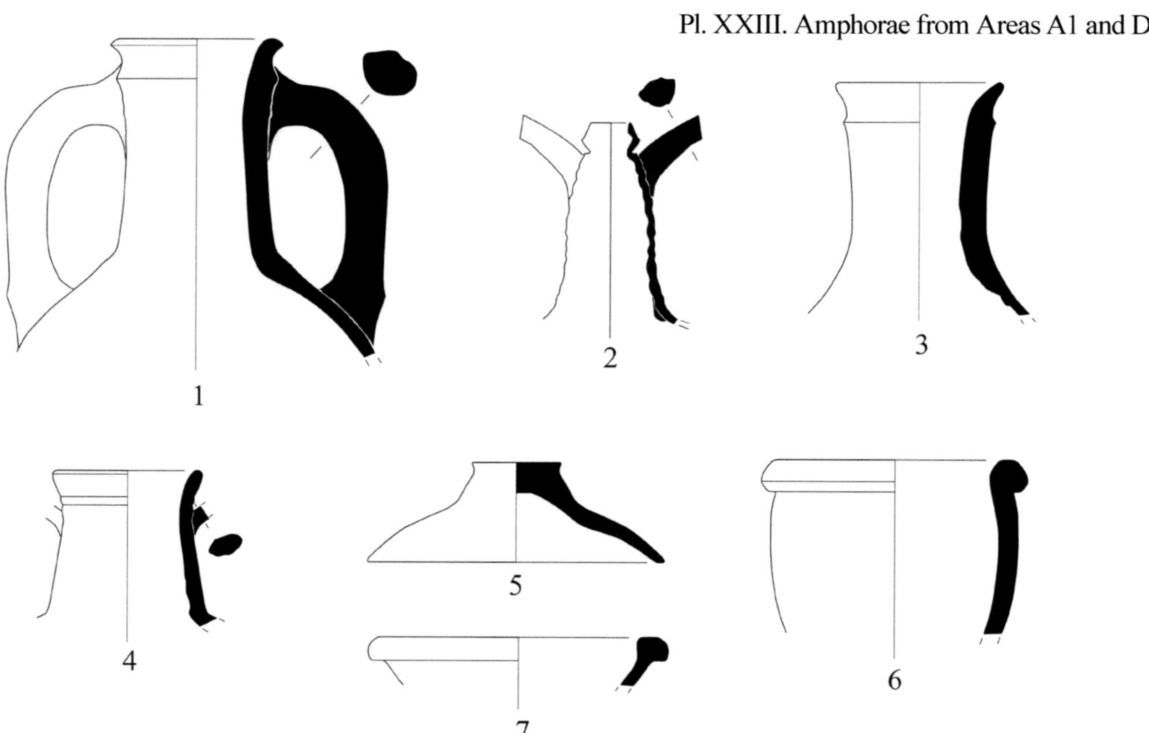

Pl. XXIV. Amphorae from Area B

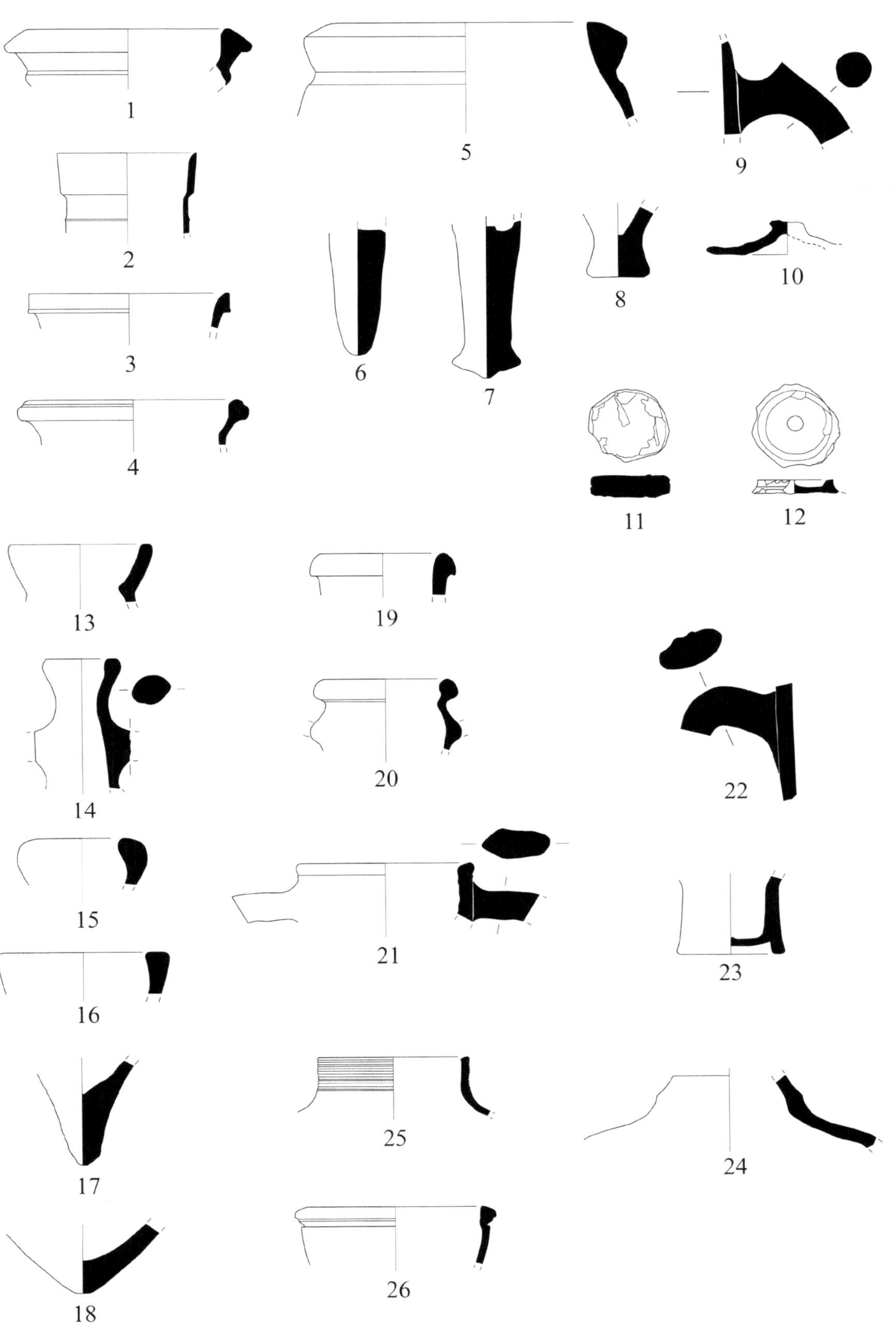

Pl. XXV. Amphorae from Area B

Pl. XXVI. Amphorae from Areas C2 and F

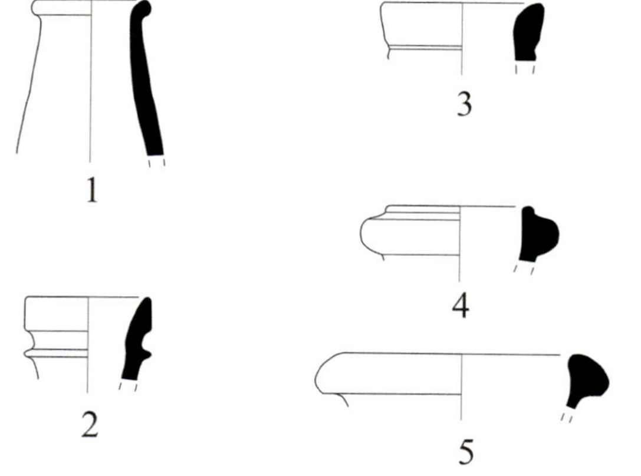

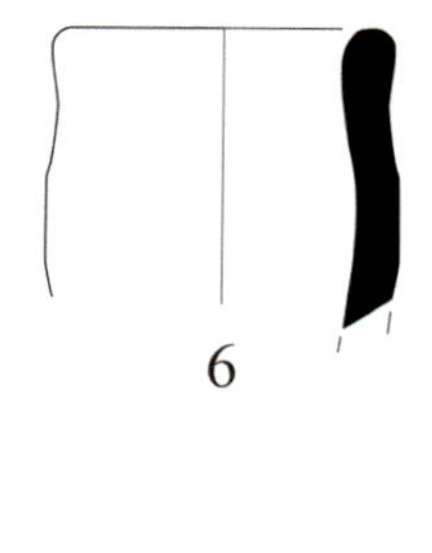

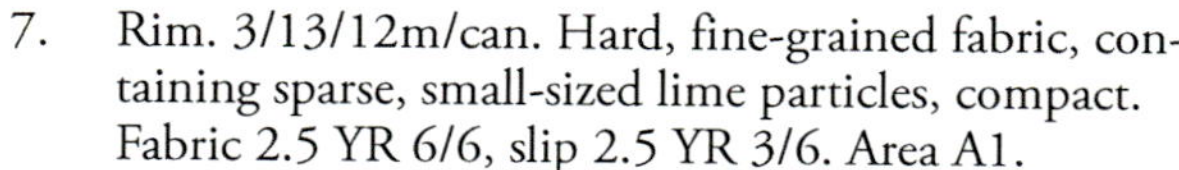

7. Rim. 3/13/12m/can. Hard, fine-grained fabric, containing sparse, small-sized lime particles, compact. Fabric 2.5 YR 6/6, slip 2.5 YR 3/6. Area A1.

Pl. XXIV. Area B

1. Rim. 111/4/00/OM. Hard fabric containing medium amount of large lime particles, small amount of silver mica flakes, tempered with coarse sand, rather dense. Fabric and surface 7.5 YR 7/4.
2. Rim. 33/3/00/OM. Hard fabric containing small amount of medium-sized lime particles, tempered with fine-grained sand, rough surface. Fabric and surface 5 R 6/6.
3. Rim. 2/2/13m/OM. Medium-hard, rather dense fabric without visible tempers. Fabric and surface 5 YR 7/1.
4. Rim. 13/6/00/OM. Medium-hard, fine-grained fabric without visible inclusions. Fabric 5 YR 6/6, slip 2.5 YR 5/8.

5. Rim. 119/4/00/OM. Hard fabric containing small amount of small-sized lime particles, tempered with small amount of fine-grained sand, slightly porous. Fabric 7.5 YR 7/4, surface 2.5 YR 6/4.
6. Base. 2/2A/13m/OM. Hard fabric containing sparse lime particles, slightly porous, rough surface. Fabric 5 R 6/6.
7. Base. 11/2/14m/OM. Hard, rather dense, well-sorted fabric with coated rough surface. Fabric 10 R 6/8, surface 2.5 YR 6/8.
8. Base. 78/2A/00/OM. Hard fabric with small amount of medium-sized lime particles, large amount of small-sized silver mica flakes, rather dense, surface rough. Fabric and surface 2.5 YR 6/8.
9. Handle. 119/4A/00/OM. Fragment of a handle. Medium-hard fabric without visible inclusions, slightly porous, smooth surface covered with coating. Fabric 5 YR 7/6, surface 7.5 YR 7.
10. Stopper. 11/d1/00/OM. Hard fabric containing small amount of small-sized lime particles, large amount of small-sized silver mica flakes, tempered with fine-grained sand, surface uneven, rough, with lime sediment. Fabric and surface 5 YR 6/6.
11. Stopper made from secondarily used brick. 2/4/00/OM.
12. Stopper made from secondarily used bottom of a vessel. 4/2/00/OM. Fabric and surface 5 YR 6/6.
13. Rim. 160/1/00/OM. Hard fabric containing small amount of small-sized lime particles. Fabric 5 YR 5/8, surface 5 YR 6/4.
14. Rim, neck and fragments of two handles. 160/1A/00/OM. Hard fabric tempered with medium amount of fine-grained sand, rough. Fabric 5 YR 5/8, surface 5 YR 7/4.
15. Rim. 9/4/00/OM. Hard fabric containing large amount of coarse lime particles, sparse pyroxene, slightly porous. Fabric 2.5 YR 7/4, surface 7.5 YR 7/4.
16. Rim. 45/6A/00/OM. Hard fabric containing small amount of silver mica flakes and lime particles, tempered with fine-grained sand, slightly porous; rough surface. Fabric 7.5 YR 7/4, surface 5 YR 7/4.
17. Base. 4/1/00/OM. Hard fabric containing medium amount of lime particles, tempered with fine-grained sand, porous; rough surface. Fabric 7.5 YR 6/4, surface 2.5 Y 7/3.
18. Bottom. 119/5/00/OM. Hard fabric containing medium amount of large lime and dark particles, tempered with medium amount of coarse sand, slightly porous. Fabric 7.5 YR 7/4, surface 2.5 YR 6/4.
19. Rim. 126/2/00/OM. Hard fabric tempered with medium amount of fine-grained sand, slightly porous; rough surface. Fabric and surface 10 YR 6/2.
20. Rim. 130/79/OM. Hard micaceous fabric with lime particles, tempered with fine-grained sand, slightly porous. Fabric and surface 5 YR 6/6.
21. Rim with fragments of two handles. 8/1/14m/OM. Medium-hard fabric with medium-sized lime particles, powdery surface. Fabric and surface 7.5 YR 7/1.
22. Handle. 11/d2/00/OM. Hard fabric containing medium amount of medium- and large-sized lime particles, small amount of small silver mica flakes and medium-sized pyroxene particles, tempered with coarse sand with brownish inclusions, porous; uneven surface. Fabric and surface 10 YR 8/3.
23. Base. 10/d2/00/OM. Hard fabric containing medium amount of medium- and large-sized lime particles, small amount of small silver mica flakes and medium-sized pyroxene particles, tempered with sand with small and medium-sized stones and brown inclusions, porous; uneven surface. Fabric and surface 10 YR 7/3.
24. Fragment of a shoulder. 160/4/00/OM. Hard fabric containing sparse lime particles and silver mica flakes, rather dense. Fabric G1 3/N – 4/N, surface 2.5 Y 6/2
25. Rim and neck. 64/2/00/OM. Hard fabric containing medium amount of silver mica flakes and large amount of lime particles, porous. Fabric G2 5/5 PB, surface 2.5 YR 6/6.
26. Rim. 164/1/00/OM. Hard fabric with medium-sized limestone inclusions. Fabric 5 YR 5/8, slip 5 YR 6/8.

Pl. XXV. Area B

27. Rim. 127/79/OM. Fabric pinkish, slip light brownish.
28. Rim. 70/4/00/OM. Ware XI. Fabric 7.5 YR 6/8, slip 2.5 YR 5/8.
29. Rim. 6/1/00/OM. Ware XI. Fabric 10 YR 8/4, slip 10 YR 4/2.
30. Rim and neck. 5/9/14m/OM. Ware XI. Fabric 7.5 YR 6/8, slip 2.5 YR 5/8.
31. Rim. 1/3/00/OM. Ware XI. Fabric 5 YR 7/6, slip 5 YR 5/4.
32. Rim. 8/6/00/OM. Ware XI. Fabric 2.5 YR 6/6, slip 2.5 YR 5/6.
37. Rim. 21/6/00/OM. Ware XI? Well-sorted fabric, dense, with small limestone inclusions and red particles. Fabric 7.5 YR 6/4, surface 7.5 YR 5/4.
38. Upper part. 41/1/13m/OM. Ware XI? Hard fabric, tempered with coarse sand, rather porous. Fabric and surface 5 R 5/8 (red).
39. Rim. 24/3/00/OM. Ware XI. Fabric and slip 7.5 YR 7/4. Published: Tomas 2006, cat. no. 20, Fig. 14.8.

Pl. XXVI. Area C2 and F

Area C2

1. Rim. 4/60/13m/can. Hard fabric containing small amount of small-sized lime particles, tempered with small amount of fine-grained sand; slightly porous. Fabric and surface 2.5 YR 4/1.
2. Rim. 4/69/13m/can. Fabric and surface 2.5 YR 5/8.
3. Rim. 4/70/13m/can. Fabric 2.5 YR 6/6, surface 10 YR 8/4.
4. Rim. 4/73/13m/can.
5. Rim. 4/75/13m/can. Ware XI.

Area F

6. Rim of an amphora. 2/7/14m/Kč. Clay containing large percentage of small-sized lime, small quantity of mica flakes and red round particles. Very hard and porous fabric with middle-grained sand. Surface rough. Fabric and surface 1 FOR GLEY 7/N.

4. Glass finds and evidence of glass manufacturing

Agnieszka Tomas

Fragments of ancient window panes, glass oil lamps and glass vessels are very often found, both inside the fortress and in the extramural area, in all occupation layers. This fact is well-reflected in the old name of the locality where the ruins of Novae are situated – Stuklen (Bulg. *stuklo* means glass). Glass finds from the fortress have been quite well studied; thus, no thorough attempt was made to collect the fragments from the area of the annexe. It seems much more valuable to present the finds from the *vicus* (Area B), where glass finds are numerous and have never been the subject of publication. The following commentary to the catalogue should be regarded as an overview of the finds from this site, while identifying some problems which concern attested glass production in Novae.

Roman glass is a soda-lime-silica glass comprising three major components, where silica is the basic component in the compound form of silicon dioxide (SiO_2), in nature occurring as quartz sand containing some alumina.[1] Pure quartz melts at a temperature of 1700°C, and such high temperatures were unobtainable for ancient workshops, so the glassmakers added a flux of sodium dioxide in the form of mineral soda (*natron*, Na_2O) to lower the melting temperature of quartz sand.[2] In Antiquity, mineral soda was imported from places where salt was readily available, particularly Wadi el-Natrun in Egypt, or created using halophytic plants containing sodium, which were burnt to obtain ash.[3] Laboratory analyses and discoveries of large raw glass slabs in the Middle East indicate that not *natron* itself was imported, but rather raw glass containing soda, which was crushed and redistributed throughout the Mediterranean and Europe, where it was re-melted.[4] The use of cullet is also mentioned by ancient authors.[5] Glass made from quartz sand mixed with soda is soluble and requires a stabilizer, usually calcium oxide (CaO), appearing naturally in beach sand, or sometimes magnesia. Ancient glass metal containing iron impurities is naturally pale green or pale blue. To obtain colourless glass, specific oxides were added to neutralize other impurities present in the batch. Coloured (monochromatic) glass was obtained by the addition of specific oxides, such as magnesium oxide (MgO) or aluminium oxide (Al_2O_3).[6]

Glass finds from Novae have been published in a series of articles and a monograph by Jerzy Olczak.[7] A wider monograph which included Novae has been published recently by Teresa Stawiarska.[8] The finds from the nearby sites, Iatrus, Nicopolis, and Sturmen on Yantra in particular, produced analogous, well-published material helpful for the elaboration of the present finds.[9]

The chemical analysis of glass from Novae shows that natron glass was dominant in Novae, and it was usually naturally coloured by iron oxide achieving a pale green or pale blue tint.[10] Soda-lime-silica glass metal containing alumina was the prevailing technology from the 3rd to the end of the 6th century, and soda-lime-silica technology was used from the 4th to the 5th/6th centuries. In the 4th century, soda-lime-silica glass containing alumina and magnesium was also noticeable, but this technology never played an important role. In the 4th–5th centuries, the glassmakers used glass metal containing potash from plants or wood to produce soda-lime-silica glass containing potassium and magnesium oxides. This type of glass metal was probably imported, perhaps as cullet used in the local workshops.[11]

The glass from Novae is badly preserved. Acid soil conditions and weathering have caused corrosion and the flaking of the surface. The earliest dated remains of glass-work, i.e., colourless window panes and pale greenish bracelets, come from the late 2nd–early 3rd centuries AD. Products dated to a later period mainly include pale green glassware, window panes, and lamps. Monochrome glass, usually dark blue, green or red, was used to make bracelets, mostly in the 4th and 5th centuries AD, but the best-quality monochromatic glass products are dated to the 2nd– 4th centuries AD.[12]

Bracelets made from dark blue glass (**Pl. XXVII, 1–6**) were made in Novae and they are dated to the mid-2nd century AD.[13] This type of jewellery must have been quite common, since it is found in all places

1. Freestone 2008, 83.
2. Stern 1990, 37.
3. Freestone 2005; Henderson 2013, 22–55.
4. Freestone 2008, 78–79; Shortland et al. 2006.
5. Shepherd 1999, 302; Freestone 2008, 82–83.
6. Jackson 2005, 763–65; Henderson 2013, 2–3; Shepherd 1999, 301.
7. Olczak 1998 with literature, esp. 119–20.
8. Stawiarska 2014, esp. 56–63.
9. Dekówna 1975; Gomolka 1979; Shepherd 1999.
10. Olczak 1998, 88–89; Stawiarska 2014, 61–62, and 115–16.
11. Stawiarska 2013, 62.
12. Olczak 1998, 120–21.
13. Olczak 1998, 54.

within the fortress and its vicinity.[14] A black bracelet (**Pl. XXVII, 7**) was perhaps also made locally. A relatively big fragment of a pale greenish and red bracelet (**Pl. XXVII, 10**) attracts special attention due to its quality. A dark brown-red fragment of a bracelet (**Pl. XXVII, 8**) is rather unique for Novae, both in its form and colours.

An upper part of a jug and a rim (**Pl. XXVIII, 11–12**) could belong to the popular Isings 50 form, widespread from the 1st to the beginning of the 3rd century AD, and they were particularly common in the late 1st century.[15] Analogous jugs dated to the Flavian period are known from Novae, and some later examples from Nicopolis.[16]

A stemmed goblet is a distinctive form commonly found at Roman sites (Isings form 111). The earliest finds of stemmed goblets are dated to the 3rd century.[17] Stemmed goblets had very thin body walls, which corroded and shattered; therefore, stems are the fragments of these vessels that have most frequently been preserved.[18] They are very numerous in the late Roman layers of the fortress in Novae. The earliest stemmed goblets from Novae are dated to the end of the 3rd – beginning of the 4th century AD, and they were produced until the end of Roman presence at the fortress.[19]

Stem goblets from Novae have been the subject of several publications. The classification created by Maria Dekówna was later further developed by Galina Dankova, who defined three basic groups divided into further sub-groups. Another classification was created by Alicja Turno, who defined 5 types, but her classification was based on a small group of finds.[20] Therefore, the dating based on this typology should be treated very cautiously.

Various types, differing in their diameters and manufacturing technology, have been collected at the site (**Pl. XXVIII, 13–16**). One fragment, which is relatively massive when compared to other items, made from decolourized glass metal (**Pl. XXVIII, 13**), would fit the Turno 1.2 type, dated to the 3rd and 4th centuries, but – according to Dankova – this would be an item belonging to Group III dated to the 4th–5th centuries.[21] Similar bases were found in the *principia*, but in a context dated to the 6th century.[22] A stem with a base ring (**Pl. XXVIII, 14**) fits a type classified by Dankova as Group IIa2 dated to the 4th–5th century AD, while Turno, who classified such vessels as type 4.3.2, offered a more precise dating to the 5th century.[23] The items found in Nicopolis were dated to the 5th century,[24] but in Dichin they were dated to the 6th century,[25] while those in the *principia* to between the 4th century and the 6th century.[26] A bottom made in the same way as an item from Area B (**Pl. XXVIII, 15**) was found in Dichin in a layer dated to the 6th century.[27] This confusing dating indicates that this type of glass item was produced throughout the entire late Roman period and many such specimens were found in secondary contexts. According to J. Olczak, in the 6th century stem goblets were manufactured in a broader variety than in the preceding period.[28]

Two other bases (**Pl. XXVIII, 16–17**) were most probably made by the same masters as the stemmed goblets. A form analogous to the first item was found in Nicopolis (context dated to AD 300–450) and a second one in Dichin.[29]

Some cup bottoms with an applied base ring collected in Area B (**Pl. XXVIII, 18–20**) have analogies in forms known from fortress layers dated to AD 280 – the first half of the 4th century AD.[30] In Nicopolis, the earliest bottom of an similar form is dated by its context to AD 150–250,[31] although later dated items look very similar.[32]

Twenty percent of the glass finds at Novae are oil lamps produced locally and they are found in contexts dated to the 3rd – beginning of the 7th century AD.[33] Classifications of the lamps from Novae were proposed by A. Turno, who defined four types, and by J. Olczak,

14. Olczak 1981, 63–64, Tab. IX, 1–7; Vulov 1965, 29, Fig. 4.
15. Cholakova 2006a, 214, Tab. IV, 1–6.
16. Gencheva 2002, 46, Tab. XLVII, 3; Shepherd 1999, 367, no. 83.
17. Isings 1967, 262,3; Gomolka 1979, 161–164; Turno 1989, 165; Olczak 1995, 59.
18. Turno 1989, 163.
19. Dankova 1993, 100, no. 19 and 103, no. 29; Olczak 1998, 48.
20. Turno 1989, 164–65; cf. Olczak 1995, 59–60.
21. Dankova 1993, 113–17, nos. 56–68, Tab. VI; cf. Turno 1989, 165, Abb. 1, 1.2.
22. Olczak 1995, 62–64, Tab. 2, 11, 16.
23. Dankova 1993, 110–13, nos. 49–56, Tab. V; cf. Turno 1989, 165, Abb. 1, 4.3.2.
24. Shepherd 1999, 337–38, Fig. 11.12, 271–73.
25. Cholakova 2005, nos. 27–30.
26. Olczak 1995, Tab. 2.7–8; Tab. 3.4, 6, 10, 13–18.
27. Cholakova 2005, no. 31.
28. Olczak 1995, 76.
29. Shepherd 1999, 354, no, 662, Tab. 11.17; Cholakova 2005, 732 and Fig. on p. 737, no. 16.
30. Dyczek 1999, 102–03, Fig. 3, esp. nos. 8–10.
31. Shepherd 1999, 334, Fig. 11.11, no. 243.
32. Shepherd 1999, 349–50, Fig. 11.16, 591–653.
33. Olczak 1998, 49.

who defined three types.[34] Surprisingly, no fragments which could be identified as lamps have been found in Area B.

Glass vessels are represented by 5 diagnostic fragments. A fragment of a thick flat bottom (**Pl. XXVIII, 21**) could have belonged to a beaker, jug or flask. A flask with a similar shape of its bottom found in Novae was dated to the 2nd–3rd centuries.[35] Two bowl rims (**Pl. XXVIII, 22, 23**) have close analogies in Nicopolis, where they were found in a context dated to the 4th and 5th centuries.[36] The third rim, which is everted, much thicker and bears a small fragment of an ornament stuck to the outer surface, belonged to a bowl. Base rings of vessels with wide bottoms could have been made using the same technique as the goblets and cups discussed above (**Pl. XXVIII, 25** cf. **17**). Applied base rings were also made in such vessels (**Pl. XXVIII, 26**).

Several fragments of window panes have been collected in Area B (**Pl. XXIX, 27–36**). In the fortress, fragments of window panes are frequent in layers dated to the 5th and 6th centuries AD, though the earliest finds related to window production are dated to the mid-2nd century AD.[37] The 2nd–3rd-century window panes from Novae are colourless, while the later ones were naturally pale green in colour.[38] Less than half of them are cast, while the rest are blown, and these two techniques were both used in the 2nd and in the 4th centuries. It is worth noting that more than half of the finds are only 0.1–0.2 cm thick.[39]

The distribution of glass finds and glass-making waste in Area B indicates possible glass manufacturing carried out there (**Fig. 67**). Several pieces of glass-making waste, namely slag (**Fig. 66**), was collected at the site in 2000.[40] Glass production is well attested in Novae, but only in the fortress. Several glass furnaces dated to the first half of the 4th century were discovered to the north and to the east of the episcopal basilica (*basilica maior*) and in the ruins of the military hospital (in its northern part).[41] The discovered furnaces served for melting glass (tank furnaces) and for shaping products ("domed" furnaces).[42] The earliest furnaces are dated by their context to the 2nd century, and the latest to the end of the 6th century.[43] The questions formulated by Jerzy Olczak concerning where the glass masters working in Novae came from, about the origins of the raw glass metal, and – last but not least – whether the Novae products were exported elsewhere[44] must remain open. Nevertheless, Teresa Stawiarska made a very interesting observation concerning the use of antimony as a decolourant in late Roman Novae, while it seems unlikely that it was used elsewhere at that time. According to the Polish scholar, this

34. Turno 1989, 166; Olczak 1995, 31–32.
35. Turno 1989, 168–169, Abb. 3.5.
36. Shepherd 1999, 346, nos. 483–97, Fig. 11.14, 483; 497.
37. Olczak 1995, 26; 1998, 54; cf. Turno 1989, 168 (the earliest finds date to the second half of the 3rd c. AD).
38. Olczak 1998, 120–21; Stawiarska 2014, 60.
39. Turno 1989, 168 and Tab. 6.
40. Tomas 2006, 117.
41. Olczak 1998, 13, fn. 2 and 76–87; Nawracki 1999; Dyczek 1999.
42. Olczak 1998, 23ff.; Biernacki et al. 1991, 110; Dyczek 1999, 101; Stawiarska 2013, 59.
43. Olczak 1998, 13 and 87–88; Stawiarska 2013, 62.
44. Olczak 1998, 89.

Fig. 66. Ostrite Mogili (Area B). Glass production waste collected in 2014 (photo by A. Tomas).

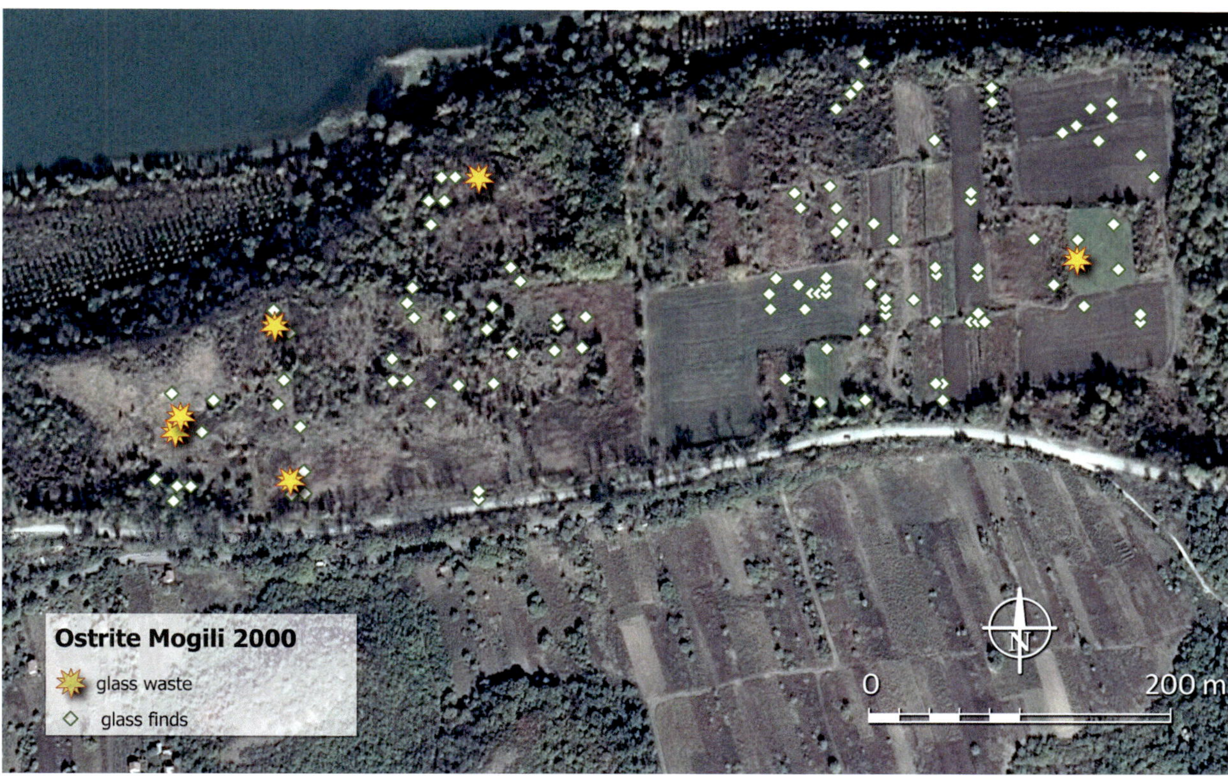

Fig. 67. Ostrite Mogili (Area B). The map of glass finds and glass production waste based on the results of surveys in 2000 (by A. Tomas).

can be explained by the fact that the same chemical component was used by Dacian craftsmen before the evacuation of Dacia, and glass production could have been linked to the Dacian tradition.[45]

It is not possible to state whether the window panes collected in Area B (**Pl. XXIX**) were produced in the *vicus* or installed in some building. Although the archaeological findings are neither rich nor conclusive,[46] iconographic representations show that glazed windows were found both in public and private buildings.[47] Glass vessels from Area B are mostly dated to the Late Roman and Early Byzantine periods, while window panes are dated to the Early Roman times. It is possible that some of them were produced on site, and the glass-making waste found there during the surveys provides evidence for this hypothesis.

Catalogue of glass finds

Pl. XXVII. Area B. Bracelets

1. Fragment of a bracelet. 9/00w/OM. Dark blue glass with opalescent corrosion on its surface. Published: Tomas 2006, cat. no. 48, Fig. 18.3.
2. Fragment of a bracelet. 16/00w/OM. Slightly twisted roll. Dark blue glass with opalescent corrosion on its surface. Published: Tomas 2006, cat. no. 47, Fig. 18.2.
3. Fragment of a bracelet. 22/00w/OM. Dark blue glass with white limestone sediment on its surface.
4. Fragment of a bracelet. 28/00/OM. Irregular oval roll. Dark blue glass with opalescent corrosion on surface.
5. Fragment of a bracelet. 29/00/OM. Dark blue glass with opalescent corrosion on its surface.
6. Fragment of a bracelet. 39a/00/OM. Dark blue glass with opalescent corrosion on its surface. Published: Tomas 2006, cat. no. 46, Fig. 18.1.
7. Fragment of a bracelet. 39b/00/OM. Two perpendicular rolls stuck together. Black glass.
8. Fragment of a bracelet. 60/00/OM. Slightly twisted roll. Brown glass with two red stripes.
9. Fragment of a bracelet. 46/00w/OM. Pale green translucent glass.
10. Fragment of a bracelet. 35/14w/OM. Regular circle of two strongly twisted rolls of green and red glass.

Pl. XXVIII. Area B. Glass vessels

11. Upper part of a jug with a handle. 17/00/OM. A rim and a neck made from one layer of glass. The preserved upper part of a handle was made of a wide, flat ribbon of glass with two perpendicular grooves. The handle was stuck under the rim and along the neck. Pale green translucent glass with numerous air-bubbles. *Published*: Tomas 2006, cat. no. 12, Fig. 13.12.

45. Stawiarska 2014, 63.
46. Harden 1961, Tab. V; Michielin 2019, 98–99.
47. Velo-Gala and Garriguet Mata 2017.

Pl. XXVII. Glass bracelets from Area B

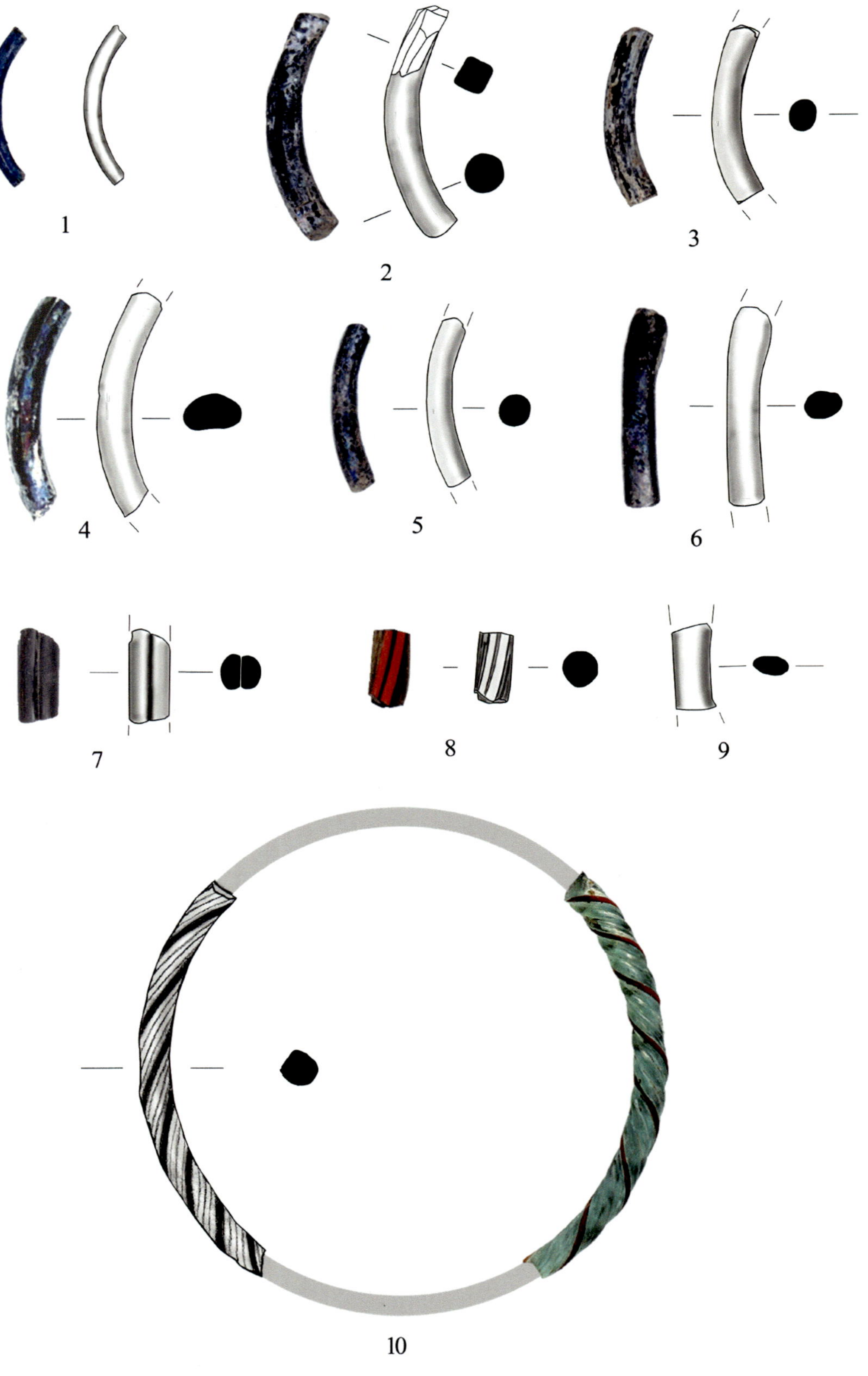

Pl. XXVIII. Glass vessels from Area B

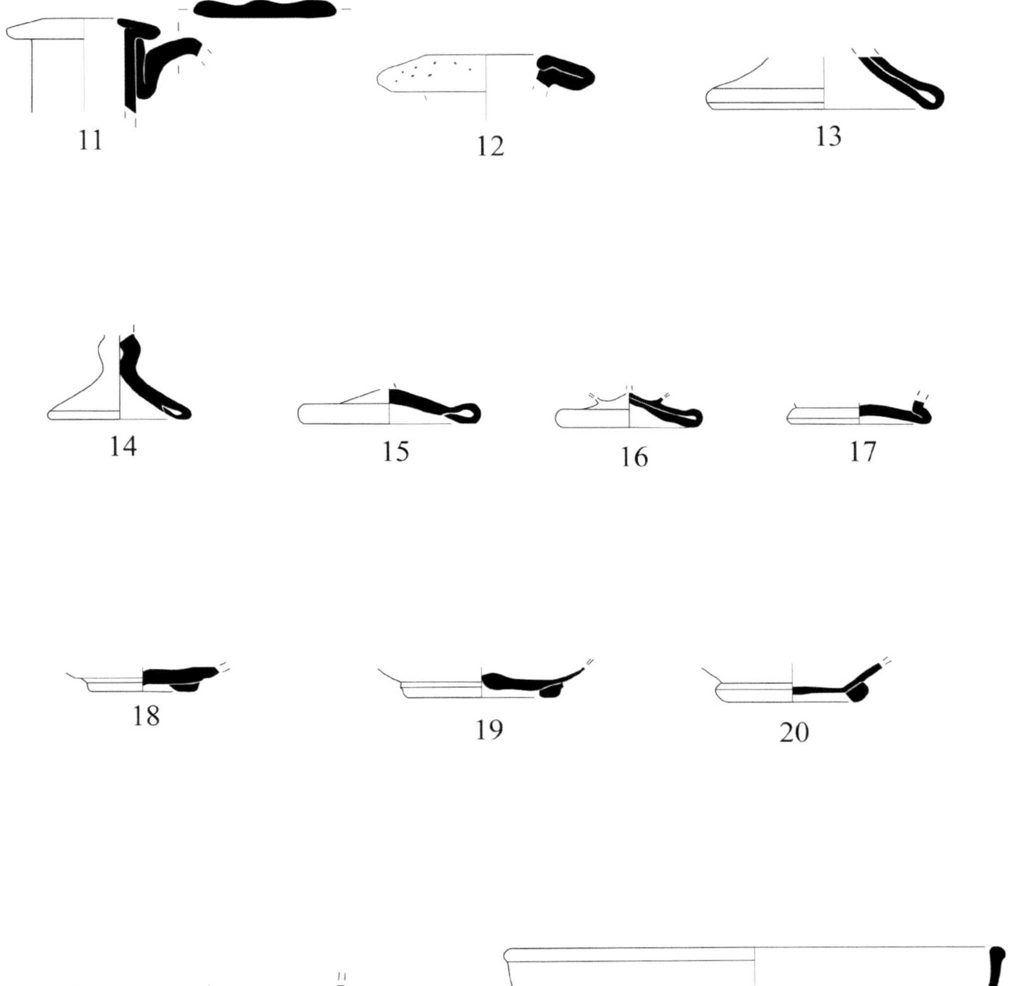

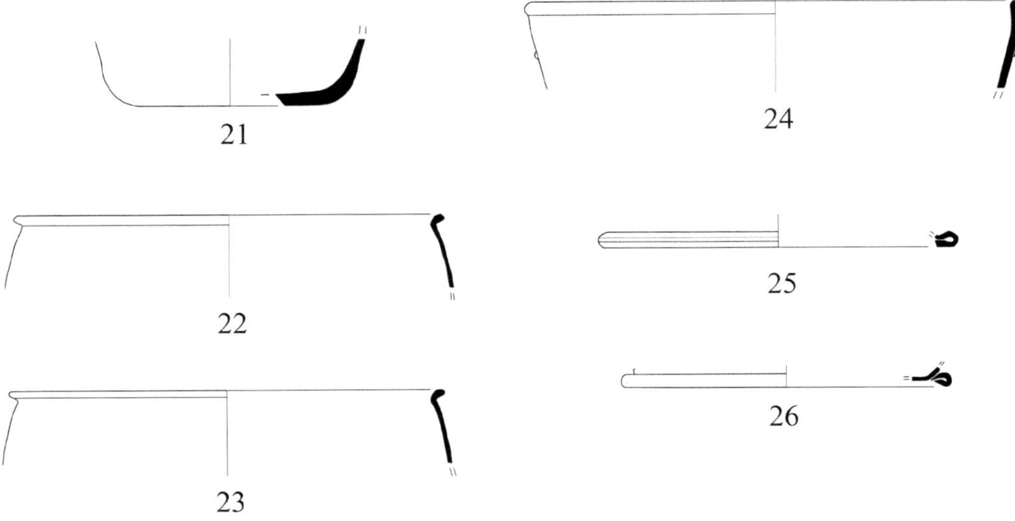

12. Rim of a jug. 69/00w/OM. Rim made from one layer of glass. Blue translucent glass with air-bubbles.
13. Stem of a goblet. 8b/00w/OM. Found with no. 14. Base made from two layers of glass pulled inwards. Colourless translucent glass with air-bubbles.
14. Stem of a goblet. 40/00w/OM. Profiled conical base made from two layers of glass pulled inwards. Pale green translucent glass with air-bubbles. *Published*: Tomas 2006, cat. no. 10, Fig. 13.10
15. Stem of a goblet. 68/00w/OM. Flat base made from two layers of glass pulled inwards and stuck under the outer edge. Colourless translucent glass with sparse air-bubbles.
16. Stem of a goblet. 23/00w/OM. Flat base made from two layers of glass pulled inwards. Pale blue translucent glass with air-bubbles.
17. Bottom of a cup. 12/10/00m/OM. Bottom made from one layer of glass with everted edge forming a base. Colourless translucent glass with air-bubbles.
18. Bottom of a cup with a base ring. 133/1/00m/OM. Bottom made from one layer of glass with applied base ring. Pale green translucent glass without visible air-bubbles.
19. Bottom of a vessel with a base ring. 48/00w/OM. Bottom made from one layer of glass with applied base ring. Pale green translucent glass with air-bubbles.
20. Bottom of a cup with a base ring. 19/00/OM. Bottom made from one layer of glass with applied base ring. Pale green translucent glass with numerous air-bubbles.
21. Bottom of a jug or beaker(?). 57/3/00m/OM. A flat bottom and fragment of a body. Pale green translucent glass with air bubbles.
22. Rim of a beaker. 43/00w/OM. Colourless translucent glass. Karanis 274.
23. Upper part of a vessel. 2/00w/OM. Colourless translucent glass with air bubbles.
24. Upper part of a vessel. 18/00w/OM. Colourless translucent glass with air bubbles.
25. Base of a bowl. 8a/00w/OM. Found with no. 4. Fragment of a hollow base formed by a layer of glass everted inwards. Pale green translucent glass with air bubbles.
26. Fragment of the bottom of a bowl with a base ring. 57/00w/OM. Pushed-in base made from one layer of glass with a hollow tubular base ring. Pale green translucent glass with air-bubbles. *Published*: Tomas 2006, cat. no. 11, Fig. 13.11.

PL. XXIX. Area B. Window glass

27–36. Fragments of translucent colourless window glass collected in 2000, in the western part of the site. Stretched air bubbles are visible in all pieces. Photo by J. Recław. Some of the fragments were published by Tomas 2006, Fig. 15.

Pl. XXIX. Window glass from Area B

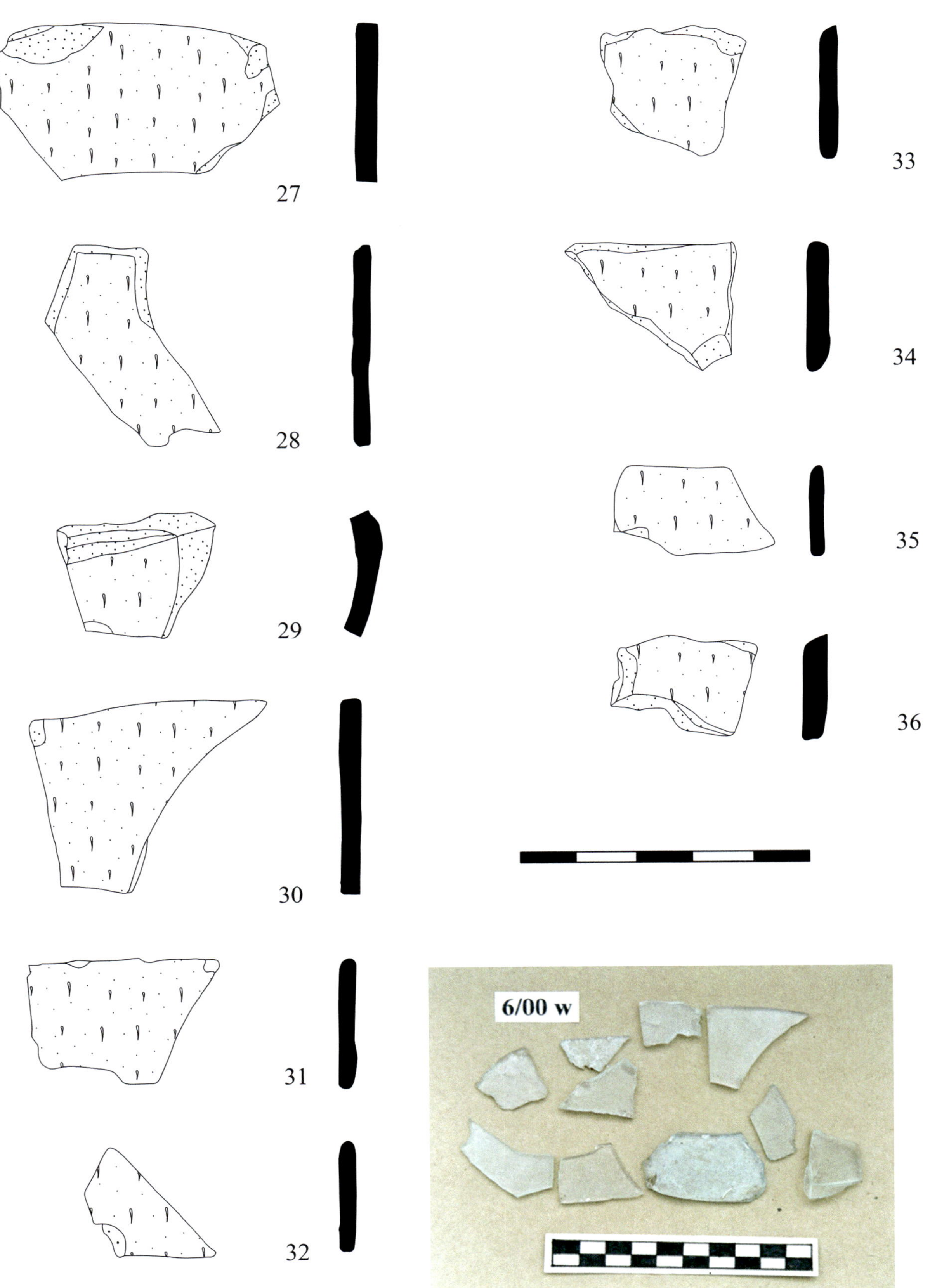

5. Weapons, armour, and other equipment

Bartosz Kontny

Thirty-five metal finds were related to military activities. Among them, arrowheads made of iron are the most numerous group of finds in the collection (24). They were found in almost all areas: in Area A1 (11), Area B (10) and E (3). Other finds related to military equipment and armour were found only in the vicinity of the camp (Area A1), and they are represented by 11 finds.

Arrowheads

Eleven arrowheads have been collected from the annexe (Area A1, **Fig. 68**), ten from the *vicus* (Area B, **Fig. 70**) and three from another small settlement (Area E, **Fig. 71**). Among them, one may indicate three trilobate, tanged specimens (**Pl. XXX, 1–3**). Such forms are also known from earlier excavations in Novae.[1] They may be tentatively attributed to W. Zanier's Type 3 (1988), i.e., ones with rhombic blades, although the lobes are not complete here. The chronology of this form has not been established with much precision; thus, it encompasses the time-span from the Republican Period until the 3rd century AD.[2] Such specimens were very typical for military contexts. Easy to produce,[3] they served military purposes, often in conjunction with reflex composite bows.[4] The three blades made their flight more stable, i.e., less vulnerable to gusts of wind, than in the case of flat arrowheads.[5] Trilobate arrowheads were common in the Roman world, which is proven by numerous finds from the western provinces (Britannia, Germania and Raetia), while they were less popular in the Danube area, i.e., Noricum, Pannonia, Moesia and Dacia, and quite unique in Asia Minor and the Middle East; however, the examples from the last two places may be of local, non-Roman origin.[6] They were attested even as far as south-east Arabia, here plausibly as Parthian imports.[7] Trilobate arrowheads from the Roman military camps are linked with archers from auxiliary forces, specifically in the north-western provinces.[8] It seems more

1. Gacuta 1987, 167, 169–70, Pl. XXXII:2, 6–8, 12–14; 1993, 37–38, Pl. XXIII:1–4, 6–8, 12–15.

2. Zanier 1988, 6.
3. Zanier 1995.
4. Delrue 2007, 246–47.
5. Delrue 2007, 245.
6. Zanier 1988, 7–9, Fig. 2.
7. Delrue 2007.
8. Zanier 1988, 9–13, Fig. 4.

Fig. 68. Novae, Area A1 (annexe). Finds of arrowheads from 2012–14 (by A. Tomas).

Fig. 69. Novae, Area A1 (annexe). Finds of other military equipment from 2012–14 (by A. Tomas).

difficult to understand why *sagitarii* troops from Dacia, Pannonia and Moesia left so few arrowheads, but we may have a distorted view of the issue due to the state of research (see the finds of arrowheads Type Gudea B III from Dacia[9] or the ones from Novae).

Theoretically, the rhombic trilobate arrowheads may also be later. Such forms are well known in the nomadic milieu in the Migration Period. They were taken over from the nomadic Huns by the Germanic peoples, e.g., the Gepids, Thuringians, Heruls, Bavarians, Alamanni or even the Lombards (in this case Avaric influence is also possible) in the Early Migration Period. Such forms were also in use among the nomadic Alans from the same period, as well as in Eastern Europe: in the Kiev culture, Moshchino culture, among the Dnieper Balts, on the upper Don River (Type Chertovitskoe III sites) or in the Tsebelda culture in the east Pontic zone.[10] Therefore, one cannot exclude that the trilobate arrowheads from Novae should be attributed to 5th-century barbarians, e.g., the Hunnic invaders from the first half of the 5th century or the settlement of the Goths there under Theodoric the Great in the 480s.

The next group consists of bodkin-type arrowheads, i.e., rectangular (**Pl. XXX, 5–7, 9–11; XXXI, 1, 2**) or triangular (**Pl. XXX, 8**) in cross-section, all tanged. Such forms were documented in Novae.[11] They were very simple to produce, and possessed quite a good piercing capacity. They could have been used for target practice, as proven by the find of an ox skull in Northumberland with several small, punched square holes.[12] However, their popularity was highest in the 3rd century in Germania.[13] Similar forms but with a conical blade (**Pl. XXXII, 1**) are known from the Early Principate.[14] Once again, one cannot state definitely that they are not of different origin, as bodkin-type arrowheads constituted a very effective element of the Germanic military archery in Scandinavia and northern Germany from the 3rd century onwards.[15] We know of them also from the Middle

9. Gudea 1994, Fig. 5.
10. Bitner-Wróblewska and Kontny 2006, with further literature.

11. Gacuta 1987, 169, Pl. XXXII:3–4.
12. Coulston 1985, 265.
13. Bishop and Coulston 2006, 166, Figs. 106:6, 8–11.
14. Bishop and Coulston 2006, 88, Figs. 46:8, 10, 12.
15. Raddatz 1963; Pauli Jensen 2009; Pauli Jensen and Nørbach 2009, 68–77, Figs. 57, 59.

Ages in different parts of Europe.[16] One should not neglect the possibility that at least in the case of certain poorly preserved specimens we may be dealing with another function (**Pl. XXXI.8, 9**). Maybe we should also add one iron item (**Pl. XXXII, 1**) to this group, but this is highly hypothetical because of its fragmentary state of preservation.

Leaf-bladed arrowheads supplemented with tang are another significant group. The shape of the blades is rhomboid (**XXX.4; XXXI.5-7, 10; XXXII.3**), and one possesses a ring-shaped widening at the base of the blade (**Pl. XXXI, 3**). Arrowheads of this type were also unearthed in Novae earlier.[17] In this case, we are dealing with quite simple forms, but not typical of Antiquity, although they were documented in the north European Barbaricum in the Younger Roman and Migration Period, i.e., late 2nd–6th centuries, but this refers to the non-rhombic-like form Subtype 1A1.[18] However, the specimens from Novae should most probably be attributed to the Medieval Period,[19] and linked with eastern nomadic influences, e.g. the Pechneg, Hungarians[20] or Tartars.[21] However, it is very difficult to reach any conclusions when dealing with materials out of context. At times, scholars conclude that such a form should be associated with Antiquity,[22] which is proved by finds from grave 2/2006 in Singidunum IV, where a Germanic warrior was buried together with both trilobate and leaf-shaped tanged arrowheads with rhombic blades, showing the direct influence of the nomadic milieu.[23] In the discussed case of the Novae finds, it is possible that they represent early nomadic arrowheads of that type, but it seems even more probable that we are dealing with the remains of Hungarian raids against Great Moravia, as they were typical for these nomads.[24] Such arrowheads were frequently found at the Great Moravian ringforts on the Danube. Moreover, neither the territory of the Great Moravia nor their earlier Frankish counterparts delivered firmly dated earlier or local examples of such items. Theoretically, it is justified to treat them as elements of the Pechnegs' armament but their archaeological context within strongholds makes such a supposition less likely.[25] The same interpretation may be applicable in the case of another tanged arrowhead (**Pl. XXXI, 1**), which resembles a bodkin type, but its narrow blade is flat and slightly rhombic in shape. It finds very good parallels in the Magyar material from attacked forts in Medieval Bulgaria, e.g., Pliska, dated to the 10th–11th centuries.[26]

Belt elements

Other finds of military equipment are known exclusively from the annexe (**Fig. 69**). A single-strap terminal pendant was found that is lanceolate in form (teardrop-shaped), with a loop for fastening in its upper part and a knob at the bottom (**Pl. XXX, 12**). Such endings were widespread across the limes provinces of the Roman Empire[27] in the late 2nd–3rd centuries, occasionally also at the beginning of the 4th century.[28] They were generally worn in pairs, at the ends of belt terminals, specifically terminating apron straps,[29] but are also encountered as pendants on horse harnesses.[30] Although the majority of the terminals are associated with the military sphere, one cannot exclude the possibility that civilians also sometimes used them, since they were documented in female graves.[31] Theoretically, they could have been used on baldrics,[32] though so far we cannot prove this hypothesis.

Another element of the belt is an elongated, copper-alloy belt mount with transverse, slightly diagonal grooves (**Pl. XXX, 13**). It is supplemented by two rivets and an oblong washer. Items similar in form are assigned to belt mounts, but there is a possibility that they were used also as horse harness mounts.[33] Their chronology covers the time-span from the beginning of the 2nd until the early 3rd centuries, but mainly in the mid-2nd century.[34]

The peltiform stud (**Pl. XXX, 21**) found at the site is an example of a simple decoration used to adorn leather

16. See, e.g.: Kazakevičius 2004, 116, Figs. 19:9–10, Figs. 27–28; Creighton and Wright 2016, 171, Fig. 6.4; see English arrowheads types M5, M6, M7 according to Jessop 1999, 198, Fig. 1.
17. Gacuta 1987, 169, Pl. XXXII:9–11.
18. Pauli Jensen and Nørbach 2009, 56–57, 105, Fig. 40.
19. Kazakevičius 2004, 114–15, Figs. 20–22; 2.
20. Henning 2011.
21. Medvedev 1966, 54–60; Świętosławski 1997, *passim*.
22. See, e.g., Gardun / *Tiliurium* – Sanader and Tončinić 2010, 58.
23. Ivanišević and Kazanski 2007, 116–25, Fig. 7:43–45. The authors date the interment to Phase D1 but I tend to situate it in Phase D2, i.e., in the second third of the 5th c., see: the chronology of Asian type spathae – Kontny and Mączyńska 2015, 245–49.
24. See the finds from the Bulgarian city at Pliska – Henning 2007, 667, Pl. I:11–12.
25. Henning 2011, 251–52.
26. Henning 2007, 667, Pl. II:16.
27. Also in Novae – see Gencheva 2000, 67, Pl. V:6.
28. Oldenstein 1977, 143–44, Pl. 36:291–304; see also, e.g., Chapman 2005, 147; Radman-Livaja 2008, 301.
29. Bishop and Coulston 2006, 110, Fig. 63:1.
30. Palágyi 1997, 467.
31. Oldenstein 1977, 144.
32. Radman-Livaja 2008, 301.
33. Oldenstein 1977, 189, Pl. 58:727–29.
34. Oldenstein 1977, 189–90; see Chapman 2005, 129–30, Pl. Sr50–54.

Fig. 70. Ostrite Mogili (Area B). Finds of arrowheads from 2000 and 2014 (by A. Tomas).

Fig. 71. Chehlarski geran (Area E). Finds of arrowheads from 2014 (by A. Tomas).

straps (i.a., belts), which is inferred from the length of the rivet (one or two). They are dated to the second half of the 2nd century, but were also encountered in the 3rd century,[35] while the ones with a triangularly segmented upper part, like in the case in question, are mainly dated to the 3rd–4th centuries.[36] Such items are linked sometimes with horse harness sets.[37] The piece

35. Oldenstein 1977, 178–79, Pl. 53:627–29.

36. Radman-Livaja 2004, 117.

37. Radman-Livaja 2004, 117; 2009, 1501, Fig. 2:18.

in question, with a horizontal cross-bar, represents Aurrecoechea-Fernández's Type I3c.[38]

Another specimen is a strongly profiled terminal (**Pl. XXX, 20**), preserved fragmentarily so its precise function cannot be established unequivocally. A similar strap is found at the end of Madyda-Legutko's Type 1 from the 1st–early 2nd century. Such terminals were very popular among the Barbarians, namely those from Central Europe.[39] They existed to reinforce the free ends of straps and to provide some extra weight to help the strap to hang properly.[40] However, one cannot exclude that they were used as horse harness elements.[41] Generally, such forms ended with a rivet plate split into two, but some were equipped with a single short rivet plate. Thus, it is assumed that they served also as mounts for furniture, caskets or doors.[42] This seems probable in the discussed case, as its dimensions are quite big for a strap end. The Barbarian strap ends, much more popular, do not differ significantly from the Roman ones; the chronology of the latter is assumed to indicate the 1st and 2nd centuries.[43]

Attempts have been made to identify the function of a discovered copper-alloy decorative plate (**Pl. XXX, 14**). Such specimens are included in the group of belt mounts; however, in this particular case, we are dealing with only a small fragment. It seems to be strongly profiled, which is typical of the Early Principate belt fittings, but also of horse harness strap terminals or links.[44] Therefore, there are some doubts as to the precise identification of the plate from Novae.

Finally, there is one item which cannot be identified precisely (**Pl. XXX, 19**). Made of iron, it consists of a roughly rectangular plate with a rod, slightly bent inwards, from which the button terminal projects; the rod is situated on the edge of the plate. On its back, the plate is supplemented with two oval terminals most probably used to fix it to the ground (the holes in the terminals seem to have been meant for placing a toggle inside). However, the item looks a little like a girdle plate tie-loop of a *lorica segmentata* (they used to be made of copper alloy but also of iron), but it does not have the characteristic details, such as a strongly bent terminal, ended without a button. It is also less slender and tie-loops do not have oval terminals on their backs.[45] Ostensibly, it seems more reasonable to interpret the specimen from Novae as a belt fitting (belt clasp?). Two similar items, parts of openwork belt mounts, were found in the amphitheatre at Caerleon in Wales.[46] Unfortunately, in our case, there is no such decoration and moreover the terminals are too long for them to have been used conveniently on a belt.

Nails

There are three copper-alloy nails with hut-shaped heads in the collection (**Pl. XXX, 15–17**). Along with similarly shaped rivets, they are one of the most popular categories of finds in the Roman military context, although their exact function is not clear. It is assumed that some of them were mounted on leather straps.[47] Oldenstein mentions their use in Barbaricum as a means to fasten shield-edge mounts,[48] which is obviously false (see different forms of rivets for fixing edge mounts).[49] However, almost identical items (mostly rivets, not nails), also ones made completely of copper alloy, served to mount shield grips and shield bosses on Barbarian shields (Type C by Zieling), specifically in the late 1st–early 2nd centuries.[50] However, this form of rivets is also known as specimens used to fix different elements, e.g. ornamental casket mounts from the Przeworsk culture cemetery at Opatów, Grave 1229.[51] Concluding, the purpose of the nails from Novae has not been fully determined, but their chronology should be set most probably to the times of the Early Principate.

Shafted weapons

There is one piece found at a certain distance from the fortress (Area E) that may be assigned to the iron blade of the head of a shafted weapon (**Pl. XXXII, 4**). It is fragmentarily preserved (only part of the blade has survived), so its exact chronology and cultural affiliation is impossible to establish.

38. Aurrecoechea-Fernández 2007, Fig. 3.
39. Madyda-Legutko 2011, 17–31, Maps 3–4.
40. Chapman 2005, 124.
41. Bishop 1988, Pl. 52:1a.
42. Franke 2009, 52, Pl. 46:933.
43. Oldenstein 1977, 144–46, Pl. 36:310–14; see, e.g., Chapman 2005, 124, Fig. Sp01–02.
44. See, e.g., Unz and Deschler-Erb 1997, Pl. 61:1697–1705, 62:1713–14, 1723–26, 1751–52, 64:1820–23; Franke 2009, Pl. 13, 19.
45. Bishop 2002, 39, Fig. 5.6:4; Thomas 2003, 91–93, Fig. 61.
46. Chapman 2005, 109–10, Pl. Sc10–11; see also Oldenstein 1977, Pl. 62:800, 63:807.
47. Oldenstein 1977, 166–67, Pl. 46:451–68.
48. Oldenstein 1977, 166.
49. Zieling 1989, 227–39, Pl. 32.
50. Zieling 1989, 258–59, Pl. 34:5–6.
51. Madyda-Legutko, Rodzińska-Nowak, and Zagórska-Telega 2011, 253, Pl. CCCXCI:9.0.

Conclusions

The militaria from the collection includes items quite widely dated, yet firmly linked with the Roman military fortress. Among them, we have generally identified trilobate and bodkin-type arrowheads, a few nails, and belt or horse harness mounts (Area A1). Only a couple of the tanged arrowheads with a rhombic flat blade seem to document later events that occurred at the site, i.e., a possible Magyar appearance in the region in the Middle Ages. The rhombic arrowheads were concentrated at Area B (*vicus*), which was not secured and where numerous finds proving a Medieval settlement phase were spotted.

In contrast, the majority of the bodkin type and trilobate arrowheads, were found in Area A1 (annexe), together with typically Roman small finds, like a peltiform stud, nails, a belt mount, an appliqué or a lanceolate strap end. Despite doubts as to the identification of particular specimens as expressed above, one may state that their context speaks for their Roman origin. Therefore, it may be concluded that they are connected with the phase of Roman presence, and the chronology of the mentioned finds does not contradict the general chronology of the site. The appearance of the trilobate arrowheads in the area seems to prove the existence of a *sagittarii* unit as part of the Roman military forces here.

Area E is definitely underrepresented as refers to militaria (only one unequivocally identified find). However, this should not be surprising if we take into consideration the character of the place, i.e., a farmhouse.

Catalogue of weapons, armour, and other equipment

Pl. XXX. Area A1

1. Trilobate arrowhead, iron. 8/13w/can.
2. Trilobate arrowhead, iron. 14/13w/can.
3. Trilobate arrowhead. 27/13w/can.
4. Leaf-bladed arrowhead, iron. 51/12w/can.
5. Bodkin type arrowhead, iron. 50/12w/can.
6. Bodkin type arrowhead, iron. 9/13w/can.
7. Bodkin type arrowhead, iron. 11/13w/can.
8. Bodkin type arrowhead, iron. 28/13w/can.
9. Bodkin type arrowhead, iron. 3/14w/can. To the east of the eastern camp's wall. Selected from among the mass finds; without an exact findspot.
10. Bodkin type arrowhead?, iron. 7/13w/can.
11. Bodkin type arrowhead, iron. 24/13w/can.
12. Lanceolate strap end, copper alloy. 41/12w/can.
13. Belt mount, copper alloy. 38/12w/can.
14. Decorative plate, copper alloy. 42/12w/can.
15. Nail, copper alloy. 56/12w/can.
16. Nail, copper alloy. 30/13w/can. To the east of the eastern camp's wall. Selected from among the mass finds; without an exact findspot.
17. Nail, copper alloy. 22/13w/can.
18. Copper alloy fitting (?). 40/12w/can.
19. Appliqué, iron. 3/13w/can.
20. Mount, iron. 45/12w/can.
21. Peltiform stud, copper alloy. 39/12w/can.
22. Iron item (belt buckle?). 19/13w/can. To the east of the eastern camp's wall. Selected from among the mass finds; without an exact findspot.

Pl. XXXI. Area B – Ostrite Mogili

1. Bodkin type arrowhead, iron. 5/00w/OM.
2. Bodkin type arrowhead, iron. 10/00w/OM.
3. Leaf-bladed arrowhead, iron. 7/14w/OM.
4. Bodkin type arrowhead, iron. 33/14w/OM.
5. Leaf-bladed arrowhead, iron. 70/00w/OM.
6. Leaf-bladed arrowhead, iron. 23/14w/OM.
7. Leaf-bladed arrowhead, iron. 51/13w/OM.
8. Bodkin type arrowhead?, iron. 14/14w/OM.
9. Bodkin type arrowhead?, iron. 57/13w/OM.
10. Leaf-bladed arrowhead, iron. 4/00/OM.

Pl. XXXII. Area E

1. Bodkin type arrowhead, iron. 116/14w/OM3.
2. Leaf-bladed arrowhead?, iron. 117/14w/OM3.
3. Leaf-bladed arrowhead, iron. 30/14w/OM3.
4. Spearhead fragment (?), iron. 36/14w/OM.

Pl. XXX. Weapons, armour and other military equipment from Area A1

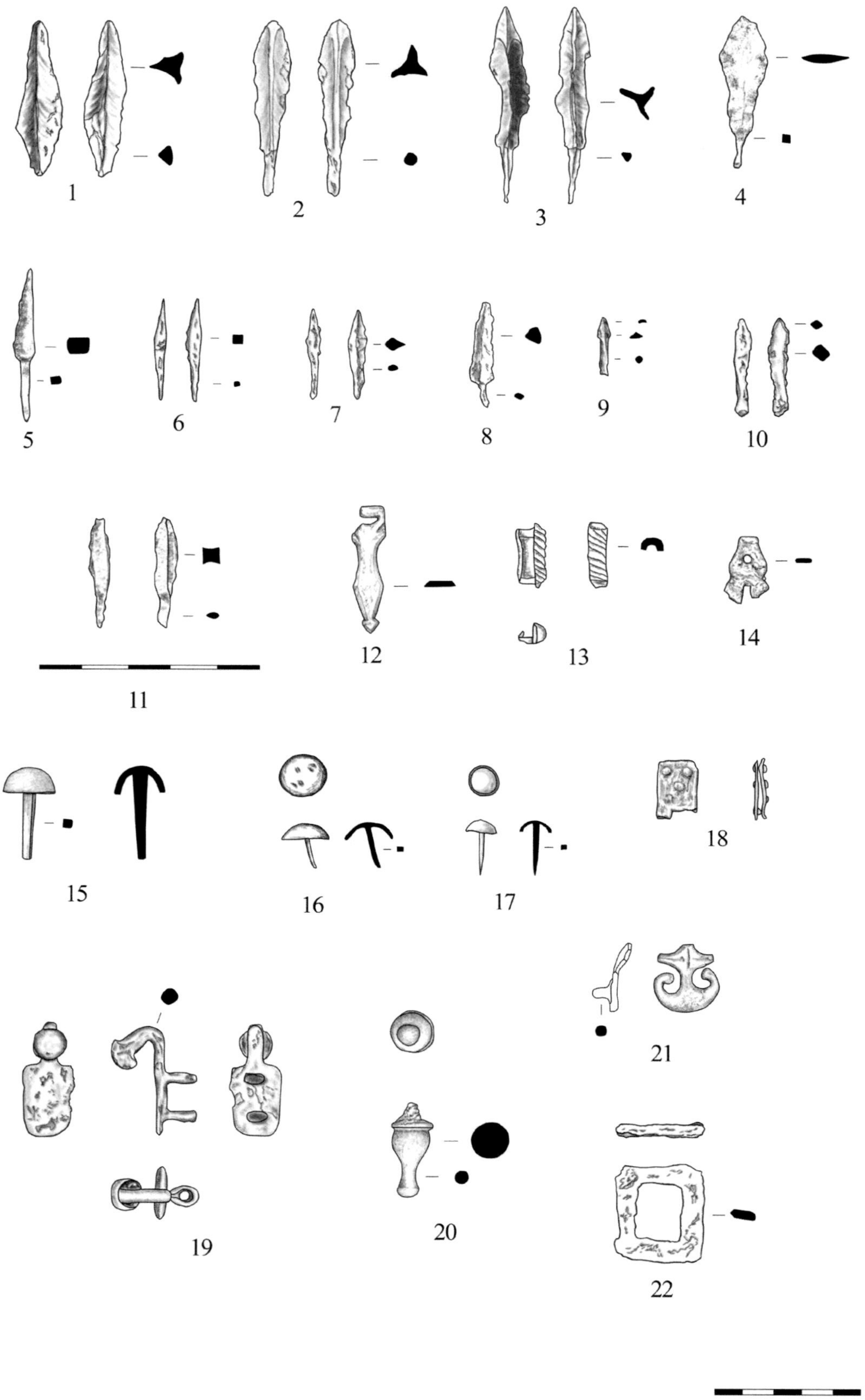

1 2 3 4

5 6 7 8 9 10

11 12 13 14

15 16 17 18

19 20 21 22

Pl. XXXI. Arrowheads from Area B

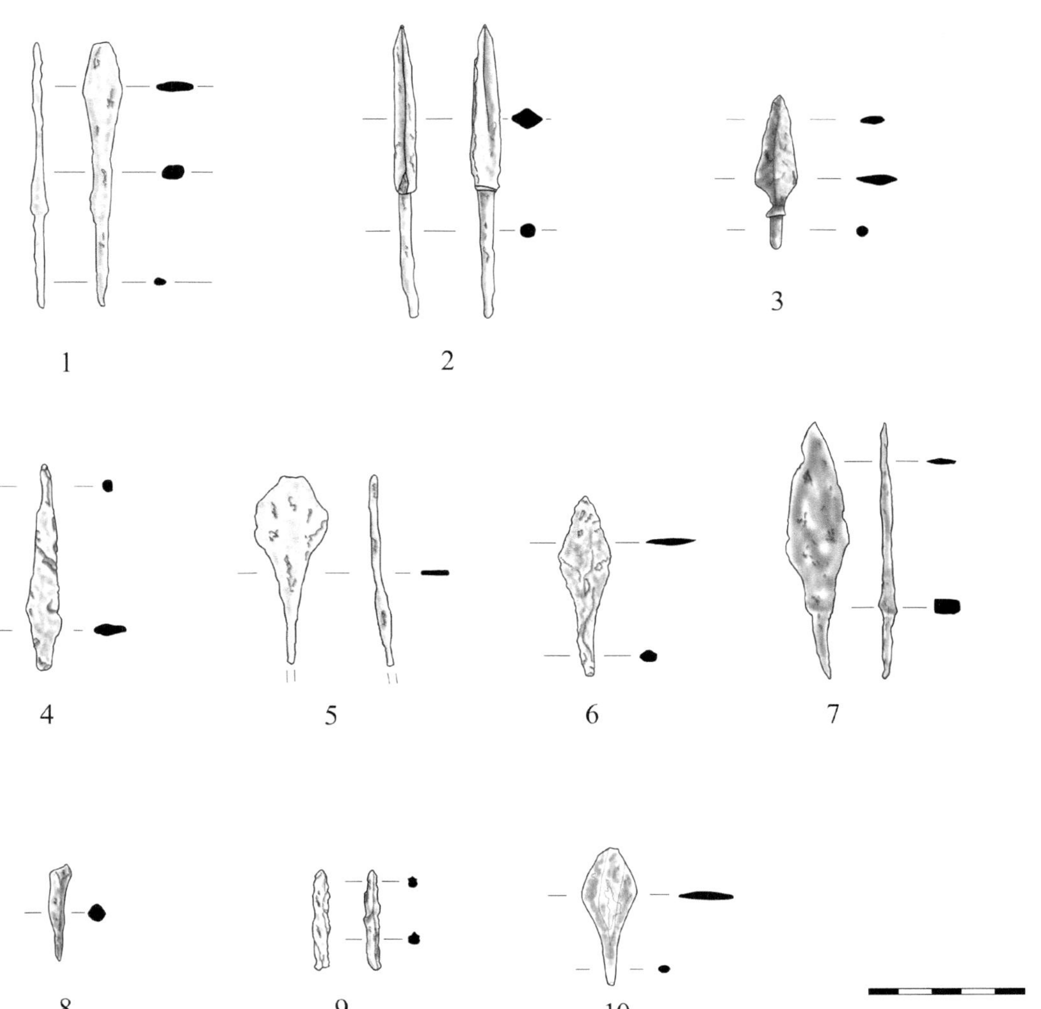

Pl. XXXII. Area E. Weapons from Area E

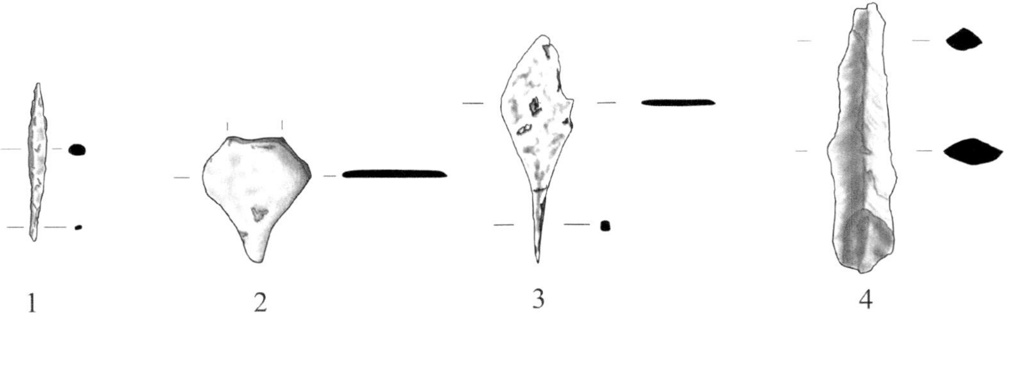

6. Jewellery and cosmetic items

Evgenia Gencheva, Agnieszka Tomas

Jewellery was rarely found during our surveys in the extramural area. This results from the fact that small finds of this kind, especially those made from non-ferrous metals, are attractive for looters. Iron finds are more frequent, because their material is regarded as less attractive and ignored as unwanted.

The surveys in the annexe (Area A1) provided eight pieces of jewellery and three mirror fragments (**Fig. 72**). The pieces of jewellery were rather modest, i.e., two copper alloy brooches, two iron brooches, and one fragment of a copper alloy brooch (Area A1, **Pl. XXXIII, 1–5**), one iron finger ring (**Pl. XXXIII, 6**), one fragment of a copper alloy hairpin (**Pl. XXXIII, 7**), and a copper alloy locket pendant (**Pl. XXXIII, 11**).

The copper alloy brooch (**Pl. XXXIII, 1**) is a type of fibula with a tucked foot. It belongs to a rare type with a triangular catchplate with a loop winding around its axle. The type always has a spring with a spring chord at the bottom; however, in this case, the element has not been preserved. The discussed specimen was described by Gh. Diaconu (1971), and in the literature on the subject it is known as the "Dacian" type.

The variant with the triangular catchplate is very rarely encountered. So far, in Lower Moesia, it has only been found in Novae. It seems that these were locally produced brooches, modelled on specimens from south-western Muntenia in Romania, where "Dacian"-type fibulae are most frequently encountered.[1] Unfortunately, the variant with the triangular catchplate is also not found in the neighbouring Roman provinces – in Dacia and Upper Moesia.[2]

"Dacian"-type brooches are dated to between the first half and the end of the 3rd century,[3] while in Serbia – even to the 4th century.[4] In Novae, a similar brooch has been found in a layer of burnt material, left behind after the invasion of the Goths in the mid- or second half of the 3rd century.[5]

The second copper alloy brooch (**Pl. XXXIII, 2**) belongs to a type derived from the Aucissa-type fibulae with a high catchplate. Fibulae of this type are widespread in northern Bulgaria (Lower Moesia areas), while they are practically not found in the south of the country (the Thracian province). Their place of production remains unknown. They are characterized by the borrowing of various features from Aucissa-type fibulae and from other strongly profiled fibulae. In the front part of the brooch, they have a rectangular plate above the hinge structure of the pin, similar to the Aucissa type. In turn, the ring in the centre of the hoop and the knob at the end of the foot are characteristic for strongly profiled fibulae. A feature that distinguishes the discussed type is its high catch.

These fibulae are prevalent in Upper and Lower Moesia and Dacia, but they are also found – less frequently – in Pannonia.[6] The dating of the fibulae is determined on the basis of the high catch, characteristic of the second half of the 2nd century and the first half of the 3rd century. In Lower Moesia and in Dacia, fibulae are dated to the period between the second half of the 2nd century and the first half of the 3rd century.[7] Only in Upper Moesia does the dating of this fibulae reach as late as the 4th century.[8] The fibulae are made from high-quality copper alloy and are found together with much later material from the 4th century.

A copper alloy fragment (**Pl. XXXIII, 5**) belongs to a strongly profiled fibula. Only the foot has been preserved along with part of the catchplate. It can be concluded based on the fragment that it belonged to a strongly profiled brooch with a high catchplate, which is a variant of proper strongly profiled fibulae. The type was produced in local workshops and they are dated slightly later than their prototype. The high catchplate is characteristic of the second half of the 2nd century, and most probably this is the period from which the discovered fragment originates.[9]

Two iron brooches (**Pl. XXXIII, 3–4**) were discovered during our surveys. The first fibula (**Pl. XXXIII, 3**) belongs to Almgren's group VII, series 4, known from the northern part of the Barbaricum.[10] These are what is referred to as Armbrustfibeln with the catchplate coming directly out of the spring. As the name itself indicates, they have a spring with a bottom chord, which usually winds around the long axle.

Fibulae of this type mainly occur in the north of Europe – along the Elbe, in Denmark, in southern Sweden, sporadically also within the territory of the Roman Empire – for example, along the *limes Germaniae*.[11] Their presence in Novae might be the effect of military actions or soldier mobility.

1. Diaconu 1971, 262; Bichir 1984, 50–51.
2. Cociş 2004, 142–47; Petković 2010, 307–12.
3. Protase 1976, 64; Bichir 1984, 50–51; Cociş 2004, 147.
4. Petković 2010, 310.
5. Gencheva 2004, 54.
6. Gencheva 2004, 44–45; Cociş 2004, 79–83; Petković 2010, 67–68.
7. Gencheva 2004, 45; Cociş 2004, 83.
8. Petković 2010, 68.
9. Gencheva 2004, 30.
10. Böhme 1972, Abb. 4.
11. Böhme 1972, 34.

Fig. 72. Novae 2012–14. Area A1 (the annexe and its vicinity). Jewellery and cosmetic finds (by A. Tomas).

The dating of these brooches in the Roman provinces is limited to the end of the 2nd century,[12] but they are dated to a slightly later period in the Barbaricum.[13] It is difficult to adopt a precise dating for the artifact from Novae, because it is an exceptional find.

The second iron brooch (**Pl. XXXIII, 4**) is a military or legionary type – referred to as Type A15. This is variant with an evenly cut-off foot. All such fibulae are unilateral and they have a short spring with a bottom spring chord. In the relevant academic literature, they are referred to as military fibulae, because they have most frequently been discovered within the territory of Roman military bases; however, in recent times, this term is avoided as specimens of the type have also been found in women's burials.

Brooches of this type are found along the entire limes from the mid-1st to the mid-2nd century, but they most often occur together with Trajan's coins.[14] Individual specimens are found in contexts dated to the end of the 2nd century.[15] In neighbouring Upper Moesia, fibulae of this type are also dated to the 1st–2nd century.[16]

The iron finger ring (**Pl. XXXIII, 6**) is quite primitive and its 2.3 cm diameter indicates that it was rather worn by a man as a signet ring. The central part of the ring has traces of a concave place for a gem. It is very doubtful that the iron ring was adorned with a precious stone, but glass paste is possible, perhaps with an intaglio sign. Only copper alloy finger rings from Novae have been published so far.[17] The finger ring is very badly preserved, but its form is close to gold and silver rings classified by L. Ruseva-Slokoska as Type V, typical for the 3rd century AD.[18] The bronze hairpin found in the annexe (**Pl. XXXIII, 7**) has a simplified globular ending which does not allow for its precise dating.

The locket pendant (**Pl. XXXIII, 11**) is a coin-sized piece of jewellery, decorated on one side. The image resembles a schematic portrait of a bearded warrior (Mars?), but the state of preservation and

12. Böhme 1972, 35.
13. Peškař 1972, 111–12.
14. Böhme 1972, 14.
15. Ettlinger 1973, 41.
16. Petković 2010, 34.
17. Gacuta 1987, 163–64, nos. 337–42, Tab. XXXI, 1–6; 1993, 44–47, nos. 98–101, 106, 110–11, Tab. XXXI, 5, 6, 8–11, 18. The identification of nos. 5, 8, 9 and 11 should be treated with caution. Copper alloy rings may have been used as parts of various items.
18. Ruseva-Slokoska 1991, 75, 99.

the simplified image on the pendant makes this identification very uncertain.

Two fragments of mirror frames (**Pl. XXXIII, 9–10**) belong to a well-identified group of cast frames known from north Italy and Lower Danubian provinces,[19] among others from Sucidava and Drobeta in Dacia Inferior, where they were manufactured in the 2nd and 3rd centuries.[20] Similar frames were discovered in Durostorum.[21] The size of two mirrors from Novae is similar, but the decoration is different. The first one (**cat. no. 9**) is decorated on both sides, while the second – only on one side (**cat. no. 10**). Two pieces (**Pl. XXXIII, 8, 10**) were made using a technique of copper alloy casting and coating with lead. No. 8 has strongly polished surface. The mirror plate was intentionally cut into a shape resembling a gaming token. Other examples of mirrors from Novae were made from copper alloy cast.[22]

Only three finds which can be attributed to the discussed group were made at Ostrite Mogili (**Fig. 73**). The first is a fragment of a copper alloy strigil found in the *vicus* at Ostrite Mogili (Area B, **Pl. XXXIV, 1**). A similar fragment was found in the vicinity of the camp (Area C2, **Pl. XXXIV, 3**). The second was a copper alloy bracelet discovered south-west of the *vicus* (Area E, **Pl. XXXIV, 4**). This is a piece of high-quality jewellery, carefully manufactured and finished. The open-end bracelet was made of a thick wire round in section, thinned at the ends and twisted several times around the endings. Such decoration is simplified but quite common.[23] Similar finds were discovered at the necropolis in Sucidava.[24] Most bracelets were found in graves in the territory of Bulgaria, mainly in Thrace,[25] but some male graves in the necropolis at Sucidava also contained bracelets.[26] A dating to the second half of the 4th century has been suggested,[27] but the concept behind such decoration was known earlier. Pieces of jewellery made using a similar technique but from a more solid piece of metal were discovered in a child's grave at the *vicus* necropolis at Ostrite Mogili together with a coin of Faustina the Younger (147–175).[28] The thick wire of the bracelet seems to have been intentionally bent as if it was secondarily used as a loop or simply bereft of its original function.

19. Mușețeanu and Elefterescu 2012, 108.
20. Tudor 1959; 1966, 16 and Fig. 26; Mușețeanu and Elefterescu 2012, 109.
21. Mușețeanu and Elefterescu 2012, esp. Fig. 2.4a-b, generally dated to between the 2nd and the 4th century.
22. Gacuta 1993, 47, nos. 112, 113 and Tab. XXX, 1 and 2.
23. Ruseva-Slokoska 1991, 60, 166–68, cat. nos. 140–75. For the closest analogy see p. 98, type VII.
24. Popilian and Bondoc 2012, 247–248 and Pl. XXXIV–XXXVI, Graves 211, 275, 324, 351, 381.
25. Ruseva-Slokoska 1991, 60.
26. Popilian and Bondoc 2012, 247.
27. Ruseva-Slokoska 1991, cat. Nos. 169–70; Popilian and Bondoc 2012, 247.
28. Vulov 1965, 32, cat. Nos. 5, 6 and Fig. 12.

Fig. 73. Ostrite Mogili and Chechlarski geran 2014. Jewellery and cosmetic finds (by A. Tomas).

Pl. XXXIII. Jewellery and cosmetic items from Area A1

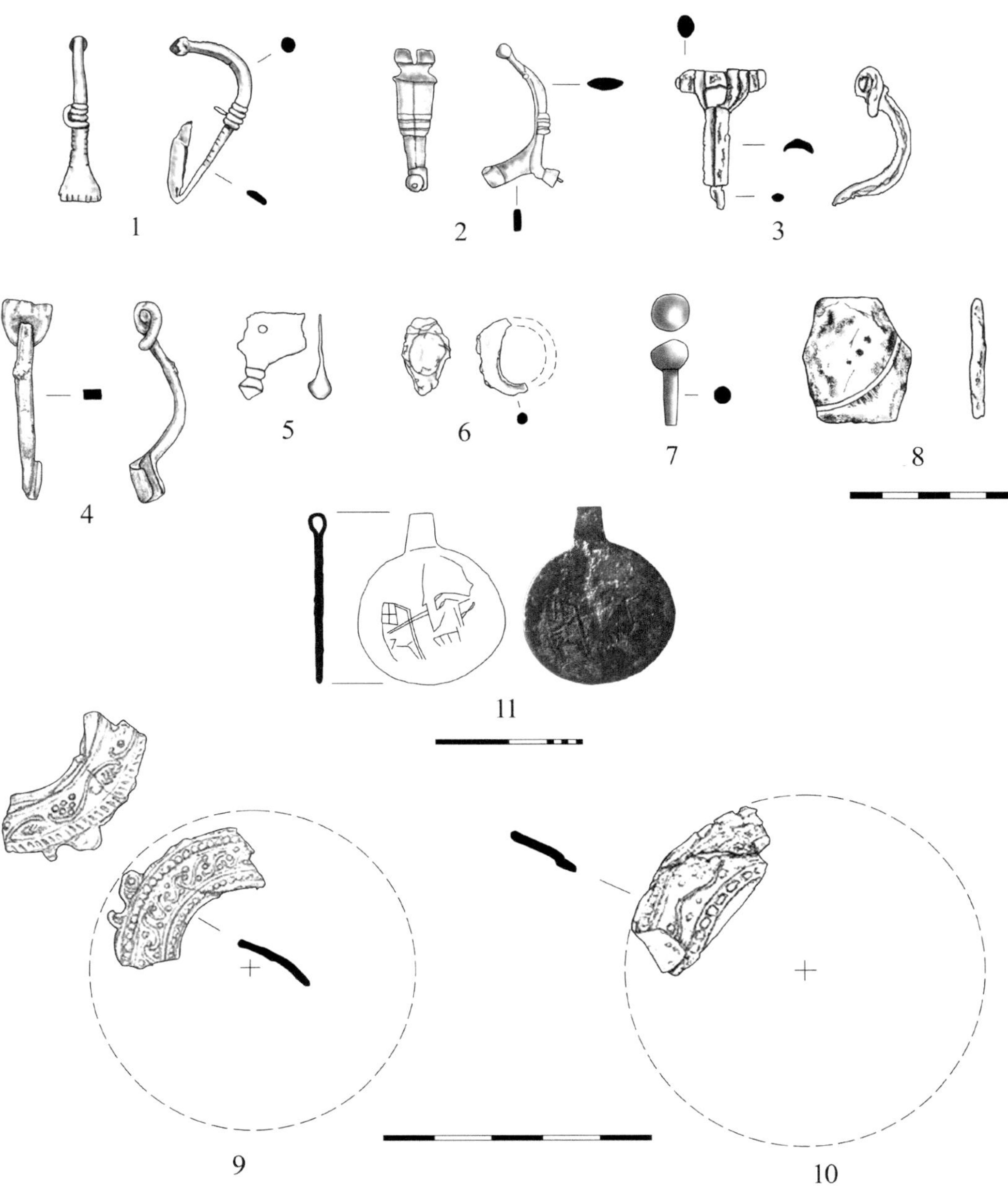

The last item is a small decoration (2.5 cm high and 1.5 cm wide) in the form of a bird with a ring attached to its head (**Pl. XXXIV, 2**). The ring with the back is joined by a handle imitating twisted hair(?). The bird figure seems to be the ending of a pin. However, this specific find may be a fragment of well-known copper alloy sticks with representations of birds interpreted as doves.[29] They are usually interpreted as sticks of unknown function, but the religious and symbolic meaning of the Christian dove or cosmetic purpose was taken into account.[30] Metal pins or sticks ending with a bird on one side and a ring on the other constitute a specific group of finds known from the Late Roman context from the sites in the western and the eastern part of the Empire; therefore, they are sometimes linked with the Goths or other barbarian groups.[31] Their religious purpose, however, was not explained, and their practical use as jewellery items cannot be excluded.

29. E.g. Madgearu 2008; Bondoc 2009, 253–54, Pl. 1, 2–3; Dohijo 2016.

30. Madgearu 2008, 221–23.

31. Madgearu 2008, 221–22.

Pl. XXXIV. Jewellery and cosmetic items from Areas B, C2 and E

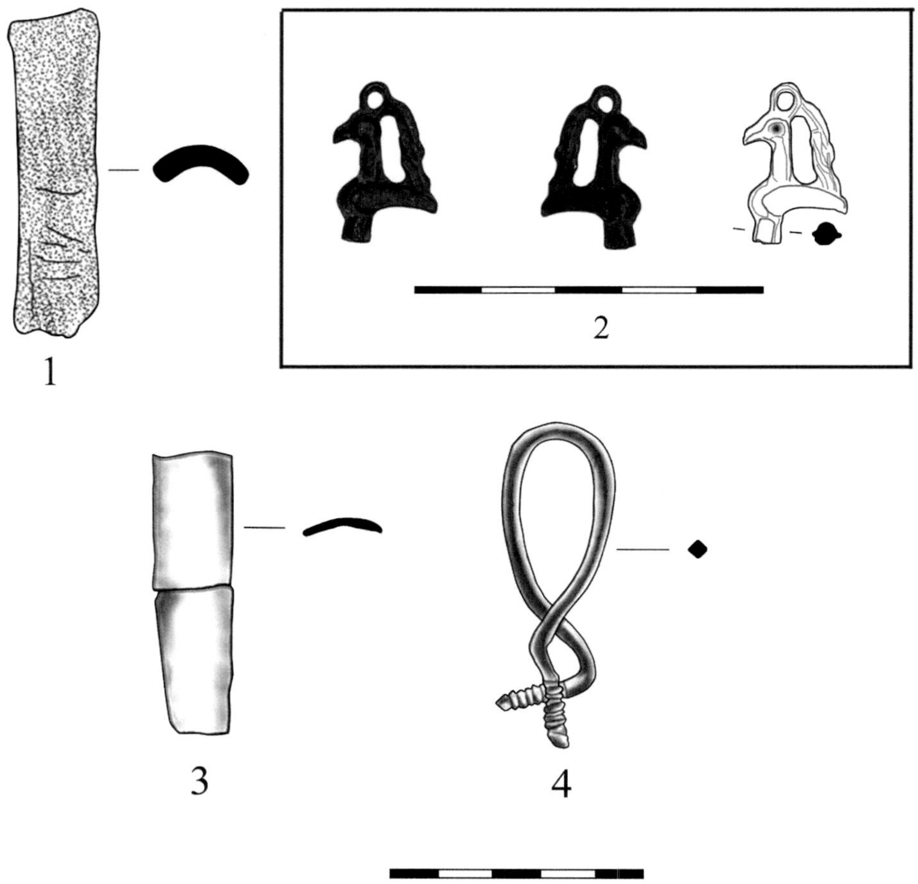

1

2

3

4

Catalogue of jewellery and cosmetic items

Pl. XXXIII. Area A1

1. Copper alloy brooch. 29/13w/can.
2. Copper alloy brooch. 37/13w/can.
3. Iron brooch. 26/13w/can.
4. Iron brooch. 43/12w/can.
5. Copper alloy fragment of a brooch (?).
6. Iron finger ring. 23/13w/can.
7. Fragment of a copper alloy hairpin. 2/14w/can.
8. Fragment of a lead mirror frame. 60/13w/can. Thick copper alloy plate with lead coating and strongly polished surface. The plate was cut out in the form of an irregular hexagon.
9. Fragment of a lead mirror frame. 36/12w/can. Cast relief decoration on both sides.
10. Fragment of a copper alloy mirror coated with lead. 37/12w/can. Cast relief decoration.
11. Copper alloy pendant. 46/12w/can. Cast relief decoration.

Pl. XXXIV. Areas B, C2 and E

Area B-Ostrite Mogili

1. Fragment of a copper alloy strigil. 33/00w/OM. Thin plate broken at both ends.
2. Bronze decoration in the form of a bird. 50/13w/OM. Square 1.

Area C2

3. Fragment of a copper alloy strigil. 81/13w/can. Thin plate broken at both ends.

Area E

4. Copper alloy bracelet. 118/14w/OM3. Thick wire round in section, thinned at the ends, and twisted several times around the endings.

7. Other metal finds

Szymon Modzelewski

At the moment of discovery, each metal find was classified as a mass or selected item. Mass finds were described at the defined surveyed areas, while each selected find received its precise location established with a hand-held GPS receiver.[1] Iron finds were the most frequent, but they were usually very corroded. In many cases, it was difficult to establish whether an iron object was ancient, mediaeval or modern. These problems applied, for example, to iron rings, knives or tools which do not change their forms through the ages.[2] Several categories of metal finds, such as weapons and military equipment, jewellery and cosmetic items, coins, lead seals, and the evidence of metal processing are discussed separately. This chapter presents copper alloy, iron and lead finds which have not been classified into the above-mentioned groups. It also briefly presents mass finds, which were documented only photographically.

Mapping metal finds was done in the central and southern parts of the annexe (Area A1) and the western part of the *vicus* (Area B). Area A1 provided 414 mass metal finds, of which 72 were selected for more detailed documentation. Modern metal waste was surprisingly not so numerous. One of the most interesting copper alloy finds from Area A1 is a fragment of a statue which was probably cut for remelting (**Pl. XXXV, 23**). Fragments of bronze statues cut and collected for further processing were found in the headquarters' *aerarium* in Novae.[3]

Among other collected copper alloy items, there is a part of a full cast handle, without traces of any decoration (**Pl. XXXV, 1**), and an item spherical in shape with traces of having been attached (**Pl. XXXV, 2**). Other metal objects are rather common, although some of them deserve comments. Copper alloy and iron needles are known at Novae,[4] but the find collected during prospection (**Pl. XXXV, 6**) is a high-quality product. Three copper alloy rings (**Pl. XXXV, 7, 8, 9**) could have been elements of various objects (including *lorica hamata*), and their classification as possibly ancient was based on their material and state of preservation. Two styluses have been found in Area A1, one copper alloy specimen and one iron (**Pl. XXXV, 10, 11**). Analogous writing tools are known from Novae and other sites.[5]

1. For more details concerning the methods of surveying, see Chapter III.
2. Kolendo and Kowal 2015.
3. Gacuta and Sarnowski 1981; 1982.
4. Gacuta 1987, 105, Tab. XV, 4, 6; 1993: 145, Tab. XXXIV; 5, 6, 10, 11, 17, 18.
5. Dimitrova-Milcheva 2006, 99; Atkinson and Preston 2015, Figs. 530, 531.11–27.

Fig. 74. Novae 2012–14. Other metal finds from Area A1 – the annexe (by A. Tomas).

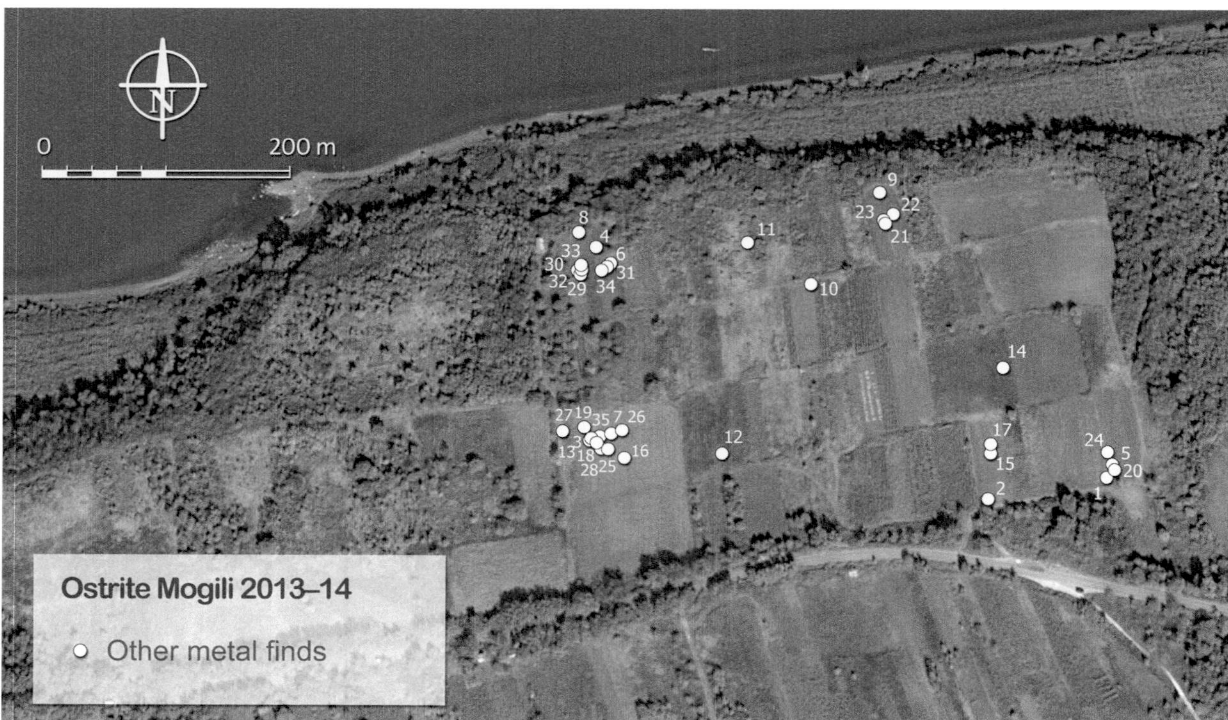

Fig. 75. Ostrite Mogili 2013–14. Other metal finds from Area B (by A. Tomas).

A lead weight for fishing nets (**Pl. XXXV, 21**) has a typical shape known from other Roman sites.[6] One of the most numerous and common iron finds in Novae are knives,[7] and three such items were found in Area A1 (**Pl. XXXV, 16–19**). They cannot be attributed to any particular type, apart from one specimen (**Pl. XXXV, 16**), which may be an example of the *Griffzungenmesser mit geschweifter Klinge* type, according to Heimo Dolenz.[8]

A long iron nail could have been used for the construction of a building's wooden element (**Pl. XXXV, 24**). A fragment of an iron hobnail was probably used in a smaller wooden object (**Pl. XXXV, 15**). Iron nails are very common finds at Novae,[9] which is evidence of the widespread use of wood. One of the iron objects (**Pl. XXXV, 14**) could have been part of some scissors or an agricultural tool, the same as no. 5. A small lead token or a washer has a unique shape which can be trace of its use (**Pl. XXXV, 22**).

Area A1 provided the most numerous ancient mass metal finds, mainly medium-sized iron nails, pieces of tools and fittings. In the surveyed clusters, they were mixed with random modern metal waste (**Fig. 74**).

The finds from the *vicus* (Area B) are more varied, since the site was not so intensively looted as the fortress annexe. The clusters selected for intensive metal find mapping provided 575 mass metal finds, but almost half of them (210 pieces) were modern metal waste (**Fig.** 77).

Among those identified as ancient, 80 were selected for further detailed documentation. A copper alloy rosette appliqué (**Pl. XXXVI, 4**) could have been the decoration of a leather clothing element, e.g., a belt or a cap. It could also have been part of a sword scabbard mount or even elements of armour.[10] A globular copper alloy item may have been a pendant (**Pl. XXXVI, 6**). Iron tools, among them a tinder-box, a hook, a sickle blade, and a ferrule (?), are not so numerous for the type of investigated site (**Pl. XXXVI, 11–13 and 16**). They were documented, since they were found at the site, but their identification as ancient should be approached with caution as various agricultural activities have been carried out at the site in modern times. The same applies to the significant number of iron knives (**Pl. XXXVI, 10, 20–29; XXXVII, 30–35; XXXVIII, 1–3**) and nails (**Fig.** 77). It is quite possible that some of the knives are mediaeval or modern. However, some knives found here may be attributed to the Roman period, since they resemble examples from the Upper Danubian provinces of the Roman Empire. One knife (**Pl. XXXVI, 10**) is similar to the iron knives from Magdalensberg in Noricum.[11] It belongs to a specific

6. Atkinson and Preston 2015, Figs. 524, 526–29.
7. Gacuta 1987: 97–98, Tab. VII, VIII; 1993, 166, Tab. LV.
8. Dolenz 1992, 102–03, Taf. 3.
9. Gacuta 1987, 91–94, Tab. I–IV; 1993, 172–74, Tab. LXI–LXV.
10. Bishop and Coulston 2006, 99, Figs. 56.7, 9, 10, 11; 160, Fig. 101.3; Atkinson and Preston 2015, Fig. 546.35.
11. Dolenz 1992, 102–07, Taf. 3, 4.

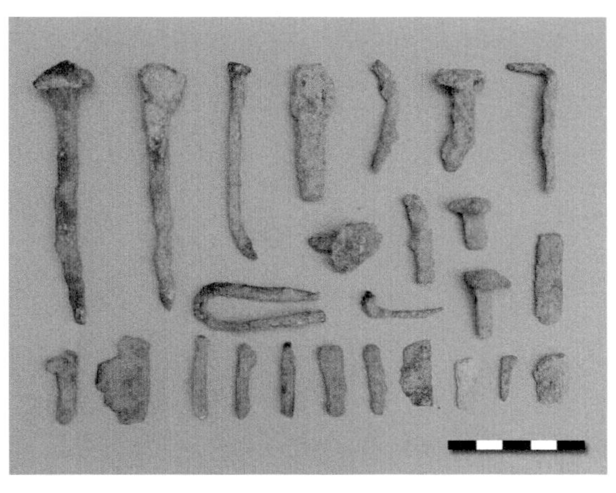

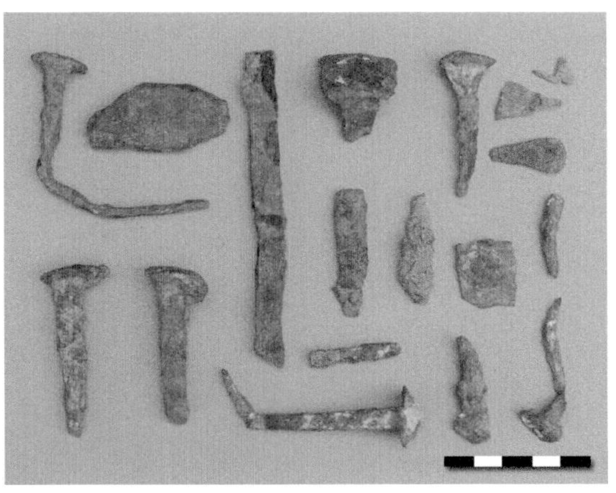

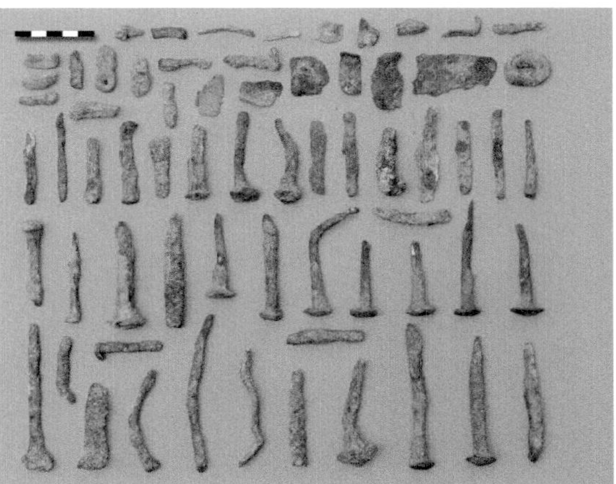

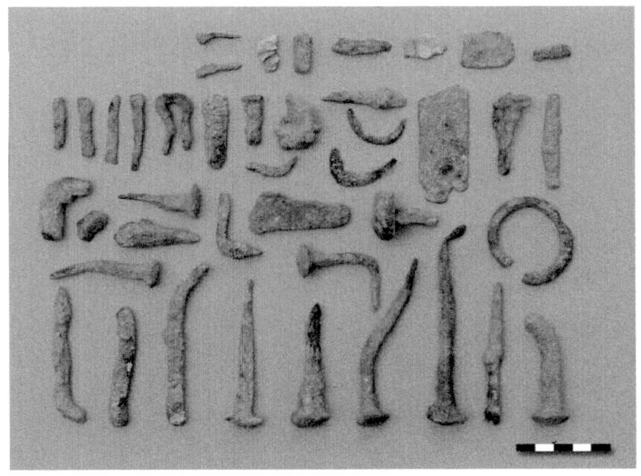

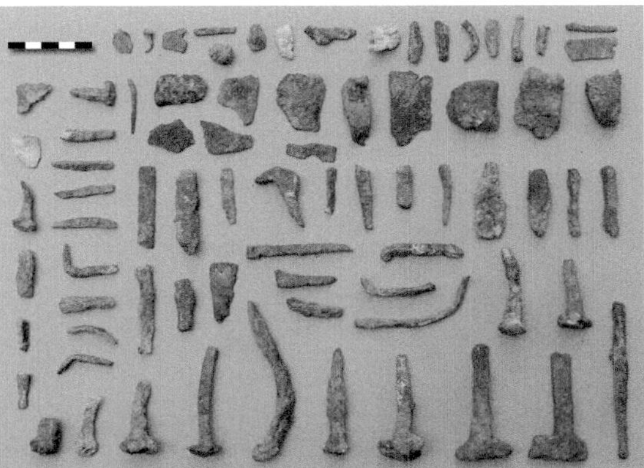

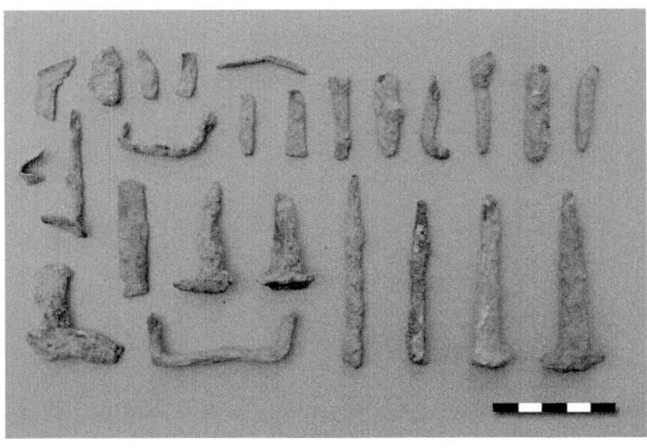

Fig. 76. Novae 2012–14. Metal mass finds from Area A1 (photo by P. Jaworski).

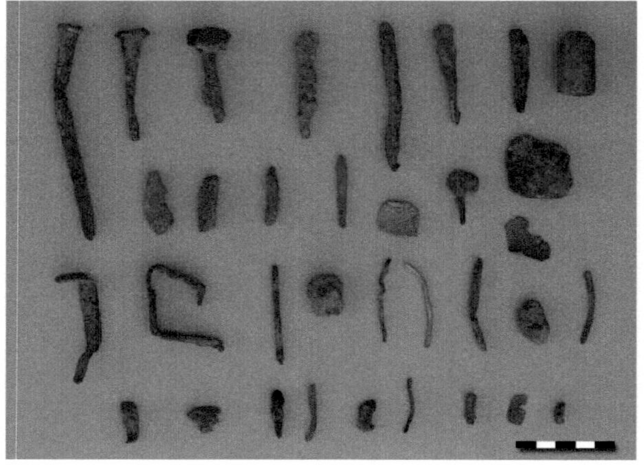
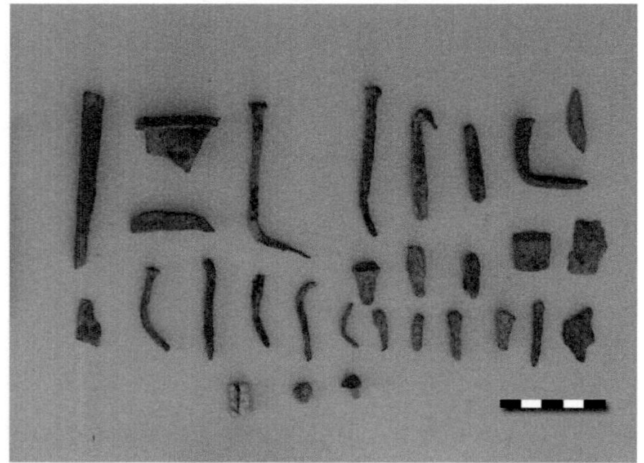
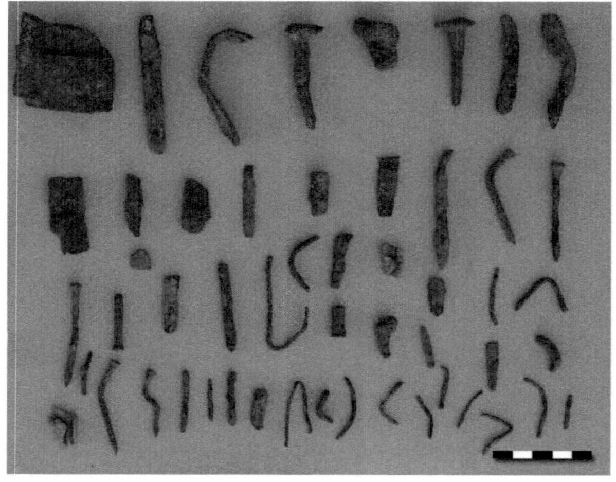
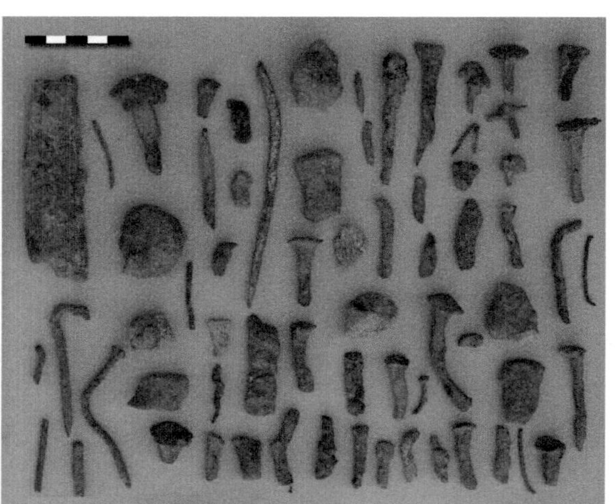
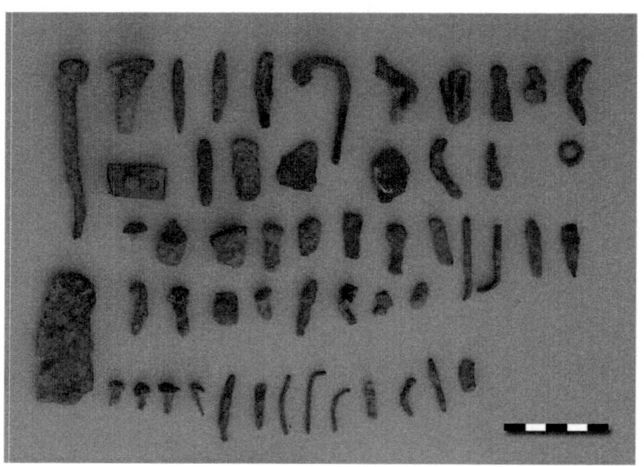
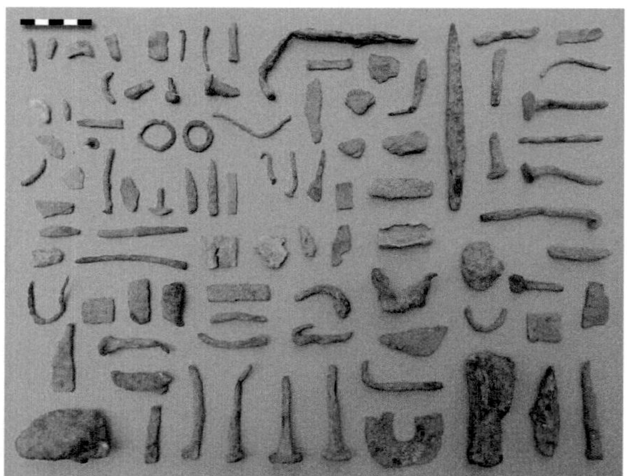

Fig. 77. Ostrite Mogili 2013–14. Metal mass finds from Area B (photo by P. Jaworski).

type which is referred to as *Griffzungenmesser mit geschweifter Klinge*, following H. Dolenz. This type of tool was widespread in the Alps and the Danube Valley, and its shape comes from the Hallstatt period.

Area E provided 247 metal objects, mainly mass iron objects (239) and one copper alloy unspecified item which was included into the mass finds. More than half of them were modern, and only 76 were classified as ancient or hypothetically ancient (**Fig. 78**). The only interesting find was a copper alloy bracelet (discussed in Chapter VI.6). The mass iron finds were very corroded, and three knives were the only items it was possible to identify (**Pl. XXXVIII, 1–2**).

Area F was also polluted by modern waste and only twelve iron finds out of a total of 47 were identified as hypothetically Roman or Mediaeval,

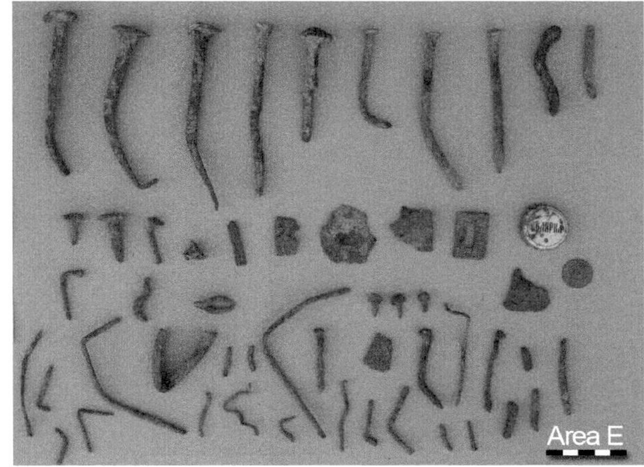

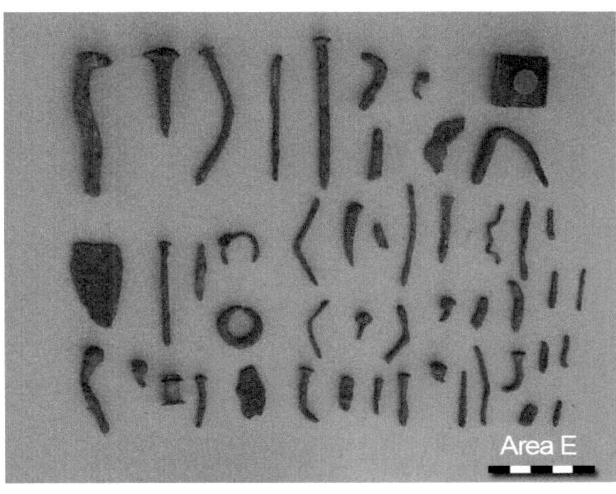

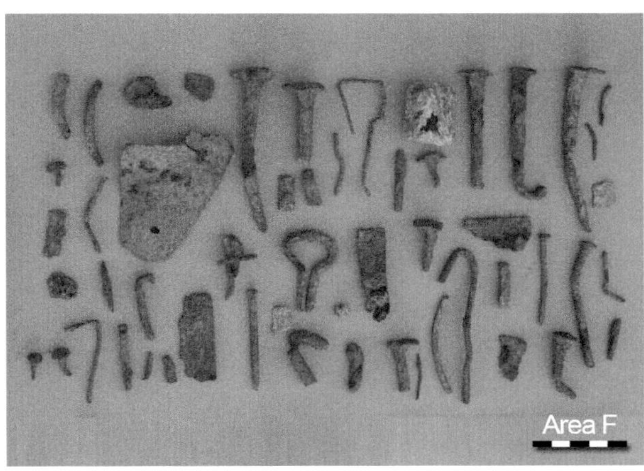

Fig. 78. Novae 2012–14. Metal mass finds from Areas E and F (photo by P. Jaworski).

among them five nails (**Fig. 78**). Only one iron knife was documented in detail (**Pl. XXXVIII, 3**).

Catalogue of other metal finds

Pl. XXXV. Area A1 (the annexe)

1. Copper alloy handle of a vessel. 44/12w/can.
2. Copper alloy lump. 45/12w/can.
3. Copper alloy item. 52/12w/can.
4. Copper alloy item (bead?). 55/12w/can.
5. Copper alloy item. 54/12w/can.
6. Copper alloy needle. 13/13w/can.
7. Copper alloy ring. 25/13w/can.
8. Copper alloy ring. 6/13w/can.
9. Copper alloy ring. 15/13w/can.
10. Copper alloy stylus. 58/12w/can.
11. Iron tool (stylus? spatula?). 32/13w/can.
12. Square iron fitting(?). 19/13w/can. Selected from mass finds, no specific findspot.
13. Iron item. 31/13w/can.
14. Iron scissors(?). 53/12w/can
15. Iron nail. 49/12w/can.
16. Iron knife. 2/13w/can.
17. Iron knife. 12/13w/can.
18. Iron knife. 4/13w/can.
19. Iron knife. 10/13w/can.
20. Lead fitting. 59/12w/can.
21. Lead weight for fishing net. 20/13w/can.
22. Lead token(?). 1/13w/can.
23. Fragment of a copper alloy sculpture. 57/12w/can.
24. Iron building nail. 34/12w/can.

Pl. XXXVI. Area B - Ostrite Mogili

1. Copper alloy hinge. 41/13w/OM.
2. Appliqué, iron. 49/13w/OM.
3. Fragment unspecified item, lead. 15/14w/OM.
4. Copper alloy appliqué. 39/14w/OM.
5. Copper alloy token. 43/13w/OM.
6. Copper alloy globule. 26/14w/OM.
7. Copper alloy lump. 6/14w/OM.
8. Copper alloy rivet. 55/13w/OM.
9. Lead weight for fishing net. 59/13w/OM.
10. Iron knife. 41/00m/OM.
11. Iron tool. 32/00m/OM.

Pl. XXXV. Area A1. Other metal finds

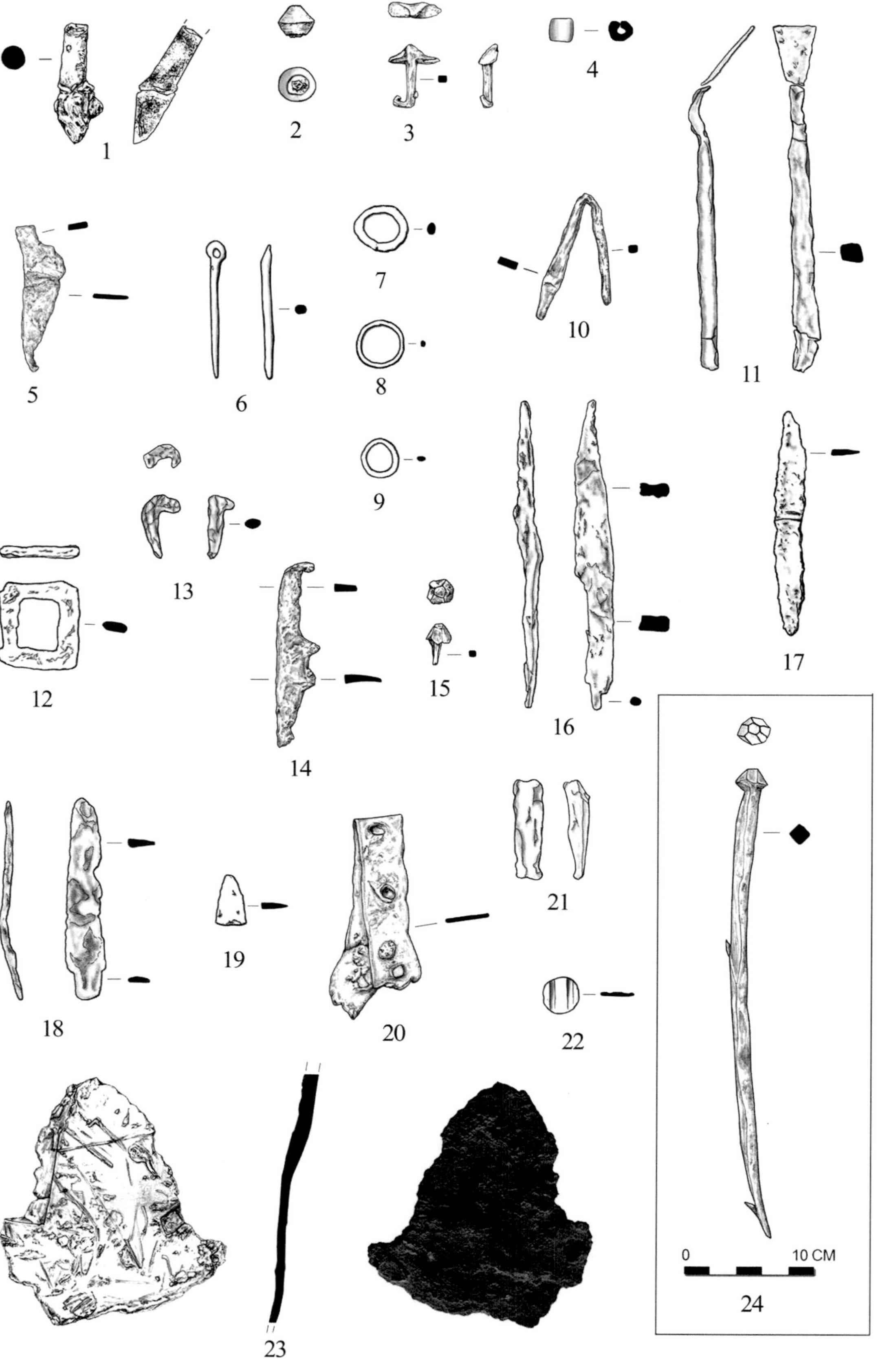

Pl. XXXVI. Area B. Other metal finds

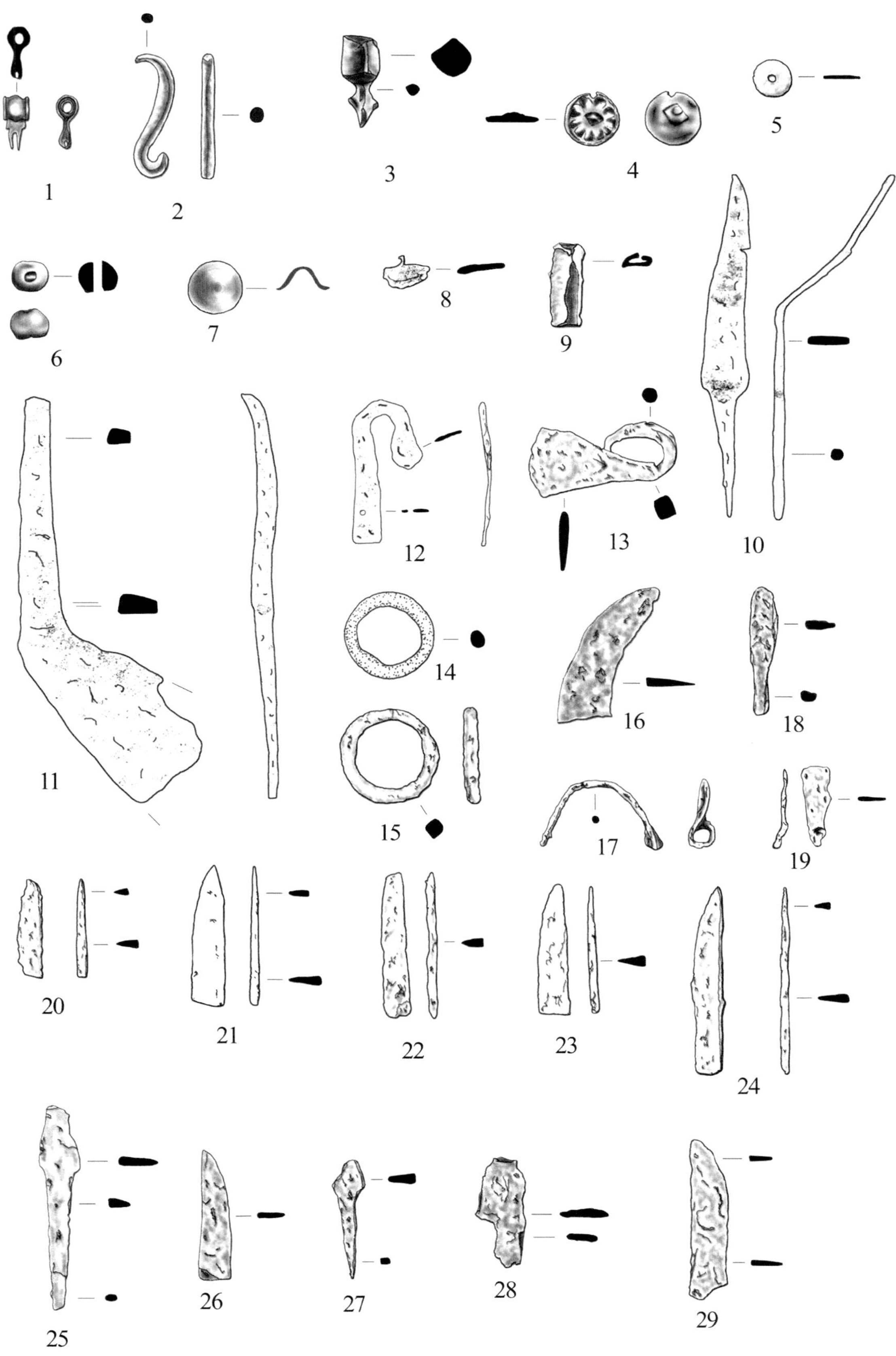

12. Iron tool. 14/00m/OM.
13. Iron item. 9/14w/OM.
14. Iron ring. 44/00m/OM.
15. Iron ring. 48/13w/OM.
16. Iron scythe. 20/14w/OM.
17. Iron item. 47/13w/OM.
18. Iron item. 22/14w/OM.
19. Iron spatula. 21/14w/OM.
20. Iron knife. 40/13w/OM.
21. Iron knife. 53/13w/OM.
22. Iron knife. 54/13w/OM.
23. Iron knife. 58/13w/OM.
24. Iron knife. 39/13w/OM.
25. Iron knife. 5/14w/OM.
26. Iron knife. 13/14w/OM.
27. Iron knife. 16/14w/OM.
28. Iron knife. 17/14w/OM.
29. Iron knife. 24/14w/OM.

Pl. XXXVII. Area B - Ostrite Mogili

30. Iron knife. 115/14w/OM.
31. Iron knife. 25/14w/OM.
32. Iron knife. 31/14w/OM.
33. Iron knife. 34/14w/OM.
34. Iron knife. 32/14w/OM.
35. Iron knife. 18/14w/OM.

Pl. XXXVIII. Areas E and F

1. Iron knife. 27/14w/OM3. Area E.
2. Iron knife. 28/14w/OM3. Area E.
3. Iron knife. 37/14w/OM2. Area F.

Pl. XXXVII. Area B. Other metal finds

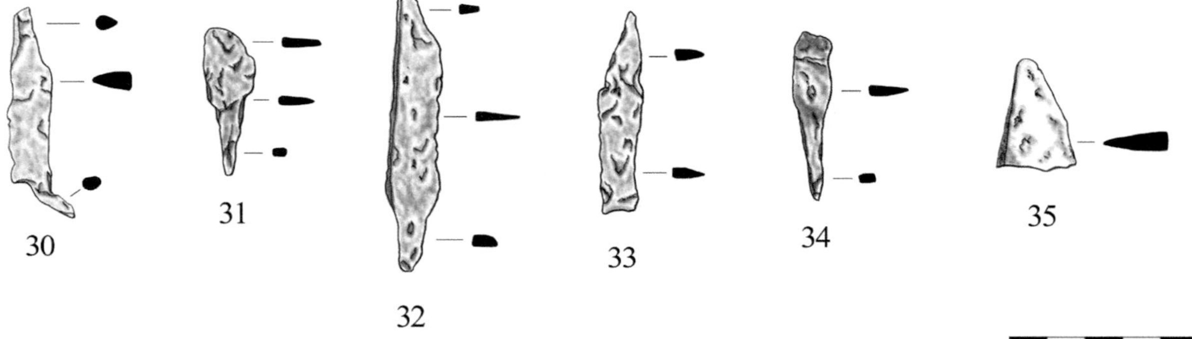

Pl. XXXVIII. Areas E and F. Other metal finds

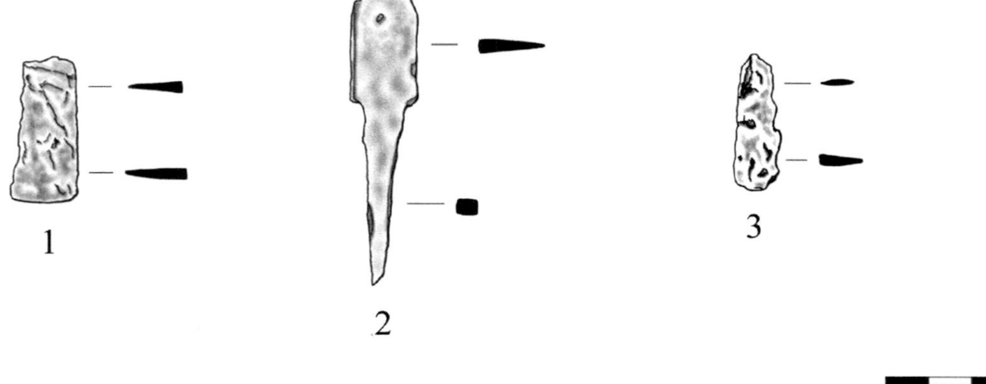

8. Evidence of local metal processing

Szymon Modzelewski

Slag is very often an underestimated or even neglected find, while remains of metal processing provide information about the production activities and define areas where such manufacturing could have taken place.

Local copper alloy production was performed both in the fortress and outside of it. Copper alloy waste, i.e., a fragment of a bronze sculpture found in the annexe (see Chapter VI.7, **Pl. XXXV, 23**), indicates that local production was performed there. The objects were probably cut in order to acquire raw material. A fragment of a statue probably cut for remelting went through the same process as copper alloy waste, including fragments of bronze statues, discovered in the *aerarium* of the fortress headquarters.[1] Bronze and copper alloy scraps collected as raw material[2] were found along with items connected with metalworking, such as a chisel and pincers. Melting pots of the same type were found in the Flavian pits in the legionary fortress.[3] Analogous evidence of metal processing and metallurgical activities are known from other legionary bases.[4]

Lead was also processed and small pieces of metal waste were found during prospection (**Fig. 79, 1–2**). Iron slag lumps are direct proof of metal processing in the Novae area. They were found both in the annexe and at the Ostrite Mogili site. Metal processing tools and iron lumps have also been found inside the walls of the legionary fortress.[5] Iron slag from the annexe (**Fig. 79, 3–6**) and from Ostrite Mogili (**Fig. 79, 7–10**) is typical iron processing waste. The lumps are probably iron-smelting or iron processing slags, i.e., the remains left after the process of smelting iron ore in bloomery furnaces or reheating iron lumps or iron forging and smithing. These operations were necessary to obtain iron suitable for further processing.[6]

Small-scale production in private workshops must have flourished throughout Antiquity. Craftsmen designed and produced mostly items necessary for soldiers, but also for the inhabitants of both settlements. A small melting pot found at Ostrite Mogili (**Fig. 79, 11**) indicates the local production of small metal items in the *vicus*. The technological knowledge and abilities of blacksmiths from the vicinity of Novae did not differ from those of the average craftsmen from the Danube provinces. Metal processing and metallurgical activities were also attested at Nicopolis ad Istrum and they are similar in quality.[7] Iron and copper alloy tools, weapons and implements were used in every field of the economic and social life of its inhabitants.

Iron items and slags from Novae and Iatrus (Krivina) were subjected to metallographic tests.[8] Metallographic examination proved the metal processing technology used by artisans in Novae was quite sophisticated. Craftsmen were able to handle both iron and copper alloys. They used both forging and casting methods. Metallurgists and blacksmiths often used carburizing and hardening to strengthen the structure of iron objects. They knew the methods of intensive carburizing and hardening, which allowed them to produce iron items characterized by considerable hardness and abrasion resistance. Copper alloy items were reinforced by cold forging. Some of the copper alloy items were made using the lost-wax casting method.

Knowledge of such advanced metallurgical techniques was necessary to produce high-quality metal objects. The iron obtained by the reduction process in a smelting furnace had an uneven carburization level. It was porous and heavily contaminated with slag. It required forging and reheating. A secondary carburizing process was necessary to obtain highly carburized, hard iron items. Only high-quality "wootz" steel imported to the Roman Empire from India had a high and even carburization level. A good example of such an imported piece of high-carbon crucible steel is a bloom from the Roman trade emporium at Risan.[9] Iron or steel of comparable quality was not available to artisans from Novae. Techniques of artificial carburization, reheating and heat-treatment were well known in the Roman world.[10]

1. Gacuta and Sarnowski 1982; Sarnowski 1985a.
2. Gacuta and Sarnowski 1982, 132–33, 141, Tab. III, 9–10; Sarnowski 1985a, 531, Abb. 8; Gacuta 1993, 128, 132, 147, 163, Tab. XVII, XXI, XXXVI, LII.
3. The publication of the pits is in preparation. The melting pots have been elaborated by M. Natuniewicz-Sekuła.
4. Bishop and Coulston 2006, 233–40.
5. Gacuta 1987, 104, Tab. XIV; Sarnowski 1985a, 531–33, Abb. 9.
6. Biborski and Stępiński 2014, 263–64; Pleiner 2000, 215–16; 230–31.
7. Cholakova 2006b.
8. Głowacki 1975, 279; Piaskowski 1991.
9. Biborski and Stępiński 2014, 272–75.
10. Tylecotte 2002, 65–66.

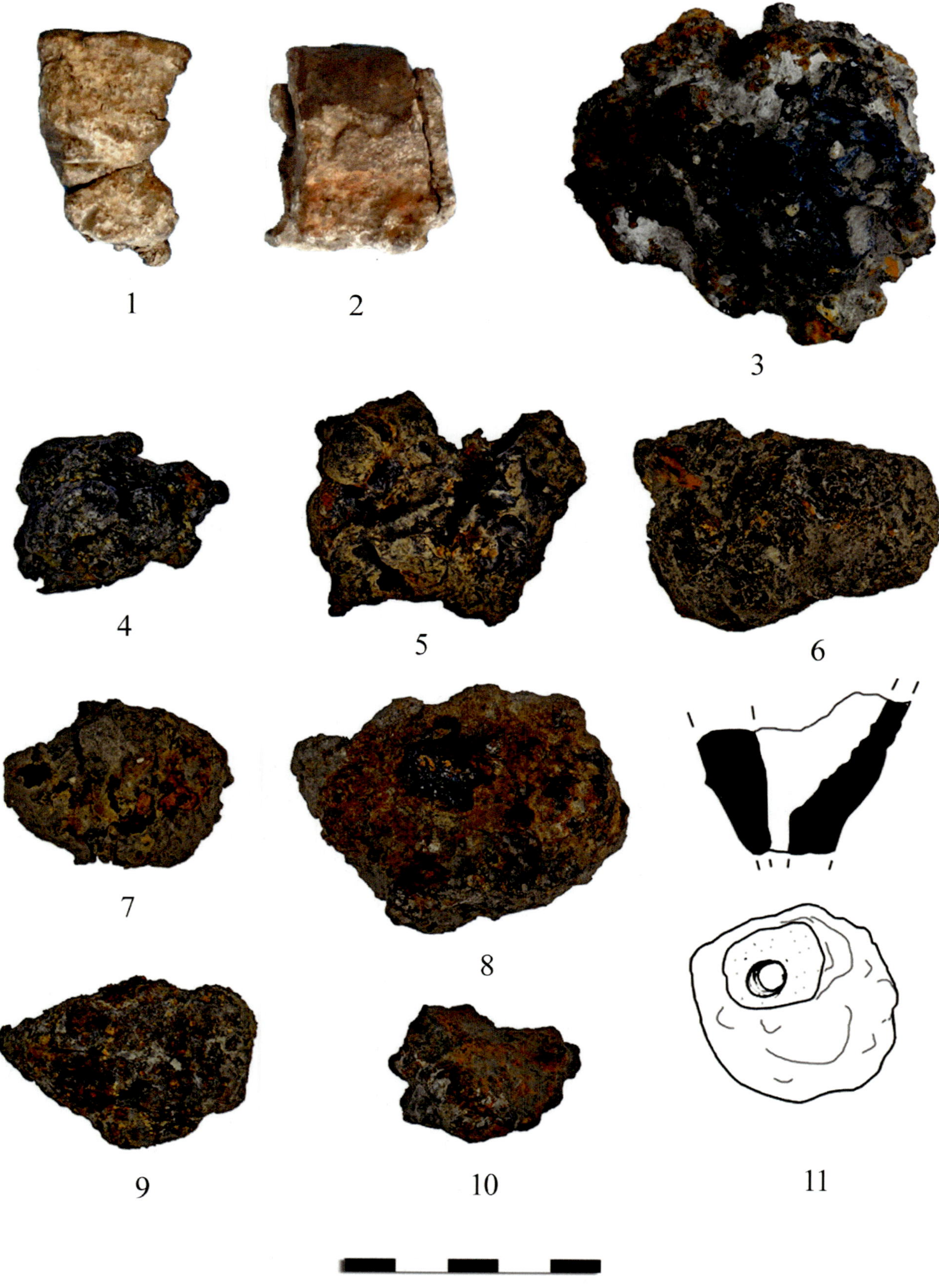

Fig. 79. Novae and Ostrite Mogili 2012–14. Finds related to metal processing. Area A1: 1–6; Area B: 7–11. (photo and drawing by A. Tomas).

9. Roman and Early Byzantine coin finds

Piotr Jaworski

I. Introduction

Monetary finds from non-invasive surveys conducted in the annexe of Novae and its immediate vicinity (Area A1) and the Ostrite Mogili site (Area B)[1] show some variation in the chronological structure, although they do not differ substantially from the general characteristics of the monetary mass circulating in the Roman legionary camp and the late Roman town of Novae.[2] In the numismatic material from the annexe, which is dated between the 1st and the end of the 6th centuries, the dominance of the coins of the 4th and the first half of the 5th century is visible. The finds from Ostrite Mogili are characterized by a slight predominance of coins from the first half of the 3rd century. The lack of coins minted after the mid-5th century can be observed.

The main difference between the coins from the annexe and Ostrite Mogili lies in the lack of Medieval coins in the first of these sites, while the 13th-century emissions are predominant among the monetary finds from the latter (cf. **Fig. 98** in Chapter VI.16). Moreover, the saturation with finds in Ostrite Mogili, similarly to the neighboring Chehlarski geran site – Area F (only two specimens), with the exception of the above-mentioned Medieval coins, is much lower than in the annexe (cf. **Figs. 80–82** and **83–84**). All the coins discovered in Novae were made of copper alloy, while the finds from Ostrite Mogili include a Geta denarius (cat. no. 7), as well as a perforated denarius *subaeratus* (cat. no. 9).

The numismatic material obtained during the non-invasive research conducted in Novae and Ostrite Mogili can be divided into two basic chronological groups: coins of the Roman Empire period (63 specimens) and the Early Byzantine coins (2 specimens). The chronological and topographic structure of the finds is presented in Table 1.

The set of Roman coins consists of two main categories: coins from the mint of Rome and other central mints operating in the late Roman period, and provincial coins struck in the cities of Thrace and Moesia Inferior. Although the oldest of the identified coins from the Roman period

1. The Roman and Early Byzantine coins discussed in the present chapter were discovered during the research carried out in 2012–14 under the supervision of Agnieszka Tomas and the finds from the survey carried out in 2000 at the Ostrite Mogili by Piotr Dyczek. I would like to express my gratitude to the above-mentioned researchers who made coins from their research available to me for publication.
2. Cf., among others: Dimitrov 2013b; Ciołek 2011; Dimitrov 2011; Kunisz 1992.

Fig. 80. Novae 2012–14. Early Roman coin finds from Area A1 (by A. Tomas).

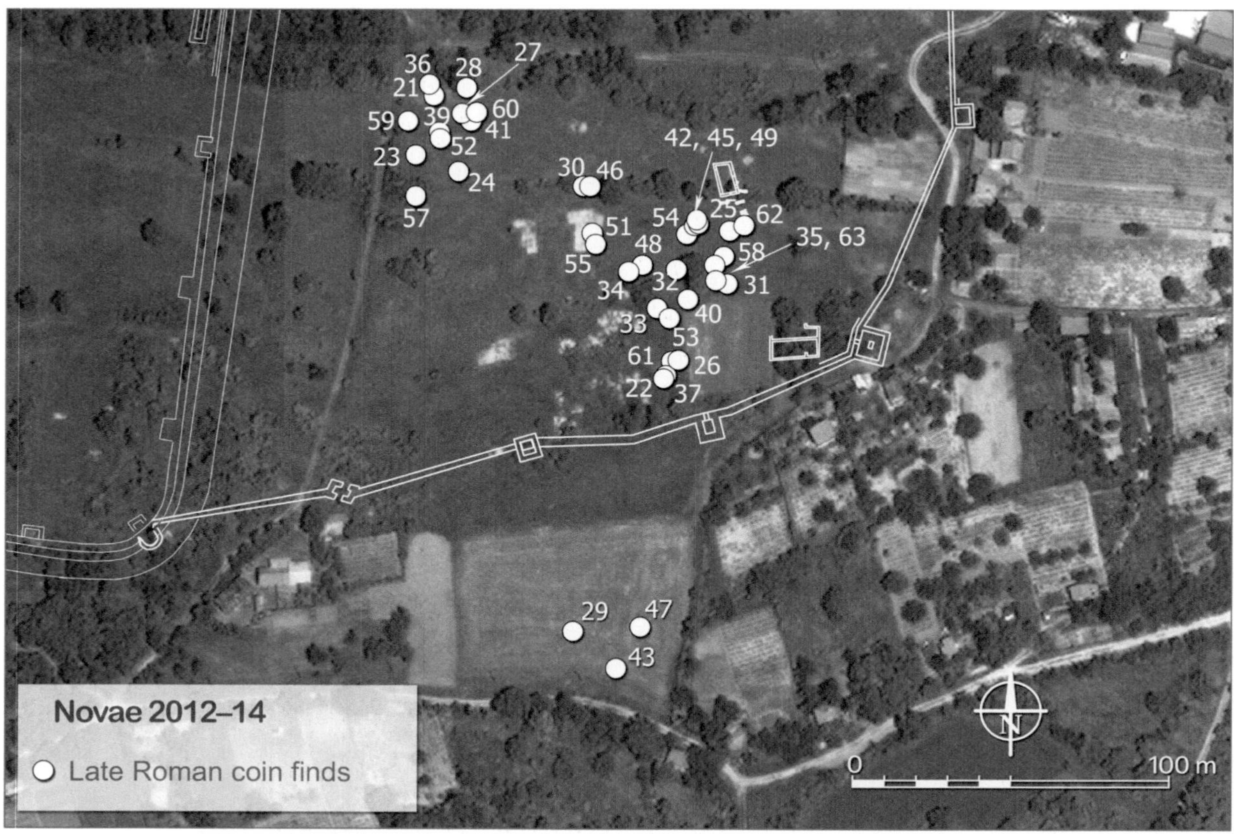

Fig. 81. Novae 2012–14. Late Roman coin finds from Area A1 (by A. Tomas).

Date	Issuer	Area A1 (1)	Area D	Area A1 (2)	Area B (1)	Area B (2)	Area B (3)	Area E	Total
			Roman Coinage						
1st–mid 3rd c.	Commodus						1		1
	Septimius Severus		1		1			1	3
	Caracalla	2							2
	Geta				1	1			2
	uncertain issuers	2	1		1	4			8
2nd half of the 3rd c.	Gallienus	1					1		2
	Probus		1				1		2
	Diocletian	1							1
4th–half of the 5th c.	Constantinopolis	3							3
	Constantius II (caesar)	1							1
	Constantine I (posthumous)	2							2
	Constans	1							1
	Constantius II	10	3		1				14
	Constantius Gallus (caesar)		1				1		2
	Gallus or Julian (caesares)	1							1
	Julian II	1							1
	Valentinian I		1						1
	Valentinian II	1							1
	Theodosius I	2		1		1			4
	Theodosius II	2		1					3
	uncertain issuers	7						1	8
			Byzantine Coinage						
6th c.	Justin I or Justinian	1	-	-	-	-	-	-	1
	Maurice Tiberius	1	-	-	-	-	-	-	1
	Total	39	8	2	4	6	4	2	65

Table 1. Chronological structure of the coin finds from field surveys conducted in 2000 and 2012–14 (according to investigated area): Area A1(1): southern part of the annexe; Area D: to the south of the annexe; Area A1(2): northern part of the annexe, from the illegal trench containing wall remains; Area B(1): Ostrite Mogili – eastern part; Area B(2): Ostrite Mogili – western part; Area B(3): Ostrite Mogili – field surveys in 2000; Area E: Chehlarski geran.

Fig. 82. Novae 2012–14. Early Byzantine coin finds from Area A1 (by A. Tomas).

was minted during the reign of Commodus (cat. no. 1*), the presence of older coins in the obtained material, including those minted in the 1st century AD, is confirmed by the two ases cut in half (cat. nos. 10, 11). The practice of cutting bronze coins in the provinces began in the first decades of the Roman Empire to obtain lower-denominations currency, which was lacking in circulation.[3] In the discussed numismatic material, however, there are no coins from the pre-Roman and the Republican periods.[4]

The vast majority, namely 3/4 of the coins minted until the middle of the 3rd century (12 specimens) are provincial coins struck in the cities of Thrace (Pautalia, Philippopolis, Anchialus) and Moesia Inferior (Nicopolis ad Istrum, Marcianopolis). Among them, the most numerous are small bronzes minted in Nicopolis during the Severan period. Only five coins are dated to the second half of the 3rd century.[5]

Coins minted in the years 330–435 constitute the most numerous group among the finds from Novae and Ostrite Mogili (42 specimens).[6] Coins struck during the reign of Constantius II (14 specimens) are predominant. Among the late Roman coins with legible mint marks, the mints operating in Thessalonica, Constantinople and Nicomedia are prevailing. Coins dated to the Early Byzantine period are only two (cat. nos. 64, 65), and they represent the denominations of 5 and 40 nummi. Both, most probably, were minted in Constantinople in the 6th century.

Coins discovered in the southern part of the annexe are the most numerous (39 specimens) group of finds from the surveys conducted in and around Novae. This group is dominated by the coins of the 4th and the first half of the 5th century (31 specimens). Two Early Byzantine coins mentioned above were also discovered within the annexe. Among eight coins found outside the annexe, those minted in the 4th century make up the majority (5 specimens). In a small trench left by the robbers, located in the northern part of the annexe, one coin of Theodosius I and one of Theodosius II were also discovered. The eastern part of the Ostrite Mogili site have

3. On the phenomenon of fragmenting the coins under the Julio-Claudian dynasty, see i.a.: Kunisz 1984; Buttrey 1972.

4. Finds of pre-Roman and republican coins from Novae are discussed in: Paunov 2014; Dimitrov 2013a.

5. On the circulation of coins in the second half of the 3rd century in Novae: Dimitrov 1980; cf. Dimitrov 2005b.

6. Finds of the 4th and 5th-century coins from Novae were discussed, among others in: Dimitrov 2014; Biernacki and Dimitrov 2008; Dimitrov 2005a; cf. Kunisz 1987.

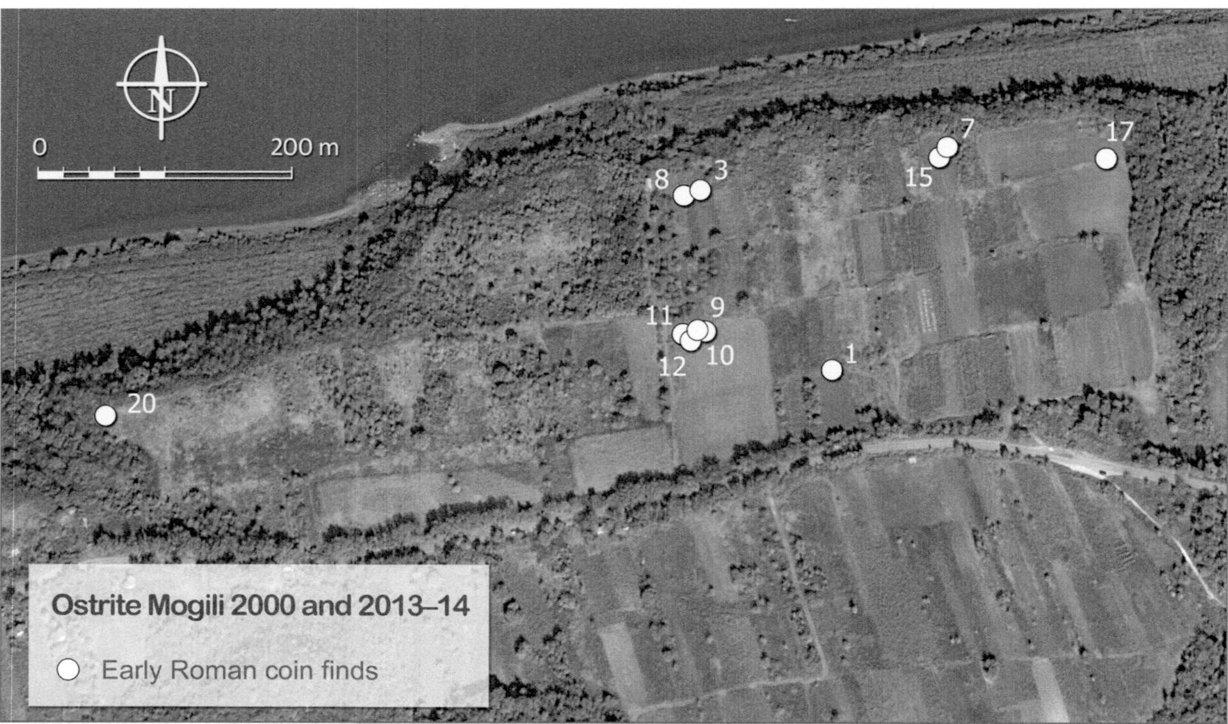

Fig. 83. Ostrite Mogili 2000 and 2013–14. Early Roman coin finds (by A. Tomas).

brought only 4 finds of ancient coins, out of which three are dated to the first half of the 3rd century, and one to the late Roman period. Six coins were found in the western part of the site, five of which were minted before the middle of the 3rd century, and one in the end of the 4th century. Among the Roman coins discovered on this site during the surveys in 2000, two were minted in the second half of the 3rd century. Only two coins were found at the neighboring site of Chehlarski geran – Area E: the coin of Septimius Severus struck in Philippopolis (cat. no. 2) and the coin dated to ca. 364–367 (cat. no. 56).

Fig. 84. Ostrite Mogili 2000 and 2013–14. Late Roman and early Byzantine coin finds (by A. Tomas).

Mint	265–296	330–363	364–395	408–435	Total
Rome	2	-	-	-	2
Siscia	1	-	1	-	2
Thessalonica	-	5	-	-	5
Heraclea	1	1	-	-	2
Constantinople	-	3	-	-	3
Nicomedia	-	2	2	-	4
Cyzicus	-	-	-	1	1
Antioch	-	1	1	-	2
Total	4	12	4	1	21

Table 2. Late Roman coins found during field surveys 2000 and 2012–14, according to mints.

II. Catalogue

The present catalogue contains descriptions of all the Roman and Byzantine coins found during the non-invasive survey conducted in the area located to the east and to the south-east of the legionary fortress (Area A1), at the site of Chehlarski geran (Area E), as well as at the Ostrite Mogili site (Area B) in 2012–14. The catalogue also presents coins found during the survey carried out at the latter site in 2000,[7] with these catalogue entries additionally marked with an asterisk (*) symbol. The coins in the catalogue are arranged according to the chronological and typological order, divided into Roman (including Roman provincial coins) and Byzantine coins. The numismatic material obtained from several separate research areas is treated here as a whole, but with information on the area in which individual coins were discovered. More detailed topographic information is provided by the attached maps, where the exact location of each specimen is marked. Information on the chronology of finds within individual areas covered by the research has been discussed in the text, and also presented collectively in Table 1.

Within individual catalogue notes, the elements of the description were provided in the following order: the sequence number within the catalogue and the field inventory number of small finds, the inventory number of the Museum in Svishtov (only for coins found at Ostrite Mogili in 2000), the date of issue (if possible to determine), the mint and denomination (if it was impossible to determine — the module or metal, for instance 'AE' for bronze coins made of copper alloys), the description of the obverse and the reverse, together with information on the state of preservation of the individual monetary legends (using square brackets), the denotation of the type, metrological data (weight, diameter, the die axis expressed in hours, additional comments on the state of preservation), as well as the find location. In addition, in the description of the coins found at Ostrite Mogili in 2000, information about which was provided in previous publications, references were made to the literature. In cases where the same issue or series is represented by several specimens, the entries have been ordered according to the state of preservation. All catalogue entries are accompanied by black and white photographs in a 1:1 scale, compiled on separate plates.

The figures in the present chapter show distribution of coin finds in the surveyed areas in chronological division: Area A1 – **Figs. 80–82**, Area B – **Figs 83** and **84**. The number on the two plates (**Pl. XXXIX** and **XL**) refer to the catalogue numbers.

Abbreviations

AMNG	Die antiken Münzen Nord-Griechenlands, vol. I: B. Pick, K. Regling. Die antiken Münzen von Dacien und Moesien, Berlin 1898
GIC	I. Varbanov, Greek Imperial Coins, vol. I–III, Bourgas 2005–2007
MIB	W. Hahn, Moneta Imperii Byzantini. Rekonstruktion des Prägeaufbaues auf synoptisch-tabellarischer Grundlage, vol. I-II, Wien 1973–1975
RIC	The Roman Imperial Coinage, vol. I.2–II.2, London 1984–2007, vol. III–X, London 1930–1994
cuir.	cuirassed
diad.	diademed
dr.	draped
ex.	exergue
l.	left
laur.	laureated
obv.	obverse
r.	right
rad.	radiated

7. Tomas 2017, 79; Tomas 2006, 119, 123.

rev.	reverse
std.	seated
stg.	standing
var.	variant

Location of finds

Area A1 (1)	the annexe
Area A1 (2)	outside the annexe
Area A1 (3)	the annexe – illegal trench containing remains of wall
Area B (1)	Ostrite Mogili – eastern part
Area B (2)	Ostrite Mogili – western part
Area B (3)	Ostrite Mogili – field survey 2000
Area E	Chehlarski geran

I. ROMAN COINAGE

COMMODUS (180–192)

1*. Inv. № 47/00w (= Svishtov Museum, inv. № 3418)
Thrace, Pautalia mint, AE
Obv. Laur., dr. bearded bust r., [AY KAI M]AP AY[P KOMO]Δ[OC]
Rev. Female figure stg. l. by altar (?), ΟVΛΠΙΑC ΠΑVΤΑΛΙΑC
Uncertain type
6,92 g; 23 mm; 1 h
Area B (3)
References: Tomas 2006, no. 37, p. 123 (as Elagabalus)

SEPTIMIUS SEVERUS (193–211)

2. Inv. № 102/14w/OM
Thrace, Philippopolis mint; AE
Obv. Laur. bust r., [AY K Λ C CEVEPOC] (?)
Rev. Bunch of grapes, ΦΙΛΙΠΠ[ΟΠΟΛΕΙΤΩΝ]
GIC III, 1261
3,62 g; 17 mm; 12 h
Area E

3. Inv. № 61/14w/OM
Moesia Inferior, Nicopolis ad Istrum mint; AE
Obv. Laur. bust r., AY KAI [CEVH]POC
Rev. Winged Thanatos stg. r. with legs crossed, leaning on inverted torch set on altar, [NIKOΠOΛI] ΠPOC ICTP
AMNG I 1366 (var.)
2,78 g; 17 mm; 8 h
Area B (1)

4. Inv. № 5/12w/can
Undetermined provincial mint; AE
Obv. Laur. bust r., [...] CЄVEPOC
Rev. Prize urn, [...]
Uncertain type
1,01 g; 13 mm; 8 h
Area A1 (2)

CARACALLA (211–217)

5. Inv. № 26/12w/can
Moesia Inferior, Marcianopolis mint; AE
Obv. Laur. bust r., AY K M AVP ANTONINOC Π AV
Rev. Homonoia stg. l., holding cornucopia and sacrificing with patera over altar to l., MAPKIANOΠOΛITΩN (AP in ligature)
GIC I, 906
6,56 g; 22 mm; 2 h
Area A1 (1)

6. Inv. № 69/13w/can
Moesia Inferior, Nicopolis ad Istrum mint; AE
Obv. Laur. bust r., [AV K] M A[V] ANTΩN[INOC]
Rev. Crescent and three stars, [...N]IKOΠ[OΛ...]
GIC I, 3020-3021 (var.)
4,09 g; 17 mm; 5 h
Area A1 (1)

GETA (209–212 n.e.)

7. Inv. № 78/13w/OM
Ca. 203–208 (under Septimius Severus), Rome mint; denarius
Obv. Bareheaded, dr. bust r., [P] SEPTIMIVS GETA CAES
Rev. Liberalitas stg. l., holding abacus and cornucopiae, LIBERALITAS AVG V[I]
RIC IV.1, 44
1,90 g; 17 mm; 6 h
Area B (1)

8. Inv. № 57/14w/OM
Thrace, Anchialus mint; AE
Obv. Bareheaded, dr. cuir. bust r., [...] ΓETA[C]
Rev. Altar, AΓX[IA]ΛEΩN
Uncertain type
1,50 g; 15 mm;1 h
Area B (2)

UNCERTAIN ISSUERS (1ST–MID-3RD C.)

9. Inv. № 79/14w/OM
Rome mint (?); denarius subaeratus (perforated)
Obv. Laur. bust r., [...]NVS [...]
Rev. Female figure stg. l., [...]
Uncertain type
1,85 g; 20 mm; 6 h
Area B (2)

10. Inv. № 111/14w/OM
Rome mint; 1/2 of cut as
Obv. Illegible
Rev. Illegible
Uncertain type
2,05 g; 26 mm; ?
Area B (2)

11. Inv. № 92/14w/OM
Rome mint (?); 1/2 of cut as (?)
Obv. Illegible
Rev. Illegible
Uncertain type
1,67 g; 24 mm; ?
Area B (2)

12. Inv. № 83/14w/OM
Moesia Inferior, Nicopolis ad Istrum mint (?); AE
Obv. Laur. bust r., [...]
Rev. Lion walking r., [...]
Uncertain type
2,98 g; 16,5 mm; 1 h
Area B (2)

13. Inv. № 70/13w/can
Moesia Inferior, Nicopolis ad Istrum mint (?); AE
Obv. Laur. bust r., [...]
Rev. Club, [...]
Uncertain type
1,57 g; 15 mm; 4 h
Area A1 (1)

14. Inv. № 30/12w/can
Undetermined provincial mint; AE
Obv. Bust r., [...]
Rev. Wreath, [...]
Uncertain type
2,83 g; 19 mm; ?
Area A1 (1)

15. Inv. № 79/13w/OM
Undetermined provincial mint; AE
Obv. Laurel bust r., [...]
Rev. Coiled serpent, [...]
Uncertain type
3,60 g; 17 mm; 6 h
Area B (1)

16. Inv. № 6/12w/can
Undetermined provincial mint; AE
Obv. Bust r., [...]
Rew.: lion leaping r. (?), [...]
Uncertain type
3,52 g; 16 mm; 6 h (?)
Area A1 (2)

GALLIENUS (253–268)

17*. Inv. № 12/00w (= Svištov Museum, inv. № 3408)
Ca. 265–267; Rome mint; antoninianus
Obv. Rad. head l., [... GAL]L[IENVS ...]
Rev. Providentia stg. l., holding baton and cornucopiae, globe at foot, [PRO]VIDENT[IA AVG], in r. field: X
RIC V.1, 267 or 269
3,80 g; 20 mm; 6 h
Area B (3)
References: Tomas 2006, no. 38, p. 123 (as mid-3rd c. undetermined Roman provincial coin)

18. Inv. № 32/12w/can
Undetermined mint; 1/4 of cut antoninianus
Obv. Rad. head r., [... G]ALLIENV[S ...]
Rev. Illegible
Uncertain type
1,68 g; > 16 mm; ?
Area A1 (1)

PROBUS (276–282)

19. Inv. № 1/12w/can
Rome mint; ca. 2/3 of cut antoninianus
Obv. Rad. cuir. bust r., [IMP PRO]BVS AVG (?)
Rev. Roma std. in temple, holding Victory and sceptre, ROMAE [AETER], in ex.: R ‿ [?]
RIC V.2, 186–187 (var.)
2,47 g; 21 mm; 12 h
Area A1 (2)

20*. Inv. № 62/00w (= Svishtov Museum, inv. № 3402)
Siscia mint, antoninianus
Obv. Rad. dr. cuir. bust r., IMP C M AVR PROBVS AVG
Rev. Emperor stg. r., receiving globe from Jupiter stg. l., CLEMENTIA TEMP, in field between: A•, in ex.: XXI
RIC V.2, 644 (var.)
3,01 g; 22 mm; 11 h
Area B (3)
References: Tomas 2006, no. 36, p. 123, fig. 16.8 (pl. 130)

DIOCLETIAN (284–305)

21. Inv. № 65/13w/can
Ca. 284–296; Heraclea mint; antoninianus
Obv. Rad. dr. cuir. bust r., IMP C C VAL DIOCLETIANVS P F AVG
Rev. Emperor stg. r., receiving Victory from Jupiter stg. l., CONCORDIA MILITVM, in field between: HA, in ex.: [•XXI•] (?)
RIC V.2, 284
3,27 g; 21 mm; 1 h
Area A1 (1)

CONSTANTINOPOLIS SERIES

22. Inv. № 12/12w/can
330–333; Thessalonica mint; AE
Obv. Laur. helmeted bust of Constantinople l., CONSTANTINOPOLIS
Rev. Victory stg. l. on prow with spear and shield, in ex.: SMTSЄ
RIC VII, 188
1,36 g; 16 mm; 12 h
Area A1 (1)

23. Inv. № 76/13w/can
333–336; Heraclea mint; AE
Obv. Laur. helmeted bust of Constantinople l., CONSTANTINOPOLI
Rev. Victory stg. l. on prow with spear and shield, in ex.: SMHA*
RIC VII, 144
2,46 g; 20 mm; 5 h
Area A1 (1)

24. Inv. № 75/13w/can
336–337; undetermined mint; AE
Obv. Laur. helmeted bust of Constantinople l., CONSTANTINO[POLI]
Rev. Two soldiers stg., between them one standard, GLORIA EXERCITVS, mint-mark in ex. uncertain
Uncertain type
1,40 g; 15 mm; 11h
Area A1 (1)

CONSTANTIUS II (CAESAR)

25. Inv. № 14/12w/can
336–337; Thessalonica mint; AE
Obv. Laur. dr. cuir. bust r., FL IVL CONSTANTIVS NOB C
Rev. Two soldiers stg., between them one standard, GLORIA EXERCITVS, in ex.: SMTSΓ
RIC VII, 224
1,43 g; 17 mm; 8 h
Area A1 (1)

CONSTANTINE I (POSTHUMOUS)

26. Inv. № 13/12w/can
337–340; Nicomedia mint; AE
Obv. Veiled head r., DV CONSTANTINVS PT AVGG
Rev. Emperor, veiled, in quadriga to r., the hand of God reaches down to him, in ex.: SMNS
RIC VIII, 18
1,77 g; 13 mm; 4 h
Area A1 (1)

27. Inv. № 63/13w/can
337–340; undetermined mint; AE
Obv. Veiled head r., DV CONSTANTINVS PT AVGG
Rev. Emperor, veiled, in quadriga to r., the hand of God reaches down to him, mint-mark in ex. uncertain
Uncertain type
1,76 g; 16 mm; 11 h
Area A1 (1)

CONSTANS (337–350)

28. Inv. № 66a/13w/can
337–340; Nicomedia mint; AE
Obv. Laur. head r., [D N] CONS[TA]NS P F AVG
Rev. Two soldiers stg., between them one standard, GL[ORIA E]XE[RC]ITVS, in ex.: SMNS
RIC VIII, 12 (var.)
1,15 g; 17 mm; 12 h
Area A1 (1)

CONSTANTIUS II (337–361)

29. Inv. № 3/12w/can
337–340; Thessalonica mint; AE
Obv. Laur. diad. cuir. dr. bust r., CONSTANTIVS P F AVG
Rev. Two soldiers stg., between them one standard, [GLO]RI[A EXER]CITVS, in ex.: SMTSB
RIC VIII, 56
1,21 g; 16 mm; 8 h
Area A1 (2)

30. Inv. № 24/12w/can
337–340; Constantinople mint; AE
Obv. Diad. head r., D N CONSTANTIVS P F AVG
Rev. Two soldiers stg., between them one standard, GLORIA EXERCITVS, in ex.: CONSH
RIC VIII, 27
1,79 g; 15 mm; 6 h
Area A1 (1)

31. Inv. № 20/12w/can
337–347; Antioch mint; AE
Obv. Diad. head r., CONSTANTI[VS AVG]
Rev. Two soldiers stg., between them one standard, [GLO]RIA EXERCITVS, in field: • | •, in ex.: SMANAI
RIC VIII, 54
1,17 g; 17 mm; 12 h
Area A1 (1)

32. Inv. № 18/12w/can
347–348; Constantinople mint; AE
Obv. Diad. head r., D N CONST[ANTI]VS P F AVG
Rev. [VOT/X]X/MVLT/XXX within wreath, in ex.: CONSIA
RIC VIII, 69
0,88 g; 16 mm; 12 h
Area A1 (1)

33. Inv. № 16/12w/can
347–348; undetermined mint; AE
Obv. Diad. head r., D N CONSTA[NTIVS P F AVG]
Rev. VOT/XX/MVLT/XXX within wreath, mint-mark in ex. uncertain
Uncertain type
1,67 g; 15 mm; 2 h
Area A1 (1)

34. Inv. № 19/12w/can
347–348; undetermined mint; AE
Obv. Diad. head r., [D N CONSTANTIVS P] F A[VG]
Rev. VOT/X[X]/MVLT/XXX within wreath, mint-mark in ex. uncertain
Uncertain type
1,51 g; 14 mm; 12 h
Area A1 (1)

35. Inv. № 7/12w/can
351–361; Thessalonica mint; AE
Obv. Diad. head r., [D N CON]STANTIVS [P F AVG]
Rev. Soldier spearing falling horseman, [FEL TEMP REPARATIO], in ex.: SMTS
Uncertain type
1,42 g; 15 mm; 4 h
Area A1 (1)

36. Inv. № 74/13w/can
351–361; undetermined mint, AE
Obv. Diad. dr. cuir. bust r., [D N CON]STAN[TIVS P F AVG]
Rev. Soldier spearing falling horseman, [FEL TEMP REPARATIO], in l. field: • S •, mint-mark in ex. uncertain
Uncertain type
3,94 g; 18 mm; 12 h
Area A1 (1)

37. Inv. № 23/12w/can
351–361; undetermined mint; AE
Obv. Diad. dr. cuir. bust r., D N CONSTAN[TIVS P F AVG]
Rev. Soldier spearing falling horseman, [FEL TEMP REPARATIO], mint-mark in ex. uncertain
Uncertain type
2,65 g; 17 mm; 12 h
Area A1 (1)

38. Inv. № 77/13w/OM
351–361; undetermined mint; AE
Obv. Diad. dr. cuir. bust r., D N CONSTANTIVS P F AVG
Rev. Soldier spearing falling horseman, FEL TEMP [REPARATIO],

in l. field: B, mint-mark in ex. uncertain
Uncertain type
2,23 g; 17 mm; 12 h
Area B (1)

39. Inv. № 73/13w/can
351–361; undetermined mint; AE
Obv. Diad. dr. cuir. bust r., [D N] CONSTANTIVS P F AVG
Rev. Soldier spearing falling horseman, [FEL TEMP REPA] RATIO, mint-mark in ex. uncertain
Uncertain type
1,99 g; 17 mm; 11 h
Area A1 (1)

40. Inv. № 10/12w/can
351–361; undetermined mint; AE
Obv. Diad. head r., [D N CONSTAN]TIVS [P F AVG]
Rev. Soldier spearing falling horseman, in l. field: II (?), mint-mark in ex. uncertain
Uncertain type
1,55 g; 18 mm; 4 h
Area A1 (1)

41. Inv. № 64/13w/can
351–361; undetermined mint; AE
Obv. Diad. dr. cuir. bust r., [D N CONSTANTIVS P F AVG]
Rev. Soldier spearing falling horseman, [FEL TEMP REPARATIO], mint-mark in ex. uncertain
Uncertain type
1,12 g; 14 mm; 7 h
Area A1 (1)

42. Inv. № 21/12w/can
355–361; Thessalonica mint; AE
Obv. Diad. dr. cuir. bust r., D N [CO]NST[ANT]IVS P F AVG
Rev. Emperor stg. l., holding globe and spear, SPES REI [P] VBLICE, in ex.: SMTSB (?)
RIC VIII, 213
1,79 g; 16 mm; 4 h
Area A1 (1)

CONSTANTIUS GALLUS (CAESAR)

43. Inv. № 4/12w/can
351–354; Constantinople mint; AE
Obv. Bareheaded dr. cuir. bust r., D N FL CL C[ONST]ANTIVS NOB [CAES]
Rev. Soldier spearing falling horseman, [F]EL TEMP REPARAT[IO], in l. field: x•, in ex.: CONS[?]
RIC VIII, 124
2,40 g; 17 mm; 4 h
Area A1 (2)

44*. Inv. № 21/00w (= Svishtov Museum, inv. № 3405)
351–354; undetermined mint; AE
Obv. Bareheaded bust r., DN CONS[TANTIVS NOB CAES]
Rev. Soldier spearing falling horseman, FEL TEM REPA[RATIO], in ex.: SM[...]
Uncertain type
2,12 g; 16 mm; 5 h
Area B (3)

CONSTANTIUS GALLUS OR JULIAN II (CAESARES)

45. Inv. № 22/12w/can
351–361; undetermined mint, AE
Obv. Bareheaded bust r., [...]
Rev. Soldier spearing falling horseman, [FEL TEMP REPARATIO], mint-mark in ex. uncertain
Uncertain type
3,02 g; 14 mm; 10 h
Area A1 (1)

JULIAN II (361–363)

46. Inv. № 31/12w/can
Undetermined mint; AE
Obv. Diad. dr. cuir. bust r., D N FL CL IVLIANVS P F AVG
Rev. Emperor stg. l., holding globe and spear, SPES REI [PVBLICE], mint-mark in ex. uncertain
Uncertain type
1,79 g; 15 mm; 12 h
Area A1 (1)

VALENTINIAN I (364–375)

47. Inv. № 2/12w/can
364–367; Nicomedia mint; AE
Obv. Diad. dr. cuir. bust r., [D N V]ALENT[INIANVS P] F AVG
Rev. Emperor advancing r., with r. hand dragging captive and holding labarum in l., GLORIA [RO]MANORVM, in ex.: SMNA
RIC IX, 9a
1,60 g; 16 mm; 6 h
Area A1 (2)

VALENTINIAN II (375–392)

48. Inv. № 27/12w/can
378–383; Siscia mint; AE
Obv. Diad. dr. cuir. bust r., D N VALENTINIANVS P F AVG
Rev. Roma std. facing, head l., holding globe and reversed spear, CONCORDIA AVGGG, in ex.: BSISC
RIC IX, 27b
2,40 g; 17 mm; 8 h
Area A1 (1)

THEODOSIUS I (379–395)

49. Inv. № 8/12w/can
383–392; Antioch mint; AE
Obv. Diad. dr. cuir. bust r., DN THEODO[SIV]S P F AVG
Rev. Victory advancing l., holding trophy on shoulder with r. hand and dragging captive with l., SALVS REIPVBLICAE, in l. field: +, in ex.: ANTA
RIC IX, 67b (var.)
1,39 g; 13 mm; 4 h
Area A1 (1)

ARCADIUS (AUGUSTUS UNDER THEODOSIUS I)

50. Inv. № 63/14w/OM
Ca. 388–395; undetermined mint: AE
Obv. Diad. dr. cuir. bust r., D N ARCA[DIVS P F AVG]
Rev. Victory advancing l., holding trophy on shoulder with r. hand and dragging captive with l., [SALVS REIPVBLICAE], mint-mark in field and ex. uncertain
Uncertain type
1,06 g; 14 mm; 4 h
Area B (2)

51. Inv. № 76/14w/can
Ca. 388–395; undetermined mint: AE
Obv. Diad. dr. cuir. bust r., [D N ARCA]DIVS P [F AVG]
Rev. Victory advancing l., holding trophy on shoulder with r. hand and dragging captive with l., [SALVS REIPVBLICAE], mint-mark in field and ex. uncertain
Uncertain type
1,00 g; 11,5 mm; 6 h
Area A1 (3)

HONORIUS (AUGUSTUS UNDER THEODOSIUS I)

52. Inv. № 71/13w/can
Ca. 388–395; undetermined mint: AE
Obv. Diad. dr. cuir. bust r., [D]N HONO[RIVS P F AVG]
Rev. Victory advancing l., holding trophy on shoulder with r. hand and dragging captive with l., [SALVS REIPVBLICAE], mint-mark in field and ex. uncertain
Uncertain type
1,14 g; 12 mm; 6 h
Area A1 (1)

THEODOSIUS II (408–450)

53. Inv. № 15/12w/can
408–423; undetermined mint; AE
Obv. Diad. dr. cuir. bust r., [D N THEODOSIVS P F AVG]
Rev. Two emperors stg. facing, heads turned to one another, each holding spear and supporting between them a globe, [GLORIA ROMANORVM], mint-mark in ex. uncertain
Uncertain type (RIC X, 407-418)
2,13 g; 13 mm; 10 h
Area A1 (1)

54. Inv. № 66b/13w/can
408–423; undetermined mint; AE
Obv. Diad. dr. cuir. bust r., [D N THEODOSIVS P F AVG]
Rev. Two emperors stg. facing, heads turned to one another, each holding spear and supporting between them a globe, [GLORIA ROMANORVM], mint-mark in ex. uncertain
Uncertain type (RIC X, 407-418)
1,58 g; 14 mm; 5 h (?)
Area A1 (1)

55. Inv. № 75/14w/can
425–435; Cyzicus mint; AE
Obv. Diad. dr. cuir. bust r., [D N T]HEODOSIVS P F [AVG]
Rev. Cross within wreath, no legend, in ex.: SMKA
RIC X, 451
1,10 g; 11,5 mm; 12 h
Area A1 (3)

UNCERTAIN ISSUERS, (4TH–1ST HALF OF 5TH C.)

56. Inv. № 100/14w/OM
Ca. 364–367; undetermined mint; AE
Obv. Diad. dr. cuir. bust r., […]
Rev. Emperor advancing r., with r. hand dragging captive and holding labarum in l., [GLORIA ROMANORVM], mint-mark in ex. uncertain
Uncertain type
2,13 g; 18 mm; 2 h
Area E

57. Inv. № 72/13w/can
378–383; Nicomedia mint; AE
Obv. Diad. dr. cuir. bust r., […]V[S P F AVG]
Rev. VOT/XX/MVLT/XXX within wreath, in ex.: SMNA
Uncertain type
0,96 g; 14 mm; 12 h
Area A1 (1)

58. Inv. № 28/12w/can
Ca. 383–388; undetermined mint; AE
Obv. Diad. dr. cuir. bust r., […]
Rev. VOT/V within wreath, mint-mark in ex. uncertain
Uncertain type
1,48 g; 12 mm; 12 h
Area A1 (1)

59. Inv. № 68/13w/can
392–395; undetermined mint; AE (>1/2 of cut coin)
Obv. Diad. dr. cuir. bust r., [… P] F AVG
Rev. Emperor on horseback r., raising r. hand, [GLORIA ROMANORVM], mint-mark in ex. uncertain
Uncertain type
1,76 g (broken); 16 mm; 6 h
Area A1 (1)

60. Inv. № 67/13w/can
425–435; undetermined mint; AE
Obv. Diad. dr. cuir. bust r., […] P F AVG
Rev. Cross within wreath, no legend, mint-mark in ex. uncertain
Uncertain type
1,03 g; 12 mm; 6 h
Area A1 (1)

61. Inv. № 11/12w/can
425–435; undetermined mint; AE
Obv. Diad. dr. cuir. bust r., […]
Rev. Cross within wreath, no legend, mint-mark in ex. uncertain
Uncertain type
0,93 g; 11 mm; 10 h
Area A1 (1)

62. Inv. № 25/12w/can
Undetermined mint; AE
Obv. Illegible
Rev.: Illegible
Uncertain type
0,78 g; 10 mm; 6 h (?)
Area A1 (1)

63. Inv. № 17/12w/can
Undetermined mint; AE (ca. 1/2 of broken coin)
Obv. Illegible
Rev.: Illegible
Uncertain type
0,80 g; 13 mm; ?
Area A1 (1)

II. BYZANTINE COINAGE

JUSTIN I (518–527) OR JUSTINIAN I (527–565)

64. Inv. № 29/12w/can
Ca. 522–537; Constantinople or Nicomedia mint; 5 nummi
Obv. Diad. dr. cuir. bust r., […]

Rev. Large Chi-Rho symbol, in r. field: Є, letter in l. field illegible
Uncertain type
1,84 g; 12 mm; 6 h
Area A1 (1)

MAURICE (582–602)

65. Inv. № 9/12w/can
587/588; Constantinople mint; 40 nummi
Obv. Helmeted and cuir. bust facing, holding globus cruciger and shield, D N MAVR C TIBЄR P P AVC
Rev.: Large M, cross above, Є below, in l. field: A/N/N/O, in r. field: ч, in ex.: CON
MIB II, 67d
12,16 g; 30 mm; 6 h
Area A1 (1)

Pl. XXXIX. Roman coin finds

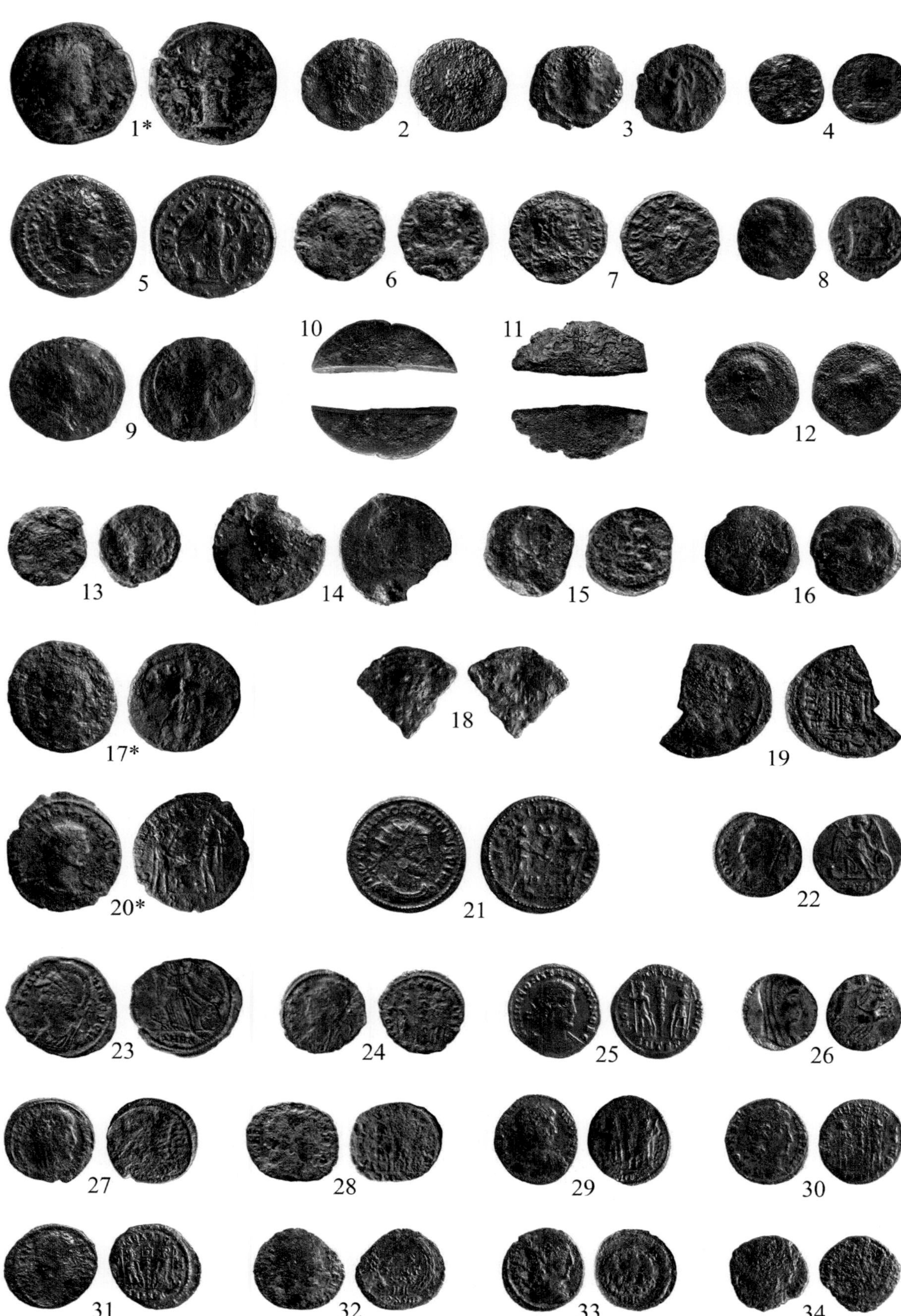

Pl. XL. Roman coin finds

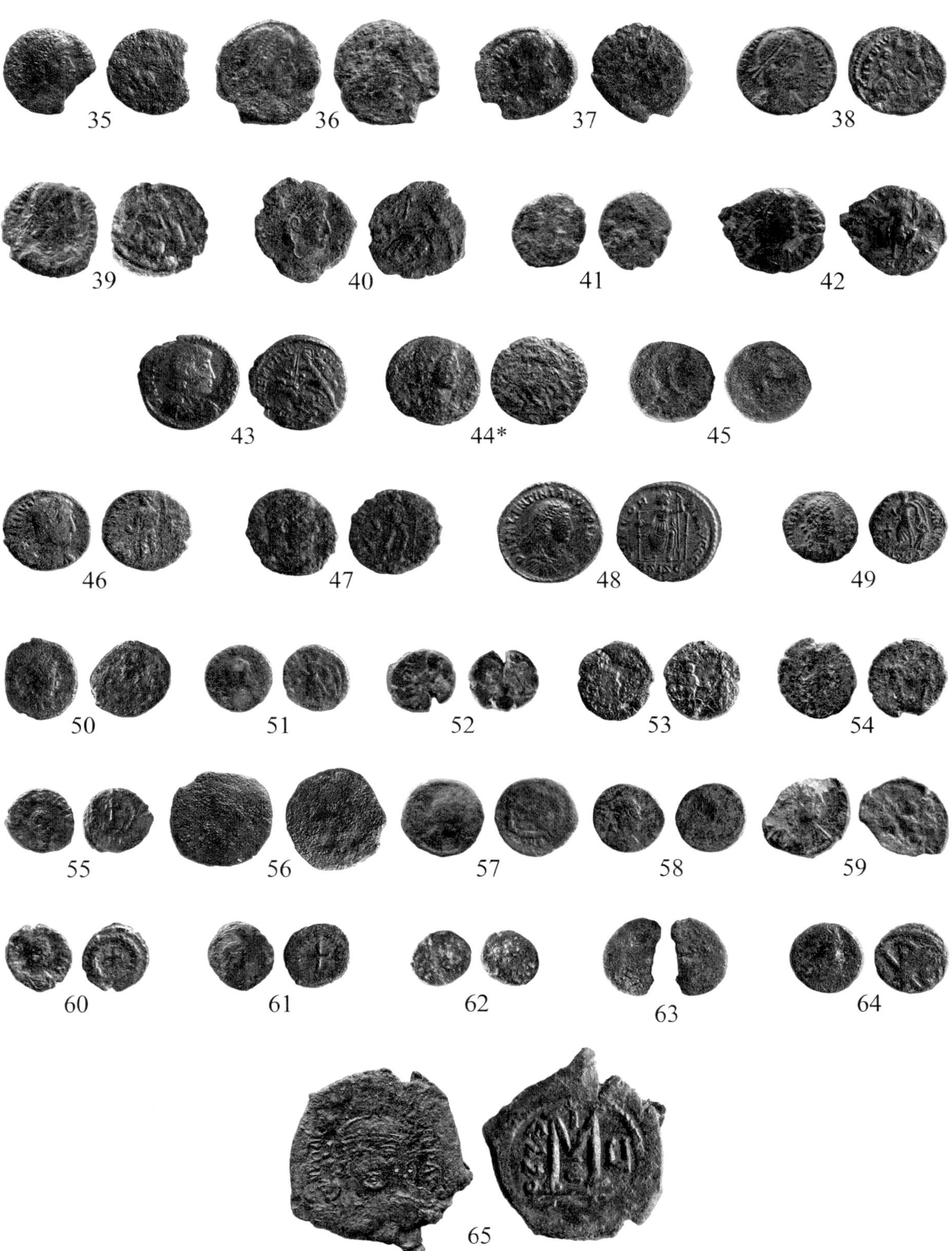

10. Lead seals

Piotr Jaworski

Among the finds from Novae, Roman and Byzantine lead seals belong to the group of artifacts that have been the least studied. This situation is a reflection of the generally insufficient state of research on this extremely important category of finds,[1] although thanks to a series of publications in recent years by Bulgarian and Romanian researchers, our knowledge in this field has improved dramatically. The oldest publication mentioning the finds of seals from Novae dates back to 1965.[2] Leszek Mrozewicz is the author of the first publication devoted entirely to this category of finds, in which 19 specimens were discussed.[3] These seals have recently been republished,[4] along with ten others once thought to have been lost, but which have since been found during an inventory conducted at the Svishtov Museum in 1981,[5] as well as five specimens from later excavations.[6] Some of the seals in the Svishtov Museum's collection come from donations and other sources, originating not only from Novae itself but also from its immediate surroundings, while others were discovered during excavations at the site.[7]

In 2012, in the course of mapping metal finds in the southern part of the Novae annexe, two lead artifacts of an epigraphic character were found using a metal detector (**Fig. 85, Pl. XLI, 1–2**). The third artifact, bearing a figural representation (**Pl. XLI, 3**), was found in 2014 at the Ostrite Mogili site (Area B). Each of them represents a different function and dating.

1. Inv. no. 40/12w/can (**Pl. XLI, 1**).
   Provincial seal. Pamphylia, second half of the 4th c.
   Round-shaped, one-sided. Diam. 19 mm. W. 5.43 g.
   Obv. PAM/FV/LON (in three lines), between two palm branches.
   Rev. Blank; conical-shaped central nipple.[8]
   References: Chiriac and Munteanu 2014, no. 50 (Type V); RLS, no. 0316; after: Culică 1975, no. 104; cf. Culică 1976, Pl. IX (cf. Fig. 1).

The artifact comes from Pamphylia, located in the southwestern part of Asia Minor, which was previously part of the administrative structures of a few Roman provinces (Cilicia, Asia, Galatia); as of Vespasian's times, it co-formed a joint province together with Lycia, while finally in AD

1. Chiriac and Munteanu 2014, 299; cf. Still 1993, 403.
2. Zhuglev 1965, 250, nos. 250, 255.
3. Mrozewicz 1981a.
4. Recław 2009, 1560–65, nos. 1–19.
5. Recław 2009, 1565–67, nos. 20–29; cf. Recław 2005, 47.
6. Recław 2009, 1567–68, nos. 30–34; cf. Recław 2005, 47.
7. Recław 2009, 1559.
8. Still 1995, Type 8.

Fig. 85. Novae 2012. Places in the annexe where lead seals were found (by A. Tomas).

Pl. XLI. Areas A1 and B. Lead seals

1

2

3

314 or 325 achieving the status of a separate province.[9] The seal bears a legend in Greek, written in the plural genitive, but expressed with Latin letters (PAMFVLON). In this form, widespread in legends placed on Greek coins, it referred to the inhabitants of Pamphylia (Παμφύλων). In this sense, as Michael Still has pointed out, it was a traditional ethnicon, not a reference to the name of a province.[10] According to Still, the use of Latin may indicate that these seals were used by the Roman provincial administration.[11] It should be mentioned that a certain type of seal from this period also bears the same legend, though written in Greek: ΠΑΜΦΥΛΩΝ.[12]

Considering the iconographic motifs and legends placed on the obverses of one-sided late Antiquity Pamphylian seals found in Dobruja, Costel Chiriac and Lucian Munteanu divided them into five basic types:[13]

Type I. Lion walking right, ΠΑΜΦΥ.

1 specimen found in Izvoarele (Sucidava), Museum of National History and Archaeology, Constanţa.[14]

Type II. ΠΑΜ/ΦΥΛ/•Α• (in three lines).

1 specimen found in southern Dobruja, Regional History Museum, Dobrich.[15]

Type III. Draped female bust right, ΠΑΜΦΥ–ΛΙΑC.

1 specimen found in Oltina (Altinum), National History Museum of Romania, Bucharest.[16]

Type IV. Draped female figure standing to the front, holding cornucopiae (?) in the left hand, a patera (?) in the right one, ΠΑΜ–ΦΥΛΩΝ.

3 specimens found in Izvoarele (Sucidava), Museum of National History and Archaeology, Constanţa (2), Lower Danube Museum, Călăraşi (1).[17]

Type V. PAM/FY/L[IA] (in three lines), palm branch in left field.

1 specimen found in Izvoarele (Sucidava), Museum of National History and Archaeology, Constanţa **(Fig. 86)**.[18]

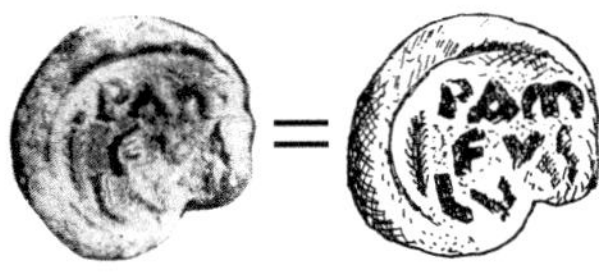

Fig. 86. Late Roman lead seal from Pamphylia found in Izvoarele (Sucidava). After: Culică 1976, Pl. IX (picture on the left), Culică 1975, 252 (drawing on the right).

On the basis of the above typology developed by Chiriac and Munteanu, it can be concluded that the seal from Novae belongs to type V, although there are some – easily explainable – discrepancies in the description of the two specimens. The stamp on the specimen discovered in Sucidava (cf. **Fig. 86**) was impressed off-centrically, leaving the right field partially invisible, making it impossible to read it correctly. Vasile Culică reconstructed the two missing letters as PAM/FY/L[IA],[19] while Michael Still decided to leave the lacuna: PAM/FV/L[—].[20] The specimen from Novae, on which the stamp was placed centrically, dispels any doubts, making it possible to read the legend in its entirety as PAM/FV/LON. In addition, in the right field, similarly as in the left one, one can observe a palm

9. Martini 2000, 218.
10. Still 1995, 316.
11. Still 1995, 315.
12. Chiriac and Munteanu 2014, 316 – Type IV.
13. Chiriac and Munteanu 2014, 315 f.
14. Culică 1975, 251, no. 85, Pl. VIII, XIV; 1976, Pl. VIII; Still 1995, 544, no. 1596; Chiriac and Munteanu 2014, 315, no. 44.
15. Chiriac and Munteanu 2014, 316, no. 45, Pl. II.4.
16. Barnea 1990, 318, no. 3; Chiriac and Munteanu 2014, 316, no. 46.
17. Culică 1975, 241, nos. 28–29, Pl. III, XII; 1976, Pl. III; 1979, 147, no. 139, Figs. 1–3; Still 1995, 316 f., no. 0319; Chiriac and Munteanu 2014, 315, no. 44. There is probably an additional specimen of this type (although the figure is described as Tyche), of uncertain provenance, in the Récamier collection in Lyon: Still 1995, 315, no. 0315A.
18. Culică 1975, 253, no. 104, Pl. IX, XV; 1976, Pl. IX; Still 1995, 315 f., no. 0316; Chiriac and Munteanu 2014, 316, no. 50.
19. Culică 1975, 253.
20. Still 1995, 315.

leaf. Thus, this element should be added to the description of type V.

The seal found in Novae belongs to the broadly understood group of late Antique trade seals, referred to as provincial ones, i.e., seals containing the name of the province. Along with the Asia Minor municipal seals (i.e., seals bearing the names of cities), Pamphylia seals constitute a quite numerous group of finds from Roman Danubian sites, consisting of over 50 published specimens.[21] These seals were found in areas that during the Principate period made up part of the Roman province of Moesia Inferior, especially in Dobruja and its nearest vicinity.[22] Almost all of the municipal seals found represent 17 cities of the western part of Asia Minor, primarily in Ionia (including Smyrna, Ephesus) and Lydia (including Hypaepa, Koloe).[23] A Pamphylia seal should also be noted, of an unknown type, found in Tomis.[24] In addition to the West Pontic area, specimens of seals from cities in Asia Minor have been discovered at sites further west in Moesia Inferior, as well as in Thrace, Pannonia, and even in Gaul and Britannia.[25]

Nevertheless, the fact that the number of finds of Asia Minor seals in the Western Pontic area, especially in the Danube area, is so dense has led researchers dealing with this group of artifacts to formulate some interesting observations. Upon analysing the majority of contemporary seals from the cities of western Asia Minor, which were epigraphic in character and devoid of figural elements, M. Still, quoting the opinions of various authors, drew attention to the similarity in the arrangement of the rectangular incused field of the stamp. On this basis, he formulated a conclusion about the existence of a system for providing supplies to the Danube garrisons organised by representatives of state administration (*comes sacrarum largitionum*) in the second half of the 4th century.[26] City seals, affixed to transported containers, would mark batches of quotas delivered by individual cities and provinces of western Asia Minor that passed customs inspection at Ephesus, a centre that played a key role in the *annona* system.[27] According to Still, this type of system of supplying the Danube garrisons was not associated with any specific events in the region.

In turn, C. Chiriac and L. Munteanu have gone further in their conclusions, pointing to the events of AD 366-369 and the involvement of the Roman army in the Balkans under Valens' command in the war against the Goths, which required a substantial and organized victualling effort. A trace of these efforts can be observed in the large influx of lead seals from Asia Minor to the Danube centres.[28] According to the authors, the supplies were executed for a few years, even though they did not exclude its functioning until the defeat at Hadrianopolis in AD 378. Noviodunum and Sucidava were to play an important role in the supply system, and after the peace with the Goths in AD 369 acted as open markets.[29]

The Asia Minor urban and provincial seals from Pamphylia form a distinct group of finds and provide material evidence of processes of an interregional nature. They occurred in a specific geopolitical context of the Balkans, i.e., during the period of Valens' Gothic wars. It should be noted that the Pamphylia seal discovered in Novae is not an isolated find. Two earlier finds should be noted of conical one-sided seals from Asia Minor, currently in the Svištov Museum collection:

– an urban seal from Magnesia by Meander, with the legend MAΓ/NHT/Є/M in a rectangular field.[30] An analogous seal, as in the case of the Pamphylia seal, was found in Sucidava.[31]

– a Smyrna urban seal, with the legend CMY/PNA in a rectangular field.[32] In his publication, J. Recław read its content as EMS/PNA or PNA/PNA; however, the comparison of the drawing of the artifact he published[33] with a series of known similar finds,[34] does not leave any doubts as to the identification of this find. The highest amount, because as many as 10 from among the 14 Smyrna seals discovered in the western Pontic area, come from Sucidava, including 6 type I specimens[35] and 4 specimens belonging to Chiriac and Munteanu's type II, with the PNA/CMY variant of the legend.[36] Three specimens are supposed to have originated from Tomis,[37] while one specimen was found in Cius.[38]

21. Chiriac and Munteanu 2014, 309–18.
22. Cf. Chiriac and Munteanu 2014, 304–05; 329, Pl. V.
23. Chiriac and Munteanu 2014, 304.
24. Barnea 1990, 317.
25. Chiriac and Munteanu 2014, 305.
26. Still 1995, 94 f.; cf. Kritzinger and Zimmermann 2019, 299–302.
27. Still 1995, 95.
28. Chiriac and Munteanu 2014, 306–08.
29. Chiriac and Munteanu 2014, 306.
30. Mrozewicz 1981a, 82, no. 18; Still 1995, 326 f., no. 0351.
31. Culică 1975, 246, no. 61, Pl. VI, XIV; 1976, Pl. VI; Still 1995, 323, no. 0338; Chiriac and Munteanu 2014, 312, no. 24.
32. Recław 2009, 1567, no. 27.
33. Recław 2009, 1561, Fig. 1.
34. Type I according to Chiriac and Munteanu 2014, 313–14, nos. 28–37; cf. ibidem, 326, Pl. II.1.
35. Culică 1975, 244, 255, nos. 49–53, 116, Pl. V, X, XIII, XV; 1976, Pl. V, X; Still 1995, 323–325, nos. 0339–44; Chiriac and Munteanu 2014, 313–14, nos. 30–34, 37.
36. Culică 1975, 244, nos. 54–56, Pl. V, XIII; 1976, Pl. V; Still 1995, 325 f., nos. 0345–47; Chiriac and Munteanu 2014, 314–15, nos. 38–41; Barnea 1996, 215 f., nos. 2, 217, Fig. 1.2.
37. Still 1995, 329, no. 0358–60; Chiriac and Munteanu 2014, 313–14, nos. 28–29, 36.
38. Chiriac and Ungureanu 2004, 236–38, Fig. 4.a–b, Pl. II.1, 6; Chiriac and Munteanu 2014, 314, no. 35.

Fig. 87. Justinian I lead seal. Scale 1:1. CNG Electronic Auction 440, Lot: 540: Classical Numismatic Group (www.cngcoins.com).

We have a relatively small number of finds from Novae that fall into the discussed group of seals from Asia Minor. Therefore, it seems too early at the present stage of research to directly link them to the phenomenon discussed above, which for sites located in the western Pontic areas is already well identified. It is hoped that future archaeological research at Novae, including the eastern annexe area, and especially the processing of the material acquired at the site in recent years, will provide new information about the finds of Late Roman seals from Asia Minor. These will perhaps in the future allow for a better understanding of the role Novae played in the economic and geopolitical processes taking place during the period of Valens' Gothic wars, the effects of which were severe on this Danube fortress, as well as on the entire region.

2. Inv. no. 39/12w/can (**Pl. XLI, 2**).
Imperial seal of Justinian I, 527–565.
Irregular in shape, two-sided. Diam. 21 mm. W. 6,18 g.
Obv. Nimbate bust of Justinian I facing forward, wearing a helmet with a diadem, [D N I]VSTIN[IANVS PP AVG].
Rev. Winged Victory advancing frontward, wearing a long chiton and holding a wreath in each hand (left wreath invisible), a cross on the right (the cross on the left is not visible).
References: DOC Seals, vol. 6, no. 4.1–4.15; BLS, no. 3 (Type B).

This artifact belongs to the relatively narrow group of Justinian I seals.[39] It consists of only three types,[40] among which only one type is categorized without any doubts among the seals of this emperor, represented by a specimen found in the area of what is referred to as the annexe in Novae, known in two variants.[41] Its identification with Justinian I is possible thanks to the legend visible on the obverse side, on the discussed specimen from Novae fragmentarily preserved: [*D(ominus) n(oster) I*]*ustin*[*ianus p(er) p(etuus) aug(ustus)*)].[42] In this case, the imperial titulature was assumed based on Justinian I monetary issuance.

The iconography of the seal is also similar, though not identical, to the representations known from this emperor's coins,[43] which seems to indicate certain possibilities for narrowing its dating. Primarily, the frontal representation of the emperor's bust on the obverses of coins appeared in the silver minting of Justinian I as early as at the end of AD 537 (MIB, no. 42–43), while it was predominant in the gold and bronze issuances since the introduction of the monetary reform of AD 538.

It should be noted that the presence of a nimbus above Justinian I's frontal bust (**Fig. 87**), which is a characteristic feature for the representations on the seals and is not present on his monetary busts during the long period of this emperor's independent governance, is not a reliable feature for dating. Indeed, the nimbus appears in minting as early as between April and August 527, on the joint issuances of gold and bronze coins of Justin I and Justinian I,[44] on which both emperors are presented frontally: full-body representations of the emperors seated on thrones (solids: MIB, no. 1–3) or in the form of busts (half-follis issued by a mint in Antioch: MIB, no. 11). The famous medallion of Justinian I, once in the collection of the Bibliothèque nationale de France in Paris, on the obverse of which there is a bust of the emperor wearing armour and facing forward, with his head in a nimbus, 3/4 visible, is perhaps of an even earlier dating.[45] The figure of Justinian himself in a nimbus appears on gold coins minted in Constantinople during the first years of his independent reign, on obverses (seated on a throne: MIB, no. 4) and reverses (standing facing to the left: MIB, no. 2). Meanwhile, the standing emperor in nimbus appears on the reverses of silver coins minted in Constantinople during most of his reign (MIB, no. 42–47, 49–50).

Finds of Justinian I seals have been noted in various places across the Byzantine Empire,[46] including in Ephesus[47] or Chersoneses, where four specimens were found.[48] A marked concentration of finds of Justinian's seals, contrasting with the very modest number of seals discovered of other 6th-century emperors,[49] can be noted in the north-eastern and eastern

39. DOC Seals, 7-14.
40. Zacos and Veglery 1972, vol. I.1, type A–C, 6–8, nos. 2–4.
41. Ibidem, type B, 7–8, no. 3; cf. Nesbitt 2009, 7–8, 13, no. 4.1–4.15, 5.1.
42. Cf. Nesbitt 2009, 8.
43. Nesbitt 2009, 1, 8–9.
44. Hahn 1973, 44f.
45. Morrisson 1970, 69, Pl. VIII.1.
46. For the list of older finds, see: Seibt 1978, 58f., no. 6.
47. Cheynet 1999, 318, no. 1.
48. Sokolova 1991, 204, no. 2; Alekseenko 1999, 146 f., nos. 2–5.
49. Cf. Curta 2016, 312, Tab. 2.

Balkan region.[50] However, finds of this emperor's seals in the rest of the Balkan interior are rare. A rather exceptional example here is a specimen from Zvechan in Kosovo,[51] as well as two specimens discovered in Izvor in western Bulgaria, and one from Haskovo in the south of this country.[52] In sum, almost 50 Justinian I seals have been registered in modern-day Bulgaria.[53] Just over 20 of these have a defined provenance.

Four of the Justinian I seals published thus far were found along the lower Danube River, including in Noviodunum (Isaccea),[54] Sucidava (Izvoarele),[55] Durostorum (Silistra),[56] as well as in Krasen, ca. 10 km to the south of Sexaginta Prista (Ruse).[57] Novae would thus currently be the westernmost place of discovery of this emperor's seals by the Danube River.

This fact may have some bearing on the interpretation of the find discussed here, especially in the context of the hypothesis formulated for lead seals by Florin Curta in 2002 and republished in a slightly modified form a few years ago.[58] The researcher studied a rich sigillographic resource, which consisted of nearly 240 diverse seals, dated to the 6th–7th centuries with an established provenance in the Balkans, including 20 Justinian I seals.[59] The author drew attention to the fact that the sites where the majority of the 6th–7th-century seals were found, including imperial, those belonging to government officials of various levels and private commercial seals, are concentrated in the north-central, central, and north-eastern Balkans and overlap significantly with the area of the two provinces of the Thrace Diocese: Scythia Minor and Moesia Secunda.[60] Moreover, Curta noted that the planigraphy of early Byzantine seals, discovered at many fortified sites, largely corresponds to the distribution map of Late Roman amphora type 2.[61] This type of amphora, produced since the 4th century in the Peloponnese under the control of the central government,[62] was originally intended for the transport of oil from southern Greece and the Aegean basin, while in the 6th century it was distributed to the Danube borderlands, to the provinces of Scythia Minor and Moesia Secunda, in order to supply the garrisons stationed there with oil and other necessary foodstuffs, as part of the army's tax obligations in kind (*annona militaris*) collected, e.g., from Caria, Cyprus and the Aegean area.[63] Supplies under the *annona militaris* for the Danube garrisons deployed in the Balkans and engaged in the defence of the Empire's borderlands during the Slavic-Avar invasions were provided within the framework of the *quaestura exercitus*, a new administrative unit established by Justinian I in AD 536 that included Moesia II, Scythia, Caria, Cyprus and the Cyclades Islands.[64] The organisation of supplies was the responsibility of Justinian's army quaestor (*quaestor Iustinianus Exercitus*) in Odessos, while according to Florian Curta the role of "point of entry for the military *annona* collected overseas" was performed by Tomis, where large amounts of type LR2 amphora have been discovered.[65]

The smooth functioning of the new model of the administrative structure was possible thanks to sea and river transportation, with a special role performed by the Danube.[66] According to Curta, in the 6th century, the goods were transported from the rich provinces by individual entrepreneurs, and then redistributed inside the *quaestura exercitus* and to the neighbouring provinces on the limes and beyond.[67] Thus, the finds of LR2 amphora and seals, originating both from individual entrepreneurs and officials of various levels, from Scythia Minor and Moesia Secunda, reflect the routes used for transporting supplies, as well as the destinations of their distribution.[68] According to Curta, seals bearing the names and honorary titles of imperial administration officials can be interpreted as evidence of the involvement of provincial administration officials in the *annona* distribution network organized as part of the officials' *quaestura exercitus*, as well as proof of the interest shown by the imperial administration and the emperor himself.[69]

Justinian I's seals were probably attached to letters and instructions addressed to the officials and military commanders of the Balkan Danube provinces, operating within the *quaestura exercitus* structure.[70] However, the imperial correspondence did not necessarily refer only to matters of supply. It should be remembered that the transformation of the administrative structure was accompanied in the Balkan provinces by an extensive construction campaign aimed at reorganizing

50. Cf. Curta 2016, 312, Tab. 2; 313, Fig. 3.
51. Gaj-Popović 1980, 165; Stamenković and Ivanišević 2013, 247 f., no. 11.
52. Curta 2016, 320f.
53. Yordanov 2012, 61 f., nos. 4–44, 44.a–f; Yordanov 2011, no. 44.v–e.
54. Curta 2016, 324, no. 153.
55. Curta 2016, 324, no. 160.
56. Yordanov 2012, 61, no. 5; Curta 2016, no. 218.
57. Yordanov 2012, 62, no. 22; Curta 2016, 325, no. 172.
58. Jones 1964, 280; Curta 2002; 2016.
59. Curta 2016, 324–26, no. 139–41, 144, 153, 160, 169, 171, 173–74, 177, 188, 195, 200, 203, 205, 218, 228–29, 234.
60. Curta 2002, 14 f.; 2016, 319.
61. Curta 2016, 308–11, Fig. 1; cf. Curta 2002, 12f.
62. Karagiorgou 2001, 146, 150; cf. Curta 2016, 309.
63. Curta 2002, 12. On the *annona militaris*, see Rizos 2015.
64. Jones 1964, 280; Torbatov 1997, 78; Curta 2002, 11f.; 2016, 316.
65. Curta 2016, 316f.; cf. Karagiorgou 2001.
66. Curta 2002, 11.
67. Curta 2002, 15.
68. Curta 2016, 319.
69. Curta 2016, 319. For more on the subject, see Gkoutzioukostas 2008.
70. Curta 2002, 15.

Fig. 88. Lead tessera, 1st–3rd century AD. Asia Minor (Ionia?). Scale 1:1. CNG Electronic Auction 368, Lot: 251: Classical Numismatic Group (www.cngcoins.com).

the settlement space towards its militarization. Novae, as a peripheral *quaestura exercitus* outpost, was undoubtedly part of Justinian I's plans to strengthen the defence of the Balkan area along the Danube line. This is evidenced not only by numerous traces of building activities, but also by the increased influx of this emperor's coins.[71] It seems reasonable to assume that the imperial seal discovered during surface excavations in the area of the eastern annexe is also related to the delivery of supplies to Novae as part of the *quaestura exercitus*.

Justinian I's seal from Novae is not the only such seal from the 6th–7th century discovered in this place. One of the commercial seals, containing a cross monogram, probably bearing the name Komentiolos,[72] was published without any identification by L. Mrozewicz.[73] In addition, three more, thus far unidentified, early Byzantine seals from Novae were published by J. Recław.[74] A seal bearing the name Ioannes also supposedly originates from Svishtov.[75]

3. Inv. no. 29/14w/OM (**Pl. XLI, 3**).
Appliqué/pendant/amulet (?). Unknown provenance, 1st–3rd century AD (?)
Round-shaped, one-sided. Diam. 14 mm. W. –.
Obv. Head of Medusa facing forward (?).
Rev. Blank; irregular swelling across flan.
References: similar to Turcan 1987, no. 856.

Due to the stamp impression on the obverse and the bulging shape of the reverse surface, for the purposes of this publication this item has been associated with two specimens representing a related category of lead seals. Nevertheless, the identification of the utilitarian function it represents must raise some doubts.

The identification of the head depicted on the obverse of the relic as Medusa seems most probable, because of the frontal representation of the head as a mask, as well as due to the puffed-out cheeks and protruding tongue, which are difficult to observe due to the poor state of preservation of the surface. The last-mentioned iconographic feature is practically absent in Roman plastic arts,[76] which would bring the find from Novae close to the Greek tradition of representations. The stamp was impressed on a small lead disc, but it is possible that its edges were trimmed. Therefore, the outer outline of the hair (including possible snakes) and the wings on either side of the head are not visible.

According to Michail Rostovtzeff, who published the Roman lead *tesserae* with a representation of Medusa's face from the Ermitage collections,[77] in Roman times the discussed iconographic motif primarily had an apotropaic meaning. It is worth emphasizing that the motif of a Medusa mask, quite common on lead anepigraphic *tesserae*, both one-sided[78] (**Fig. 88**) and two-sided,[79] is exceptionally rare in the repertoire of iconographic lead seals.[80] Michael Still, in his monumental work on Roman lead seals, did not take into account any specimens with a representation of Medusa.[81]

The Gorgoneion motif was also present on lead items decorated with a seal impression, representing other purposes, such as amulets,[82] with in this case doubtless an apotropaic function. The find from Novae can be considered as part of this rather broadly-understood category of artifacts. The lack of clear traces of a tube, which would be a remnant of an attachment typical for seals, seems to exclude it from this category, just as the one-sided decoration and the uneven reverse seem to exclude it from the *tesserae* category. The irregularly shaped bulge on the reverse could be a remnant of a pin used to attach the piece in question as an appliqué or for hanging it, for example, as a necklace. A specimen from the Lyon Museum collection seems to be a close similarity to the Novae artifact,[83] with a similar small diameter (12 mm) and equally "closely" trimmed edges. However, Robert Turcan, who considered the face depicted *en face* to be covered with male stubble, described it as a "personnage dionysiaque".[84]

The anepigraphic character of this find makes it impossible to date it with any precision; however, due to the archaeological context of the findspot and the iconographic motif of the Medusa's mask applied on the obverse side, the date of its production should be narrowed down to the Principate period (1st–3rd century AD).

71. Salamon 2008, 184 f.
72. Cf. Feind 2010, 267; Yordanov 2012, nos. 2288–92; Yordanov and Zhekova 2007, nos. 466–67, Curta 2016, nos. 132–34.
73. Mrozewicz 1981a, 82, no. 19; cf. Recław 2009, 1565, no. 19.
74. Recław 2009, nos. 23, 24, 28.
75. Yordanov 2012, no. 2286.
76. Cf. Paoletti 1988, *passim*.
77. Rostovtzeff 1903, 224–25; nos. 2632–34.
78. For example, the ones found in Ephesus: Gülbay and Kireç 2008, no. 191–92.
79. Cf. Turcan 1987, nos. 442–43; Pl. 21.
80. P.ex. Turcan 1987, no. 53.
81. Cf. Still 1995, *passim*.
82. P.ex. Turcan 1987, no. 854; Pl. 32.
83. Turcan 1987, no. 856; Pl. 32.
84. Turcan 1987, 173.

11. Epigraphic finds

Agnieszka Tomas

During the prospection in 2013, three fragments of inscriptions were found, i.e., one small fragment was found to the west of the fortress (Area C2), and two others – at the Ostrite Mogili site (Area B).

Numerous illegal robbery trenches were localised at the Ostrite Mogili site, some of them in a dense forest on the Danubian scarp (**Fig. 89**). One of the trenches measuring 1.85×1.25 m contained a section of a 0.60-m-thick, quite solid masonry wall (**Fig. 90**).[1] The wall was built from local sandstone, pieces of limestone and random ceramic tiles, joined with grey mortar. After cleaning, it turned out that the limestone fragments are reused pieces of a broken inscription and a fragment of a cornice (**Fig. 91, Pl. XLII**). The material from which the cornice and the inscription were made differ in colour – the cornice was cut from greyish limestone and it is much thicker (w. 0.36×h. 0.27×th. 0.11–0.16 m), while the inscribed fragments were carved in a slightly porous white-yellowish limestone slab. The inscription was first published in 2014 as follows:[2]

a) Fragment of the inscription (**Pl. XLII, 1**), inv. no. 61/13w/OMa, dimensions: width 24 cm, height 39.5 cm, thickness 9–10 cm, letter height: line 2: 7.5–8 cm; line 3: 6.3–7 cm, line 4: 5.9 cm. White-yellowish limestone.

ỊM[---]
2 RO PI[---]
ADIAḄ[---]
4 ỊII • IṂ[---]
[.]ṢIP[---]

b) Fragment of the inscription (**Pl. XLII, 2**), inv. No. 61/13w/OMb, dimensions: width 32 cm, height 28 cm, thickness 9–10 cm, letter height 7.5, 5.8–6.0 cm. White-yellowish limestone.

[---]ṬENACỊ [---]
[---]ṆT • M[---]
[---]Ṣ • II • [---]

In the first publication, the following reconstruction of the text was suggested:

Ịm[p(eratori) Caes(ari) L(ucio) Septimio Seue]-
2 *ro Pi[o Per]ṭenacị [Aug(usto) Arab(ico)]*
Adiaḅ(enico) [p(atri) p(atriae) po]ṇt(ifici)
m[(aximo) tr(ibunicia) pot(estate)]
4 *ỊII · iṃ[p(eratori) VIII co(n)]ṣ(uli) II* [---]
[.]*ṣip*[---]

1. Tomas 2017, 77–79.
2. Tomas 2014. The present text is an important correction of the reading.

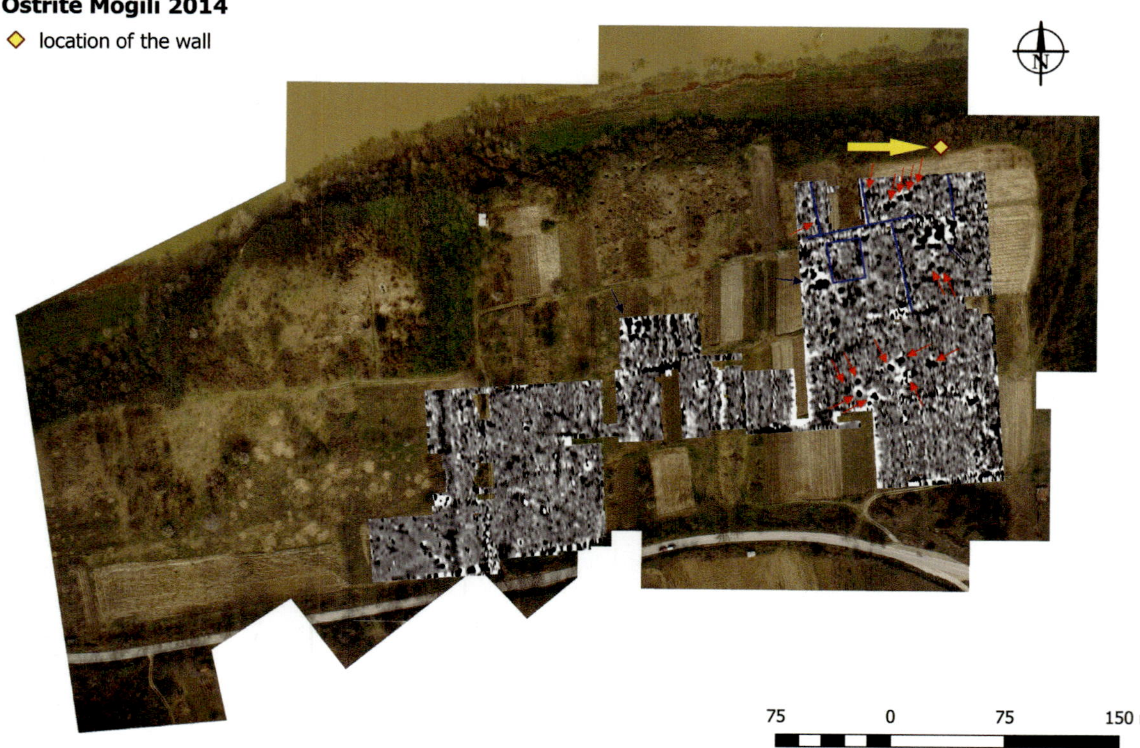

Fig. 89. Area B (Ostrite Mogili). The location of the wall with the reused inscription and cornice (by A. Tomas).

Further analysis of line 5 preserved in the first fragment shows that the reading of the first letter as "S" (as presented in my earlier publications) was wrong.[3] The combination of these three letters in Latin epigraphy is very rare. The re-examination of the preserved fragment of the letter makes it possible to state that the letters "C" or "T" are far more probable (**Fig. 92**). The comparison with the lettering of other inscriptions from Novae could suggest, e.g. the reading *ex s]tip(endiis)* or [--- *muni]cip*[---]. The Ostrite Mogili site is considered by some scholars as a settlement which was possibly granted municipal rights.[4]

However, a letter "C" in the fragment *a* could also belong to the word [--- *prin]cip[i* ---], therefore the new reading should be as follows:

ỊM[---]
2 RO PI[---]
ADIAḄ[---]
4 ỊII • IṂ[---]
ÇIP[---]

Furthermore, the closer analysis of the fragment *b* fragment shows that the letter "O" is partly preserved:

[---]ṬENACỊ [---]
[---]ṆT • M[---]
[---]Ṣ • II • Ọ[---]

Thus, the preserved fragment of the inscription should be reconstructed as follows:

Ịm[p(eratori) Caes(ari) L(ucio) Septimio Seue]-
2 *ro Piọ[Per]ṭenaci [Aug(usto) Arab(ico)*
Adiaḅ(enico) p(atri) p(atriae) po]ṇt(ifici)
m[(aximo) tr(ibunicia) pot(estate)]
4 *Ịll iṃ[p(eratori) VIII co(n)]*
ṣ(uli) II [optimo prin]-
ç ip(i)

In line 4, *im[p(eratori) VII* cannot be excluded. After the title of consul in line 4, the title of proconsul is omitted.[5]

Immediately after the end of the First Parthian War, which took place in the first half of AD 195, the titulature of Septimius Severus contained double triumphal cognomina, i.e., *Parthicus Arabicus* and *Parthicus Adiabenicus*.[6] According to SHA[7] and the abbreviations on some coins,[8] the emperor soon abandoned the title of Parthicus and used the abbreviated form *Arabicus Adiabenicus*, and this title would fit the discussed text as there is no space for a longer text. In January 198, after the victorious end of the Second Parthian War, the emperor assumed the title of *Parthicus maximus*.[9] Therefore, the monument must have been erected between the second half of 195 and January 198.

Fig. 90. Area B (Ostrite Mogili). A fragment of a wall in one of the illegal trenches (photo by S. Rzeźnik).

The beginning of line 4 should start with the number of the *tribunicia potestas*. The preserved end of the number "II" can be part of III, IIII or VII. In the referred period, Severus held his *tribunicia potestas* for the third time (10th Dec. 195 – 9th Dec. 196), the fourth time (10th Dec. 196 – 9th Dec. 197) and the fifth time (10th Dec. 197 – 9th Dec. 198),[10] but the seventh (held after the discussed period) can be excluded.

In the second half of AD 195, Severus held the title of emperor for the seventh time after the wars with the Adiabeni, and the eighth time after the fall of Byzantion.[11] As stated above, only the abbreviated titulature *Arabicus Adiabenicus* would fit on the recreated epigraphic field of the stone; therefore, the following possibilities can be taken into account:

1) imp. VII shortly before 28th Aug. 195 (with the titulature *Arabicus Adiabenicus*)

3. I would like to thank to Dr Florian Matei-Popescu for his valuable comments and kind advice in reading the inscription.

4. Gerov 1964, 128–133; Gerov 1977, 300, fn. 4; (*canabae*, late 2nd or early 3rd c.); Poulter 1983, 84 (*canabae*, Severan period); J. Kolendo in IGLNov, p. 17 (unknown place; M. Aur.); Mrozewicz 2008, 681 (Severan period). Initially, I considered vicus to have possibly been granted municipal rights, but later I came to support the *canabae* option: Tomas 2006, esp. 127–128 (vicus?, M. Aur.?), cf. Tomas 2012, 159; 2017, 161–64 (*canabae*, beginning of the 3rd c.).

5. Cf. e.g., CIL VIII 8835; VIII 12402; XIV 5331.

6. Kneissl 1969, 126–38; Kienast, Eck, Heil 2017, 151; Hasebroek 1921, 81.

7. SHA, Sever. IX 9–10; Mrav 2013, 211.

8. The abbreviation ARAB ADIAB appears with IMP V, VI, VII and VIII. See Kneissl 1969, 129.

9. Kneissl 1969, 142–48; Kienast, Eck, Heil 2017, 151.

10. He held the title of imperator for the seventh time in the period from the summer to December 195, and for the eighth time from December 195 (after the fall of Byzantion) to the 19th of February 197; Hasebroek 1921, 80; Kienast, Eck, Heil 2017, 150; Kneissl 1969, 135–36 and cf. with supplements and remarks given by C. Ando (2012, 31–32, n. 9).

11. Kneissl 1969, 135.

2) imp. VIII from December 195 to 19th Feb. 197 (with the titulature as above)

Consequently, the following dates can be taken into account:

1) trib. pot. III, imp. VII – after the war with the Adiabeni, during the civil war (the summer of 195: before 28th Aug. 195);
2) trib. pot. III, imp. VIII – before or just after(?)[12] the fall of Byzantium (the autumn of 195: after 28th Aug., but before 10th Dec. 195);
3) trib. pot. IIII, imp. VIII – after the civil war, during his fourth *tribunicia* (the winter of 195 to the autumn of 196: from 10th Dec. 195 to 9th Dec. 196).

The space at the beginning of line 4, where the beginning of the number of *tribunicia* is missing, is not wide enough for a number four marked as "IIII", and the shape of the upper horizontal line suggests the same. In conclusion, it is quite safe to state that the monument was raised during the emperor's third *tribunicia*; therefore, between the summer of AD 195 and 10th December 195.[13]

The two discussed fragments of the inscription come from a dedication as the titulature is given in Dativus. The entire inscription must have been quite large and taken up a space of about 50×125 cm. Such a monument needs a correspondingly large, public space.

Although the thickness of the stone is considerable for the cladding of the monument, it fits well with a horse statue. The recreated size (40×140 cm), the height of the letters, and the name of the emperor in Dativus indicate rather to a honorific, not a building inscription.[14] Eight dedications for Septimius Severus have been identified

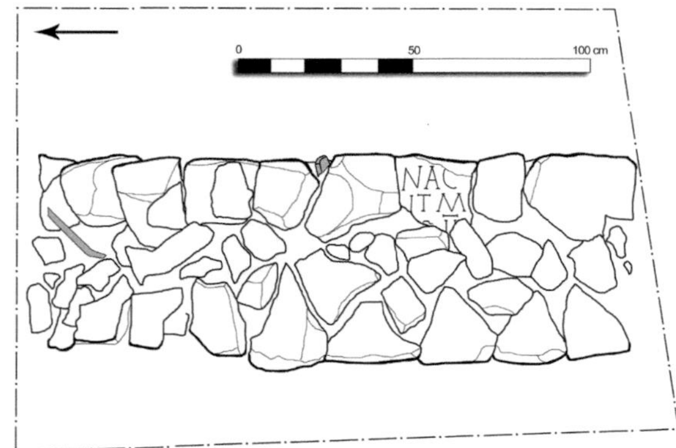

Fig. 91. Area B (Ostrite Mogili). A fragment of the wall with the reused inscription (drawing by A. Tomas).

in Novae,[15] with the best known being one made by *primi ordines et centuriones* in AD 196,[16] during the fourth *tribunicia potestas* of Septimius Severus. It was found in the legionary headquarters, which is not surprising since the dedicants are the military. This almost contemporary inscription was carved on a large limestone block (h./w./l.) 82×73.5×[34] cm, which originally could have been even 1.5 m long. Until recently, it was the only dedication from Novae dated to the early period of his rule. The monument discussed here could have been erected earlier, so it is the earliest known dedication to Septimius Severus from Novae and – generally – from among all such identified dedications. Official dedications made for Septimius Severus before AD 197 are less frequent than those made after AD 198, due to intensified building and foundation activities after that date and a final consolidation of Septimius' position upon defeating his rivals.[17]

In AD 193, when Septimius Severus rose to power, Lucius Marius Maximus Perpetuus Aurelianus was a legate of the *legio I Italica*. When the war with Pescenius Niger, governor of Syria, broke out that same year, Marius Maximus took the side of Septimius Severus and – as the inscription from

12. The precise date of the fall of Byzantion is not known, but scholars mostly agree at the end of AD 195; see Hasebroek 1921, 79–80; Kienast, Eck, Heil 2017, 1496; Birley 1999, 119, 121. Based on the analysis of numismatic finds, D. Boteva proposed a hypothesis concerning an earlier chronology of events. According to Boteva, Clodius Albinus was declared public enemy on 15th December 194, not a year later, as had been hitherto assumed; see Boteva 1999, 23–28.

13. In 2014, I suggested the more precise dating of between 28th August and 10th December 195 (Tomas 2014, 82). During the discussed period, Cosconius Gentianus was the governor of Lower Moesia, and not Pollienus Auspex; *PIR*² C 1526 and cf. C 951, 952; Leunissen 1989, 250; Boteva 1996, 239–47, esp. 240–41; 1997, 163–64, 331; cf. Doruţiu-Boilă 1985, 197–203; Birley 1999, 122.

14. Building inscriptions with the name of an emperor in Dativus are attested, but they are extremely rare; see Horster 2001, 15 and cf. 41–42.

15. IGLNov 47 (dedication to the *signum originis*, AD 208), IGLNov 57bis (dedication by the *primi ordines* and *centuriones*, AD 196), IGLNov 58 (dedication for S. Severus or Caracalla, AD 206/215), IGLNov 59 (building inscription with the names of S. Severus and his sons, AD 198/209) IGLNov 60 and 61 (dedicated to S. Severus and his sons, AD 198/209), IGLNov 62 (dedicated to S. Severus and his family, AD 202/205), IGLNov 63 (dedicated to the Severs, AD 198); Bunsch, Kolendo, and Żelazowski, 2004, 57, no. 4 (fragment with the imperial titulature of S. Severus).

16. Sarnowski 1993 (=IGLNov 57bis), with the historical circumstances discussed on p. 211. For a further discussion of the text, see Speidel 1994 and Sarnowski 1996. The term *primi ordines* is known from three other inscriptions: from Mogontiacum (CIL XIII 6801, AD 204) and from Lambaesis (CIL VIII 2532; AD 128 and VIII 18065, AD 162).

17. Platnauer 1918, 27 and fn. 2; Mrav 2013, 227–29. Other early dated inscriptions from Lower Moesia: CIL III 766=6153, Tomis, AD 194; AÉ 1954, 35, Sexaginta Prista, AD 196; AÉ 1922, 69, AD 195; AÉ 1980, 813, AD 196, vicus Clementiani.

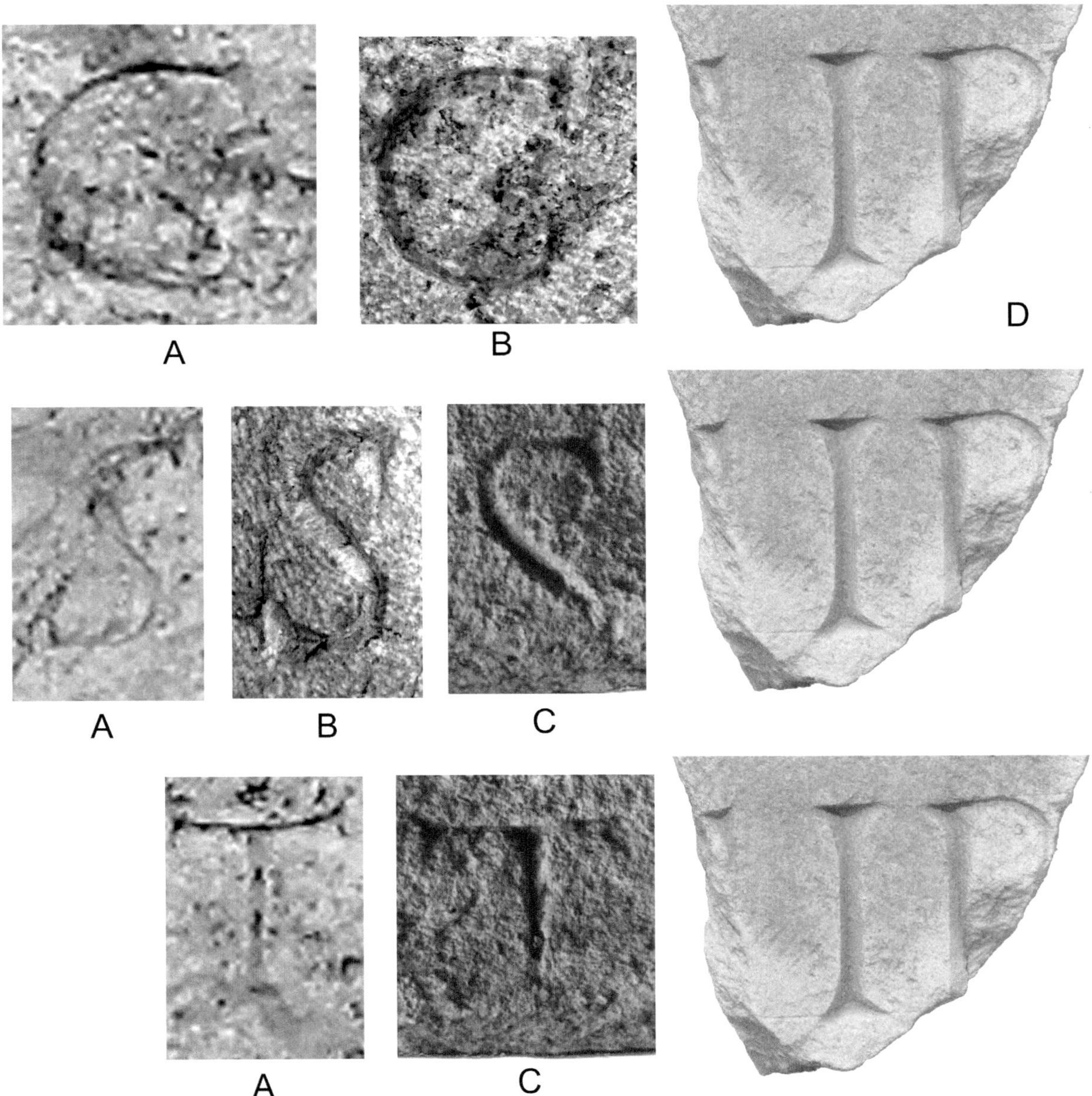

Fig. 92. The comparison of line 4 on the piece found at Ostrite Mogili with the engraved texts on other stones from Novae. A – IGLNov 46 (AD 184); B – AE 2008, 1185 (2nd–3rd c.); C – IGLNov 77 (AD 201–250); D – letters C̣IP in the fragment *a* from Ostrite Mogili (selection by A. Tomas). Not to scale.

Rome informs – led the army to fight the enemy in Thrace and to besiege Byzantion,[18] where Niger had his headquarters. In May 194, Niger was defeated at Issus and beheaded thereafter, but Byzantion refused to surrender and the siege continued. In spring 195, Septimius started campaigns against Niger's supporters and marched to the East. For his success, the senate granted him the titles of Parthicus Arabicus and Parthicus Adiabenicus. After the capitulation of Byzantion at the end of AD 195 and a three-month march, on 6th April 196, the emperor arrived in Viminacium,[19] after passing through Thrace and Moesia.[20] At the same time, the army of Marius Maximus returned from Byzantion to the Danube.[21] Rome witnessed the punishment of Niger's supporters

18. CIL VI 1450 (dux exercitus Mysiaci aput Byzantium) and see Barnes 1967, 101. A. Birley maintains that he is identical with the author of the archetype of the first part of SHA; see Birley 1997, 2678–2757.

19. SHA, Sev. X, p. 395; Hasebroek 1921, 86–87; Birley 1999, 121–22.

20. The shortest route between Byzantion and Novae (according to the interactive map of the Roman world ORBIS, prepared by W. Scheidel et al., at www.orbis.stanford.edu) led via Hadrianopolis and Philippopolis to Oescus. However, no honorification inscription dedicated to Septimius Severus has been found at Oescus so far.

21. Birley 1999, 121.

Fig. 93. Novae (Area C2): a marble fragment with a letter (inv. no. 1/14w/can). Phot. by A. Tomas.

and the execution of his family. In AD 195, when the monument was erected, the First Italic legion was probably still in Thrace.[22]

The discussed inscription is the first find of this type discovered in the vicus of Ostrite Mogili. It is very probable, however, that the stone was brought from the fortress and secondarily-used in the wall, which can be dated certainly after the early 3rd century.

The second fragment of an inscription, was found in the western part of the *canabae* (Area C2) between the private lots. A small piece of marble was found on the ground, probably unearthed during spring agricultural fieldwork as the surface is not corroded by atmospheric factors. The inscription was carved on a 4.5 cm thick white-greyish marble slab **(Fig. 93)**. The preserved

Fig. 94. Novae (Area A1). Fragment of a lead item with carved signs (drawing by A. Tomas).

Fig. 95. Novae (Area A1). Fragment of a lead item with carved signs (photo by P. Jaworski)

lower part of a letter could belong to the letters "I", "P", "T", "F". Its shape suggests that it was made no later than in the 3rd century.[23] It was very carefully engraved and its original dimensions (about 10 cm) indicate that the text had an official character and was presented in some public space.

The third find raises doubts in interpretation. It is a piece of lead bearing visible carvings on one of its sides in a way resembling lead *tesserae* related to textile production.[24] However, the carvings on the find from Novae cannot be read as a meaningful text **(Fig. 94)**.

Catalogue of epigraphic finds

Pl. XLII. Area B - Ostrite Mogli

1. Fragment of a white-yellowish limestone slab with an inscription. 61a/13w/OM. Area B. Width 24 cm, height 39.5 cm, thickness 9–10 cm, letter height 7.5, 6.3, 5.9 cm. ỊM [---] / RO PI [---] / ADIAḄ[---] / ỊII • IṂ[---] / ÇIP[---]. *Published*: Tomas 2014.
2. Fragment of a white-yellowish limestone slab with an inscription. 61b/13w/OM. Area B. Width 32 cm, height 28 cm, thickness 9-10 cm, letter height 7.5, 5.8–6.0 cm. [---] ṬENACỊ [---] / [---] ṆT • M [---] / [---] Ṣ • II • O[---]. *Published*: Tomas 2014.
3. Fragment of a cornice. 61c/13w/OM. Area B. Greyish limestone. Width 36 cm, height 27 cm, thickness 11–16 cm. The cornice was discovered with cat. nos. 1 and 2, but the stone differs in colour and finishing. *Published*: Tomas 2014.
4. Reconstructed text of an inscription found at Ostrite Mogili. *Published*: Tomas 2014.

22. Sarnowski 1993, 211.

23. For the shape of the carved letters in Novae, see Mrozewicz 2010, esp. 92, nos. B3, 5, 11; 93, B21–23, A5–7; 94–95, B27, 36–37; 96, C13; 97, B51.

24. Martijnse 1993; Gostenčik 2012, 67 and Figs. 2.6 and 2.11,

Pl. XLII. Areas B and C2. Epigraphic finds

5. Fragment of a marble plate with partly preserved letter (I? P? T? F?). 1/14w/can. Area C2. Thickness 4 cm. Drawing by A. Tomas, photo by P. Jaworski. **Fig. 93**.

6. Fragment of a lead item with carved signs. 4/14w/can. Selected from the mass finds from 2013. **Figs. 94, 95**.

12. Brick and tile-stamps

Tadeusz Sarnowski (†)

The field surveys carried out by Polish archaeological teams in the vicinity of Novae in 1979, 1981 and 2000 (Ostrite Mogili, archaeological site on the Danube, 2.5 km to the east of Novae) as well as in 2012–14 in the extramural settlement (*canabae*) produced nine stamped tiles.[1] The most frequently represented include the following:

Stamps of the legio I Italica

1. Inv. No. 10/14c, a fragment of a tegula found in 2014 in the spoils from a trench dug by treasure hunters in the annexe (Area A1) (*canabae*) (**Pl. XLIII, 1**)
   Stamped: LEG̣IITAL

   Leg̣(ionis) I (primae) Ital(icae)

   Type: Sarnowski 1983a, VI, variant 135–137; Matuszewska 2006, VI-80-82 ?
2. Inv. No. 12/14c, a fragment of a tegula found in 2014 in spoils from a trench dug by treasure hunters in the annexe (Area A1) (*canabae*) (**Pl. XLIII, 2**)
   Stamped: [LEG]ỊỊTAL

   [Leg(ionis)] Ị (primae) Ịtal(icae)

   Type: Sarnowski 1983a, VI, variant ?; Matuszewska 2006, VI-105 ?
3. Inv. No. 2/79c, an unstratified fragment of a tegula found in 1979 during a survey at Ostrite Mogili (**Pl. XLIII, 3**)
   Tomas 2006, 122, cat. No, 23, Fig. 15: 2.
   Stamped: [.]ẸGII[...]

   [L]ẹg(ionis) I (primae) I[tal(icae)]

   Type: Sarnowski 1983a, VI, variant ?; Matuszewska 2006, VI, variant ?
4. Inv. No. 1/00c, an unstratified fragment of a tegula found in 2000 during a survey at Ostrite Mogili (**Pl. XLIII, 4**)
   Tomas 2006, 122, cat. No. 24, Fig. 15: 3.
   Stamped: [....]ỊTAL

   [Leg(ionis) Ị (primae)] I[tal(icae)]

   Type: Sarnowski 1983a, VI, variant ?; Matuszewska 2006, variant ?
5. Inv. No. GR/6/00c, a fragment of a tegula found in 2000 in a grave situated in the western part of the Ostrite Mogili site (**Pl. XLIII, 5**)
   Tomas 2006, 122, cat. No. 34, Fig. 16: 3.
   Stamped: LEGIITAḶ

   Leg(ionis) I (primae) Itaḷ(icae)

   Type: Sarnowski 1983a, VI, variant 135–37; Matuszewska 2006, VI-94c

All the stamps belong to the longest used and most common Sarnowski VI type. In two cases, it is possible to approximately identify the type-variants. Unfortunately, these are not among the stamps that can be dated with precision of up to a quarter or even a half of a century. Thus, we must be content with the statement that our finds were tiled in the 2nd or 3rd centuries. The *I Italica* undoubtedly has the richest list of publications and studies on its stamps among all the legions, which of course results from more than fifty years of excavations in Novae, the legion's military base on the Lower Danube. These have been discussed in two recent papers by M. Duch.[2] He focused on the finds from Novae, to which the stamped bricks and tiles from other Roman strongholds along the lower course of the Danube should be added,[3] the Trajanic forts in Wallachia, mainly from Drajna de Sus,[4] and finally also from Tyras and Charax on the northern Black Sea coast.[5] The first typology of the stamps from Novae, with 37 types and many variants, was created in 1983.[6] The attempt to simplify it by N. Gudea,[7] who without seeing the finds divided the *legio I Italica* stamp types into several groups, did not bring any significant modifications.[8] The usefulness of the first typology is confirmed by the fact that it is still used by archaeologists working in Novae,[9] and its correctness and compatibility with similar studies from other provinces has been demonstrated by R. Kurzmann.[10] The study by M. Matuszewska is also very important, who – not without some inaccuracies – supplemented the 1983 typology with new variants.[11] Stratigraphic observations made in Novae in the Flavian bath and in the Trajanic hospital built in the same spot have made it possible to identify a small group of type VI stamps (LEG I ITAL), which were in use in their primary function during the Flavian/Trajanic period.[12] They also had a secondary usage together with the tiles

1. I would very much like to thank Dr hab. A. Tomas for entrusting me with the publication of the stamps on bricks and roof tiles from her investigations in and around Novae.

2. See Duch 2011; 2017.
3. See above all Ivanov 2002; Torbatov 2010; 2012; Gudea 2006.
4. Zahariade and Dvorski 1997.
5. Sarnowski 1987b; 2006a.
6. Sarnowski 1983a.
7. Gudea 2003b.
8. I do not know where my Romanian colleague saw the new LEG I ITAL S type (Gudea 2003b, 208, fig. 9), which should be dated to the reign of Severus Alexander. To the list of stamps of the First Italic legion, he adds the CEMEL stamps from Novae and Iatrus, read by him in an astonishing manner as *Ce(nturia; ae ...) M(o)e(siae) l(egionibus)*; see Gudea 2003a, 328.
9. See also Torbatov 2010; 2012.
10. Kurzmann 2006.
11. Matuszewska 2006; 2013.
12. Duch 2012.

Pl. XLIII. Stamped building materials from Areas A1 and B

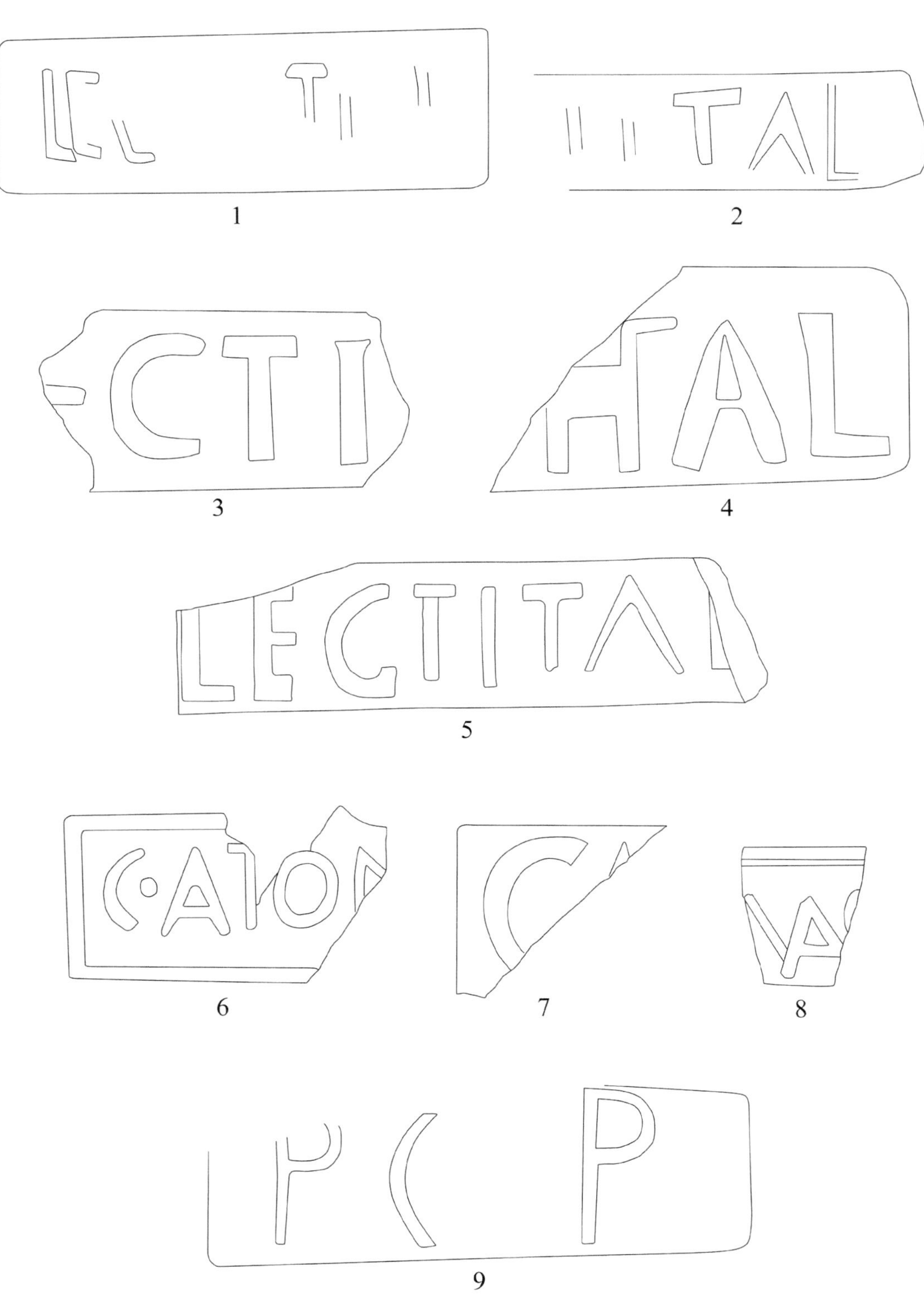

stamped by the *XI Claudia* and *I Minervia* legions during the construction of the hospital around AD 101 or in the period between Trajan's two Dacian wars (AD 102–105).[13]

The similarity of the clay paste used in the tiles stamped by the *XI Claudia*, *I Minervia* and *I Italica* legions and their archaeological context in Novae allowed me to assume that they were made in a tilery shared by work groups sent by several legionary detachments of the Moesian or Lower Moesian army.[14] Without submitting any decisive arguments, K. Strobel criticized my hypothesis,[15] while – in turn – it was met with a positive response from R. Kurzmann.[16]

The existence of tileries shared by various units of the Lower Moesian army is testified by a fragmentary tile from Aliobrix stamped by the *classis Moesica* and bearing also the graffitto *le(gionis) vex(illatio* or *-illationi)*.[17] In this critical context, it is interesting to point out the settlement name Tegulicium, originating from the Latin word *tegula* (= tile). The settlement is situated not far from Durostorum (present-day Silistra). Another candidate may be the so far unlocalized Lucernaria burgus (formerly Lapidaria), probably near Oescus, perhaps near Somovit. In addition to the quarries, there must have been some good clay deposits somewhere in the vicinity, which enabled the production of terracotta lamps during the Late Empire.[18] The problem of the possible existence of a centralized form of military brick production in some areas and periods in Moesia/Lower Moesia finds perhaps its expression in the enigmatic stamp TRA'EX with traces of another letter on the terracotta pipe found near the *castellum aquae* just over 100 m west of the north-western corner of the legionary fortress at Novae.[19].

On the basis of the tile stamps from the Lower Rhine documenting the existence of *Tegularia transrhenana*,[20] I am inclined to read the stamp from Novae (*Tegularia* or *Figlina*) *tra(nsdanubiana) Ex(ercitus) M(oesiae* or *M(oesiae inferioris)*. Between Trajan's two Dacian wars, such communal brickwork of the Italica and V Macedonica legions operated in Transdanubia in Buridava on the Olt River.[21] If my guess is correct, the outlined situation would explain well why the custom of stamping tiles and bricks appeared in Moesia during the Flavian period. Brick stamping took place not so much in order to prevent unauthorized use but to separate larger batches of bricks and tiles made for various legions, not necessarily by the legions whose name was on the stamps.

Name stamps

6. Inv. No. 1/79c, an unstratified fragment of a tegula found in 1979 during a survey at Ostrite Mogili **(Pl. XLIII, 6)**
Tomas 2006, 122, cat. No. 28, Fig. 15: 7.
Stamped (double frame): C·ATOṆ

G(ai) · A(n)toṇ[(ii) Mag(ni)]

7. Inv. No. 4/k1/00m, an unstratified fragment of a tegula found in 2000 during a survey at Ostrite Mogili **(Pl. XLIII, 7)**
Tomas 2006, 122, cat. No. 27, Fig. 15: 6.
Stamped: ÇẠ

Ģ(ai) Ạ[(n)ton(ii) Mag(ni)]

8. Inv. No. 3/00c, an unstratified fragment of a tegula found in 1979 during a survey at Ostrite Mogili **(Pl. XLIII, 8)**
Tomas 2006, 122, cat. No. 26, Fig. 15: 5.
Stamped (double frame): ṂAÇ

[G(ai) A(n)ton(ii)] Ṃag(ni) or [- - -*V*]*Maç[ri]*

In the latter case, it might be a Late Roman military stamp of the Fifth Macedonian legion.

9. Inv. No. 2/00c, an unstratified fragment of a tegula found in 1979 during a survey at Ostrite Mogili **(Pl. XLIII, 9)**
Tomas 2006, 122, cat. No. 25, Fig. 15: 4.
Stamped: PC P

P(ublius ?) *C*(---) *P*(---)

The three letters in No. 9 are probably the abbreviated *tria nomina* of someone (a legionary soldier or an officer?) responsible for the manufacture of roof tiles or for the construction project, which could also have involved the normal repair of a roof, or for both. In addition to the find from Ostrite Mogili, we know of two such stamps in Novae. Since they come from the rubble in the hospital,[22] where the tile was probably present in its primary usage, one should think that we are dealing with a military person. Certain doubts arise in connection with a very similar stamp found in the sanctuary of Apollo in Ruse (Sexaginta Prista).

13. Sarnowski 1987a; Strobel 1988.
14. Sarnowski 1987a, 110.
15. Strobel 1988, 502, n. 10.
16. Kurzmann 2006, 115.
17. Sarnowski 1997, 498.
18. Cf. Kolendo 1981, 55–57.
19. Kolendo and Kowal, 2011, 72, Figs.7 and 8.
20. Lehner 1904, 291–96; Hanel 2002.
21. *IDR* III 559; Strobel 1987, 282–84.
22. Duch 2017, 102, type IV.1 and 114. [This text had been prepared in 2018 before the further analogies were found, see Duch 2021 – A.T.].

The archaeological context dates it back to the first half or middle of the 2nd century AD.[23]

The situation with the group of stamps bearing the inscription G.ANTON.MAGNI is far more complex. According to the calculations made by J. Żelazowski, we know of as many as 16 stamps by Antonius Magnus from Novae and Ostrite Mogili.[24] The stamp is also present in the material from Dimum (today Belene), an auxiliary fort located about 20 km upstream from Novae. In the legionary base at Novae, the stamp is present among the finds from the hospital, the bathhouse, the west and east gates, the officer's house in the *scamnum tribunorum*, and from the very close vicinity of the ramparts. The relatively large number of finds and different stamp forms indicate that the name Antonius Magnus appeared on several delivery batches of tiles and bricks, which also travelled quite far from Novae. The stratigraphic context makes it possible to date two fragmentary *tegulae* from the valetudinarium at Novae to the first half of the 3rd century. We do not know if they were used primarily. In any case, it is more probable we are dealing with an example of the roof being repaired. Until recently, the stamps bearing the name G. Antonius Magnus were considered to have been those of a private tiler stamping also for the army. J. Żelazowski believes that it is equally possible that Magnus was a military specialist who did not necessarily act as a production organizer, but rather – for example – as a person responsible for the implementation of a building project or projects, and as such as a recipient of the bricks and tiles sent by the brickyard.[25] Based on the fairly sophisticated form of the stamp, the scattering of the finds and their amount, my intuition tells me that Antonius Magnus was probably like M. Aurelius Statianus,[26] i.e., a veteran engaged by the legion to carry out some important projects. A similar status could possibly have been held by M. Arrius Clemens and C. Cocceius Capito, whose names are on two terracotta pipes from the late 1st or early 2nd century from the officer's house in the *scamnum tribunorum* at Novae.[27] The *nomen gentile* Arrius is also present on other pipes from the Flavian bath under the Trajanic *valetudinarium*.[28] J. Kolendo and T. Kowal saw him as a private manufacturer, perhaps from the ceramic production centre in Boutovo. Only the comparative laboratory analysis of the clay used to make the pipes and raw clay material from Boutovo can bring more clarity to the issue. If my reading of the two new stamps is correct,[29] then Arrius Clemens and Cocceius Capito were rather manufacturers or production organisers, not entrepreneurs specializing in water supply systems.

At Ostrite Mogili, located just over 2 km east of Novae and interpreted as a *vicus* raised probably under Marcus Aurelius to a *municipium* status,[30] our German and Bulgarian colleagues found a few more stamps,[31] namely ANTON.MAG, LEG I ITAL, one stamp of the I Minervia legion, MACRI[32] and LEPIFICOR = *Le(gionis) p(rimae) I(talicae) fi(glina) co(hor)tis* from the Constantinian period. [33] Two fragments of the AD 196 building inscription found in secondary use and Late Roman stamps indicate that Ostrite Mogili was inhabited at the end of the 3rd and in the 4th century and that some construction work took place there at that time. Stamped building ceramics, which unfortunately came only from stray finds, appear there either in primary or secondary use. We are dealing with quite a different situation in the eastern annexe, i.e., in the eastern part of the extramural settlement in times of the Principate. In addition to stray finds with LEG I ITAL stamps, twenty LEPIFICOR stamps were found near the south gate of the annexe, as well as a MARCI stamp.[34] Late Roman bricks stamped LEPIFICOR were most likely used primarily in the late-3rd-century defensive walls of the annexe or in their not much later thickening.

23. Torbatov 2012, 184, Fig. 3:12. Torbatov reads the inscription as PO, but the photograph of the find shows both O and C are possible.

24. Żelazowski 2015, 251.

25. Żelazowski 2015, 253.

26. Tomas and Sarnowski 2007.

27. A full publication is being planned. [A separate publication was planned by T. Sarnowski and M. Lemke, but never undertaken; see Lemke 2021, 189, fn. 21.– A.T.]

28. Kolendo and Kowal 2011, 69, Figs. 3–5.

29. LEG·I·ITAL/M·ARRIVS/CLEMENS·FECIT = *Leg(ioni) I Ital(icae) / M. Arrius / Clemens fecit*; LEG·I·ITAL / C·COCCEIVS/ CAPITO·FECIT = *Leg(ioni) I Ital(icae) / C. Cocceius Capito / fecit*. Courtesy of prof. E. Gencheva, Director of the Bulgarian Expedition at Novae.

30. Initially A. Tomas shared my opinion (Tomas 2006), but now is inclined to argue that the *canabae* was a settlement which was granted municipal rights (see Tomas 2017, 159–62).

31. Ivanov 2002, 119.

32. Ivanov (2002, 119) reads the inscription as MARCI, but the drawing 87 on p. 123 shows ---] V MACRI. In such a case, the reading *[leg(ionis)] V (quintae) Ma(cedonicae) c(oho) r(s) I (prima)* seems appropriate; cf. Sarnowski 1985b, 121 Tab.1; Gudea and Zahariade 2016, 42 (e.g.: Stamps from Sucidava – Celei).

33. On the reading and dating of this stamp, see Sarnowski 1985b, 117. I can only guess that this is the stamp that provided P. Dyczek with the basis (2011, 85f., 90) for conceiving a new *cohors figlinorum* = a *cohors* of ceramic workers (?) or of tileries (? sic!).

34. Ivanov 2002, 117.

13. Terracotta and ceramic items

Agnieszka Tomas

In Area B, five spindle whorls (cat. nos. 1–5) were found in the western part of the site, four of which were discovered within an area of 50 sq. m., so it is possible they could have belonged to one household (**Fig. 96**). All are made from clay. Three of them are bigger and two smaller (**Pl. XLIV, 1–5**).

A spindle whorl is put on a wooden shaft, which is a stick between 3 and 10 mm in diameter. The only function of the whorl is to weigh the spindle at its bottom, middle or top. Spinning whorls are usually spherical, semicircular or in the form of a disc. They can be made out of a variety of materials, such as wood, metal, glass, stone, clay or bone, but clay items are the most common. The shape, size and weight of a whorl affects the momentum of a spindle and leads to it maintaining a constant speed for a long time. This has a direct impact on the thickness and twist of the thread. A properly documented spinning whorl should be weighed.

Two of the discovered spinning whorls are similar in shape and size, while one of them has a row for a thread which may be a trace of thread guiding (**Pl. XLIV, 1, 2**). The spherical whorl (**Pl. XLIV, 3**) was very carefully made from good quality clay, possibly with some admixture, since it was marked in the documentation as heavier than the other specimens. The size of these three spinning whorls is quite ordinary, and they could have been used for spinning wool. Two small clay whorls were used for weaving a delicate thread (**Pl. XLIV, 4, 5**). Their presence should be followed by loom weights and distaffs, which could have been made out of bone or wood. Wood does not preserve at Novae, and only bone distaffs have been found at the fortress. The surveys at Ostrite Mogili did not provide any distaffs, so it is possible that here they were made more often from wood.

Spindle whorls have a universal shape, which does not allow for dating them more precisely, but they provide clear evidence for textile manufacturing at the site. The small size of the spindles indicates finer yarn and higher expertise.

Weights could serve various purposes in the household. Two such items (**Pl. XLIV, 6, 7**) were found in Area B not far from the spinning whorls (**Fig. 96**), so their function as loom weights cannot be excluded. Clay weights were frequently made from secondarily used bricks or tiles.[1]

---

1. Kowal 2011, 129 and Tab. 1.

Fig. 96. Ostrite Mogili. Terracotta and clay finds from 2000 and 2014 (by A. Tomas).

Pl. XLIV. Areas B and C2. Terraccota and clay items

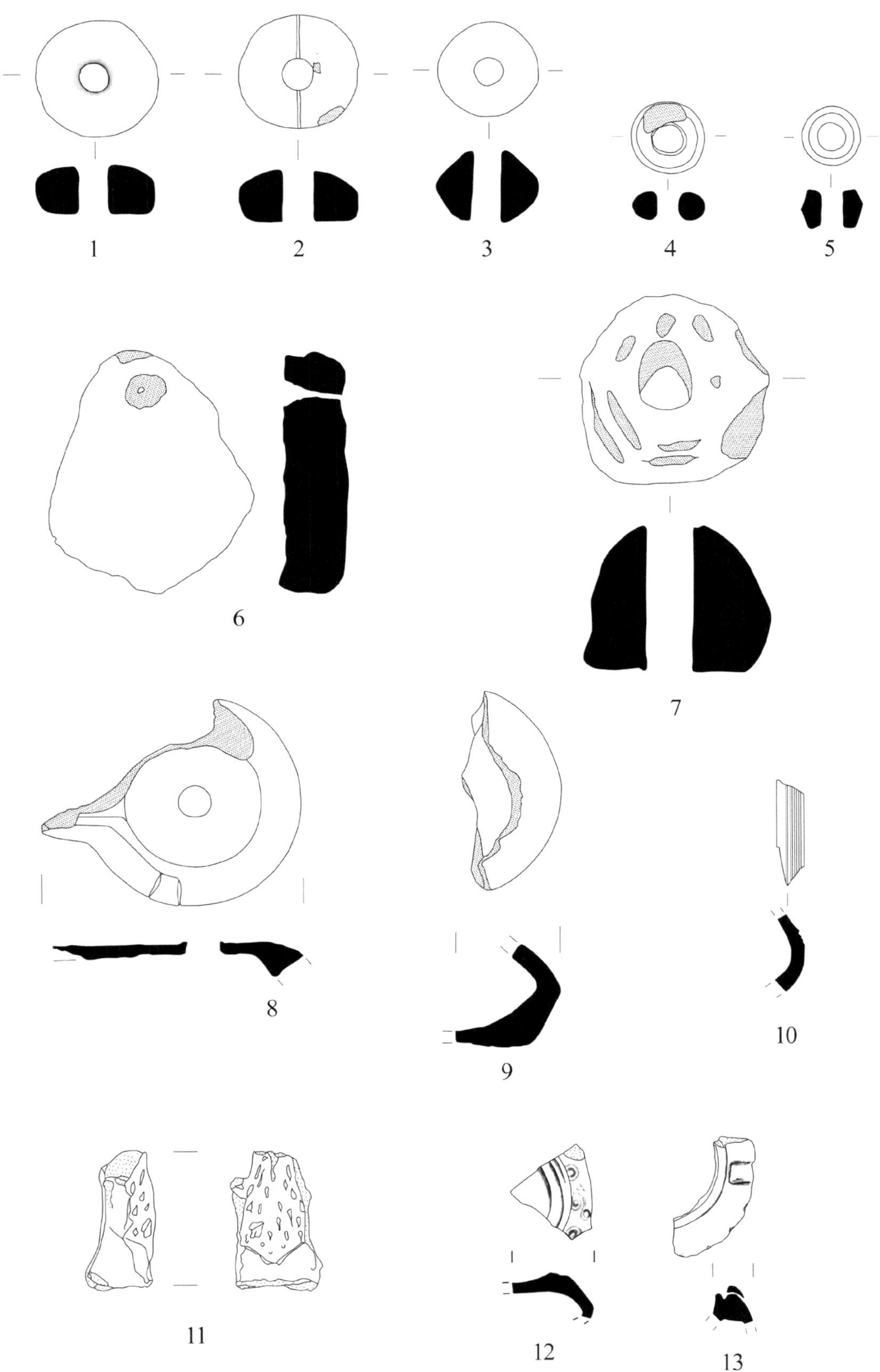

Only four fragments of terracotta oil lamps were collected in Area B (cat. nos. 8–10), and all of them were preserved very fragmentarily (**Pl. XLIV, 8–10**). Two can be recognized as imported *Firmalampen* or *Factory Lamps* (**Pl. XLIV, 8, 9**).[2]

Originally, Firmalampen were manufactured in Northern Italy (near Modena), possibly originating from the second half of the 1st century, but provincial production of the Italic prototypes continued throughout the 2nd century, while in some parts of the Balkan provinces it was continued until the late 4th century AD.[3] The lamps of this group have a circular reservoir with a flat hollowed discus and a raised ring around it, which forms an elongated channel at the nose rising towards the wick-hole. The nozzle is elongated, with an angular profile. Early types were not equipped with a handle, while later specimens had ring-shaped ones. In Lower Moesia, all the imported Firmalampen belong to the Loeschcke IX (=Buchi IX)[4] type (with three subtypes – a, b and c).[5] Cat. no. 8 seems to be a fragment of a Buchi IX type (most probably variant a or b), and similar lamps were found in Novae.[6]

A fragment of a ribbed base of a lamp (**Pl. XLIV, 10**) is very badly preserved, so it is difficult to identify its type, but it is possible that it belonged to some other local form. Clay vessels and lamps were also manufactured at Novae. Local production is testified by kilns, and by pottery and clay lamp moulds discovered in Novae.[7]

Two fragments of terracotta oil lamps were found in the *canabae* (Area C2), both of them were manufactured locally in Boutovo/Pavlikeni centres (**Pl. XLIV, 12, 13**). In Pavlikeni, lamps were produced from the mid-2nd century and in the Boutovo centre they were manufactured in 50 types with the earliest examples dated to the first decade of the 2nd century, while the latest to the mid-4th century.[8] Round lamps, very often decorated on their shoulders, are a broad group described as "Lower Danubian lamps with a rounded nozzle", which were produced from the beginning of the 3rd century.[9] These locally manufactured lamps had a rounded shape and a short nozzle imitating the Greek type of oil lamps, very often decorated with floral or geometric motifs, and such motifs are visible on one of the discussed fragments (cat. no. 13).

The most interesting terracotta find is the torso of a terracotta eagle (**Pl. XLIV, 11**). The fabric is typical for Boutovo/Pavlikeni centres, where terracotta products, including statuettes, were also manufactured.[10]

The concentration of terracotta finds in the western part of Ostrite Mogili is remarkable (**Fig. 96**), and their function (lighting and household items) definitely proves that at least one household existed in this part of the site.

Catalogue of terracotta finds

Pl. XLIV. Terracotta and clay items

Area B: Ostrite Mogili

1. Clay spindle. 73/8/00m/OM. Fabric containing small amounts of small-sized silver mica flakes and lime particles, slightly porous; slightly rough surface. Fabric 7.5 YR 6/4. Found in the western part of the site.
2. Clay spindle. 7/00w/OM. Found in the western part of the site.
3. Clay spindle. 53/00w/OM. Found in the western part of the site. Good-quality clay. Heavy.
4. Clay spindle. 99/00w/OM. Found in the western part of the site.
5. Clay spindle. 13/00w/OM. Smooth surface, fabric 5 YR 3/3. Found in the western part of the site.
6. Loom or fishing weight made from a piece of brick. 126/4/00m/OM. Found in the western part of the site.
7. Clay weight. 24/00w/OM. Fabric tempered with medium-sized sand, 7.5 YR 6/4. *Published*: Kowal 2011, No. 26, Tab. II, 26. Found in the western part of the site.
8. Terracotta lamp. 20/00w/OM. Well-sorted fabric, 7.5 YR 6/6. Found in the western part of the site.
9. Terracotta lamp. Fragment of the body and bottom. 15/00w/OM. Well-sorted fabric, 10 YR 7/2. Found in the western part of the site.
10. Terracotta lamp. 101/1/00m/OM. Fragment of the body decorated with horizontal grooves. Fabric well-sorted, containing sparse fine silver mica, fracture slightly porous. Surface 5 YR 6/4, fabric 5 YR 6/3. Found in the western part of the site.
11. Torso of a terracotta eagle. 63/00w/OM. *Published*: Tomas 2006, No. 35, Fig. 16.7. Found in the eastern part of the site.

Area C2

12. Terracotta lamp. 4/6/13m/can. Area C2. Fabric XI/XII.
13. Terracotta lamp. 4/4/13m/can. Area C2. Fabric XI/XII.

2. I would like to thank Maria Jaworska for her valuable comments and suggestions concerning terracotta oil lamps.
3. Kouzmanov and Minchev 2018, 244; Chrzanovski 2020, 216.
4. For the typologies of Firmalampen, see: Loeschcke 1919, 255–57; Buchi 1975, XXIII–XXVIII.
5. Chrzanovski 2019, 286.
6. Chichikova 1974, 157–58; Chrzanovski 2019, 287–88, cat. no. 17 and Fig. on p. 287 or 18 and Fig. on p. 287.
7. Chichikova 1950, 150–51, Figs. 1, 2, 7, 8; Dyczek 2005, 301; Tomas 2015c, 67–69.
8. Soultov 1962, 30, Fig. 6 and 7; 1985, 91–93; Soultova 1991, 116; Vladkova 2011, 108–36.
9. Soultova 1991, 116; Vladkova 2011, 111–12.
10. Soultov 1962, 30; 1977, 40–41; 1985, 93; Soultova 1992.

14. Stone finds

Agnieszka Tomas

Sandstone and soft limestone were quarried in the surroundings of Novae, but basalt was also available. Sandstone naturally appears in loess layers, while outcrops of soft white limestone are abundant in the whole area, e.g., at the mouth of the Yantra River. Sandstone was usually used as building material for rustic walls in private dwellings, while the buildings in the legionary fortress were more often built from limestone.[1] Harder metamorphosed greyish limestone was quarried near the present-day village of Hotnitsa, in the *chora* of the ancient Nicopolis, while basalt was quarried from the basalt hills in several places to the south of Novae.[2]

The stone mortar found in Area A1 was made from soft limestone (**Pl. XLV, 1**). Limestone and marble were usually used for making mortars in Novae, although sandstone mortars have also been identified.[3] The shape of the mortar is rather primitive and comparable to the find discovered in the late fortress layers in 1962.[4]

The limestone cross discovered in Area A1 (cat. no. 2) was made from metamorphosed Hotnitsa limestone. It is roughly hewn and has no traces of signs or letters, but its surface shows signs of chiseling (**Pl. XLV, 2**). The cross is a Christian symbol and the treated surface indicates that its function was not technical but undoubtedly religious.

The piece of a marble found on the Danubian riverbank, at the foot of the Ostrite Mogili site (cat. no. 3) is a fragment of a votive tablet on which one can see the remains of a depiction: the foot of a rider (**Pl. XLV, 3**). The preserved fragment is very similar to the representations of the Thracian horseman (Heros) and Artemis (Diana) hunting depicted as a rider, known from the surroundings of Novae and Nicopolis.[5] Both cults were very popular in Novae and its hinterlands.[6] Ten votive reliefs with representations of the Thracian horseman have been identified in Novae, while three of Diana-Artemis, but only the Thracian horseman from Novae is shown as a rider.[7]

Three whetstones were collected during the surveys, two in Area B (cat. nos. 4 and 5) and one in Area F (cat. no. 8). All of them were made of local pale green basalt (**Pl. XLV, 4, 5, 8**). One (cat. no. 5) was provided with a small hole, possibly to thread twine through it. Similar basalt whetsones are quite common at Novae and in its vicinity.[8] The opinion presented in the past that it was forbidden to export whetstones (*coti*) to Barbaricum along with weapons has been very convincingly rejected by Boris Rankov.[9] The new interpretation presented by Rankov of a passage from Paulus included in *Digesta* seems to confirm that whetstones were very common items.[10]

The sandstone weight found in Area B (**Pl. XLV, 6**) might have been used for drying fishing nets, but other farming or household activities, including spinning, are also possibilities.[11]

The stone vessel found in Area B (**Pl. XLV, 7**) might have been used as a kitchen mortar or a multi-functional stone vessel. Stone vessels, including a smaller one similar in shape, were found in Nicopolis ad Istrum.[12]

Catalogue of stone finds

Pl. XLV. Stone finds from Areas A1, B, and F

Area A1: The annexe

1. Mortar. 33/13w/can. Soft, lumpy limestone. Found in a robbery trench.
2. Fragment of a cross. 11/14c/can. Hotnitsa limestone. The fire traces are modern. Found in a robbery trench.

Area B: Ostrite Mogili

3. Fragment of a votive tablet. A/79/OM. Soft, greyish marble. Preserved fragment of a leg. Found on the Danubian riverbank, at the foot of the Ostrite Mogili site.
4. Whetstone. 27/00w/OM. Pale green basalt.
5. Whetstone. 44/13w/OM. Pale green basalt.
6. Stone weight. 98/79w/OM. Greyish sandstone.
7. Stone vessel (mortar?). 17/00w. Eastern part of the site. Hard, Hotnitsa limestone.

Area F

8. Whetstone. 11/1/14m/can. Pale green basalt.

1. Tomas 2017, 54.
2. Tomas 2016, 6, 37–39 and Fig. 19.
3. Misiewicz and Tumidajewicz 1987.
4. Majewski 1964, 164, Fig. 28 (found with a brick stamped LEPIFICOR shown on Fig. 29).
5. E.g., Kovacheva 1985, 48 (=ILBulg 244); Stoyanov 1984, 39–40, Fig. 1e, g (= IGBulg 709–710); Tomas 2016, 78, Fig. 24.1.
6. Tomas 2016, 77–78.
7. Tomas 2017, 68–69, Fig. 31, A–B (Thracian horseman) and 64–65, Fig. 32, A–B (Diana/Artemis).
8. Tomas 2016, 39.
9. Vismara 1947, 444; Dąbrowski and Kolendo 1972, 86; Kerr 1991, 442; Thompson 2002, 10; cf. Rankov 1999.
10. Dig. 39.4.11 ("Cotem ferro subigendo necessariam hostibus quoque venundari, ut ferrum et frumentum et sales, non sine periculo capitis licet.") and see Rankov 1999.
11. Kowal 2011, esp. 131 and 133.
12. Tsurov 1987, 50–51, cat. nos. 24–31, Tab. VI/1.

Pl. XLV. Stone finds from Areas A1, B and F

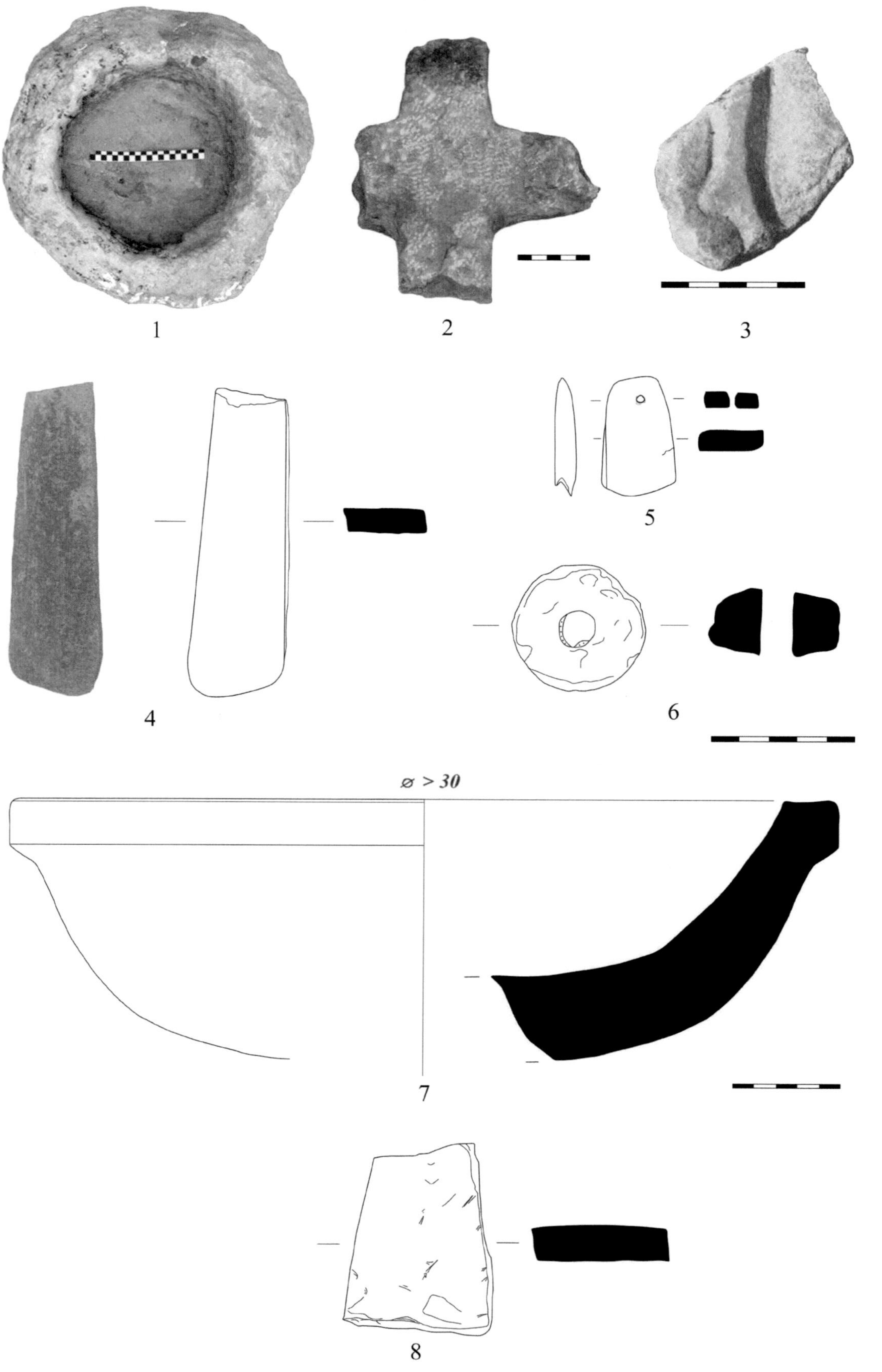

15. Medieval and post-Medieval pottery

Paweł Janik

In 1960, when Polish archaeologists started their preliminary reconnaissance of the area where Novae was located, Ostrite Mogili along with Novae itself became a subject of interest for Professor Witold Hensel, interested in early Slavic settlement. The same year Polish archaeologists conducted excavations at a spot situated some 50 m to the west of the West Gate (Sector III) where they expected to find the remains of a Slavic settlement.[1] The results were not very promising, so the team began reconnaissance in a broader area, including Ostrite Mogili, as well as Kaleto hill in Svishtov, where the excavations were conducted.[2] Finally, Hensel's team decided to carry out longer excavations at what in their opinion was the most promising site – Sturmen on the Yantra River, ca. 30 km to the south-east from Novae.[3]

Zofia Hilczerówna (after marriage Kurnatowska) who made the surveys at Ostrite Mogili in the autumn 1960s defined three Medieval sites within the prospected area, and four others near Vardim.[4] Medieval pottery sherds were also found during the investigations in 1977, 1999 and 2000, but the latter field walkings brought also metal finds and Early Byzantine coins discovered with the use of metal detectors.[5] The most numerous finds dated to the Medieval period were collected in the springs of 2013 and 2014. The coins and a copper alloy fitting found in 2014 are presented separately in the next chapters.

During prospection we have noticed that the total area of the Medieval settlement at Ostrite Mogili is larger than that of the Roman site. Pottery sherds were very fragmented due to their poor quality. However, they were numerous enough to recreate the size of the site, which could have covered up to 25 ha and was located on both sides of the gully giving access to the Danube (**Fig. 97**).

The finds from Ostrite Mogili dating to the Medieval period can be linked to the period when the Slavs and Eurasian nomads, principally Proto-Bulgarians and Avars, appeared on the Lower Danube. Slavs began to migrate to the Lower Danubian lands as early as in the 6th century AD, but by the beginning of the 7th century AD these areas were to a greater or lesser extent under Byzantine control. The turning point is considered to be the beginning of Heraclius' reign, when, due to various factors, the Roman army and administration were gradually withdrawn, from towns, including Novae and Durostorum.[6] The Proto-Bulgarians,[7] who started to appear on the Lower Danube from the 680s, strengthened their rule in northeastern Bulgaria shortly after their

1. Majewski 1962, 106–13.
2. Hensel et al. 1965, 262–84.
3. Hensel 1980.
4. Hensel et al. 1965, 284–86.
5. Tomas 2006 with literature.
6. Madgearu 2006; Atanasov 2014, 529
7. Curta 2013, 148.

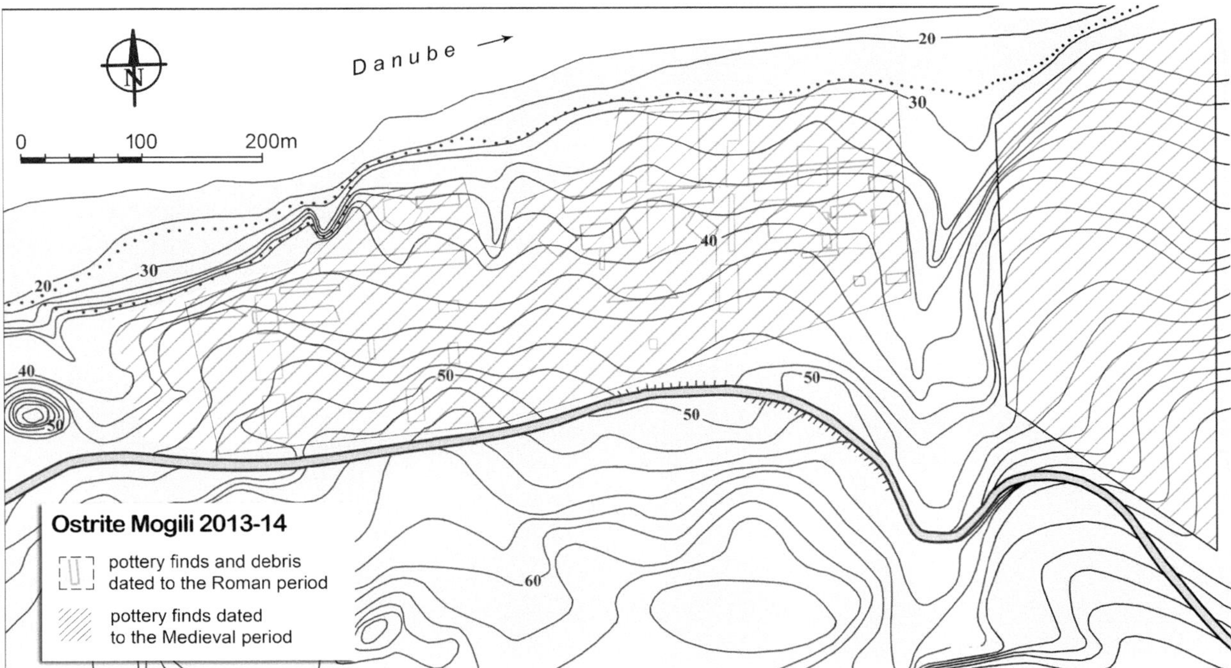

Fig. 97. Ostrite Mogili. The area of the early Medieval site compared to the Roman site (drawing by A. Tomas).

arrival and formed the First Bulgarian State. The lands around Novae (present-day Svishtov) fell within its borders.[8] The Avars first demanded the lands south of the Lower Danube, but were prevented from getting them by the Byzantines, and ultimately came to control the lands to the north of the Middle and Lower Danube, forming there the Avar Khaganate.

Ware XVIII: Early Medieval pottery

The analysed pottery sherds were found during the prospections carried out in 1979, 2000, and 2012–14. They belonged to large ovoid pots with a wavy decoration, which – based on their shape and adornments – are linked mainly to the Slavic ethnos. Their fabric is quite recognizable as well and it was described in Table I included in Chapter VI.2 as Ware XVIII. The vessels were hand-formed and wheel-thrown, had a rough and uneven surface and sharp endings on the prominent edges of the ornaments. Numerous examples were found in the *vicus* (**Pl. XLVII–XLIX**). A few sherds were collected in Areas E and F to the south from Ostrite Mogili (**Pl. L–LI**).

Due to the fragmentary state of preservation, in most cases it is impossible to recreate the original shape of the vessels (i.e. all dimensions), but in many cases these are fragments of spouts and fragments of decorated bellies, where the dating element may be a type of ornament.

Uwe Fiedler, who studied the burials dated to the 6th–9th centuries on the Lower Danubian lands created a typology of pottery forms and decorations. Among the discussed pottery sherds from Ostrite Mogili, the following types of ornamentation according to Fiedler's typology have been found:

Type I – horizontal, straight, densely spaced lines (**Pl. XLVI, 8; XLVII, 24**). Vessels decorated with Type I motif are known, among others from Durostorum, where they are dated at the end of the 8th and the first half of the 9th century,[9] Sturmen on the Yantra and Morava to the south of Novae,[10] and from the vicinity of Novae – from Ostrite Mogili and Vardim,[11] as well as from Romania – Păuleasca in Teleorman district.[12]

Type III – horizontal, but sparsely spaced, straight lines (**Pl. XLVI, 1; XLVIII, 36**). Vessels decorated with Type III decorations are known from Durostorum,[13] from the rural areas to the south of Novae – Alexandrovo, Morava, Novgrad and Vardim,[14] as well as from the Romanian sites – Dulceanca,[15] Sturmen,[16] Păuleasca, and Satu Nou.[17]

Type VI – horizontal, quite densely spaced, straight lines in the lower part of the vessel and horizontal wavy lines (in the form of several lined waves) under the spout (**Pl. XLVI, 3, 5, 7, 12, 22; XLVII, 26**). This type of decoration appears on vessels known from the sites to the south of Novae – Alexandrovo, Morava and Sturmen on the Yantra,[18] as well as from the sites on the Danube – Vardim near Novae and Belene (Roman Dimum),[19] and from the Romanian sites of Păuleasca[20] and Satu Nou.[21]

Type VII – horizontal, alternating rows of wavy lines (in the form of waves composed of several dashes) and quite densely spaced straight lines (**Pl. XLVI, 20**). This type of decoration is known from Alexandrovo,[22] Dulceanca,[23] and Sturmen.[24]

Type XI – horizontal waves (made up of several lines) overlapping with horizontal, densely spaced, straight lines (**Pl. XLVI, 7 and 16**).[25] Type XI is known, among others, from sites to the east and west of Novae – Novgrad, Belene and Ostrite Mogili,[26] as well as to the south – Morava and Sturmen.[27]

In addition to the above-mentioned types of decorations, Uwe Fiedler defined additional ornamental motifs, which accompanied the above-mentioned decorations:

Ornament type 8 – lines, the position of which can be considered more vertical (although they go diagonally), appearing alone or overlapping other ornamental motifs (**Pl. XLVI, 9, 11, 14–15, 17–18**). Ornaments of this type appear, among others, at Sturmen on the Yantra[28] and

8. Giuzelev 1986, 32–38; Panayotov 1998, 49–68.
9. Atanasov 2014, 532, Fig. 44.2.
10. Hensel et al. 1980, 182, Tab. III (Sturmen); Hensel et al. 1965, 249–50 and 255, Figs. 10.17 and 13.7 (Morava).
11. Hensel et al. 1965, 283, Fig. 34.1 (Ostrite Mogili); 285, Fig. 36.1 (Vardim).
12. Fiedler 1992, Teil 2, Tab. 1.4; 2.3.
13. Atanasov 2014, 532.
14. Hensel et al. 1965, 238–39, Fig. 2.6 (Alexandrovo); 249–50 and 254–55, Figs. 10.13 and 26;12.2 and 4; 13.5 (Morava); 260–61, Fig. 17.8, Fig. 18.19–29 (Novgrad); 285, Fig. 36.3, 8 and 12 (Vardim).
15. Harhoiu 2005, 186, Abb. 22.B2.
16. Hensel 1980, 195–96, Tab. XVI-XVII.
17. Fiedler 1992, Teil 2, Tab. 1.2-3 (Păuleasca); Tab.5.4–5 (Satu Nou).
18. Hensel et al. 1965, 238–39, Fig. 2.3 (Alexandrovo); 249–50, Fig. 10.16 (Morava); Hensel et al. 1980, 180–81, Tab. I–II (Sturmen).
19. Hensel et al. 1965, 285, Figs. 36.9 and 14 (Vardim); 239–40, Figs. 3.1 and 8–9 (Belene).
20. Fiedler 1992, Teil 2, Tab.1.1; 2.2.
21. Fiedler 1992, Teil 2, Tab. 3.6.
22. Hensel et al. 1965, 238–39, Fig. 2.2.
23. Harhoiu 2005: 186, Abb. 22. B2.
24. Hensel 1980, 182, 201, 233, Tab. III, XXII, LIV.
25. Fiedler 1992, Teil 1, 151, Abb. 34.
26. Hensel et al. 1965, 260, Fig. 17.6 (Novgrad); 239–40, Fig. 3.4 (Belene); 283–84, Fig. 35.6 (Ostrite Mogili).
27. Hensel et al. 1965, 249–50, Fig. 10.8 (Morava); Hensel et al. 1980, 181–82, 213, Tab. II–III, XXXIV (Sturmen).
28. Hensel 1980, 181, 216, 229, 235, 238, 244, Tab. II; XXXVII; L; LVI; LIX; LXVI.

Novgrad near Novae,[29] from the Dolni Lukovit site in Pleven district,[30] in Histria on the Black Sea,[31] and at the sites of Satu Nou[32] and Izvorul (Giurgiu district).[33]

Ornament type 10 – obliquely arranged straight or crescent-shaped or half-nail-shaped grooves, usually occurring around the spout (**Pl. XLVI, 6; XLVII, 25, 29–30; XLVIII, 31–32**).[34] Ornaments of this type are known from Sturmen,[35] Izvorul[36] and Dolni Lukovit.[37]

The above set of additional ornaments collected at Ostrite Mogili corresponds very well with the ornaments known from Sturmen on the Yantra.[38] Based on the dated finds from the latter site and other similarities cited above, the discussed pottery fragments can be dated to the 8th / 9th century AD.

Among the finds from Ostrite Mogili, there is a piece of a vessel bottom with a potter's stamp (**Pl. XLVII, 27**). It has the form of three overlapping squares forming a triple broken swastika pattern. This type of stamp was defined by Fiedler as type XV/1.[39] Similar finds are known, among others, from Sturmen on the Yantra.[40] Pottery stamps were very characteristic for Slavic pottery in the 9th and 10th centuries,[41] although the above type of stamp was also found at the bottom of a Proto-Bulgarian jug from Kamenyak near Shoumen.[42]

The next, but less numerous group, are pottery fragments which can be linked to the nomads. These include very characteristic vessels with what is referred to as "attaches" (**Pl. XLIX**). Such fragments were also found, e.g., in Sturmen.[43] Vessels provided with "attaches" were defined by Fiedler as the D.IX type dated to the 9th century.[44] Such vessels are rarely found inside the territory of Bulgaria (Dolni Lukovit) and Romania (Histria).[45]

Fragments decorated with "smoothened" ornamental motifs, characteristic for Proto-Bulgarian pottery have also been identified among the finds from Ostrite Mogili (**Pl. XLVI, 10, 13**), although their number is small. These are fragments with type I decoration according to Fiedler's typology – in the form of diagonal, straight lines forming a grid of rectangles.[46] They often appeared on Proto-Bulgarian type F jugs according to Fiedler's typology.[47] Similar vessels are known from other Lower Danubian sites, such as Dolni Lukovit, Razdelna, Devnya, Kyulevcha, Novi Pazar, Varna and Shoumen,[48] as well as from Volga Bulgaria[49] and the areas of the Saltovo-Mayaki culture.[50] However, this type of ornament appears also on other forms as evidenced by the vessel found in Razdelna near Varna,[51] with decoration possibly inspired by the type F jugs.

The majority of the pottery fragments collected at Ostrite Mogili (with the exception of the D.IX type vessels and the sherds with "smoothened" ornamental motifs discussed above) consists of Slavic pottery, which has analogies from present-day Bulgaria and Romania.[52] Such pottery is very frequent in the surroundings of Novae.[53] Analogous sherds were found in Nicopolis in contexts dated after the 6th century.[54] Their forms and finishing is also known from the broad areas occupied by Slavic cultures in the 8th to the 10th century.[55] The pottery fragments discussed above indicate that the site at Ostrite Mogili was intensively settled in this period.

Ware XIX: Byzantine Medieval and post-Medieval glazed pottery

Fragments of medieval and post-Medieval glazed pottery were collected during the field walkings in 1979, 2000 and 2014. This group consists of various types of medieval and post-medieval glazed pottery. Vessels of this type were usually made from fabric, which at first glance seems to form one group (see Chapter VI.2, Tab. I, ware XIX). The sherds are not very frequently found in Novae. The most numerous examples originate from Area E (**Pl. L**), but a few were found also at Ostrite Moglili (**Pl. XLVIII, 37–39**), including the Byzantine glazed sgraffito pottery

29. Hensel et al. 1965, 260–61, Fig. 17.5; 18.9.
30. Fiedler 1992, Teil 2, Tab. 53.6.
31. Fiedler 1992, Teil 2, Tab.18.9.
32. Fiedler 1992, Teil 2, Tab.3.8.
33. Fiedler 1992, Teil 2, Tab. 38.19.
34. Fiedler 1992, Teil 1, 151, 155, Abb. 34; 36.
35. Hensel 1980, 181–82, 190, 192, 199, Tab. II–III; XI; XIII; XX.
36. Fiedler 1992, Teil 2, Tab. 36.17.
37. Fiedler 1992, Teil 2, Tab. 52.3; 54.6; 55.4.
38. Hensel 1980, 77–78, 128, Fig. 9; 36.
39. Fiedler 1992, Teil 1, 159, Abb. 37.
40. Hensel 1980, 136, Figs. 43.20, 22 and 31.
41. Buko 1990, Fig. 65.
42. Fiedler 1992, Teil 2, Taff. 115.2.
43. Hensel 1980, 134–35, Fig. 41–42.
44. Fiedler 1992, Teil 1, 141, Abb. 27.
45. Fiedler 1992, Teil 2, Taff. 34.7; 54.1.
46. Fiedler 1992, Teil 1, 155, Abb. 36.
47. Fiedler 1992, Teil 1, 144, Abb. 29.
48. Fiedler 1992, Teil 2, Taff. 52.1; 54.3; 61.2; 97.13; 103.18; 23; 108.11; 112.5, 8; 114.16; 115.1.
49. Genning and Halikov 1964, Tab. VIII,1.
50. Pletneva 1981, Figs. 46.30, 36.
51. Fiedler 1992, Teil 2, Taf. 68.58.
52. Fiedler 1992, Teil 2, Taff. 1–117.
53. Hensel et al. 1965.
54. Falkner 1999, 91 (Ware 43).
55. Gardawski 1970, 93–103, Tab. 1–81; Szymański 1973, 114–15; Leciejewicz 1976, 86–87; Kurnatowska 1977, 70–71.

Pl. XLVI. Medieval pottery decorations

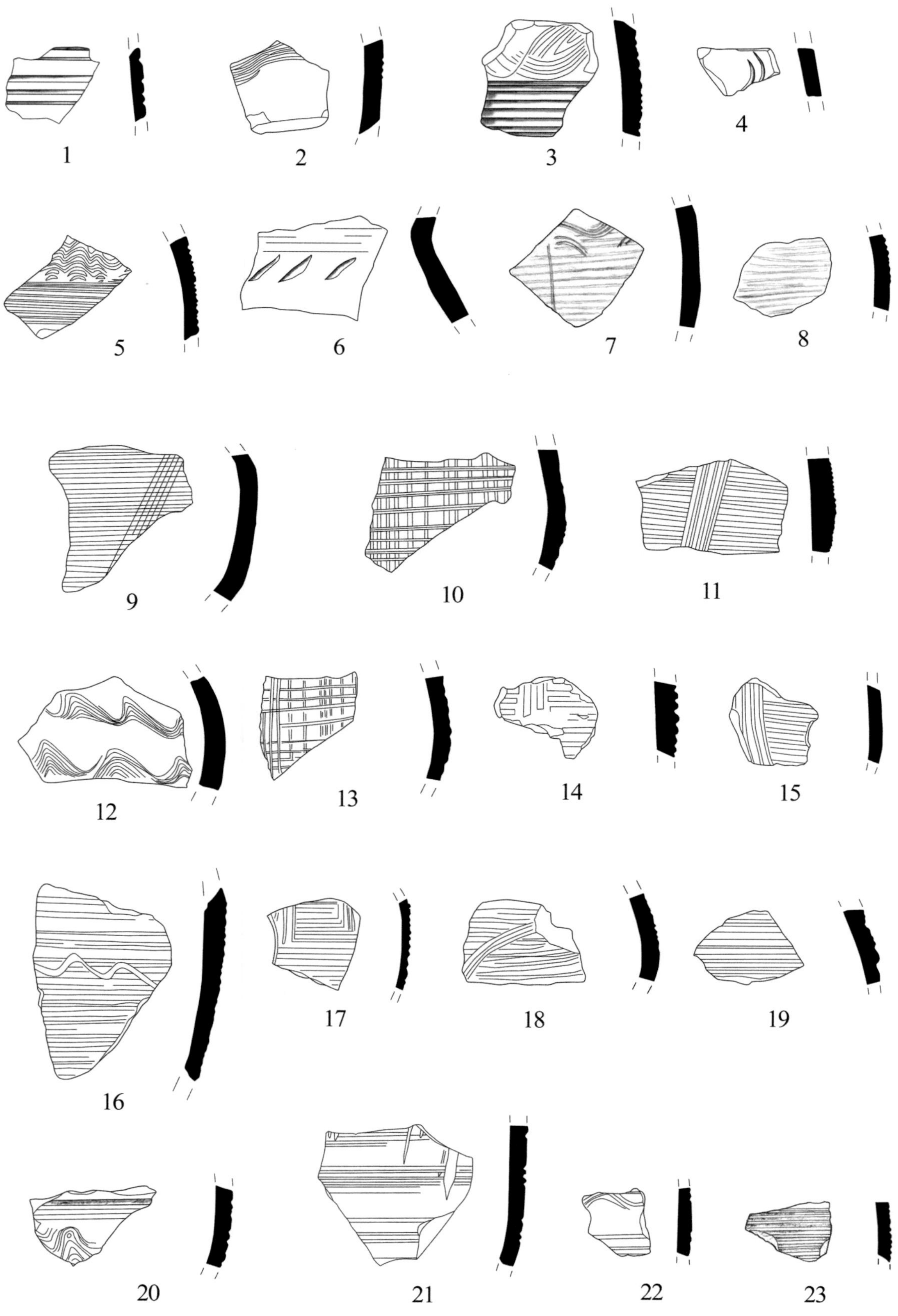

(**Pl. XLVIII, 37–38**). Examples of sgraffito pottery were found also in Nicopolis, where they are dated to the period of the Second Bulgarian Empire.[56]

Catalogue of Medieval and post-Medieval pottery

Pl. XLVI. Area B. Early Medieval pottery decorations

(all fragments were classified as fabric Class XVIII; description of finds from 1979 is given after the original documentation)

1. Fragment of a body with grooved ornament. 5/16/13m/OM.
2. Fragment of a body with grooved wave ornament. 5/10/13m/OM.
3. Fragment of a body with grooved ornament. 5/9/13m/OM.
4. Fragment of a body with grooved ornament. 5/13/13m/OM.
5. Fragment of a body with grooved and incised ornament. 5/5/13m/OM.
6. Fragment of a body with incised ornament. 7/5/13m/OM.
7. Fragment of a body with grooved ornament. 7/3/13m/OM.
8. Fragment of a body with grooved ornament. 6/1/13m/OM.
9. Fragment of a body with grooved ornament. 11/00/OM.
10. Fragment of a body with grooved ornament. 59/00/OM.
11. Fragment of a body with ornament. 131/2/00/OM.
12. Fragment of a body with grooved ornament. 20/d1/00/OM. Published: Tomas 2006, cat. no. 51, fig. 18.6.
13. Fragment of a body with grooved ornament. 59/3/00/OM.
14. Fragment of a body with grooved ornament. 6/79/OM. Fabric tempered with coarse sand, brownish grey fabric and surface.
15. Fragment of a body with grooved ornament. 7/79/OM. Fabric tempered with fine-grained sand, brownish grey fabric and surface.
16. Fragment of a body with grooved ornament. 1/79/OM. Fabric tempered with coarse sand, brownish grey fabric and surface.
17. Fragment of a body with grooved ornament. 4/79/OM. Fabric tempered with small amount of fine grained sand, brownish grey fabric and surface.
18. Fragment of a body with grooved ornament. 131/00/OM.
19. Fragment of a body with grooved ornament. 5/14/13m/OM.
20. Fragment of a body with grooved ornament. 5/3/13m/OM.
21. Fragment of a body with grooved ornament. 5/3/13m/OM.
22. Fragment of a body with grooved ornament. 5/12/13m/OM.
23. Fragment of a body with grooved ornament. 9/5/13m/OM.

Pl. XLVII. Area B. Early Medieval pottery

(all fragments were classified as fabric Class XVIII; description of published fragments is given after the publication)

24. Upper part with grooved ornament. 12/1/13m/OM.
25. Upper part with grooved and incised ornament. 13/1a/00/OM. Hard fabric, porous. Fabric black, surface beige, with traces of fire. *Published:* Tomas 2006, cat. no. 50, fig. 18.5.
26. Upper part with grooved decoration. 10/1/13m/OM.
27. Bottom with a potter's stamp in form of a relief swastika. 23/1a/00/OM. Hard fabric containing large amount of coarse sand with translucent grids, lime particles, small-sized silver mica flakes and red particles, porous, rough surface. Fabric black, surface greyish-beige. *Published:* Tomas 2006, cat. no. 53, fig. 18.8.
28. Upper part with grooved ornament. 14a/k1/00/OM. Hard fabric containing large amount of lime and silver mica flakes, tempered with large amount of fine-grained sand, porous, rough surface. Fabric and surface greyish-beige. *Published:* Tomas 2006, cat. no. 52, fig. 18.7.
29. Rim with incised ornament. 24/2/13m/OM.
30. Upper part with incised decoration. 5/79/00/OM. Fabric tempered with large amount of coarse sand, brownish grey.

Pl. XLVIII. Area B. Byzantine Medieval and post-Medieval pottery

(all fragments were classified as fabric Class XVIII unless otherwise stated; description of finds from 1979 is given after the original documentation)

31. Upper part with grooved and incised decoration. 19/79/OM. Fabric tempered with coarse sand, fabric brownish red, greenish beige glaze.
32. Upper part with grooved and incised decoration. 64/3/00/OM.
33. Fragment of a pot-pad (?) with grooved decoration. 89/2/00/OM. Hard fabric containing small amount of silver mica flakes, slightly porous, tempered with medium amount of small-sized sand. Fabric 7.5 YR 5/3.
34. Fragment of a rim. 30/4/00/OM.
35. Fragment of a rim. 11/2/13m/OM.
36. Upper part of a vessel. 24/1/13m/OM. Grooved ornament and glazed surface.
37. Bottom of an opened vessel. 89/9/00/OM. Greenish glaze, ornament of dark green incised lines. Ware XIX.
38. Fragment of a vessel. 125/1/00/OM. Greenish glaze, ornament of dark green incised lines. Ware XIX.
39. Rim. 96/79. Fabric tempered with coarse sand, fabric brownish red, greenish beige glaze. Ware XIX.

56. Falkner 1999, 91–92 (Ware II).

Pl. XLVII. Medieval pottery from Area B

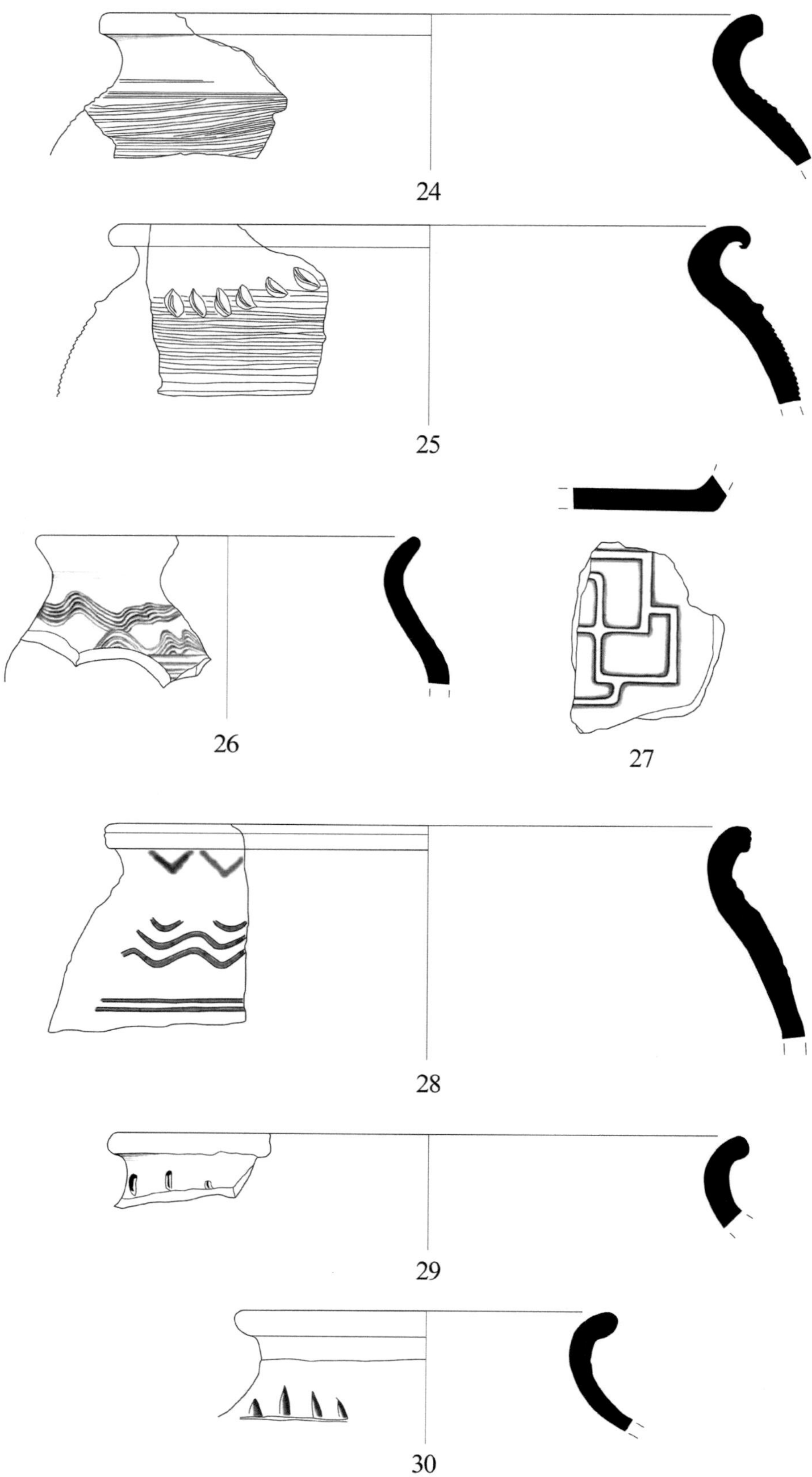

Pl. XLVIII. Medieval pottery from Area B

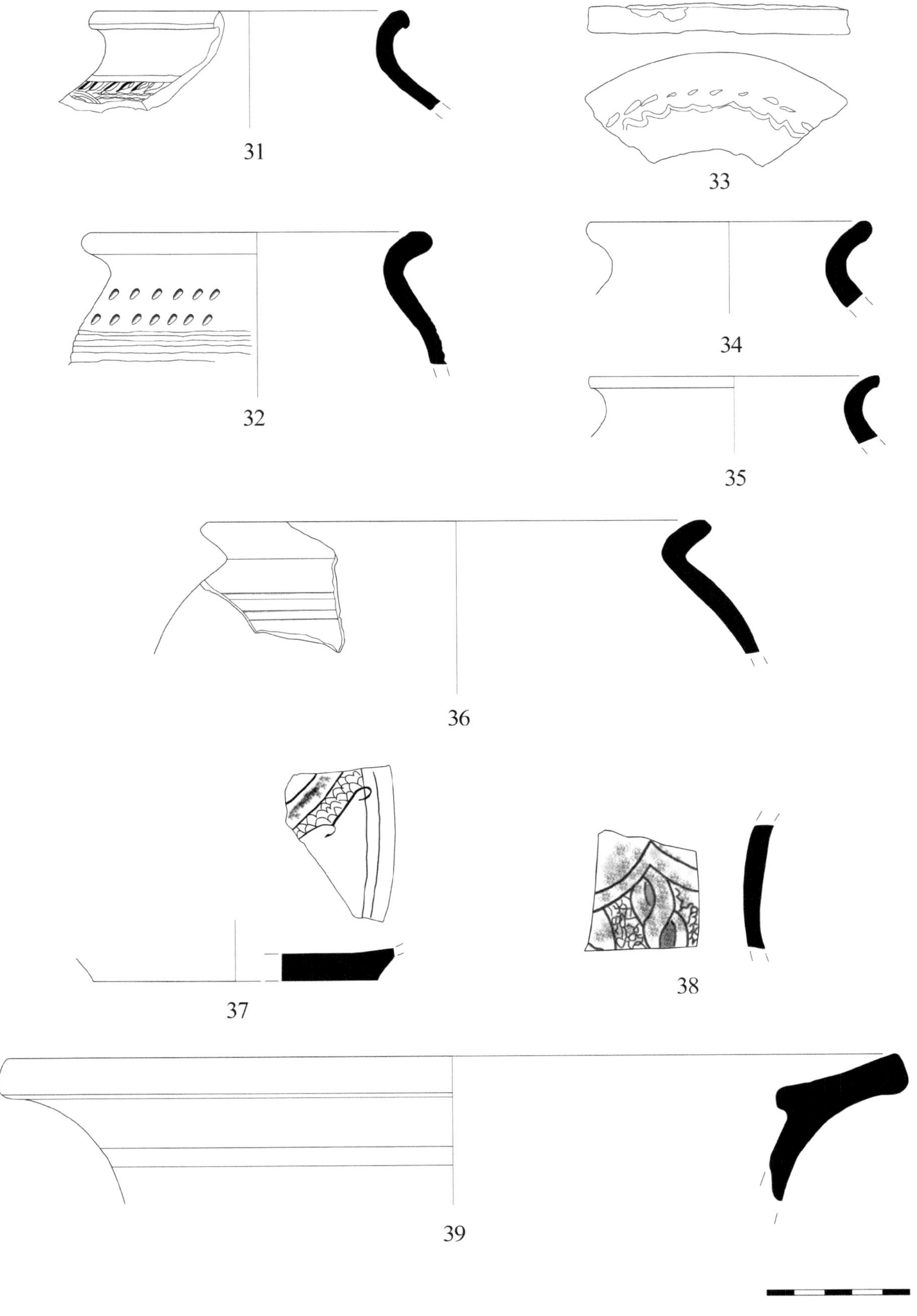

Pl. XLIX. Medieval pottery from Area B

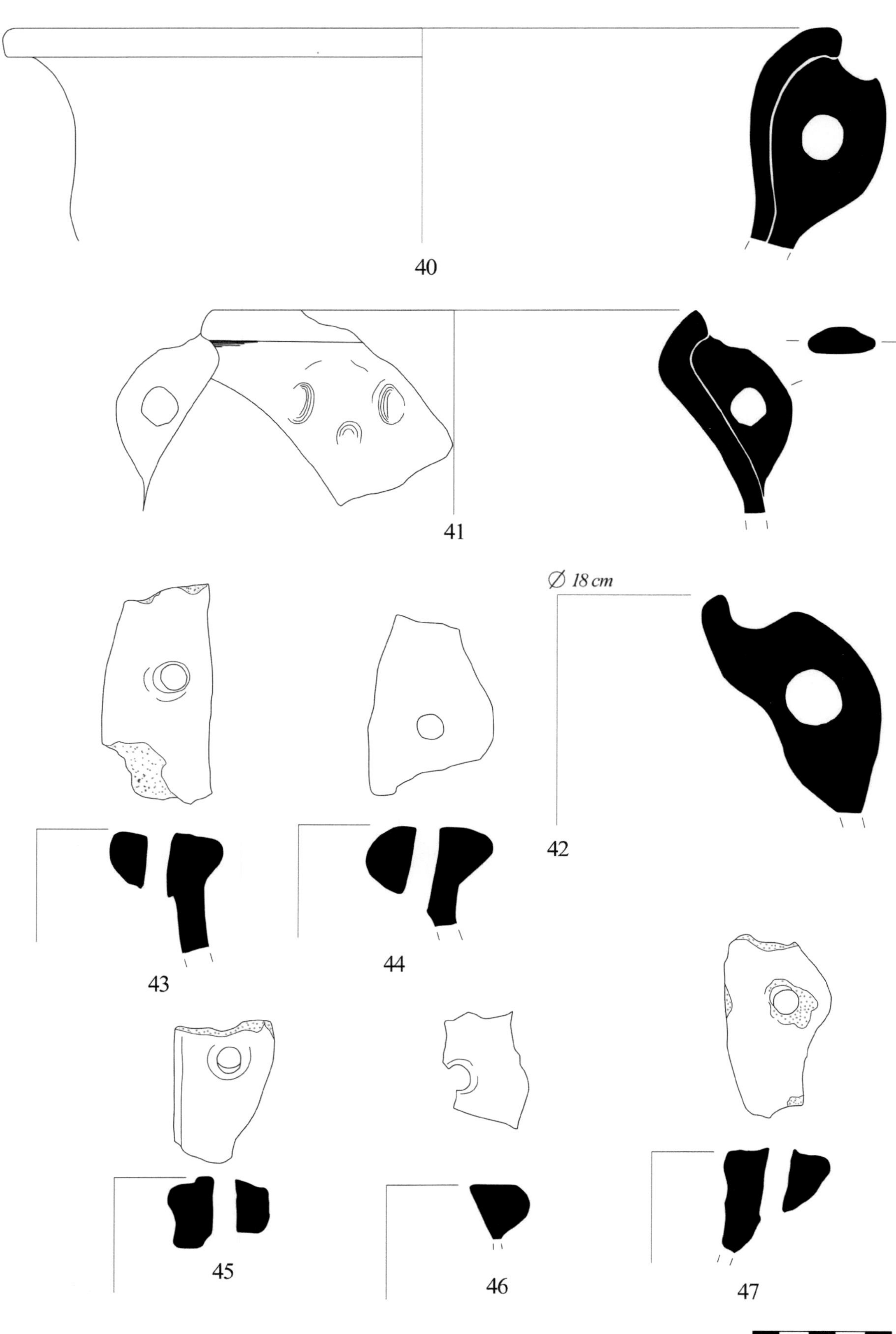

Pl. L. Byzantine and post-Medieval pottery from Areas E and F

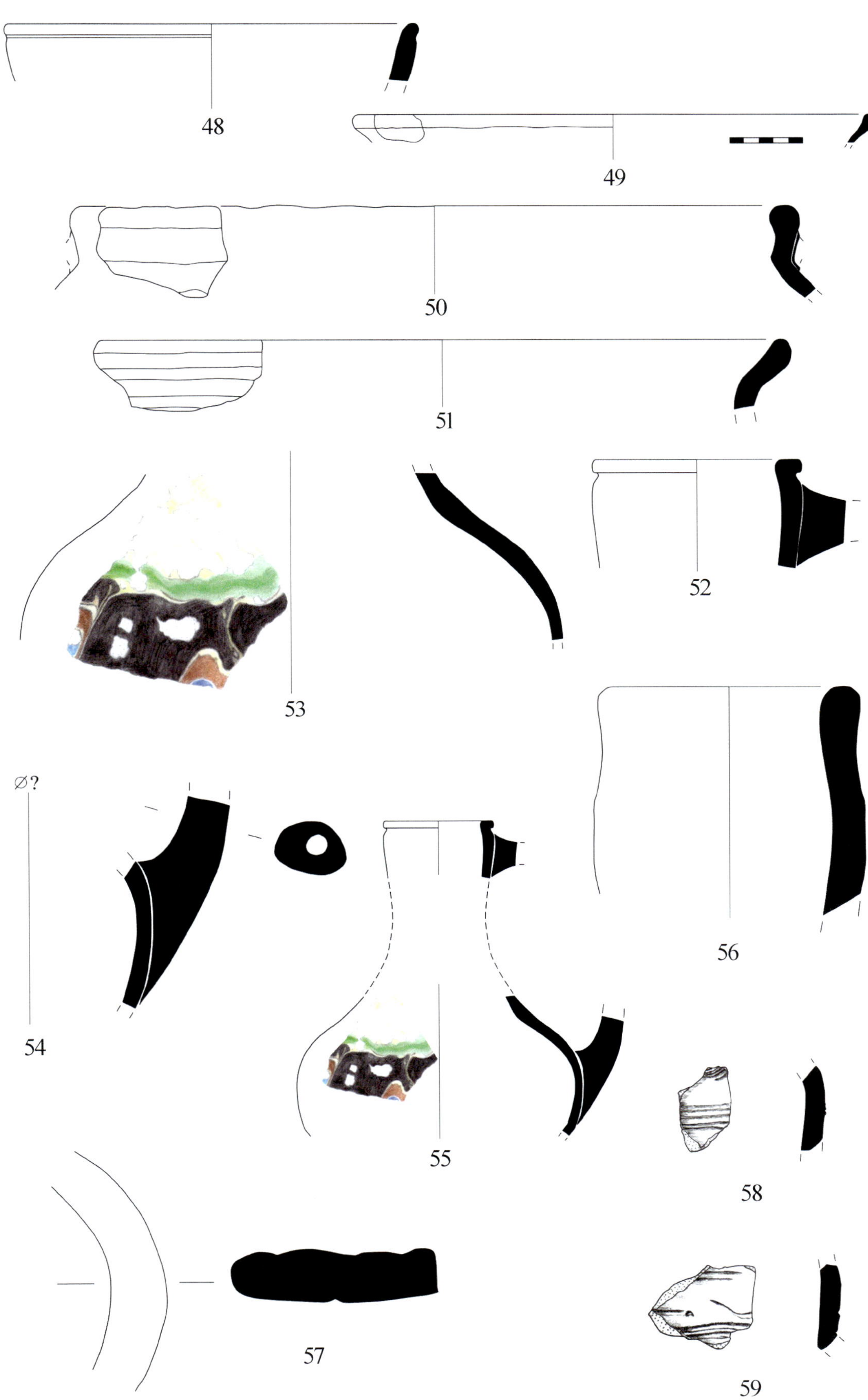

Pl. XLIX. Area B. Byzantine pottery

(description of finds from 1979 is given according to the original documentation)

40. Upper part with a handle. 129/3/00/OM.
41. Upper part with a handle. 19/d1/00/OM.
42. Fragment of a rim with a handle. 111/7/00/OM.
43. Fragment of a handle. 24/d1/00/OM.
44. Fragment of a handle. 19/3/00/OM.
45. Fragment of a handle. 151/79/OM. Fabric tempered with coarse sand, brownish-orange.
46. Fragment of a handle. 138/2/00/OM.
47. Fragment of a handle. 152/79/OM. Fabric tempered with coarse sand, brownish-orange.

Pl. L. Area E. Byzantine pottery and post-Medieval pottery

Ware XIX

48. Rim of a glazed vessel. 3/9/14m/OMS. Green glaze. Medium-hard, fine-grained fabric with no visible inclusions, dense; glazed surface. Fabric 10 YR 5/3, glaze 6 GY N8/6.
49. Rim of a bowl. 1/3/14m/OMS. Hard fabric containing medium amount of small-sized lime particles and large amount of small-sized silver mica flakes. Fabric 5 Y 5/4, glaze 10 Y 5/4.
50. Rim. 1/2/14m/OMS. Hard fabric containing medium amount of small-sized lime particles and large amount of small-sized silver mica flakes and small-sized red particles. Fabric 5 Y 5/6, glaze 10 Y 5/4.
51. Rim. 2/3/14m/OMS. Fabric 10 YR 5/3, glaze 6 GY N8/6. Ware XIX.
52. Rim of a jug. 1/9/14m/OMS. Fabric 10 YR 5/3, glaze 6 GY N8/6. Post-medieval.
53. Fragment of a glazed body. 2/1/14m/OMS. Post-medieval.
54. Fragment of a jug with a handle or a spout. 3/5/14m/OMS. Post-medieval.
55. Possible reconstruction of a jug based on fragments cat. nos. 52–54. Not to scale.

Area F. Byzantine and Medieval pottery

56. Amphora rim with a neck and fragment of a handle. 2/1/14m/Kč. Very hard fabric containing medium amount of medium-sized sand particles, big amount of small-sized lime, small amount of silver mica and red round particles. Rough, concrete-like surface. Fabric and surface 10 GY 6/2.
57. Amphora(?) handle. 2/2/14m/Kč. Fabric and colour similar to cat. no. 56.
58. Fragment of a pot decorated with horizontal and angled grooves. 3/1/14m/Kč. Ware XVIII.
59. Fragment of a pot decorated with horizontal waved grooves. 3/2/14m/Kč. Ware XVIII.

16. Medieval coins found at Ostrite Mogili

Piotr Jaworski

Billon trachea dated to the 13th century, when Veliko Turnovo, the nearby capital of the Second Bulgarian Empire was rapidly developing, constitute the most numerous group of coins, consisting of 62 specimens found at the Ostrite Mogili site and in its immediate vicinity[1] during non-invasive research conducted in 2013 and 2014 (**Fig. 98**). Coins from the 1st century to the first half of the 5th century AD[2] constitute a much smaller group among the finds from Ostrite Mogili than at the annexe in Novae, while there are no finds representing early Byzantine coinage of the 6th – early 7th centuries (**Fig. 100**). Earlier, during field surveys carried out at this site in 2000, 19 billon trachea were found,[3] three of which have been included in this paper,[4] while an anonymous class A2 follis was also discovered at that time:[5]

Fig. 99. Ostrite Mogili 2000. Anonymous follis found during prospection (photo by P. Jaworski).

Anonymous issuer; 976 (?) – ca. 1030/35; Constantinople mint; *follis* (**Fig. 99**)
Inv. № 25/00w (=Svishtov Museum, Inv. № 3403)
Obv. Bust of Christ Pantocrator, facing forward [+] ЄMMAN[OVHΛ], in field: IC–XC
Rev. [+] IhSUS/XRISTUS/bASILЄU/bASILЄ
DOC III.2: class A2kk, var. 40, 666–667
14.78 g; 33 mm; 6 h
Area B: Ostrite Mogili
References: Tomas 2006, 123, no. 49, Fig. 18.4 (Pl. 132).

Although the finds of anonymous folles in Bulgaria are relatively numerous,[6] and they have also been re-

1. The coins were found at the Ostrite Mogili site (Area B) and the Chehlarski geran site (Area E) located south of the Svishtov–Vardim road. At the latter spot, one specimen was found of a coin dated to the 13th century (cat. no. 53).
2. Coins minted during the Roman period are presented in Chapter VI.9 of this volume. It is worth adding that in Ostrite Mogili, coins dating back to the Hellenistic period were also discovered, mainly from Illyria, Macedonia and Thrace, as well as Roman republican *denarii* from the end of the 2nd–1st century BC, although this information should be treated with great caution, since most of these coins are in private possession (Svishtov), cf. Dimitrov 2013a, 731–37; Tomas 2006, 119; Tomas 2017, 79.
3. "Mostly concaved bronze coins" (Tomas 2006, ibidem).
4. Cat. nos. 2, 17, 26.
5. Tomas 2006, 123, cat. no. 49, Fig. 18.4 (pl. 132).
6. Morrisson 2002, 960.

Fig. 98. Ostrite Mogili 2014. Finds of 13th-century billon trachea (by A. Tomas).

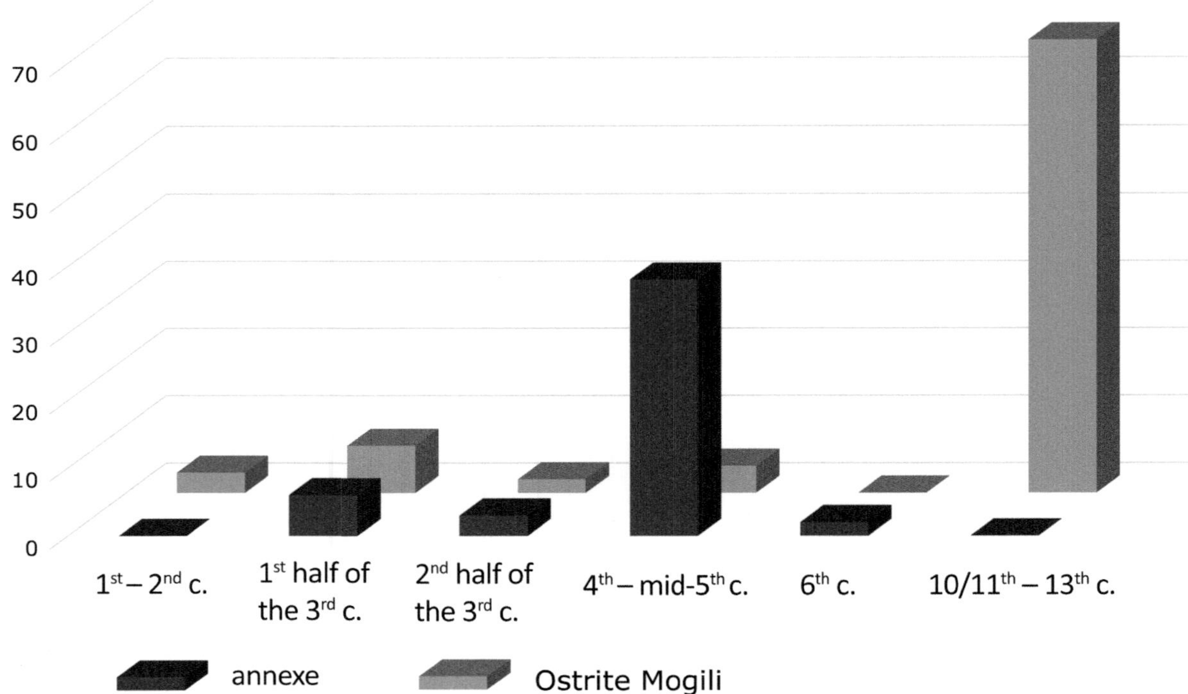

Fig. 100. Comparison between the chronological structure of the coins found at the annexe in Novae and at Ostrite Mogili during surveys in 2000 and 2012–14 (by P. Jaworski).

corded in the vicinity of Ostrite Mogili,[7] the presence of the above specimen among very homogeneous material from the 13th century seems particularly interesting in the context of the ongoing discussion regarding the possible later dating of the circulation of these series of coins.[8]

With the exception of the anonymous Byzantine follis mentioned above, all the remaining medieval coins discovered at Ostrite Mogili can be classified into the billon trachea coin category, although the vast majority of specimens have only trace amounts of silver or they are made purely of copper. The characteristic concave shape of most of these coins, largely representing small modules, and – above all – the carelessness of the stamps used, often completely worn, as well as the irregular shapes of the coins, in many cases clipped, allow them to be considered as belonging to the imitative coinage of the first three decades of the 13th century (**Pl. LI** and **Pl. LII**).[9] Scyphates found at Ostrite Mogili can be divided into the following groups (**Fig. 101**): 1. "Bulgarian" imitations (1200–18); 2. Latin imitations (Constantinople mint; 1208–41); 3. Latin imitations (Thessaloniki mint; 1208–24); 4. Latin imitations difficult to classify due to their state of preservation, 5. other billon trachea, including two specimens of Theodore I Lascaris coinage (Nicaea mint; 1208–22) and one Theodore Comnenus-Dukas coin (Thessaloniki mint; 1224–30). Many specimens underwent weight reduction treatments by having their edges clipped and various shaped pieces being cut off (**Table I**). It is worth noting the lack of officially regulated coinage of Bulgarian rulers, which are a characteristic part of the monetary mass circulating in medieval Bulgaria.[10]

In the first half of the 13th century, the lands included in the Asenid Kingdom of Bulgaria continued to be part of the Byzantine monetary zone.[11] After the conquest of Constantinople in 1204 by the Crusaders and the establishment of the Latin Empire, the monetary circulation in individual parts of the former Byzantine Empire was dominated by imitative billon trachea coinage of the types minted in the 12th century, with minor changes and errors.[12] These imitations gradually replaced the older Byzantine coins. In the following decades, there was a further reduction in the value of the billon currency in the former Empire while the state administration was not fully in control of coin production.

The market was flooded by large amounts of small module coins repeating the imitative types issued by the mints operating in Constantinople and

7. For instance, in Iatrus, cf. Schönert-Geiss 2007, 381, cat. no. 1623; see also nos. 1624–26, or in Svishtov (Kaleto), cf. Hensel et al. 1965, 264, Fig. 20.2.

8. Salamon 1987, 243.

9. Cf. Hendy 1969, 200.

10. See Dimitrova-Chudilova 2008.

11. Hendy 1985, 519, 520; cf. Laiou 2012; Salamon 1987, 278.

12. Yordanov 1984, 59–66; Hendy 1969, 199–217.

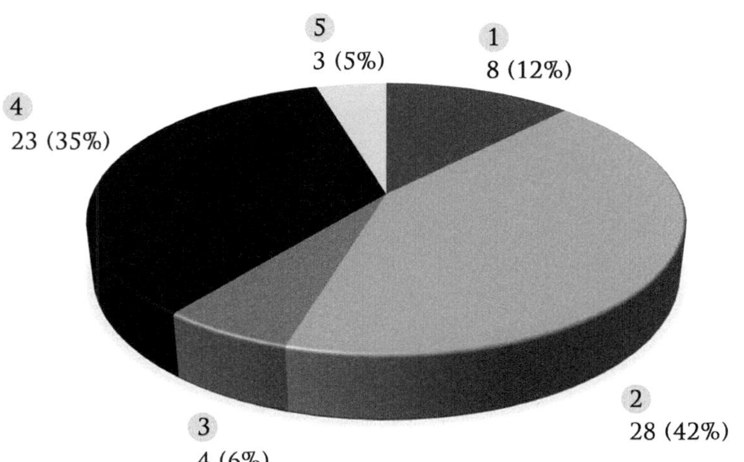

Fig. 101. Structure of the billon trachea found at Ostrite Mogili in 2000 and 2014 (by P. Jaworski).

Thessaloniki. Moreover, in the Kingdom of Bulgaria, considerable amounts of imitations of metropolitan emissions of Manuel I, Isaac II and Alexios III[13] were introduced into circulation, collectively referred to as "Bulgarian" imitations. According to I. Yordanov, imitations constitute at least 90% of the coins in circulation in Bulgaria in 1203–61.[14]

All the billon trachea from ca. 1200–41 discovered at Ostrite Mogili were found in the western part of the site, where a significant number of medieval pottery fragments was also noted,[15] in two small ploughed fields explored through metal detector searches. The saturation of both fields with scyphates was very high (**Fig. 98**), sometimes creating the impression that we were dealing here with a hoard scattered on the surface as a result of agricultural activities. Although the hoard from Svishtov (**Table II**), consisting of 300 billon trachea,[16] shows some similarities with the group of finds from Ostrite Mogili, the above presumption is not currently based on sufficiently strong grounds.

An attempt to define, even approximately, the chronological range for the circulation of the coins discovered at Ostrite Mogili which could support the dating of the settlement functioning there in the Middle Ages[17] requires some explanation. Among the single finds from the Veliko Turnovo area, where the coin appears around 1150 after a break,[18] one can notice, as in the case of the finds from Ostrite Mogili, an increased influx of the billon trachea minted in the years 1208–30.[19] A characteristic feature of the coin finds from this period in Bulgaria is the existence of evidence for the progressive devaluation of billon denominations, due to the lack of effective state control over imitative production. According to Yordanov, a further deterioration in the quality of the coin alloy in the 13th century, in practice already made of copper, became impossible. Therefore, practices aimed at reducing the weight of coins were introduced, involving cutting their edges (in the 1230s) and fragmentation (in the 1250s and 1260s).[20] In extreme cases, the smallest trachea fractions weigh 0.4–0.5 g (in Ostrite Mogili even 0.33 g). After 1241, hoards containing clipped and fragmented coins were concentrated primarily in central, northern, and southern Bulgaria.[21] The widespread use of this small change in everyday transactions in even small settlements is confirmed, for example, in Seuthopolis.[22] It seems reasonable to assume that a similar manifestation of the monetization of the local market is also present at the Ostrite Mogili settlement. According to Yordanov, the crisis of coin denominations was overcome only in the 1270s and 1280s, with the introduction of coins into circulation under Micho and Constantine Asen in Bulgaria and Michael VIII Palaiologos in Byzantium.[23] Taking into account the fragmentation of a significant part of the coin finds from Ostrite Mogili (cf. **Table I**), as well as the lack in the discussed evidence of the Byzantine series from the 12th century, issues minted by the Bulgarian rulers in the second half of the 13th century or any other later coins, it is possible to date the use of the coins in the settlement at Ostrite

13. Hendy 1969, 219; Yordanov 1984, 60, 61.
14. Yordanov 1984, 59.
15. Tomas 2006, 116.
16. Yordanov 1984, 203, 204 (no. 159).
17. On certain aspects of the Medieval past of Novae and its surroundings, including Ostrite Mogili, see, i.a., Tomas 2017, 78; Dyczek 2008; Tomas 2006, *passim*; Lemke 2005; Hensel et al. 1965, *passim*.
18. Morrisson 2002, Fig. 6.13.
19. Dochev 1992, 22–68; Yordanov 1984, 106, 107 and 114; see Table IV.
20. Yordanov 1984, 116.
21. Among others, a hoard from Draganovo (Buchvarov 1983).
22. Yordanov 1984, 118.
23. Ibidem.

Mogili with some caution to between the fourth and sixth decades of the 13th century.[24] This dating, made on the basis of the interpretation of monetary finds, may to some extent provide a premise for further reflections on the dating of the Medieval settlement at this site.

24. Cf. the dating of Bulgarian hoards deposited in 1230–61: Yordanov 1984, 117 (Table VI).

Table I. Weight structure of the billon trachea finds from Ostrite Mogili (L – larger module. M – middle module. S – smaller module).

Group	Total number			Condition						Average weight (g)						Weight range (g)					
	Module			Full			Clipped/ cut			Full			Clipped/cut			Full			Clipped/cut		
	L	M	S	L	M	S	L	M	S	L	M	S	L	M	S	L	M	S	L	M	S
„Bulgarian" imitative	–	–	8	–	–	4	–	–	4	–	–	1.43	–	–	0.98	–	–	0.63–2,05	–	–	0.67–1.32
Latin imitative Constantinople	9	1	18	–	1	9	6	–	12	–	2.06	1.12	0.86	–	0.73	–	2,06	0.71–2,01	0.43–1.27	–	0.33–1.46
Latin imitative Thessalonica	–	–	4	–	–	4	–	–	–	–	–	1.21	–	–	–	–	–	1.03–1.36	–	–	–
Latin imitative uncertain	–	–	23	–	–	5	–	–	18	–	–	1.09	–	–	0.48	–	–	0,66–1.78	–	–	0.17–0.84
Theodore I Lascaris, Nicaea	–	–	2	–	–	2	–	–	–	–	–	0.85	–	–	–	–	–	0,60–1.09	–	–	–
Theodore, Thessalonica	1	–	–	–	–	–	1	–	–	–	–	–	0.77	–	–	–	–	–	0.77	–	–

Table II. Identifiable billon trachea from the hoard found in Svishtov (after Yordanov 1984).

Type	Module	Number of specimens	Remarks
"Bulgarian" imitative			
C	S	6	–
Latin imitative – Constantinople			
A	S	60	–
B	S	2	–
C	S	3	–
E	S	1	–
H	L	1	–
N	L	1	clipped
P	L	1	–
R	L	2	clipped
S	S	1	–
T	S	5	–
III	S	1	–
VI	S	1	–
Latin imitative - Thessalonica			
A	S	1	–
C	S	2	–
Theodore I, Lascaris – Nicaea			
1st coinage	S	2	–
Theodore I, Lascaria – Magnesia			
B	S	1	–
John III, Ducas-Vatatzes - Magnesia			
G	L	1	–
Theodore, Comnenus-Ducas – Thessalonica			
A	M	1	–
B	L	1	cut (1/2)
Manuel, Comnenus-Ducas – Thessalonica			
G	M	1	–
G	S	1	–

Catalogue

The catalogue (**Table III**) contains descriptions of all coins belonging to the category of billon trachea dated to the first half of the 13th century found during the field surveys carried out in Ostrite Mogili in 2000 and 2014 by the expeditions of the University of Warsaw. The coins were divided into four main groups: 1. "Bulgarian" imitations (1200–18); Latin imitations from mints operating in: 2. Constantinople (1208–41) and 3. Thessaloniki (1208–24); 4. Latin imitations, whose typological attribution and provenance could not be determined due to their state of preservation. At the end of the list, there are two specimens of the Theodore Laskaris coin type issued in Nicaea (1208–22) and one specimen representing the coinage of Theodore Komnenos Doukas in Thessaloniki (1224–30). Each catalogue note contains the consecutive number, the field inventory number of the small finds, information about the module and the type represented, the weight and dimensions (measured along the short and long axes of the item), as well as comments on the condition of individual specimens. The catalogue is preceded by a list of abbreviations and the types of coins represented, along with a simplified description of the iconographic motifs on the obverse and reverse, as well as basic bibliographic references (Yordanov 1984, Hendy 1969). Photographs of all the copies were included in a 1:1 scale in separate tables, in the order used in this catalogue.

Abbreviations

l. – left
r. – right
Obv. – obverse
Rev. – reverse
L – larger module
M – medium-sized module
S – smaller module

List of types recorded at Ostrite Mogili

"Bulgarian" imitative (1200–1218)

S / Yordanov C/b; Hendy C	Obv. bust of Christ, scroll in l. hand Rev. emperor and St. Constantine, holding a globus cruciger between them, each holding a labarum-headed sceptre (either a scepter cruciger or a jewelled one) (Yordanov 1984, 52, 53, Pl. XXI.7–9; Hendy 1969, 218,Pl. 25.1–5)

Latin imitative – Constantinople (1208–1241)

S / Yordanov A/b; Hendy A	Obv. Virgin seated upon a throne Rev. emperor, holding a labarum on a long shaft in r. hand, and an anexikakia in the l. one (Yordanov 1984, 53, Pl. XXII.3; Hendy 1969, 198, Pl. 29.1–3)
L / Yordanov A/a; Hendy A	Obv. ditto Rev. ditto (Yordanov 1984, 53, Pl. XXII.1; Hendy 1969, 191, Pl. 25.6–10)
S / Yordanov B/b; Hendy B	Obv. Christ seated upon a throne Rev. emperor, holing a sword in r. hand, pointed downwards, and a globus cruciger in the l. one (Yordanov 1984, 53, 54, Pl. XXII.5; cf. Hendy 1969, 198, Pl. 29.4–6)
S / Yordanov D/b; Hendy –	Obv. bust of Christ, scroll in l. hand Rev. emperor, holding a scepter cruciger in r. hand, and a globus cruciger in the l. one (Yordanov 1984, 54, Pl. XXII.9; cf. Hendy 1969, 192, Pl. 25.14, 15)
L / Yordanov E/b; Hendy E	Obv. bust of Christ, scroll in l. hand Rev. emperor, holding a labarum-headed scepter in r. hand, and a globus surmounted by a patriarchal cross in the l. one (Yordanov 1984, 54, Pl. XXIII.1; cf. Hendy 1969, 192, Pl. 26.1)
S / Yordanov H/b; Hendy –	Obv. Virgin seated upon a throne Rev. emperor being crowned by Christ, holding labarum-headed scepter in r. hand, and a globus cruciger in l. one; Christ holding Gospels in l. hand (Yordanov 1984, 55, Pl. XXIII.8; cf. Hendy 1969, 193, Pl. 26.4, 5)
S / Yordanov N/b; Hendy –	Obv. Virgin orans Rev. emperor and St. George, holding between them a patriarchal cross on a long shaft and three steps; Saint holding sword, pointed downward (Yordanov 1984, 56, Pl. XXIV.6; cf. Hendy 1969, 194, 195, Pl. 26.14, 15)
L / Yordanov N/b; Hendy N	Obv. ditto Rev. ditto (Yordanov 1984, 56, Pl. XXIV.5; Hendy 1969, 194, 195, Pl. 26.14, 15)
M / Yordanov O/b; Hendy –	Obv. Christ standing on a dais, r. hand raised in benediction, Gospels in l. hand Rev. emperor, holding a labarum on a long shaft in r. hand, and a globus cruciger in the l. one (Yordanov 1984, 56, Pl. XXIV.8; cf. Hendy 1969, 195, Pl. 27.1, 2)

S / Yordanov P/b; Hendy –	Obv. bust of Christ, scroll in l. hand Rev. Archangel Michael, holding a jewelled scepter in r. hand, and a globus cruciger in the l. one (Yordanov 1984, 56, Pl. XXIV.10; cf. Hendy 1969, 195, Pl. 27.3, 4)
L / Yordanov R; Hendy R	Obv. Christ seated upon throne Rev. Virgin orans (Yordanov 1984, 56, Pl. XXIV.11; Hendy 1969, 196, Pl. 27.6, 7)
S / Yordanov III; Hendy –	Obv. Archangel Michael, holding a spear in r. hand, and a shield in the l. one Rev. emperor seated upon throne, holding a scepter in r. hand, and a globus cruciger in the l. one (Yordanov 1984, 58, Pl. XXVI.5, 6)

Latin imitative – Thessaloniki (1208–1224)

S / Yordanov A/b; Hendy D	Obv. Christ seated upon throne Rev. half-length figure of emperor, holding a scepter cruciger in r. hand, and a globus cruciger in the l. one (Yordanov 1984, 57, pl. XXV.7, cf. XXXIX.7; Hendy 1969, 198, Pl. 29.10–12)
S / Yordanov B/b; Hendy E	Obv. bust of Christ Emmanuel (bearded), scroll in l. hand Rev. emperor, holding a labarum-headed scepter in r. hand, and a globus cruciger in the l. one (Yordanov 1984, 57, Pl. XXV.10; Hendy 1969, 198, Pl. 29.13–15)

Theodore I, Lascaris – Nicaea (1208–1222)

S / Yordanov, 1st coinage/b;	Obv. Virgin seated upon throne Hendy G (Latin imitative) Rev. emperor and St. Theodore, holding a patriarchal cross on a long shaft between them; emperor holding a labarum-headed scepter in r. hand, saint holding a spear in l. hand, resting on his shoulder (Yordanov 1984, 66, 67, Pl. XVII.2; Hendy 1969, 199, Pl. 29.19, 20)

Theodore, Comnenus-Ducas – Thessalonike (1224–1230)

L / Yordanov A; Hendy A	Obv. bust of Christ Emmanuel (beardless), scroll in l. hand Rev. emperor and St. Demetrius, holding a cross within a circle between them, surmounting a triangular decoration on a long shaft; Saint holding a sword in l. hand, resting on his shoulder (Yordanov 1984, 78, 79, Pl. XXXII.1, 2; Hendy 1969, 269, Pl. 37.7–9)

Table III. Catalogue of billon trachea found at Ostrite Mogili.

No	Inv. No	Module	Type	Weight (g)	Dim. (mm)	Remarks
"Bulgarian" imitative						
1	54/14w	S	Yordanov C/b; Hendy C	2.05	17 × 19	–
2	36/00w	S	ditto	1.73	14 × 16	–
3	88/14w	S	ditto	1.31	20 × 20	–
4	71/14w	S	ditto	1.32	14 × 18	clipped
5	97/14w	S	ditto	1.20	13 × 18	clipped
6	69/14w	S	ditto	0.74	11 × 15	clipped
7	62/14w	S	ditto	0.67	11 × 13	overstruck, clipped
8	65/14w	S	ditto	0.63	18 × 20	overstruck
Latin imitative – Constantinople						
9	48/14w	S	Yordanov A/b; Hendy A	1.29	17 × 18	–
10	49/14w	S	ditto	1.17	15 × 21	–
11	98/14w	S	ditto	0.92	15 × 20	–
12	40/14w	S	ditto	0.71	14 × 17	–
13	91/14w	S	ditto	0.87	16 × 17	clipped
14	109/14w	L	Yordanov A/a; Hendy A	1.03	13 × 18	folded edge, clipped
15	95/14w	S	Yordanov B/b; Hendy B	0.79	17 × 20	reverse double struck
16	67/14w	S	ditto	0.57	12 × 15	clipped
17	34/00w	S	Yordanov D/b; Hendy –	1.46	17 × 18	clipped
18	80/14w	S	ditto	1.12	13 × 16	clipped
19	66/14w	S	ditto	0.86	12 × 13	clipped

20	84/14w	S	ditto	0.53	9 × 15	clipped
21	60/14w	S	ditto	0.45	10 × 15	clipped
22	55/14w	S	ditto	0.39	10 × 12	folded edge, clipped
23	110/14w	L	Yordanov E/b; Hendy E	0.43	11 × 13	cut (1/4)
24	50/14w	S	Yordanov H/b; Hendy –	0.39	10 × 18	clipped
25	112/14w	S	Yordanov N/b; Hendy –	1.21	16 × 17	–
26	37/00w	S	ditto	1.05	12 × 15	–
27	52/14w	S	ditto	0.90	15 × 16	–
28	81/14w	L	Yordanov N/b; Hendy N	1.03	13 × 15	clipped
29	51/14w	M	Yordanov O/b; Hendy –	2.06	24 × 25	–
30	41/14w	S	ditto	2.01	20 × 22	–
31	74/14w	S	Yordanov P/b; Hendy –	1.30	15 × 16	clipped
32	68/14w	S	ditto	0.56	9 × 16	clipped
33	86/14w	L	Yordanov R; Hendy R	1.27	13 × 18	clipped
34	53/14w	L	ditto	0.75	12 × 13	clipped
35	113/14w	L	ditto	0.65	15 × 16	clipped
36	73/14w	S	Yordanov III; Hendy –	0.33	10 × 12	clipped
Latin imitative – Thessaloniki						
37	43/14w	S	Yordanov A/b; Hendy D	1.33	19 × 22	–
38	38/14w	S	ditto	1.14	17 × 19	–
39	96/14w	S	ditto	1.03	15 × 20	–
40	46/14w	S	Yordanov B/b; Hendy E	1.36	15 × 20	–
Latin imitative – uncertain mint and type						
41	44/14w	S	–	0.91	15 × 16	Rev.: emperor and saint (?)
42	42/14w	S	–	0.66	13 × 16	Rev.: emperor holds globus cruciger
43	77/14w	S	–	0.35	10 × 16	Rev. emperor holds labarum, clipped
44	90/14w	S	–	0,93	13 × 15	Rev. emperor (?)
45	93/14w	S	–	0,70	17 × 21	Rev. emperor (?), clipped
46	47/14w	S	–	0,51	11 × 14	Rev. emperor (?), clipped
47	72/14w	S	–	0,39	10 × 18	Rev. emperor (?), clipped
48	70/14w	S	–	0,23	9 × 20	Rev. emperor (?), clipped
49	59/14w	S	–	0,84	14 × 19	Obv. Archangel (?), folded edge, clipped
50	89/14w	S	–	0,68	10 × 11	Obv. bust of Christ, clipped
51	85/14w	S	–	0,54	11 × 11	Obv. bust of Christ, clipped
52	64/14w	S	–	1,78	13 × 18	struck off center
53	101/14w	S	–	1,16	16 × 16	–
54	114/14w	S	–	0,78	15 × 15	folded edge, clipped
55	103/14w	S	–	0,54	16 × 17	folded edge, clipped
56	87/14w	S	–	0,54	11 × 14	clipped
57	78/14w	S	–	0,47	9 × 9	clipped
58	99/14w	S	–	0,44	9 × 13	clipped
59	108/14w	S	–	0,41	10 × 14	folded edge, clipped
60	106/14w	S	–	0,36	8 × 10	clipped
61	104/14w	S	–	0,35	7 × 11	folded edge, clipped
62	105/14w	S	–	0,35	11 × 15	clipped
63	107/14w	S	–	0,17	10 × 13	clipped, broken
Theodore I, Lascaris – Nicaea						
64	58/14w	S	Yordanov, 1st coinage/b; Hendy G (Latin imit.)	1,09	18 × 19	–
65	82/14w	S	ditto	0,60	15 × 16	–
Theodore, Comnenus-Ducas – Thessaloniki						
66	45/14w	L	Yordanov A; Hendy A	0,77	12 × 17	clipped

Pl. LI. Billon trachea from Area B

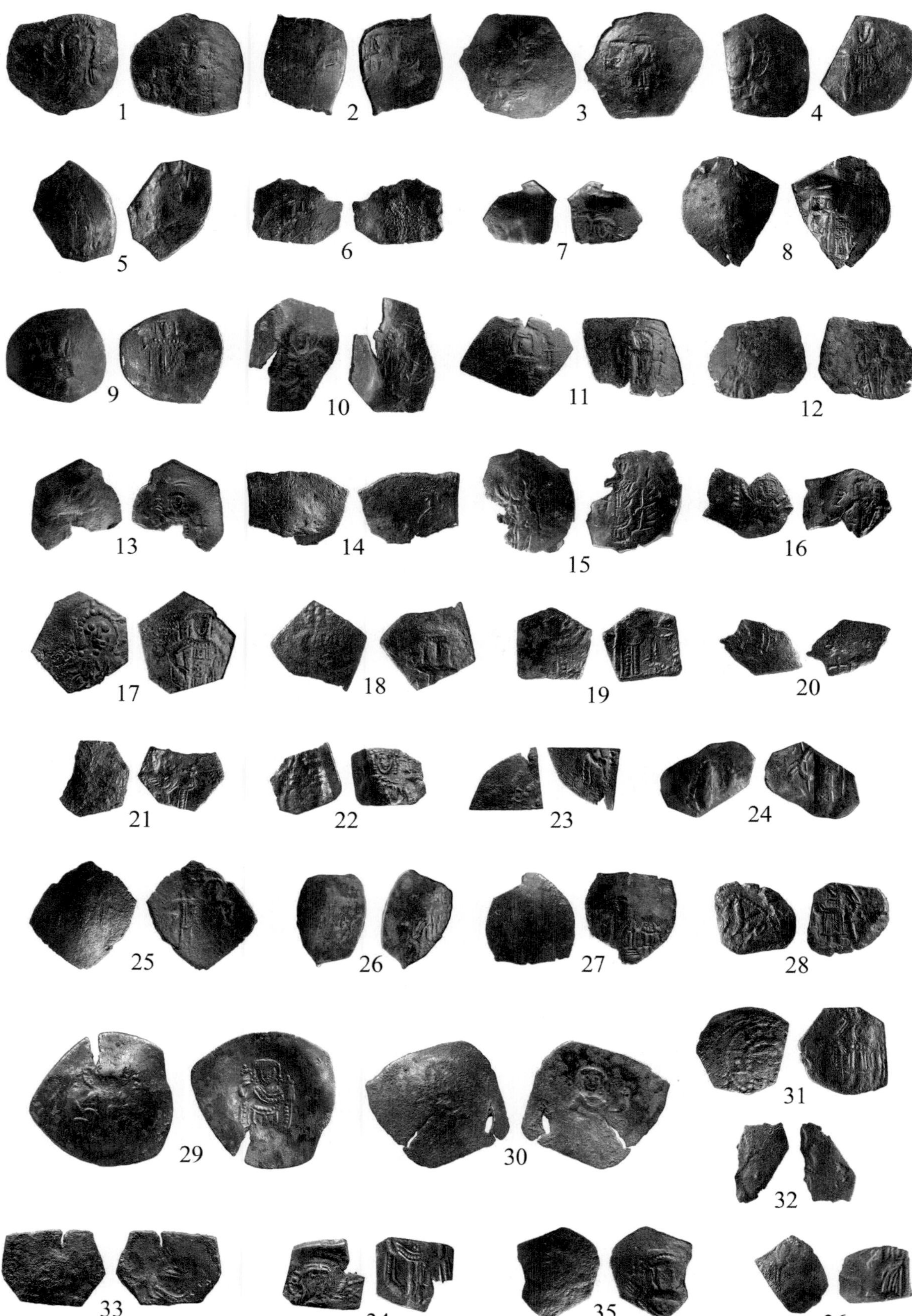

Pl. LII. Billon trachea from Area B

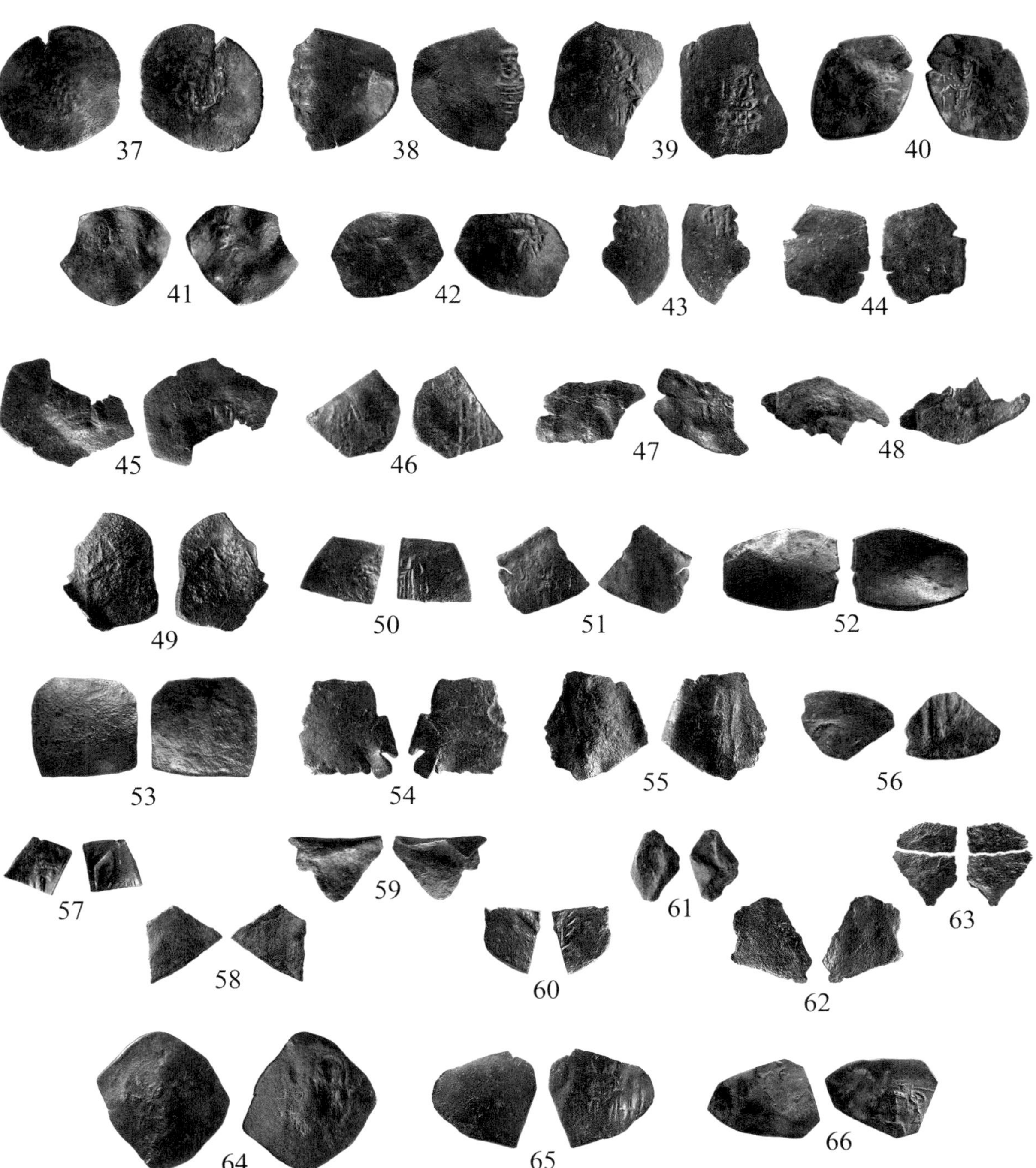

17. Medieval heart-shaped copper alloy find from Ostrite Mogili

Paweł Janik

One copper alloy item found in 2013 might be attributed to non-Roman settlement. The attribution of this find is difficult and disputable, for example, due to the fact that it was collected with metal detectors from a humus layer; however, its shape and decoration has some analogies with non-Roman finds. Therefore, it can be linked rather to nomads than to Roman settlement.

The find under discussion is a heart-shaped copper alloy cast appliqué, which is 1.3 cm high and 1.6 cm wide (**Fig. 102**). On the front side, its edges are bold and the central part is slightly convex. Most probably the concavity is a poorly preserved palmetto or antithetic floral ornament. On the back side, it is provided with two protruding spikes, which could have been used for attaching.

Decorated belts were very distinctive and important element of the material culture of nomads in Medieval Europe. A belt and various utensils attached to it (like drinking horns, bags, scabbards, quivers, etc.) were indicators of their owner's social position and were decorated with metal or organic appliqués. In the Danubian lands, heart-shaped decorations found, for example, in Pliska, Preslav,[1] the early Medieval site of Gradishteto near Yakimovo village[2] (**Fig. 104A**) or Sturmen on the Yantra foothills,[3] and are dated to as early as the beginning of the 9th century. They remained in fashion until the 11th century, when belt decorations were especially popular. Although places of manufacturing heart-shaped appliqués have been identified in present-day Bulgaria near the villages of Nadarevo, Novosel and Zlatar in the Shoumen district,[4] they are not considered local forms, typical for the Danubian lands. However, the metal find should not be considered as certain proof of proto-Bulgarian

Fig. 102. Heart-shaped fitting from Ostrite Mogili; copper alloy (phot. P. Jaworski).

1. Vitlyanov 2003, 429 and 436, Figs. 3.19 and 28.
2. Milchev 1963, 34, Fig.12.
3. Hensel 1980,124, 152, Fig. 53.182.
4. Nikolov 2011.

Fig. 103. Heart-shaped fittings. Geszteréd, Szabolcs-Szatmár-Bereg county, Hungary (grave find); silver (after Fodor 1996, 80-81, Fig. 9.). Not to scale.

Fig. 104. Heart-shaped fittings. A. Gradishteto near Yakimovo village, Bulgaria (find from the foothill); gilded bronze (after Milchev 1963, 34, Fig. 12; B - Heart-shaped fittings. Nagykörü, Jász-Nagykun-Szolnok county, Hungary (unknown context); silver (after Fodor 1996, 243, Fig. 4.). Not to scale.

presence on the site. It might be a local imitation. The appliqué from Ostrite Mogili resembles belt decorations known, e.g., from Geszteréd[5] (**Fig. 103**), Nagykörü[6] (**Fig. 104B**), Szolnok,[7] and Kecel[8] in Hungary. Proto-Bulgarians most probably copied heart-shaped decorations, extremely popular among the culture of north and north-eastern nomads. The most numerous finds are known from areas related to nomadic Hungarians in the Carpathian Valley and Eastern Europe,[9] the Khazaria,[10] and Rus.[11]

According to Doncheva-Petkova, heart-shaped appliqués were symbols of their owners' military position,[12] but it is very difficult to verify such a hypothesis. Most probably they were simply decorations, which may have indicated their owners' social position. Items made from gold or silver have also been identified. Most frequently, however, such items were copper alloy cast.

Fittings of this kind, along with other decorated items, such as head decorations (*prochelniki*) from south-eastern Bulgaria and Macedonia,[13] belong to the 9th–10th-century palmette style horizon, distinctive for nomadic Hungarians,[14] Khazaria, i.e., the Saltovo-Mayaki culture,[15] Volga Bulgaria,[16] and Rus.[17]

One cannot exclude that the popularity of such plaques was the result of contacts with Kievan Rus, which had strong connections with the Magyars, expressed, for example, in many jewellery finds.[18]

Despite the fact that this fitting has analogies in many areas and is very similar to the Hungarian ones, in my opinion, this plaque probably is of Danubian proto-Bulgarian origin or is a local (Danubian Slavs/autochthons) imitation, because this kind of ornament was produced (manufactured?) in the First Bulgarian Empire. Taking into consideration the fact that a Medieval settlement at Ostrite Mogili is also attested by finds of pottery and coins, the discussed appliqué can be attributed to the proto-Bulgarian and nomadic traditions. The appliqué, similarly as with the discovered coins, but contrary to the pottery made on the spot, may have been brought from more distant places.

5. Fodor 1996, 80–81, Fig. 9.
6. Fodor 1996, 243, Fig. 4.
7. Fodor 1996, 284, Fig.2.
8. Fodor 1996, 324–25, Fig.2.
9. Genning and Halikov 1964, 78, Fig. 21.17; Milchev 1963, 33.
10. Pletneva 1967, 163, Fig. 44.18 and 165, Fig. 45.7.
11. Sedov 1982, 282, Tab. LXIX,7; Fodor 1977, Taf. XII.5
12. Doncheva-Petkova 1992, 210.
13. Grigorov 2003, 29–38; 2004, 61–62.
14. Fodor 1996, 32–35.
15. Pletneva 1967, 163, Fig. 44.
16. Halikov 1985, 99, Tab. XXXVII.
17. Sedov 1982, 282, Tab. LXIX.
18. Dąbrowska 1979, 163; Fodor 1996, 33.

VII

Summary and conclusions

Agnieszka Tomas

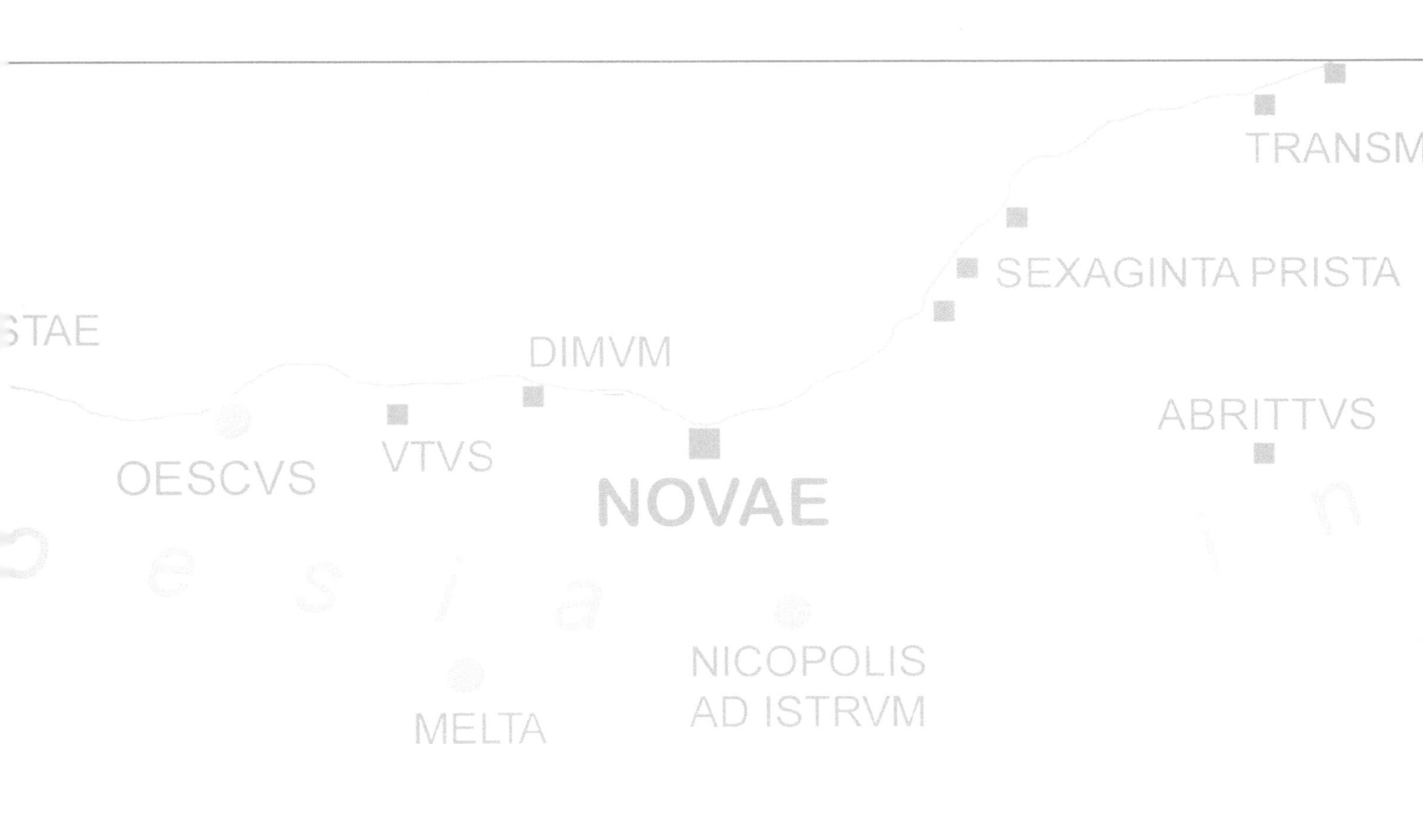

1. Summary

After an attempt to depict the rural hinterland of Novae in 2016,[1] it was a natural choice to take a closer look at the vicinity of the fortress. Novae is an extremely difficult site for non-invasive methods (see Chapter I), especially geophysical measurements, which turned out to not bring the unequivocal results we had expected. However, the surroundings deserve to be surveyed, since no fortress can function without an environment that provides a logistic base (for general remarks, see Chapter II). The vicinity of the fortress provides data necessary to develop a true and complete picture of the economic, social and strategic importance of the military base. Credible conclusions concerning the history of Novae and of its close surroundings require many years of multi-faceted research. We hope that despite the limits imposed on us during the research project, the data we obtained over a six-week period will be helpful in reconstructing the past of Novae and its people.

The past environment

The continental climate with a dry and very warm summer and cold winter has not changed much since Antiquity.[2] The palaeo-environmental analyses (Chapter III) show that the ancient fauna and flora at Novae during the Roman period has also not changed significantly since then. Enclaves of mixed oak-hornbeam forests and mixed broadleaf forests with clusters of pine, oak, linden and hornbeam grew on the hills to the south of the fortress, while alluvial forests with oak, elm, ash and willows grew in the valleys, the same as today (**Fig. 8**). Dry, open steppe vegetation attested in the ancient layers could be observed to the south of Novae, while the pollen of plants growing on wet meadows and pastures is typical for the other side of the Danube.

Apart from conifer, which grows on the nearby hills even today, other conifers – fir trees and spruce, as well as beech present in the samples dated to the late Flavian and Trajanic periods could have floated downriver from mountainous areas, e.g., from the Iron Gates. The wood of trees growing in the mountains could have been used for the roofing in the Flavian wood-and-earth camp and in investments made during Trajanic building activities. Common local trees, such as pine, oak and linden, were used in the 4th century, while the long-distance transport of trees is attested only by the presence of spruce.

The analyses of a sample taken from the layer considered to be virgin soil were most surprising. The almost pure yellowish or light brownish loess identified in the *retentura* (**Fig. 10**) as a geological layer[3] turned out to contain the seeds of olives, lentil and grapes. Burials dated to the Bronze Age and the Early Iron Age finds were recorded during the excavations of the eastern defensive walls in the 1960s.[4] However, finds which could be related to pre-Roman settlement are dated to no later than the 3rd century BC, while the period preceding Roman conquest is marked only by single tetradrachms commissioned by the Romans between the second half of the 2nd century and the 80s BC with no structural remains of settlement.[5] These inconclusive results require further analysis.

The layers dated to the 1st century AD show that cereals and grapes were cultivated here both before and after the arrival of the Romans. The hand-formed vessel found in the Flavian context in the *retentura* (**Fig. 11**) most probably contained grapes. Millet and peas were also known before the arrival of the Romans, but buckwheat found in the same sample indicates rather Roman trade with the northern Black Sea region. Lettuce found in the earliest dated layer near the northern defensive wall (**Fig. 9**)[6] could have been brought there and cultivated by the Romans. Olives and figs were commonly traded by the Romans and transported in amphorae from the Mediterranean areas.[7] The various cereals and legumes (lentil, peas) found in almost all the layers at Novae can be regarded as quite common in the Roman diet, especially the military one.[8]

The goals and the methods

The goals of our investigations were twofold: 1) to collect the broadest possible spectrum of archaeological data to create a database of the settlement remains; and 2) to find out whether the idea of an applied settlement pattern, where two civil settlements develop near a legionary fortress outside an area with a radius of 1 *leuga* (2.22 km),[9] could be

1. Tomas 2016. This book published in 2016, which collected the available publications on the topic, was based on my PhD thesis completed in 2007 at the University of Warsaw under the supervision of Prof. Tadeusz Sarnowski.
2. Tomas 2016, 7–8.
3. For the results of these excavations, see Sarnowski et al. 2016, 188.
4. Chichikova 1980, 60.
5. Tomas 2017, 38; Tomas 2018, 13–15; cf. Dimitrov 2013a, 728–30; Paunov 2013, Fig. 5.2.
6. On the excavations in this sector, see Sarnowski, Kovalevskaja, and Tomas 2010.
7. Davies 1971, 128–31; Thomas and Stalibrass 2008, 5.
8. Davies 1971, 126 and 133; Roth 1999, 18–24 and 25–26.
9. An idea first presented by Ioan Piso (1991), and later discussed in other scholarly literature, presented here in Chapter II.

traced archaeologically at Novae. To achieve these aims, we analysed sattellite imagery, collected finds, verified the places where archaeological remains had been previously reported, and chose particular sites to make more detailed investigations.

Due to the obstacles caused by the present shape of the terrain, agricultural and human activities, at the beginning of the project we had to establish a combination of various methods that would be applied in different places and prepare a research programme for the six weeks of our planned fieldwork (Chapter IV). With two weeks and 14 people available in all the three seasons, this task was extremely difficult, but we felt motivated by the critical situation the site was facing. 2012 was the last year before the creation of the Archaeological Park which changed the character of the central part of Novae. In addition, in 2012, a great part of the Ostrite Mogili site, which back in 2000 had been an open field (**Fig. 41**), was already divided into smaller private lots, making archaeological investigations more difficult. Over the last twenty years, we have also observed the dramatic effects of looting, both inside and outside the fortress, as well as at Ostrite Mogili.

The analysis of the satellite imagery, aerial photographs and personal visits to the site enabled the choice of several spots for further investigation. These places were named as follows: Area A1 (the southern part of the annexe and a field just outside it), Area B (the *vicus* at Ostrite Mogili), Areas C1 and C2 (the *canabae* outside the West Gate), Area D (the fields on both sides of the Dermen dere), Area E (the Chehlarski geran site to the south of Ostrite Mogili) and Area F (Kanlu cheshme, the hypothetical farmhouse to the south-east of the fortress). Additionally, Area A2 was defined as encompassing some grassy terrain in the *retentura dextra* for the purpose of carrying out geophysical measurements, which would allow us to verify the effectiveness of the method. Large fields to the south of Novae, which turned out to be settlement voids, came to be referred to as N1 and N2 (**Fig. 15**). In 2012–14, a total area covering ca. 90 ha was investigated, including 13.95 ha of geophysical investigations and 2 ha of detailed mapping.

Ceramic vessel sherds were so numerous in many of the surveyed areas that we decided not to map them during our surveys and collected only distinct fragments showing the variety of finds and groups of fabric. The pottery was elaborated according to the standards used during the excavations of the Faculty of Archaeology University of Warsaw Expedition. The groups of wares were defined during excavations before the start of our project and applied during fieldwalking surveys (Chapter VI.2, **Tab. I**). Glass and terracotta finds were mapped, as were metal finds collected with the use of metal detectors on a chosen set of grids (**Fig. 21**). Metal waste was also collected in order to estimate the level of metal pollution.

General prospection results

The results of geophyscial prospection, as well as the remains of architecture and other more significant mapped finds were put into a GIS database. Such a database required developing a new precise plan of the site, in particular of the late Roman fortifications excavated until the late 1960s and never measured with modern measuring instruments. Aerial orthophotomaps (**Figs. 23–26**) were very helpful in estimating the condition of the site, as well as in finding architectural remains not visible on the ground (**Fig. 33**). Additionally, they verified the old plans. Accurate measurements with the use of GPS RTK and total station continued up to 2018, and the figures included in this publication show the plan of the fortress recreated up to that year (**Figs. 5, 6 and 28**). The measurements taken along the late Roman fortifications of the annexe allowed the area they surrounded to be established as amounting to 8.85 ha, which added to the surface of the former *castra* (17.99 ha) corresponds to about 26.84 ha of the late Roman Novae (**Figs. 5, 28**). A town with such an area can be categorized among the group of medium-sized late Roman urban settlements: in Gaul, towns occupied only a part of the former towns of Principate and were comparable to Novae – Orleans 30 ha, Lyon 21, Vienne 20, Arles perhaps 17.[10] When compared to other Moesian towns of the provincial interior, Novae is among the bigger towns (but not the biggest), along with Nicopolis ad Istrum, whose size has not changed since its foundation (22.55 ha): Abritus covered an area of 10 ha, Tropaeum Traiani – 10.5, Ibida – 17, while Oescus enlarged its area (28 ha).[11]

Simultaneously, we have tried to estimate the size of the *canabae*. The field walkings around the fortress done systematically since the autumn of 2011 with the use of a hand-held GPS receiver, enabled the surface of the area to be established where the archaeological materials are visible on the ground as ca. 70–80 ha (**Fig. 27**).[12] This area, however, does not correspond to the size of the *canabae*, but only to the spread of the finds. It is not possible to estimate how big the fortress settlement was, but at least

10. Poulter 1983-84, 110; Liebeschuetz 2001, 84.
11. Poulter 1983-84, 111, 121; Ivanov and Kovacheva 2002, 32.
12. Tomas 2017, 41–42.

30–40 ha is quite possible. The settlement stretched along the roads outside *porta principalis sinistra* (West Gate) and *porta decumana* (South Gate).

The survey of the areas outside the West and South Gates was very limited due to the presence of private properties, but we were able to investigate some open fields placed among these properties (Areas C1, C2, **Fig. 30**), as well as to see pottery sherds and worked stone along the roads and inside the properties. On the Danubian bank, we found the remains of a structure which most probably belonged to the western aqueduct (**Figs. 31, 32**), the same as two other structures documented earlier.[13] The southern part of the annexe and the extramural areas outside of it were the most easily available for the investigations in 2012–14 (**Fig. 34**). The annexe (Area A2) together with a part of the *retentura dextra (*Area A1) were the subject of geophysical investigations, while Area A2 also of a more detailed mapping of metal finds. Some architectural remains were documented in the illegal trenches (**Fig. 35, 38**). The remains of the mithraeum, located to the south-east of the fortress and excavated in the 1980s, were again unearthed and documented precisely (**Fig. 39, 40**).[14]

Settlement duality is observed at Novae, with the second settlement 2.7 km east of the locus gromae (2.5 km outside the East Gate) when measured in a straight line (Area B). It is quite obvious that the distance between the fortress and the *vicus* definitely does not correspond either with one leuga (2.22 km) or 1.5 of a Roman mile, which would be the equivalent of one *leuga*. Secondly, the shape of the terrain at the mouth of the Dermen dere does not allow for building a straight road. If the ancient road ran more or less the same course as today, for a pedestrian another 500–700 m must be added, which makes 3–3.2 km the real distance from the East Gate to Ostrite Mogili (**Fig. 7**).

The *vicus* was not large – it must have covered no more than 15 ha, perhaps even less (**Figs. 41, 44**). The presence of buildings is confirmed by the increased amount of building materials recorded in the eastern and central parts of the site (**Figs. 42, 43**) and the anomalies visible on the image obtained from the geophysical measurements, while a burial was found in the western part, near the road (**Fig. 106**). Illegal trenches were recorded all over the site (**Fig. 25**), with one of them containing the remains of a wall with two fragments of an inscription (**Fig. 45**). However, it is worth noting that some settlements had been reported in the past, including near Tsarevets, 3 km to the south of Novae, but now this area has been overbuilt and the sites destroyed.[15] The area was not included in our project; thus, it cannot be excluded that some *vicus* existed to the south of Novae, especially since one of the bigger water conduits supplied the liquid to some unknown place to the south of Novae.[16]

Although the existence of other sites near Novae was marked in older publications and their location was not very precise, some places are still locatable today and we have tried to find them and to measure the distances from the *castra*. Traces of settlement were found in a spot located at a distance of 800 m to the south-west of the *vicus* (Area E). Some pottery, building materials and other finds were collected there; it is possible there was a farmhouse which existed there in the Early Roman period. In turn, the hypothetical farmhouse at Kanlu cheshme (Area F, **Fig. 46**), surveyed in 1977, where two funerary monuments – one dated to the Severan period and one unepigraphic – were found,[17] lies ca. 2 km to the east of the South Gate. The verification of the site was disappointing – the remains are very modest now. The remains of a Dionysus shrine excavated by D. Mitova-Dzhonova in 1961[18] seem to be located some 2.1–2.2 km to the south-east of the South Gate in a straight line, which would be 1.5 Roman mile. But again, the shape of the terrain makes this distance longer for the pedestrian, up to 2.5 km. This place turned out to be completely unavailable for prospection.

In spring 2013, during the rescue excavations carried out in the *principia* before the construction of the Archaeological Park, a skeletal burial was unearthed. The grave was documented (**Figs. 47, 48**) and tentatively dated to the 5th–6th century AD, but it will be the subject of a more detailed publication.

Geophysical investigations conducted in the *retentura* (Area A2) were promising (**Fig. 49**). The image obtained from the anomalies showed a street grid and the remains of buildings arranged in accordance with the fortress axis (**Fig. 50**). In the annexe (Area A1), the results were not so unequivocal. The anomalies were numerous, and the remains of buildings and of the occurrence of a fire were suggested, but the image turned out to be very difficult to interpret (**Figs. 51, 52**). Due to the high number of illegal trenches, geophysical investigations at Ostrite

13. For a discussion, see Tomas 2017, 54 with further literature.

14. Tomas and Lemke 2015.

15. Stefanov 1956, *passim;* Tomas 2016, 138–39.

16. Tomas 2016, 67 and Fig. 26A.

17. IGLNov 82; T. Sarnowski 1979.

18. Dzhonova 1961.

Mogili (Area B) were possible only in the eastern part of the site (**Fig. 53**). Architectural remains seem to be concentrated in the north-eastern part of the site, where we found the remains of a wall in one of the illegal trenches (**Figs. 54, 104**). Traces of robbery were also detected in this part of the site.

The more time-consuming electrical resistivity methods were applied on small lots near the extramural residence (Area C1, **Fig. 55**) and among the private lots to the south-west of the camp (Area C2, **Fig. 56**). The results were more easily readable and they showed the remains of some structures, including some buildings (**Fig. 57**). Geomagnetic methods were used on one of the fields to the south-east of the annexe (Area D, **Fig. 59**), but only traces of contemporary anthropogenic activities were detected. The same methods applied in Area E enabled the detection of some anomalies concentrated in one spot (**Figs. 60, 61**). Area F (Kanlu cheshme) provided plentiful anomalies, which can be presumed to be the relics of architecture in advanced stages of destruction (**Figs. 62, 63**). This stands in contrast with the almost complete lack of archaeological material visible on the ground.

The images acquired from the geophysical investigations inside the fortress are more easily readable than those from the extramural area, except for the electrical resistivity surveys conducted in the western part of the *canabae*. Perhaps one of the most important conclusions is that the poor readability of the images obtained in the extramural areas results from the fact that sandstone mixed with broken bricks was used in the extramural architecture, while the limestone used in the buildings inside the camp provides clearer images. Illegal trenching is an additional serious obstacle for geophysical methods.

Discussion on the finds related to the Roman occupation

Pottery was the most numerous group of finds collected during field surveys (Chapter VI.2, **Pl. II–XXII**). Fragments of handmade vessels (ware I), which are the same as those found in the 1st-century layers and pits in the camp, are proof of contacts between the Romans and the broadly understood indigenous population. Some of the fragments found during our prospection were hand-formed and wheel-thrown vessels (ware I). New technologies combined with Iron Age forms are good examples of acculturation, well known from the Boutovo pottery centre.[19]

This local hand-made pottery can be seen as proof of continuous local settlement at Novae and its environs before and after the Roman conquest.[20] Very similar vessels have been found in Oltenia on the other side of the Danube. At Novae, the same as in Upper Moesia, such pottery was found in the Flavian context. No such finds have been recorded in the 2nd-century layers at Novae, while they appear in the interior. From the first decades of the 2nd century onwards, pottery formed and decorated in the same manner was manufactured in the Boutovo and Pavlikeni centres, while also appearing in Nicopolis. This fact seems to be convergent with the Dacian names appearing in the area of Nicopolis ad Istrum, Novae and Durostorum.[21] Therefore, it is not without grounds that it can be concluded that the 1st-century handmade pottery found in Novae and its close surroundings were the product of displaced peoples moved from across the Danube in the 1st century AD,[22] and later resettled in the interior. On the northern side of the Danube, this type of pottery continued to be manufactured in the 2nd and 3rd centuries AD.[23]

Ware VI (burnished pottery) may also be linked to the trans-Danubian ethnos. In Novae it is much less frequent than ware I. This pottery is known from Muntenia, especially at sites identified with what is referred to as the Chilia-Militari culture.

Early tableware and kitchenware (wares II, III, V, and VIII) – both produced on the spot and imported – were collected from the areas outside the fortress. Wares II and III were most probably produced locally in the *canabae*, while wares V (*Orange burnished*) and VIII (*Norico-Pannonian coarse ware*), present in the early Flavian pits, may have been brought there from the Norico-Pannonian area.

Pottery and tableware produced in the Boutovo / Pavlikeni centres (wares XI – XIII) are the most numerous finds collected during our research, and they are also the most numerous finds obtained during excavations. In the 2nd century AD, another type of kitchenware appears, namely ware XIV (*Lower Danube Kaolin ware*), the mass quantities of which seem to have come from some none-too-distant manufacturing centre flourishing in the late 2nd and 3rd century AD. It is possible that these vessels were also produced in the *chora* of Nicopolis.

Although several fragments of late Roman pottery (wares XV–XVII) were collected in the *vicus* and nearby sites, they are very rare finds,

19. Soultov 1984, 186; 1985, 87–88; Tab. XLV.

20. Sarnowski 1986; Sarnowski 2009, 18–19; Chichikova 2013, esp. 228–34.

21. Matei-Popescu 2017, 149; Tomas 2017, 151

22. Tomas 2018.

23. Popilian 1976.

and this fact unequivocally indicates the shrinking of the extramural settlement and the collapse of the sites within a 3-km radius of the fortress.

Chapter VI.3, presenting the amphora fragments, presents a small sample only partially illustrating the variety of ceramic containers to be found at Novae (**Pl. XXIII–XXVI**).[24] The earliest amphorae are dated to the Flavian period, while the latest, and the least numerous, come from the 6th century. The most common types are amphorae Zeest 90 = Dressel 24 *similis* and Kapitän II originating from Asia Minor and the Aegean region. The second group is formed by local Soultov 1 type table amphorae/pitchers and amphorae with twisted-handles produced in the province. The high number of amphorae found in the *vicus* can be divided into two groups: locally manufactured Moesian containers and those imported from outside the province. The amphorae of the second group originate from distant areas – Spain, through the Adriatic coast, up to the Pontic coast, and Asia Minor.

Glass finds (Chapter VI.4, **Pl. XXVII–XXIX**) collected from the surface are usually in poor condition. Contrary to the past, when the area where Novae is located was referred to as Stuklen (in Bulgarian "stuklo" meaning "glass"), most probably due to the number of glass pieces visible on the surface, now ancient glass has become an increasingly less frequent surface find, mainly as a result of corrosion and human activity. In 2000, at Ostrite Mogili, production waste and glass fragments were mapped (**Fig. 67**), but in 2014 they were very rare. Glass finds were not collected in the annexe, as the fragments visible in 2012 were not diagnostic. The most durable of such items, and the most frequent, include goblet stems, as well as glass bracelet and window pane fragments.

Weapons and armour (Chapter VI.5, **Pl. XXX–XXXII**) are not surprising finds for a military site, but the distribution of the collected finds warrants some attention. Among the weapons, arrowheads are the most numerous finds, from the vicinity of the fortress (Areas A1, C2, **Fig. 68**), the *vicus* (Area B, **Fig. 70**), and the site to the south of it (Area E, **Fig. 71**). They form two quite well-recognizable groups in all these places dated to the late Roman period (3rd–6th century) and the Medieval period (10–11th century). Armour elements were found only in the annexe (**Fig. 69**), and they are dated to the 2nd and 3rd centuries AD.

24. Dyczek 2001.

Jewellery and cosmetic items (Chapter VI.6, **Pl. XXXIII–XXXIV**) were found in Area A1, B and E, but surprisingly the majority were collected in the annexe (**Figs. 72**, cf. **73**). Apart from jewellery finds typical for the region (lead mirrors, a ring, a hairpin, a bracelet), the discovered 2nd-century iron brooch of definitely Barbarian character was found. The bird-shaped ending of a pin or a stick found in the *vicus* is probably also related to the Gothic (or Barbarian in general) ethnos, but regrettably we do not understand its function. The copper alloy bracelet found in Area E was the best-quality find preserved there.

Other metal finds (Chapter VI.7, **Pl. XXXV–XXXVIII**) were very numerous and they seem to have been scattered across all of the investigated areas. Their concentrations visible in Areas A1 and B result from the fact that they come from the surveyed grids (**Figs. 74, 75**). Among these finds, knives and metal tools (especially from Area B) seem to be the most common. The remaining mass finds (almost all of them iron and lead), including metal waste were counted and photographed (**Figs. 76–78**). Surprisingly, modern metal pollution was mostly found in the extramural areas (Areas B, C2, E, F), but not in the annexe (Area A1), although the place has been used for agricultural purposes in modern times. It is quite noteworthy that local metal processing has been attested both in the fortress and in the *vicus* (Chapter VI.8, **Fig. 79**). Copper alloy processing is also attested indirectly by finds of cut metal objects.

Roman and Early Byzantine coins (Chapter VI.9, **Pl. XXXIX–XL**) have been analysed separately from the Medieval billon trachea (Chapter VI.16). Eight coins dated to the late 2nd and 3rd century were found in Area A2; their distribution shows that both the area of the later annexe and the terrain at its foot were used during the Principate period (**Fig. 80**). The 2000 and 2013–14 surveys conducted at Ostrite Mogili provided eleven coins dated to the same horizon, mainly in the eastern part of the site (**Fig. 83**). The most numerous are issues from the Severan period. Interestingly, in both cases the latest coins from the 3rd century were issued by Gallienus and Probus. Late Roman coins are prevalent in the annexe (**Fig. 81, 82**), while only three were found in the *vicus,* all of them from the 4th–mid 5th century (**Fig. 84**).

The finds of two lead seals (Chapter VI.10, **Pl. XLI**), both of them discovered in the annexe (**Fig. 85**), are of special importance, as they are evidence of military provisioning. The first is a Pamphylian provincial seal dated to the second half of the 4th century. Such seals would mark batches of goods delivered by individual cities or provinces obliged to secure provisions for the army through taxation in kind (*annona*). Sealing must have been performed in port-towns, which functioned as gathering places and the seats of inspection centres controlling the fulfilment of obligations.[25] The late Roman civilian officials (*primipilarii*) assigned to particular legions had an obligation (*munus*) secured by their entire properties to organise transports (*prosecutio annonae* / *παραπομπή*) from these centres to the frontier garrisons. This task was referred to as *pastus militum* or *pastus primipili*.[26] The activities of the *primipilarii* are attested by inscribed monuments raised after their duties had been fulfilled (*post pastum militum*) for garrisons at Oescus and Novae.[27] Lycia and Pamphylia (which under Diocletian split into two provinces) was an imperial province that – according to the epigraphic evidence – played an important role in supplying the army during the 3rd century,[28] and – as the lead seals show – also later.

The second find is a seal of Justinian I (527–565). Similarly to the Pamphylia seal, this imperial seal may be testimony of military provisions realised within the framework of the *quaestura exercitus*, the provisioning system established by Justinian I in AD 536, which definitely functioned until AD 575 or slightly later.[29] It combined several provinces, which included Mediterranean producers of goods (Caria, Cyprus, and the Cyclades Islands) and frontier recipients (Moesia II and Scythia). The provisioning was coordinated by the office in Odessos (today Varna) with his *quaestor Iustinianus exercitus* equal in rank to a *praefectus praetorio*.[30] So far, the majority of the seals dated to this period have been found in Scythia (today Dobruja).[31]

The most important epigraphic find is a fragment of an inscription reused in a wall at the Ostrite Mogili site (the *vicus*), 2.5 km from the fortress (Chapter VI.11, **Figs. 89–91**). The inscription is dated to AD 195 (**Pl. XLII**). Among all the known dedications to Septimius Severus found in Novae,[32] this seems to be the earliest one, also – more generally – from among all such identified dedications in the Empire. In my first reading of the text proposed in 2014, I suggested [.]*ṣip*[---] in the last line.[33] However, the first preserved letter is very damaged, and a closer analysis of the stone inclined me to change my opinion and propose a new reading, which would be [.]*cip*[---], with the possible reconstruction of the text as *prin*]*cip*[*i* ---], as a part of the imperial titulature (see **Pl. XLII** and **Fig. 92**). The name and titulature of Septimius Severus given in Dativus, as well as the recreated size of the inscription (40×140 cm) indicates to a statue base, probably on a horse.

The two other finds do not provide so much information. The piece of a marble plate found in the *canabae* (Area C2, **Fig. 93**) belonged to a monumental inscription. Marble plate fragments found in Novae in the past bear monumental or official inscriptions.[34] A small piece of lead with some marks (**Fig. 94**) found in the annexe has the shape of a lead *tessera* related to textile production, but the marks cannot be read as a meaningful text.

The finds of brick and tile stamps elaborated by Tadeusz Sarnowski (Chapter VI.12, **Pl. XLIII**) can be divided into two groups: military stamps and name stamps. Five fragments classified to the first group are the stamps of the First Italic Legion (LEG I ITAL) tiled in the 2nd or 3rd century. Eight stamps of a certain Caius Antonius Magnus(?) were found outside the fortress. According to Sarnowski, C. Antonius Magnus could have been a veteran engaged by the legion to carry out some important projects, as in the case of some other men known from stamps found in Novae: M. Aurelius Statianus,[35] M. Arrius Clemens,[36] and C. Cocceius Capito (see T. Sarnowski, fn. 29 in this book). The three-letter stamp P C P found in Ostrite Mogili is also understood by T. Sarnowski as an abbreviation of a name *P*(*ublius* ?) *C*(---) *P*(---), but in this case he suggested that the producer might have been a military person,

25. Rizos 2015.
26. Under Principate, this was the obligation of a *primus pilus* – a commander of the first cohort and the chief centurion of the Roman legion. This obligation was later passed on to civilian notables referred to as *primipilarii* (sing. *primipilarius*). On the *pastus militum* and *primipilarii*, see Sarnowski 2013, 142–43 and fn. 39; also Łajtar 2013, 105 and fn. 33 and Faure 2019 with further literature in these papers.
27. Łajtar 2013; 2015; 2021.
28. Rizos 2015, 291.
29. Procop., *De aed.* IV, 7, 11; Iust. *Nov.* XLI. On *quaestura exercitus* and the controversies around the role of the office in Odessos, see Torbatov 1997; Curta 2002, and cf. Wiewiórowski 2006. The last records of the office are dated to AD 575, but there are some indications that it might have continued to exist later; see Torbatov 1997, 85.
30. A discussion of the sources has been presented by Torbatov (1997, 90).
31. Curta 2002, 14.
32. Eight dedications to Septimius Severus have been identified in Novae: IGLNov 47; 57bis; 58–63; Bunsch, Kolendo, and Żelazowski, 2004, 57, no. 4 (fragment with Septimius Severus' imperial titulature). The discussed inscription would be the ninth one.
33. Tomas 2014.
34. IGLNov 58; AE 2012, 1265 and inv. no. 32/95 and 76/95 w (unpublished).
35. Tomas and Sarnowski 2007.
36. Kolendo and Kowal, 2011, 72.

based on the fact that his stamps have been found only in Novae, including in the military hospital.

The terracotta and ceramic items (Chapter VI.13) found at Novae include spindle whorls, fragmentarily preserved oil lamps and a terracotta figure of an eagle (**Pl. XLIV**). Apart from the eagle and the oil lamp fragment, all the terracotta finds were discovered in the eastern part of the site (**Fig. 96**). The majority of stone finds, all of them related to household activities (Chapter VI.14, **Pl. XLV**), were collected in Area B (the *vicus).*

Finds dated to the Medieval period

During our investigations, we collected pottery sherds (Chapter VI.15), coins (VI.16) and metal finds, including a copper alloy heart-shaped fitting (VI.17) and leaf-bladed arrowheads dated to the Medieval period (Chapter VI.5). The finds dated to the post-Roman era found at Ostrite Mogili are not homogenous: pottery is mostly identified with the 8th–10th-century Slavic settlement. The size of the early Medieval Slavic settlement covers an area of 25 ha, including the whole surface of the former Roman Ostrite Mogili and part of the right side of the Kouru dere – a small gully on the eastern edge of the site (**Fig. 97**). The next group of finds comes from the 10th–11th century, namely one Early Byzantine coin, and possibly some arrowheads discussed in Chapter VI.5. The last chronological group is formed by coins (billon trachea) issued in the first half of the 14th century and a few sherds of Byzantine sgraffito pottery. Arrowheads related to the Medieval period were found also in the annexe.

2. Conclusions

The investigated sites have provided information about human presence dated to as early as the Paleolithic period (Ostrite Mogili site). The period of Roman occupation is that of the most intensive development of settlements in the vicinity of the fortress (the *canabae,* the annexe), as well as to the east of it – at the Ostrite Mogili site (Area B) and to its south (Area E). Medieval settlement has also been attested, but it was not as intensive, and should probably be seen as of secondary importance.

Prehistoric sites at Novae and in its vicinity

Human presence in the surroundings of Novae is dated to as early as the Gravettian and Epigravettian horizon (Chapter VI.1), but finds dated to the Bronze Age and the Early Iron Age are also attested, including in the area of the fortress.[37] The various factors that attracted humans to the area included favorable settlement conditions, the proximity of a large river, which was not only a source of food, but also a communication route. The prehistory of the site and its vicinity is still not very well identified and it definitely requires further investigations.

Roman occupation

Although the area outside the West Gate was not available for broadscale investigations, which were limited to small lots (C1 and C2), the research has provided quite interesting materials, including those dated to the earliest period – possibly Flavian times – when the canabae started to develop.[38] The results from Area C1 near the extramural residence show that this part of the site still covers solid buildings. Small finds collected from Area C2 (**Pl. LIV**) included imported tableware and a fragment of a strigil, possibly a trace of a bathing facility. These finds, although few, seem to be evidence of a relatively high living standard (**Pl LV**). Glass and iron were abundant in Area C2, but very fragmentarily preserved. The architectural remains visible on the ground are scarce. Apart from the mithraeum documented in 2015, only the remains of some water facility, (possibly a water collector) related to the western aqueduct visible on the Danubian escarpment, were documented 250 m to the west of the West Gate. These remains are in very bad condition, and in the next 10 years they will probably be completely destroyed.

The improved plan of the fortress' annexe, accurate position of the extramural residence and the mithraeum, as well as the spread of finds outside the fortress allowed us to create the accurate plan of the site (**Fig. 105**). The southern part of the late Roman annexe and its vicinity (Areas A1 and D) provided a low amount of pottery fragments, but this does not reflect well the extent of land use in Antiquity. The investigated area is covered with high grass and bushes, crisscrossed with tens of illegal trenches. The collected pottery sherds were found mainly in these trenches. Amphorae and local tableware and kitchenware are prevalent, with a small quantity of hand-formed and wheel-thrown vessels, discovered just outside the annexe, which seem to be the developed version of hand-formed pottery found in the 1st-century contexts in the camp (ware I). This type of pottery must have been produced in the *canabae* during the existence of the fortress.

37. Stefanov 1955; Chichikova 2013.
38. Tomas 2017, 150.

Pl. LIII. Selected finds from the eastern side of the fortress (Areas A1 and D)

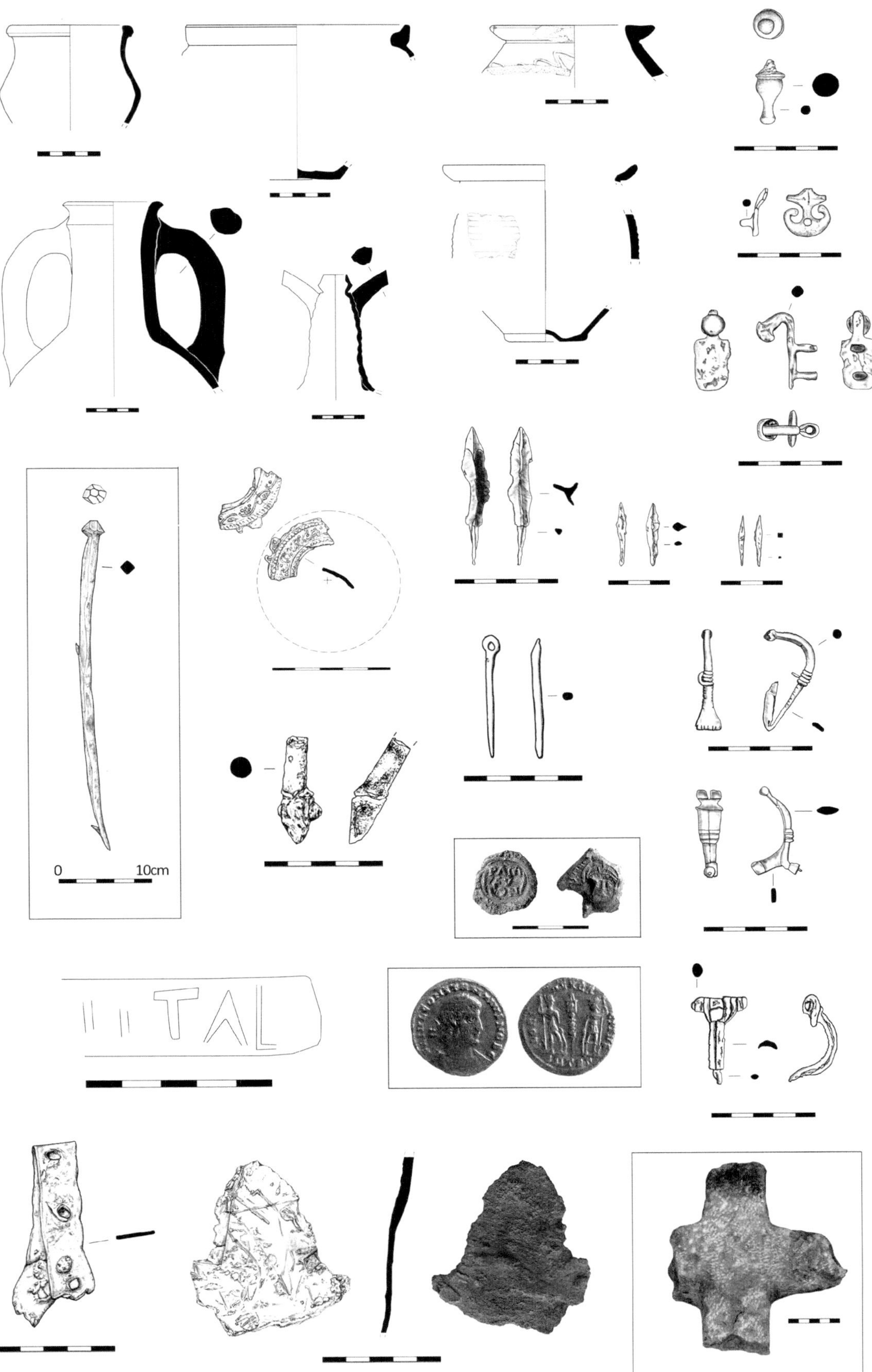

The early Roman finds collected in Area A1 include pieces of jewellery, elements of armour dated to the 2nd–3rd centuries, two fragments of building materials stamped LEG I ITAL and eight coins (dated to between the reign of Septimius Severus and Probus). These finds were few, but at the time of our investigation, it was difficult to conclude whether their low amount resulted from the poor availability of the terrain or the character of this part of the site.

The presence of cut metal items seems to indicate metal manufacturing done on the spot. Some copper alloy pieces found in the annexe (the fragment of a statue, a handle) were most probably cut for remelting. Local metal processing is also evidenced by slag. The small finds seem to confirm that manufacturing was carried out there, although some military function of the annexe cannot be excluded. Arrowheads of different types were collected in the annexe, with the earliest one dated to no later than the 3rd century AD and the remaining majority in use in late Antiquity (4th–6th centuries).

The military finds from the annexe can generally be linked to the military character of the site, and should most probably be dated to the late Roman period when the fortress defenders could have included not only infantry soldiers, but also archers. The presence of a *sagittarii* unit as part of the Roman military forces at Novae is a very interesting conclusion. Perhaps such a unit could have supported the legionaries remaining at Novae after the partition of the legion during Diocletian's reforms. On the other hand, some of these finds, attributed to the Germanic ethnos, could have been traces of Barbarian attacks on Novae, in the 3rd century in particular. This supposition seems to be confirmed by two brooches of possible Barbarian (one of them even of Scandinavian) origin. They may be evidence of Barbarian raids, but the temporary presence of some auxiliary troops cannot be excluded.

Late Roman coins make up the majority of numismatic finds from the annexe. The early Roman coinage is represented by ten coins issued within the timespan between the reign of Commodus (180–192) and Probus (276–282). Late Roman issues come from the period between the reign of Diocletian (284–305) and Maurice (582–602). Among them the coins of Constantius II (337–361) clearly dominate in number (14). It is possible that they reflect some building activity in this part of the site.

The majority of amphorae found in the annexe are dated to the late Roman period, and this results from the fact that they were found in illegal trenches, which are dug into the late Roman layers. Although LR2 amphorae were not collected there, they must be present, as they are very frequent in Novae and in Iatrus.[39] At least some of the goods transported from the eastern Aegean in accordance with the obligations performed by *primipilarii* must have been transported in LR 2 amphorae.[40] A 4th-century lead seal found in the annexe may be evidence of the redistribution

39. Biernacki and Klenina 2015, 105. The numerous fragments of Zeest 90 = Dressel 24 *similis* amphorae found in Novae would indicate these containers could have been used for such a purpose during the Principate period.

40. Karagiorgou 2001; Opaiţ 2004, 295.

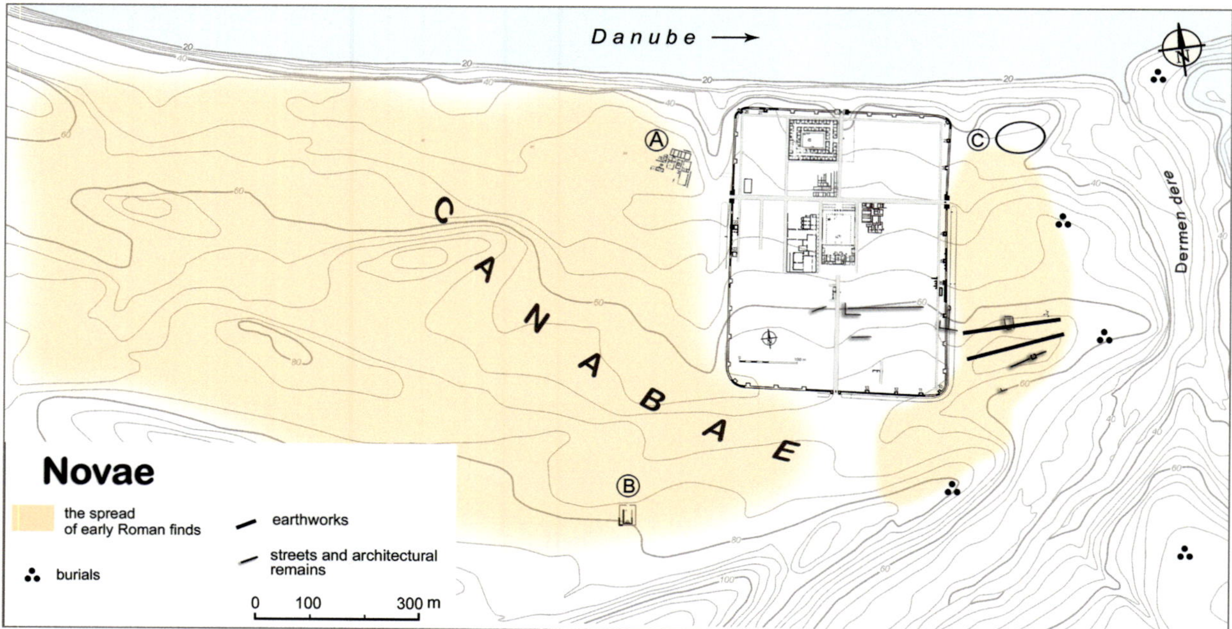

Fig. 105. Novae. Plan of the fortress and its vicinity showing the spread of archaeological material and the location of the known and hypothetical architectural remains (by A. Tomas).

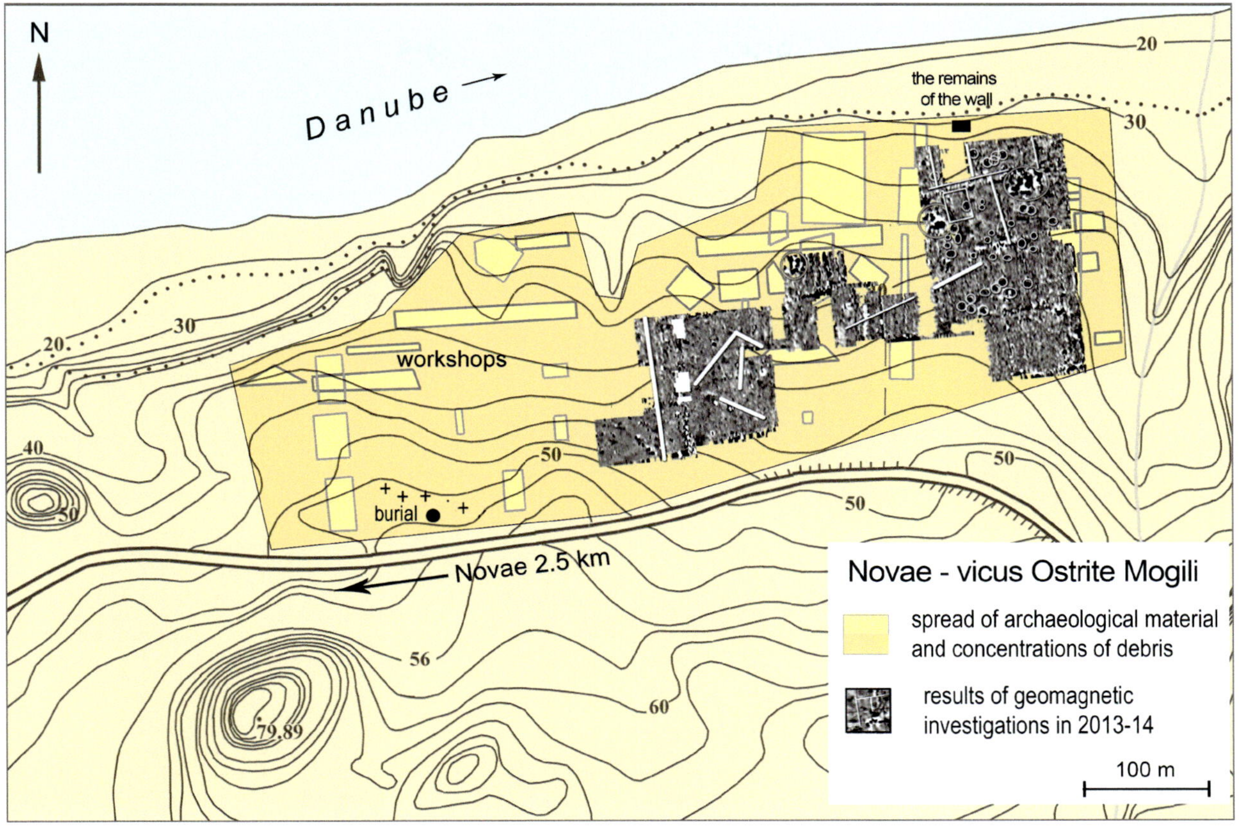

Fig. 106. Ostrite Mogili. Plan of the site showing the spread of archaeological material and the location of the known and hypothetical architectural remains (by A. Tomas).

Pl. LIV. Selected finds from the *canabae* (Area C2)

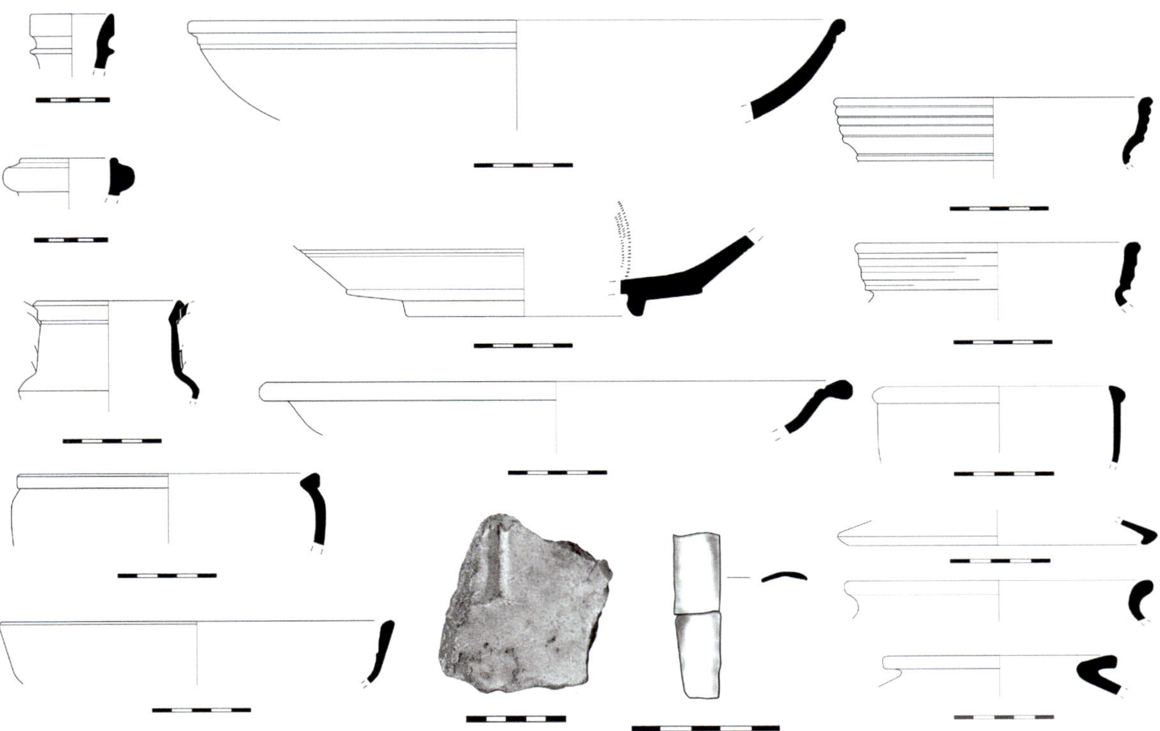

of goods conducted there. Military provisioning is also attested by Justinian's imperial seal and the 6th-century amphorae present at the annexe. At least one of the containers used for these provisions was a LR 1 amphora, which first occur in the 4th century, and start to be particularly numerous in the 5th–6th-century contexts on the Lower Danube,[41] including Novae. Fragments of these amphorae (or their late imitations)[42] were collected from the annexe (**Pl. XXIII,1**, 3 and possibly 4).

The *vicus* at Ostrite Mogili (Area B) provided the highest number of finds (**Pl. LVI–LVIII**). Although the majority of the finds were collected in 2014, the present book includes unpublished finds and results from 1979 and 2000. The finds from Ostrite Mogili show that during the Roman occupation the settlement was intensively inhabited from the Flavian period up to the mid-3rd century. It seems that the main part of the settlement was on the eastern side, where more concentrations of debris and pottery sherds were recorded (**Fig. 42**), as well as coins dated to the 2nd and 3rd centuries (**Fig. 83**). The interpretation of geophysical measurements may suggest that the site was cut with oblique roads, while the maps of finds allow to create the image which shows how the site was used (**Fig. 106**).

41. Empereur and Picon 1989, 236; Opaiţ 2004, 294 and 306–07.

The site flourished in the 2nd and 3rd centuries, which is well reflected by the abundant quantity of tableware and kitchenware, mainly produced in the local Moesian pottery centres. Locally manufactured amphorae are very well attested, but those imported from distant areas are also numerous. Although it cannot be ruled out that some of the sherds originate from containers imported to the legionary fortress and later reused outside of it, some may be evidence of the trade of their inhabitants. Such distant regions from which products were imported to such a small town may indicate that its role was also to supply the camp and the surrounding areas with imported products.

The finds of window panes from the *vicus* are quite interesting, which can be dated to the early Roman period. It is possible that they are evidence of on-site glass manufacturing. A higher quantity of glass waste in the western part of the site can be related to this activity (**Fig. 67**). Metal processing is also attested by finds of slag and a melting pot.

The non-military nature of the site is clearly confirmed by finds like stone weights, whetstones and a stone vessel, as well as a fragment of a votive tablet, most probably showing a Thracian Horseman worshipped in the surroundings

Pl. LV. Selected amphorae from the *vicus* (Area B)

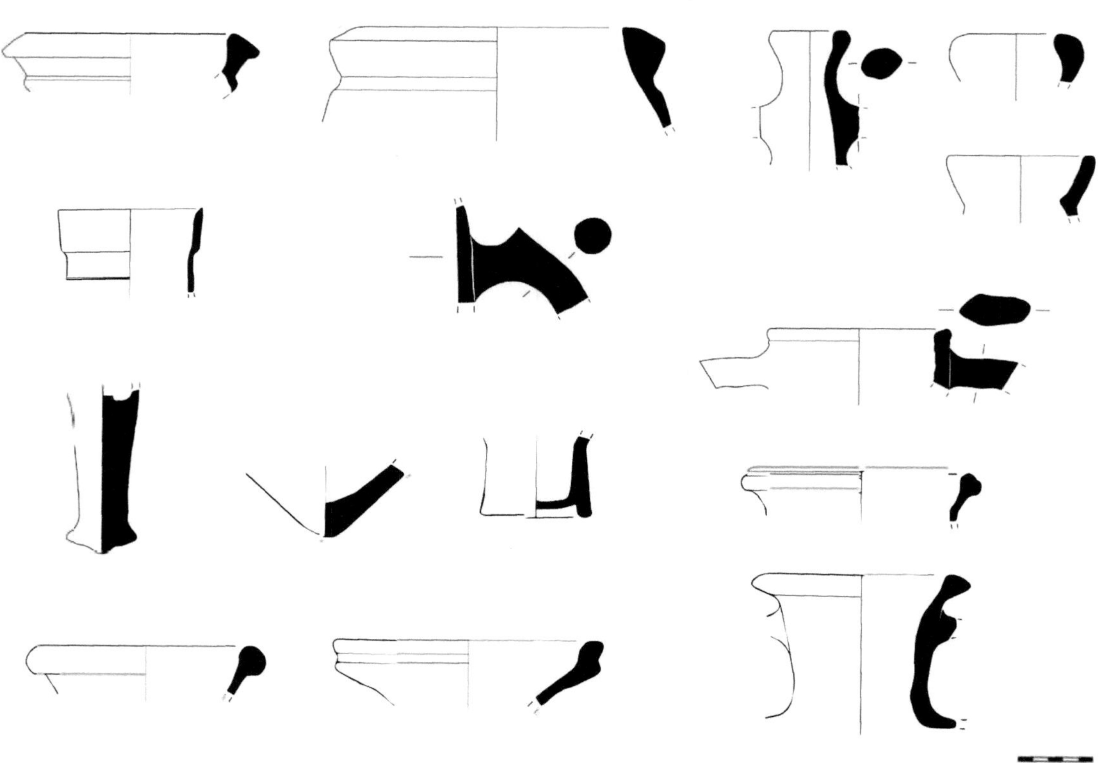

42. Opaiţ 2004, 307–08.

Pl. LVI. Selected tableware and kitchenware from the *vicus* (Area B)

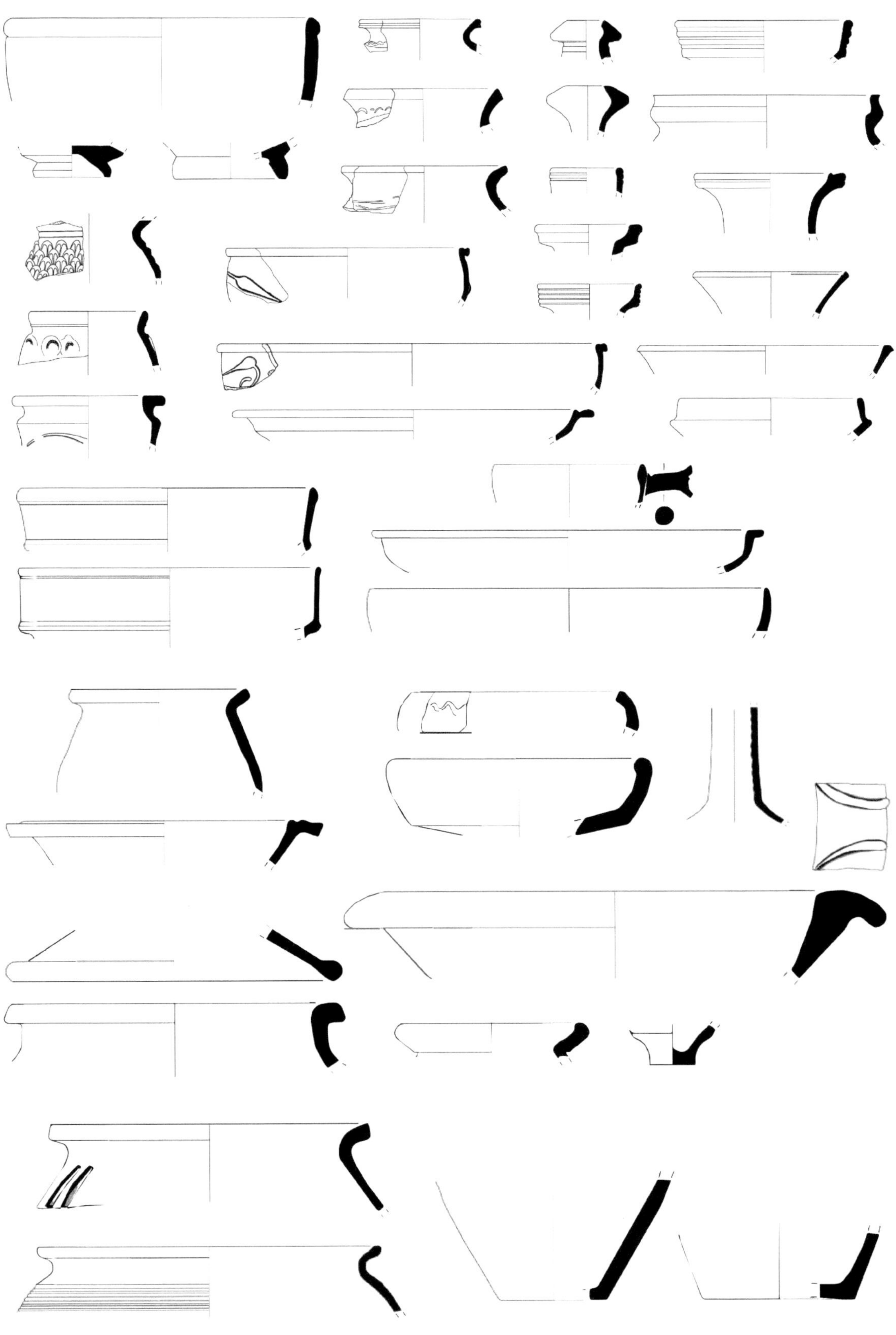

Pl. LVII. Selected finds from the *vicus* (Area B)

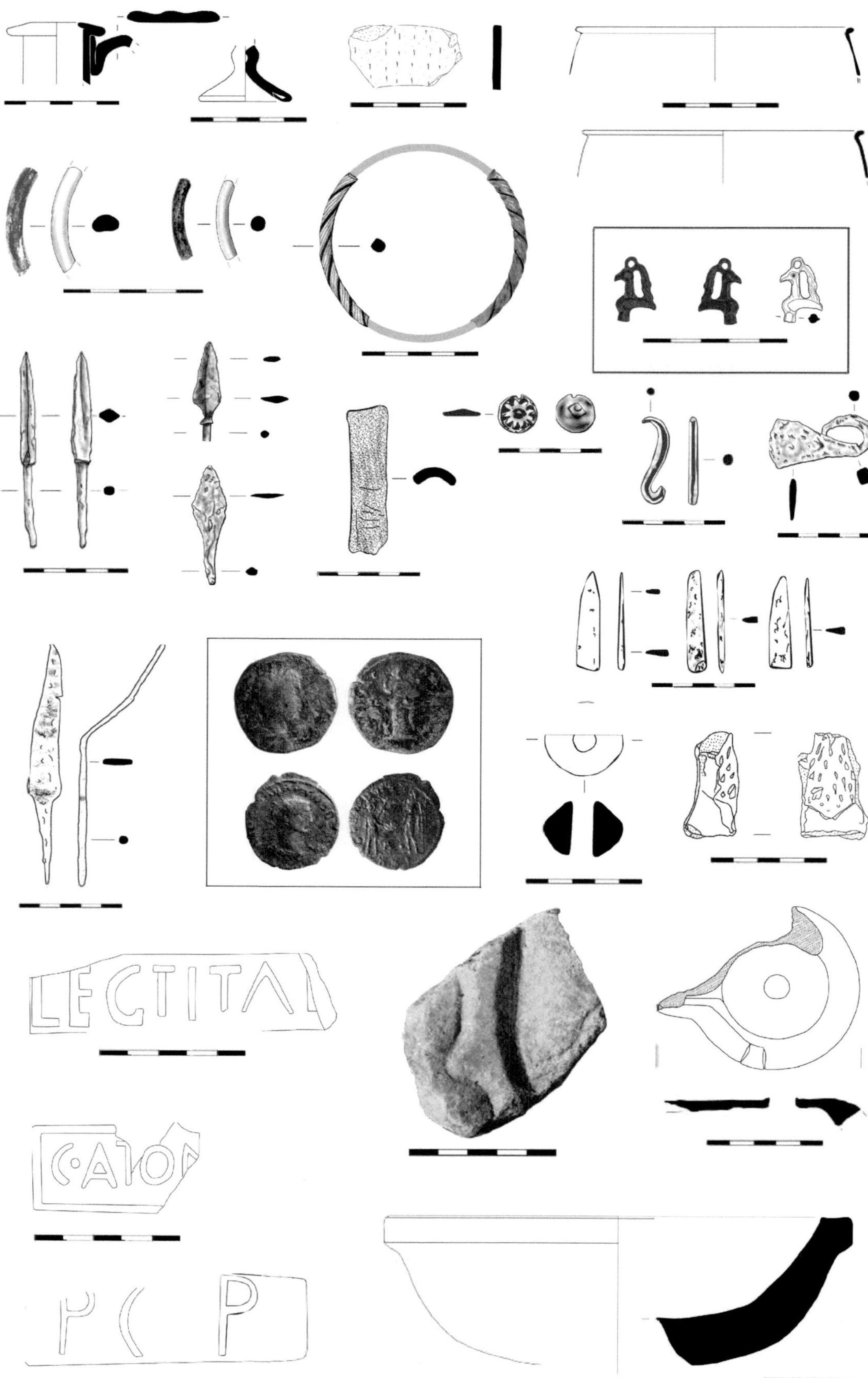

of Novae. The concentration of terracotta finds related to lighting and household activities in the western part of the *vicus* at Ostrite Mogili is another argument for the presence of residential houses. The fragment of a strigil is possibly a trace of some bathing facility.

Two fragments of an inscription embedded in a wall belonged to a monument of an official character, which most probably stood in the fortress. The nature of the finds from the *vicus* and its size indicate the existence of a small-sized settlement, but not a town with municipal rights.[43] The new reading of the inscription would point to its military context.

Interestingly, elements of military equipment in the *vicus* are lacking, while arrowheads have been recorded. The lack of equipment seems to indicate the non-military character of the site, if we agree that the presence of arrowheads is a trace of the Barbarian raids. However, building material stamped LEG I ITAL have been found there, as well as those of the late Roman LEPIFICOR type.[44] The presence of stamped military building materials may be the result of the vicinity of the fortress. The sale of stamped military building material to civilians is unlikely, but its secondary use in civilian context is not out of the question. Otherwise, its presence in the *vicus* may be a testimony of military building activity on the spot. It is more likely that stamped military bricks and tiles could have been thrown away after renovation works and reused by the local population as a cheap building material. The secondary use of such materials is attested in civil contexts, e.g., at cemeteries near Novae.[45] Name stamps found at the site may be reused or bought by the inhabitants. It cannot be excluded that some of these materials were a private commodity, but it is possible that private producers and the military operated in the same tileries, based on some agreement; therefore, the question of the name of their producer will never be fully answered.

Late Roman finds at Ostrite Mogili are less frequent. Only three coins were identifed as late Roman issues and all of them belong to 4th-century minting and only several fragments of late Roman pottery (wares XV–XVII) were found, along with some amphora fragments. We can add to this the possible LEPIFICOR stamps mentioned in R. Ivanov's publication.[46] Late Roman pottery is not abundant in the broader surroundings of Novae, and this fact unequivocally indicates the shrinking or even collapse of the settlement within a 3-km radius of the fortress. The moment it happened is difficult to establish without excavations. The presence of these materials may indicate some form of activity at the site, but definitely not the continuity of habitation in a previous form. In this context, the late Roman bird-shaped ending of a pin or a stick, probably related to the Gothic (or Barbarian in general) ethnos, is a very interesting item. Its presence may be explained by the closeness of the fort at Iatrus manned by the Barbarian *foederati*.

Small settlements to the east of Novae, which were named Areas E and F, have brought interesting observations concerning the results obtained thanks to various non-intrusive methods. The prospection at Area E provided some materials collected from the surface which were promising for geophysical investigations, but the results turned out to be very modest. In contrast, the image obtained from the magnetic measurements in Area F, where finds were almost non-existent, shows a number of anomalies which testify to intensive human activity.

The site at Chehlarski geran (Area E) provided some finds (**Pl. LIX**) that may indicate a possible farmhouse with perhaps a necropolis existing from the turn of the 1st and 2nd centuries up to the Severan period or slightly later. One fragment of a vessel attributed to ware II dated to the end of the 1st – early 2nd century AD found there, and a coin of Septimius Severus, were probably related to this habitation. It is possible that a well-preserved bracelet found at the site, which was intentionally bent into the form of a loop, was actually bereft of its original function and put into a grave, since it would be difficult to accept that such a precious item was used for everyday activities. The late Roman presence is not so well attested, but there is one uncertain coin dated to the late Roman period.

Area F (referred to in the literature as Kulna cheshma, properly Kanlu cheshme) seems to be a site which is in the process of being destroyed, as the surface finds are very few (**Pl. LX**), although in the late 1970s the finds were numerous.[47] How-

43. The question of which settlement near Novae (the *canabae* or the *vicus*) was granted municipal rights has been a matter long debated, and presented more extensively in my book (Tomas 2017, 159–162). I share the opinion presented by A.G. Poulter in 1983 (Poulter 1983-84, 112) that it was the *canabae*.

44. Ivanov 2002, 119. R. Ivanov also mentions a stamp of *legio I Minervia*, but the book does not include a drawing or the circumstances of its finding.

45. Vulov 1965.

46. Ivanov 2002, 119 and Fig. 87.

47. T. Sarnowski 1979.

Pl. LVIII. Selected finds from the Chehlarski geran site (Area E)

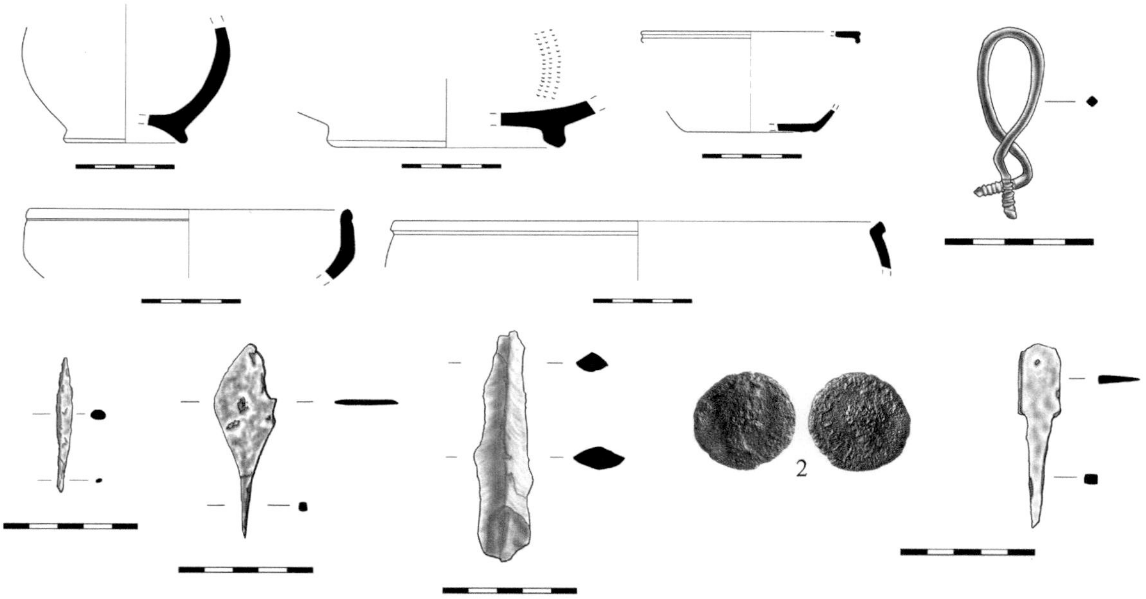

Pl. LIX. Selected finds froma Kanlu cheshme (Area F)

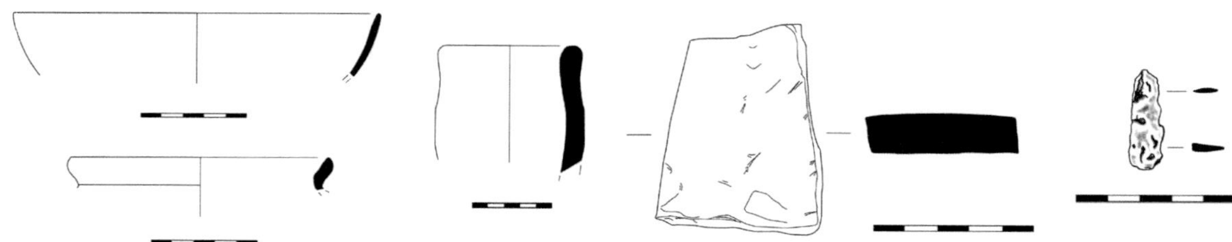

ever, it is possible that some structures have survived underground.

Medieval settlement

The Lower Danubian lands were settled by the Slavs from the beginning of the 7th century onwards. In 611, they ravaged Moesia II and soon the lands between the Lower Danube and the Rhodopes started to be referred as to Slaviniya, Sklavenia or Sclavonia, while the tribes as Severtsite.[48] Traces of Medieval settlement were found 5 km away in Svishtov and on the other side of the Danube in Fîntînele.[49] Medieval settlement is also indirectly attested at Novae. A Medieval necropolis was unearthed in the ruins of a late Roman residence, overbuilding the ruins of the legionary hospital, but where exactly the Medieval settlement existed during this period remains a mystery. The jewellery found in the graves was dated to the 8th–11th centuries.[50]

The Slavic pottery discovered at Ostrite Mogili (**Pl. LXI**) is dated to the same period as the Medieval necropolis at Novae, but their mutual relationship is difficult to establish. The *follis* of an anonymous issuer dated to AD 1030 found at Ostrite Mogili seems to be convergent with the presence of arrowheads and the end of this settlement.

The billon trachea found at Ostrite Mogili are dated to the first three decades of the 13th century, when the Second Bulgarian Empire existed (1185–1396). They were found in the entire area of the site. In 2000, they were collected in the western part, which could suggest that we were dealing with a hoard, but two concentrations were discovered in 2014 in the eastern part of the site (**Fig. 98**).

48. Mikov 1946–47, 144–46.

49. Comşa 1969.

50. Lemke 2006.

Pl. LX. Selected finds from the Medieval site at Ostrite Mogili (Area B)

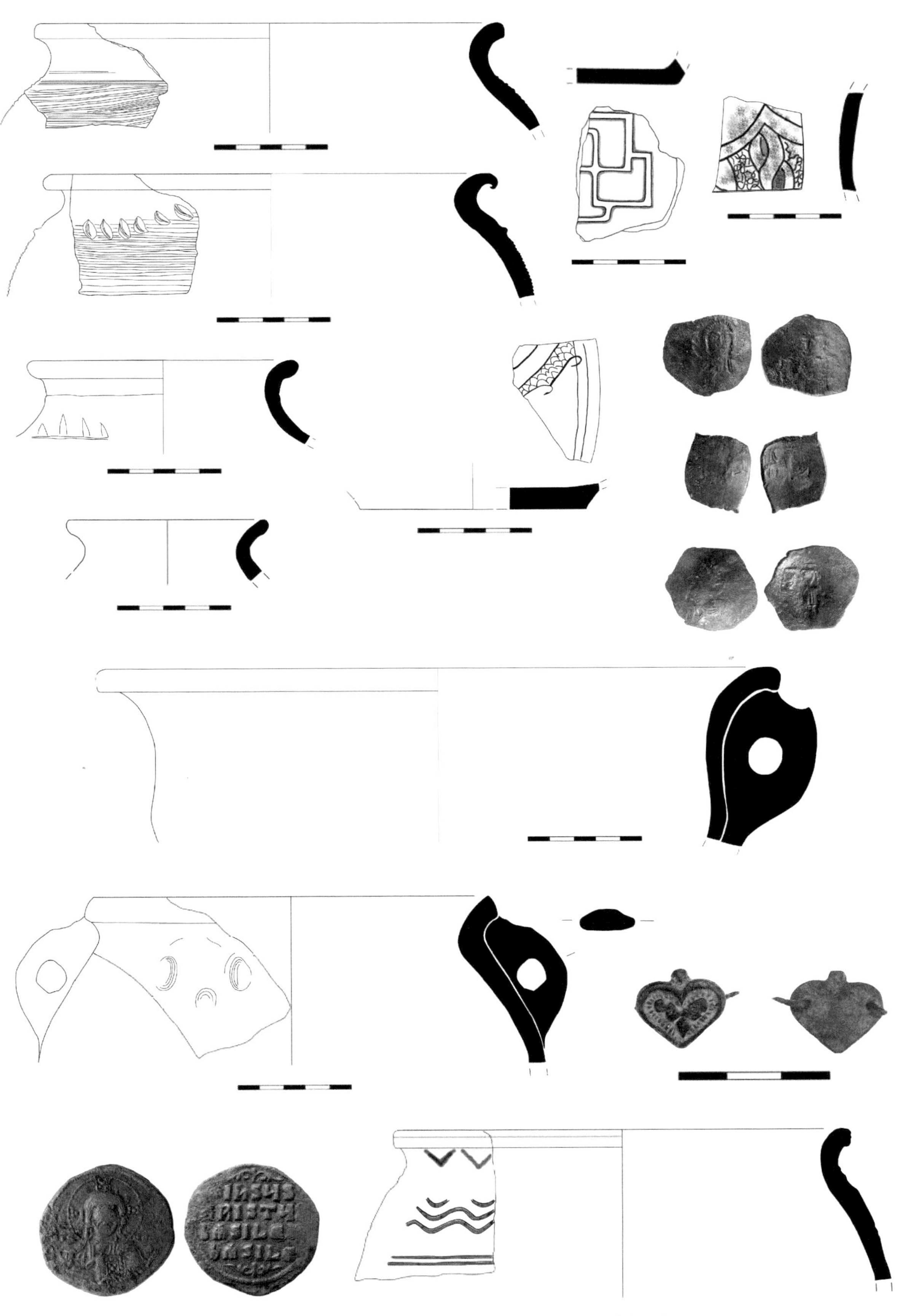

Fig. 107. Novae 2012. Illegal trenches in the southern part of the annexe (photo by M. Pisz).

This may lead to the conclusion that their presence is not accidental and not just related to a hoard. According to P. Jaworski, they could have been used between the fourth and sixth decade of the 13th century. This monetary evidence stands in some contrast, however, to the lack of other Medieval finds from this period. Perhaps the billon trachea along with some pottery sherds, including two *sgraffito* vessels, can be linked to some temporary habitation, e.g., related to the wars that took place at that time.

Evaluation of the detrimental factors harmful to the site

Nature is the first, though not the most dangerous factor that has some influence on archaeological remains. The eroding activity of the Danube is not friendly to archaeological relics. In some places along the Danubian scarp, the remains of masonry constructions are visible and we were able to document some of them, but in many other places we have seen only traces of walls visible in the high loess scarp. The erosion caused by the high waters of the Danube is harmful to the scarp, while the forest grows and spreads within the site. Over the last fifty years, trees have covered 18 out of the 28 ha of the fortress. At present, the forest grows throughout the entire northern and central part of the site. The uncontrolled forestation of the site brings damage to the stratigraphy and helps looters to remain hidden during their illegal activities.

Modern infrastructure in the form of pipes, private buildings, fencing has changed the landscape. Moreover, the presence of private lots limits the scale and possibilities of any archaeological surveys. This particularly applies to the western part of the *canabae*, which seems to be the most important for research purposes. Our estimations show that about 3 ha of the fortress are covered by modern buildings, an asphalt road, and an additional 2 ha are covered by archaeological bases. Many places excavated in the past or recently are used as waste deposits.

One of the most damaged places is the southern part of the annexe (**Fig. 107**), which is a very interesting place due to its localization and natural defensive potential used in Late Antiquity. Looting in this part of the site is very intensive and done in the form of very densely excavated small regular trenches. The number

Fig. 108. Novae 2014. Documentation of illegal trenches in the annexe (photo by A. Tomas).

of illegal trenches is too numerous to count. In 2013, we documented about two hundred trenches only in the annexe area, and this number continues to grow constantly. The same illegal activities take place at other archaeological sites in the surroundings. At some, we have documented architectural remains. Fortunately, they were not very deep (**Fig. 108**).

Fig. 109. Ostrite Mogili 2014. Illegal trenches in the western part of the site (photo by M. Pisz).

The area to the south of the fortress is also severely damaged. The number of illegal trenches seems not to be as high, but the excavated trenches are wider and deeper (**Fig. 108**). Some lots were bought purely to serve this purpose, and it is very possible that looting will be continued here with great intensity.

Illegal trenches also cover the western part of the *vicus* at Ostrite Mogili (**Fig. 109**). One such trench produced the inscription published in this volume. The smaller sites situated to the south of Ostrite Mogili seem to be less damaged by looting, although the results of our surveys show that these places could have been robbed in the past. The very intensive agricultural activities in the area are the main factor unfavourable for the archaeological remains.

Novae remains one of the 100 most endangered archaeological sites in the world. Lost finds and damaged stratigraphy are obviously the most regrettable harm done to the site. Additionally, some survey methods are not easily applied due to the damaged surface and difficulties in mapping or conducting geophysical measurements. The actions taken in recent years by the local authorities to create a new archaeological park, which was for several years partly monitored by cameras, were of great value. The central part of the site (the headquarters building and episcopal complex) is now more visible from the road, which discourages looters. In 2016, the forest was cleared of dense bushes, which limited the illegal activities, but vegetation in Novae is very intensive and grows back rapidly. Regrettably, the greater part of the site, including the extramural area, still awaits better protection.

Ancient authors

Cass. Dio — *Cassius, Dio, Roman History*, with an English Translation by H.B. Foster, and E. Cary, London–New York: Heinemann, 1914

Dig. — *Corpus iuris civilis.* Vol. 1, Institutiones; recognovit Paulus Krueger. *Digesta*; recognovit Theodorus Mommsen. Retractavit Paulus Krueger. Berolini: Apud Weidmannos, 1954.

Hyg. — *Hygini, De limitibus.* In B. Campbell, *The Writings of the Roman Land Surveyors. Introduction, Text, Translation and Commentary*, 76–102. London 2000: Society for the Promotion of Roman Studies.

SHA — *The Scriptores Historiae Augustae*, vol. I, edited by H. Peter, with an English translation by D. Magie, Cambridge (Mass.)-London: Harvard University Press, 1921.

Strabo — *Strabo, The Geography*, with an English translation by H.L. Jones, W. Heinemann, in eight volumes, London – Cambridge (Mass.) 1917–1967.

Tac. *Ann.*, Tac. *Hist.* — *Tacitus in five volumes. The Histories.* Translation by C.H. Moore (*Histories*), and J. Jackson (*Annals*). Loeb Classical Library. Harvard: Harvard University Press, 1925–1937.

Abbreviations

Ad fines — *Ad fines imperii Romani. Studia Thaddaeo Sarnowski ab amicis, collegis discipulisque dedicata*, edited by A. Tomas, Warszawa: Institute of Archaeology, University of Warsaw, 2015.

AÉ — *L'année épigraphique*. Paris: Presses universitaires de France.

AMNG — *Die antiken Münzen Nord-Griechenlands*, vol. I: B. Pick, and K. Regling, *Die antiken Münzen von Dacien und Moesien*. Berlin: G. Reimer, 1898.

ANRW — *Aufstieg und Niedergang der römischen Welt*. Berlin–Boston: de Gruyter.

AOR — *Arheologicheski otkritiya i razkopki*

ArchBulg — *Archaeologia Bulgarica*

B.A.R. Int. Ser. — British Archaeological Reports, International Series

B.A.R. Br. Ser. — British Archaeological Reports, British Series

Beiträge Gerov — B. Gerov, *Beiträge zur Geschichte der römischen Provinzen Mösien und Thrakien, Gesammelte Aufsätze*, 1980. Amsterdam: Hakkert.

BJb — *Bonner Jahrbücher*

BLS — *Byzantine Lead Seals* (= Zacos, G., Veglery, A. 1972)

Carinthia I — *Zeitschrift für geschichtliche Landeskunde von Kärnten* (Klagenfurt)

CBSB — *Corpus of Byzantine Seals from Bulgaria* (= Yordanov, I. 2009)

CIL — *Corpus Inscriptionum Latinarum*, vols. I-XVII, Berlin, 1863-1986.

Companion Novae — *Novae. Legionary Fortress and Late Antique Town*, vol. I, *A Companion to the Study of Novae*, edited by T. Derda, P. Dyczek, and J. Kolendo, Warszawa: Wydawnictwa Uniwersytetu Warszawskiego, 2008.

CRAI — *Comptes rendus des séances de l'Académie des Inscriptions et Belles-Lettres*

DAGR — *Dictionnaire des Antiquités grecques et romaines*, edited by Ch. D'Aremberg and E. Saglio, Graz: Akademische Druck- und Verlagsanstalt, 1877–1919.

DE — *Dizionario epigrafico di antichità romane*, edited by E. de Ruggiero, Roma: L'Erma di Bretschneider, 1895.

DOC Coins — P. Grierson, *Catalogue of the Byzantine Coins in the Dumbarton Oaks Collection and in the Whittemore Collection*, vol. III/2, Washington, D.C.: Dumbarton Oaks Center for Byzantine Studies, 1973.

DOC Seals — J. Nesbitt, *Catalogue of Byzantine seals at Dumbarton Oaks and in the Fogg Museum of Art, vol.* VI: *Emperors, Patriarchs of Constantinople, Addenda*. Washington, D.C.: Dumburton Oaks, 2009.

Ernout-Meillet — A. Ernout, A. Meillet, *Dictionnaire étymologique de la langue latine. Histoire de mots*, Paris: Klincksieck, 1932 (2001).

GIC — I. Varbanov, *Greek Imperial Coins and Their Value*, vol. I–III. Bourgas: Adicom, 2005–2007.

GMSB — *Godishnik na muzeyte ot severna Bulgariya*

GSUIFF — *Godishnik na Sofiyskiya Universitet, Istrochesko-filozoficheski Fakultet*

I diritti locali — *I diritti locali. Atti del convegno internationale sul tema: I diritti locali nelle prov-*

	ince romane con particolare riguardo alle condizioni quiridiche del suolo, 109–124. Roma: Academia Nazionale dei Lincei.
IAI	*Izvestiya na Arheologicheskiya Institut*
Iatrus I–VI	*Iatrus-Krivina. Spätantike Befestigung und frühmittelterliche Siedlung an der unteren Donau,* vol. II: *Ergebnisse der Ausgrabungen 1966–1973,* Berlin: Akad.-Verl., 1982; vol. IV: *Ergebnisse der Ausgrabungen 1975–1981,* Berlin: Akad.-Verl., 1991; vol. VI: *Ergebnisse der Ausgrabungen 1992–2000,* Mainz: Philipp von Zabern, 2008.
IBAI	*Izvestiya na Bulgarskiya Arheologicheski Institut*
IDR	*Inscriptiones Daciae Romanae,* vol. I, I.I. Russu, *Prolegomena historica et epigraphica. Diplomata militaria, tabulae ceratae,* Bucharest 1975; vol. III. *Dacia Superior,* 2. *Ulpia Traiana Dacica (Sarmizegetusa),* I.I. Russu, in collaboration with I. Piso and V. Wollmann, Bucharest 1980.
IGLNov	J. Kolendo, V. Božilova, *Inscriptions grecques et latines de Novae (Mésie inférieure),* Bordeaux 1997.
IIMVT	*Izvestiya na Istoricheski Muzey Veliko Turnovo*
INMVarna	*Izvestiya na Narodniya Muzey Varna*
IOMVT	*Izvestiya na Okruzhniya Muzey Veliko Turnovo*
ISAW	Institute for the Study of the Ancient World
ISM I-V	*Inscriptiones Daciae et Scythiae Minoris. Series altera: Inscriptiones Scythiae Minoris Graecae et Latinae,* vol. I, *Inscriptiones Histriae et vicinae,* D.M. Pippidi (ed.), Bucharest 1983; vol. II, *Tomis et territorium,* edited by I. Stoian, Bucarest 1987; vol. III, *Callatis et son territoire,* edited by Al. Avram, Bucarest 1999; vol. V, *Capidava – Troesmis – Noviodunum,* edited by E. Doruţiu-Boilă, Bucharest 1980.
JMH	*Journal of Military History*
JRA	*Journal of Roman Archaeology*
JRMES	*Journal of Roman Military Equipment Studies*
Liddell, Scott	H.G. Liddell. R. Scott, *A Greek-English Lexicon,* revised and augmented throughout by Sir H. Stuart Jones, with the assistance of R. McKenzie, Oxford 1940.
LIMC	*Lexicon Iconographicum Mythologiae Classicae*
Limes von Diokletian	*Der Limes an der Unteren Donau von Diokletian bis Heraklios, Vorträge der Internationalen Konferentz Svištov (1.–5. September 1998),* edited by G. von Bülow, A. Milčeva. Sofia: Nous.
MIB	W. Hahn, *Moneta Imperii Byzantini. Rekonstruktion des Prägeaufbaues auf synoptisch-tabellarischer Grundlage,* vol. I–II, Wien 1973–1975: Verlag der Österreichischen Akademie der Wissenschaften.
Nicopolis I	A.G. Poulter, R.K. Falkner, and J.D. Shepherd, *Nicopolis ad Istrum: A Roman to Early Byzantine City. The Pottery and Glass,* Reports of the Research Committee of the Society of Antiquaries of London, 57, London 1999: Leicester University Press for the Society of Antiquaries of London.
Opercula	*Coperchi d'Anfora Fittili con Scritte, Segni e Grafemi dall'area Alto-Adriatica Aquileia, 14 Aprile 2012,* edited by M. Buora, S. Magnani, and P. Ventura, Quaderni Friulani di Archeologia XXII/XXIII, 2012-2013, Udine: Società Friulana di Archeologia.
PIR^2	*Prosopographia Imperii Romani,* 2. Auflage, Berlin 1933.
RCRFA	*Rei Cretariae Romanae Fautorum Acta*
RE	*Real-Encyklopädie der klassischen Altertumswissenschaft,* edited by A. Pauly, G. Wissowa, K. Kroll, K. Mittelhaus, and K. Ziegler, Stuttgart–Weimar: Meztzler, 1894–1980.
RIC	*The Roman Imperial Coinage,* vol. I^2–II^2, London 1984–2007, vol. III–X, London: Spink and Son, 1930–1994.
RLS	*Roman Lead Seals* (= Still, M.C.V. 1995)
SCIVA	*Studii şi Cercetări de Istorie Veche şi Arheologie*
TLL	*Thesaurus Linguae Latinae* online, De Gruyter. (http://www.degruyter.com/databasecontent?dbid=tll&dbsource=%2Fdb%2Ftll)
Walde-Hofmann	A. Walde, *Lateinisches Etymologisches Woerterbuch.* 3e Auflage, bearb. bei J.B. *Hoffmann,* Heidelberg: 1938, Winter.
ZPE	*Zeitschrift für Papyrologie und Epigraphik*

Literature

Alekseenko, N.A. 1999. "Provincial'nyy Herson v sfere interesov vizantiyskogo dvora po dannym imperatorskih moliv-dovulov, Drevnosti 1997–1998." *Har'kovskiy istoriko-arheologicheskiy ezhegodnik* 4: 145–60.

Alexandrescu, C-G., Chr. Gugl, and B. Kainrath, 2016. *Troesmis I. Die Forschungen von 2010–2014*. Cluj-Napoca: Mega Publishing House.

Ando, C. 2012. *Imperial Rome AD 193 to 284: The Critical Century*. Edinburgh: Edinburgh University Press.

Andreeva, P., Marinov, M., Gencheva, E., Taneva, S., Penkova, P., Dancheva, A., and N. Nikolova, 2018a. "Terenni izdurvaniya v zemlishtata na selata Tsarevets i Vardim, obshtina Svishtov." In *AOR prez 2017 g.*, 583–84. Burgas: NAIM BAN.

Andreeva, P., Marinov, M., Aleksandrov, S., Taneva, S., Dancheva, A., and T. Dyakov, 2018b. "Terenni izdurvaniya po traseto na prenosen gazoprovod do grad Svishtov." In *AOR prez 2017 g.*, 584–87. Burgas: NAIM BAN.

Andreeva, P., E. Stefanova, and M. Gurova, 2014. "Chert raw materials and artefacts from NE Bulgaria: A combined petrographic and LA-ICP-MS study." *Journal of Lithic Studies* 1: 25–45.

Asouti, E., and Ph. Austin, 2005. "Reconstructing Woodland Vegetation and its Exploitation by Past Societies, based on the Analysis and Interpretation of Archaeological Wood Charcoal Macro-Remains." *Environmental Archaeology* 10: 1–18.

Atanasov, G. 2014. *Durostorum – Dorostol – Drastar – Silistra. The Danubian Fortress (4th–19th c.)*, Corpus of Ancient and Medieval Settlements in Bulgaria, vol. 2, Thracian, Greek, Roman and Medieval Cities, Residences and Fortresses, edited by R. Ivanov, 493–587. Varna: Zograf.

Atkinson M., and S. Preston, 2015. "Heybridge: A Late Iron Age and Roman Settlement. Excavations at Elms Farm 1993–5. Volume 2." *Internet Archaeology* 40 (http://dx.doi.org/10.11141/ia.40.1)

Auriemma, R., and E. Quiri, 2004. "Importazioni di anfore orientali nell'Adriatico tra primo e medio impero." In *Transport Amphorae and Trade in the Eastern Mediterranean. Acts of the International colloquium at the Danish Institute at Athens, September 26–29, 2002*, Monographs of the Danish Institute at Athens, 5, 43–55. Aarhus: Aarhus University Press.

Aurrecoechea-Fernández, J. 2007. "Arneses equinos de época romana en Hispania." *Sautuola* 13: 321–44.

Austin, N.J.E., and N.B. Rankov, 1995. *Exploration: Military and Political Intelligence in the Roman World from the Second Punic War to the Battle of Adrianople*. London: Routledge.

Avram, Al., and M. Ionescu, 2013. "Un nuovo *patronus* della città di Callatis: Cn. Cornelius Lentulus Augur." *Il Mar Nero* 7: 167–77.

Baatz, D. 1989. "Kommandobereiche der Legionslegaten." *Germania* 67: 169–78.

Badal Garcia, E. 1992. "L'anthracologie préhistorique: à propos de certains problèmesméthodologiques." *Bulletin de la Société botanique de France. Actualités Botaniques* 139(2-4): 167–89.

Barnea, I. 1990. "Sigilii bizantine inedite din Dobrogea (III)." *Pontica* 23: 315–34.

– 1996. "Sigilii bizantine din Dobrogea." *SCIVA* 47(2): 215–20.

Barnes, T.D. 1967. "The Family and Career of Septimius Severus." *Historia* 16: 87–107.

Bărbulescu, M., and M. Buzoianu, 2014. "L'espace ouest-pontique sous l'empereur Tibère à la lumière d'un décret inédit découvert en Dobroudja." In *Interconnectivity in the Mediterranean and Pontic World during the Hellenistic and Roman Period. In Memory of Professor Heinz Heinen, The Proceedings of the International Symposium held in Constanța, July 8–12, 2013*, edited by V. Cojocaru, A. Coșcun, and M. Dana, Pontica et Mediterranea, III, 415–34. Cluj-Napoca: Mega Publishing House.

Becker, Chr., C. Constantin, C., and Fr. Villedieu, 1989. "Types d'amphores en usage à Lugdunum du Ier au VIe siècle." In *Amphores romaines et histoire économique. Dix ans de recherche. Actes du colloque de Sienne (22–24 mai 1986)*, edited by F. Zevi, Publications de l'École française de Rome, 114, 656–59. Rome: Diff. de Boccard.

Behre, K.-E. 1981. "The interpretation of anthropogenic indicators in pollen diagrams." *Pollen and Spores* 23(2): 225–245.

– 1990. "Some reflections on anthropogenic indicators and the record of prehistoric occupation phases in pollen diagrams from the Near East." In Man's Role in the Shaping of the Eastern Mediterranean Landscape, edited by S. Bottema, G. Entjes-Nieborg, and W. van Zeist, 219–230. Rotterdam – Brookfield: Balkema.

Beijerinck, W. 1947. *Zadenatlas der Nederlandische flora*. Wageningen: H. Veenman & Zonen.

Beltrán, L.M. 1970. *Las ánforas romanas en España*. Zaragoza: Zaragoza Diputación Provincial. Institución "Fernando el Católico."

Bérard, Fr. 1992. "*Territorium legionis*: camps militaires et agglomérations civiles aux premiers siècles de l'empire." *Cahiers du Centre Gustave Glotz* 3: 75–105.

Berggren, G. 1969. *Atlas of seeds and small fruits of Northwest-European plant species with morphological descriptions*. Part 2. *Cyperaceae*. Stockholm: Swedish Natural Science Research Council.

Beschaouch, A. 1979. "Eléments celtiques dans la population du pays de Carthage." *CRAI* 123(3): 394–409.

Beug, H.J. 2004. *Leitfaden der Pollenbestimmung für Mitteleuropa und angrenzende Gebiete*, München: Verlag Friedrich Pfeil.

Bezeczky, T. 1998. "Amphora types of Magdalensberg." *Arheološki vestnik* 49: 225–42.

– 2004. "Early Roman Food Import in Ephesus: Amphorae from the Tetragonos Agora." In *Transport Amphorae and Trade in the Eastern Mediterranean. Acts of the International Colloquium at the Danish Institute at Athens*, edited by J. Eiring, and J. Lund, Monographs of the Danish Institute at Athens, 5, 85–97. Aarhus: Aarhus University Press.

– 2005. "Roman Amphorae from Vindobona." In *Vindobona – Beiträg zu ausgewählten Keramikgattungen in ihrem topographiscen Kontext*, 35–109. Wien: Verlag der Österreichischen Akademie der Wissenschaften.

Biborski, M., and J. Stępiński, 2014. "Materiały do poznania metalurgii żelaza okresu rzymskiego." In *Honoratissimum assensus genus est armis laudare: studia dedykowane Profesorowi Piotrowi Kaczanowskiemu z okazji siedemdziesiątej rocznicy urodzin*, edited by R. Madyda-Legutko, and J. Rodzińska-Nowak, 263–76. Kraków: Towarzystwo Wydawnicze "Historia Iagiellonica".

Bichir, Gh. 1984. *Geto-Dacii din Muntenia în epoca romană.* Biblioteca de archeologie 43, Bucureşti: Editura Academiei Republicii Socialiste România.

Biernacki, A.B., and K. Dimitrov, 2008. *The coin hoard from the thermae legionis and the monetary circulation in Novae 330–348 AD*, Novae Studies and Materials III, Poznań: Wydawnictwa UAM.

Biernacki, A.B., and E. Klenina, 2015. "Amphorae of the 4th – 6th centuries AD from Novae (Moesia Secunda): typology and chronology." In *Per terram, per mare*, edited by S. Demesticha, 99–120. Uppsala: Åströms förlag.

Birley, A. 1997. "Marius Maximus: The Consular Biographer." In *ANRW* II/34.3, 2678–2757.

– 1999. *Septimius Severus. The African Emperor.* London: Routledge.

Bishop, M.C. 1988. "Cavalry equipment of the Roman army in the first century A.D." In *Military Equipment and the Identity of Roman Soldiers. Proceedings of the Fourth Roman Military Equipment Conference*, edited by J.C. Coulston, B.A.R. Int. Ser., 394, 67–194. Oxford: B.A.R.

– 2002. *Lorica segmentata*, vol. I: *A Handbook of Articulated Roman Plate Armour*, Journal of Military Equipment Studies Monograph, 1. Chirnside: The Armatura Press.

Bishop, M.C., and J.C.N. Coulston, 2006. *Roman Military Equipment: From the Punic Wars to the Fall of Rome.* Cambridge: Cambridge University Press.

Bitner-Wróblewska, A., and B. Kontny, 2006. "Controversy about Three-Leaf Arrowheads from Lithuania." *Archeologia Lituana* 7: 104–22.

Bohn, O. 1926. "Rheinische Lagerstädte." *Germania* 10: 25–36.

Bohn, U., Gollub, G., Hettwer, C., Neuhäuslová, Z., Raus, Th., Schlüter, H., and H. Weber, 2004. *Karte der natürlichen Vegetation Europas. Maßstab 1:2.500.000.* Interaktive CD-ROM-Erläuterungstext, Legende, Karten / *Map of the Natural Vegetation of Europe. Scale 1:2.500.000.* Interactive CD-ROM-Explanatory Text, Legend, Maps. Bon-Bad Godesberg: Bundesamt für Naturschutz.

Bondoc, D. 2009. "A Roman import from the Slavic-Age settlement in Craiova, the point "Fântâna Obedeanu." In *Near and Beyond the Roman Frontier. Proceedings of the Colloquium held in Târgovişte, 16–17 October 2008*, 253–56. Bucureşti: Conphys.

Bonifay, M., and D. Piéri, 1995. "Amphores du Ve au VIIe s. à Marseille: nouvelles données sur la typologie et le contenu." *JRA* 8: 94–120.

Bonsall, C., M. Gurova, C. Hayward, C. Nachev, and N. Pearce, 2010. "Characterization of 'Balkan flint' artefacts from Bulgaria and the Iron gates using LA-ICP-MS and EPMA." *Interdisciplinarni izsledvaniya* 22-23: 9–18.

Boteva, D. 1996. "Legati Augusti pro praetore Moesiae inferioris A.D. 193–217/218." *ZPE* 110: 239–47.

– 1999. "Two Notes on D. Clodius Albinus." *ArchBulg* 3(3): 23–28.

Bozilova, E., Tonkov, S. 1998. "Towards the vegetation and settlement history of the southern Dobrudza coastal region, north-eastern Bulgaria: A pollen diagram from Lake Durankulak." Vegetation History and Archaebotany 7: 141–148. https://doi.org/10.1007/BF01374002.

Böhme, A. 1972. "Die Fibeln der Kastelle Saalburg und Zugmantel." *Saalburg Jahrbuch* 29: 5–112.

Böttger, B. 1967. "Einglätteter Dekor auf Gefässen aus römischen Donauprovinzen." *Wissenshaftlishe Zeitshrift d. Univ. Rostock* 16: 421–23.

– 1982. "Die Gefässkeramik aus dem Kastell Iatrus." In *Iatrus II*, 33–148.

Buchvarov, I. 1983. "Kolektivna nahodka ot bilonovi skifati v rayona na s. Draganovo, velikoturnovski okrug." *Numizmatika* 17(4): 3–13.

Buchi, E. 1975. *Lucerne del museo di Aquileia.* 1. *Lucerne romane con marchio di fabbrica.* Aquileia: Pubblicazioni dell'Associazione Nazionale per Aquileia.

Buko, A. 1990. *Ceramika Wczesnopolska. Wprowadzenie do badań.* Wrocław–Warszawa–Kraków: Ossolineum.

Bunsch, E., J. Kolendo, and J. Żelazowski, 2004. "Inscriptions découvertes entre 1998 et 2002 dans les ruines du valetudinarium à Novae." *Archeologia* 54 (2003): 43–64.

Buttrey, T.V. 1972. "Halved Coins, The Augustan Reform, and Horace, Odes I.3." *American Journal of Archaeology* 76(1): 31–48.

Campana, S. 2017. "Drones in Archaeology. State-of-the-art and Future Perspectives." *Archaeological Prospection*, 24(4): 275–96. DOI: 10.1002/arp.1569.

Campbell, B. 2000. *The Writings of the Roman Land Surveyors. Introduction, Text, Translation and Commentary.* London: Society for the Promotion of Roman Studies.

Cappers, R., Bekker R., and J. Jans, 2006. *Digital seed atlas of the Netherlands*, Groningen: Barkhuis Publishing.

Carandini, A., and C. Panella, 1981. "The trading connections of Rome and Central Italy in the late second and third centuries: the evidence of the terme del Nuotatore excavations, Ostia." In *The Roman West in the Third Century*, edited by A. King, B.A.R. Int. Ser., 109, 487–503. Oxford: BAR Publishing.

Carrington, P., C. Appleby, and A. Heke (eds.), site reports by Ward, S., Mason D.J.P., and J. McPeake, 2012. *Excavations at Chester: The Western and Southern Roman Extramural Settlements. A Roman Community on the Edge of the World: Excavations 1964–1989 and Other Investigations*, Chester Archaeological Excavation and Survey Report, 15, B.A.R. Br. Ser., 533, Oxford: Archaeopress.

Carrión Marco, Y. 2005. *La vegetación mediterránea y atlántica de la Península Ibérica. Nuevassecuencias atracológicas*, S.I.P. Serie de Trabajos Varios, 104. Valencia: Diputacion Provincial de Valencia.

Chabal, L. 1988. "Pourquoi et comment prélever les charbons de bois pour la période antique: les méthodes utilisés sur sites de Lattes (Hérault)." *Lattara* 1: 187–222.

– 1997. *Forêts et sociétés en Languedos (Néolithic final, Antiquité tardive). L'anthracologie, méthode et paléoécologie*, Documents d'Archéologie Française, 63, Paris: Éditions de la Maison des sciences de l'homme.

Chabal, L., L. Fabre, J.-Fr. Terral, and I. Théry-Parisot, 1999. "L'Anthracologie." In *La Botanique*, edited by Chr. Bourquin-Mignot, J.-E. Brochier, L. Chabal, S. Crozat, L. Fabre, J.-F. Terral, and I. Théry-Parisot, Collection « Archéologiques », 43–104. Paris: Errance.

Chapman, E.M. 2005. *A Catalogue of Roman Military Equipment in the National Museum of Wales*, B.A.R. Br. Ser., 388, Oxford: Archaeopress.

Cheynet, J.-C. 1999. "Les sceaux Byzantins du musée de Selçuk." *Revue numismatique* 154: 317–52.

Chichikova, M. 1950. "Kalupi za antichni glineni lampi ot Miziya." *Godishnik na Narodniya Arheologicheski Muzej Plovdiv* 2: 145–56.

– 1974. ""Firmalampen" du limes Danubien en Bulgarie." In *Actes du IXe congrès international d'études sur les frontières romaines: Mamaia, 6–13 septembre 1972*, 155–65. Bucarest: Editura Academiei.

– 1980. Forschungen in Novae, *Klio* 62: 50–67.

– 1987. "Pottery lamps from Novae (Lower Moesia), 1st–3rd century." *IAI* 37: 153–72.

– 1992. "L'édifice à perisyle extra muros à Novae (Moesia Inferior)." In *Studia Aegea et Balcanica in honorem Lodovicae Press*, 235–241. Warszawa: Wydawnictwa Uniwersytetu Warszawskiego.

– 2013. "Trakiyskata kultura v rayona na Nove." In *Sbornik v pamet na akademik D.P. Dimitrov*, edited by K. Rabadzhiev, 227–46. Sofiya: NAIM BAN.

Chiriac, C., and L. Munteanu, 2014. "Trade Connections between Asia Minor and the Western Pontic Area in the 4th Century CE. Some Sphragistic Considerations." In *Interconnectivity in the Mediterranean and Pontic World*, edited by V. Cojocaru, A. Coşkun, and M. Dana, 299–330. Cluj-Napoca: Mega Publishing House.

Chiriac, C., and C. Ungureanu, 2004. "Cius – New Roman finds on the Danubian limes in Scythia (Dobrodja)." *Arheologia Moldovei* 27: 233–39.

Cholakova, A. 2005. "Stukleni sudove ot rannovizantiyskoto ukrepeno selishte pri Dichin, Velikoturnovsko." In *Stephanos Archaeologicos in honorem Professoris Ludmili Getov*, edited by K. Rabadzhiev, and M. Milcheva, Studia Archaeologica Universitatis Serdicensis, Suppl. IV, 729–38. Sofiya: Universitetsko izdatelstvo "Sv. Kliment Ohridski."

– 2006a. "Rimski stukleni sudove ot Bulgariya (I–III v.)." In *Arheologiya na bulgarskite zemi*, vol. 2, 209–33. Sofiya: Ivray.

– 2006b. "Metalurgichni proizvodstva v rannata istoriya na Nikopolis ad Istrum." *IAI* 39: 163–84.

Chrzanovski, L. 2019. "Lamps from the foundation pits (fossae) in the principia of the castrum of Novae." *Polish Archaeology in the Mediterranean* 28(1): 263–95.

– 2020. "Firmalampen: an abundantly-produced lamp-type almost never used? Socio-economic elements to define a new framework to study these peculiar lighting devices." *Peuce (Serie Nouă) – Studii şi cercetari de istorie şi arheologie* 18: 215–62.

Ciołek, R. 2011. "Conclusions from the inventory." In P. Dyczek and R. Ciołek, *Novae. Legionary Fortress and Late Antique Town*, vol. II, *Coins from Sector IV*, 235–78. Warszawa: Wydawnictwa Uniwersytetu Warszawskiego.

Ciotola, A., S. Picciola, R. Santangeli Valenzani, and R. Volpe, 1989. "Roma: tre contesti. 1. Via Nova-Clivo Palatino. 2. Crypta Balbi. 3. Via Sacra-Via Nova." In *Amphores romaines et histoire économique. Dix ans de recherche. Actes du colloque de Sienne (22–24 mai 1986),* 114, 604–09. Rome: École Française de Rome.

Cipriano, S., and S. Mazzocchin, 2013. "Tappi d'anfora dall'area Veneta: Tipologia, cronologia ed epigrafia." In *Opercula Inscripta. Coperchi d'anfora fittili con scritte, segni e grafemi dall'area alto–adriatica, Aquileia, 14 aprile 2012*, edited by M. Buora, S. Magnani, and P. Ventura, Quaderni Friuliani di Archeologia, 22-23, 93–100. Udine: Editreg.

Cociş, A. 2004. *Fibulele din Dacia Romana*. Cluj-Napoca: Mega.

Combourieu-Nebout, N., Peyron, O., Dormoy, I., Desperat, S., Beaudouin, C., Kotthoff, U. and F. Marret, 2009. "Rapid climatic variability in the west Mediterranean during the last 25 000 years from high resolution pollen data", *Climate of the Past* 5: 503–21 (www.clim-past.net/5/503/2009/).

Comşa, M. 1969. "Ein Begräbnis-Fundverband aus dem 9.–10. Jahrhundert in Fintînele (Kreis Teleorman)." *Dacia* 13: 417–438.

Connor, M., and D. Scott, 1998. "Metal Detector Use in Archaeology: An Introduction." *Historical Archaeology* 32(4): 76–85.

Conrad, S. 2006a. "Archaeological Survey on the Lower Danube: Results and Perspectives." In *Surveying the Greek Chora. The Black Sea Region in a Comparative Perspective. International Conference, Sandbjerg, Denmark (31 August – 3 September 2003)*, edited by P. Guldager, and V.F. Stolba, Black Sea Studies, IV, 309–31. Aarhus: Aarhus University Press.

– 2006b. "Bemerkungen zu den Votivdenkmälern des Thrakischen Reiterheros am untermösischen Donaulimes." In *Pontos Euxeinos. Beiträge zur Archäologie und Geschichte des antiken Schwarzmeer – und Balkanraumes*, edited by S. Conrad, R. Einicke, A.E. Furtwängler, H. Löhr, and A. Slawisch, ZAKSS Schriften Bd. 10. 229–35. Langenweißbach: Beier&Berlan.

Conrad, S., and D. Stančev, 2002. "Archaeological survey on the Roman frontier on the lower Danube between Novae and Sexaginta Prista. Preliminary report (1997–2000)." In *Limes XVIII. Proceedings on the XVIIIth International Congress of Roman Frontier Studies held in Amman, Jordan (September 2000)*, vol. II, edited by J. Freeman, J. Bennett, Z.T. Fiema, and B. Hoffmann, B.A.R. Int. Ser., 1084, 673–84. Oxford: Archaeopress.

Corremans, M., J. Poblome, P.M. Bes, and M. Waelkens, 2010. "The Quantification of Amphorae from Roman Sagalassos, Turkey." In *Proceedings of the 12th Annual Meeting of the European Association of Archaeologists, Krakau (Poland), 19th September 2006 – 24th September 2006*, 285–303. Kraków: The Kraków Branch of the Polish Academy of Sciences.

Coulston, J. 1985. "Roman Archery Equipment." In *The Production and Distribution of Roman Military Equipment*, edited by M.C. Bishop, B.A.R. Int. Ser., 275, 220–336. Oxford: BAR Publishing.

Creighton, O.H., and D.W. Wright, 2016. *The Anarchy. War and Status in 12th-Century Landscape of Conflict*. Liverpool: Liverpool University Press.

Crişan, I.H. 1969. *Ceramica daco-getică: cu speciala privire la Transilvania*. Bucureşti: Editura Sţintifica.

Culică, V. 1975. "Plumburi comerciale din cetatea romano-bizantină de la Izvoarele (Dobrogea)." *Pontica* 8: 215-62.

– 1976. "Plumburi comerciale din cetatea romano-bizantină de la Izvoarele." *Pontica* 9: 115-33.

– 1979. "Plumburi comerciale din cetatea romano-bizantină de la Izvoarele (Addenda et corrigenda)." *Pontica* 12: 145–49.

Curta, F. 2002. "*Quaestura exercitus*: the evidence of lead seals." *Acta Byzantina Fennica (N.S.)* 1: 9–26.

– 2013. "The Beginning of the Middle Ages in the Balkans." *Millenium* 10(1): 145–214.

– 2016. "Amphorae and Seals: The 'Sub-Byzantine' Avars and the *Quaestura Exercitus*." In *Zwischen Byzanz und der Steppe. Archäologische und historische Studien Festschrift für Csanád Bálint zum 70. Geburtstag*, edited by Á. Bollók, G. Csiky, and T. Vida, 307-34. Budapest: Institute of Archaeology, Research Centre for the Humanities, Hungarian Academy of Sciences.

Cvjetičanin, T. 2005. "Flavian limes in Upper Moesia: A ceramic viewpoint (preliminary notes)." In *Römische Städte und Festungen an der Donau Akten der regionalen Konferenz organisiert von Alexander von Humboldt-Stiftung Beograd, 16–19 Oktober 2003*, edited by M. Mirković, 145–52. Belgrade: Filozofski fakultet Beograd.

– 2006. *Late Roman glazed pottery. Glazed pottery from Moesia Prima, Dacia ripensis, Dacia Mediterranea and Dardania.* Belgrade: National Museum.

Dankova, G. 1993. "Kieliszki i unguentaria z Novae. Materiały do katalogu." *Novensia* 6: 81–130.

Daszkiewicz, M., Bobryk, E., and G. Schneider, 2006. "Some Aspects of Composition, Technology and Functional Properties of Roman and Early Byzantine Pottery from Novae (Bulgaria)." In Klenina 2006: 189–211.

Daszkiewicz, M., E. Bobryk, G. Schneider, and S. Rădan, 2010. "Composition and technology of Lower Danube Kaolin ware (LDKW) – examples from Novae (Bulgaria)." *RCRFA* 41: 34–49.

Daszkiewicz, M., R. Naumann, G. Schneider, and M. Baranowski, 2013. "Referenzgruppen für moesische sigillata mit PRFA und WD-RFA." In *Metalla. Archäometrie und Denkmalpfege 2013. Jahrestagung and der Bauhaus-Universität Weimar, 25.–28. September 2013*, edited by A. Hauptmann, O. Mecking, and M. Prange, Metalla Sonderhefte, 6, 169–72. Bochum: Deutsches Bergbau-Museum.

Davies, R.W. 1968. "The Training Grounds of Roman Cavalry." *Archaeological Journal* 125(1): 73–100.

– 1971. "The Roman Military Diet." *Britannia* 2: 122–42.

Dąbrowska, E. 1979. "Węgrzy." In E. Dąbrowska, and W. Szymański, *Awarzy, Węgrzy*, 131–250. Wrocław–Warszawa–Kraków: Ossolineum.

Dąbrowski, K., and J. Kolendo, 1972. "Les épées romaines découvertes en Europe centrale et septentrionale." *Archaeologia Polona* 13: 59–109.

Degeest, R. 2000. *The Common Wares of Sagalassos*, Studies in Eastern Mediterranean Archaeology, 3. Turnhout: Brepols.

Dekówna, M. 1975. "Wyroby szklane z grodziska w Styrmen (Bułgaria)." *Slavia Antiqua* 22: 177–277.

Delrue, P. 2007. "Trilobate Arrowheads at ed-Dur (U.A.E., Emirate of Umm l-Quaiwain)." *Arabian Archaeology and Epigraphy* 18: 239–50.

Diaconu, Gh. 1971. "Über die Fibel mit umgeschlagenem Fuss in Dazien." *Dacia* 15: 239–65.

Dichek, P. (Dyczek, P.) 2003. "Terenni obhozhdaniya i sondazhi prouchvaniya na t. nar. teatur v okolnostite na Nove." In *AOR prez 2002 g.*, 111–12. Sofiya: NAIM BAN.

Dimitrov, K. 1980. "La circulation monetaire a Novae pendant la seconde moitie du III[e] siecle (selon les trouvailles numismatiques du secteur est)." In *Pulpudeva. Semaines philippopolitaines de l'histoire et de la culture Thrace*, vol. 3, *3–17 Octobre 1980*, edited by Al. Fol, 290–95. Sofiya: Izdatelstvo BAN.

– 2005a. "Monetna tsirkulaciya v Nove (Miziya II) prez 378–612 g. Statistika i istoricheska interpretatsiya." In *Heros Hephaistos: studia in honorem Liubae Ognenova-Marinova*, edited by T. Stojanov, M. Tonkova, Chr. Preshlenov, and Chr. Popov, 346–365. Sofiya: NAIM BAN & Universitet Sv. Kliment Ohridski.

– 2005b. "Novae and the Barbaric Incursions in 238–51," *Orpheus* 15: 79–98.

– 2011. "Antichni i rannovizantiyski moneti ot sektor XI (*principia*) na Nove (Dolna i Vtora Miziya)." In *Varia Thracica. Studia in honorem Mariae Čičikova*, edited by M. Hristova, and L. Aleksiyeva, 140–216. Sofiya: Akademichno Izdatelstvo "Prof. Marin Drinov."

– 2013a. "Antichni moneti ot rayona na Nove (Miziya), secheni predi osnovaneto na rimskiya voenen lager (V v. pr. Hr.–41 g. sl. Hr.)." In *Sbornik v pamet na akademik D.P. Dimitrov*, edited by K. Rabadzhiev, 712–66. Sofiya: NAIM BAN.

– 2013b. "The *thermae legionis* in Novae (Moesia Inferior and Moesia Secunda): numismatic evidence and historical probabilities." In *Studia classica Serdicensia II. Sbornik v chest na professor Ruska Gandeva (1911–2001)*, edited by S. Yanakieva, and V. Gerdhikova, 244–61. Sofiya: Universitet Sv. Kliment Ohridski.

– 2014. "Nove (Miziya II) prez 346/8–378 g. Monetni nahodki i istoriya." In *Balkanite i svetut: modus concurrandi*, edited by L. Simeonova, Studia Balcanica, 50, 55–62. Sofiya: Institut za balkanistika s Tsentur po trakologiya BAN.

Dimitrov, D.P., Chichikova, M., Soultov, B., and A. Dimitrova, 1970. "Arheologicheski raskopki v vostochnom sektore Nove prez 1966 g.," *IAI* 32: 55–71.

Dimitrova-Chudilova, S. 2008. "Osobenosti na Bulgarskoto srednovekovno monetosechene – imitacii ili falshivi moneti?" In *Phosphorion. Studia in honorem Mariae Čičikova*, edited by D.S. Gergova, 574–80. Sofiya: Akademichno Izdatelstvo "Prof. Marin Drinov".

Dimitrova-Milcheva, M. 2006. *Die Bronzefunde aus Novae, Moesia inferior.* Warszawa: Wydawnictwa Uniwersytetu Warszawskiego.

Dobruski, V. 1900. "Materiali po arhologiya na Bulgariya." *Bulgarski pregled* 6: 3–146.

Dochev, K. 1992. *Moneti i parichno obrashtenie v Turnovo XII–XIV v.* Veliko Turnovo: Vital.

Dohijo, E. 2016. Los "osculatorios" hallados en el yacimiento de Thermes (Soria). Varillas con y sin anilla circular y remate figurado, versus removedores y/o ruecas." *Oppidum* 12: 149–183.

Dolenz, H. 1992. "Studien zu den Eisenmessern vom Magdalensberg in Kärnten." *Carinthia I*, 182: 93–134.

Domżalski, K. 1998. "Ceramika stołowa z principia w Novae. Wypełnisko jamy nr 4." *Novensia* 11: 141–55.

Doncheva-Petkova, L. 1992. "Dva modela za kolanni aplikacji." *Prinosi kum bulgarskata arheologiya* 1: 210–13.

Doneus, M., Chr. Gugl, and N. Doneus, 2013. *Die Canabae von Carnuntum – eine Modellstudie der Erforschung römischer Lagervorstädte Von der Luftbildprospektion zur siedlungsarchäologischen Synthese*, Der Römische Limes in Österreich, 47. Wien: Verlag der Österreichischen Akademie der Wissenschaften.

Donevski, P. 1991. "Razkopki v mestnostta Ostrite Mogili iztochno ot Nove." In *AOR prez 1990 g.*, 95–96. Lovech: NAIM BAN.

Doniţă, N., U. Bohn, T. Raus, and H. Wagner, 2004. "Thermophilous mixed deciduous broadleaved forests." In Bohn *et al.* 2004, 317–341.

Doruţiu-Boilă, E. 1985. "Legaten von Moesia Inferior zwischen 190 und 198." *ZPE* 58: 197–203.

Duch, M. 2011. "Polish Studies of Impressed Building Ceramics from Novae. An Attempt to Determine the Chronology of Occurrence of the 1st Italian Legion Stamps." In *Studia Lesco Mrozewicz ab amicis et discipulis dedicata*, edited by S. Ruciński, K. Królczyk, and K. Balbuza, 73–85. Poznań: Instytut Historii UAM.

– 2012. "Flawijskie stemple na cegłach i dachówkach łaźni legionowej w Novae (Moesia Inferior)." *Studia Flaviana* 2: 259–82.

– 2017. "Stamps on bricks and tiles from Novae. Outline of chronology." *Novensia* 28: 99–119.

Dyczek, P. 1999. "A Glass Atelier from Sector IV in Novae." In *Limes von Diokletian*, 99–104.

– 2001. Roman Amphorae of the 1st–3rd centuries AD Found on the Lower Danube. Typology. Warszawa: Wydawnictwa Uniwersytetu Warszawskiego.

– 2005. "A new pottery manufacturing center at Novae." In *Congressus vicesimus quartus Rei Cretariae Romanae Fautorum Namuri et Duobus Lovaniis habitus MMIV,* edited by S. Ladstätter, (= RCRFA 39), 301–06. Abingdon: Habelt-Verlag.

– 2008. "The latest settlement in Novae." In *Companion Novae,* 235–45.

– 2009. "Ceramika typu Lower Danube Kaolin wares (LDKW). Dystrybucja, datowanie, funkcja, typologia, geneza, miejsca produkcji." *Novensia* 20: 153–71.

– 2010. "Kapitän II amphorae from Novae – between east and west." In LRCW 3, Late Roman Coarse Wares, Cooking Wares and Amphorae in the Mediterranean. Archaeology and Acheometry Comparison between western and eastern Mediterranean, edited by S. Manchelli, S. Santoro, M. Pasquinucci, and G. Guiducci, B.A.R. Int. Ser. 2185(II), 993–99. Oxford: BAR Publishing.

– 2011. "Observations on Marks on Rooftiles Bricks and Ceramic Tiles from Sector in Novae (Moesia Inferior)." *Novensia* 22: 85–108.

Dzhonova, D. 1961. "Svetilishte na Dionis kray Svishtov." *Arheologiya* (Sofia) 3(2): 21–24.

Egri, M. 2007. "The Use of Amphorae for Interpreting Patterns of Consumption." *Theoretical Roman Archaeology Journal* (2006): 43–58.

Empereur, J.-Y., and M. Picon, 1989. "Les régions de production d'amphores impériales en Méditerranée orientale." In *Amphores romaines et histoire économique. Dix ans de recherche. Actes du colloque de Sienne (22–24 mai 1986)*, Publications de l'École française de Rome, 114, 223–48. Rome: École Française de Rome.

Enciu, P., D. Balteanu, and C. Dumitrica, 2015. "Contributions to the knowledge of Quaternary formations in the southwest Romanian Plain." *Quaternary International* 357: 58–69.

Ettlinger, E. 1973. *Die römischen Fibeln in der Schweiz.* Bern: Francke.

Evans, E. 2000. *The Caerleon Canabae*, Britannia Monograph Series, 16. London: Society for the Promotion of Roman Studies.

Fagan, G.G. 2002. *Bathing in Public in the Roman World.* Ann Arbor: University of Michigan Press (2nd edition).

Falkner, R.K. 1999. "The Pottery." In *Nicopolis I,* 55–296.

Faure, P. 2019. "*Accepta pariatoria* et primipilat. Nouvelles hypothèses sur un monument inscrit de Nouae." Tyche 34: 61–80.

Feind, R. 2010. *Byzantinische Monogramme und Eigennamen. Alphabetisiertes Wörterbuch.* Regenstauf: Gietl.

Fiedler, U. 1992. *Studien zu Gräberfeldern des 6. bis 9. Jahrhunderts an der unteren Donau.* Bonn: Habelt.

Filipović, D., Meadows, J., Corso, M.D., Kirleis, W., Alsleben, A., Akeret, Ö., Bittmann, F., Bosi, G., Ciută, B., Dreslerová, D., Effenberger, H., Gyulai, F., Heiss, A.G., Hellmund, M., Jahns, S., Jakobitsch, T., Kapcia, M., Klooß, S., Kohler-Schneider, M., Kroll, H., Makarowicz, P., Marinova, E., Märkle, T., Medović, A., Mercuri, A.M., Mueller-Bieniek, A., Nisbet, R., Pashkevich, G., Perego, R., Pokorný, P., Pospieszny, Ł., Przybyła, M., Reed, K., Rennwanz, J., Stika, H.-P., Stobbe, A., Tolar, T., Wasylikowa, K., Wiethold, J., and T. Zerl, 2020. "New AMS 14C dates track the arrival and spread of broomcorn millet cultivation and agricultural change in prehistoric Europe." Scientific Reports 10: 13698.

Fodor, I. 1977. *Altungarn, Bulgarotürken und Ostslawen in Südrussland (archäologische Beiträge)*, Acta Universitatis de Attila József Nominatae, Acta antiqua et archaeologica, 20, Opuscula Byzantina, 4. Szeged: JATE.

– 1996. *The Ancient Hungarians. Exhibition Catalogue.* Budapest: Magyar Nemzeti Múzeum.

Franke, R. 2009. *Römische Kleinfunde aus Burghöfe,* 3. *Militärische Aurüstungsgegestände, Pferdegeschirr, Bronzegeschirr und-gerät,* Fruhgeschichtliche und Provinzialrömische Archäologie. Materialen und Forschungen, 9. Rahden/Westf: VML.

Freestone, I. 2005. "The provenance of ancient glass through compositional analysis." In *Materials Issues in Art and Archaeology VII*, edited by P. Vandiver, J. Mass, and A. Murray, 195–208. Warrendale: Materials Research Society.

– 2008. "Pliny on Roman Glassmaking." In *Archaeology, History and Science: Integrating Approaches to Ancient Materials*, edited by M. Martinon-Torres, and Th. Rehren, 77–100. London: Routledge.

Gacuta, W. 1987. "Przedmioty metalowe z Novae – kampanie wykopaliskowe z lat 1960–1969, 1971, 1973, 1975 i 1977." *Novensia* 1: 75–176.

– 1993. "Przedmioty metalowe z Novae. 6 kampanii wykopaliskowych ekspedycji Archeologicznej w latach 1977–1987." *Novensia* 5: 7–177.

Gacuta, W., and T. Sarnowski, 1981. "Zespół zabytków metalowych z rumowiska kaplicy sztandarów i jej najbliższego otoczenia." *Archeologia* 30 (1979): 227–32.

– 1982. "Skarb brązów z zachodniego aerarium komendantury w Novae." *Archeologia* 33: 125–42.

Gaj-Popović, D. 1980. "Olovni pečat cara Iustnijana." *Numizmatičar* 3: 165–68.

Gardawski, A. 1970. *Chodlik, cz. 1. Wczesnośredniowieczny zespół osadniczy.* Wrocław–Warszawa–Kraków: Zakład im. Ossolińskich.

Gencheva (Genčeva), E. 2000. "Metalowe części wyposażenia żołnierskiego z Novae." *Novensia* 12: 49–98.

– 2001. "Terenni obhozhdaniya v hinterlanda na rimskiya voenen lager i rannovizantiyski grad Nove prez 2000 g." In *AOR prez 1999–2000 gg.*, 75–76. Sofiya: NAIM BAN.

– 2002. Purviyat voenen lager v Novae provinciya Miziya (Severna Bulgariya). Sofia–Warszawa: Wydawnictwa Uniwersytetu Warszawskiego.

– 2004. *Rimskite fibuli ot Bulgariya ot kraya na I v. pr. n.e. do kraya na VI v. na n.e.* Veliko Turnovo: Faber.

Gencheva, E., and Ya. Retslav (Recław), 2010. "Sondazhni prouchvaniya na putishta kum voeniya lager Nove." In *AOR prez 2009 g.*, 317. Sofiya: NAIM BAN.

Genning V.F., and A.H. Halikov, 1964. *Rannye Bolgary na Volge, Tarhanski mogilnik.* Moskva: Nauka.

Gerov, B. 1964. "Die Rechtsstellung der untermösischen Stadt Novae." In *Akten des 4. Internationalen Kongresses für Griechische und Lateinische Epigraphik. Wien 17. bis 22. September, 1962*, 128–33. Wien: Böhlau (reprinted in *Beiträge Gerov*, 113–18).

– 1977. "Zum Problem der Entstehung der römischen Städte am Unteren Donaulimes." *Klio* 59: 299–309.

– 1998. "Zur epigraphischen Dokumentation des publicum portorii Illyrici et ripae Thraciae." In *Beiträge Gerov*, 479–90.

Giuzelev, V. 1986. "Bułgarskie średniowiecze." In *Bułgaria. Zarys Dziejów / Kratka istoriya na Bulgariya),* edited by I. Dymitrov, and A. Kosewski, 23–54. Warszawa: Książka i Wiedza.

Gkoutzioukostas, A. 2008. "Published lead seals concerning *quaestura exercitus*". In *Yubilen sbornik 'Sto godin ot rozhdenieto na d-r Vasil Charalanov (1907–2007)'*, 109–18. Shoumen: Regionalen istoricheski muzey.

Głowacki, Z. 1975. "Badania metaloznawcze." In Novae-Sektor Zachodni 1972. Wyniki badań wykopaliskowych ekspedycji archeologicznej Uniwersytetu im. Adama Mickiewicza w Poznaniu, 275–79. Poznań: Wydawnictwa UAM.

Gomolka, G. 1979. "Die spätantike Glässer aus Iatrus." In *Iatrus I*, 145–66.

von Gonzenbach, V. 1963. "Die Verbreitung der gestempelten Ziegel der im 1. Jahrhundert n. Chr. in Vindonissa liegenden römischen Truppen." *BJb* 163: 76–150.

Gostenčik, K. 2012. "Austria: Roman Period." In *Textiles and Textile Production in Europe from Prehistory to AD 400*, edited by M. Gleba, and U. Mannering, Ancient Textiles Series, 11, 65–88. Oxbow Books: Oakville.

Grigorov, V. 2003. "Prinos kum prouchvaneto na starobulgarskata diadema (VIII–XI v.)." *Arheologiya* (Sofia) 44(1): 29–38.

– 2004. "Srednovekovna diadema-prochelnik ot Nacjonalniya arheologicheski muzey – Sofiya." *Arheologiya* (Sofia) 45(1-2): 61–62.

Grünewald, M. 1979. *Die Gefässkeramik des Legionslagers von Carnuntum (Grabungen 1968–1974)*, Der römische Limes in Österreich, 29, Wien: Österreichische Akademie der Wissenschaften.

– 1980. "Zur spätrömischen Fundstoff im Legionslager Carnuntum." In *Die Völker an der mittleren und unteren Donau im fünften und sechsten Jahrhundert*, edited by H. Wolfram, and F. Daim, Österreichische Akademie der Wissenschaften, Phil.-Hist. Klasse Denkschriften, 145, 29–32. Wien: Österreichische Akademie der Wissenschaften.

– 1983. *Die Funde aus dem Schutthügel des Legionslagers von Carnuntum, Die Baugrube Pingitzer*, Der römische Limes in Österreich, 32. Wien: Österreichische Akademie der Wissenschaften.

Gudea, N. 1994. "Römische Waffen aus den Kastellen des westlichen Limes von Dacia Porolissensis." In *Beiträge zu römischer und barbarischer Bewaffnung in der ersten vier nachchristlichen Jahrhunderten*, edited by C. von Carnap-Bornheim, 79–89. Lublin–Marburg: Vorgeschichtliches Seminar der Philipps-Universität Marburg.

– 2003a. "Contribuţii la istoria militară a provinciei Moesia inferior. 1. Propunere pentru lectura unei ştampile militare încănerezvolvate: CEMEL." *Banatica* 16: 323–32.

– 2003b. "Contribuţii la istoria militară a provinciei Moesia inferior. 2. Pentru o nouă tipologie a ştampilelor legiunii I Italica." *Ephemeris Napocensis* 13: 195–216.

– 2005. "Der untermoesische Donaulimes und die Verteidigung der moesischen Nord- und Westkuste des Schwarzen Meeres. Limes et litus Moesiae Inferioris (86–275 n. Chr.)." *Jahrbuch des Römisch-Germanischen Zentralmuseums* 52(2): 317–566.

– 2006. "Contribuţii la cunoaşterea limesului provinciei Moesia Inferior 1. Cazul Iatrus." *Revista Bistriţei* 20: 177–86.

Gudea, N., and M. Zahariade, 2016. *Dacia ripensis. Festungen an der Nordgrenze der Provinz und ihre Truppenkörper.* Amsterdam: A.M. Hakkert.

Guest, P., Luke, M., Pudney, C., Webster, P., Lewis, M., and A. Powell, 2012. *Archaeological Evaluation of the Extramural Monumental Complex ('The Southern Canabae') at Caerleon, 2011. An Interim Report*, Cardiff Studies in Archaeology, 33. Cardiff: Department of Archaeology & Conservation, School of History, Archaeology and Religion, Cardiff University.

Gugl, Chr. 2012. "Leugengrenze und juristischer Status von canabae-Siedlungen." In *Akten des 13. Österreichischen Archäologentages. Klassische und Frühägäische Archäologie. Paris – London – Universität Salzburg vom 25. bis 27. Februar 2010*, edited by C. Reinholdt, and W. Wohlmayr, 413–20. Wien: Phoibos Verlag.

Gurova, M. *et al.* 2016. "Flint raw material transfers in the prehistoric Lower Danube Basin: An integrated analytical approach." *Journal of Archaeological Science: Reports* 5: 422–41.

Gülbay, O., and H. Kireç, 2008. *Efes kursun tesseraelari / Ephesian lead tesserae.* Selçuk: Selcuk Belediyesi.

Gylybov, Zh. et al. 1960. *Fizicheskaya geografiya Bolgarii*, Moskva.

Hahn, W. 1973 (= *MIB*). *Moneta Imperii Byzantini. Rekonstruktion des Prägeaufbaues auf synoptisch-tabellarischer Grundlage*, vol. 1: *Von Anastasius I. bis Justinianus I. (491–565).* Wien: Verlag der Österreichischen Akademie der Wissenschaften.

Halikov, A.H. 1985. *Kul'tura Bilyara-Bulgorskiye orudiya truda i orshiye X–XIII vv.* Moskva: Nauka.

Hanel, N. 2007. "Military Camps, Canabae, and Vici. The Archaeological Evidence." In *A Companion to the Roman Army*, edited by P. Erdkamp, 395–416. Oxford: Wiley-Blackwell.

– 2002. "Ein Ziegelstempel der cohors XV Voluntariorum c. R. aus der Tegularia transrhenana im Flottenlager Köln-Marienburg (Alteburg)." *ZPE* 139: 293–96.

– 2013. "Zur Frage des so genannten "Militärterritoriums" in Niedergermanien." In *Imperium und Romanisierung. Neue Forschungsansätze aus Ost und West zu Ausübung, Transformation und Akzeptanz von Herrschaft im Römischen Reich*, edited by Al. Rubel, 73–84. Konstanz: Hartung-Gorre Verlag.

Harden, D.B. 1961. "Domestic Window Glass: Roman, Saxon and Medieval." In *Studies in Building History*, edited by E.M. Jope, 39–63. London: Oldhams.

Harhoiu, R. 2005. "Die untere Donau während der späten Kaiserzeit und der Völkerwanderungszeit." In *Wasserwege: Lebensadern – Trennungslinien*, edited by C. von Carnap-Bornheim, H. Friesinger, 157–91. Neumünster: Wachholtz.

Harmatta, J. 1974. "*The Problem of the Juristic Conditions of Land in* Pannonia." In *I diritti locali*, 77–88.

Hasebroek, J. 1921. *Untersuchungen zur Geschichte des Kaisers Septimius Severus.* Heidelberg: Carl Winter.

Heath, S., and B. Tekkök (eds), 2012. *Greek, Roman and Byzantine Pottery at Ilion (Troia), 2006 – 2009. Roman Period Cooking Vessels* (retrieved 12.11.2012 from http://wareics.uc.edu/troy/grbpottery/).

Henderson, J. 2013. *Ancient Glass. An Interdisciplinary Exploration.* Cambridge: Cambridge University Press.

Hendy, M.F. 1969. *Coinage and money in the Byzantine Empire 1081–1261.* Washington, D.C.: Dumbarton Oaks Center for Byzantine Studies, Trustees for Harvard University.

– 1985. *Studies in the Byzantine Monetary Economy c. 300–1450.* Cambridge: Cambridge University Press.

Henning, J. 2007. "Catalogue of archaeological finds from Pliska." In *Post-Roman Towns, Trade and Settlement in Europe and Byzantium*, vol. 2: *Byzantium, Pliska, and the Balkans*, edited by J. Henning, 601–704. Berlin–Boston: de Gruyter.

– 2011. "Pliska and Continental Europe in the later 9th to 10th c. AD. Invasions, state formation and stronghold building." In *Proceedings of the 22nd International Congress of Byzantine Studies, Sofia, 22–27 August 2011*, vol. 2: *Abstracts and Round Table Communications*, edited by Angel Nikolov with the assistance of E. Kostova, and V. Angelov, 251–52. Sofia: Bulgarian Historical Heritage Foundation.

Hensel, W. (ed.), Dymaczewski, A., Dymaczewska, U., and Z. Kurnatowska 1980. *Styrmen nad Jantrą (Bułgaria). Badania archeologiczne w latach 1961–1964 i 1967–1968.* Wrocław–Warszawa–Kraków–Gdańsk: Wydawnictwo PAN.

Hensel, W. (ed.), Dymaczewski, A., Hilczerówna, Z., and T. Wiślański, 1965. "Materiały z badań archeologicznych w Bułgarii." *Slavia Antiqua* 12: 235–87.

Horster, M., 2001. Bauinschriften römischer Kaiser. Untersuchungen zu Inschriftenpraxis und Bautätigkeit in Städten des westlichen Imperium Romanum in der Zeit des Prinzipats, Historia Einzelschriften, Bd. 157, Stuttgart: Franz Steiner Verlag.

Hristova, I., Atanassova, J., and Marinova, E., 2017. "Plant economy and vegetation of the Iron Age in Bulgaria: archaeobotanical evidence from pit deposits." *Archaeological and Anthropological Science* 9: 1481–94.

Isings, C. 1967. *Roman Glass from Dated Finds.* Groningen–Djakarta: J.B. Wolters.

Ivanišević, V., and M. Kazanski, 2007. "Nouvelle nécropole des grandes migrations de Singidunum." *Starinar* 57: 113–35.

Ivanov, R. 1993. "Ulpia Oescus – römische und frühbyzantinische Stadt in Moesia inferior (heute VR Bulgarien)." *Bulgarian Historical Review* 21(2-3): 26–28.

– 2002. *Stroitelna keramika ot Dolniya Dunav. Bricks and Tiles from the Lower Danube (Oescus – Novae – Durostorum).* Sofia: Alea.

Ivanov, R. and T. Kovacheva 2002. Ulpiya Eskus. In Rimski i rannovizantiyski gradove v Bulgariya. Vol. I, 31–58, Sofiya: NAIM BAN.

Ivanova, V. 1926. "Stari tsurkvi i manastiri vu Bulgarskit' zemi (IV–XII v.)." *Godishnik na Natsionalniya Muzey* (1922–1925): 429–582.

Jackson, C.M. 2005. "Making colourless glass in the Roman period." *Archaeometry* 47(4): 763–80.

Jessop, O. 1999. "A New Artifact Typology for the Study of Medieval Arrowheads." *Medieval Archaeology* 40: 192–205.

Jones, A.H.M. 1964. *The Later Roman Empire, 284–602. A Social, Economic and Administrative Survey*, vol. 1. Oxford: Basil Blackwell.

Kabukcu, C. 2018. "Wood charcoal analysis in archaeology." In *Environmental Archaeology. Current Theoretical and Methodological Approaches*, edited by Pişkin, E., Marciniak, A., and M. Bartkowiak, 133–54. Springer (https://doi.org/10.1007/978-3-319-75082-8).

Kabukcu, C., and L. Chabal, 2021. "Sampling and quantitative analysis methods in anthracology from archaeological contexts: Achievements and prospects." *Quaternary International* 593–94: 6–18.

Kanitz, F. 1879. *Donau Bulgarien und der Balkan. Historisch-geographisch-etnographische Reisestudien aus den Jahren 1860–1879*, vol. I-II. Zweite neu bearbeitete Auflage, Leipzig: H. Fries.

Karagiorgou, O. 2001. "LR2: a container for the military annona on the Danubian border?" In *Economy and Exchange in the East Mediterranean during Late Antiquity. Proceedings of a Conference at Somerville College, Oxford, 29th May, 1999*, edited by S. Kingsley, and M. Decker, 129–66. Oxford: Oxbow Books.

Karasiewicz-Szczypiorski, R. 1998. "Ceramika kuchenna z komendantury w Novae. Wypełnisko jamy nr 4." *Novensia* 11: 191–202.

Kats, N.Ya., Kats, S.V., and M.G. Kipiani, 1965. *Atlas i opredelitel' plodov i semyan vstrechayushchichsya v chetviertichnych otlozhenijach SSSR* (Atlas and keys of fruits and seeds occurring in the Quaternary deposits of the USSR). Moskva: Nauka.

Kazakevičius, V. 2004. *Geležies amžiaus strėlės Lietuvoje II–XIII a.*, Vilnius: Generolo Jono Žemaičio Lietuvos Karo Akad., Lietuvos Istorijos Inst.

Keay, S.J. 1984. *Late Roman amphorae in the Western Mediterranean. A typology and economic study: the Catalan evidence*, B.A.R. Int. Ser. 196, Oxford: BAR Publishing.

Kerr, W.G. 1991. "Economic Warfare on the Northern Limes: Portoria and the Germans." In *Roman Frontier Studies 1989: Proceedings of the XVth International Congress of Roman Frontier Studies*, edited by V.A. Maxfield, and M. Dobson, 442. Exeter: University of Exeter Press.

Kienast, D., Eck, W. and M. Heil, 2017. *Römische Kaisertabelle. Grundzüge einer römischen Kaiserchronologie.* 6. überarbeitete Auflage, WBG Wissen *verbindet.*

Klenina, E. 1999. "Table and Cooking Pottery of the IV – VI A.D. from the Excavation of the Episcopal Residence in Novae." In *Limes von Diokletian*, 87–94.

– 2006. *Stolovaya i kuhonnaya keramika III – VI vekov iz Nov (Severna Bolgariya) / Stołowa i kuchenna ceramika III – VI wieku z Novae (północna Bułgaria)*, Novae. Studies and Materials, II. Poznań: Wydawnictwo Wydziału Historii UAM.

Kneissl, P. 1969. *Die Siegestitulatur der römischen Kaiser. Untersuchungen zu den Siegerbeinamen des ersten und zweiten Jahrhunderts*, Hypomnemata, 23. Göttingen: Vandenhoeck et Ruprecht.

Kolendo, J. 1968. "Découvertes d'inscriptions grecques pendant la guerre russo-turque 1828–1829." *Archeologia* 18: 51–54.

– 1981. "Le centre non-identifié de production des lampes romaines sur le Bas-Danube. Lucernaria burgus ches Procope de Césarée." *Kwartalnik Historii Kultury Materialnej* 1: 55–57.

– 2008a. "Archaeological Research Prior to the Start of Excavation." In *Companion Novae*, 3–30.

– 2008b. "Novae during the Goth Raid of AD 250/1 (Iordanes, Getica 101–103)." In *Companion Novae*, 117–31.

Kolendo, J., and T. Kowal, 2011. "Stamps on Ceramic Pipes from Novae (Moesia inferior)." *Novensia* 22: 67–76.

– 2015. "Iron Components of Agricultural Tools Discovered During Excavations at Novae: Are They Always Ancient or Early Medieval in Date?" In *Ad fines*, 289–302.

Kontny, B., and M. Mączyńska, 2015. "Ein Kriegergrab aus der frühen Völkerwanderungszeit von Juszkowo in Nordpolen." In *Dying Gods. Religious beliefs in northern and eastern Europe in the time of Christianisation*, edited by Ch. Ruhmann and V. Brieske, Neue Studien zur Sachsenforschung, 5, 241–62. Hannover: Niedersächsisches Landesmusem.

Kotecki, J. 1978. "Piec garncarski w sondażu wodociągowym." In Majewski 1978, 193–200.

Kouzmanov, G. 1985. *Rannovizantiyska keramika ot Trakiya i Dakiya (IV – nachaloto na VII vek)*, Sofiya: Archeologicheski Institut i Muzey (Bulgarska Akademiya na Naukite).

Kouzmanov, G. and A. Minchev, 2018. *Antichni lampi. Kolekciya na RIM Varna*, edited by L. Vagalinski, and T. Stefanova, Sofiya: NAIM BAN.

Kovacheva, T. 1985. "Kultovi pametnici na Trakiyskija konnik ot Plevensko." *Vekove* 5: 1985, 48–49.

Kovács, P. 2000. "Consistentes intra leugam." In *Epigraphica*, 1. *Studies on epigraphy*, Hungarian Polis Studies, 6, 39–56. Debrecen: University of Debrecen.

– 2013. "*Territoria, pagi* and *vici* in Pannonia." In *Studia epigraphica in memoriam Géza Alföldy*, edited by W. Eck, B. Feher, and P. Kovács, 131–54. Bonn: Habelt.

Kowal, T. 2011. "Ciężarki z Novae (Moesia inferior) wydobyte przez Ekspedycję Archeologiczną Uniwersytetu Warszawskiego w latach 1960–2010." *Novensia* 22: 127–47.

Kowal, T., and S. Kozłowski, 2011. "Zabytki prehistoryczne z Novae i Ostrite Mogili." *Novensia* 22: 7–13.

Kozłowski, J.K., and M. Kaczanowska, 2004. „Gravettian / Epigravettian sequences in the Balkans and Anatolia." *Mediterranean Archaeology and Archaeometry* 4: 5–18.

Körber-Grohne, U. 1988. *Nutzpflanzen in Deutschland. Kulturgeschichte und Biologie*. Stuttgart: Konrad Theiss Verlag.

Kritzinger, P., and K. Zimmermann, 2019. "Die Heeresversorgung des 4. Jahrhunderts im Spiegel von Historiographie und Sphragistik." In *Aspetti di tarda antichità. Storici, storia e documenti del IV secolo d.C.*, edited by T. Gnoli, 279–316. Bologna: Pàtron.

Kunisz, A. 1992. "Le monnàie et les camps des légionnaires romains le long du bas Danube aux Ier, IIème et IIIème siecles: l'example de Novae," *Litterae Numismaticae Vindobonenses* 4: 107–14.

– 1984. *Pieniądz zastępczy i jego rola w ekonomice państwa rzymskiego w początkach Cesarstwa (27 r. p.n.e. –68 r. n.e.)*, Prace naukowe Uniwersytetu Śląskiego w Katowicach, 663. Katowice: Uniwersytet Śląski.

– 1987. *Le trésor d'antoniniens et de folles des "principia" de la legion de Novae (Bulgarie)*, Studia Antiqua, 10. Warszawa: Wydawnictwa Uniwersytetu Warszawskiego.

Kurnatowska, Z. 1977. *Słowiańszczyzna południowa*. Wrocław–Warszawa–Kraków: Zakład Narodowy im. Ossolińskich.

Kurzmann, R. 2005. "Soldier, Civilian and Military Brick Production." *Oxford Journal of Archaeology* 24: 405–13.

– 2006. *Roman Military Brick Stamps. A Comparison of Methodology*, B.A.R. Int. Ser. 1543. Oxford: Archaeopress.

Laiou, E.A. 2012. "Regional Networks in the Balkans in the Middle and Late Byzantine Periods." In *Trade and Markets in Byzantium*, edited by C. Morrisson, 125–46. Washington, D.C.: Dumbarton Oaks Research Library and Collection.

Langgut, D., Cheddadi, R., Carrión, J.S., Cavanag, M, Colombaroli, D., Eastwood, W.J., Greenberg, R., Litt, T., Mercuri, A.M., Miebach, A., Roberts, N., Woldring, H., and J. Woodbridge, 2019. "The origin and spread of olive cultivation in the Mediterranean Basin: The fossil pollen evidence." *The Holocene* 29(5): 902–922.

Latałowa, M., Tobolski, K. and D. Nalepka, 2004. "Pinus L. subgenus Pinus (subgen. Diploxylon (Koehne) Pilger) – Pine." In *Late Glacial and Holocene history of vegetation in Poland based on isopollen maps*, edited by M. Ralska-Jasiewiczowa et al., 165–178. Kraków: W. Szafer Inst. of Botany, Polish Academy of Sciences.

Leciejewicz, L. 1976. *Słowiańszczyzna zachodnia*. Wrocław: Zakład Narodowy im. Ossolińskich.

Lehner, H. 1904. "Die Einzelfunde von Novaesium. I. Die Ziegel." *BJb* 111/112: 289–306.

Lemke, M. 2005. "Kolczyki z cmentarzyska średniowiecznego w Novae." *Novensia* 17: 53–61.

– 2015. "Marsigli's Moesia: The Limes Sites in Bulgaria as Seen in the 18th Century." In *Ad fines*, 173–92.

– 2021. "Wasserversorgung mit einem Hauch von Selbstdarstellung. Zu den gestempelten flavischen Tonrohren aus Novae." In: *Antiquitas Aeterna. Classical Studies dedicated to Leszek Mrozewicz on his 70th Birthday* (=Phillippika 153), edited by: K. Balbuza, M. Duch, Z. Kaczmarek, K. Królczyk, A. Tatarkiewicz, 185–19. Wiesbaden: Harrassowitz.

LeRoux, P. 1982. *L'armée romain et l'organisation des provinces ibériques d'Auguste a l'invasion de 409*, Collection de la Maison de pays ibériques, 9, Paris: De Boccard.

Leunissen, P. 1989. *Konsulen und Konsulare in der Zeit von Commodus bis Severus Alexander. Prosopographische Untersuchungen zur senatorischen Elite im römischen Kaiserreich.* Amsterdam: J.C. Gieben.

Leveau, P. 1993. "*Territorium urbis*. Le territoire de la cité romaine et ses divisions: du vocabulaire aux réalités administratives." *Revue des Études Anciennes* (Bordeaux): 95(3-4): 460–71.

Liebeschuetz, J.H.W.G. 2001. *The Decline and Fall of the Roman City*. Oxford-New York: Oxford University Press.

Lipa, Sz. 2000. "Badania teledetekcyjne w Novae." *Novensia* 12: 133–47.

Liphschitz, N., Gophna, R., Hartman, M. and G. Biger, 1991. "The beginning of olive (Olea europaea) cultivation in the Old World: A reassessment." Journal of Archaeological Science 18: 441–453.

Lipovac Vrkljan, G., Konestra, A., and I. Ožanić Roguljić, 2013. "I tappi d'anfora dall'officina ceramica di Crikvenica." In *Opercula Inscripta. Coperchi d'anfora fittili con scritte, segni e grafemi dall'area alto–adriatica, Aquileia, 14 aprile 2012*, edited by M. Buora, S. Magnani, and P. Ventura, Quaderni Friuliani di Archeologia, 22–23, 129–35. Udine: Editreg.

Lityńska-Zając, M. 2005. *Chwasty w uprawach roślinnych w pradziejach i wczesnym średniowieczu*. Kraków: IAIE PAN.

Lityńska-Zając, M., and K. Wasylikowa, 2005. "Przewodnik do badań archeobotanicznych." In *Vademecum Geobotanicum*, edited by J.B. Faliński, 563. Poznań: Wydawnictwo Naukowe PWN.

Loeschke, S. 1912. "Sigillata-Töpfereien in Çandarlı." *Athenische Mitteilungen* 37: 344–407.

– 1919. *Lampen aus Vindonissa: Ein Betrag zur Geschichte von Vindonissa und des antiken Beleuchtungswesens*. Zurich: Peer.

Łajtar, A. 2013. "A Newly Discovered Greek Inscription at Novae (Moesia Inferior) Associated with *pastus militum*." *Tyche* 28: 97–111.

– 2015. "Another Greek Inscription from Novae (Lower Moesia) Associated with pastus militum." In Ad fines, 277–288.

– 2021. "Two Greek dedications by primipilarii recently discovered in Novae." In Ad ripam fluminis Danuvi. Papers of the 3rd International Conference on the Roman Danubian Provinces Vienna, 11th–14th November 2015, edited by Fr. Mitthoff, L. Zerbini, and Ch. Cenati, Tyche Suppl. 11, 121–130. Wien: Holzhausen.

Łuczaj, Ł. 2004. *Dzikie rośliny jadalne Polski. Przewodnik survivalowy*. Krosno: Chemigrafia.

Madgearu, Al. 2006. "The end of the Lower Danubian limes. A violent or a peaceful process?" Studia Antiqua et Archaeologica 12: 151–168

– 2008. "A stick with dove head found in Halmyris." *Cultura şi civilizaţie la Dunărea de Jos* (Călăraşi) 24: 221–30.

Madyda-Legutko, R. 2011. *Studia nad zróżnicowaniem metalowych części pasów w kulturze przeworskiej. Okucia końca pasa*. Kraków: Historia Iagiellonica.

Madyda-Legutko, R., Rodzińska-Nowak, J., and J. Zagórska-Telega, 2011. *Opatów Fpl. 1. Ein Gräberfeld der Przeworsk-Kultur im nordwestlichen Kleinpolen*, Monumenta Archeologica Barbarica, 15. Warszawa–Kraków: Uniwersytet Jagielloński, Instytut Archeologii.

Majewski, K. (ed.), 1962. "Sprawozdanie tymczasowe z wykopalisk w Novae w 1960 roku." *Archeologia* 12 (1961): 75–170.

– 1963. "Novae 1961. Tymczasowe sprawozdanie z wykopalisk Ekspedycji Archeologicznej Uniwersytetu Warszawskiego." *Archeologia* 13 (1962): 65–125.

– 1964. "Novae 1962. Tymczasowe sprawozdanie z wykopalisk Ekspedycji Archeologicznej Uniwersytetu Warszawskiego." *Archeologia* 14 (1963): 151–194.

– 1978. "Novae – Sektor zachodni, 1975. Sprawozdania tymczasowe z wykopalisk Ekspedycji Archeologicznej Uniwersytetu Warszawskiego." *Archeologia* 28 (1977): 153–203.

Marinova, E. 2003. The new pollen core Lake Durankulak-3: a contribution to the vegetation history and human impact in Northeastern Bulgaria. In *Aspects of Palynology and Palaeoecology Festschrift in honor of Elissaveta Bozilova*, edited by S. Tonkov, 279–288. Philadelphia: Pensoft Pub.

– 2007. Archaeobotanical data from the Early Neolithic of Bulgaria. In Archaeobotanical perspectives on the origin and spread of agriculture in south west Asia and Europe, edited by S. Colledge and J. Conolly, 85–98. London: UCL Press.

Marinova, E. and J. Atanassova, 2006. "Anthropogenic impact on vegetation and environment during the Bronze Age in the area of Lake Durankulak, NE Bulgaria: Pollen, microscopic charcoal, non-pollen palynomorphs and plant macrofossils." *Review of Palaeobotany and Palynology* 141/1: 165–178.

Marinova, E., Filipović, D., Obradović, D., and E. Allué, 2012/2013: "Wild plant resources and land use in the Mesolithic and early Neolithic south-east Europe: Archaeobotanical evidence from the Danube catchment of Bulgaria and Serbia." *Offa* 69-70: 467–78.

Marinova, E., and R. Krauß, 2014. "Archaeobotanical evidence on the Neolithisation of Northeast Bulgaria in the Balkan-Anatolian context: chronological framework, plant economy and land use." *Bulgarian e-Journal of Archaeology* 4: 179–94.

Marsigli, L.F. 1726. *Danubius Pannonico-Mysicus. Observationibus geographicis, astronomicis, hydrographicis, historicis, physicis perlustratus et in sex tomos digestus*, Hagae: Comitum Amstelodami.

– 1744. *Description du Danube, depuis la Montagne de Kalenberg en Autriche, jusqu'au confluent de la riviere Jantra dans la Bulgarie: contenant des observations geographiques, astronomiques, hydrographiques, historiques et physiques, traduite du latin.* La Haye: J. Swart.

Martijnse, E. 1993. *Beschriftete Bleietiketten der Römerzeit in Österreich.* PhD diss., Universität Wien: Wien (n.v.).

Martini, W. 2000. "Pamphylia." In *Der Neue Pauly. Enzyklopädie der Antike*, IX, 216–19. Stuttgart–Weimar: J.B. Metzler.

Mason, D.J.P. 1988. "*Prata legionis* in Britain." *Britannia* 19: 163–89.

Matei-Popescu, F. 2014. "The Horothesia of Dionysopolis and the Integration of the Western Pontic Greek Cities in the Roman Empire." In *Interconnectivity in the Mediterranean and Pontic World during the Hellenistic and Roman Period. In Memory of Professor Heinz Heinen, The Proceedings of the International Symposium held in Constanța, July 8–12, 2013*, edited by V. Cojocaru, A. Coscun, and G. Custurea, Pontica et Mediterranea, III, 457–72. Cluj-Napoca: Mega.

– 2017. "The Dacians from Moesia Inferior." In *Migration, Kolonisierung, Akkulturation im Balkanraum und im Osten des Mittelmeerraumes (3. Jh. v. Chr. – 6 Jh. n. Chr.)*, edited by L. Mihailescu-Bîrliba, 139–159. Konstanz: Hartung-Gorre Verlag.

Matuszewska, M. 2006. "Bemerkungen zur Typologie der Ziegelstempel aus Novae (Moesia inferior)." *ArchBulg* 10: 45–63.

– 2013. "Ceramika budowlana z Novae." In *Biskupstwo w Novae (Moesia secunda) IV–VI w. Historia – Architektura – Życie codzienne*, edited by A. B. Biernacki, and R. Czerner, 201–35. Poznań: Wydawnictwo Poznańskie.

Matuszkiewicz, J.M. 2005. *Zespoły leśne Polski*. Warszawa: Wydawnictwo Naukowe PWN.

Matuszkiewicz, W. 2004. "Mixed oak-hornbeam forests (*Carpinus betulus, Quercus robur, Q.petraea, Tilia cordata*)." In Bohn et al. 2004, 255–68.

Matuszyk, J., Szybiński, M., and T. Sarnowski, 1979. "Wyniki badań geofizycznych." *Archeologia* 30 (1977): 211–16.

Medvedev, A.F. 1966. "Tataro-mongolskie nakonechniki strel v Vostochnoj Evrope." *Sovetskaya Arheologiya* 1966(2): 50–60.

Medwecka-Kornaś, A. 1972. "Zespoły leśne i zaroślowe." In *Szata roślinna Polski*, edited by W. Szafer, and K. Zarzycki, 383–440. Warszawa: Wydawnictwo Naukowe PWN.

Mehl, A. 1986. "Eine private Weihung auf kaiserlichem Boden in Walheim am Neckar." *Fundberichte aus Baden-Württemberg* 11: 259–67.

Menke, M. 1977. "Zur Struktur und Chronologie der spätkeltischen und frührömischen Siedlungen im Reihenhaller Becken." In *Symposium zum Ausklang der Latène-zivilisation und Anfänge der germanischen Besiedlung im mittleren Donaugebiet*, edited by B. Chropovský, 223–38. Bratislava: Hartung-Gorre Verlag.

Michielin, L. 2019. *Fores et fenestrae. A computational study of doors and windows in Roman domestic space*, PhD thesis. Edinburgh: University of Edinburgh.

Mikić, M., Stojanović, V., and N. Mrdić, 2006. "Primena gradiometra za potrebe zaštitnih arheoloških istaživanja na Viminacijumu – lokalitet rit." *Archaeology and Science* 2: 21–26.

Mikov, V. 1946–47. "Starite slavyani na yug ot Dunava." *Istoricheski pregled* 1946/1947(2): 142–61.

Milchev, A. 1963. "Rannosrednovekovni bulgarski nakiti i krustove enkolpioni ot severozapadna Bulgariya." *Arheologiya* (Sofia) 5(3): 22–34.

Millet, P.B. 2015. "Novedades sobre la tipología de las ánforas Dressel 2-4 tarraconenses (New Data on Dressel 2-4 Tarraconensis Typology)." *Archivo Español de Arqueología* 88: 187–201.

Misiewicz, K., and S. Tumidajewicz, 1987. "Żarna i mortaria kamienne z Novae." *Novaensia* 1: 177–230.

Mócsy, A. 1954. "Das *territorium legionis* und die *canabae* in Pannonien." *Acta Academiae Scientiarium Hungaricae* 3: 179–200.

– 1974. Il problema delle condizioni del suolo attribuito alle unità militari nelle province Danubiane. In *I diritti locali*, 335–355.

Mommsen, Th. 1873. "Die römischen Lagerstädte." *Hermes. Zeitschrift für klassische Philologie* 7: 303–05.

Moore, P.D., Webb, J.A. and M.E. Collinson, 1991. *Pollen analysis*, Oxford: Blackwell.

Morrisson, C. 1970. *Catalogue des monnaies byzantines Catalogue de la Bibliothèque nationale, vol. I: D'Anastase Ier à Justinien II (491-711).* Paris: Brill.

– 2002. "Byzantine Money: Its Production and Circulation." In *The economic History of Byzantium: From the Seventh through the Fifteenth Century*, edited by A.E. Laiou, 909–966. Washington, D.C.: Dumbarton Oaks Research Library and Collection.

Moskal-del Hoyo, M. 2013. "Mid-Holocene forests from Eastern Hungary: new anthracological data." *Review of Palaeobotany and Palynology* 193: 70–81.

Mrav, Z. 2013. "Septimius Severus and the Cities of the Middle Danubian Provinces." In *Studia epigraphica in memoriam Géza Alföldy*, edited by W. Eck, B. Fehér, and P. Kovács, Antiquitas. Reihe I/61, 205–40. Bonn: Habelt Verlag.

Mrozewicz, L. 1981a. "Les plombs de Novae." *Archeologia* 32 (1984): 79–84.

– 1981b. "Municipium Novae: problem lokalizacji." In *Novae – Sektor Zachodni 1976, 1978: wyniki badań wykopaliskowych Ekspedycji Archeologicznej Uniwersytetu im. A. Mickiewicza w Poznaniu*, edited by S. Parnicki-Pudełko, 197–200. Poznań: Uniwersytet im. A. Mickiewicza.

– 1981c. "Stellung Novae in der Organisationsstruktur der römischen Provinz Moesia Inferior (I–III Jh)." *Eos* 69(1): 105–18.

– 1982. *Rozwój ustroju municypalnego a postępy romanizacji w Mezji Dolnej*. Poznań: UAM.

– 1984. "Ze studiów nad rolą canabae w procesie urbanizowania terenów pogranicza reńsko-dunajskiego w okresie wczesnego cesarstwa." In *Novae i kultura starożytna*, edited by W. Pająkowski, and L. Mrozewicz, Balcanica Posnaniensia, III, 285–97. Poznań: Uniwersytet im. A. Mickiewicza.

– 2008. "Municipalisation des provinces danubiennes à l'époque des Sévères." In *Epigrafia 2006. Atti della XIVe Rencontre sur l'Epigraphie in onore di Silvio Panciera con altri contributi di colleghi, allievi e collaboratori*, edited by M.L. Caldelli, G.L Gregori, and S. Orlandi, 679–86. Roma: Quasar.

– 2010. Paleography of Latin Inscriptions from Novae (Lower Moesia), Prace Komisji Historycznej, 67. Poznań: PTPN.

– 2013. "Resettlement into Roman territory across the Rhine and the Danube under the Early Empire (to the Marcomannic Wars)." *Eos C: fasciculus extra ordinem editus electronicus*: 424–42.

Mueller-Bieniek, A., Bogucki, P., Pyzel, J., Kapcia, M., Moskal-del Hoyo, M., and D. Nalepka, 2019. "The role of *Chenopodium* in the subsistence economy of pioneer agriculturalists on the northern frontier of the Linear Pottery culture in Kuyavia, central Poland." *Journal of Archaeological Science* 111 (105027). (https://doi.org/10.1016/j.jas.2019.105027).

Mușețeanu, C., and D. Elefterescu, 2012. "Oglinzi romane din plumb de la Durostorum." *Pontica* 11: 105–11.

Mušmov, N. 1934. "Vizantiyski olovni pechati ot sbirkata na Narodniya Muzey." *IBAI* 8: 331–49.

Načeva (Nacheva), V. 1981. "Étude technologique du vernis rouge de centres céramiques dans les villages Butovo et Hotnica et a Pavlikeni, departement de Veliko Tarnovo." *Arheologiya* (Sofia) 23(3): 1–7.

Nawracki, M. 1999. "Badania archeologiczne pozostałości późnoantycznej pracowni szklarskiej w Novae (Bułgaria)." *Acta Universitatus Nicolai Copernici. Archeologia* 27: 163–67.

Negru, M., Badescu, A., and R. Avram, 2003. "The Amphorae of Kapitan II Type in Dacia." *RCRFA* 38: 209–13.

Nikolov, M. 2011. *Bulgarskite ukrasi na kolani prez Srednovekovieto* (http://www.desant.net/show-news/22271/ derived 25.05.2011).

Noti, R. et al. 2009. "Mid- and late-Holocene vegetation and fire history at Biviere di Gela, a coastal lake in southern Sicily, Italy." *Vegetation History and Archeobotany* 18: 371–387.

Ntinou, M. 2002. *La Paleovegetación en el Norte de Grecia desde el Tardiglaciar hasta el Atlántico. Formaciones Vegetales, Recursos y Usos*, B.A.R. Int. Ser., 1083. Oxford: BAR Publishing.

Obidowicz, A. et al. 2003. "Abies alba Mill." In *Late Glacial and Holocene history of vegetation in Poland based on isopollen maps*, 31–38. Kraków: W. Szafer Inst. of Botany, Polish Academy of Sciences.

Olczak, J. 1981. "Wyroby szklane." In *Novae – Sektor Zachodni 1976, 1978: wyniki badań wykopaliskowych ekspedycji archeologicznej Uniwersytetu im. Adama Mickiewicza w Poznaniu*, edited by S. Parnicki-Pudełko, 55–72. Poznań: Wydawnictwa UAM.

– 1995. "Szkło rzymskie z terenu komendantury w Novae." *Novensia* 8: 15–86.

– 1998. *Produkcja szkła w rzymskim i wczesnobizantyjskim Novae* [Summary: Glass Production in Roman & Early Byzantine Novae in the Light of Archaeological Sources (Moesia Inferior)], Toruń: Uniwersytet Mikołaja Kopernika.

Oldenstein, J. 1977. "Zur Ausrüstung römischer Auxiliareinheiten." *Bericht der Römisch-Germanischen Kommission* 57 (1976): 51–284.

Opaiț, A. 1996. *Aspecte ale vietii economice din provincia Scythia (secolele IV–VI p. Ch.). Producția ceramicii locale și de import*. București: Institutul Român de Tracologie.

– 2003. "„Table" amphora versus „table" pitcher in the Roman Dobrudja." *RCRFA* 38: 215–18.

– 2004. "The Eastern Mediterranean Amphorae in the Province of Scythia." In *Transport amphorae and trade in the Eastern Mediterranean. Acts of the international colloquium at the Danish Institute at Athens, September 26–29, 2002*, edited by J. Eiring, and J. Lund, 293–308. Aarhus: Aarhus University Press.

– 2007. "A Weighty Matter: Pontic Fish Amphorae." In *The Black Sea in Antiquity: Regional and Interregional Economic Exchanges*, edited by V. Gabrielsen, and J. Lund, Black Sea Studies 6, 101–22. Aarhus: Aarhus University Press.

– 2013. "Producția și consumul de vin în ținturile dintre Carpati și Marea Neagra (sec. II a. Chr. – III p. Chr.): unele considerații." *Studii și Cercetari de Istorie Veche și Arheologie* 64(1-2): 21–65.

– 2022. "On the origin and evolution of the Kapitän II amphora type." In *Amphorae from the Eastern Mediterranean and Beyond: Production and Distribution from the Early to the Late Roman Period*, edited by A. Kaldeli, Studies in Mediterranean Archaeology and Literature, PB 191, 191–222. Nicosia: Astrom Editions.

Opaiț, A., and M. Ionescu, 2016. "Contributions to the economic life of the city of Callatis in light of new ceramic finds (2nd – 6th centuries AD)." *Arheologia Moldovei* 39: 57–112.

Opaiț, A., and A. Tsaravopoulos, 2011. "Amphorae Dressel 24 similis type in the Central Aegean area (Chios – Erythrai – Kyme)." *The Annual of the British School at Athens* 106: 275–323, 375–76.

Opaiț, A., Barnea, Al., Barnea, I., Grigoras, B., and I. Potra, 2020. "Supplying wine, olive oil and fish products to the Lower Danube frontier (2nd–7th c. AD): A case of Dinogetia." *RCRFA* 46: 159–72.

Orton, C., Tyers, P., and A. Vince, 1993. *Pottery in Archeology*. Cambridge: Cambrdige University Press.

Palágyi, S. 1997. "Rekonstruktionsmöglichkeit des Zaumzeuges aus dem Wagengrab von Kozarmisleny (Pannonia)." In *Roman Frontier Studies 1995. Proceedings of the XVIth International Congress of Roman Frontier Studies*, edited by W. Groenman-van Waateringe, E. Birley, and V. Maxfield, 467–71. Oxford: Oxbow Books.

Panayotov, P., 1998. *Istoriya na Bulgariya*. Veliko Turnovo: Abagar.

Paoletti, O. 1988. "Gorgones romanae." In *LIMC*, vol. 4.1, 345–62. Zürich-München: Artemis Verlag.

Parnicki-Pudełko, S. 1981. "Canabae Novae: problem lokalizacji." In *Novae – Sektor Zachodni 1976, 1978*: *wyniki badań wykopaliskowych Ekspedycji Archeologicznej Uniwersytetu im. A. Mickiewicza w Poznaniu*, edited by S. Parnicki-Pudełko, 201–04. Poznań: Uniwersytet im. A. Mickiewicza.

Pauli Jensen, X. 2009. "North Germanic Archery. The Practical Approach – Results and Perspectives." In *Waffen in Aktion. Akten des 16. Internationalen Roman Military Equipment Conference (ROMEC), Xanten, 13.–16. Juni 2007*, edited by H.-J. Schalles, and A.W. Busch, Xantener Berichte, 16, 369–75. Xanten: von Zabern.

Pauli Jensen, X., and L.Ch. Nørbach, 2009. *Illerup Ådal 13: Die Böger, Pfeile und Äxte*, Jutland Archaeological Society Publications, XXV/13. Moesgård: Jysk Arkæologisk Selskab.

Paunov, E.I. 2013. *From Koiné to Romanitas. The Numismatic Evidence for Roman Expansion and Settlement in Bulgaria in Antiquity (Moesia and Thrace), ca. 146 BC – 98/117 AD*, (Diss.), Cardiff University.

– 2014. "Early Roman Coins from Novae. Patterns and Observations," *Novensia* 25: 145–75.

Peacock D.P.S. 1977. "Roman amphorae: typology, fabric and origin, Méthodes classiques et méthodes formelles dans l'étude des amphores." *Collection de L'École Française de Rome* 32: 261–73.

– 1984. "The amphorae: typology and chronology." In *Excavations at Carthage: The Bristol Mission*, vol. 1/2, The avenue du Président Habib Bourguiba, Salambo. *The Pottery and other Ceramic Objects from the site*, edited by M. G. Fulford, and D.P.S. Peacock, 116–40. Sheffield: University of Sheffield for the British Academy.

Peacock, D., and D. Williams, 1991. *Amphorae and the Roman Economy: An Introductory Guide*. London: Longman.

Peškař, I. 1972. *Fibeln aus römischer Kaiserzeit in Mähren*. Praha: Dr. Rudolf Habelt GmbH.

Petković, S. 2010. *Rimske fibule u Srbiji od I do V veka n.e.* Beograd: Arheološki Institut.

von Petrikovits, H. 1979. "Militärisches Nutzland in den Grenzprovinzen des Römischen Reiches." In *Actes du VIIe Congrès International d'Épigraphie Grecque et Latine (Constanza, 9–15 septembre, 1977)*, 229–42. Constanza: Académie des Sciences Sociales et Politiques.

– 1981. "Die Canabae Legionis" In *150 Jahre Deutsches Archäologisches Institut, 1829–1979*, 163–75. Mainz: von Zabern.

Piaskowski, J. 1991. "Metallkundliche Untersuchungen antiker und frümittelalterlicher Eisengegenstände." In *Iatrus IV*, 241–60.

Picavet, P.L. 1912. "Suspension pendulaire elliptique." *La Revue du Cerf-Volant* 1, n° 8, 1er novembre 1912.

Piccottini, G. 1997. "Amphorae litteratae von Magdalensberg." In *Komos. Festschrift für Thuri Lorenz zum 65. Geburstag*, edited by G. Erath, G. Schwarz, and M. Lehner, 203–206. Wien: Phoibus.

Piéri, D. 2005. *Le commerce du vin oriental à l'époque Byzantine: le témoignage des amphores de Gaule*. Beirut: Institute Français du Proche-Orient.

Piso, I. 1991. "Die Inschriften vom Pfaffenberg und der Bereich der *canabae legionis*." *Tyche* 6: 131–69.

– 2003. *Das Heiligtum des Jupiter Optimus Maximus auf dem Pfaffenberg / Carnuntum*, edited by W. Jobst, vol. I., *Die Inschriften, Römische Limes in Österreich*, 41. Wien: Verlag der Österreichische Akademie der Wissenschaften.

Platnauer, M. 1918. *The Life and Reign of the Emperor Lucius Septimius Severus*. London: Oxford University Press.

Pleiner, R., 2000. *Iron in archaeology: The European bloomery smelters*, Prague: Archeologicky Ústav AV ČR.

Plešnicar-Gec, L. 1977. *Keramika emonskih nekropol*, Dissertationes et Monographiae, 20, 2 vols. Beograd-Ljubljana: Mestni Muzej.

Pletneva, S.A. 1967. *Ot kocheviy k gorodam*. Moskva: Nauka.

– 1981. "Saltovo-mayatskaya kul'tura." In *Stepi Evrazii v epokhu srednevekov'ya*, edited by S.A. Pletneva, 62–75. Moskva: Nauka.

Polaschek, E. 1936. "Novae" In *RE* XVII/1, col. 1125–29.

Popilian, Gh. 1976. "Traditions autochtones dans le céramique provinciale romaine de la Dacie méridionale." In *Thraco-Dacica. Recueil d'études à l'occasion du IIe Congrès International de Thracologie (Bucarest, 4–10 septembre 1976)*, edited by C. Preda, Al. Vulpe, and C. Poghirc, 279–86. București: Editura Academiei Republicii Socialiste Romania.

– 1997. "Les centres de production céramique d'Oltenie." In *Études sur la céramique romaine et daco-romaine de la Dacie et de la Mésie Inférieure*, 7–20. Timişoara: Tipografia Universităţii din Timişoara.

Popilian, G., and D. Bondoc, 2012. *The Roman and Late Roman Cemetery of Sucidava-Celei. The Excavations from 1969–1983*. Craiova: Museum of Oltenia.

Popova, T. 1999. "Palaeoethnobotanical and anthracological analysis from the Roman Times of Nicopolis ad Istrum and Late Antique Hillfort of Dichin (Northern Bulgaria)." *ArchBulg* 3(2): 69–75.

Popova, T., and E. Marinova, 2000. "Archaeobotanical and anthracological analysis of the Roman and early Byzantine castle Abritus in north-eastern Bulgaria: Some palaeoethnobotanical and environmental aspects." *ArchBulg* 4: 49–58.

Potter, D. 1997. "Empty Areas and Roman Frontier Policy." *The American Journal of Philology* 113(2): 269–74.

Poulter, A., 1983-84. "Roman towns and the problem of late Roman urbanism." *Hephaistos* 5-6, 1983-84: 109–132.

– 1999. "The excavations and the social and economic context." In Nicopolis I, 1–54.

– 2008. *The Transition to Late Antiquity, on the Danube and Beyond, Oxford*: Oxford University Press.

Protase, D. 1976. *Un cimitir dacic din epoca romana la Soporu de Cimpie. Contribuţie la problema continuităţii in Dacia.* Bucureşti: Editura Academiei Republicii Socialiste România.

Punt, W. *et al.* 1976-2009. *The Northwest European Pollen Flora (NEPF)*, vols. I– IX, 1976–2009, Amsterdam: Elsevier Science Ltd.

Raddatz, K. 1963. "Pfeilspitzen aus dem Moorfund von Nydam." *Offa* 20: 49–56.

Radman-Livaja, I. 2004. *Militaria Sisciensia. Nalazi rimske vojne opreme iz Siska u fundusu Arheološkoga muzeja u Zagrebu*. Zagreb: Arheoloski muzej u Zagreb.

– 2008. "Roman belt fittings from Burgenae." *JRMES* 16: 295–308.

– 2009. "Roman horse harness fittings from Burgenae." In *Limes XX. XX Congreso Internacional de Estudios sobre la Frontera Romana / XXth International Congress of Roman Frontier Studies*, edited by Á. Morillo, N. Hanel, and E. Martín, *Gladius* 13/3: 1499–1508.

Radulescu, A. 1975. "Contributi la cunoasterea ceramici de us comun din Dobrogea." *Pontica* 8: 331–60.

Rankov, B. 1999. "The Roman Ban on the Export of Weapons to the Barbaricum. A Misunderstanding." *JRMES* 10: 115–20.

Recław, J. 2005. "Wykorzystanie ołowiu w Novae." *Novensia* 16: 41-50.

– 2009. "Lead plombs from fortress of legio I Italica. Novae, Moesia Inferior." In *LIMES XX. XX Congreso Internacional de Estudios sobre la Frontera Romana = XXth International Congress of Roman Frontier Studies. León (España), Septiembre, 2006, Anejos de Gladius*, 13, vol. 3, edited by Á. Morillo, N. Hanel, and E. Martín, 1559–69. Madrid: Ed. Polifemo.

Reille, M. 1992-98. *Pollen et spores d'Europe et d'Afrique du nord*, Suppl. 1 and 2, Marseille: Laboratoire de Botanique historique et Palynologie.

Riley, J.A. 1979. "The coarse pottery from Berenice." In *Excavations at Sidi Khrebish Benghazi (Berenice)*, vol. II, edited by J.A. Lloyd, G. Barker, A. Bonanno, and J.A. Riley, Supplement to Libya Antiqua, 5, 91–467. Tripoli: Department of antiquites.

Rizos, E. 2015. "Remark on the logistics and infrastructure of the *annona militaris* in Eastern Mediterranean and Aegean areas." *Antiquité Tardive* 23: 287–302.

Rodwell, W. 1975. "Milestones, Civic Territories, and The Antonine Itinerary." *Britannia* 6: 76–101.

Rostovtzeff, M. 1903. *Tesserarum urbis Romae et suburbi plumbearum sylloge*. St.-Pétersbourg: Commissionnaires de l'Académie impériale des Sciences.

Roth, J. 1999. *The Logistics of the Roman Army at War (264 B.C. – A.D. 235)*, Columbia Studies in the Classical Tradition, 23, Leiden – Boston – Köln.

Rüger, C.B. 1968. *Germania inferior: Untersuchungen zur Territorial – und Verwaltungegeschichte Niedergermaniens in der Prinzipatszeit*. Köln: Böhlau.

Ruscu, L. 2014. "On the *praefectura orae maritimae* on the western coast of the Black Sea." In *The Edges of the Roman World*, edited by M.A. Janković, V.D. Mihailović, and S. Babi, 159–71. Cambridge: Cambridge Scholars Publishing.

Ruseva-Slokoska, L. 1991. *Roman Jewellery. Catalogue of National Museum in Sofia*, Sofia–London: NAIM BAN.

Rusu-Bolindeţ, V. 2007. *Ceramica romană de la Napoca*. Cluj-Napoca: Mega.

Salamon, M. 1987. *Mennictwo bizantyńskie*. Kraków: PTAiN.

– 2008. "Novae in the age of Slav invasions." In *Novae. Legionary Fortress and Late Antique Town*, vol. I, edited by P. Dyczek, 173–212. Warsaw: Wydawnictwa Uniwersytetu Warszawskiego.

Sanader, M., and D. Tončinić, 2010. "Katalog nalaza. Gradun – antički Tilurium / The Catalogue of Finds. Gardur – the Ancient Tilurium." In *Nalazi Rimske Vojne Opreme u Hrvatskoj / Finds of the Roman Military Equipment in Croatia*, edited by I. Radman-Livaja, 55–111. Zagreb: Arheološki muzej.

Sarnowski, T. 1976. "Novae jako siedziba legionu I Italskiego." *Archeologia* 27: 50–65.

– 1979. "Badania powierzchniowe w okolicy Novae." In Majewski 1979: 207-10.

– 1983a. "Die Ziegelstempel aus Novae. I. Sistematik und Typologie." *Archeologia* 34: 17–61.

– 1983b. "Odcinek XI – principia." In L. Press (ed.), "Novae – Sektor Zachodni, 1981. Sprawozdanie tymczasowe z wykopalisk Ekspedycji Archeologicznej Uniwersytetu Warszawskiego." *Archeologia* 34 (1981): 150–53 and 159.

– 1984. "Początki legionowego budownictwa w Novae i wojny dackie Domicjana i Trajana." In *Mezja – Tracja – Bałkany*, edited by S. Parnicki-Pudełko, Balcanica Posnaniensia, I, 143–69. Poznań: Uniwersytet im. A. Mickiewicza.

– 1985a. "Bronzefunde aus dem Stabsgebäude in Novae und Altmetalldepots in den römischen Kastellen und Legionslagern." *Germania* 63: 521–40.

– 1985b. "Die legio I Italica und der untere Donauabschnitt der Notitia Dignitatum." *Germania* 63: 107–27.

– 1986. "En marge de la discussion sur l'origine du nom de la ville de Novae en Mésie inférieure." *Klio* 68(1): 92–101.

– 1987a. "Zur Truppengeschichte der Dakerkriege Traians. Die Bonner Legio I Minervia und das Legionslager Novae." *Germania* 65: 107–22.

– 1987b. "Das römische Heer im Norden des Schwarzen Meeres." *Archeologia* 38: 61–97.

– 1988. *Wojsko rzymskie w Mezji Dolnej i na północnym wybrzeżu Morza Czarnego* (=*Novensia* 3), Warszawa: Wydawnictwa Uniwersytetu Warszawskiego.

– 1991. "Novae Italicae im I. Jh. N.Chr.," Études et Traveau 15: 347–55.

– 1993. "Primi ordines et centuriones legionis I Italicae und eine Dedikation an Septimius Severus aus Novae in Niedermoesien." *ZPE* 95: 205–19.

– 1996. "Promotio ex nova ordinatione eines künftigen Centurio. Zur Inschrift aus Novae in ZPE 95, 1993." *ZPE* 111: 289–90.

– 1997. "Legionsziegel an militärischen und zivilen Bauplätzen der Prinzipatszeit in Niedermoesien." In *Roman Frontier Studies 1995. Proceedings of the XVIth International Congress of Roman Frontier Studies*, edited by W. Groenman-van Waateringe, E. Birley, and V. Maxfield, 497–501. Oxford: Oxbow Books.

– 2006a. "Römische Militärziegel von der südwestlichen Krim. Probleme der Produktionstätigkeit und der Produktionsorte." *Archeologia* 56: 91–101.

– 2006b. "Ti. Plautius Silvanus, Tauric Chersonesus and classis Moesica." *Dacia* 50: 89–92.

– 2009 (with a contribution by D. Dragoyev). "The name of Novae in Lower Moeasia." *Archeologia* 58 (2007): 15–23.

– 2013. "*Accepta pariatoria* und *pastus militum*. Eine neue Statuenbasis mit zwei Inschriften aus Novae." *Tyche* 28: 135–46.

Sarnowski, T., Biernacki, A.B., Lemke, M., Tomas, A., and P. Vladkova, 2012. *Novae. An Archaeological Guide to A Roman Legionary Fortress and Early Byzantine Town on The Lower Danube (Bulgaria)*. Warszawa: Uniwersytet Warszawski.

Sarnowski, T., Kovalevskaja, L., and J. Kaniszewski, 2005. "Novae – Castra legionis, 2003–2005." *Archeologia* 56: 141–52.

Sarnowski, T., Kovalevskaja, L., and A. Tomas, 2000. "Flasze gliniane z principia w Novae." *Novensia* 12: 107–22.

– 2010. "Novae – Castra legionis, 2006–2009. Preliminary Report on the Excavations of the University of Warsaw Archaeological Expedition." *Archeologia* 59 (2008): 153–72.

Sarnowski, T., Kovalevskaja, L., Tomas, A., Chowaniec, R., and P. Zakrzewski, 2014. "Novae – castra legionis, 2010–1012. Preliminary report on the excavations of the University of Warsaw Archaeological Expedition." *Archeologia* 62-63 (2010): 75–90.

Sarnowski, T., Kovalevskaja, L., Tomas, A., Dziurdzik, T., Jęczmienowski, E., and P. Zakrzewski, 2016. "Novae – castra, canabae, vicus, 2013–15. Preliminary report on the Excavations and Prospection Surveys of the University of Warsaw Archaeological Expedition." *Archeologia* 65 (2014): 177–203.

Schmidt, A., Linford, P., Linford, N., David, A., Gaffney, C., Sarris, A., and J. Fassbinder, 2015. *EAC Guidelines for the Use of Geophysics in Archaeology: Questions to Ask and Points to Consider*. Namur: European Archaeological Council.

Schönert-Geiss, E. 2007. "Die Fundmünzen von Iatrus-Krivina." In *Iatrus VI*, 329–82. Mainz am Rhein: von Zabern.

Schulten, A. 1894. "Das Territorium legionis." *Hermes* 29(4): 481–516.

Schweingruber, F.H. 1990a. *Mikroskopische Holzanatomie*. Birmensdorf: Swiss Federal Institute for Forest, Snow and Landscape Research.

– 1990b. *Anatomie Europäischer Hölzer. Ein Atlas zur Bestimmung europäischer Baum-, Strauch – und Zwergstrauchhölzer / Anatomy of European woods. An atlas for the identification of European trees, shrubs and dwarf shrubs.* Birmensdorff-Bern: Eidgenössische Forschungsanstalt für Wald, Schnee und Landschaft; Haupt.

Sedov, V.V. 1982. *Vostochnye Slavyane v VI – XIII vv.* Moskva: Nauka.

Seibt, W. 1978. *Die Bleisiegel in Österreich, vol. I. Kaiserhof.* Vienne: Verlag der Österreichischen Akademie der Wissenschaften.

Shepard, A.O. 1976. *Ceramics for the Archeologist.* Washington: Braum-Brunfield.

Shepherd, J.D. 1999. "The Glass." In *Nicopolis I*, 297–378.

Shortland, A., Schachner, L., Freestone I., and M. Tite, 2006. "Natron as a flux in the early vitreous materials industry: sources, beginnings and reasons for decline." *Journal of Archaeological Science* 33: 521–30.

Skoczylas, J. 1995. "Differentiation of the Rock Material at Novae in the Light of Petrographic Investigations." In *Novae. Studies and Materials*, 1, edited by A.B. Biernacki, 91–99. Poznań: Uniwersytet im. Adama Mickiewicza w Poznaniu.

– 1999. "Das Gestein aus dem Steinbruch von Hotnica und die Architektonischen Elemente in den römischen Bauwerken von Niedermösien." In *Limes von Diokletian*, 127–130.

Skoczylas, J., Tcholakov (Cholakov), N., and Z. Walkiewicz, 1979. "Uwagi o pochodzeniu surowców skalnych stosowanych w budowlach Novae." In *Novae – Sektor Zachodni 1974: wyniki badań wykopaliskowych Ekspedycji Archeologicznej Uniwersytetu im. A. Mickiewicza w Poznaniu*, 2, edited by S. Parnicki-Pudełko, 131–35. Poznań: Uniwersytet im. Adama Mickiewicza w Poznaniu.

Slavova, M. 1998. "Lines 26–32 of the Horothesia of Dionysopolis (IGBulg V 5011)." *ZPE* 120: 99–106.

Sokolova, I. 1991. "Vizantiyskie pechati VI–pervoy poloviny IX v. iz Hersonesa." *Vizantijskiy Vremennik* 52: 201–13.

Sommer, C.S. 1984. *The Military Vici of Roman Britain. Aspects of their Origins, their Location and Layout, Administration, Function and End*, B.A.R. Br. Ser., 129. Oxford: Archaeopress.

– 1997. "Kastellvicus und Kastell: Modell für die Canabae legionis?" *Jahresbericht der Gesellschaft pro Vindonissa* s.n.: 41–52.

– 2004. "Intra leugam. Canabae, Kastellvici und der Obergermanisch-raetische Limes." In *Orbis Antiquus. Studia in honorem Ioannis Pisonis*, edited by L. Ruscu, R. Ardevan, and C. Ciongradi, 312–21. Cluj-Napoca: Nereamia Napocae.

Soultov, B. 1962. "Edin zanayatchiyski centur v Dolna Miziya." *Arheologiya* 4(4): 30–34.

– 1968. "Antichni grobni nahodki ot Velikoturnovski okrug." *IOMVT* 4: 41–50.

– 1977. "Pavlikenskiya kray prez antichnostta" In *Palikeni i Pavlikenskiya kray.* Sofiya: Otechesven front.

– 1983. "The typology and chronology of provincial Roman pottery from Lower Moesia." In *Ancient Bulgaria. Papers Presented to the International Symposium on the Ancient History and Archaeology of Bulgaria*, edited by A.G. Poulter, 119–28. Nottingham: Departement of Classical and Archaeological Studies (Archaeology Section).

– 1984. "Thrakische Traditionen in der Produktion der antiken Keramikzentren bei Hotnica, Pavlikeni, Butovo und Bjala Cerkva." In *Dritter Internationaler Thrakologischer Kongress zu Ehren W. Tomascheks: 2.–6. Juni 1980*, edited by D. Popov, K. Jordanov, and I. von Bredow, 184–90. Wien – Sofia: Swyat.

– 1985. *Ceramic Production on the Territory of Nicopolis ad Istrum*, (= *GSUIFF* 76(2) (1983)). Sofia: Centrum Historiae "Terra Antiqua Balcanica".

Soultova, S. 1991. "Glineni lampi tip 'Boutovo'." *IIMVT* 6: 116–28.

– 1992. "Terakotovi statuetki na Afrodita ot keramichniya centur v Boutovo (Dolna Miziya)." *IIMVT* 7: 153–58.

Speidel, A. 1994. "The Tribunes' Choice in the Promotion of Centurions." *ZPE* 100: 469–70.

Stamenković, S., and V. Ivanišević, 2013. "Rimski i ranovizantijski carski olovni pečati iz zbirke Narodnog muzeja u Beogradu." *Numizmatičar* 31: 239–52.

Stanchev, D. 2002. "Terenni arheologicheski prouchvaniya po proekt 'Istoriya na selishtnite sistemi okolo Jatrus i Nove na Dolniya Dunav'". In *AOR prez 2001 g.*, 88–89. Sofiya: NAIM BAN.

Stawiarska, T. 2014. *Roman and Early Byzantine Glass from Romania and Northern Bulgaria. Archaeological and Technological Study.* Warszawa: Polish Academy of Sciences.

Stefanov, S. 1930-1931. "Rimskite vodoprovodi na Nove." *IBAI* 6: 265–79.

– Stefanov, S. 1955. "Predrimski pametnici ot Novae." *IAI* 19: 49–54.

– 1956. *Starinite po dolniya baseyn na Jantra*, Sofiya.

– 1958. Prinos kum starata istoriya na Svishtov do sredata na XVII vek. In *Sto godini narodno chitalishte Svishtov 1856 g. – 1956 g. Jubilen sbornik*, 337–365. Svishtov.

Stern, W. B., 1990. "The composition of Roman glass: problems of non-destructive analysis." In *Annales du 11e Congrès de l'Association Internationale pour l'Histoire du Verre*, 37–41. Amsterdam: Association internationale pour l'histoire du verre.

– 1955. "Predrimski pametnici ot Nove." In *Sbornik Gavril Kacarov. Statii posveteni po slučaj na sedemdesetgodišninata mu 4 oktombri 1874 – 4 oktombri 1944*, vol. II (= *IBAI* 19), 49–54. Sofiya: Izdatelstvo BAN.

– 1958. "Prinos kum starata istoriya na Svishtov do sredata na XVII vek." In *Sto godini narodno chitalishte Svishtov 1856 g. – 1956 g. Jubilen sbornik*, edited by R.K. Kazanski, 337–65. Svishtov: Obshtina Svishtov.

Still, M.C.V. 1993. "Opening up imperial lead sealings." *JRA* 6: 403–08.

– 1995 (= RLS). *Roman Lead Sealings* (PhD thesis), vols. I–II. London: University of London.

Stopiński, W. 1968. "Wstępna analiza doświadczalnych badań elektorooporowych z wycinka miasta Novae – Sektor Zachodni." *Archeologia* (Warsaw) 18 (1967): 190–207.

Stoyanov, T. 1984. "Obrochnite relefi na Artemida (Diana)-ezdachka ot Miziya i Trakiya przez rimskata epoha." *Arheologiya* (Sofia) 26(2-3): 31–44.

Strobel, K. 1987. "Anmerkungen zur Truppengeschichte des Donauraumes in der hohen Kaiserzeit II: Die trajanischen Ziegelstempel aus Buridava-Stolniceni." *ZPE* 68: 282–84.

– 1988. "Anmerkungen zur Truppengeschichte des Donauraumes in der hohen Kaiserzeit, I: Die neuen Ziegelstempel der Legio I Minervia aus dem Lager der Legio I Italica in Novae in Moesia Inferior." *Klio* 70: 501–11.

Sugita, S., Gaillard, M.-J., Brostrom, A. 1999. "Landscape openness and pollen records: a simulation approach." *The Holocene* 9/4: 409–421.

Suszka, B. 1983. Generative propagation. In *Jodła pospolita. Abies alba Mill. Nasze drzewa leśne*, edited by S. Białobok, Monografie popularno-naukowe, 4, 175–265. Warszawa-Poznań: PWN.

Syme, R. 1999. "The Early History of Moesia." In *The provincial at Rome and Rome and the Balkans 80BC – AD14.*" edited by R. Syme, and A. Birley, 193–220. Exeter: University of Exeter Press.

Szymański, W. 1973. *Słowiańszczyzna wschodnia*. Wrocław–Warszawa–Kraków: Zakład Narodowy im. Ossolińskich.

Świętosławski, W. 1997. *Archeologiczne ślady najazdów tatarskich na Europę Środkową w XIII w.*, Łódź: IAIE PAN.

Škorpil, K. 1905. "Nekotoriye iz dorog vostochnoy Bolgarii." *Izvestiya Russkogo Arheologicheskogo Instituta v Konstantinopole* 10: 443–502.

Teodor, E. 2015. "One hundred sherds. Chilia-Militari Culture Reloaded. Alexandria pottery case." *Journal of Ancient History and Archaeology* 2(4): 90–135.

Théry-Parisot I. 2001. Économie du combustible au Paléolithique. Anthracologie, Expérimentation, Taphonomie. Dossier de Documentation Archéologique, 20. Paris: CNRS.

Thomas, M.D. 2003. *Lorica segmentata*, vol. II: *A Catalogue of Finds*, *JRMES* Monograph, 2. Chrinside: The Armatura Press.

Thomas, R. and S. Stallibrass, "For starters: producing ans supplying food to the army in the Roman north-west provinces." In *Feeding the Roman Army: The Archaeology of Production and Supply in NW Europe*, edited by R. Thomas and S. Stallibrass, 1-17. Oxford: Oxbow Books.

Thompson, E.A. 2002. *Romans and the Barbarians: the Decline of the Western Empire*. Madison (Wis.): University of Wisconsin.

Tibiletti, G. 1974. "Ager publicus e suolo provinciale." In *I diritti locali*, 99–107.

Tomas, A. 2003. "Jugs from Novae. A Study on Finds 1960–1999." *Novensia* 14: 119–84.

– 2006. "Municipium Novensium? Report on the Field Survey at Ostrite Mogili, Veliko Turnovo District." *Światowit* 47(A) (2004): 115–28.

– 2009. "*Inter Moesos et Thraces*. A Contribution to The Studies On The Rural Hinterland of Novae In Lower Moesia." *Archeologia* 58: 31–47.

– 2011. "Connecting to Public Water: The Rural Landscape and Water Supply of Lower Moesia." *ArchBulg* 15(2): 59–72.

– 2012. "Canabae legionis I Italicae: state of research on civil settlements accompanying the legionary camp in Novae (Lower Moesia) compared to relevant Lower Danubian sites." *Światowit* L(A) (2011): 155–68.

– 2013. "Pachnące miasta czy slumsy? Urządzenia sanitarne w cywilnych osiedlach przy rzymskich bazach wojskowych." In *Czystość i brud. Higiena w starożytności*, edited by W. Korpalska, and W. Ślusarczyk, 139–54. Bydgoszcz: Wydawnictwo Naukowe Uniwersytetu Mikołaja Kopernika.

– 2014. "A New Dedicatory Inscription from Novae (Lower Moesia)." *Światowit* 52(A) (2013): 79–86.

– 2015a. "Female family members related to soldiers and officers of the legio I Italica. A case study." In *Colonization and Romanization in Moesia Inferior. Premises of A Contrastive Approach*, edited by L. Mihailescu-Bîrliba, 93–124. Kaiserlautern: Harrassowitz Verlag.

– 2015b. "A New Dedicatory Inscription from Novae (Moesia inferior)." *Światowit* 52(A): 79–86.

– 2015c. "A Six-century Pottery Kiln from Novae (Moesia secunda). A Contribution to the Local Pottery Manufacturing." *ArchBulg* 19(3): 63–74.

– 2015d. "Dionysus or Liber Pater? The Evidence of the Bacchic Cult at Novae (*castra et canabae legionis*) and in its Hinterland." In *Ad fines*, 257–75.

– 2016. Inter Moesos et Thraces. *The Rural Hinterland of Novae in Lower Moesia (1st – 6th century AD)*. Oxford: Archaeopress Publishing.

– 2017. *Living with the Army I. Civil Settlements near Roman Legionary Fortresses in Lower Moesia*. Warszawa: Institute of Archaeology, University of Warsaw.

– 2018. "Pre-Roman Settlements in the Hinterland of Novae in Lower Moesia: a re-assessment of the displacements of the conquered tribes by the Romans." In *Romans in the Middle and Lower Danube Valley: Case Studies in Archaeology, Epigraphy, and History, 1st BC – 5th AD: case studies in archaeology, epigraphy and history*, edited by E. de Sena, and C. Timoc, B.A.R. Int. Ser., 2882, 13–22. Oxford: BAR Publishing.

Tomas, A., Jaskulska, E., Dworniak-Jarych, J., Jęczmienowski, E., Dziurdzik, T., and A. Mech, 2020. "The eastern necropolis at Novae." *ArchBulg* 24(3): 37–63.

Tomas, A., and M. Lemke, 2015. "The Mithraeum at Novae Revisited." In *Ad fines*, 227–47.

Tomas, A., and T. Sarnowski, T. 2007. "M. Aurelius Statianus from Lower Moesia. A Note on his Origin, Status and Business." In *The Lower Danube in Antiquity. International Archaeological Conference Bulgaria–Tutrakan, 6–7.10.2005*, edited by L. Vagalinski, 1–3. Sofia: Bulgarian Academy of Sciences, National Institute of Archaeology and Museum; Tutrakan: Tutrakan History Museum.

Torbatov, S. 1997. "Quaestura exercitus: Moesia Secunda and Scythia under Justinian." *ArchBulg* 1.3: 78–87.

– 2010. "Stroitelna keramika s pechati na I Italiyski legion ot kastela Trimamium." *Arheologiya* (Sofia) 51(3-4): 41–57.

– 2012. "Stroitelna keramika s pechati ot Sexaginta Prista." *Izvestiya na Regionalen istoricheski muzey – Ruse* 5: 162–97.

Toynbee, C.J. 1996. *Death and Burial in the Roman World*. London: JHU Press.

Trebsche, P. 2010. "Untersuchungen ze Reichweite und Bedeutung von Kontakten in der Spätlatènezeit anhand der Feinkammstrich-Keramik." In *Nord-Süd, Ost-West. Kontakte während der Eisenzeit in Europa. Akten der Internationalen Tagungen der AG Eisenzeit in Hamburg und Sopron 2002*, edited by E. Jerem, M. Schönfelder, and G. Wieland, 17, 333–48. Budapest: Archaeolingua Alapítvány.

Tschernia, A. 1986. *Le vin de l'Italie romaine*. Rome: École Française de Rome.

Tsonev, Ts. 1997. "Origin and Evolution of the Gravettian Culture in the Eastern Balkans." Archaeologia Bulgarica I(1): 1–4.

Tsurov, I. 1987. "Kamenni sudove ot Velikoturnovski okrug." *GMSB* 13: 43–51.

Tudor, D. 1959. "Le dépôt de miroirs de verre double de plomb trouve à Sucidava." *Dacia* 3: 415–32.

– 1966. *Sucidava*, Craiova: Editura Scrisul Românesc.

Turcan, R. 1987. *Nigra moneta. Sceaux, jetons, tesseres, amulettes, plombs monétaires ou monétiformes, objets divers en plomb ou en etain d'époque romaine conserves au Musée des Beaux-Arts de Lyon (Palais Saint-Pierre).* Lyon: Diffusion De Boccard.

Turno, A. 1989. "Römische und frühbyzantinische Gläser aus Novae in Bulgarien." *Kölner Jahrbuch für Vor – und Frühgeschichte* 22: 163–70.

Tylecotte, R. F., 2002. *A History of Metallurgy*, 2nd edition, London: Gordon and Breach Science Publishers.

Unz, Ch. and E. Deschler-Erb, 1997. *Katalog der Militaria aus Vindonissa. Militärische Funde, Pferdegeschirr und Jochteile bis 1976*, Veröffentlichungen der Gesellschaft pro Vindonissa, 14, Brugg: Gesellschaft pro Vindonissa.

Vagalinski, L. 2007. *Izluskana keramika ot I – nachalo na VII vekjuzhno ot dolen Dunav (Bulgariya) / Burnished Pottery from the First Century to the Beginning of the Seventh Century AD from the Region South of the Lower Danube (Bulgaria)*, Sofia: NOUS.

Vagalinski, L., Stanchev, D, von Bülow, G., and S. Conrad, 2001a. "Bulgaro-nemski terenni prouchvaniya v Jatrus-Krivina prez 1999 g." In *AOR prez 1999–2000 gg.*, 76–79. Sofiya: NAIM BAN.

– 2001b. "Bulgaro-nemski arheologicheski prouchvaniya v kusnoantichnata krepost Jatrus kray s. Krivina, rusensko, i v neynata okolnost prez 2000 g." In *AOR prez 1999–2000 gg.*, 79–82. Sofiya: NAIM BAN.

Vanhanen, S., 2012. "Archaeobotanical study of a late Iron Age agricultural complex at Orijärvi, Eastern Finland." *Fennoscandia Archaeologica* 29: 55–72.

Velichkevich, F.Yu., and E. Zastawniak, 2006. *Atlas of Pleistocene vascular plant macroremains of Central and Eastern Europe*, Part I – *Pteridophytes and monocotyledons*, 224. Kraków: Institute of Botany, Polish Academy of Sciences.

– 2008. *Atlas of vascular plant macroremains from the Pleistocene of central and eastern Europe*, Part II – *Herbaceous dicotyledons*, 379. Kraków: Institute of Botany, Polish Academy of Sciences.

Velo-Gala, A., and J.A. Garriguet Mata, 2017. "Roman window glass: an approach to its study through iconography." *Lucentum* 36: 159–76.

Vismara, G. 1947. "Limitazione al commercio internazionale nell' impero romano e nella communitá cristiana medioevale." In *Studi in onore di Contardo Ferrini pubblicati in occasione della sua beatificazione*, edited by G.G. Archi, and C. Ferrini, vol. I, Milano: Vita e pensiero.

Vitlyanov, S. 2003. "Novootkriti nakitni predmeti i elementi na oblekloto ot Veliki Preslav." *Preslavska knizhovna shkola* 7: 426–37.

Vittinghoff, F. 1971. "Die rechtliche Stellung der canabae legionis und die Herkunftsangabe castris." *Chiron* 1: 299–318.

– 1974. "Das Problem des Militarterritoriums in der vorseverischen Keiserzeit." In *I diritti locali*, 109–24. Roma: Academia Nazionale dei Lincei.

Vladkova, P. 2003. "The Portico Building *extra muros* in Novae. Investigations and Problems." *Novensia* 14: 221–30.

– 2006. "Nekropol kray Novae ot vremeto na Teodorih Veliki." In *Goterna – current aspects of the Gothic historical and cultural heritage in Bulgaria*, edited by R. Milev, 57–70. Sofia: Balkanmedia.

– 2011. *Antichen proizvodstven centur pri Pavlikeni (Dolna Miziya)*, Veliko Turnovo: Dar-RH.

– 2015. "Free-standing Towers West of Novae." In *Limes XXII. Proceedings of the 22nd International Congress of Roman Frontier Studies Ruse, Bulgaria, September 2012,* edited by L. Vagalinski, and N. Sharankov, 187–94. Sofia: NAIM BAN.

Vnukov, S. 2003. *Prichernomorskie amfory I v. do n.e. – II v. n.e. (morfologia)*, Moskva: Nauka.

– 2004. "Pan-Roman amphora types produced in the Black Sea region." In *Transport amphorae and the trade in the eastern Mediterranean. Acts of the International Colloquium at the Danish Institute at Athens, September 26–29, 2002*, edited by J. Eiring, and J. Lund, Monographs of the Danish Institute at Athens, 5, Aarhus, 407–16. Aarhus: Aarhus University Press.

– 2011. "Sinopean amphorae of the Roman period." *Ancient civilizations from Scythia to Siberia* 16 (2010): 361–70.

– 2016. "Eshcho raz o tipologii, evoljutsii i hronologii svetloglinianyh (pozdnegeraklejskih) uzkogorlyh amfor (On the typology, evolution and chronology of light-clay (late Heraclean) narrow-necked amphorae)." *Rossiyskaya Arheologiya* 2016(2): 36–47.

Vulov, V. 1965. "Antichni nekropoli v Svishtovsko." *Archeologiya* (Sofia) 7(1): 27–34.

Wheeler, E. 2010. "Rome's Dacian Wars: Domitian, Trajan, and Strategy on the Danube, vol. I." *JMH* 74(4): 1185–1227.

– 2011. "Rome's Dacian Wars: Domitian, Trajan, and Strategy on the Danube, vol. II." *JMH* 75(1): 191–219.

Wieland, G. 1993 "Spätkeltische Traditionen in Form und Verzierung römischer Grobkeramik." *Fundberichte aus Baden-Württemberg* 18: 61–70.

Wiewiórowski, J. 2006. "Quaestor Iustinianus exercitus – A Late Roman Army Commander?", *Eos* 93: 317–340.

Wilkes, J.J. 1969. *Dalmatia*, London: Routledge & Kegan Paul.

Wilmans, J.C. 1981. "Die Doppelurkunde von Rottweil und ihr Beitrag zum Städtewesen in Obergermanien." *Epigraphische Studien* 12: 1–182.

Yordanov, I. 1984. *Moneti i monetno obrashtenie v srednovekovna Bulgaria 1081–1261*. Sofiya: Nauka i izkutstvo.

– 2009 (= *CBSB*). *Corpus of Byzantine Seals from Bulgaria*, vol. 3. Sofia: Agato Publishers.

– 2011. "Corpus of Byzantine Seals from Bulgaria, vols. 1–3, Sofia, 2003, 2006, 2009. Addenda et corrigenda." *Numizmatika, sfragistika i epigrafika* 7: 189–228.

– 2012. "The Diocese of Thrace (5th – 7th c.) According to the Sigillographic Data." *ArchBulg* 16/3: 57–76.

Yordanov, I., and Z. Zhekova, 2007. *Catalogue of Medieval Seals at the Regional Historical Museum of Shumen*. Shumen: Historical Museum of Shumen.

Zacos, G., and A. Veglery, 1972 (= *BLS*). *Byzantine Lead Seals*. Basel: J.J. Augustin.

Zahariade, M., and T. Dvorski, 1997. *The Lower Moesian Army in Northern Wallachia*, Bucharest: The Sylvi Publishing House.

Zanier, W. 1988. "Römische dreiflügelige Pfeilspitzen." *Saalburg Jahrbuch* 44: 5–27.

– 1995. "Zur Herstellung römischer dreiflügeliger Pfeilspitzen." *Saalburg Jahrbuch* 48: 19–25.

Zeest, I.B. 1960. "Keramicheskaya tara Bospora." Materialy i issledovaniya po arheologii SSSR, 83, Moskva: Nauka.

Zhuglev, K. 1965. "Ikonomicheskoto polozhenie v Trakiya Miziya i turgovskite im otnosheniya s Italia prez I–II v. ot n.e." *GSUIFF* 59(3): 187–395.

Zieling, N. 1989. *Studien zu germanischen Schilden der Spätlatène – und der römischen Kaiserzeit im freien Germanien*, B.A.R. Int. Ser., 505, Oxford: BAR Publishing.

Zohary, D., and M. Hopf, 2000. *Domestication of Plant in the Old World. The Origin and Spread of Cultivated Plants in West Asia, Europe and Nile Valley*, 316. Oxford: Oxford University Press.

Zohary, D. and P. Spiegel-Roy, 1975. "Beginning of fruit growing in the Old World." Science. 187: 319–327.

Żelazowski, J. 2012. "A New Name Stamp from the Army Camp at Novae." *Novensia* 23: 158–66.

– 2015. "New Examples of the Name Stamp (Sarnowski type XXV) from the Legionary Fortress at Novae (Lower Moesia)." In *Ad fines*, 249–56.

List of figures and tables in the text

Chapter I

Chapter III

tudinal tangential section – Layer (f); 4. *Fraxinus* sp.: transverse section – Layer (f); 5. *Acer* sp.: a. transverse section, b. longitudinal tangential section – Thracian vessel; 6. *Pinus* sp. type sylvestris-nigra: transverse section – Layer (f); 7. *Vitis vinifera*: a. transverse section, b. longitudinal tangential section, c. longitudinal radial section – Layer F. Scale bar: 300 μm (1a), 100 μm (1b, 3b, 7a, 7b, 7c), 1.00 mm (2), 400 μm (3a), 200 μm (4, 5a, 5b, 6). Sample 1: 1 and 5; Sample 3: 2 and 3; Sample 5: 4, 6 and 7 (by M. Moskal-del Hoyo).

Fig. 14. Taxonomic curve presenting the dependency in three samples between the amounts of taxa determined and the number of analysed charcoal fragments (by M. Moskal-del Hoyo).

Table I. Novae 2013. *Retentura sinistra*. Palynological samples and the basis for their dating. Quantitative values (by H. Winter).

Table II. Novae 2013. *Retentura sinistra*. Palynological samples and the basis for their dating. Percentage values (by H. Winter).

Table III. Novae 2013. *Retentura sinistra*. The archaeobotanical samples and the basis for their dating (by R. Stachowicz-Rybka).

Table IV. Novae 2013. *Retentura sinistra*. List of identified seeds and fruits and the basis for their dating (min. – mineralised; charr. – charred). Quantitative values (by R. Stachowicz-Rybka).

Table V. Novae 2013. *Retentura sinistra*. List of taxa identified in anthracological assemblages. Number of charcoal fragments and their percentage value (by M. Moskal-del Hoyo).

Chapter IV

Fig. 15. Google Earth satellite image with the georeferenced layout of Novae. The areas chosen for the prospection are marked with the letters. A – *retentura* and the southern annexe; B – Ostrite Mogili; C1 – extramural residence quarter; C2 – *canabae*; D – field to the south-west of the fortress; E – fields to the south of Ostrite Mogili; F – presumed villa at Kanlu cheshme (by A. Tomas).

Fig. 16a. Sampling pattern presented on exemplary 10×10 m grid. Left: 1. Widely used today 1×1 m sampling resolution profiles along one axis; 2. Sampling pattern applied in the principia area – 1×2 m, 2 m intervals between profiles measured along two axes; 3. Sampling pattern applied in the extra mural area – 1×5 m, 5 m intervals between profiles measured along two axes (by M. Pisz).

Fig. 16b. Electrical resistivity survey sampling pattern over hypothetical high-contrasting architectural remains. With (1×1 m) samples marked. Grey-coloured grids represent theoretical highly resistive response measured by the instrument. 1 – 1×1 m sampling; 2 –1×2 m sampling; 3 –1×5 m sampling; 4 –0.5×0.5 m sampling (M. Pisz).

Fig. 17. Scheme of the extensive field walking (transect) method implemented in 2012–14 (by A. Tomas).

Fig. 18. Novae 2012–14. Label used during field walkings in 2012–14 (by A. Tomas).

Fig. 19. Scheme of intensive field walkings (grid) method implemented in 2012–14 (by A. Tomas).

Fig. 20. Novae 2013. Hexacopter DJI S800 equipped with a Canon 5D MkII camera with a 14–70 mm lens (photo by M. Pisz).

Fig. 21. Novae 2014. Parallel transects used for mapping finds with the use of metal detectors (photo by P. Jaworski).

Chapter V

Fig. 22. Novae 2012. The southern part of the annexe and the view on the Dermen dere Valley (photo by M. Pisz).

Fig. 23. Novae 2011–12. The orthophotomap presenting the site with the fortress' schematic layout marked in yellow (by M. Pisz).

Fig. 24. Novae 2013. The orthophotomap of the site superimposed over satellite imagery (by M. Pisz).

Fig. 25. Ostrite Mogili 2014. The orthophotomap of the site (by M. Pisz).

Fig. 26. Novae 2013. The orthophotomap of the southern part of the annexe (by M. Pisz).

Fig. 27. Novae. The surveyed areas in the close vicinity of the fortress (by A. Tomas).

Fig. 28. Novae 2014. Plan of the *castra* and the outline of the annexe's eastern defensive walls (by A. Tomas, E. Jęczmienowski).

Fig. 29. Novae 2012–14. Fields surveyed in Area D (by A. Tomas).Fig. 30. Novae 2013. Area C2 (photo by A. Tomas).

Fig. 30. Novae 2013. Area C2 (photo by A. Tomas).

Fig. 31. Novae 2013. Area C1. The arrows mark the remains of walls, a possible line of the western aqueduct of Novae (photo by M. Pisz).

Fig. 32. Novae 2013. Area C1. The remains of a wall (photo by S. Rzeźnik).

Fig. 33. Novae 2012. Northern part of the annexe. Thick arrows mark towers 1 and 2 and thin arrows mark the line of the annexe's defensive walls (photo by M. Pisz).

Fig. 34. Novae 2012. Southern part of the annexe. The view from the west (photo by M. Pisz).

Fig. 35. Novae 2012. Illegal trenches in the annexe (photo by S. Rzeźnik).

Fig. 36. Novae 2013. The location of a stone structure and the remains visible in the high scarp of the Dermen dere Valley (by A. Tomas).

Fig. 37. Novae 2013. The view on the southern part of the *canabae* (photo by M. Pisz).

Fig. 38. Novae 2011. Illegal excavations in the southern *canabae* photo by A. Tomas).

Fig. 39. Novae 2014. The remains of the mithreum. The view from the east (photo by M. Lemke).

Fig. 40. Novae 2014. The finds from the mithraeum and plan of the building. A – stamped bricks; B – fragments of clay lamps; C – plan of the mithraeum (photo by A. Tomas, drawing by E. Jęczmienowski, A. Tomas).

Fig. 41. Ostrite Mogili 2000. The view from the west (photo by A. Tomas).

Fig. 42. Ostrite Mogili 1977 and 2000. A – the spread of debris; B – stone finds (drawing and photo by A. Tomas).

Fig. 43. Ostrite Mogili 1977 and 2000. A – the spread of pottery; B – the spread of other finds (drawing and photo by A. Tomas).

Fig. 44. Ostrite Mogili. Hypothetical reconstruction of the site (by A. Tomas).

Fig. 45. Ostrite Mogili 2014. Stone wall in the western part of the site (photo by S. Rzeźnik).

Chapter VI

Chapter VII

List of Plates